BUSINESS ECONOMICS

N. GREGORY MANKIW, MARK P. TAYLOR, ANDREW ASHWIN

FOURTH EDITION

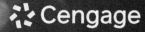

Cengage

Australia • Brazil • Canada • Mexico • Singapore • United Kingdom • United States

Business Economics, Fourth Edition
US authors: N. Gregory Mankiw
Adapting Authors: Mark P. Taylor and
Andrew Ashwin

Publisher: Annabel Ainscow

Development Editor: Yasmin Goosey

Marketing Manager: Louise Corless

Content Project Manager: Jyotsna Ojha

Manufacturing Buyer: Elaine Bevan

Manufacturing Manager: Eyvett Davis

Typesetter: Lumina Datamatics, Inc.

Cover Design: Varpu Lauchlan

Cover Image(s): © gettyimages / Simple
Reflection / EyeEm

For product information and technology assistance, contact us at
emea.info@cengage.com

For permission to use material from this text or
product and for permission queries, email
emea.permissions@cengage.com

British Library Cataloguing-in-Publication Data

A catalogue record for this book is available
from the British Library.

ISBN: 978-1-4737-9131-2

Cengage Learning, EMEA
Cheriton House, North Way
Andover, Hampshire, SP10 5BE
United Kingdom

Cengage Learning is a leading provider of customized learning
solutions with employees residing in nearly 40 different
countries and sales in more than 125 countries around the
world. Find your local representative at: **cengage.uk**

To learn more about Cengage platforms and services, register
or access your online learning solution, or purchase materials
for your course, visit **cengage.uk**

Printed in United Kingdom by Ashford Colour Press Ltd
Print Number: 01   Print Year: 2024

BRIEF CONTENTS

CONTENTS

PART 4
MICROECONOMICS: THE ECONOMICS OF FIRMS IN MARKETS 161

PART 5
MICROECONOMICS: FACTOR MARKETS 331

ABOUT THE AUTHORS

N. GREGORY MANKIW is Robert M. Beren Professor of Economics at Harvard University. As a student, he studied economics at Princeton University and the Massachusetts Institute of Technology. As a teacher he has taught macroeconomics, microeconomics, statistics and principles of economics. Professor Mankiw is a prolific writer and a regular participant in academic and policy debates. His work has been published in scholarly journals such as the *American Economic Review, Journal of Political Economy* and *Quarterly Journal of Economics.* In addition to his teaching, research and writing, Professor Mankiw has been a research associate of the National Bureau of Economic Research, an advisor to the Federal Reserve Banks of Boston and New York, and the Congressional Budget Office. From 2003 to 2005 he served as chairman of the US President's Council of Economic Advisors.

MARK P. TAYLOR is the Donald Danforth, Jr Distinguished Professor of Finance at the Olin Business School at Washington University in St Louis, USA. He was previously Dean of the Olin Business School and, before that, Dean and Professor of Finance and Economics at Warwick Business School at the University of Warwick, UK. He obtained his first degree in philosophy, politics and economics from Oxford University and his Master's and Doctoral degrees in economics and finance from London University. Professor Taylor has taught economics and finance at various universities (including Oxford, New York, Bordeaux and Aix-Marseille) and at various levels (including principles courses and advanced undergraduate and postgraduate courses). He has also worked as a senior economist at the International Monetary Fund and at the Bank of England and as a managing director at BlackRock, the world's largest financial asset manager, where he ran a global investment fund based on macroeconomic analysis. His research has been extensively published in scholarly journals and he is today one of the most highly cited economists in the world.

ANDREW ASHWIN is an associate lecturer at the University of Lincoln where he teaches on MBA and MSc courses in leadership and commercial and operations management. He has an MBA from the University of Hull, UK, and a PhD from the University of Leicester, UK. Andrew is an experienced author writing a number of texts on economics and business for students at different levels and publications related to his PhD research. Andrew was Chair of Examiners for a major awarding body in England and Wales for Business and Economics and is a former editor of the *Economics, Business and Enterprise Association* (EBEA) journal. Andrew is also a subject expert for economics to the qualifications regulator in England and Wales and is a Chartered Educational Assessor and a Fellow of the Chartered Institute of Educational Assessors.

PREFACE

How much of business is economics and how much of economics is business? This is a difficult question to answer but perhaps what is at the heart of both is decision making. This book is about decision making. Alfred Marshall, the great nineteenth-century British economist, in his textbook, *Principles of Economics* published in 1890 wrote: 'Economics is a study of mankind in the ordinary business of life.' For many people, the ordinary business of life is interwoven with relationships with business. Every single day, billions of people around the world make decisions. When we make decisions, we are being economists. A great proportion of these decisions are made by people in the context of their work which in turn is part of business, so business and economics are very closely linked.

A study of economics in a business context will help you understand the world in which you live. There are many questions about businesses and the economy that might spark your curiosity. Why do airlines charge less for a return ticket if the traveller stays over a Saturday night? Why are movie businesses prepared to pay some actors extremely large sums to star in films, while others struggle to even get a bit part? Why are living standards so meagre in many African countries? Why do some countries have high rates of inflation while others have stable prices? Why do businesses produce many products that are so similar? Surely they succeed only in cannibalizing their market? Why is it so important to have a better understanding of how consumers behave? Why have some European countries adopted a common currency? These are just a few of the questions that a course in Business Economics will help you answer.

The second reason to study Business Economics is that it will make you a more astute participant in the economy and in business. As you go about your life, you make many economic decisions. While you are a student, you decide how many years to stay in full-time education. When you have completed your degree, you will have to decide on a career path and find a job (which may be difficult despite being highly qualified). Once you take a job, you decide how much of your income to spend, how much to save and how to invest your savings. In your daily work, you will have to make many decisions and respond to an ever-changing environment. One day you may find yourself running your own small business or a large firm, and you will decide what prices to charge for your products and what products to offer for sale. The insights developed in the coming chapters will give you a new perspective on how best to make these decisions.

A study of Business Economics will give you a better understanding of the potential and limits of economic policy and how such policy can influence business behaviour. In your business career, you may find yourself asking various questions about economics. What are the burdens associated with alternative forms of taxation? What are the effects of free trade with other countries? To what extent do businesses have a responsibility to protect the environment? How does the government budget deficit affect the economy and thus your business?

A study of Business Economics will go some way towards helping you make more sense of the world, your place in it and how business is affected and behaves as a consequence.

FOR WHOM IS THIS BOOK WRITTEN?

The book has been written for the non-specialist who has to embark on a course of study in economics as part of a degree in Business. Your degree might be Business Economics, it might be Business Management or it might be Sports Coaching and Management. An increasing number of degree courses will include some coverage of economic principles, and this book is designed for just such courses. We have tried to put ourselves in the position of someone seeing economics for the first time and not necessarily looking forward to the prospect. Our goal has been to emphasize the material that *students* should and do find interesting about the study of the economy and business.

One result is that this book is briefer than many books used to introduce students to economics. Throughout this book we have tried to return to applications and policy questions as often as possible. All the chapters include a case study which illustrates how the principles of economics are applied. In addition, 'In the News' boxes offer highlights from news events showing how economic ideas shed light on current issues facing business and society, along with questions to help you apply your knowledge to new contexts – a vitally important part of learning.

Readers should note that part of this book is adapted from Greg Mankiw's best-selling US undergraduate *Principles of Economics* text. The adaptation to Professor Mankiw's text takes into account the needs of students and lecturers in the EMEA region and as such, may reflect different views to those in the original US text. Responsibility for the adaptation lies with Cengage EMEA.

LEARNING TOOLS

The purpose of this book is to help you learn the fundamental lessons of economics and to apply these lessons to a business context. Towards that end, we have used various learning tools that recur throughout the book.

- *Case Studies.* Economic theory is useful and interesting only if it can be applied to understanding actual events and policies. This book, therefore, contains numerous case studies that apply the theory that has just been developed in a business context. Questions have been provided to help encourage your thinking and writing skills.
- *'In the News' boxes.* One benefit that students gain from studying economics is a new perspective and greater understanding about news from around the world. To highlight this benefit, we have incorporated discussions of news events from around Europe, and the wider world. These articles, together with our brief introductions, show how basic economic theory can be applied and raise important questions for discussion in business. To help further develop application skills we have included some questions at the end which can either be used as practice for self-study or as the basis for seminar or tutorial discussion.
- *'FYI' boxes.* These boxes provide additional material 'for your information'. Some of them offer a glimpse into the history of economic thought. Others clarify technical issues. Still others discuss supplementary topics that instructors might choose either to discuss or skip in their lectures but which students should find useful in supplementing their knowledge and understanding.
- *Definitions of key concepts.* When key concepts are introduced in the chapter, they are presented in bold typeface. In addition, their definitions are placed in a box in the page. This treatment is designed to help with learning and reviewing the material.
- *Pitfall Prevention boxes.* The authors have used their collective teaching wisdom to outline areas where students make frequent mistakes and which can be a cause of confusion. The Pitfall Prevention boxes alert you to the potential for these mistakes.
- *Jeopardy Problem boxes.* These are problems designed to help you think as an economist. You will be given end-points or solutions and you must think through the different ways in which the solutions or end-point given might have been arrived at using your knowledge of economics and business.
- *What if...? boxes.* Questions designed to get you thinking about different scenarios in business and economics.
- *Self-Test Questions.* After most major sections, you are offered a 'self-test' to check your comprehension of what you have just learned. If you cannot readily answer these questions, you should stop and reread material before continuing.
- *Chapter summaries.* Each chapter ends with a brief summary that reminds you of the most important lessons that you have just learned. Later in your study it offers an efficient way to revise for exams.
- *Questions for review.* At the end of each chapter are questions for review that cover the chapter's primary lessons. You can use these questions to check your comprehension and to prepare for exams.
- *Problems and applications.* Each chapter also contains a variety of problems and applications that ask you to apply the material you have learned. Some instructors may use these questions for private study assignments. Others may use them as a starting point for classroom discussions.

ACKNOWLEDGEMENTS

The authors would like to thank the following reviewers for their comments on this and previous editions:

Andrew Abbott – *University of Hull, UK*
Dr Turner Anna – *CEU Business School, Hungary*
Emanuele Bracco – *Lancaster University, UK*
Dr Yu-Fu Chen – *Dundee University, UK*
Dr Zheng Chris Cao – *Aston University, UK*
Matthew T. Col – *University College Dublin, Ireland*
Gary Cook – *University of Liverpool, UK*
Dr John Duignan – *University of the West of Scotland, UK*
Aat van Eeden – *Zuyd University of Applied Science, Netherlands*
Robert Elliott – *University of Birmingham, UK*
John Forde – *University of Salford, UK*
Richard Godfrey – *Cardiff School of Management, UK*
Marco Gundermann – *Cardiff Metropolitan University, UK*
Dr Hala Helmi El Hadidi – *British University, Egypt*
Michael Harrison – *University of East London, UK*
Juan Garcia Lara – *Universidad Carlos III Madrid, Spain*
Qamarullah Bin Tariq Islam – *Rajshahi University, Bangladesh; University of Glasgow, UK*
Paul L. Latreille – *Swansea University, UK*
Dr Alan Leonard – *University of Portsmouth, UK*
Paul Lovejoy – *University of Portsmouth, UK*
Dr Bobby Mackie – *University of the West of Scotland, UK*
Dr James Mallon – *Edinburgh Napier University, UK*
Tim Maxfield – *University of Worcester, UK*
Pedro Martins – *Queen Mary, University of London, UK*
Fearghal J. McHugh – *Galway Mayo Institute of Technology, Ireland*

Natalie Moore – *University of Nottingham, UK*
Yoko Nagase – *Oxford Brookes University, UK*
Adel Nemeth – *Jacobs University, Bremen*
Jens J. Nielsen – *The International Business Academy, Denmark*
Dr Matthew Olczak – *Aston University, UK*
Quentin Outram – *Leeds University Business School, UK*
Bruce Philp – *Nottingham Business School, UK*
Julia Planko – *Hogeschool Utrecht, Netherlands*
Robert Price – *University of Suffolk, UK*
Neil Reaich – *Business Economics Specialist, UK*
Jose R. Sanchez-Fung – *Kingston University London, UK*
Ulrich Schüle – *School of Business FH Mainz-University of Applied Sciences, Germany*
Cemil Selcuk – *Cardiff University, UK*
Vasilios Sogiakas – *University of Glasgow, UK*
Nicholas Spearman – *University of the Witwatersrand, South Africa*
Dr F Steffen – *University of Liverpool Management School, UK*
Dr Alexander Tziamalis – *Sheffield Hallam University, UK*
Michael Wood – *London South Bank University, UK*
Dr Michael Wynn-Williams – *University of Greenwich, UK*
Gaston Yalonetzky – *Leeds University Business School, UK*

DIGITAL RESOURCES

Dr Zheng Chris Cao – *Aston University,* UK
Dr Giancarlo Ianulardo – *University of Exeter Business School,* UK
Dr Alan Leonard – *University of Portsmouth,* UK
Dr Sangaralingam Ramesh – *University of Oxford and University College London,* UK
Neil Reaich – *Business Economics Specialist,* UK

Fit your coursework into your hectic life.

Make the most of your time by learning your way. Access the resources you need to succeed whenever and wherever you like.

 Study with interactive tools and resources designed to help you master key concepts and prepare you for class.

 Review your current course grade and compare your progress with your peers.

 Get the free Cengage Mobile App and learn wherever you are.

MINDTAP. POWERED BY YOU

cengage.uk/mindtap

Cengage

Teaching & Learning Support Resources

Cengage's peer-reviewed content for higher and further education courses is accompanied by a range of digital teaching and learning support resources. The resources are carefully tailored to the specific needs of the instructor, student and the course. Examples of the kind of resources provided include:

A password-protected area for instructors with, for example, a test bank, PowerPoint slides and an instructor's manual.

Lecturers: to discover the dedicated teaching digital support resources accompanying this textbook please register here for access:
account.cengage.com/login

Learn more at cengage.uk

PART 1
THE ECONOMIC AND BUSINESS ENVIRONMENT

1 WHAT IS BUSINESS ECONOMICS?

LEARNING OUTCOMES

After reading this chapter you should be able to:

- Explain what businesses do and what economics studies.
- Provide a definition and example of business activity in the public and private sectors.
- Define scarcity.
- Explain the idea of a trade-off and provide at least one example.
- Give a definition of opportunity cost and provide at least three examples relating to individual and business decision making.
- Explain the difference between capitalist and communist economic systems in how they answer the fundamental questions of society.
- Outline how prices direct resources to different economic activities.
- Explain why specialization and trade can improve people's choices.

WHAT IS BUSINESS ECONOMICS?

Business studies and economics are invariably taught as separate subjects in many schools prior to university. Business studies focuses on issues and problems related to business organizations of different types and includes business objectives, marketing, business organization, human resources management, accounting and finance, operations management and the influence of external factors including management of change. Economics focuses on the workings of markets, firm behaviour, market structures, factor markets (such as the market for labour and capital), international trade and the workings of the economy as a whole including growth, unemployment, inflation and exchange rates.

There is one thing, however, which connects the two discipline areas and that is decision making. People in businesses have to make decisions every day and the way in which they make these decisions and the outcome of those decisions can be informed by using the models, methods and tools of economics.

In addition, an understanding of the key concepts of economics is essential. The purpose of this book is to help you begin to think as an economist and to apply that thinking to business contexts to set you on the way to being a better decision maker. Businesses need people who understand the basic principles of business, who are flexible, can think in different ways and who are problem solvers who can cope with and confront change in a positive way. Having an understanding of the basic principles of economics will help in developing these skills.

What Is Business?

Business is an activity. It involves using inputs, which are broadly described as land, labour and capital, and turning them into some output which is then sold to customers. These outputs could be goods such as TVs, food, books, clothes, furniture, bricks, cars, glass and so on or services such as banking, insurance, accounting, tourism, repairs, medical care, entertainment, transportation, hotels, restaurants, etc. The customers who buy these outputs could be private individuals, other businesses or government bodies both from the domestic economy and from overseas. In the process of exchange of outputs, buyers pay a price to acquire the outputs and the money received by the seller represents the income of the business.

Business activity is carried out for different reasons. In some cases, the primary aim of a business is to ensure that the money received from selling outputs is greater than the cost of producing these outputs. In other words, the business is focused on making a profit and **profit** is the reward for the risk taken in carrying out business activity. Some business activity will be carried out with the primary intention of fulfilling a need, and while in most cases it is expected that the costs of providing the output must at the very least be covered by the income generated, any surplus that is generated is put back into the business or used for a good cause.

profit the reward for taking risk in carrying out business activity

Because business activity has different aims, the organizations that provide outputs are different. The **private sector** is made up of different types of businesses. Some are very small, one-person organizations and some are giants with operations in many different countries employing many thousands of people. The main aim of these businesses is to generate profit, but they will also have many other aims which might also include a recognition of their moral and ethical responsibilities to society as a whole. Other businesses in the private sector are set up with the primary aim of providing outputs or a service which meet a particular need. These businesses will include charitable organizations, carrying out voluntary work, fundraising and activities which have wider social and community benefits. This is referred to as the **third sector** or not-for-profit business.

private sector business activity which is owned, financed and organized by private individuals
third sector business activity owned, financed and organized by private individuals, but with the primary aim of providing needs and not making profit

In many countries a large amount of business activity is carried out by the government on behalf of the population as a whole. This is referred to as the **public sector**. The finance for public sector activity comes from tax payers, from government borrowing and from the income that can be generated from the activity itself. Public sector activity is focused on providing goods and services to the public as a whole, and in doing so maximizing the opportunities for access. Balancing the cost of providing education, health, legal, welfare, emergency services, roads and transport and so on with the demand for these services is a considerable challenge to any government but, fundamentally, it might be expected that the cost of provision is at least met by the funds available.

public sector business activity owned, financed and organized by the state on behalf of the population as a whole

One of the main decisions facing businesses is what the aims of the business should be. If the primary aim is to make profit, decisions made may be different, but related to those which are made if the primary aim of the business is to provide a perceived social benefit. Public sector organizations have to make difficult decisions about the provision of services because funds may be limited.

In most business activity, decisions might include any or all of the following:

- How many people to employ.
- What each of those people will do to contribute to the business.
- How much employees get in return for their labour.
- Who should receive a bonus scheme and who should not.
- How to increase output per worker.
- How best to manage costs.
- When to invest.
- How much to invest and where best to get the funds to invest from.
- What products to produce.
- What products not to produce.
- When to stop producing products.
- When to expand.
- When to contract.
- How best to manage the sales process and customer relations.
- Whether to be environmentally friendly or whether to give the impression of being so.
- How to deal with competitors.
- Whether to charge a high price or a low price (or one in-between).

It is important to note at the outset that there are rarely simple and identifiable 'right' and 'wrong' answers in business. However meticulous the analysis carried out and data collected, ultimately judgements have to be made. When the judgements lead to positive outcomes, the decision makers are praised and may be lauded as having some special skill or insight, but when the judgement leads to negative outcomes decision makers are criticized and may find themselves out of a job.

Decision makers will seek to use many different techniques and methods to help them make better decisions, that lead to the positive outcomes desired. A knowledge of the methods, tools and models of economics may be one way in which decision makers can understand the problems and issues they face and be in a better position to make decisions as a result. It is important to emphasize, however, that having a good understanding of economics is not going to automatically lead to business success, however that success is defined.

Types of Economic System Businesses operate as part of society. Typically, business activity forms part of a society that is based on capitalist principles where resources are owned by private individuals, and trade and exchange is carried out largely for the purposes of making a profit. In some societies, resources are owned by the state and business activity is carried out for social, economic and political reasons, which may include a fundamental belief that society ought to be organized along more egalitarian lines than those which exist in capitalist societies. These are referred to as **communist economies** (and more generally as 'command economies'). Inequality is an outcome of **capitalist economies** and the gaps between the rich and poor and those who have and have not form fundamental areas of disagreement in decision making.

> **communist economies** systems where resource inputs are largely owned by the state, and exchange and trade are based on social, political and economic motives which may be primarily based on a belief of greater equality
> **capitalist economies** systems where resource inputs are largely owned by private individuals and where the motive for exchange takes place primarily for profit

The Fundamental Questions of Society

Regardless of the economic system in place, any country has some fundamental questions to answer. These questions are:

- What products will be produced?
- How will products be produced?
- Who will get the products that are produced?

These are profound questions and have equally profound implications. In any society, human beings have wants and needs; at the most basic level these wants and needs are food, clothing and shelter. To provide for these needs, resources, which we have classified as land, labour and capital, have to be organized to generate the products that society needs to answer the first question, 'What is to be produced?'

There are many different ways in which products can be produced, and who gets access is determined by the economic system that is adopted in a country. In a capitalist system, those who own resources may get access to a far greater proportion of the products produced than those who do not, whereas in a non-capitalist system resources are owned by the state, and the state may determine a far greater degree of equality of access. Decisions made in capitalist economies will be based on different beliefs and priorities to those made in communist or command economies.

What Is Economics?

At its simplest, **economics** is the study of how society manages its resources. The management of society's resources is important because resources are scarce. **Scarcity** means that society has limited resources and therefore cannot produce all the products people desire. Just as a household cannot give every member everything they want, a society cannot give every individual the highest standard of living to which they might aspire.

economics the study of how society makes decisions in managing scarce resources
scarcity the limited nature of society's resources in relation to wants and needs

In capitalist societies, the fundamental questions of what is to be produced, how products are to be produced, and who gets access to the products produced are answered through the combined actions of millions of households and firms. Economists therefore study how people make decisions: how much they work, what they buy, how much they save and how they invest their savings. Economists also study how people and people in businesses interact with one another. Economists analyze forces and trends that affect the economy as a whole, including the growth in average income, the fraction of the population that cannot find work and the rate at which prices change.

In communist societies, the fundamental questions are answered by the state making judgements about resource use. These judgements will be based on different belief systems from those in capitalist societies. Economists study how decisions are made in these societies and the implications of these decisions. In many countries, private individuals and the state operate together in answering the fundamental questions. These are referred to as **mixed economies**. The proportion of economic activity that is carried out by the private sector and public sector varies, but there are few instances of countries where the private and public sector do not coexist in addressing the fundamental questions.

mixed economies economic systems that include elements of both private and public ownership of resources to answer the fundamental questions

In a sense, economics can be described as the science of decision making. In thinking as an economist in the context of business, there are particular concepts, models and methods that have developed within the discipline of economics. These can be applied and help in the analysis of business problems and issues.

SOME KEY IDEAS IN ECONOMICS

We use the term 'the economy' on a regular basis, but have you ever stopped to think about what the term really means? Whether we are talking about the economy of a group of countries, such as the European Union (EU) or the Middle East, or the economy of one particular country, such as South Africa or the United Kingdom (UK), or of the whole world, an economy is just a group of people interacting with one another as they go about their lives. This interaction is invariably through a process of exchange.

Whether it be an individual buying a coffee, a business buying several hundred tonnes of steel for a construction project or a government funding a higher education institution, the interaction consists of millions of individuals all making decisions and together we describe these interactions as **the economy**.

the economy the collective interaction between individuals in the process of production and exchange in a defined area

There are some fundamental ideas that are associated with economics which will appear consistently throughout our analysis in this book. These are introduced below.

Idea 1: Decision Making Involves Trade-Offs

When individuals, businesses or governments make decisions, they have to make a judgement between two or more courses of action. Each course of action will have certain benefits. If one course of action is chosen, the benefits of that action can be gained, but usually making that decision involves having to give up the benefits of the other courses of action. The benefits that have to be given up are said to be the **trade-offs** of a decision. Making decisions requires trading off the benefits of one action against the benefits of another.

trade-off the loss of the benefits from a decision to forego or sacrifice one option, balanced against the benefits incurred from the choice made

Consider a business manager who must decide how to allocate their most valuable resource: their time. They can spend all of their time reflecting on strategy in their office which, if implemented successfully, could bring benefits to the business. Equally, they could spend all of their time walking around the premises talking to staff, gaining a better understanding of the business and motivating workers, which may bring benefits of improved productivity and efficiency; or they can divide their time between the two fields. For every hour they spend reflecting and strategizing, they give up the benefits that could be gained for an hour they could have used talking to staff.

Similarly, consider employees of this business deciding how to spend the income they receive from working at the business. They can buy food, clothing or a family holiday, each of which bring certain benefits. Or they can save some of the family income for retirement, which brings benefits in the future. If the family decides to save an extra €100 a month for retirement, then they have to trade-off the benefits this brings in the future for the benefits incurred by spending that €100 on products today.

When people are grouped into societies, they face different kinds of trade-offs. Resources devoted to consumer goods such as clothing, food, cars, washing machines and so on could also be used for producing capital goods, equipment and machinery that is used for the production of other goods. The more society spends on consumer goods that bring benefits to people, the less we can spend on capital goods that bring the benefits of raising standards of living at some point in the future.

Also important in modern society is the trade-off between a clean environment and a high level of income. Laws that require firms to reduce pollution might raise the cost of production but bring the benefit to society as a whole (and possibly to the firm in the form of good publicity). Because of the higher costs, these firms may end up earning smaller profits, paying lower wages, charging higher prices or some combination of these three. Thus, while pollution regulations give us the benefit of a cleaner environment and the improved levels of health that come with it, they reduce the benefits that higher incomes would bring to firms' owners, workers and customers.

Recognizing that people and businesses face trade-offs does not by itself tell us what decisions they will or should make. A chief executive officer (CEO) should not abandon time set aside for reflection and thinking just because doing so would increase the time available to talk to workers. Society should not stop protecting the environment just because environmental regulations reduce our material standard of living. Nevertheless, acknowledging trade-offs is important because people and businesses are likely to make good decisions only if they understand the options that they have available and can quantify them in some way to make informed decisions.

Idea 2: The Cost of Something Is What You Give Up to Get It

Because people and businesses face trade-offs, making decisions requires comparing not only the benefits but also the costs of alternative courses of action. In many cases, however, these costs and benefits are not as obvious as might first appear.

Consider the decision by a business to cease production of a product that is not selling very well. The benefit is that resources can be made available to invest in other parts of the business that are more successful. But what is the cost? To answer this question, you might be tempted to add up the money the business has to pay in redundancy to workers who may no longer be needed, to close down the plant and get rid of defunct machinery and equipment. Yet this total does not truly represent what the business gives up when it ceases production of a product. First, it ignores many wider issues that the business might face as a result of its decision. How do competitors view the decision? Will they seek to use it as an example of the decline of the business? What about customers? Will they be disappointed that the product has disappeared? A number of businesses have found themselves under pressure to bring back much loved products that may not have been financially viable and have incurred disappointment from customers and possible loss of loyalty as a result. Then there is the attitude among workers. Is this closure the first of others? Does it send negative signals to the rest of the workforce resulting in a decline in motivation and increases in staff turnover as workers seek to get out before they are pushed out? Second, it does not include the lost revenue from sales of the product. It may be that sales were low and not very profitable, rather than it was not viable to continue with production, i.e. that the business was making a loss. Assuming that sales were not zero, there will have been some revenue being generated and this will now be lost. This has to be taken into consideration.

The decision, therefore, has costs far greater than pure money costs. The cost of loss of goodwill, worker and customer loyalty and bad publicity also has to be taken into consideration in assessing the costs of the decision and these may not be immediately obvious and sometimes not easy to work out.

The **opportunity cost** of an action is what you give up to pursue that course of action. When making any decision, such as whether to close down production of a product, decision makers should be aware of the opportunity costs that accompany each possible action.

opportunity cost the cost expressed in terms of the benefits sacrificed of the next best alternative

> **SELF TEST** You may have heard the adage 'There is no such thing as a free lunch'. What do you think this means in the context of trade-offs and opportunity cost?

Idea 3: Rational People and Businesses Think at the Margin

There are many aspects of economics which are based on assumptions. One such assumption is that people behave rationally. In this context, behaving rationally means doing the best you can given the circumstances. The extent to which this is indeed the case is debatable but, in some cases, businesses and individuals do make decisions based on a rational assessment (as far as is possible) of different options. The decision by a company worker of whether to put in the extra hour at the end of the working day might be based on the perceived costs and benefits of completing a task before going home. A publisher may have to make a decision about whether to print an extra 1,000 copies of a textbook when it is not certain that all these extra books will sell. Economists use the term **marginal changes** to describe small incremental adjustments to an existing plan of action. Keep in mind that 'margin' means 'edge', so marginal changes are adjustments around the edges of what you are doing. In many situations, people can make sensible decisions by thinking at the margin.

marginal changes small incremental adjustments to a plan of action

Consider an airline company deciding how much to charge passengers. Suppose that flying a 200-seat aeroplane from London to Warsaw costs the airline €50,000. In this case, the average cost of each seat is

€50,000/200, which is €250. You might be tempted to conclude that the airline should never sell a ticket for less than €250. If the airline thinks at the margin, it could raise its profits. Imagine that 24 hours before the plane is due to depart, there are still ten empty seats. Last-minute passengers accessing the booking area on the airline's website might be willing to pay €200 for a seat. Should the airline sell it to them? If the plane has empty seats, the cost of adding one more passenger is minuscule. Although the *average* cost of flying a passenger is €250, the *marginal* cost is merely the cost of the airline meal that the extra passenger will consume (which may have gone to waste in any case if it was provided) and possibly a slight increase in the amount of aircraft fuel used. As long as the late booking passengers pay more than the marginal cost, selling them a ticket can be profitable. We assume that a rational decision maker takes an action if the marginal benefit of the action exceeds the marginal cost.

Idea 4: People and Businesses Respond to Incentives

If people and businesses make decisions by comparing costs and benefits, their behaviour may change when the costs or benefits change. That is, people respond to incentives. When the price of an apple rises, for instance, some people decide to eat more pears and fewer apples because the price paid to buy an apple is higher. At the same time, apple orchards decide to hire more workers and harvest more apples, because the benefit of selling an apple is also higher. The effect of price on the behaviour of buyers and sellers in a market is crucial for understanding how the economy works.

Public policy makers should never forget about incentives, because many policies change the costs or benefits that people face and, therefore, alter behaviour. Concerns over the environment and climate change have led some governments to pass legislation around the future production of vehicles using internal combustion engines. This, along with other business related factors, has encouraged manufacturers to invest more in the production of electric vehicles and for consumers to consider going electric when changing their vehicles. This in turn has led to new firms developing around the provision of the infrastructure needed, which includes more widespread and accessible public charging points and the provision of charging points in private homes.

When policy makers fail to consider how their policies affect incentives, they often end up with results they did not intend. These are referred to as **unintended consequences**. For example, if a government decided to make the wearing of safety helmets for cyclists a legal requirement, the primary focus of the law might be to help reduce the incidents of serious head injuries for cyclists. The unintended consequences might be that people decide not to cycle in the numbers they used to because wearing a cycle helmet is unfashionable. The number of people suffering head injuries might fall because fewer people are now cycling but, in addition, society loses the positive health benefits that cycling can bring, and businesses manufacturing and servicing bicycles might see demand fall. Public transport and roads may become busier because people switch to using buses and cars rather than cycling to work.

> **unintended consequences** the outcomes of decision making or policy changes which are not anticipated and are unforeseen

This is an example of the general principle that people respond to incentives. When analysing any policy or business decision, we must consider not only the direct effects but also the indirect effects that work through incentives. If the decision changes incentives, it will cause people to alter their behaviour.

SELF TEST The emphasis on road safety throughout Europe has increased since the early 1990s. Not only are cars packed with safety technology and devices, but roads are also designed to be safer with the use of safety barriers and better road surfaces, for example. Is there a case for believing that if people feel they are safer in their cars there is an incentive to drive faster because the marginal cost is now outweighed by the marginal benefit?

CASE STUDY   Technology and Decision Making

One of the major debating points in economics is around how humans make decisions. Economics has a history of assuming that humans make decisions based on the principle of rationality. This is highlighted in the ideas we have discussed in this chapter. Many models in economics are based around the assumption of rational behaviour, that is people making decisions to do the best they can given their circumstances. However, research has shown that humans can often make irrational decisions partly due to their inability to comprehend and process the amount of data needed to make better decisions.

Technology, however, is being developed to help humans, and in particular humans who work in businesses, to analyze and process data to improve decision making. Artificial intelligence (AI) is technology that enables machines to perform with human-like capabilities in solving problems and making decisions. AI covers a wide range of technologies but includes machine learning where systems can process information and establish patterns which enable the system to improve performance in the future. Many of us will have experience of AI through the use of smart speakers, digital assistants on websites, face recognition on smartphones, the personalized information we are fed through social media accounts, spell checks on computer devices, travel and weather apps, and banking services. Much of the time, AI is working in the background to process the data we provide and to understand us better to provide more personalized experiences in many areas of our lives.

In business, AI is becoming increasingly important. In manufacturing, AI can be used to monitor production processes and systems and to identify potential problems and rectify them before they happen.

Many businesses now collect massive amounts of data which humans would not be able to process effectively but machines can. The analysis of data can provide information to help improve decision making, to better understand customers and their behaviour, to understand their operations more effectively and to make improvements which generate greater efficiency. At this stage in the development of the technology, AI is not replacing humans but working with humans to facilitate improved decision making.

AI can make decision-making more efficient but to what extent should it replace human judgement?

Questions

1   Give an example of a 'rational' business decision. What is it about the decision that makes it 'rational'?
2   The case study provides a definition of AI. Do you think it is important for software developers working on AI to find ways to take into account opportunity costs in making decisions? Explain.
3   How important do you think it is that AI does not replace humans but that business decision making continues to rely on human judgement? Explain.

Idea 5: Trade Can Make Everyone Better Off

The United States, South Africa and Japan are often mentioned in the news as being competitors to Europe in the world economy. In some ways this is true, because US, South African and Japanese firms do produce many of the same goods as European firms. Airbus and Boeing compete for the same customers in the market for aircraft. Toyota and Citroën compete for the same customers in the market for cars. South African and US fruit growers compete in the same market as European fruit growers, and South African and US wine producers compete in the same market as French, Spanish and Italian wine makers.

Yet it is easy to be misled when thinking about competition among countries. Trade between Europe and South Africa or the United States, or between Europe and Japan, is not like a sports contest where one side wins and the other side loses (a zero-sum game). Trade between two economies can make each economy better off.

In the private sector in a capitalist system, when a business produces a product it competes against other businesses that are producing similar products. Despite this competition, a business would not be better off isolating itself from all other businesses. If it did, the business would have to supply all its own raw materials and components, find its own staff, arrange its own insurance, do its own banking, arrange its own security and so on. Businesses can benefit from their ability to trade with others. Trade allows each business to specialize in the activities it does best, whether it is farming, making clothes or home building. By trading with others, businesses can buy a greater variety of goods and services at lower cost and therefore (potentially) increase efficiency.

Countries as well as businesses benefit from the ability to trade with one another. Trade allows countries to specialize in production of certain goods and services which they have developed an efficiency in for some reason. This might be because of resource endowments, for example parts of the Arab world have significant reserves of oil. It could also be because they have developed experience, infrastructure and skill in finance, such as the City of London or Frankfurt. The production of these goods and services can be traded so that citizens are able to enjoy a greater variety of goods and services. The Japanese and Americans, as well as the Egyptians and Brazilians, are as much partners in the world economy as they are competitors. While trade can bring benefits it must be borne in mind that with any trade there can be winners and losers.

Idea 6: Markets Can Be a Good Way to Organize Economic Activity

Communist economic systems have central planners in the government who guide economic activity. These planners decide what goods and services are produced, how much is produced and who produces and consumes these goods and services. Those who support central planning might argue that only the government can organize economic activity in a way that promotes economic well-being for the country as a whole.

In a capitalist system, the private ownership of resources means that individuals making millions of decisions every day determine economic activity. The interaction of buyers and sellers in markets allocates resources to different uses and addresses the fundamental economic questions. In a **market economy**, firms decide who to hire and what to make; individuals supplying labour decide which firms to work for and what to buy with their incomes. These individuals (collectively referred to as households) and firms interact in the marketplace, where prices and self-interest guide their decisions. The process of exchange in market economies is facilitated by prices that provide signals to consumers and producers, and lead to resources moving to different uses, all of which are based on the self-interests of firms and households. Prices reflect both the value of a good to society and the cost to society of making the good.

> **market economy** an economy that allocates resources through the decentralized decisions of many firms and households as they interact in markets for goods and services

In a pure market economy (one with no state involvement), no individual is considering the economic well-being of society as a whole. Yet, despite self-interested decision makers, market economies have proven remarkably successful in organizing economic activity, and the vast majority of countries around the world base their economies on a market system to a greater or lesser degree. Proponents of market economies argue that they are the most effective way yet devised in allocating resources and improving standards of living. However, note the caveat in this idea. Markets *can be* a good way to organize economic activity. We emphasize *can be* because markets are not devoid of problems. Events since 2019 have highlighted the fragility of market systems and how disruption to the flow of goods and services in market systems can cause widespread problems. We will look at the reasons why markets may not work properly in later chapters.

FYI

Adam Smith and the Invisible Hand

Adam Smith's *The Wealth of Nations* is a landmark in economics. It reflected a point of view that was typical of so-called 'enlightenment' writers at the end of the eighteenth century, that individuals are usually best left to their own devices, without government guiding their actions. This political philosophy provided the intellectual basis for the market economy summed up in the following description by Adam Smith of how people interact:

> *Man* (sic) *has almost constant occasion for the help of his brethren, and it is vain for him to expect it from their benevolence only. He will be more likely to prevail if he can interest their self-love in his favour, and show them that it is for their own advantage to do for him what he requires of them... It is not from the benevolence of the butcher, the brewer, or the baker that we expect our dinner, but from their regard to their own interest. ... Every individual... neither intends to promote the public interest, nor knows how much he is promoting it. ... He intends only his own gain, and he is in this, as in many other cases, led by an invisible hand to promote an end which was no part of his intention. Nor is it always the worse for the society that it was no part of it. By pursuing his own interest he frequently promotes that of the society more effectually than when he really intends to promote it.*
>
> *The Wealth of Nations* 1776

Economists have interpreted this as Smith arguing that participants in the economy are motivated by self-interest and that the 'invisible hand' of the marketplace guides this self-interest into promoting general economic well-being. For many years the 'invisible hand' has been cited as an example of the way in which markets are the most appropriate way yet devised to address the fundamental economic questions. Not everyone, however, believes this to be the case. Some economists argue that Smith was writing in the particular context of his day and that the world and economies are very different today and have different belief systems that may mean markets do not always lead to improvements in overall well-being.

Idea 7: Governments Can Sometimes Improve Market Outcomes

Markets only work if certain assumptions are upheld. One of these assumptions is that an effective system of property rights exists. **Property rights** are linked to the idea of ownership of resources, which forms the basis of the capitalist system. If an individual owns property, then there has to be some system in place to ensure that the rights associated with owning that property can be enforced. These rights might include the exclusive right to use and exploit the good to generate income and the right to transfer ownership to another individual or organization. A farmer will not grow food if they expect their crop to be stolen, and a restaurant will not serve meals unless it is assured that customers will pay before they leave. A market-based system has to rely on the legal system and police to enforce rights over the things we produce and these are provided by the state.

 property rights the exclusive right of an individual, group or organization to determine how a resource is used

A pure market system can lead to outcomes that may not be deemed desirable. Specifically, market outcomes may be seen as being inefficient or inequitable. Governments step in to promote efficiency and equity by seeking to either enlarge the economic cake or change the way in which the cake is divided.

When market outcomes fail to lead to an efficient allocation of resources, economists call this **market failure**. One possible cause of market failure is an **externality**, which is the uncompensated impact of one person's actions on the well-being of a bystander or third party. For instance, the classic example of an external cost is pollution. Another possible cause of market failure is **market power**, which refers to the ability of a single person (or small group) to unduly influence market prices. For example, if everyone in a remote village in the Scottish Highlands needs water but there is only one well, the owner of the well may act in their own self-interest and in doing so make decisions that have wide social and economic implications.

market failure a situation in which a market left on its own fails to allocate resources efficiently
externality the uncompensated impact of one person's actions on the well-being of a bystander or third party
market power the ability of a single economic agent (or small group of agents) to have a substantial influence on market prices

> **?** ■ **WHAT IF...** the intervention by government actually leads to a worse outcome than if it had not done anything in the first place? Does this mean government should never interfere in the market?

Market systems may also fail to ensure that economic prosperity is distributed equitably. A market economy rewards people according to their ability to produce things for which other people are willing to pay. The world's best footballer earns more than the world's best chess player simply because people are willing to pay more to watch football than chess. The invisible hand does not ensure that everyone has sufficient food, decent clothing and adequate health care. Many public policies, such as income tax and the social security system, aim to achieve a more equitable distribution of economic well-being.

To say that the government *can* improve on market outcomes at times does not mean that it always *will*. Public policy is made by a political process that is far from perfect. Sometimes policies are designed simply to reward the politically powerful (which might include business leaders). Sometimes they are made by well-intentioned leaders who are not fully informed or who are unduly swayed by lobbying from businesses with a great deal of influence and power. Well-intentioned policies can have unintended consequences. Thinking as an economist helps you to judge when a government policy is justifiable to promote efficiency or equity, and when it is not.

The Economy as a Whole As noted earlier, individuals make decisions and also interact with one another with these collective decisions and interactions making up 'the economy'. A key concept in Business Economics is **economic growth**: the percentage increase in the number of goods and services produced in an economy over a period of time, usually expressed over a quarter and annually.

economic growth the increase in the amount of goods and services in an economy over a period of time

Idea 8: An Economy's Standard of Living Depends on Its Ability to Produce Goods and Services

Economic growth is important because it relates to the amount of goods and services produced by a country in a period and can be used as a reflection of the **standard of living** that citizens of that country enjoy. Economic growth can be measured by looking at the change in the value of goods and services a country produces each year, its **gross domestic product (GDP)**. Citizens in countries with high levels of GDP tend to have more goods and services such as housing, TVs, internet access, cars, household white goods and so on, which can make life more comfortable, as well as access to better nutrition, better health care and longer life expectancy than citizens of low GDP countries. In addition, many of these high income countries have more robust legal systems which enforce the law and reduce the incidences of corruption, which is important in ensuring that businesses are governed appropriately and behave to high standards.

Taking the GDP of a country and dividing the figure by the population gives **gross domestic product (GDP) per head** or per capita. GDP per head is used as one measure of the standard of living of citizens in a country as it reflects the amount of goods and services people are able to access. It can be argued that countries with higher GDP per head tend to enjoy a higher standard of living compared to countries with low GDP per head, although there may be other measures of well-being that can be used rather than the amount of goods and services which can be bought.

> **standard of living** a measure of welfare based on the amount of goods and services a person's income can buy
> **gross domestic product (GDP)** the market value of all final goods and services produced within a country in a given period of time
> **gross domestic product (GDP) per head** the market value of all final goods and services produced within a country in a given period of time divided by the population of a country to give a per capita figure

One of the main factors influencing the rate at which an economy grows over time is productivity. **Productivity** is the amount of goods and services produced from each hour of a worker's or another factor of production's time. In nations where workers or other factors can produce a large quantity of goods and services per unit of time, people tend to enjoy a high standard of living; in nations where workers or other factors are less productive, people tend to endure a more meagre existence. Similarly, the growth rate of a nation's productivity determines the growth rate of its average income. Productivity is not only important to a country's well-being but is also vital to that of businesses.

> **productivity** the quantity of goods and services produced from each hour of a worker, or other factor of production's, time

The relationship between productivity and living standards has profound implications for public policy. When thinking about how any policy will affect living standards, the key question is how it will affect a country's ability to produce goods and services. To boost living standards, policy makers need to raise productivity by ensuring that workers are well educated, have the tools needed to produce goods and services, and have access to the best available technology. These policies are important in providing the resource infrastructure that businesses need to be able to thrive. Without well-educated workers with high levels of employability skills, business costs would be higher because they would have to pay to train workers in these skills themselves. Without an adequate transport and communications network, business activity is hampered and again costs are higher and productivity lower.

SUMMARY

- The fundamental lessons about individual decision making are that people and businesses face trade-offs among alternative goals, that the cost of any action is measured in terms of foregone opportunities, that rational people and businesses make decisions by comparing marginal costs and marginal benefits, and that people and businesses change their behaviour in response to the incentives they face.
- The fundamental lessons about interactions among people and businesses are that trade can be mutually beneficial, that markets are usually a good way of coordinating trade among people and businesses, and that the government can potentially improve market outcomes if there is some market failure or if the market outcome is inequitable.
- The fundamental lesson about the economy as a whole is that productivity is the ultimate source of living standards.

IN THE NEWS

The Business of Music Festivals

Music festivals are big business. Like any business they have costs and must meet those costs by generating sales that provide revenue sufficient to cover the costs and make a profit. Where those profits go may be dependent on the business aims of the organizers, but regardless, if a festival has costs higher than revenues, then it is simply not viable.

Following the Covid-19 pandemic, 2022 was the year when things were supposed to get back to some sort of normality. Lockdowns and restrictions meant that many festivals were cancelled in 2020 and 2021. In June 2022, festival goers once again poured through the gates onto Worthy Farm for the Glastonbury festival and the Reading and Leeds festivals were both sold out. However, such a success story was not the case for all festivals and there were reports than many were struggling to survive as both micro and macroeconomic factors affected them.

The festival industry is reported to be worth around £1.76 billion (€2.04 billion) to the UK economy and around 85,000 jobs are related to the industry. The post-pandemic world was expected to see a rise in demand for certain hedonistic goods and services – holidays, social events and so on, but circumstances meant that many people faced having to make careful choices about how to allocate their income. The price of a number of goods and services rose sharply and supply chain problems, partly caused by the after-effects of the pandemic and conflict in Ukraine, meant that the cost of living rose for many people. Some festival organizers saw a drop-off in demand for tickets and with the cost of staging festivals rising some became commercially unviable and had to be cancelled. Cost pressures arose from shortages of raw materials such as wood and steel to build the stages and facilities that form the backbone of festivals, the cost of fuel increased affecting transport costs and some festivals say they experienced challenges in recruiting labour to help set up and stage their festivals. Some estimates put the increase in costs at around 30 per cent.

In addition to the challenges of staging an event, there have also been criticism of artists, especially those that are the bigger draws at such events, who have sought to make up for lost incomes during lockdowns by charging higher fees. There have been calls for artists and their agents to moderate their fees to help festivals remain viable. There is a question around what drives ticket sales; artists may argue that they are the ones that drive ticket sales, but equally, festival organizers argue they provide the outlet for artists and provide them with considerable revenues.

It may also be the case that the festival market has outgrown itself. The popularity of major festivals like Glastonbury has seen the growth of this type of entertainment, and most weekends during the late spring and summer will see some festival or other taking place at a number of venues around the UK and also across Europe. Artists may travel around these different festivals, but ultimately, are there sufficient customers willing and able to pay to go to all of these events? According to some in the industry, that is clearly not the case and they fear for the future of the industry.

Festivals have become more popular in recent years but not all are guaranteed to be successful and financially viable.

(Continued)

Questions

1 **Explain why the staging of a music festival can be described as a business. Are such businesses part of the public sector or the private sector?**

2 **Imagine a festival organizer is looking at artists to headline their event. What trade-offs might they have to consider in their decision making over who to book?**

3 **How is the concept of opportunity cost related to the decisions people make about going to a festival given the economic climate that existed in 2022?**

4 **Given the value of the festival industry and its impact on the economy as a whole, should government be more involved in supporting the industry? Explain your reasoning.**

5 **What might be the business arguments of asking artists and their agents to lower their fees, and how do these arguments highlight some of the key issues facing businesses in general?**

References: https://accessaa.co.uk/artist-fees-the-elephant-in-the-room/ (accessed 6 June 2023).
www.theguardian.com/music/2022/jun/04/uk-summer-music-festivals-forced-to-close-as-cost-of-living-crisis-hits-home (accessed 6 June 2023).

QUESTIONS FOR REVIEW

1 Give three examples of trade-offs that a business manufacturing washing machines might have to face.

2 What is the opportunity cost to a business of purchasing a new IT system to manage its accounting at a cost of €55,000?

3 A business in the construction industry is considering investing in building ten new houses on the edge of a small town. How might it use thinking at the margin to make a decision whether to go ahead with the investment?

4 Why should policy makers think about incentives?

5 If trade is beneficial, why do some countries seek to put up barriers to trade?

6 Why might trade among countries have some winners but also some losers?

7 What is it claimed the 'invisible hand' of the marketplace does?

8 Explain the two main causes of market failure and give an example of each.

9 How can an increase in productivity reduce business costs?

10 Why is an increase in productivity important in helping to improve the standard of living in a country?

PROBLEMS AND APPLICATIONS

1 Describe some of the trade-offs faced by each of the following:

a. An entrepreneur starting a small business deciding to borrow some start-up capital from a bank or raise the funds through borrowing from friends and relations.

b. A member of the government deciding how much to spend on some new military hardware for the defence industry.

c. A CEO deciding whether to invest in a new more efficient heating system for the company's headquarters.

d. A worker in a hotel deciding whether to accept the offer by their manager of extra shifts in the restaurant.

2 You work in a bank and were planning to spend Saturday going to watch your local football team with some friends. However, your boss has asked you if you would help prepare some important financial data for some new regulations that are being introduced by the government. It is not compulsory to come in over the weekend but it is made clear it would be looked upon favourably.

a. If you decide to go to the football match, what is the true cost to you of that decision?

b. If you decide to go into work for the weekend to help out your boss, what is the true cost of that decision?

3 A business operated by a sole trader generates €20,000 in profits and has the option of retaining the amount to reinvest into the business or putting the sum into a bank which would generate 2 per cent interest a year. What would your decision be, why, and what is the opportunity cost of your decision?

4 A smartphone manufacturer has invested €20 million in developing a new phone design and interface, but the development is not quite finished. At a recent meeting, your sales people report that a rival has just released a new phone which is estimated to reduce the expected sales of your new product to €12 million. If it would cost €4 million to finish development and make the product, should you go ahead and do so? What is the most that you should pay to complete development? Explain your answer.

5 Three members of the operations management team at a plant manufacturing steel tubing for construction projects are discussing a possible increase in production. Each suggests a way to make this decision.

   a. Team member 1: We should base the decision on whether labour productivity would rise if we increased output.
   b. Team member 2: We need to focus more on cutting our average cost per tube. This will help us to be more competitive against our rivals.
   c. Team member 3: We should only increase output if the extra revenue from selling the additional tubes would be greater than the extra costs.

   Who do you think is right? Why?

6 The Covid-19 pandemic caused a significant disruption to economies across the world and impacted millions of people. Does this experience mean that governments should take a more active role in managing economic activity?

7 Suppose the EU adopted central planning for its economy, and you became the chief planner. Among the millions of decisions that you need to make for next year are: how much food to produce, what land to use, who should receive the food produced and in what quantities.

   a. To make these decisions intelligently, what information would you need about the food industry?
   b. What information would you need about each of the people in the countries making up the EU?
   c. How would your decisions about food affect some of your other decisions, such as how much farm equipment to produce, how much labour to employ on farms and how much fertilizer to use? How might some of your other decisions about the economy change your views about food?

8 Explain whether each of the following government activities is motivated by a concern about equity or a concern about efficiency. In the case of efficiency, discuss the type of market failure involved.

   a. Regulating gas prices.
   b. Regulating advertising.
   c. Providing students with vouchers that can be used to buy university education.

9 Discuss each of the following statements from the standpoints of equity and efficiency.

   a. 'All students should have free access to higher education.'
   b. 'Businesses making workers redundant should be made to provide at least six months' pay as a redundancy payment to enable those affected time to find a new job.'
   c. 'Businesses should be made to pay more into workers' pension schemes to ensure that people have a decent standard of living when they retire.'

10 Countries have to address the fundamental economic questions and in doing so most have a role for the public sector and a role for the private sector. In some countries the public sector plays a larger role in determining what is produced, how it is produced and who gets what is produced.

   a. How do you think the extent of the division between the role the public sector and the private sector plays has come about?
   b. What role might belief systems play in determining the division?
   c. Do you think business operates more effectively under private ownership than public ownership? Justify your reasoning.

2 ECONOMICS AND BUSINESS DECISION MAKING

LEARNING OUTCOMES

After reading this chapter you should be able to:

- Give examples of unconscious and conscious decisions by consumers and businesses.
- Explain the basic economic problem of scarce resources and unlimited wants.
- Give examples about how informed decision making can be based on assumptions about weighing up the value of costs and benefits.
- State at least two examples of the difficulties businesses face in accurately valuing costs and benefits.
- Explain the importance to businesses of decisions on investment, growth and expansion, using appropriate examples.
- Show why acquiring and keeping customers are important decisions for a business.
- Give an example to show how making decisions on keeping customers needs to be assessed carefully.

ECONOMICS: THE SCIENCE (OR ART) OF DECISION MAKING

In every walk of life humans have to make decisions. In business, this is no different. Every day millions of people working in businesses at many different levels make decisions. Decisions arise because there is a choice of different actions. A business might have to make a decision about whether and how far to change price, whether to invest in new technology, hire or release workers, spend money on an advertising campaign and so on. In each case, it will have to weigh up the costs and benefits of making the decision and in doing so consider other possible options as part of the decision making process. These decisions between alternatives arise because resources are usually scarce relative to the demand. This is the heart of the economic problem.

The Economic Problem: Scarce Resources and Unlimited Wants and Needs

The central economic problem is one of scarce resources for unlimited wants and needs. The Earth is blessed with resources of all kinds: some we know about and some we still do not know exist. Oil, metals, land, minerals, plants, animals and so on all provide humans with the means to satisfy our needs; the essentials of life such as food, water, clothing and shelter, without which it would be difficult to survive, and our wants, all the things we would like to have which we believe make our lives more comfortable and happy.

However, these resources are scarce. By scarce resources we mean that they are insufficient in quantity relative to the demand for them. Few businesses have so much money that they can afford to satisfy all their wants and needs. As a result, businesses have to make decisions about how they allocate income and scarce resources to different uses.

 WHAT IF... you are living inside the Arctic Circle and are having some guests round to your house for a party. You go to a store which is selling packaged ice cubes in its freezer. Would you buy them? If so why and if not, why not?

When consumers choose between buying one product or another they undertake both conscious and subconscious processing. Understanding how consumers behave is important for businesses. Economists attempt to model decision making behaviour and in building these models have to make assumptions. One such assumption is that humans weigh up the value of the costs and benefits of a decision. If the value of the benefits of a decision is greater than the value of the costs, then this can be a reasonable basis on which to make a purchasing decision.

This assumption of rational behaviour, that is individuals and businesses doing the best they can given their circumstances, may be relevant in many cases; it could be argued that businesses in particular have developed sophisticated ways of making rational decisions by identifying and quantifying costs and benefits to help them make decisions. Management accounting techniques, in particular, have been developed with the primary intention of assisting in decision making. Since the early 1990s, advances in technology and research in the field of neuroscience and psychology have opened up new information as to how and why humans make decisions. The developments in the analysis of 'big data' is also revealing consumer behavioural traits and habits in increasingly sophisticated ways. This information is being used by businesses to help understand consumer behaviour and this can help in the design and development of new products as well as in the way in which existing products are marketed.

The Effect of Human Decision Making on Businesses

When consumers go to the supermarket, many will fill up the shopping trolley with similar products to those purchased on the last visit, almost on autopilot. Some might be tempted by the end-of-aisle or point-of-sale offers that seek to persuade consumers to give up hard earned cash in order to acquire the good in question, but this involves a little bit more mental computation than simply buying on autopilot. Does the consumer really need (or want) the item concerned and does the amount of money being asked for the product (the price) represent value for money; in other words, will buying the product bring adequate benefits? Every time an individual makes a decision about the purchase of a product it has an effect on a business.

Consider the following example.

A new student walks into a university bookshop and looks at the copy of Mankiw, Taylor and Ashwin, which has been recommended by their lecturer. The student looks at the book, thinks it looks impressive but when they look at the price they think it is a little high. Giving up €60 at that moment in time makes them think twice. They think about the freshers' welcome party for new members of the sports team which they are planning on going to, not to mention the freshers' ball at the end of the week. They put the book back on the shelf and decide they will try their luck in the library instead.

The effect of this decision is that the bookshop will not receive €60 from the sale of the book. This is just another in a long line of decisions being made by students which has seen sales at the bookshop declining. At the end of the month the bookshop returns the unsold stock back to the publisher, Cengage Learning. The publisher has to adjust its inventories (stocks) and now has more stock of the book than it had anticipated. The bookshop may find that if it cannot encourage more students to use its facilities rather than spending their money on other things, or even buying their books second hand or online, then it may not be able to cover the costs of stock, staffing, lighting and heating, administrative costs and rent for the premises. It may have to close down as a result. Indeed, this story is a familiar one for campus bookshops, many of which have now closed down.

For the publisher, the increase in stock means that it will not have to reprint the book at the time it planned to do so. The printing company finds that the reprint order it was expecting does not arrive and as a result it cuts back on the amount of paper and ink it orders from its suppliers. For paper manufacturers the fall in the order for paper means that they now do not need to hire as many workers and so some workers are made redundant.

These workers find their incomes are now much lower and so have to cut back on the family spending. They used to eat out at least once every two weeks but now decide they have to cut that out altogether. The restaurant where they used to eat notices a drop in the number of people walking through the door to eat and so does not need to order as many supplies of ingredients as previously…

And so on.

The simple decision by the student on its own may not seem to be that important, but the combined effect of millions of decisions made every day by millions of people around the world does have significant effects on businesses. These decisions are important in other ways too.

Value for Money

A decision to buy this book is a message to the publisher and the authors that the book has some value. It helps with study, it makes the subject easier to understand, the support resources are helpful in getting through assessments, and ultimately the students can get the grade they are looking for. In other words, a decision to buy this book implies the buyer feels it will give value for money. We can define **value for money** as a situation where the satisfaction gained from using the book (however we choose to measure that satisfaction) is at least equal to or greater than the amount of money the individual had to hand over to acquire it (the price).

> **value for money** a situation (mostly subjective) where the satisfaction gained from purchasing and consuming a product is equal to or greater than the amount of money the individual had to hand over to acquire it (the price)

If enough students make such a decision this book will be very successful. The authors will be pleased because they will get royalties from the sale of each book and the publisher will be pleased because each sale represents revenue. If enough books are sold to more than cover the total costs of producing and selling the book, it will make a profit.

However, the decision to buy this book has an effect on other books which could have been bought for a Business Economics course. When you are in a book shop or looking at the choices on a website, choosing one book is an endorsement for the producer of that book, but what about the one you decide not to buy? If enough people make the choice to buy this book and not another, then the rival publisher may decide that its book does not have a market and declares the book out of print. The author is likely to get very few, if any, royalties and those people that worked hard to help produce the book may find their jobs in jeopardy if something similar happens to other books they are involved with.

This is why economists spend a great deal of time looking at the working of markets. A market is made up of two parties, buyers (consumers) and sellers (producers), coming together to agree on exchange. Businesses make products available and consumers make decisions about whether to buy these products. Every individual consumer decision is important in its own right, but in order to get an understanding of the market as a whole we look at the effects of the aggregation of those decisions.

Why consumers make the decisions they do is the subject of continued debate and academic research. The developments in imaging technologies have revealed in part (there is still much we do not know) how the brain functions when we make decisions. It is opening up fascinating new lines of enquiry and understanding. Neuroscience and developments in psychology are playing their part in helping economists to understand human behaviour in a variety of contexts, including how they make purchasing decisions. Behavioural economics is becoming an increasingly important branch of the discipline and is being utilized not only by academic economists but also by businesses in a bid to understand decision making and human behaviour.

BUSINESS DECISION MAKING

Businesses are also interested in how they, themselves, make decisions about a whole host of things such as who to hire, when to hire, what to invest in, what not to invest in, how to improve productivity, whether to pursue an acquisition or not, whether to conduct an advertising campaign and if so how much to spend on it and when, among others. There are stakeholder decisions that affect the business and need to be understood, for example why some employees may be less committed to their work or to the principles and values of the business. How do governments make decisions and what impact will they have on businesses? What decision making processes take place at suppliers? Are the decisions managers and owners make compatible, and if so how will these decisions affect local communities and the environment?

SELF TEST Think about a recent purchase decision you made. What were the other options you could have chosen instead? Articulate the reasons why you eventually made the decision to purchase the product you did.

There are three important areas for business where decision making has to be considered carefully.

Investment

One of the key decisions that has to be made relates to investment. **Investment**, in this context, is about a business making money available to develop a project that will generate future returns, including increasing future productive capacity. Examples of business investment might include:

- A chemical engineering firm deciding to hire a specialist chemist to work on the development of a particular process for a client.
- A tool-making firm investing in a new piece of machinery which helps make the firm more productive.
- A food manufacturing plant buying a new oven which helps improve temperature regulation of the cooking process or helps to increase the volume of ingredients being processed at any one time.
- A farmer considering whether to install a new milking parlour to replace an existing facility. The new parlour might provide the farmer with more information about the volume and quality of the milk being given by the herd, as well as automating some procedures which mean that more cows can be milked in a shorter amount of time. This might then free up the farmer to do other important jobs around the farm.
- A Chinese restaurant owner having to make a decision about which insurance company to use to renew its insurance policies to cover it for fire, theft, loss of profits, public liability (in case any customer or member of the public is injured or suffers in some way as a result of the business's actions), employers' liability (injury to employees), damage or loss to machinery and equipment and many other possible risks. Does it stick with its existing insurer who has provided good service but is quite expensive, or go with a new insurer with an unknown reputation but which is much cheaper?
- A road haulage company considering investing in a computerized monitoring system for all its fleet of vehicles which travel around Europe to help it improve its logistical planning, adherence to health and safety regulations and help improve tracking in the event of theft.

investment making money available to develop a project which will generate future returns including increasing future productive capacity

There are some key characteristics which are common to this sort of investment decision. Any decision will bring with it some costs, both financial and otherwise, and will also bring with it benefits. These benefits could be to the business itself and to those who have an interest in the business (**stakeholders**) and wider society. These costs and benefits have to be weighed up and we assume that a decision is worth taking if the value of the accrued benefits to the business outweighs the value of the total costs of the decision.

stakeholders groups or individuals with an interest in a business, such as workers, managers, suppliers, the local community, customers and owners

WHAT IF... a business values two options equally? How might it make a decision which to invest in if it can only afford one of them?

Economists would argue that in order to make any informed decision we have to have some idea of the value of the relative costs and benefits. Calculating the financial cost of building and operating a new assembly plant for a manufacturing firm, and estimating the financial benefits from the resulting expansion in production, might be relatively straightforward. What is not so easy is calculating the cost of the new plant on the ecosystem, or the damage to the visual amenity of the area around which the plant will be built. The more accurately these sorts of costs can be calculated the more informed the decision. Economists try to find effective ways of calculating costs and benefits more accurately, but ultimately there is always going to be some error term and a lack of information which will make the calculations and estimates less than perfect.

JEOPARDY PROBLEM In the UK, there is a fierce ongoing debate about the building of a new high-speed rail route connecting London with towns and cities further north. Phase one of the project from London to the West Midlands has begun, but there is still debate around subsequent phases, in particular the connections to Leeds. The decisions will affect many businesses in different ways. What factors would businesses take into account in agreeing with the decision to invest in extending HS2 to places like Derby and Leeds? How and why might other stakeholders view the decision to go ahead differently?

Growth and Expansion

At some point in time, a business will have to make a decision about growth and expansion. It could be argued that a new business start-up is as much a part of growth and expansion as a decision by a large multinational business to acquire a new business by merger or takeover.

These decisions involve considerable risk to a business. **Risk** is the extent to which a decision leading to a course of action will result in some loss, damage, adverse effect or otherwise undesirable outcome to the decision maker. One of the first questions many businesses may ask themselves when making a decision is 'What could go wrong?' and decisions relating to growth and expansion are no different.

risk the extent to which a decision leading to a course of action will result in some loss, damage, adverse effect or otherwise undesirable outcome to the decision maker

A business might grow through internal or external means. Internal growth comes from the business generating sufficient profits to be able to reinvest back into the business. This reinvestment might be in buying new premises, new plant and equipment, taking on more staff, more efficient computer systems or hiring a consultant to help identify new systems and processes of working which allow the business to sell more.

External growth by contrast is generally much quicker. A firm can grow by either taking over or merging with another business. Merger and acquisition activity (M&A) tends to fluctuate with the swings in economic activity; when the economy is growing, M&A activity tends to be higher and vice versa. There are often grand claims made by business leaders about the benefits to the business of any such external growth. The word 'synergies' is used to describe how anticipated benefits will accrue to the business. **Synergy** refers to a situation where the combination of two or more businesses or business operations brings total benefits which are greater than those that would arise from the separate business entities. The idea of 2 + 2 = 5 is often used to exemplify the principle.

synergy a situation where the combination of two or more businesses or business operations brings total benefits which are greater than those which would arise from the separate business entities

The reality tends to be less spectacular. There have been a number of very high-profile mergers and takeovers which have promised huge benefits to shareholders and customers alike which have proved to be illusory. Some estimates put the success rate of M&A at between 20 and 45 per cent. If we take the lower end of these estimates, then only one in five M&As are successful. This, of course, depends on what we mean by 'success'. If the M&A did not bring the benefits promised at the outset, then the process could be classed as not being successful, although the business might still be in a better position than it was prior to the M&A.

> **PITFALL PREVENTION** Terms such as 'success' or 'failure' are relative. This means that we have to be careful how we make judgements in relation to these terms. If a business tells its shareholders that a merger will yield a 40 per cent increase in efficiency within five years, but in the event efficiency only increases by 20 per cent, should this be classed as a failure? Always make sure that you are clear in your definition of what is meant by 'success' or 'failure' when discussing business activity.

Acquiring and Keeping Customers

For any business to survive it must have customers, whether these customers are other businesses or final consumers. Acquiring customers involves some cost: marketing, advertising, promotion, putting in place appropriate services, having the right product in the right place at the right time and ensuring that the product meets the expectations of customers in terms of quality. It will also involve making decisions about how much money should be devoted to acquiring new customers. How much budget should a new advertising or promotion campaign be given? What is the best and most efficient way in which customers can be reached and persuaded to try the business's products?

Once a business has acquired customers, there are also decisions to be made about how these customers can be retained and at what cost. What emphasis should the business put on keeping customers in relation to acquiring new ones? Should it be 80:20, 70:30, 60:40, 50:50 or some other proportion?

At what point is it appropriate to lose a customer? In principle, the answer can be given by reference to thinking at the margin. It might be worth losing a customer if the cost of retaining that customer becomes higher than the benefits that the customer brings. In other words, the revenue being generated by the customer is less than the cost of retaining that customer.

The balance between the cost of acquiring and keeping customers changes, depending in part on the wider economic environment. It is often said that it is much cheaper to keep existing customers than find new ones. The Chartered Institute of Marketing notes that the cost of acquiring a new customer depends on the industry or market sector, but that in general it is between four and ten times the cost of keeping an existing one. There are a number of factors that can affect the cost of both these things, including the rate at which new competitors enter the industry, the extent to which existing competitors bring out new products and how close a substitute they are, pricing tactics being adopted and levels of customer service. The latter can be important in retaining customers and includes such things as the expectations of customers not being met, the quality of the product in terms of how easy it is to use and how resilient it is, errors in billing customers and general customer service issues like the length of time customers have to wait to speak to someone, how knowledgeable customer service operatives are, the ease of accessing technical help, and how easy a website is to navigate.

All these factors are affected to a greater and lesser extent by the decisions a firm makes. Someone in the organization, for example, makes a decision about what telephone system to use, how many people there are to staff the system, where it is located and what its perceived role is. On the basis of this decision, the company could win and lose customers. Giving customers a frustrating time at the end of a phone but at low unit cost could be false economy.

CASE STUDY   Decision Making and the Pandemic

Perhaps one of the things we take for granted is the extent of business interdependency. The Covid-19 pandemic helped to highlight the importance of this interdependency. When governments across Europe introduced lockdowns to try to control the spread of the virus, many coffee shops and sandwich bars suffered. Decisions around where to locate these types of businesses are often dependent on the availability of customers, so it is no surprise to see such businesses located in and around busy town and city centre areas. Many rely on office workers and the travelling public for their business. The existence of other businesses and how they operate, therefore, is an essential prerequisite for other businesses. Coffee shops, for example, might rely on workers commuting to their offices and places of work for passing trade. Once lockdown happened, many found their revenues dried up. The British Coffee Association, for example, noted that revenue from sales fell from around £363 million in March 2020 to £51 million in April of that year. A Covid-19 impact study by the World Coffee Portal suggested that 87 per cent of coffee shop operators interviewed said that the pandemic negatively impacted their business and 72 per cent believed that changes in consumer behaviour as a result of the pandemic will impact their business in some way. Sandwich shops fared little better. Sales prior to the pandemic were estimated at around £7.85 billion a year but estimates suggest sales fell by around 60 per cent in 2020 compared to equivalent periods in 2019.

Some sandwich bars and coffee shops are one and the same thing and many are small, independent businesses. Some of the larger branded coffee shops may have been in a better position to cope with the effects of the pandemic and some were able to move some of their business online. This was partly designed to take advantage of the decision by consumers to purchase coffee making machines for the home and thus required supplies of coffee beans, ground coffee and pods. Some retailers offered a delivery service, and some sought to retain customers through a subscription service – pay a monthly subscription and get access to a certain number of drinks each day.

As lockdowns ended and life began to return to some sort of normality, many coffee shops and sandwich bars may have been hoping for customers and sales to return. This has not always been the case, however. Many businesses have changed their working practices following the pandemic and an increasing number

of people now work from home permanently or have far greater flexibility as to when they go into the office. This will undoubtedly have an effect on retailers, not just coffee shops and sandwich bars but other businesses that rely on footfall through towns and cities for their business. In September 2022, the cake and pastries retailer Patisserie Valerie announced that it was closing nine sites across the UK, including sites in Belfast, Victoria Station in London, Windsor, Dundee, Glasgow, Eastbourne and Exeter because the sites had not been able to recover sufficiently from the pandemic. In 2017, Patisserie Valerie had almost 200 sites; by 2023 this had fallen to just 30. Some businesses did not survive the pandemic and some have had to think very hard about how they structure and run their business post-pandemic.

Many businesses rely on others for their business and the pandemic highlighted the extent of business interdependency.

Questions

1 What do you understand by the term 'business interdependency' and why is it important for the potential success or failure of a business (you might also want to include a clear definition about what you mean by 'success' and 'failure' in this context).

2 How do the decisions made by businesses post-pandemic about how to organize their operations highlight the importance of human decision making on business?

3 Consider some of the strategies being used by coffee shops and sandwich bars to capture and retain customers outlined in the article and consider the possible factors they may be taking into account when making decisions around these strategies.

References: https://britishcoffeeassociation.org/covids-impact-on-coffee-sales/ (accessed 6 June 2023).
www.wired.co.uk/article/coronavirus-sad-sandwich (accessed 6 June 2023).
www.worldcoffeeportal.com/Latest/InsightAnalysis/2020/UK-coffee-shops-The-Coronavirus-Impact-Study (accessed 6 June 2023).
www.bighospitality.co.uk/Article/2022/09/02/patisserie-valerie-to-close-nine-sites (accessed 6 June 2023).
www.mylondon.news/whats-on/food-drink-news/starbucks-costa-pret-manger-pure-20247635 (accessed 6 June 2023).

> **SELF TEST** What factors might a business have to consider in making a decision to outsource customer service operations to a low labour cost economy?

CONCLUSION

Economics can be seen as being a science of decision making. Because we are all affected in some way by scarce resources and unlimited wants and needs, we have to allocate resources to different uses and thus make choices. In making these choices we have to make decisions. There are increasingly more sophisticated ways of looking at how individuals and businesses make decisions, but in order to analyze how economies work we make basic assumptions about behaviour. In making these assumptions we can then observe deviations and seek to develop more sophisticated models to understand why, which lead to better theories to help make predictions.

Every individual consumer decision is important in its own right because that decision sends messages to a business about how the consumer values the products on offer. A decision to purchase can be taken as a positive message while a decision to purchase another product is a message that somehow the rival product is more valuable to the consumer for some reason. This collective individual decision making has major effects on the extent to which businesses are successful or not.

Businesses have to understand these reasons in order to improve their offering. In responding to changes or to the messages they receive from consumers, businesses also make decisions every day. These decisions can range from seemingly mundane ones such as whether to order reams of paper from one supplier or another, right through to major decisions on new plant and equipment or whether to acquire another business to help meet consumer needs more effectively. Each is important in its own right.

We can look at business decision making in three main areas: decisions on investment in new productive capacity, on growth and expansion, and on acquiring and keeping customers. Collectively these decisions are related and will have knock-on effects on other decisions businesses have to make. For example, if a decision is taken to introduce an enterprise resource planning (ERP) system (a system that brings together management information from inside and outside the business to the whole organization, which helps improve flows of information within the business), this might then lead to decisions having to be taken on hiring new staff, maybe reducing staffing in some areas, decisions on training needs and how to manage some of the disruption that will occur during transition.

We work on the basic assumption that businesses will weigh up the costs and benefits of a decision, attempting to quantify as far as possible these costs and benefits, and then making a decision based on the assessment of the value of the benefits in relation to the value of the costs. One of the problems businesses face in making decisions based on this principle is accurately valuing all the costs and benefits.

SUMMARY

- Decision making is at the heart of economics.
- Millions of decisions are made every day by businesses and consumers and these decisions affect businesses in different ways.
- Businesses have to make decisions focused on three main areas:
  - investment
  - growth and expansion
  - acquiring and keeping customers.
- Assessing the value of the costs and benefits is a basis for making decisions.
- If the value of the benefits is greater than the value of the costs, then the decision can be justified.
- It is not always easy to quantify the value of all the costs and benefits in making a decision.
- Neuroscience and psychology are revealing new ways in which people and businesses make decisions which may not always reflect a rational decision based on the value of costs and benefits.

IN THE NEWS

Mergers

Mergers and acquisitions (M&A) are often touted as being the source of improved business performance, increased efficiency, better quality products, increased customer experience and, of course, more profits for the merged organization's owners and shareholders. These were some of the advantages put forward by publishers Cengage Learning and McGraw-Hill when they announced plans to merge in 2019. Both are global operators producing textbooks, digital products and other educational resources. According to Statista, Cengage's global revenue in 2021 was around $1.24 billion (£1.03 billion, €1.21 billion) and McGraw-Hill's, around $1.54 billion (£1.28 billion, €1.50 billion). The merged entity would have accounted for around 45 per cent of the market. Merging two such large organizations always carried risks not just in terms of whether the two companies could work together and whether the merger would result in synergies but also in arousing the concerns of competition authorities and other stakeholder groups opposed to the dominance of large publishers.

Both companies invested large sums of money in planning for how the merged entity would look and operate post-merger and also in providing information to the relevant competition authorities around the world. Around one year after the initial announcement of the plans to merge, the two companies issued a statement in May 2020 saying that they had agreed to call off the merger. Investigations into the merger by the Department of Justice in the United States, the Competition and Markets Authority in the UK, and regulatory authorities in Australia and New Zealand raised concerns about the market power of the merged entity. It was reported that Cengage and McGraw-Hill had been requested to divest assets to avoid compromising competition in the industry. According to sources from the two companies, the amount of the assets to be sold off was too great and would have impacted on the economic viability of the merged entity. There were also consumer groups that opposed the merger and had campaigned against it arguing that the merger would reduce competition and lead to students having to pay higher prices. Both Cengage and McGraw-Hill had argued strongly that this would not be the case and that students would benefit from the merger.

Mergers are not always successful and there are numerous challenges to overcome.

Questions

1 Explain how and why mergers and/or acquisitions can result in improved performance for the resulting entity.
2 How do you think the proponents of the proposed merger between the two companies estimated and assessed the costs and benefits of the merger?
3 What do you think was the major reason for the proposed merger – growth and expansion or acquiring and keeping customers?
4 The cost of textbooks in the United States can be in excess of $300 in some cases and across the UK and Europe a textbook for a first-year undergraduate module can be anything up to £100. How would you, as a student, assess the value for money provided by textbooks from publishers like Cengage and McGraw-Hill?
5 Given the relative sizes of Cengage and McGraw-Hill, do you think that the risk that the proposed merger would be blocked in some way by regulators should have been more obvious and taken into consideration by the leaders of the respective organizations?

References: www.insidehighered.com/news/2020/05/05/cengage-and-mcgraw-hill-cancel-merger-plans (accessed 6 June 2023).
www.statista.com/statistics/801199/cengage-revenue/ (accessed 6 June 2023).
www.statista.com/statistics/800771/mcgraw-hill-education-revenue/ (accessed 6 June 2023).
https://sparcopen.org/news/2019/qa-cengage-mcgraw-hill-merger/ (accessed 6 June 2023).

QUESTIONS FOR REVIEW

1 Explain the difference between a conscious and a subconscious purchasing decision. Which do you think is more reliable and why?

2 Oil is a commodity and there are billions of barrels still waiting to be exploited. Why, then, do we refer to oil as a scarce resource?

3 Using some specific examples, explain the difference between wants and needs.

4 Explain what economists mean by 'making an informed, rational decision'.

5 Explain how a decision by a student to take a bus to a guest lecture by a famous economist at a nearby town hall, rather than a taxi, affects both transport businesses.

6 You buy a new t-shirt from Hollister and have to pay €25 for it. How would you measure the value for money of this t-shirt?

7 Why is it difficult to accurately assess the costs and benefits of a decision such as whether to grant permission to a leisure business to open a new theme park on the outskirts of a town?

8 What is risk in the context of decision making by a business?

9 Why do you think the cost to businesses of acquiring customers is generally much higher than retaining them?

10 Using an appropriate example, outline three factors which could lead to an increase in the cost of keeping customers.

PROBLEMS AND APPLICATIONS

1 When you go into a shop to buy a product, how often do you make decisions based on conscious and subconscious factors?

2 You have to arrange a flight from Amsterdam to Rome and look at a travel website for the choices available to you. List the range of factors you will want to consider in making your choice about which airline to choose to make the flight. To what extent is the decision you arrive at 'rational'?

3 Food is essential for human life. Does this mean that all food items should be classed as 'needs' and not 'wants'?

4 A customer of a mobile phone network contacts the provider to explain that they are changing to another provider. To what extent should the provider be concerned about this decision by the customer? Explain your answer.

5 Two student friends attend a gig showcasing a new band which has had rave reviews from music journalists. At the end of the evening they talk about their experience; one says they thought the band lived up to expectations and the €20 ticket was 'more than worth it'. The other thinks the evening was a 'waste of money'. Give some possible explanations about why each student had a different perception of value for money in this instance.

6 Some business leaders put faith in 'gut instinct' in making decisions. To what extent would you advise basing decisions on gut instincts rather than 'rational' analysis?

7 Explain how investment in new productive capacity can help a business grow internally.

8 Evaluate the case for a builders' merchant spending more money on retaining its existing customers rather than acquiring new ones.

9 A business calculates that the cost of acquiring a new customer is €250 and the average yearly revenue received from each customer is €260. Should the business go ahead with its customer acquisition spending on this basis? Explain using concepts covered in this chapter.

10 'There is a science to decision making and a business should take notice of this science in helping to make its own decisions.' To what extent do you agree with this statement?

3 THE BUSINESS ENVIRONMENT

THE TRANSFORMATION PROCESS

Decision making will be a recurring theme throughout our journey into Business Economics. Successful business is all about making decisions that help meet aims and objectives, and, as we have seen, economics can be seen as being a 'science' of decision making. We have seen how business activity involves taking a series of inputs and producing an output. The business might provide the output (goods and services) to someone who consumes the good or service (the final consumer). This is referred to as **B2C business**. **B2B business** is the term used when businesses sell goods or services to another business who is termed a 'customer', who may either act as an intermediary in getting goods and services to the final consumer, or who will do something to those goods and services before selling them on to a final consumer.

> **B2C business** business activity where the business sells goods and services to a final consumer
> **B2B business** business activity where the business sells goods and services to another business

In recent years there are also other forms of activity that could be classed as business activity where consumers interact with other consumers via social networking sites or specialist websites such as eBay, Amazon Marketplace, eBid, uBid and Overstock, which facilitate this type of trade. This is referred to as **C2C business**.

> **C2C business** business activity where consumers exchange goods and services, often facilitated by a third party such as an online auction site

PITFALL PREVENTION The term 'business' in a question is generic. When considering answers to questions be sure to specify what type of business you are referring to so that you contextualize your answers and show some awareness that different businesses may be affected in different ways.

Factors of Production

A common feature that characterizes business activity is the **transformation process**. Any business must utilize inputs, referred to as **factors of production**, and do something with them to produce an output, a semi-finished product or commodity (raw materials such as rubber, cocoa, coffee, wheat, tin, ores, etc.), which is then sold on to another business for producing a finished product which is sold to a consumer. It is also important to consider that many businesses provide a service which equally involves a transformation process but may use different combinations of factors of production from manufacturing organizations.

> **transformation process** the process in which businesses take factor inputs and process them to produce outputs which are then sold
> **factors of production** a classification of inputs used in business activity which includes land, labour, capital and enterprise

Economists classify these factors of production in four main ways, although there are some that argue for only three factors of production. The four are land, labour, capital and enterprise. Some class enterprise as a specialist form of labour, but we will assume it is a separate factor of production. We will look at the role of entrepreneurs in more detail later in our journey.

Land **Land** is a term that includes all the natural resources of the Earth, and so might not only include pieces of land on which factories or offices are built, or which is farmed, but also things such as fish in the sea, minerals and ores from the ground, and so on.

> **land** all the natural resources of the Earth which can be used in production

Labour **Labour** is all the physical and mental effort provided by humans in production. This includes human activity ranging from the work of a chief executive officer (CEO) at the head of a large public company right through to the person who cleans the toilets.

> **labour** all the human effort, mental and physical, which is used in production

Capital In everyday language we use the term **capital** to refer to money. Economists use the term capital in a different way, although the two are linked. Capital refers to anything that is not used for its own sake but which contributes to production. This might include equipment and machinery, buildings, offices, shops, computers, mainframes, desks, chairs, etc. Of course to get capital, businesses need money, but economists view money as a medium of exchange and so it is often more informative to look at the opportunity cost, which can tell us a great deal about the relative values that businesses put on decision making.

> **capital** any item used in production which is not used for its own sake but for what it contributes to production

---

SELF TEST Choose one good or service and write down some specific examples of the three factors of production covered so far which are used in the production of the good or service chosen.

Enterprise Factors of production like land, labour and capital need organizing before they combine to produce outputs. Iron ore in the ground is useless until someone organizes the labour and capital to extract it and process it ready for another business to use in many different ways. A chemical company will not discover new processes unless humans combine with land and capital to work out what these processes might be and design them so that they are cost effective and viable. As individuals, we would have problems cutting and styling our own hair unless someone with the necessary skill brings together the factors of production to enable us to sit and watch as our hair is transformed. This requires land for the salon building, equipment such as sinks, taps, chairs, scissors, dryers, colourings, chemicals, etc., not to mention someone or a group of people taking the risk of setting up the business in the first place.

This is the factor of **enterprise**. Entrepreneurs take the risk of organizing factors of production to generate business activity, and in return hope to get a number of rewards which might include profit but might also be less obvious things such as self-satisfaction, a social objective, personal challenge and the desire to take more control over their life.

enterprise the act of taking risks in the organization of factors of production to generate business activity

We might often think of entrepreneurs as being exceptional individuals who have seemingly become incredibly successful and very wealthy. The names usually quoted in the same breath as the term 'entrepreneur' include Sergey Brin and Larry Page, Richard Branson, Mark Zuckerberg, Debbie Fields, Azim Premji and Lakshmi Mittal, among others, but these tend to be extreme examples. The reality is that the world is full of millions of people being entrepreneurial. They might include an individual who has set themselves up in business as a painter and decorator, an electrician, builder, plumber, florist, carpet fitter, a child in a poverty-stricken area of India making some money out of recycling rubbish in some way, a farmer running a dairy herd, a financial advisor, tyre fitter and many other examples.

The skills necessary to be an entrepreneur are well documented, but the extent to which individuals possess and utilize these skills varies in each case. The reasons why some entrepreneurs go on to make millions while others struggle to barely make a living is not simply to do with the degree of determination, initiative, planning, access to finance, asking the right questions, acting on hunches, taking risks, being willing to work hard and make things happen, thinking ahead and thinking creatively; it is also to do with being in the right place at the right time and having a large degree of luck.

Entrepreneurs take risks and many of them fail: the rate of business failure in the three to five years after start-up is estimated to be around 30 per cent, although getting precise data is difficult because we must be careful how we define 'business failure'. It is clear that a business fails if it has to file for insolvency or, in the case of a sole trader, bankruptcy, but if the owner sells on the business after a few years because they do not feel they are getting enough of a return, is that also an example of failure?

 WHAT IF... the number of business failures rises above 50 per cent, would this mean that it is not worth taking the risks to start up a new business?

Setting up a new business is challenging. Potentially high failure rates do not put off millions of people around the world from starting businesses and many will try again after (sometimes many) failures in the hope that lessons have been learned and the next time will see things work. The skills and qualities of entrepreneurs are many, but perhaps the most important is the willingness to take risks. This is one reason why some economists prefer to class enterprise as a factor of production in its own right rather than seeing it as just another form of labour.

Business activity is about bringing factors of production together to generate a product which is then sold. It is essentially a transformation process, therefore, with some types of business activity being very much more complex and risky than others. This is one reason why prices might be higher for some products compared to others and why some types of labour generate more income than do others.

Adding Value

How these factors are brought together, in what proportions and how they work together in the transformation process, could be very different, even in the same type of business operating in the same industry. Rarely are two firms producing cars or chemicals the same, although they may have many similarities. One of the key elements of the transformation process is adding value and this could be at any stage in this process.

Added value is what a business does to inputs to convert them to outputs which customers (businesses or final consumers) are prepared to pay for. Adding value could be in the form of a piece of technology that makes a consumer's life much easier in some way, or does the job the product is designed for more effectively or more stylishly than other rival products on the market. It might even be that a business creates a product or service that no one has thought of before and which people are prepared to pay enough money for, and over a long enough period (often repeatedly), to enable the business to cover the costs of producing that product and to provide a sufficient return to those who own the business to persuade them to keep producing. There is a great deal of complexity that arises out of this relatively simple statement but it is at the heart of what business activity is about and how a business can survive. If it cannot add value, then the business will ultimately fail.

> **added value** the difference between the cost of factor inputs into production and the amount consumers are prepared to pay (the value placed on the product by consumers)

Some products will fail because they do not meet market needs. There are not enough people willing to pay a price which is sufficient to cover the costs of production and provide the return. The entrepreneur may have thought there was a market, and while there invariably are some people who will buy the product, the key is whether there are *enough* people or businesses willing to pay for the product over time.

In other cases, a perfectly good product which has a market will fail because some other business comes along and offers a product which does something more, and better. It could be that the product may fail because times have changed and there is simply no need for that product any more. Business activity is dynamic.

The transition in mobile phone technology is an excellent example of this dynamic process. The very idea of having a phone that can be used anywhere is relatively new, perhaps only since the early 1990s, but the changes over that period in what these products look like, their size and what they can do, have been significant. Initially, merely being able to contact and speak to another person away from the house was a major step forwards.

Then being able to send short messages was seen as revolutionary. After that, combining a mobile phone with a device that could access the internet was a goal of businesses in this industry, but very quickly it became not only accessing the internet but being able to send emails, record and transmit videos, watch TV, play music, record voices, download and read books, act as a calculator, a personal messaging system, diary, satellite navigation system and so on, which have all become part of our mobile phone, to the extent that in many cases making phone calls represents only a fraction of their overall use. It is difficult to imagine the many hours of development and technological change that have led us to the situation we are currently at with mobile phones, and it is probably even harder for us to imagine what these devices might be like in 10 years' time. However, the point is that somebody has sat and thought about these things; they have asked what else could the technology allow us to do, what new technologies do we need to enable us to provide some even more wonderful things in the future? What sort of things do people want from these devices and perhaps, equally important, what do they not want?

There were probably many different cases of products, phones and technologies that never actually made it past the design or market research stage. Many ideas probably never worked, but businesses in the industry took risks, marshalled the factors of production and made the transformations necessary to create a dynamic process. Competition has led to new products and new technologies which we are prepared to pay for and that we presumably think improve our lives (although there are always going to be disadvantages). If the advantages or benefits outweigh the disadvantages or costs, then we tend to buy them and businesses will produce products as a result.

CASE STUDY   A Complex Transformation Process

It is entirely possible that you might be reading this case study on a computer device of some kind, perhaps a laptop, a smartphone, tablet, etc. One of the key elements of these technologies is the silicon chip. Intel is one of the largest chip makers in the world and the following case gives some indication as to the complexity of the transformation process.

One of the main inputs is sand, which includes large amounts of silicon. The silicon is purified by being melted and then cooled into an ingot, a cylindrical shape around 300 mm in diameter weighing 100 kg. This process is undertaken in Japan by companies such as Toshiba Ceramics. Other companies then take these ingots and slice them into thin wafers around 1 mm thick. Each wafer is then polished and Intel buys them in this state ready for manufacturing at its plants in Arizona and Oregon in the United States.

At these plants (called 'fabs'), which, incidentally, are identical in design and building orientation, the wafers are etched with integrated circuits which build layers and are the result of hundreds of individual processes. Once these processes are complete the wafers are then shipped to Intel's assembly and test plants in Malaysia. Here the wafers are tested and then sliced into pieces called dies and tested again to ensure they work. Those that do not pass this test are discarded, and the ones that do are packaged and sent back to warehouses in Arizona. At this stage the packaging is anonymous so that it is not clear that they are from Intel, to help reduce the risk of theft in transportation. From the warehouses in Arizona the chips are then shipped to computer manufacturing plants across the world and to different

manufacturers. The plants can be in Brazil, Taiwan, China, Malaysia, Ireland and other parts of the United States such as Texas and Tennessee, depending on the manufacturer. Once the chips are put into the device this may then be shipped either to a retail outlet or direct to the customer. The humble chip in your device is likely to have travelled thousands of kilometres during its production process as it is transformed from sand into an extremely sophisticated electronic component capable of helping process millions of operations in a short amount of time.

Many technology products travel many thousands of kilometres around the world before getting into the consumer's hands.

Questions

1 **Comment on the manufacture of silicon chips from the perspective of the transformation process outlined in the chapter so far.**

2 **Illustrate how the production of silicon chips illustrates the concept of added value.**

3 **The manufacture of silicon chips is carried out by large business organizations. Does this mean that there are no entrepreneurs involved in their production? Explain.**

THE PESTLE FRAMEWORK

Change will be happening all the time in any business and how it adapts to this change will be an important part of the extent to which the business is a success. In responding to change, there are some factors which the business will have some control over and others which it will not. The business can have some control over the inputs it buys and how it combines those inputs to produce its outputs. However, there are a number of external factors over which it has very little control, but to which it has to respond and react.

To help understand and analyze these external factors, a framework is used which summarizes a number of broad, sometimes highly related and interacting areas, which business has to work within. This framework is referred to as the PESTLE framework with the acronym standing for:

- political
- economic
- social
- technological
- legal
- environmental

We will take a brief look at each one in turn.

Political

Politics refers to power. Who has power, who makes decisions and how it affects individuals and business. Power can be wielded by local governments, national governments and supranational governments, where decision making or laws are made by groups or states outside national boundaries, such as the EU. In some countries power lies in the hands of a relatively small number of people, possibly linked to a royal family, tribal or religious group. In others, the military may be an important element in the way in which political authority is framed.

In most countries in the EU government is democratic, with political parties submitting themselves for election periodically. Different systems determine who forms governments, but one particular party or group of parties in coalition may have been given the power by the people to make decisions, policies and laws that affect individuals and businesses in various ways. In other countries, it is a ruling elite or the military who make decisions and establish laws, and the people in the country may have a very limited, or no say, in the political process. In still other countries, the rule of law may barely exist and in this case business activity may be very difficult to carry out.

Changes to laws, directions in policy or regulations can all affect businesses in different ways. Laws on employment, employee rights and responsibilities, health and safety, taxation, planning, trade, advertising and business governance, among many other things, all affect business and invariably raise the cost of doing business by involving the business in additional time, form filling or procedures. In some cases, laws or regulations may be passed with the aim of helping a business by giving grants or special dispensation to operate. In this case, there may also be a cost in terms of certain conditions to which the business has to adhere to get the benefit. For example, there may be a relaxation of planning regulations which mean a business can establish new premises more quickly but the *quid pro quo* (something given in return for something) is that the business must remain at the premises for a certain period of time or employ a certain number of people.

Economic

Businesses operate within an economic environment. This relates to the extent of economic activity in different 'economies', which could include a very local economy, a regional economy, a national or supranational economy or the global economy. There are also bodies which have supernational powers, the authority to act across different nations, such as the International Monetary Fund (IMF).

Economic activity, as we have seen, refers to the amount of buying and selling that takes place. This activity can be looked at within a local area, a region, a nation or on a global scale. The rate at which buying and selling takes place (or the number of transactions) varies at different time periods for different reasons as we will see in more detail in later chapters.

Businesses are affected by these fluctuations in economic activity. For example, a restaurant will be affected by decisions of people to go out for a meal, which may, in turn, be affected by how confident these people feel that they will continue to have a job in the future, whether they feel they can afford to go out, or whether they have recently lost their job. If a restaurant finds that the number of people they serve in a week is falling, then they must adjust the supplies that they purchase and this will have an effect on other businesses. Those supplying wine, soft drinks, fresh fruit and vegetables and other ingredients will be affected by falling sales.

Such an example might be characteristic of a decline in the local economy and can often happen when an area is highly dependent on a single employer who may either scale-back operations or even close down. A similar case will occur over regions and whole countries. The south of Italy, for example, suffers from a lower level of economic activity than the north, with standards of living, opportunities for employment and growth lower as a consequence. There are similar situations which occur in parts of the former East Germany and the Middle East. In the Palestinian territories, for example, economic activity is significantly affected by the ongoing political situation and this means that this region has a lower level of economic activity.

The Financial Crisis of 2007–09 had a major impact on businesses and individuals across Europe. Governments imposed policies to cut public spending and increase taxes to reduce deficits and the reliance on borrowing. Small firms complained that they found it difficult to get access to capital that was priced reasonably. Many larger firms delayed investment programmes, citing the uncertain economic climate as a key reason. In the post-pandemic world, many countries experienced supply chain challenges, and conflict in Eastern Europe resulted in accelerating inflation and higher interest rates as a result. Businesses found their costs rising and had to pass on some of these costs to customers and consumers in the form of higher prices. What we can see from this is that businesses are affected by the swings in economic activity both locally, nationally and globally. In many cases these swings might be triggered by political instability such as that witnessed in Ukraine, or by changes in interest rates, or by crises in the banking system, but the effects are magnified by the changes in confidence levels in individuals, businesses and governments.

It is possible to classify these effects as microeconomic or macroeconomic. The **microeconomic environment** refers to factors and issues that affect an individual firm operating in a particular market or industry. Changes in economic activity can affect some firms in a positive way and others in a negative way. For example, regardless of the level of economic activity, funeral directors may experience relatively stable levels of trade, although in times of economic slowdown families may choose to spend smaller amounts on funerals or choose cheaper options than they may do when the economy is performing more strongly.

microeconomic environment factors and issues that affect an individual firm operating in a particular market or industry

In times of weak economic growth retail businesses such as supermarkets may also find that while there may be changes to the type of products people buy, the volume of trade does not decline that much, meaning they are relatively insulated from declines in economic activity. Retail businesses which sell high-end products such as electronic goods or fashion items, however, may find that they are very badly hit by economic slowdown and sales may fall dramatically, while other businesses, such as second-hand shops, pawn shops or low-price discount stores, may find their business increases. These are all examples of specific businesses in particular markets.

The **macroeconomic environment** refers to the national or global economy within which the business operates. The things which can affect businesses from macroeconomic changes include variations in exchange rates, interest rates (which may be linked), policies on taxation, planning, competition and so on. Changes in these macroeconomic factors can affect the level of economic activity in the economy as a whole, and as a result impact on businesses. As exchange rates change, businesses will be affected in different ways depending on the extent to which they buy and sell products from abroad and in what proportions. Costs could rise or fall (or a combination of the two), demand could also rise or fall, and the effects can be highly complex in businesses which trade extensively across different regions of the world.

macroeconomic environment the national or global economy within which the business operates

Social

Businesses are affected by various trends, fashions, moods and changes in society. The move to improving the equality between men and women, and diversity and inclusion in the workplace, for example, has led to businesses having to adapt their processes and their attitudes to employment, the way their businesses operate and how they monitor the attitudes and behaviour of workers.

Social changes affect our attitudes to things like sustainability, recycling and the publicity which has been given to the problem of climate change and/or global warming. These issues have resulted in many businesses reporting on the extent to which they have taken steps to monitor energy use, recycling, the use of natural resources, where they source raw materials and their policies on diversity and inclusion. Building and office construction is changing to try to find ways to improve efficiency and make them 'greener'.

There are broad social changes that are also having an impact, such as the changing structure of the population. Many European and Middle Eastern economies, for example, are experiencing an ageing population with an increasing proportion of the population over the age of 65. This creates both opportunities and threats to businesses. Retirement ages may well rise in countries as governments struggle to afford state pensions and this changes employment dynamics. Businesses that offer pension support have already found that they must adjust the type of pension they offer. Final salary schemes, where the pension the employees receive is based on a proportion of their salary at retirement, have been phased out and replaced by contributory pension schemes, simply because some businesses were finding that they could not afford to sustain final salary schemes as people were living longer.

For some businesses, the ageing population provides opportunities to develop products and services which are targeted at the needs of the growing number of people who are over 65, who tend to be more affluent and who are still relatively healthy and active. The pattern of housing demand changes, with smaller homes required to take account not only of single pensioners but also the rising number of single families, which has followed rising divorce rates in many countries. Manufacturers are looking to develop vehicles which cater for the needs of older drivers through the provision of more intuitive technologies such as automatic parallel parking, sensors which mean the car can effectively 'see round corners', active safety systems which warn of potential hazards or danger ahead, voice operated functions and wi-fi capability in the car.

Other social changes such as the growth in the use of social networking sites, viral messaging and the internet have opened up opportunities but also present threats. Social media sites such as Facebook, Twitter, TikTok and Instagram provide the chance for businesses to showcase themselves and have their brand and message spread to large numbers of people very quickly and at low cost. The flipside of this is that the degree of control a business has over messaging and the reporting of the business is limited.

Employees can, sometimes innocently, compromise the business and damage the brand or reputation simply through an injudicious use of 280 characters or an ill-judged piece of behaviour, which is subsequently broadcast to millions. Many businesses, especially small and medium sized businesses, may not fully understand social networking and how to utilize it effectively, whereas larger firms may be able to employ specialists in exploiting the benefits of social networking while limiting the disadvantages in its use. The problem is that social networking tends to change more quickly than the ability of some businesses to understand it and work out how to use it most effectively.

Technological

It is tempting to think of technology as some electronic gadget, but the definition of technology is much wider. **Technology** is the use of knowledge in some way that enables individuals or businesses to have greater control over their environment. Businesses constantly think of ways in which they can employ knowledge in this way because it can help to reduce costs and improve efficiency. Technology can also help give a firm competitive advantage which is both distinctive and defensible.

technology the application or use of knowledge in some way which enables individuals or businesses to have greater control over their environment

Since the early 1970s there has been an explosion in technological developments that have provided both opportunities and threats for businesses. Developments in 'industry 4.0' technologies, which include artificial intelligence, augmented reality, machine learning, blockchain and the internet of things, will have far reaching effects on businesses in the coming years. How businesses respond to these is crucial. Technological developments can also help to provide some answers to the most pressing problems that humans face, including the effect on the environment of business activity, how to feed the human population, how to provide access to the essentials of life such as water, how to treat killer diseases, save animals and plants from extinction and tackle global poverty.

> **SELF TEST** Outline two examples where you think technology has improved our lives and two examples where you think technology has not led to an improvement in human welfare.

Legal

Laws and regulation can be national or supranational. The legal framework covers all aspects of society, and businesses must abide by these laws. A strong legal system that is respected is fundamental to the principle of good governance, and helps provide confidence in the way in which a business operates and promotes trade. As we have seen in Chapter 1, trade can be beneficial but businesses will be reluctant to trade and customers put off buying if they lack confidence. For example, customers want to know that if they buy a litre of fuel from a petrol station they do get a litre of fuel dispensed from the pump; investors need to know that the information on which they base decisions is as accurate and truthful as possible, and that if a business comes up with a new idea, process or invention that they can protect the investment in the time, money and intellectual capital that they have made. Confidence between businesses, between businesses and customers, and with a legal and regulatory framework that is adhered to by most and which builds in adequate incentives to be adhered to, is important in facilitating business activity.

Laws and regulation govern the way in which financial accounts are reported, how labour markets work, what health and safety measures businesses need to put in place, how they can describe and advertise products, what information consumers must be given, what minimum standards must be met, how much pollution a business can create and much more. While a strong and respected legal and regulatory framework provides confidence, it also comes at a cost. Businesses must pay to implement legal and regulatory requirements, and this not only means higher costs for them and possibly an effect on margins, but might also mean higher prices or more inconvenience for consumers. For example, data protection laws mean that people often get frustrated at the fact that a business will not discuss issues relating to a spouse or partner.

> **WHAT IF...** a business sees an opportunity to sell its goods into a new market in an emerging economy but a report tells them that governance and the rule of law is weak. Should the business enter that market?

Environmental

It is now rare for any business to fail to recognize the impact of its operations on the environment. This awareness may be because of a conscious policy decision to manage its operations to take account of that impact, or through being forced by law or regulation to do so. Economic growth across many countries around the world has meant that resource use is expanding and, as we saw in Chapter 1, resources are scarce in relation to demand. There is also concern about how we use resources in terms of efficiency, and how we manage the results of resource use in terms of the waste products generated and the impact on ecosystems and land use.

One of the major themes since the early 1990s has been a growing concern that the consequences of human activity could be having a negative effect on the wider ecosystem. There are plenty of studies to suggest that carbon emissions, largely produced by human activity, have been a direct cause of a gradual rise in average global temperatures, which in turn could lead to greater volatility in global weather patterns, and bring about a thawing of polar ice caps, rising sea levels and subsequent effects on those living in low-lying areas of the world. Major efforts have been made to gain global agreement on reducing carbon emissions and finding more environmentally friendly ways of producing goods, services and energy. This has not been easy to achieve. One of the reasons is that the richer countries, which have been accused of being historically responsible for these carbon emissions, are now asking for everyone to take the pain and cost of adjustment, and poorer countries are suggesting that such a move would jeopardize their efforts to grow and better provide for their people. They argue that the rich nations are the ones who caused the problems so the rich nations should be the ones who take most of the pain. To counter this, the rich nations say that there is little point in them acting to reduce emissions if the emerging nations are going to more than replace any reductions they might make several times over in the coming years as they grow rapidly. It seems that while there is some consensus that the planet does face a problem, who is responsible and how it should be tackled is less clear.

One aspect of thinking like an economist is the necessity of thinking critically, of not accepting everything you hear or read without questioning its validity and reliability. In many countries in Europe, recycling is an obvious and significant feature of everyday life. Almost every business has recycling policies and facilities, universities vie with one another to be the 'greenest' institution, households, local government and businesses are required to recycle and to meet targets set by national and supranational government.

As business economists, we need to be thinking about the costs and benefits of recycling and thus whether it makes economic sense. Not all recycling is 'good'; if the amount of resources necessary to recycle metal cans into other products was greater than the cost of producing the cans from scratch, would it be a sensible business or economic decision to do it and would it also be sensible from an environmental perspective?

Equally, we need to remember to critically examine claims from 'scientists' about carbon emissions and climate change. If businesses are going to be required to make what are quite possibly very expensive and significant decisions on resource use and allocation, are the reasons for making those decisions based on sound information? How reliable are the studies carried out into the causes and effects of rising carbon emissions? How reliable and accurate are the assumptions used in models of climate change? Does the idea of 'global average temperature' actually mean anything? Simply, businesses must ask the right questions to get the right information in order to make more informed decisions.

PITFALL PREVENTION While we classify external factors using the PESTLE framework, in analysing real business situations it is often not easy to simply classify factors affecting a business in a simple way. The factors tend to be interrelated, and cause and effect are not readily identifiable.

SHAREHOLDER VALUE AND STAKEHOLDERS

We have seen how business activity is a transformation process, but we must ask ourselves why businesses carry out this activity and for whom? We can use two concepts to provide at least part of the answer: shareholder value and stakeholders.

Let us assume that 'shareholders' is a term used to represent business owners as a whole rather than simply those people who have purchased shares in a business and become part owners in that business, because the principle is the same. Whoever runs the business on a day-to-day basis, be it managers or in smaller enterprises the owners themselves, the imperative is to seek growth in a variety of things which may include earnings and, in larger businesses, dividends and share price. Businesses must take decisions which help to increase earnings while keeping costs under control. These decisions may include what to invest in (and what not) and when to invest, as well as how much and what the perceived returns might be. If investment decisions help to generate returns over a period, then **shareholder value** will increase. Shareholder value is not simply profit; it is also the potential for the business to continue making profits over a period of time and to grow the profits.

> **shareholder value** the overall value delivered to the owners of business in the form of cash generated and the reputation and potential of the business to continue growing over time

Investment decisions can be made that will secure short-term profit growth quickly, but which might damage the future capacity of the business to compete and survive in the longer term. Poor decision making can lead to damage in lots of ways, for example signing up a celebrity to endorse products might help boost sales and earnings in the short term, but could lead to longer-term damage if the celebrity happens to get involved in something that affects the reputation of the business. A business could dispose of waste at very low cost and secure short-term profit gains, but if that method of waste disposal damages the environment then the longer-term earnings generation potential of the business could be affected in a negative way. In the two examples given, shareholder value could potentially decline in the future.

In addition to considering shareholder value, businesses increasingly take into account the fact that their operations affect a much wider group of people or individuals than simply owners. Employees, customers, managers, suppliers, the local community, government and the environment all have an interest in a business from different perspectives.

Most businesses will recognize the effect of its operations on these different stakeholders and take their, often conflicting, perspectives into account when making decisions and running the business. For example, it might be tempting for a business to source new supplies from cheaper operators in emerging economies, but in so doing it must consider how this might affect its wider stakeholders. Consumers might be supportive of such moves if it meant that prices are lower but quality is maintained. Suppliers in the domestic economy who lose contracts will be unlikely to support such a decision; some employees might be concerned about losing their jobs as a result, and the local community might have a view about the ethical and moral basis for such a decision. Managers may feel the decision is justified if it enhances their reputation for managing complex change projects, but owners/shareholders may want to be convinced that the decision really will lead to long-term as well as short-term benefits. Reconciling the often conflicting interests of stakeholders is one of the most challenging aspects of any business, and economics can help in not only identifying the potential costs and benefits but also quantifying these costs and benefits to enable more informed decision making. Many of these decisions involve trade-offs and involve various shades of grey rather than being neat, clean decisions.

CONCLUSION

In this chapter we have provided an outline of what business is and how it has to operate in an environment. We have looked at how it takes in resources and transforms them into outputs which are then sold, either to other businesses or final consumers. As part of this transformation process, businesses operate in both an internal and an external environment. The internal environment includes factors over which the business has some control. The business can, for example, take action to change its prices, get a better understanding about its customers and markets, seek cheaper raw materials, outsource parts of its operations to countries with cheaper costs, negotiate with its bankers for cheaper finance and so on.

However, the business has little control over its external environment. We classify this external environment into a number of different areas represented by the acronym PESTLE. Understanding the political, economic, social, technological, legal and environmental influences enables decision makers to be able to analyze the position of the business and devise tactics and strategies to combat them, or to put them in a better position to compete and win customers.

While we break down these factors to facilitate ease of analysis, in reality businesses have to deal with all of these factors at the same time and it is often difficult to distinguish which factor is the most significant or which need greater emphasis.

For example, a train-operating company knows that it has to invest in high quality engines and rolling stock to provide a service to its customers that is perceived as representing value for money. It may know that there is a trend for more people to use trains, but is this a social trend, an economic one or a political one? Are customers deliberately making decisions to use rail transport because they believe it is more environmentally friendly, or are they doing it because the roads are too congested? Or is it because work patterns are changing, or because people have more disposable income and can afford to travel for business and for leisure? Have governments made decisions to increase the price of fuel to try to encourage reductions in the use of fossil fuels to help reduce the impact on the environment, or have they done so to raise money in the form of higher taxes? Has this political decision driven consumers to switch to rail use?

Rail companies will also have to consider the legal and regulatory framework. Safety on the rail networks is a key element of how train operators make decisions. They know that when accidents occur the loss of life and injury can be significant. Should they aim to meet minimum legal and regulatory standards, or should they aim to go well beyond them? How much are customers prepared to pay to feel safe when they travel?

They also know that when accidents happen governments tend to tighten regulations and laws to meet increased public concerns. Any increase in legislation on safety will have microeconomic effects on the business. Costs will be higher and so fares might have to increase. Technology may be employed to improve train and network safety, but businesses will be looking at the balance between the costs of improving safety and the benefits and relative value of both.

If a train operating company invests in new, more efficient rolling stock and engines, should it buy the equipment from a local or national provider or from the supplier who offers the cheapest price for the quality it requires? How far will these sorts of decisions be influenced by political groups? Does the business have a responsibility to its domestic workers or to its supranational workers or to its shareholders? If the cheaper option also happens to be the most environmentally friendly one, should this override national employment considerations?

We can see that any decision is not going to be purely driven or influenced by one factor alone, but by a mixture of them all. If decision making was easy, then we would all be able to make the right decisions all the time. The fact that businesses ultimately must make decisions and judgements based on what might possibly be imperfect information will inevitably lead to mistakes being made and less than efficient outcomes as a result.

SUMMARY

- Business activity involves using factors of production and transforming them into products which are bought either by other businesses or final consumers.
- Business activity takes place within an environment which is both internal and external.
- Businesses have some control over the internal environment, but sometimes limited control over the external environment.
- The external environment can be looked at through the PESTLE framework: political, economic, social, technological, legal and environmental.
- Changes in the external environment can provide both opportunities and threats.
- Businesses have a responsibility to a wide range of stakeholders who have some direct or indirect interest in the business.

IN THE NEWS

The External Environment

Consider an example of a small business that set up as a hot drink and sandwich bar in 2017. The business is located in a busy street near a number of large office blocks and not far from the town's main railway station. Between 2017 and 2019, the business sought to establish itself and managed to achieve a degree of stability in terms of its revenue and costs and generate a small but encouraging profit. However, in 2020, things changed. The pandemic led to the shop having to close down as lockdown restrictions were imposed, and it was early 2022 before the owner was able

(Continued)

to fully reopen. However, they noticed that footfall was down compared to the pre-pandemic period as a number of the businesses retained a working from home policy for its staff. In February 2022, the owner read of the conflict in Ukraine and within a few months noticed that costs had risen considerably. The Office for National Statistics (ONS) reported that the average price of an 800 gram sliced white loaf rose from £1.08 in January 2022 to £1.20 in June of that year, an increase of around 11 per cent. The average price of 100 grams of instant coffee rose from £3.06 to £3.25 over the same period, a rise of just over 6 per cent. The Bank of England announced that it was forecasting inflation would reach 13 per cent by the end of 2022 and increased interest rates in August 2022 to 1.75 per cent with many analysts predicting that it would have to increase rates further to combat inflation, and indeed rates rose to 5.0 per cent by mid- 2023.

Part of the reason for the accelerating inflation was the rise in energy prices due in part to the post-pandemic increase in demand and also to the conflict in Ukraine. Gas and electricity prices rose rapidly in 2021–2022 with the ONS noting that the wholesale price of gas was around four times higher in 2022 compared to 2021. In addition to the rising costs of operating, demand fluctuated further. The rising cost of living seemed to be having an effect on people's choices and the owner noticed that fewer people were paying for coffee and sandwiches, relying instead on drinks provided by their workplace and bringing in their own lunches. Decisions by rail workers in the UK to take industrial action over pay and working conditions led to a number of days of strike action and on those days, footfall was significantly reduced.

External influences on business are often out of the control of businesses – strikes closing transport networks, for example.

All in all, the owner felt that there were enough challenges around setting up a business without all these external effects over which they felt they had little control. However, they knew that to survive, they had to address these external pressures somehow and find ways to keep the business viable.

Questions

1 Comment on the factors of production that would be needed to set up and operate a coffee bar and sandwich shop in a location as outlined in the article. What decisions might the owner have to make about the combination of factors employed? (Hint: think about different ways in which sandwiches and hot drinks such as coffee can be made.)

2 In what ways does a business like a coffee bar and sandwich shop add value?

3 Consider the PESTLE framework used to analyze the external environment. Given the issues outlined in the article that the business owner was facing, which of the PESTLE framework categories do you think these issues would come under and why?

4 How does the article highlight the external challenges facing businesses such as the one in the article?

5 Consider some of the decisions that the business owner in the article might adopt in confronting the external challenges they face. What is the relevance of trade-offs in the decisions that the business owner might have to make in keeping their business viable?

References: www.ons.gov.uk/economy/inflationandpriceindices/articles/energypricesandtheireffectonhouseholds/2022-02-01 (accessed 6 June 2023).
www.bankofengland.co.uk/ (accessed 6 June 2023).
www.ons.gov.uk/economy/inflationandpriceindices/timeseries/cznp/mm23 (accessed 6 June 2023).
www.ons.gov.uk/economy/inflationandpriceindices/timeseries/czoh/mm23 (accessed 6 June 2023).

QUESTIONS FOR REVIEW

1 Using an example of a product of your choice, explain the principle of business activity.

2 Think about a business producing bottled spa water. Identify some examples of the four factors of production which are necessary to produce the output of that business.

3 Why do some economists argue for enterprise to be a separate factor of production rather than a specialist form of labour?

4 Think of a good and a service with which you are familiar and sketch a diagram, accompanied by a brief description, of the transformation process which takes place to produce each.

5 Describe the value added at each stage of production of a loaf of bread up to the point it is purchased by the consumer.

6 In a country with a democratic political system, why might a business be concerned about a change in government?

7 Explain the possible differences between the microeconomic and macroeconomic environment effects on a business producing costume jewellery.

8 Explain how a concern over the effect on the environment of business activity can lead to not only environmental change but also technological, social and legal changes which could affect a business.

9 Explain how an investment decision might affect shareholder value in a positive way both in the short and long run.

10 Describe how a plan by a business to increase the price of its goods might cause a conflict between the interests of managers, shareholders, employees and customers.

PROBLEMS AND APPLICATIONS

1 Is there such a thing as a 'science of decision making'? Explain your answer in relation to business decision making.

2 To what extent is it the case that value added is always higher in a B2C business than a B2B business because businesses are more aware of value for money than are consumers?

3 Industries that use large amounts of capital in relation to other factors of production are said to be capital intensive. Is it necessarily the case that capital intensive businesses are more efficient than labour intensive ones? Explain your answer using relevant examples.

4 What do you think are the most important factors which separate those entrepreneurs that are deemed massively successful because they are worth millions, and those who just about manage to survive running their own business?

5 What do you think is the main reason for the relatively high rate of business failures five years after start-up? Justify your answer.

6 The price of a high quality diamond ring used for weddings is €250. The price of a tonne of steel is €25. Does this mean that the transformation process in making a diamond ring is ten times more complex and costly than in making a tonne of steel? Explain your answer using the concept of added value.

7 A business making high quality ball-point pens faces a number of challenges in the next year. It is concerned that a slowdown in the European economy along with a shift to the use of laptops and tablet devices by young people will begin to damage its long-term viability. What advice would you give the owners of this business to respond to these two external challenges? Explain your reasoning.

8 Should businesses be allowed to regulate their own activities or should governments legislate to force them to meet their social and environmental responsibilities? Explain your reasoning and use appropriate examples to illustrate your answer.

9 A pharmaceutical business reads a research report published by a leading university that suggests consumers are 20 per cent less likely to use over-the-counter medicines if these have not been advertised on TV over the last 12 months. What questions might the business want to ask about the research conducted before making any decision on whether to advertise?

10 Do you think that it is ever possible for a business to satisfy the conflicting demands of all stakeholders? Justify your reasoning.

PART 2
MICROECONOMICS:
THE MARKET SYSTEM

4 SUPPLY AND DEMAND: HOW MARKETS WORK

LEARNING OUTCOMES

After reading this chapter you should be able to:

- List at least two characteristics of a competitive market.
- List the factors that affect the amount that producers wish to sell in a market.
- List the factors that affect the amount that consumers wish to buy in a market.
- Draw a graph of supply and demand in a market and find the equilibrium price and quantity.
- Shift supply and demand curves in response to an economic event and find the new equilibrium price and quantity.
- Describe the process by which a new equilibrium is reached.
- Explain how price acts as a signal to both producers and consumers.

THE MARKET FORCES OF SUPPLY AND DEMAND

- Poor weather conditions in parts of Europe can influence the yield of wheat crops and, as a result, businesses using wheat in food products face higher costs.
- Slowing levels of economic growth in China cause the demand for steel to fall, and this reduces prices for businesses across the rest of the world, meaning the price of both semi-finished and finished products where steel is a component part in production falls.
- If a report is published linking food products with health risks, firms producing these foods face falling prices and a possible collapse in their markets.
- A change in exchange rates for currencies can have different effects on different businesses, depending on the extent to which they trade with other businesses and customers abroad.
- Airlines know that they can charge higher prices at certain times of the year to certain destinations than at other times, when they may have to cut fares to fill aircraft.

What do these events have in common? They are all related to markets containing buyers and sellers. In this chapter, we are going to look at a fundamental aspect of business economics, the operation of markets and the interaction between the 'forces' of supply and demand.

Supply and demand are referred to as forces because they act in different ways and put pressure on prices to change. This chapter introduces the theory of supply and demand using a model of markets which has some predictive power. It considers how sellers and buyers behave and how they interact with one another. Price signals influence both buyers and sellers to change behaviour and go some way to allocating the economy's scarce resources.

At this point it is important to note a fundamental distinction. We use the terms 'price' and 'cost' regularly in everyday life, often interchangeably. In this book, we will refer to the two terms in a distinct way. **Price** is the amount of money a buyer (a business or a consumer) must give up to acquire something. **Cost** refers to the payment to factor inputs in production. When we discuss suppliers, we will be referring to cost in this sense.

> **price** the amount of money a buyer (a business or a consumer) must give up to acquire something
> **cost** the payment to factor inputs in production

Assumptions of the Model of Supply and Demand

Economists use models to represent reality. No model is perfect and no model describes every situation. The model of supply and demand is built on several assumptions and is referred to as the *competitive market* model. It is important to always keep these assumptions in mind when using the model to analyze markets.

Assumption 1: Many Buyers and Sellers In a competitive market there are many buyers and sellers, each of whom is responsible for buying or selling only a very small proportion of the total market. Buyers and sellers are assumed to be price takers. They must accept the existing market price and neither can do anything to influence or set price; a seller cannot withhold supply in the hope of forcing price upwards and a buyer cannot influence price by varying the amount they choose to buy.

Assumption 2: Homogeneous Goods Goods in the market are assumed to be identical and not subject to differentiation, so buyers have no preference for the products of one supplier over another. This also implies that sellers will each charge the same price, as there is no incentive for any seller to charge a price higher or lower than any other.

Assumption 3: Perfect Information Buyers and sellers are assumed to have perfect information, in that they know all prices that exist, they know and understand the attributes of a product, and sellers know and understand the production processes and capabilities in the market. Sellers are also assumed to be able to access the resources they need to produce a good.

Assumption 4: Freedom of Entry and Exit There are no barriers to entry or exit in any industry, meaning that firms are free to switch resources to alternative production at any time.

Assumption 5: Buyers and Sellers Are Clearly Defined The actions of buyers and sellers are completely independent of each other. Sellers cannot influence demand and buyers cannot influence supply. The factors that influence buyers and sellers are thus distinct and independent.

Assumption 6: Clearly Defined Property Rights The rights of ownership of resources and property are clear to all and enforced. This means that the decisions taken by buyers and sellers consider all the associated costs and benefits. The amount buyers are willing to pay and suppliers willing to supply takes account of all these costs and benefits.

Assumption 7: Zero Transaction Costs In facilitating an exchange, it is assumed that the buyer and the seller have no transaction costs. Transaction costs include the time taken to find appropriate goods, legal fees associated with transactions, transport costs associated with a purchase or fees charged by financial institutions such as interest rates on loans.

Assumption 8: Rational Behaviour Buyers and sellers are assumed to act rationally. The term 'rational' in this context means individuals doing the best they can, given their circumstances. Buyers are seeking to maximize the utility or satisfaction from their purchases and sellers are seeking to maximize profits.

You might be thinking that these assumptions are absurd and are so unrealistic as to make the model redundant before you have even looked at it. Indeed, there are many who cast doubt on the validity of using a model which relies on so many unrealistic assumptions. They suggest that its predictive powers are so limited as to be useless. In using the model of supply and demand, we must be mindful of these assumptions. We can then look at different contexts, gain insight, and understand behaviour and outcomes that might be different from that predicted by the model. While these assumptions are unrealistic, the model of supply and demand does allow us to make some predictions. It provides an approximation to many everyday experiences and a means of assessing how markets might behave differently when these assumptions are relaxed.

MARKETS AND COMPETITION

The terms *supply* and *demand* refer to the behaviour of businesses and people as they interact with one another in markets. A **market** is a group of sellers and buyers of a good or service. The sellers as a group determine the supply of the product, and the buyers as a group determine the demand for the product. Before discussing how sellers and buyers behave, let us first consider more fully what we mean by a 'market', and the various types of markets we observe in the economy.

market a group of buyers and sellers of a good or service who come together to agree a price for exchange

Types of Markets

Markets take many forms. Sometimes markets are highly organized and some of the assumptions outlined above do hold. Markets for many agricultural commodities and for metals are two examples. In these markets, buyers and sellers meet at a specific time and place, where an auctioneer helps set prices and arrange sales. Many businesses rely on these highly organized markets, and are affected by them because they have little control over the prices they have to pay for these products, which can affect their costs and margins considerably, both in a positive and a negative way. In agricultural markets, there can be a large number of small farmers who are price takers and have to accept the reigning market price for their output.

More often, markets are less organized. For example, consider the market for perfume. Here many of the assumptions outlined are redundant. Businesses manufacturing and selling perfume are often very large and there are a relatively small number of sellers in the industry. Each seller seeks to offer differentiated products for sale, which they hope will be distinctive and popular. The buyers of perfume do not all meet at any one time. These buyers are individuals, all of whom have different tastes. One person's ideal fragrance is another person's obnoxious smell, and they do not all gather together in a room to shout out the prices they are willing to pay. There is no auctioneer calling out the price of perfume. Each seller of perfume posts a price for a bottle of perfume (which may be uncannily similar), and each buyer makes purchasing decisions based on a number of different factors, many of which may be affected by limitations in knowledge and the peculiarities of human behaviour. In addition, buyers and sellers in these markets are not necessarily independent. Sellers may have successfully (often over many years) attempted to influence buyer behaviour. In the perfectly competitive model this is not the case.

Even though it is not organized, the group of perfume sellers and buyers forms a market. Each seller is aware that their product is similar to, but different from, that offered by other sellers. Each buyer knows that there are several sellers from which to choose. The price of perfume and the quantity of perfume sold are not determined by any single buyer or seller. Ultimately, the seller knows that if the price it is charging does not represent value for money in the eyes of the consumer, then the product will not generate the returns expected and the product may have to be modified or withdrawn from sale. Market forces still have an impact.

Competition exists when two or more firms are rivals for customers. The market for perfume, like most markets in the economy, is competitive according to this definition. Each firm strives to gain the attention and custom of buyers in the market. Economists, however, use the term *competitive market* in a different way, to mean something very specific, based on the assumptions presented earlier.

 competition a market situation when two or more firms are rivals for customers

Competition: Perfect and Otherwise

The assumptions of the model of supply and demand refer to *perfectly competitive* markets. There are some markets in which the assumption of perfect competition applies to a degree. In the wheat market, for example, there are tens of thousands of farmers who sell wheat, and millions of consumers who use wheat and wheat products. Because no single buyer or seller can influence the price of wheat, each takes the price as given. The reason for making this assumption is so that we can look at how markets operate under these 'ideal' conditions and what the expected outcomes are. If we then observe in reality that these outcomes do not occur as we expect, then we can analyze what imperfections exist which help to explain this behaviour.

It is clear that not all goods and services are sold in perfectly competitive markets. Some markets have only one seller, and this seller sets the price. Such a seller is called a *monopoly*. Your local water company, for instance, may be a monopoly. Residents in your area probably have only one water company from which to buy this service. Some markets fall between the extremes of perfect competition and monopoly. One such market, called an *oligopoly*, has a few sellers that do not always compete aggressively. Airline routes are an example. If a route between two cities is serviced by only two or three carriers, the carriers may avoid rigorous competition so they can keep prices high. Another type of market is *monopolistic* or *imperfectly competitive*; it contains many sellers, but each offers a slightly different product. Because the products are not the same, each seller has some ability to set the price for its own product. An example is the market for magazines. Magazines compete with one another for readers, and anyone can enter the market by starting a new one, but each magazine offers different articles and can set its own price.

Despite the diversity of market types we find in the world, we begin by studying perfect competition. Perfectly competitive markets are the easiest to analyze. Moreover, because some degree of competition is present in most markets, many of the lessons that we learn by studying supply and demand under perfect competition apply in more complicated markets as well.

SUPPLY

We are going to begin our look at markets by considering producers and examining the behaviour of sellers. To focus our thinking and provide a context for our analysis, let us consider producers of rapeseed, which is primarily used to make cooking oil and biofuels. Rapeseed, characterized by acres of bright yellow flowers, is grown widely across many parts of the world including Canada, China, India, France, Germany, Australia, the UK, Poland, Ukraine, the USA, the Czech Republic, Russia, Belarus, Lithuania and Denmark. Some of the assumptions of the market model apply to the market for rapeseed, including the fact that there are many sellers, each of whom supplies a relatively small proportion of the total market and the product is largely homogeneous.

The Supply Curve: The Relationship Between Price and Quantity Supplied

The quantity supplied of any good or service is the amount that sellers are willing and able to sell. There are many determinants of quantity supplied, but price plays a special role in our analysis. When the price of rapeseed is high, selling rapeseed is profitable, and so sellers are willing to supply more. Sellers of rapeseed work longer hours, devote more planting to rapeseed, invest in research and development on improvements to rapeseed growing and hire extra workers in order to ensure supplies to the market rise. By contrast, when the price of rapeseed is low, the business is less profitable, and so growers are less willing to plant rapeseed. At a low price, some growers may even choose to shut down, and their **quantity supplied** falls to zero. Because the quantity supplied rises as the price rises, and falls as the price falls, we say that the quantity supplied is *positively related* to the price of the good. This relationship between price and quantity supplied is called the **law of supply**: other things being equal, when the price of a good rises, the quantity producers are willing to supply also rises, and when the price falls, the quantity supplied falls as well.

> **quantity supplied** the amount of a good that sellers are willing and able to sell
> **law of supply** the claim that, other things being equal, the quantity supplied of a good rises when its price rises

The table in Figure 4.1 shows the quantity Tramontana, a rapeseed grower, is willing to supply at various prices of rapeseed. By convention, price is on the vertical axis and the quantity supplied on the horizontal axis.

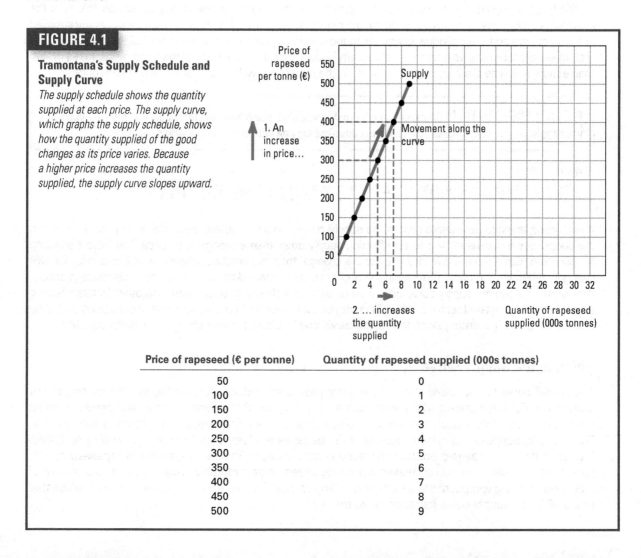

FIGURE 4.1

Tramontana's Supply Schedule and Supply Curve
The supply schedule shows the quantity supplied at each price. The supply curve, which graphs the supply schedule, shows how the quantity supplied of the good changes as its price varies. Because a higher price increases the quantity supplied, the supply curve slopes upward.

Price of rapeseed (€ per tonne)	Quantity of rapeseed supplied (000s tonnes)
50	0
100	1
150	2
200	3
250	4
300	5
350	6
400	7
450	8
500	9

At a price below €50 per tonne, Tramontana does not supply any rapeseed at all. As the price rises, it is willing to supply a greater and greater quantity. This is the **supply schedule**, a table that shows the relationship between the price of a good and the quantity supplied, holding constant everything else that influences how much producers of the good want to sell.

 supply schedule a table that shows the relationship between the price of a good and the quantity supplied

The graph in Figure 4.1 uses the numbers from the table to illustrate the law of supply. The curve relating price and quantity supplied is called the supply curve. The **supply curve** slopes upwards because, other things being equal, a higher price means a greater quantity supplied.

 supply curve a graph of the relationship between the price of a good and the quantity supplied

Market Supply Versus Individual Supply

Market supply is the sum of the supplies of all sellers. The table in Figure 4.2 shows the supply schedules for two rapeseed producers, Tramontana and Sedona. At any price, Tramontana's supply schedule tells us the quantity of rapeseed Tramontana is willing to supply, and Sedona's supply schedule tells us the quantity of rapeseed Sedona is willing to supply. The market supply is the sum of the two individual supplies.

The graph in Figure 4.2 shows the supply curves that correspond to the supply schedules. We sum the individual supply curves *horizontally* to obtain the market supply curve. That is, to find the total quantity supplied at any price, we add the individual quantities found on the horizontal axis of the individual supply curves. The market supply curve shows how the total quantity supplied varies as the price of the good varies. In reality, the market supply will be the amount all producers in the market are willing to offer for sale at each price.

PITFALL PREVENTION Be careful to ensure that you distinguish between individual and market supply in your analysis. The behaviour of one individual business may be different from the whole industry.

SHIFTS VERSUS MOVEMENTS ALONG THE SUPPLY CURVE

A distinction is made between a shift in the supply curve and a movement along the supply curve. A shift in the supply curve is caused by a factor affecting supply other than a change in its price. The factors affecting supply are outlined next. If any of these factors change, then the amount sellers are willing to offer for sale changes, whatever the price. The shift in the supply curve is referred to as an *increase or decrease in supply*. A movement along the supply curve occurs when there is a change in price, assuming other factors affecting supply are held constant (*ceteris paribus*). This may occur because of a change in demand conditions. A change in price leads to a movement along the supply curve, and is referred to as a *change in quantity supplied*.

Shifts in the Supply Curve

The supply curve for rapeseed shows how much rapeseed producers are willing to offer for sale at any given price, holding constant all the other factors beyond price that influence producers' decisions about how much to sell. This relationship can change over time, and is represented by a shift in the supply curve. For example, suppose the price of fertilizer falls. Because fertilizer is an input into producing rapeseed, the fall in its price means producing rapeseed is now cheaper. The same quantity of rapeseed can be harvested at lower cost, which makes selling rapeseed more profitable. This increases the supply of rapeseed: at any given price, sellers are now willing to offer for sale a larger quantity. This is represented as a shift in the supply curve for rapeseed to the right.

FIGURE 4.2

Market Supply as the Sum of Individual Supplies

The quantity supplied in a market is the sum of the quantities supplied by all the sellers at each price. Thus, the market supply curve is found by adding horizontally the individual supply curves. At a price of €250 per tonne, Tramontana is willing to supply 4,000 tonnes of rapeseed and Sedona is willing to supply 10,000 tonnes. The quantity supplied in the market at this price is 14,000 tonnes of rapeseed.

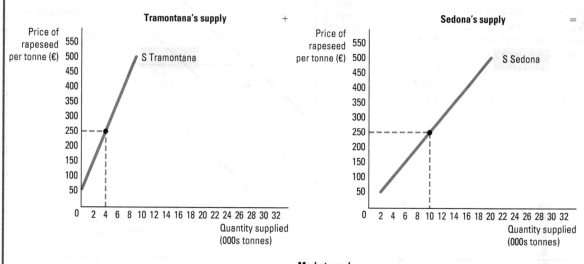

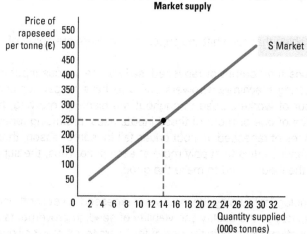

Price of rapeseed (€ per tonne)	Tramontana (000s)		Sedona (000s)		Market (000s)
0	0	+	0	=	0
50	0		2		2
100	1		4		5
150	2		6		8
200	3		8		11
250	4		10		14
300	5		12		17
350	6		14		20
400	7		16		23
450	8		18		26
500	9		20		29

Figure 4.3 illustrates shifts in supply. Any change that raises quantity supplied at every price, such as a fall in the price of fertilizer, shifts the supply curve to the right and is called an *increase in supply*. Similarly, any change that reduces the quantity supplied at every price shifts the supply curve to the left and is called a *decrease in supply*.

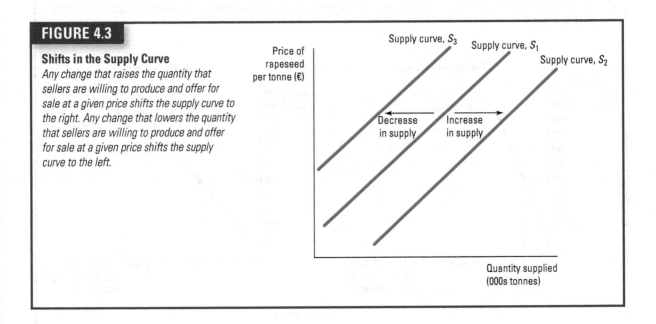

FIGURE 4.3

Shifts in the Supply Curve
Any change that raises the quantity that sellers are willing to produce and offer for sale at a given price shifts the supply curve to the right. Any change that lowers the quantity that sellers are willing to produce and offer for sale at a given price shifts the supply curve to the left.

There are many variables that can shift the supply curve. Here are some of the most important.

Input Prices To produce their output of rapeseed, sellers use various inputs: fertilizer, fuel for tractors, weed killer and harvesting machines. Growers will also have to pay for computers, machinery, farm buildings and the labour of workers used throughout the planting, growing, harvesting and distribution process. When the price of one or more of these inputs rises, producing rapeseed is less profitable and firms supply fewer tonnes of rapeseed. If input prices fall for some reason, then production may be more profitable and there is an incentive to supply more at each price. Thus, the supply of a good is negatively related to the price of the inputs used to make the good.

Technology The technology for turning the inputs into rapeseed is yet another determinant of supply. This technology might be related to the quality and viability of seed, improvements in plant breeding to create more uniform and productive plants, or in the use of fertilizers to improve soil quality and growth. Advances in technology increase productivity, allowing more to be produced using fewer factor inputs. Computer analysis of yield can help build up a database which is then fed to computers on board the tractor and can determine the amount of seed sown in different areas of the field, thus improving efficiency and managing costs. As a result, costs, both total and unit, may fall and supply increases. The invention of harvesting machines, for example, reduces the amount of labour necessary to gather and process rapeseed. By reducing firms' costs, the advance in technology raises the supply of rapeseed.

Expectations The amount of rapeseed firms supply today may depend on their expectations of the future. For example, if growers expect the price of rapeseed to rise in the future, they may put some of their current stock into storage and supply less to the market today. If government reports suggest that using cooking oil made from rapeseed reduces the chance of heart disease, then producers might reasonably expect an increase in sales and so plant more fields to rapeseed in anticipation.

The Number of Sellers Market supply will be affected by the number of firms in the industry. In the EU, around 18 million tonnes of rapeseed are harvested a year, and at an average price (as of August 2022) of approximately €714 per tonne, this means a market value around €12.8 billion. If there were more farmers switching to rapeseed production, then the amount of rapeseed produced would be likely to rise. Equally, if some of the growers that currently plant rapeseed closed down their operations, the amount of rapeseed produced would be likely to fall each year.

Natural/Social Factors There are often many natural or social factors that affect supply. These include such things as the weather affecting crops, natural disasters, pestilence and disease, changing attitudes and social expectations (for example, over the production of organic food, the disposal of waste, reducing carbon emissions, ethical supply sourcing and so on), which can all have an influence on production decisions. Some or all of these may have an influence on the cost of inputs into production.

Summary

The supply curve shows what happens to the quantity supplied of a good when its price varies, holding constant all the other variables that influence sellers. When one of these other variables changes, the supply curve shifts. Table 4.1 lists all the variables that influence how much producers choose to sell of a good.

TABLE 4.1 **Variables That Influence Sellers**

This table lists the variables that affect how much producers choose to sell of any good. Notice the special role that the price of the good plays: a change in the good's price represents a movement along the supply curve, whereas a change in one of the other variables shifts the supply curve.

Variable	A change in this variable...
Price	... is represented as a movement along the supply curve
Input prices	... shifts the supply curve
Technology	... shifts the supply curve
Expectations	... shifts the supply curve
Number of sellers	... shifts the supply curve

SELF TEST Make up an example of a supply schedule for apples, and graph the implied supply curve. Give an example of something that would shift this supply curve. Would a change in the price of apples shift this supply curve? Explain.

DEMAND

We now turn to the other side of the market and examine the behaviour of buyers. We will continue using the market for rapeseed as our context.

The Demand Curve: The Relationship Between Price and Quantity Demanded

The **quantity demanded** of any good is the amount of the good that buyers are willing and able to purchase. As we shall see, many things determine the quantity demanded of any good, but when analysing how markets work, one determinant plays a central role: the price of the good. If the price of rapeseed rose, people would buy fewer tonnes of rapeseed. Food manufacturers and retailers might switch to another form of cooking oil, such as sunflower oil. If the price of rapeseed fell to €50 per tonne, people would buy more. Because the quantity demanded falls as the price rises and rises as the price falls, we say that the quantity demanded is *negatively related* to the price. This relationship between price and quantity demanded is true for most goods in the economy and, in fact, is so pervasive that economists call it the **law of demand**.

quantity demanded the amount of a good buyers are willing and able to purchase at different prices
law of demand the claim that, other things being equal, the quantity demanded of a good falls when the price of the good rises

The table in Figure 4.4 shows how many tonnes of rapeseed Hanse, a food processor, is willing and able to buy each year at different prices of rapeseed. If rapeseed were free, Hanse would be willing to acquire 10,000 tonnes of rapeseed. At €200 per tonne, Hanse would be willing to buy 6,000 tonnes of rapeseed. As the price rises further, Hanse is willing to buy fewer and fewer tonnes of rapeseed. When the price reaches €500 per tonne, Hanse would not be prepared to buy any rapeseed at all. This table is a **demand schedule**, a table that shows the relationship between the price of a good and the quantity demanded, holding constant everything else that influences how much consumers of the good want to buy.

demand schedule a table that shows the relationship between the price of a good and the quantity demanded

The graph in Figure 4.4 uses the numbers from the table to illustrate the law of demand. The price of rapeseed is on the vertical axis, and the quantity of rapeseed demanded is on the horizontal axis. The downward sloping line relating price and quantity demanded is called the **demand curve**.

demand curve a graph of the relationship between the price of a good and the quantity demanded

FIGURE 4.4

Hanse's Demand Schedule and Demand Curve

The demand schedule shows the quantity demanded at each price. The demand curve, which graphs the demand schedule, shows how the quantity demanded of the good changes as its price varies. Because a lower price increases the quantity demanded, the demand curve slopes downwards.

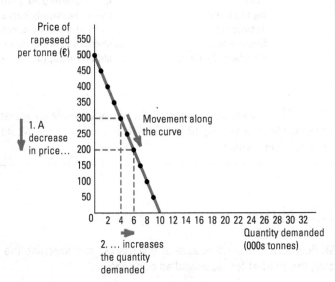

Price of rapeseed (€ per tonne)	Quantity of rapeseed demanded (000s tonnes)
0	10
50	9
100	8
150	7
200	6
250	5
300	4
350	3
400	2
450	1
500	0

Market Demand Versus Individual Demand

The demand curve in Figure 4.4 shows an individual's demand for a product. To analyze how markets work, we need to determine the *market demand*, which is the sum of all the individual demands for a particular good or service.

The table in Figure 4.5 shows the demand schedules for rapeseed of two food processers, Hanse and Michelle. At any price, Hanse's demand schedule tells us how many tonnes of rapeseed he would be willing and able to buy at different prices, and Michelle's demand schedule tells us how many tonnes of rapeseed she is willing and able to buy. The market demand at each price is the sum of the two individual demands.

The graph in Figure 4.5 shows the demand curves that correspond to these demand schedules. As we did with the market supply, we sum the individual demand curves *horizontally* to obtain the market demand curve.

Because we are interested in analysing how markets work, we shall work most often with the market demand curve. The market demand curve shows how the total quantity demanded of a good changes as the price of the good varies, while all the other factors that affect how much consumers want to buy, such as incomes and taste, among other things, are held constant.

SHIFTS VERSUS MOVEMENTS ALONG THE DEMAND CURVE

A shift in the demand curve is caused by a factor affecting demand other than a change in price. The factors affecting demand are outlined next. If any of these factors change, then the amount consumers wish to purchase changes, whatever the price. The shift in the demand curve is referred to as an *increase* or *decrease in demand*. A movement along the demand curve occurs when there is a change in price. This may occur because of a change in supply conditions, and the factors affecting demand are assumed to be held constant. A change in price leads to a movement along the demand curve and is referred to as a *change in quantity demanded*.

Movement Along the Demand Curve

We are going to briefly look at the economics behind a movement along the demand curve. Let us assume that the price of a particular variety of rapeseed (Excalibur) falls, while all other rapeseed varieties' (Vision, Dimension, Vistive and Fashion) prices remain constant. We know that the fall in price will lead to an increase in quantity demanded. There are two reasons for this increase:

1. **The income effect.** If we assume that incomes remain constant, then a fall in the price of Excalibur means that growers who buy this variety can now afford to buy more with their income. In other words, their *real income*, what a given amount of money can buy at any point in time, has increased and part of the increase in quantity demanded can be put down to this effect.
2. **The substitution effect.** Now that Excalibur is lower in price compared to other rapeseed varieties, some growers will choose to substitute the more expensive varieties with the now cheaper Excalibur. This switch accounts for the remaining part of the increase in quantity demanded.

Shifts in the Demand Curve

The demand curve for rapeseed shows how many tonnes of rapeseed buyers are willing to buy at any given price, holding constant the many other factors beyond price that influence consumers' buying decisions. As a result, this demand curve need not be stable over time. If something happens to alter the demand at any given price, the demand curve shifts. For example, suppose European health authorities discovered that people who regularly use rapeseed oil live longer, healthier lives. The discovery would be likely to raise the demand for rapeseed. At any given price, buyers would now want to purchase a larger quantity of rapeseed at all prices, and the demand curve for rapeseed would shift.

FIGURE 4.5

Market Demand as the Sum of Individual Demands

The quantity demanded in a market is the sum of the quantities demanded by all the buyers at each price. Thus, the market demand curve is found by adding horizontally the individual demand curves. At a price of €200, Hanse would like to buy 6,000 tonnes of rapeseed and Michelle would be prepared to buy 12,000 tonnes of rapeseed. The quantity demanded in the market at this price, therefore, is 18,000 tonnes of rapeseed.

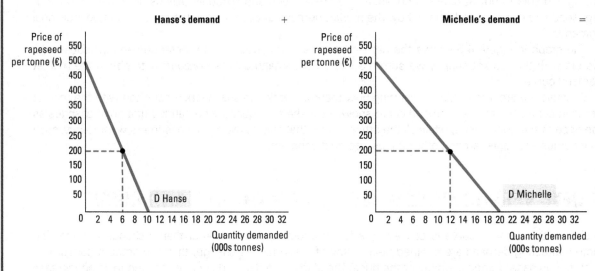

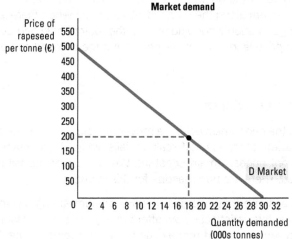

Price of rapeseed (€ per tonne)	Hanse (000s tonnes)		Michelle (000s tonnes)		Market (000s tonnes)
0	10	+	20	=	30
50	9		18		27
100	8		16		24
150	7		14		21
200	6		12		18
250	5		10		15
300	4		8		12
350	3		6		9
400	2		4		6
450	1		2		3
500	0		0		0

Figure 4.6 illustrates shifts in demand. Any change that increases the quantity demanded at every price, such as our imaginary discovery by the European health authorities, shifts the demand curve to the right and is called an *increase in demand*. Any change that reduces the demand at every price shifts the demand curve to the left and is called a *decrease in demand*.

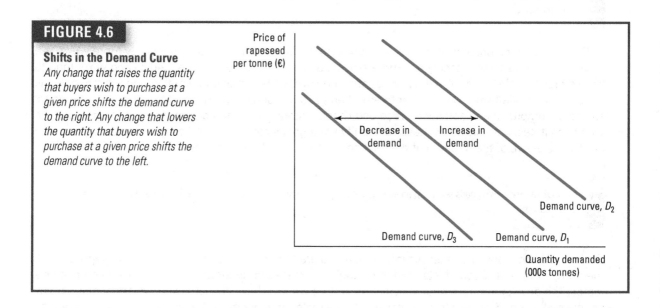

FIGURE 4.6

Shifts in the Demand Curve
Any change that raises the quantity that buyers wish to purchase at a given price shifts the demand curve to the right. Any change that lowers the quantity that buyers wish to purchase at a given price shifts the demand curve to the left.

There are many variables that can shift the demand curve. Here are the most important.

Income What would happen to the demand for rapeseed if unemployment increases? Most likely, it would fall (how much it would fall is another question, and will be dealt with in the next chapter) because of lower incomes. Lower incomes mean that people have less to spend in total, so they are likely to spend less on some, and probably most, goods. If the demand for a good falls when income falls, the good is called a **normal good**.

> **normal good** a good for which, other things being equal, an increase in income leads to an increase in demand (and vice versa)

Not all goods are normal goods. If the demand for a good rises when income falls, the good is called an **inferior good**. An example of an inferior good might be bus rides. As income falls, people are less likely to buy a car or take a taxi, and more likely to take the bus. As income falls, therefore, demand for bus rides tends to increase.

> **inferior good** a good for which, other things being equal, an increase in income leads to a decrease in demand (and vice versa)

Prices of Related Goods Suppose that the price of sunflower seed oil falls. The law of demand says that people will buy more sunflower seed oil. At the same time, people will probably buy less rapeseed oil. Because sunflower seed oil and rapeseed oil can both be used for cooking, they satisfy similar functions. When a fall in the price of one good reduces the demand for another good, the two goods are called **substitutes**. Substitutes are often pairs of goods that are used in place of each other, such as beef steak and Wiener schnitzel, pullovers and sweatshirts, and cinema tickets and movie streaming. The more closely related substitute products are, the more effect we might see on demand if the price of one of the substitutes changes.

> **substitutes** two goods for which an increase in the price of one leads to an increase in the demand for the other (and vice versa)

Suppose that the price of woks falls. According to the law of demand, people will buy more woks. Yet, in this case, people will probably buy more rapeseed oil as well, because rapeseed oil and woks tend to be used together. When a fall in the price of one good raises the demand for another good, the two goods are called **complements**. Complements are often pairs of goods that are used together, such as petrol and cars, computers and software, bread and cheese, strawberries and cream, and bacon and eggs. As with substitutes, not only do we need to identify what goods can be classed as complementary, we also need to be aware of the strength of the relationship between the two goods.

> **complements** two goods for which an increase in the price of one leads to a decrease in the demand for the other (and vice versa)

Tastes The most obvious determinants of demand are tastes and fashions. If people like rapeseed oil, they buy more of it. Economists are increasingly interested in understanding and explaining people's tastes. The developments in neuroscience mean that we now have an increasing understanding of why people make decisions, and this has come into the realm of economics. This helps economists examine what happens, and why, when tastes change. This knowledge is also very important to businesses seeking to get a better understanding of their market, how consumers behave and why they behave in the ways they do.

Expectations Buyers' expectations about the future may affect their demand for a good or service today. For example, if food processors and manufacturers who use rapeseed oil in their production expect to earn higher revenues next month, they may be more willing to spend some of their current cash reserves buying rapeseed oil. As another example, if buyers expect the price of rapeseed to fall tomorrow, they may be less willing to buy rapeseed at today's price.

The Size and Structure of the Population A larger population, other things being equal, will mean a higher demand for all goods and services. Changes in the way the population is structured also influences demand. Many European countries have an ageing population, and goods and services required by the elderly see an increase in demand. The demand for retirement homes, insurance policies suitable for elderly drivers and smaller cars, for example, may increase.

> **PITFALL PREVENTION** Many students confuse movements along and shifts in demand and supply curves. Using the correct phrasing (*change in supply/demand* refers to a shift in the curve; *change in quantity supplied/ demanded* refers to a movement along the curve) is one way to help prevent this confusion.

Summary

The demand curve shows what happens to the *quantity demanded* of a good when its price varies, holding constant all the other variables that influence buyers. When one or more of these other variables changes, the demand curve shifts, leading to an *increase* or *decrease in demand*. Table 4.2 lists all the variables that influence how much consumers choose to buy of a good.

TABLE 4.2	**Variables That Influence Buyers**

This table lists the variables that affect how much consumers choose to buy of any good. Notice the special role that the price of the good plays: a change in the good's price represents a movement along the demand curve, whereas a change in one of the other variables shifts the demand curve.

Variable	A change in this variable...
Price	... is represented as a movement along the demand curve
Income	... shifts the demand curve
Prices of related goods	... shifts the demand curve
Tastes	... shifts the demand curve
Expectations	... shifts the demand curve
Number of buyers	... shifts the demand curve

SELF TEST Make up an example of a demand schedule for pizza, and graph the implied demand curve. Give an example of something that would shift this demand curve. Would a change in the price of pizza shift this demand curve? Explain.

DEMAND AND SUPPLY TOGETHER

Having analyzed supply and demand separately, we now combine them to see how they determine the quantity of a good bought and sold in a competitive market and its price.

Equilibrium

Figure 4.7 shows the market supply curve and market demand curve together. Equilibrium is defined as a state of rest, a point where there is no force acting for change. Economists refer to supply and demand as being *market forces*. In any market the relationship between supply and demand exerts force on price. If supply is greater than demand or vice versa, then there is pressure on price to change. Notice, however, that there is one point at which the supply and demand curves intersect. This point is called the **market equilibrium**. The price at this intersection is called the **equilibrium price** or **market clearing price**, and the quantity is called the **equilibrium quantity**. Here the equilibrium price is €200 per tonne, and the equilibrium quantity is 7,000 tonnes bought and sold.

FIGURE 4.7	

The Equilibrium of Supply and Demand
The equilibrium is found where the supply and demand curves intersect. At the equilibrium price, the quantity supplied equals the quantity demanded. Here the equilibrium price is €200: at this price, 7,000 tonnes of rapeseed are supplied and 7,000 tonnes are demanded.

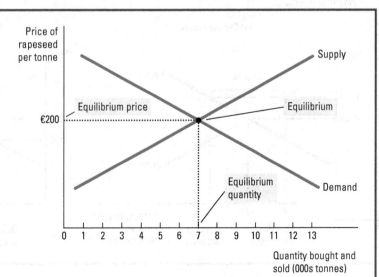

market equilibrium a situation in which the price has reached the level where quantity supplied equals quantity demanded

equilibrium price the price that balances quantity supplied and quantity demanded, otherwise known as market clearing price

market clearing price the price that balances quantity demanded and quantity supplied, otherwise known as equilibrium price

equilibrium quantity the quantity supplied and the quantity demanded at the equilibrium price

At the equilibrium price, the quantity of the good that buyers are willing and able to buy exactly balances the quantity that sellers are willing and able to sell. The equilibrium price is sometimes called the *market clearing price* because, at this price, everyone in the market has been satisfied: buyers have bought all they want to buy, and sellers have sold all they want to sell. There is neither a shortage nor a surplus.

The actions of buyers and sellers in a competitive market naturally move towards the equilibrium of supply and demand. To see why, consider what happens when the market price is not equal to the equilibrium price.

Suppose first that the market price is above the equilibrium price, as in panel (a) of Figure 4.8. At a price of €250 per tonne, the quantity suppliers would like to sell at this price (10,000 tonnes) exceeds the quantity which buyers are willing to purchase (4,000 tonnes). There is a **surplus** of the good: suppliers are unable to sell all they want at the going price. A surplus is sometimes called a situation of *excess supply*. When there is a surplus in the rapeseed market, sellers of rapeseed find they cannot sell all the supplies they have, and so the market responds to the surplus by cutting prices. Falling prices, in turn, increase the quantity demanded and decrease the quantity supplied. Prices continue to fall until the market reaches the equilibrium.

surplus a situation in which quantity supplied is greater than quantity demanded

FIGURE 4.8

Markets Not in Equilibrium

In panel (a), there is a surplus. Because the market price of €250 is above the equilibrium price, the quantity supplied (10,000 tonnes) exceeds the quantity demanded (4,000 tonnes). The excess supply results in downward pressure on the price of rapeseed, and this moves the price towards its equilibrium level. In panel (b), there is a shortage. Because the market price of €150 is below the equilibrium price, the quantity demanded (10,000 tonnes) exceeds the quantity supplied (4,000 tonnes). With too many buyers chasing too few goods, there is pressure on price to rise. Hence, in both cases, the price adjustment moves the market towards the equilibrium of supply and demand.

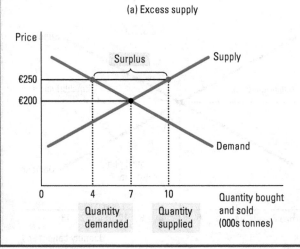

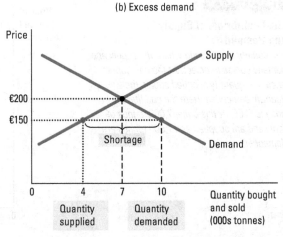

Suppose now that the market price is below the equilibrium price, as in panel (b) of Figure 4.8. In this case, the price is €150 per tonne, and the quantity of the good demanded exceeds the quantity supplied. There is a **shortage** of the good: buyers are unable to buy all they want at the going price. A shortage is sometimes called a situation of *excess demand*. When a shortage occurs in the rapeseed market, buyers may find they cannot acquire all the supplies they need. With too many buyers chasing too few goods, the suppliers respond to the shortage by raising prices without losing sales. As the price rises, quantity demanded falls, quantity supplied rises and the market once again moves towards the equilibrium.

shortage a situation in which quantity demanded is greater than quantity supplied

The activities of the many buyers and sellers push the market price towards the equilibrium price. Once the market reaches its equilibrium, all buyers and sellers are satisfied, and there is no upward or downward pressure on the price. How quickly equilibrium is reached varies from market to market, depending on how quickly prices adjust. In most free markets (which includes all the assumptions outlined earlier) surpluses and shortages are only temporary, because prices eventually move towards their equilibrium levels. Indeed, this phenomenon is so pervasive that it is called the **law of supply and demand**: the price of any good adjusts to bring the quantity supplied and quantity demanded for that good into balance.

law of supply and demand the claim that the price of any good adjusts to bring the quantity supplied and the quantity demanded for that good into balance

JEOPARDY PROBLEM The market for bicycles has seen falling prices, but not a change in the number of bicycles bought and sold. Explain how this situation might have come about. Use diagrams to illustrate.

FYI

This FYI will be helpful if you must use maths in your course. If you do not have to use maths, then you can safely move on to the next section without affecting your overall understanding of this chapter.

Functions

In economics a lot of use is made of functions. Demand and supply equations are two examples of functions. Typically, functions are expressed as:

$$Y = f(x)$$

or simply $f(x)$

This means that the value of Y is dependent on the value of the terms in the bracket. In our example above there is only one value, x, so the value of Y is dependent on the value of x.

We know from this chapter that there are several factors affecting demand and supply. The general form of the function in such a case would look like:

$$Y = f(x_1 \ldots \ldots x_n)$$

where $x_1 \ldots \ldots x_n$ represents a range of variables.

(*Continued*)

Given the determinants of demand and supply we could write the demand and supply functions as:

$$D = f(P_n, P_n \ldots P_{n-1}, Y, T, P, A, E)$$

Where:

- P_n = Price
- $P_n \ldots P_{n-1}$ = Prices of other goods (substitutes and complements)
- Y = Incomes (the level and distribution of income)
- T = Tastes and fashions
- P = The level and structure of the population
- A = Advertising
- E = Expectations of consumers

And:

$$S = f(P_n, P_n \ldots P_{n-1}, H, N, F_1 \ldots F_m, E, S_f)$$

Where:

- P_n = Price
- $P_n \ldots P_{n-1}$ = Profitability of other goods in production and prices of goods in joint supply
- H = Technology
- N = Natural shocks
- $F_1 \ldots F_m$ = Costs of production
- E = Expectations of producers
- S_f = Social factors

Linear Equations

Both demand and supply functions can be represented as linear equations, and be drawn as straight line graphs. A linear equation normally looks like:

$$y = a + bx$$

In this equation, y is the value plotted on the vertical axis (the dependent variable), x is the value on the horizontal axis (the independent variable), a is a constant and b is the slope of the line (its gradient). Remember that demand looks at the relationship between price and the quantity demanded, and supply is the relationship between price and the quantity supplied. In both cases, the quantity demanded and supplied are dependent on the price. In this case, price is the independent variable and the quantity the dependent variable.

Students of pure maths will notice that in economics, supply and demand graphs are the wrong way around. Normally, the vertical Y axis represents the dependent variable and the X axis the independent variable. In supply and demand graphs, price, the independent variable, is drawn on the Y axis and quantity demanded and supplied, the dependent variable, on the X axis. The switch is attributed to Alfred Marshall (1842–1924), among others, who developed supply and demand analysis in the latter part of the nineteenth century. It is important, therefore, to remember which is the dependent variable and which the independent variable as we progress through the analysis.

Applying the relationship between price and quantity demanded and supplied, we get typical equations such as:

$$Q_d = 2,100 - 2.5P$$
$$Q_s = -10 + 6P$$

In the case of the demand curve, the minus sign in front of the price variable tells us that there is a negative relationship between price and quantity demanded, whereas the plus sign in front of the price in the supply equation tells us that there is a positive relationship between price and quantity supplied.

You may also see demand and supply equations which look like:

$$P = 840 - 0.4Q_d$$

or:

$$P = -120 + 0.8Q_s$$

The equation $P = 840 - 0.4Q_d$ is the inverse of the demand equation $Q_d = 2,100 - 2.5P$. We found this by adopting the following method:

$$Q_d = 2,100 - 2.5P$$
$$Q_d + 2.5P = 2,100$$
$$2.5P = 2,100 - Q_d$$
$$\frac{2.5P}{2.5} = \frac{2,100 - Q_d}{2.5}$$
$$P = 840 - 0.4Q_d$$

The important thing to remember when manipulating linear equations of this sort is that whatever you do to one side of the equation (multiply, add, divide or subtract a number or element) you must do the same thing to the other side.

Finding Price and Quantity

If we take the original two equations:

$$Q_d = 2,100 - 2.5P$$
$$Q_s = -10 + 6P$$

We can dissect them in a bit more detail in relation to the standard $y = a + bx$ linear equation we first introduced. In our equations, the quantity demanded and supplied are variables in the equations. In this case, they are dependent variables. Their value depends upon the price, the independent variable. In the case of the demand curve, the quantity demanded will be 2,100 minus 2.5 times whatever the price is. If price is €6 then quantity demanded will be $2,100 - 2.5(6) = 2,085$. If price is €16 then quantity demanded will be $2,100 - 2.5(16) = 2,060$.

Looking at supply, if the price were €8 then the quantity supplied would be $-10 + 6(8) = 38$ and if price were €16 then quantity supplied would be $-10 + 6(16) = 86$.

If we used the other two equations we looked at:

$$P = 840 - 0.4Q_d$$

or:

$$P = -120 + 0.8Q_s$$

Then we can arrive at values for P or Q assuming we have at least one of these two variables.

For demand, if $P = $ €6 then the quantity demanded would be:

$$P = 840 - 0.4Q_d$$
$$0.4Q_d = 840 - 6$$
$$\frac{0.4Q_d}{0.4} = \frac{834}{0.4}$$
$$Q_d = 2,085$$

In the case of supply, if price = €8:

$$P = -120 + 0.8Q_s$$
$$8 = -120 + 0.8Q_s$$
$$\frac{8}{0.8} = \frac{-120 + 0.8Q_s}{0.8}$$
$$10 = -150 + Q_s$$
$$10 + 150 = Q_s$$
$$Q_s = 160$$

(*Continued*)

Finding Market Equilibrium

The Substitution Method We know that in equilibrium, demand equals supply (D = S). To find the market equilibrium, therefore, we set the demand and supply equations equal to each other and solve for P and Q.

Take the following demand and supply equations:

$$Q_d = 32 - 3P$$
$$Q_s = 20 + 4P$$

We know that in equilibrium: $Q_d = Q_s$, so, equilibrium in this market will be where:

$$32 - 3P = 20 + 4P$$

This now allows us to solve for P and so find the equilibrium price. Subtract 20 from both sides and add $3P$ to both sides to get:

$$32 - 20 = 4P + 3P$$
$$12 = 7P$$

$$P = €1.71 \text{ (rounded to the nearest whole cent)}.$$

We can now substitute the equilibrium price into our two equations to find the equilibrium quantity, rounded to the nearest whole number:

$$Q_d = 32 - 3P$$
$$Q_d = 32 - 3(1.71)$$
$$Q_d = 32 - 5.13$$
$$Q_d = 26.87$$
$$Q_d = 27$$
$$Q_s = 20 + 4P$$
$$Q_s = 20 + 4(1.71)$$
$$Q_s = 20 + 6.84$$
$$Q_s = 26.84$$
$$Q_s = 27$$

Note the figures for Q_d and Q_s before rounding, differ slightly because we had to round the price. Now look at this example:

$$P = 3 + 0.25Q_s$$
$$P = 15 - 0.75Q_d$$

In this case the equations are defined in terms of price, but the principle of working out equilibrium is the same as we have used above. First, set the two equations equal to each other:

$$3 + 0.25Q_s = 15 - 0.75Q_d$$

Then solve for Q:

Add $0.75Q_d$ to both sides and subtract 3 from both sides to get:

$$0.75Q_d + 0.25Q_s = 15 - 3$$
$$Q = 12$$

Substitute $Q = 12$ into one of the equations to find P:

$$P = 3 + 0.25Q_s$$
$$P = 3 + 0.25(12)$$
$$P = 6$$

To check, also substitute into the demand equation:

$$P = 15 - 0.75Q_d$$
$$P = 15 - 0.75(12)$$
$$P = 15 - 9$$
$$P = 6$$

There is another way to find both the quantity and the price, and that is through adopting the approach of solving simultaneous equations. Simultaneous equations require us to find two unknowns: price and quantity.

The Elimination Method Look at the following two equations:

$$Q_d = 20 - 2P$$
$$Q_s = 2 + 2P$$

In this case, the terms are all neatly aligned above each other, so it is a relatively simple task to add the two together. Note that we are trying to find equilibrium where $Q_d = Q_s$ so the value of Q is the same. Adding the two together we get:

$$Q_d = 20 - 2P$$
$$Q_s = 2 + 2P$$
$$2Q = 22$$
$$Q = 11$$

Notice that in the above equations we have a very convenient fact that the coefficient of P in each case is the same but with opposite signs. This makes this example very easy to eliminate P to isolate the Q value. This is not always the case, however, but it is important to remember that having two equal values with opposite signs allows us to get rid of them! We will come back to this later. We can now use the fact that we know Q, to find the equilibrium price by substituting Q into one of the equations thus:

$$Q_d = 20 - 2P$$
$$11 = 20 - 2P$$
$$2P = 20 - 11$$
$$2P = 9$$
$$P = 4.5$$

It is always worth checking your answer to make sure you have made no mistakes along the way, so in this case we will substitute our known value of Q into the second equation to check we get the same answer ($P = 4.5$):

$$Q_s = 2 + 2P$$
$$11 = 2 + 2P$$
$$11 - 2 = 2P$$
$$9 = 2P$$
$$P = 4.5$$

Sometimes we may have equations where the P and Q values are both on the same side of the equation. In this case, we have to use a development of the elimination method.
Take the following two equations:

$$-3P + 4Q = 5 \tag{1}$$
$$2P - 5Q = -15 \tag{2}$$

We have labelled these two equations (1) and (2) to allow us to keep track of what we are doing and reduce the risk of making an error. Remember above when we noted the fact that having a nice convenient equation, where the coefficient was equal but the signs opposite, enabled us to be able to eliminate one of the values to help solve the equation for the other unknown. That is what we need to do with these two equations. We must

(*Continued*)

manipulate the two equations to make either the 'P' terms or the 'Q' terms have the same coefficient but opposite signs. A knowledge of factors and lowest common denominators is useful here!

In this example, we are going to manipulate the equations to get rid of the 'P' terms. This allows us to isolate the 'Q' terms and thus solve for Q and then find P:

$$-3P + 4Q = 5 \tag{1}$$
$$2P - 5Q = -15 \tag{2}$$

To eliminate P, multiply (1) by 2 and (2) by 3:

$$-6P + 8Q = 10 \tag{3}$$
$$6P - 15Q = -45 \tag{4}$$

Add together (3) and (4):

$$-6P + 8Q = 10 \tag{3}$$
$$6P - 15Q = -45 \tag{4}$$
$$-7Q = -35$$

Divide both sides by -7:

$$Q = 5$$

We can now substitute Q into equations (1) and (2) to find (and check) P. If $Q = 5$ then:

$$-3P + 4(5) = 5$$
$$-3P + 20 = 5$$
$$20 - 5 = 3P$$
$$15 = 3P$$
$$P = 5$$
$$2P - 5(5) = -15$$
$$2P - 25 = -15$$
$$2P = -15 + 25$$
$$2P = 10$$
$$P = 5$$

In this case the equilibrium price is €5 and the equilibrium quantity is 5.

Three Steps to Analysing Changes in Equilibrium

So far, we have seen how supply and demand together determine a market's equilibrium, which in turn determines the price of the good and the amount of the good that buyers purchase and sellers produce. Markets are dynamic. Demand and supply change all the time, and in some markets these changes may be almost every second of every day, in foreign exchange markets, for example. The equilibrium price and quantity depend on the position of the supply and demand curves. When some event shifts one (or both) of these curves, the equilibrium in the market changes. The analysis of such a change is called *comparative statics* because it involves comparing two unchanging situations: an initial and a new equilibrium.

When analysing how some event affects a market, we proceed in three steps.

Step 1: Decide whether the event shifts the supply curve, the demand curve or, in some cases, both curves.

Step 2: Decide whether the curve shifts to the right or to the left.

Step 3: Use the supply and demand diagram to compare the initial and the new equilibrium, which shows how the shift affects the equilibrium price and quantity.

It is important in the analysis that the process by which equilibrium changes is understood. The changes involved are not instantaneous, although some schools of thought do refer to instantaneous changes in markets. Some markets will take longer to adjust to changes than others. Table 4.3 summarizes the three steps.

TABLE 4.3	**A Three-Step Programme for Analysing Changes in Equilibrium**
	1. Decide whether the event shifts the supply or demand curve (or perhaps both).
	2. Decide in which direction the curve shifts.
	3. Use the supply and demand.

To see how this recipe is used, let us consider various events that might affect the market for rapeseed.

Example: A Change in Demand Suppose that a government-sponsored research project finds that using rapeseed oil helps reduce the risk of heart disease and strokes. How does this event affect the market for rapeseed? To answer this question, let us follow our three steps:

1. The news has a direct effect on the demand curve by changing people's taste for rapeseed oil. That is, the report changes the amount of rapeseed oil that consumers want to buy at any given price.
2. Because the report incentivizes people to use more rapeseed oil, the demand curve SHIFTS to the right. Figure 4.9 shows this increase in demand as the shift in the demand curve from D_1 to D_2. This shift indicates that the quantity of rapeseed oil demanded is higher at every price. The shift in demand has led to a shortage of rapeseed oil in the market. At a price of €200 buyers now want to buy 26,000 tonnes of rapeseed, but sellers are only offering 12,000 tonnes for sale at this price. There is a shortage of 14,000 tonnes.

FIGURE 4.9

How an Increase in Demand Affects the Equilibrium
An event that raises quantity demanded at any given price shifts the demand curve to the right. The equilibrium price and the equilibrium quantity both rise. Here, the report linking using rapeseed oil to reductions in risk of ill health causes buyers to demand more rapeseed. The demand curve shifts from D_1 to D_2, which causes the equilibrium price to rise from €200 to €300 and the equilibrium quantity to rise from 12,000 to 20,000 tonnes.

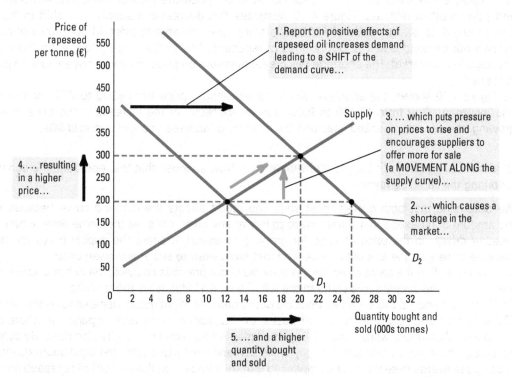

3. As Figure 4.9 shows, the shortage starts to force up prices and encourages growers to offer more rapeseed for sale, which is represented as a MOVEMENT ALONG the supply curve. The additional production incurs extra costs and so a higher price is required to compensate sellers. This raises the equilibrium price from €200 to €300 and the equilibrium quantity from 12,000 to 20,000 tonnes. In other words, the report increases the price of rapeseed and the quantity of rapeseed bought and sold.

Shifts in Curves Versus Movements Along Curves: A Reminder When the report drives up the price of rapeseed, the quantity of rapeseed that growers supply rises, but the supply curve remains in the same position. Economists say there has been an increase in 'quantity supplied' but no *change* in 'supply'.

'Supply' refers to the position of the supply curve, whereas the 'quantity supplied' refers to the amount suppliers wish to sell at different prices. In this example, we assumed supply does not change. Instead, the report alters consumers' desire to buy at any given price, and thereby shifts the demand curve. The increase in demand creates a shortage. The shortage means there are more buyers looking to purchase rapeseed than there are sellers willing to sell. As a result, price starts to creep up as buyers are prepared to pay higher prices to get products. When the price rises growers are willing to offer more rapeseed for sale, and so the quantity supplied rises. This increase in quantity supplied is represented by the movement along the supply curve. The shortage will continue to be competed away by price rising until supply and demand are once again brought into equilibrium. The result will be a rise in equilibrium price and in the amount bought and sold.

Example: A Change in Supply Suppose that, during another summer, bad weather destroys part of the seed crop for rapeseed, and drives up the world price of rapeseed for planting. How does this event affect the market for rapeseed?

1. The change in the price of seed, an input needed to grow rapeseed, affects the supply curve. By raising the costs of production, it reduces the amount of rapeseed that firms produce and sell at any given price. The demand curve does not change because the higher cost of inputs does not directly affect the amount of rapeseed buyers wish to buy.
2. The supply curve shifts to the left because, at every price the total amount that firms are willing and able to sell is reduced. Figure 4.10 illustrates this decrease in supply as a shift in the supply curve from S_1 to S_2. At a price of €200 sellers are now only able to offer 4,000 tonnes of rapeseed for sale but demand is still 12,000 tonnes of rapeseed. The shift in supply to the left has created a shortage in the market. The shortage will create pressure on price to rise as buyers look to purchase rapeseed.
3. As Figure 4.10 shows, the shortage raises the equilibrium price from €200 to €250 and lowers the equilibrium quantity from 12,000 to 9,000 tonnes. Because of the increase in the price of seed for growing, the price of rapeseed rises and the quantity of rapeseed bought and sold falls.

Example: A Change in Both Supply and Demand (i) Now suppose that the report and the bad weather occur during the same summer.

1. We determine that both curves must shift. The report affects the demand curve because it alters the amount of rapeseed that buyers want to buy at any given price. At the same time, when the bad weather drives up the price of seed for growing rapeseed, it alters the supply curve for rapeseed because it changes the amount of rapeseed that firms want to sell at any given price.
2. The curves shift in the same directions as they did in our previous analysis: the demand curve shifts to the right, and the supply curve shifts to the left. Figure 4.11 illustrates these shifts.
3. As Figure 4.11 shows, there are two possible outcomes that might result, depending on the relative size of the demand and supply shifts. In both cases, the equilibrium price rises. In panel (a), where demand increases substantially while supply falls just a little, the equilibrium quantity also rises. By contrast, in panel (b), where supply falls substantially while demand rises just a little, the equilibrium quantity falls. Thus, these events raise the price of rapeseed, but their impact on the amount of rapeseed bought and sold is ambiguous (that is, it could go either way).

FIGURE 4.10

How a Decrease in Supply Affects the Equilibrium

An event that reduces supply at any given price shifts the supply curve to the left. The equilibrium price rises and the equilibrium quantity falls. Here, an increase in the price of seed for growing rapeseed plants (an input) causes sellers to supply less rapeseed. The supply curve shifts from S_1 to S_2, which causes the equilibrium price of rapeseed to rise from €200 to €250 and the equilibrium quantity to fall from 12,000 to 9,000 tonnes.

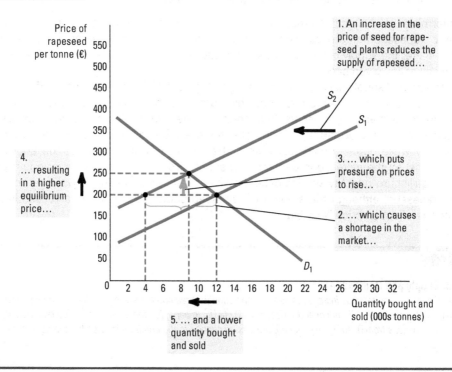

1. An increase in the price of seed for rapeseed plants reduces the supply of rapeseed...

3. ... which puts pressure on prices to rise...

2. ... which causes a shortage in the market...

4. ... resulting in a higher equilibrium price...

5. ... and a lower quantity bought and sold

FIGURE 4.11

A Shift in Both Supply and Demand (i)

Here we observe a simultaneous increase in demand and decrease in supply. Two outcomes are possible. In panel (a), the equilibrium price rises from P_1 to P_2, and the equilibrium quantity rises from Q_1 to Q_2. In panel (b), the equilibrium price again rises from P_1 to P_2, but the equilibrium quantity falls from Q_1 to Q_2.

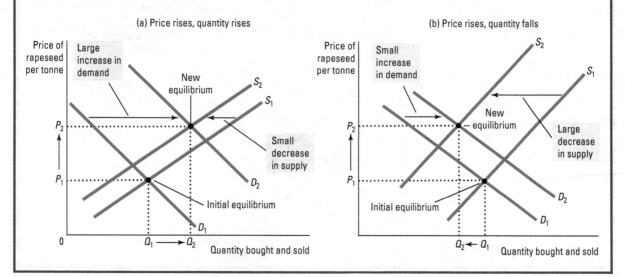

(a) Price rises, quantity rises

(b) Price rises, quantity falls

Example: A Change in Both Supply and Demand (ii) We are now going to look at a slightly different scenario, but still with both supply and demand changing together. Assume that the details of the report have been leaked prior to official publication and the findings publicized on TV news stations. We know that the report is likely to increase demand for rapeseed and so the demand curve will shift to the right. However, sellers' expectations that sales of rapeseed will increase because of the forecasts mean that they take steps to expand production of rapeseed. This would lead to a shift of the supply curve to the right. More rapeseed is now offered for sale at every price.

1. We determine that both curves must shift. The report affects the demand curve because it alters the amount of rapeseed that buyers want to buy at any given price. At the same time, the expectations of producers alter the supply curve for rapeseed because they change the amount of rapeseed that firms want to sell at any given price.
2. Both demand and supply curves shift to the right: Figure 4.12 illustrates these shifts.
3. As Figure 4.12 shows, there are three possible outcomes that might result, depending on the relative size of the demand and supply shifts. In panel (a), where demand increases substantially while supply rises just a little, the equilibrium price and quantity rises. By contrast, in panel (b), where supply rises substantially while demand rises just a little, the equilibrium price falls but the equilibrium quantity rises. In panel (c) the increase in demand and supply are identical and so equilibrium price does not change. Equilibrium quantity will increase, however. Thus these events have different effects on the price of rapeseed, although the amount of rapeseed bought and sold in each case is higher. In this instance the effect on price is ambiguous.

FIGURE 4.12

A Shift in Both Supply and Demand (ii)
Here, again, we observe a simultaneous increase in demand and supply. Three outcomes are possible. In panel (a) the equilibrium price rises from P_1 to P_2 and the equilibrium quantity rises from Q_1 to Q_2. In panel (b), the equilibrium price falls from P_1 to P_2 but the equilibrium quantity rises from Q_1 to Q_2. In panel (c), there is no change to the equilibrium price but the equilibrium quantity rises from Q_1 to Q_2.

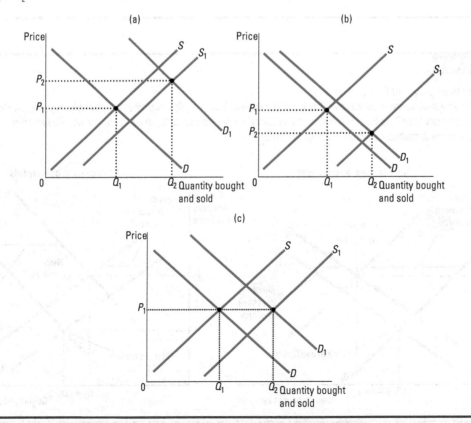

CASE STUDY   The Rapeseed Oil Market

In our discussion so far, we have been using rapeseed as an example, partly because this product fulfils some of the criteria for a competitive market model. In this Case Study, we will look at what has happened to the rapeseed oil market in recent years. Figures published by the Agriculture and Horticulture Development Board (AHDB) show falls in the global supply of rapeseed oil between 2017 and 2019, partly driven by reduced yields per acre and through farmers switching from growing rapeseed to other products. One of the reasons for this has been the impact of cabbage stem flea beetle which has damaged crop yield. The beetle

The price of rapeseed oil is dependent on the demand and supply of rapeseed.

has developed a resistance to chemical sprays and bans on certain types of pesticide sprays have also made growing the crop more challenging. Average price in pounds per tonne fell from £334 to £319 between 2016 and 2017 recovering slightly to reach £394 in 2020. However, since that point prices have risen sharply reaching an average of £603 per tonne in 2021 and around £800 per tonne in 2022. The price of rapeseed is partly determined by futures contracts where buyers will agree to enter into a contract to buy a specified amount at an agreed price in advance. Some May 2022 futures contracts settled at around £864 per tonne, for example.

What factors have driven these changing prices? One important factor has been the growth in popularity of rapeseed oil in cooking and other uses such as biofuels. Rapeseed oil is lower in saturated fat than one of its substitutes, olive oil, and contains chemicals which assist with blood circulation. Demand for rapeseed oil has, therefore, shifted to the right. However, at the same time, there have been supply constraints with harvests from countries like Canada and Australia lower than in previous years. In Canada drought was a factor in a reduced crop in 2021–22 but it was expected that supply would increase in 2022–23. In Australia, production and exports of rapeseed oil were expected to be down 22 per cent and 17 per cent, respectively, in 2022. Another major factor was the conflict in Ukraine. There were forecasts that production would be lower by around 6 per cent in 2022 compared to 2021, and there were also uncertainties around how much rapeseed oil would be exported given the political turmoil surrounding the conflict.

Questions

1 Use supply and demand diagrams to illustrate the following:
   a The effect on rapeseed oil prices of an increase in infestations of cabbage stem flea beetle, which reduces yields.
   b An increase in demand for rapeseed as a substitute for sunflower seed oil, the supply of which has been compromised as a result of the conflict in Ukraine.
   c An increase in both demand for rapeseed oil and a reduction in supply – you can provide different illustrations depending on the extent of the changes in both demand and supply.
2 To what extent do you think the rapeseed oil market is a good example of a competitive market as outlined in this chapter?
3 Why do you think that buyers enter into futures contracts to buy commodities like rapeseed oil? What are the potential advantages and disadvantages of using forward contracts?

References: https://ahdb.org.uk/news/what-will-happen-to-rapeseed-prices-next-year-grain-market-daily (accessed 6 June 2023).
https://ahdb.org.uk/knowledge-library/cabbage-stem-flea-beetle-csfb-and-its-management-in-oilseed-rape (accessed 6 June 2023).

? ▪ **WHAT IF...** Malmo FF, a Swedish football team, is taken over by a rich Middle East backer? The team is strengthened and produces a series of excellent results, which propel them to the top of the Swedish Allsvenskan. Demand for tickets to the 24,000 capacity stadium increases dramatically. Draw a supply and demand diagram to illustrate this market situation. Would the club increase ticket prices? If so, what might fans' reaction be? If the club does not increase prices, why might it make this decision? What do you think would be the practical effect on fans and the prices they must pay for tickets if prices were held at the original level? Assuming the improvement in the club's fortunes continues for several seasons, what might the long-term market situation look like?

FYI

Prices as Signals

Our analysis so far has only brushed the surface of the way markets operate. Economists have conducted extensive research into the nature and determinants of both demand and supply. It is beyond the scope of this book to go into too much detail on these issues, but it is useful to have a little bit of background knowledge on this to help understand markets more effectively.

At the heart of research into demand and supply is why buyers and sellers behave as they do. The development of magnetic resonance imaging (MRI) techniques has allowed researchers to investigate how the brain responds to different stimuli when making purchasing decisions (the application of tools and understanding in neuroscience to economic research is referred to as *neuroeconomics*). As time goes by, our understanding of buyer and seller behaviour will improve, and theories must be adapted to accommodate this new understanding.

However, much of the theory behind how markets work relies on the assumption of rational behaviour, defined in terms of humans preferring more to less and considering information prior to making a decision. The main function of price in a free market is to act as a signal to both buyers and sellers to help in decision making.

For buyers, price tells them something about what they must give up to acquire the benefits that having the good will confer on them. These benefits are referred to as the *utility* (satisfaction) derived from consumption. If you are willing to pay €10 to go and watch a film, then economists will assume that the value of the benefits you gain from watching the film is greater than the next best alternative you could have spent your €10 on. We have noted in Chapter 1 that people face trade-offs, and that the cost of something is what you must give up to acquire it. This is fundamental to the law of demand. At higher prices, the sacrifice being made in terms of the value of the benefits gained from alternatives is greater, and so we may be less willing to do so as a result. If the price of a ticket for the film was €20 (other things being equal), then it might have to be a very good film to persuade us that giving up what else €20 could buy is worth it.

For sellers, price acts as a signal in relation to the profitability of production. For most sellers, increasing the amount of a good produced will incur some additional input costs. A higher price is required to compensate for the additional cost and to also enable the producer to gain some reward from the risk they are taking in production. That reward is termed profit.

If prices are rising in a free market, then this acts as a different but related signal to buyers and sellers. Rising prices to a seller means that there is a shortage, and thus there is an incentive to expand production because the seller knows that they will be able to sell what they produce. For buyers, a rising price changes the nature of the trade-off they face. They will now have to give up more to acquire the good, and they must decide whether the value of the benefits they will gain from acquiring the good is worth the extra price they must pay.

What we do know is that for both buyers and sellers, there are many complex processes that occur in decision making. While we do not fully understand all these processes yet, economists are constantly searching for new insights that might help them understand the workings of markets more fully. All of us go through these complex processes every time we make a purchasing decision, although we may not realize it! Having some appreciation of these processes is fundamental to thinking like an economist.

Summary

We have just seen four examples of how to use supply and demand curves to analyze a change in equilibrium. Whenever an event shifts the supply curve, the demand curve, or perhaps both curves, you can use these tools to predict how the event will alter the amount bought and sold in equilibrium and the price at which the good is bought and sold. Table 4.4 shows the predicted outcome for any combination of shifts in the two curves. To make sure you understand how to use the tools of supply and demand, pick a few entries in this table and make sure you can explain to yourself why the table contains the prediction it does.

TABLE 4.4	**What Happens to Price and Quantity When Supply or Demand Shifts?**

As a self test, make sure you can explain each of the entries in this table using a supply and demand diagram.

	No change in supply	An increase in supply	A decrease in supply
No change in demand	P same	P down	P up
	Q same	Q up	Q down
An increase in demand	P up	P ambiguous	P up
	Q up	Q up	Q ambiguous
A decrease in demand	P down	P down	P ambiguous
	Q down	Q ambiguous	Q down

HOW PRICES ALLOCATE RESOURCES

This chapter has analyzed supply and demand in a single market. Although our discussion has centred on the market for rapeseed, the lessons learned here apply in many other markets as well. Whenever you go to a shop to buy something, you are contributing to the demand for that item. Whenever you look for a job, you are contributing to the supply of labour services. Because supply and demand are such pervasive economic phenomena, the model of supply and demand is a powerful tool for analysis. We shall be using this model repeatedly in the chapters which follow.

In this chapter, we have begun to see how markets work. In any economic system, scarce resources must be allocated among competing uses. Market economies harness the forces of supply and demand to serve that end. Supply and demand together determine the prices of the economy's many different goods and services; prices in turn are the signals that guide the allocation of resources. Consider the allocation of property on the seafront in a seaside resort. Because the amount of this property is limited, not everyone can enjoy the luxury of living by the beach. Who gets this resource? The answer is: whoever is willing and able to pay the price. The price of seafront property adjusts until the quantity of property demanded exactly balances the quantity supplied. Thus, in market economies, prices are the mechanism for rationing scarce resources.

Similarly, prices determine who produces each good and how much is produced. For instance, consider farming. Because we need food to survive, it is crucial that some people work on farms. What determines who is a farmer and who is not? The allocation of workers to farms is based on the job decisions of millions of workers. This system works because decisions depend on prices. The prices of food and the wages of farm workers (the price of their labour) adjust to ensure that (hopefully) enough people choose to be farmers.

SUMMARY

- Economists use the model of supply and demand to analyze competitive markets. In a competitive market, there are many buyers and sellers, each of whom has little or no influence on the market price.

- The supply curve shows how the quantity of a good supplied depends on the price. According to the law of supply, as the price of a good rises, the quantity supplied rises. Therefore, the supply curve slopes upward.

- In addition to price, other determinants of how much producers want to sell include input prices, technology, expectations, the number of sellers, and natural and social factors. If one of these factors changes, the supply curve shifts.

- The demand curve shows how the quantity of a good demanded depends on the price. According to the law of demand, as the price of a good falls, the quantity demanded rises. Therefore, the demand curve slopes downward.

- In addition to price, other determinants of how much consumers want to buy include income, the prices of substitutes and complements, tastes, expectations and the number of buyers. If one of these factors changes, the demand curve shifts.

- The intersection of the supply and demand curves determines the market equilibrium. At the equilibrium price, the quantity supplied equals the quantity demanded.

- The behaviour of sellers and buyers drives markets towards their equilibrium. When the market price is above the equilibrium price, there is a surplus of the good, which causes the market price to fall. When the market price is below the equilibrium price, there is a shortage, which causes the market price to rise.

- To analyze how any event influences a market, we use supply and demand diagrams to examine how the event affects the equilibrium price and quantity. To do this we follow three steps. First, we decide whether the event shifts the supply curve or the demand curve (or both). Second, we decide which direction the curve shifts. Third, we compare the new equilibrium with the initial equilibrium.

- In market economies, prices are the signals that guide economic decisions and thereby allocate scarce resources. Changes in prices help bring supply and demand into some sort of balance. The equilibrium price then determines how much of the good buyers choose to purchase and how much sellers choose to produce.

IN THE NEWS

Saving Rhinos From Extinction

The rhinoceros is an endangered species. The incentives for poachers to kill rhinos for their horn is significant. Rhino horns can sell for up to €250,000 each. The reason for the high prices is partly because the demand exceeds the available supply, and because of the risk premium built into the price because poaching rhino horn is illegal. To protect rhinos, there are strict international regulations on the trade in rhino horns. There have also been education programmes designed to reduce demand by pointing out that the beliefs over the properties of rhino horn are without foundation. Controls over supply and demand, however, do not seem to be working. The number of rhinos in the wild continues to decline. According to Save the Rhino, the number of black rhino fell from around 70,000 in 1970 to around 2,400 in 1995. Conservation

If controls on poaching of rhinos are not working, could making available legitimate supplies of this product help save this endangered species?

efforts have seen numbers recover to an extent, and it is estimated in 2022 that there are around 5,500 individuals. In Indonesia, there are now fewer than 80 Sumatran rhinos and around 75 Javan rhinos.

One suggestion to help save the rhino is to allow some legitimate market transactions in rhino horn. If the supply of rhino horn were to increase, the price would fall and the incentives to poach would be reduced. The South African government has reportedly contemplated the idea of some regulated legitimate market transactions in rhino horn. There are farmers who look after rhino, who de-horn the animals on a regular basis to reduce the chance of poaching. These supplies of rhino horn could be made available through a legal market to help satisfy the demand.

(Continued)

In another move to increase the supply of rhino horn, a biotech company, Pembient, run by Matthew Markus is manufacturing synthetic rhino horn. It says that if this was supplied into the market it would help drive down the price. Pembient's mission is 'to use biotechnology to grow horns larger than animals can produce' and to supply these to artisans who use them to produce curios for sale. Critics argue that legitimizing the trade in rhino horn in any way would be dangerous and send out the wrong signals. Continued bans, stronger global information sharing among police authorities and harsher punishments for poachers should be at the heart of the battle to save the rhino. Market enthusiasts claim this will simply not work and would be a recipe for hastening extinction. A study of the economics of synthetic rhino horns by Frederick Chen of Wake Forest University in North Carolina, notes, 'whether the availability of synthetic horns would decrease the equilibrium supply of wild horns – and how much the reduction would be – depends on market structure, i.e. how competitive the synthetic horn production sector is – and on how substitutable the synthetic horns are for wild horns.' Chen also notes that it is important to ensure there is competition in the market for synthetic horn to try to keep prices low otherwise there might be an incentive to keep prices too high, which would not deter poaching.

Questions

1 **Draw a supply and demand diagram to illustrate the market for rhino horn. Use the diagram to show and explain why the price of rhino horn is so high. Think about the shape of the demand and supply curves in your diagram.**
2 **Using a diagram, show how an increase in supply and a successful education programme on the claims made for rhino horn could help reduce prices for rhino horn.**
3 **The market for rhino horn is one example of how incentives drive behaviour. Why are poachers incentivized to take part in the illegal trade in rhino horn?**
4 **To what extent do you think that flooding the market with synthetic rhino horn would succeed in helping protect wild rhinos?**
5 **Consider the view that legalizing trade in rhino horn would be a more effective way of protecting wild rhinos compared to bans, increased regulation and international policing of trade in rhino horn. Use supply and demand diagrams to help illustrate your arguments.**

Sources: www.pembient.com/conservation
www.savetherhino.org/rhino-info/population-figures/
www.rhinoresourcecenter.com/pdf_files/151/1517810559.pdf

QUESTIONS FOR REVIEW

1 What determines the quantity of a good that sellers supply?
2 What are the supply schedule and the supply curve, and how are they related? Why does the supply curve slope upwards?
3 Does a change in producers' technology lead to a movement along the supply curve or a shift in the supply curve? Does a change in price lead to a movement along the supply curve or a shift in the supply curve?
4 What determines the quantity of a good that buyers demand?
5 What are the demand schedule and the demand curve, and how are they related? Why does the demand curve slope downwards?
6 Does a change in consumers' tastes lead to a movement along the demand curve or a shift in the demand curve? Does a change in price lead to a movement along the demand curve or a shift in the demand curve?
7 Carlos prefers asparagus to spinach. His income declines, and he buys more spinach. Is spinach an inferior or a normal good to Carlos? Explain your answer.
8 Define the equilibrium of a market. Describe the forces that move a market towards its equilibrium.
9 Cheese and wine are complements because they are often enjoyed together. When the price of wine rises, use the tools of supply and demand to predict what happens to the supply, demand, quantity supplied, quantity demanded and the price in the market for cheese.
10 Describe the role of prices in market economies.

PROBLEMS AND APPLICATIONS

1 Explain each of the following statements using supply and demand diagrams.

   a. When there is a drought in southern Europe, the price of olive oil rises in supermarkets throughout Europe.
   b. A slowdown in economic activity in China causes a fall in the price of steel on world markets.
   c. The price of skiing holidays rises dramatically during the two weeks in which schools have breaks in February.

2 'An increase in the demand for mozzarella cheese raises the quantity of mozzarella demanded, but not the quantity supplied.' Is this statement true or false? Explain.

3 Consider the market for large family saloon cars. For each of the events listed here, identify which of the determinants of supply or demand is affected, and indicate whether supply or demand is increased or decreased. Then show the effect on the price and quantity of large family saloon cars.

   a. People decide to have more children.
   b. A strike by steel workers raises steel prices.
   c. Engineers develop new automated machinery for the production of cars.
   d. The price of estate cars rises.
   e. A stock market crash lowers peoples' wealth.

4 During the 1990s, technological advances reduced the cost of computer chips. How do you think this affected the market for computers? For computer software? For manual typewriters?

5 Using supply and demand diagrams, show the effect of the following events on the market for sweatshirts.

   a. A drought in Egypt damages the cotton crop.
   b. The price of leather jackets falls.
   c. All universities require students to attend morning exercise classes in appropriate attire.
   d. New knitting machines are invented.

6 Suppose that in the year 2019 the number of births is temporarily high. How might this baby boom affect the price of baby-sitting services in 2024 and 2034? (Hint: 5-year-olds need babysitters, whereas 15-year-olds can be babysitters.)

7 The market for pizza has the following demand and supply schedules:

Price (€)	Quantity demanded	Quantity supplied
4	135	26
5	104	53
6	81	81
7	68	98
8	53	110
9	39	121

Graph the demand and supply curves. What is the equilibrium price and quantity in this market? If the actual price in this market were above the equilibrium price, what would drive the market towards the equilibrium? If the actual price in this market were below the equilibrium price, what would drive the market towards the equilibrium?

8 Suppose that the price of tickets to see your local football team play at home is determined by market forces. Currently, the demand and supply schedules are as follows:

Price (€)	Quantity demanded	Quantity supplied
10	50,000	30,000
20	40,000	30,000
30	30,000	30,000
40	20,000	30,000
50	10,000	30,000

a. Draw the demand and supply curves. What is unusual about this supply curve? Why might this be true?

b. What are the equilibrium price and quantity of tickets?

c. Your team plans to increase total capacity in its stadium by 10,000 seats next season. What admission price should it charge?

9 Market research has revealed the following information about the market for chocolate bars: the demand schedule can be represented by the equation $Q_d = 1,600 - 300P$, where Q_d is the quantity demanded and P is the price. The supply schedule can be represented by the equation $Q_s = 1,400 + 700P$, where Q_s is the quantity supplied. Calculate the equilibrium price and quantity in the market for chocolate bars. (Note: if you do not need to go into the maths around markets then this question can be viewed as optional.)

10 What do we mean by a perfectly competitive market? Do you think that the example of rapeseed used in this chapter fits this description? Is there another type of market that better characterizes the market for rapeseed?

5 ELASTICITY AND ITS APPLICATIONS

LEARNING OUTCOMES

After reading this chapter you should be able to:

- Calculate elasticity using the midpoint method.
- Calculate the price elasticity of supply and demand.
- Distinguish between an inelastic and elastic supply and demand curve.
- Distinguish between the price elasticity of demand for necessities and luxuries.
- Calculate different elasticities: price, income and cross.
- Demonstrate the impact of the price elasticity of demand on total expenditure and total revenue under conditions of different demand elasticities.

ELASTICITY AND ITS APPLICATION

For businesses, the price they charge for the products they produce is a vital part of their product positioning: what the product offering is in relation to competitors. We have seen in Chapter 4 how markets are dynamic, and that price acts as a signal to both sellers and buyers; when prices change, the signal is altered and producer and consumer behaviour changes.

Imagine a business producing silicon chips for use in personal computers, laptops and a variety of other electronic devices. Because the business earns all its income from selling silicon chips, it devotes much effort to making the factory as productive as it can be. It monitors how production is organized, staff recruitment and motivation levels, checks suppliers for cost effectiveness and quality, and studies the latest advances in technology. The business knows that the more chips it manufactures, the more will be available to sell, and the higher will be its income (assuming it can sell them).

One day a local university announces a major discovery. Scientists have devised a new material to produce chips which would help to increase computing power by 50 per cent. How should the business react to this news? Should it use the new material? Does this discovery make the business better off or worse off than before? In this chapter, we will see that these questions can have surprising answers. The surprise will come from applying the most basic tools of economics, supply and demand, to the market for computer chips.

To carry out this analysis we will use the concept of *elasticity,* also referred to as *price sensitivity.* We know from Chapter 4 that when price rises, demand falls and supply rises. What we did not discuss in the chapter was *how far* demand and supply change in response to changes in price. In other words, how sensitive supply and demand are to a change in prices. When studying how some event or policy affects a market, we can discuss not only the direction of the effects but their magnitude as well. **Elasticity**, a measure of how much buyers and sellers respond to changes in market conditions, allows us to turn statements about quantity supplied and demanded from the qualitative to the quantitative, with the result that the analysis will have greater precision.

> **elasticity** a measure of the responsiveness of quantity supplied or quantity demanded to one of its determinants

PRICE ELASTICITY OF SUPPLY

The Price Elasticity of Supply and Its Determinants

The law of supply states that higher prices raise the quantity supplied. **Price elasticity of supply** measures how much the quantity supplied responds to changes in the price. Supply of a good is said to be *elastic* (or price sensitive) if the quantity supplied responds substantially to changes in the price. Supply is said to be *inelastic* (or price insensitive) if the quantity supplied responds only slightly to changes in the price.

> **price elasticity of supply** a measure of how much the quantity supplied of a good responds to a change in the price of that good, computed as the percentage change in quantity supplied divided by the percentage change in price

The price elasticity of supply depends on the flexibility of sellers to change the amount of the good they produce. For example, seafront property has an inelastic supply, because it is almost impossible to produce more of it quickly. Supply is not very sensitive to changes in price. By contrast, manufactured goods, such as books, cars and television sets, have relatively elastic supplies because the firms that produce them can run their production facilities longer in response to a higher price. Supply is more sensitive to changes in price.

Elasticity can take any value greater than or equal to zero. The closer to zero the more inelastic, and the closer to infinity the more elastic.

PITFALL PREVENTION Throughout this chapter we will use the term 'relative' quite a lot. We do so because we are comparing different situations and degrees of elasticity, so it is important to be aware that we may be talking about, for example, two goods that are both inelastic but one is more inelastic than the other and so its elasticity is relative to something else.

The Determinants of Price Elasticity of Supply

The Time Period In most markets, a key determinant of the price elasticity of supply is the time period being considered. Supply is usually more elastic in the long run than in the short run. We can further distinguish between the short run and the very short run. Over very short periods of time, firms may find it impossible to respond to a change in price by changing output. In the short run, firms cannot easily change productive capacity to make more or less of a good, but may have some flexibility. For example, it might take a month to employ new labour, but after that time some increase in output can be accommodated. Overall, in the short run, the quantity supplied is not very responsive to the price. By contrast, over longer periods, firms can build new factories or close old ones, hire new staff and buy in more capital and equipment. In addition, new firms can enter a market and old firms can shut down. Thus, in the long run, the quantity supplied can respond substantially to price changes.

Productive Capacity Most businesses, in the short run, will have a finite capacity, an upper limit to the amount that they can produce at any one time determined by the quantity of factor inputs they possess. How far they are using this capacity depends, in turn, on the state of the economy. In periods of strong economic growth, firms may be operating at or near full capacity. If demand and prices are rising for the product they produce, it may be difficult for the firm to expand output, and so supply may be inelastic.

When the economy is growing slowly or is contracting, some firms may find they must cut back output and may only be operating at 60 per cent of full capacity. In this situation, if demand later increased and prices started to rise, it may be much easier for the firm to expand output relatively quickly and so supply would be more elastic.

The Size of the Firm/Industry It is possible that, as a general rule, supply may be more elastic in smaller firms or industries than in larger ones. For example, consider a small independent furniture manufacturer. Demand for its products may rise and in response the firm may be able to buy in raw materials (wood, for example) to meet this increase in demand. While the firm will incur a cost in buying in this timber, it is unlikely that the unit cost for the material will increase significantly. Compare this to a situation where a steel manufacturer increases its purchase of raw materials (iron ore, for example). Buying large quantities of iron ore on global commodity markets can drive up unit price and, by association, unit costs.

The response of supply to changes in price in large firms/industries, therefore, may be less elastic than in smaller firms/industries. This is also related to the number of firms in the industry. The more firms there are in the industry the easier it is to increase supply, other things being equal.

The Mobility of Factors of Production Consider a farmer whose land is currently devoted to producing wheat. A sharp rise in the price of rapeseed might encourage the farmer to switch use of their land from wheat to rapeseed relatively easily. The mobility of the factor of production land, in this case, is relatively high and so supply of rapeseed may be relatively elastic.

Many multinational firms that have plants in different parts of the world now build each plant to be identical. What this means is that if there is disruption to one plant the firm can more easily transfer operations to another plant elsewhere and continue production 'seamlessly'. Car manufacturers utilize such an interchangeability of parts and operations. The chassis, for example, may be identical across a range of branded car models. This is the case with some Audi, Volkswagen, Seat and Skoda models. This means that the supply may be more elastic as a result.

Compare this to the supply of highly skilled oncology consultants. An increase in the wages of oncology consultants (suggesting a shortage exists) will not mean that a renal consultant or other doctors can suddenly switch to take advantage of the higher wages and increase the supply of oncology consultants. In this example, the mobility of labour to switch between different uses is limited, and so the supply of these specialist consultants is likely to be relatively inelastic.

Ease of Storing Stock/Inventory In some firms, stocks can be built up to enable the firm to respond more flexibly to changes in prices. In industries where inventory build-up is relatively easy and cheap, the price elasticity of supply is more elastic than in industries where it is much harder to do this. Consider the fresh fruit industry, for example. Storing fresh fruit is not easy because it is perishable, and so the price elasticity of supply in this industry may be more inelastic.

Computing the Price Elasticity of Supply

Economists compute the price elasticity of supply as the percentage change in the quantity supplied divided by the percentage change in the price. That is:

$$\text{Price elasticity of supply} = \frac{\text{Percentage change in quantity supplied}}{\text{Percentage change in price}}$$

For example, suppose that an increase in the price of milk from €0.20 to €0.25 a litre raises the amount that dairy farmers produce from 90,000 to 106,875 litres per month. We calculate the percentage change in price as:

$$\text{Percentage change in price} = (0.25 - 0.20)/0.20 \times 100 = 25\%$$

Similarly, we calculate the percentage change in quantity supplied as the change in supply (16,875 litres) divided by the original amount (90,000 litres) multiplied by 100:

$$\text{Percentage change in quantity supplied} = 16,875/90,000 \times 100 = 18.75\%$$

In this case, the price elasticity of supply is:

Price elasticity of supply = 18.75/25 = 0.75

In this example, the elasticity of 0.75 reflects the fact that the quantity supplied changes proportionately three-quarters as much as the price. If price rose by 15 per cent, for example, supply would rise by 0.75 × 15 = 11.25%. In this example, the price elasticity of the supply of milk would be classed as 'inelastic' because the percentage change in supply is less than the percentage change in price.

The Midpoint Method of Calculating Percentage Changes and Elasticities

If you try calculating the price elasticity of supply between two points on a supply curve, you may notice an annoying problem: the elasticity for a movement from point A to point B seems different from the elasticity for a movement from point B to point A. For example, consider these numbers:

Point A: Price = €4 Quantity Supplied = 80
Point B: Price = €6 Quantity Supplied = 125

Going from point A to point B, the price rises by 50 per cent, the change in price divided by the original price × 100 (2/4 × 100), and the quantity rises by 56.25 per cent (the change in quantity supplied divided by the original supply × 100: 45/80 × 100), indicating that the price elasticity of supply is 56.25/50 or 1.125.

By contrast, going from point B to point A, the price falls by 33 per cent (2/6 × 100), and the quantity falls by 36 per cent (45/125 × 100), indicating that the price elasticity of supply is 36/33 or 1.09.

Note, in the working above we have rounded the fall in price to the nearest whole number (33 per cent).

One way to avoid this problem is to use the *midpoint method* for calculating elasticities. In the example above we used a standard way to compute a percentage change: divide the change by the initial level and multiply by 100. By contrast, the midpoint method computes a percentage change by dividing the change by the midpoint (or average) of the initial and final levels. In our example, the midpoint between point A and point B is:

Midpoint: Price = €5 Quantity = 102.5

€5 is the midpoint of €4 and €6. Therefore, according to the midpoint method, a change from €4 to €6 is considered a 40 per cent rise, because ((6 − 4)/5) × 100 = 40. Similarly, a change from €6 to €4 is considered a 40 per cent fall ((4 − 6)/5) × 100 = −40. Looking at the quantity, moving from point A to point B gives (125 − 80)/102.5 × 100 = 43.9% and for a price fall (80 − 125)/102.5 × 100 = −43.9%.

Because the midpoint method gives the same answer regardless of the direction of change (as indicated by the negative sign), it is often used when calculating price elasticities between two points.

According to the midpoint method, when going from point A to point B, the price rises by 40 per cent, and the quantity rises by 43.9 per cent. Similarly, when going from point B to point A, the price falls by 40 per cent, and the quantity falls by 43.9 per cent. In both directions, the price elasticity of supply equals 1.0975 (1.1 to 1 decimal place).

We can express the midpoint method with the following formula for the price elasticity of supply between two points, denoted (Q_1, P_1) and (Q_2, P_2):

$$\text{Price elasticity of supply} = \frac{(Q_2 - Q_1)/([Q_2 + Q_1]/2)}{(P_2 - P_1)/([P_2 + P_1]/2)}$$

The numerator is the percentage change in quantity computed using the midpoint method, and the denominator is the percentage change in price computed using the midpoint method.

The Variety of Supply Curves

Because the price elasticity of supply measures the responsiveness of quantity supplied to the change in price, it is reflected in the appearance of the supply curve (assuming we are using similar scales on the axes of diagrams being used). Figure 5.1 shows five cases. In the extreme case of a zero elasticity, as shown in panel (a), supply is *perfectly inelastic* and the supply curve is vertical.

FIGURE 5.1

The Price Elasticity of Supply

The price elasticity of supply determines whether the supply curve is steep or flat (assuming that the scale used for the axes is the same). Note that all percentage changes are calculated using the midpoint method.

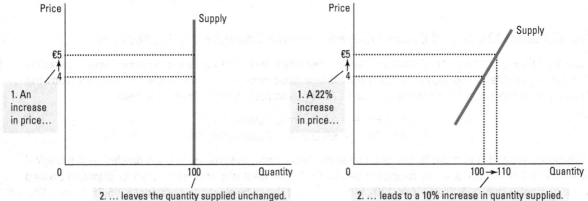

(a) Perfectly inelastic supply: Elasticity equals 0

1. An increase in price...

2. ... leaves the quantity supplied unchanged.

(b) Inelastic supply: Elasticity is less than 1

1. A 22% increase in price...

2. ... leads to a 10% increase in quantity supplied.

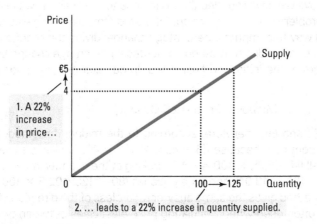

(c) Unit elastic supply: Elasticity equals 1

1. A 22% increase in price...

2. ... leads to a 22% increase in quantity supplied.

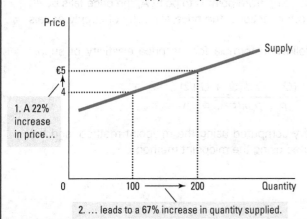

(d) Elastic supply: Elasticity is greater than 1

1. A 22% increase in price...

2. ... leads to a 67% increase in quantity supplied.

(e) Perfectly elastic supply: Elasticity equals infinity

1. At any price above €4, quantity supplied is infinite.

2. At exactly €4, producers will supply any quantity.

3. At a price below €4, quantity supplied is zero.

In this case, the quantity supplied is the same regardless of the price. As the elasticity rises, the supply curve gets flatter, which shows that the quantity supplied responds more to changes in the price. At the opposite extreme, shown in panel (e), supply is *perfectly elastic*. This occurs as the price elasticity of supply approaches infinity and the supply curve becomes horizontal, meaning that very small changes in the price lead to very large changes in the quantity supplied.

In some markets, the elasticity of supply is not constant, but varies over the supply curve. Figure 5.2 shows a typical case for an industry in which firms have factories with a limited capacity for production. For low levels of quantity supplied, the elasticity of supply is high, indicating that firms respond substantially to changes in the price. In this region, firms have capacity for production that is not being used, such as buildings and machinery sitting idle for all or part of the day. Small increases in price make it profitable for firms to begin using this idle capacity. As the quantity supplied rises, firms begin to reach capacity. Once capacity is fully used, increasing production further requires the construction of new factories. To induce firms to incur this extra expense, the price must rise substantially, so supply becomes less elastic.

Figure 5.2 presents a numerical example of this phenomenon. Each case uses the midpoint method and the numbers have been rounded for convenience. When the price rises from €3 to €4 (a 29 per cent increase), the quantity supplied rises from 100 to 200 (a 67 per cent increase). Because quantity supplied moves proportionately more than the price, the supply curve has elasticity greater than 1. By contrast, when the price rises from €12 to €15 (a 22 per cent increase), the quantity supplied rises from 500 to 525 (a 5 per cent increase). In this case, quantity supplied moves proportionately less than the price, so the elasticity is less than 1.

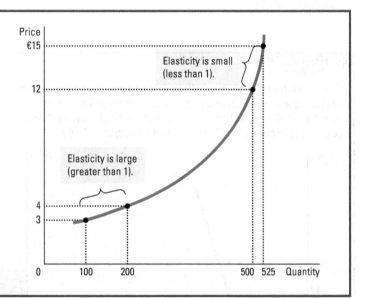

FIGURE 5.2

How the Price Elasticity of Supply Can Vary
Because firms often have a maximum capacity for production, the elasticity of supply may be very high at low levels of quantity supplied and very low at high levels of quantity supplied. Here, an increase in price from €3 to €4 increases the quantity supplied from 100 to 200. Because the increase in quantity supplied of 67 per cent (computed using the midpoint method) is larger than the increase in price of 29 per cent, the supply curve is elastic in this range. By contrast, when the price rises from €12 to €15, the quantity supplied rises only from 500 to 525. Because the increase in quantity supplied of 5 per cent (rounded up) is smaller than the increase in price of 22 per cent, the supply curve is inelastic in this range.

Total Revenue and the Price Elasticity of Supply

When studying changes in supply in a market we are often interested in the resulting changes in the **total revenue** received by producers. In any market, total revenue received by sellers is the price of the good times the quantity of the good sold ($P \times Q$). This is highlighted in Figure 5.3, which shows an upward sloping supply curve with an assumed price of €5 and a supply of 100 units. The height of the box under the supply curve is P and the width is Q. The area of this box, $P \times Q$, equals the total revenue received in this market. In Figure 5.3, where $P = €5$ and $Q = 100$, total revenue is €5 × 100, or €500.

> **total revenue** the amount received by sellers of a good, computed as the price of the good times the quantity sold

---

FIGURE 5.3

The Supply Curve and Total Revenue
The total amount received by sellers equals the area of the box under the supply curve, P × Q. Here, at a price of €5, the quantity supplied is 100 and the total revenue is €500.

The change in total revenue as a result of a price change will depend on the price elasticity of supply. If supply is inelastic, as in Figure 5.4, then an increase in the price which is proportionately larger causes an increase in total revenue. Here an increase in price from €4 to €5 (a 25 per cent increase) causes the quantity supplied to rise from 90 to 100 (an increase of 11.1 per cent), and so total revenue rises from €360 to €500.

FIGURE 5.4

How Total Revenue Changes When Price Changes: Inelastic Supply
With an inelastic supply curve, an increase in the price leads to an increase in quantity supplied that is proportionately smaller. Therefore, total revenue (the product of price and quantity) increases. Here, an increase in the price from €4 to €5 causes the quantity supplied to rise from 90 to 100, and total revenue rises from €360 to €500.

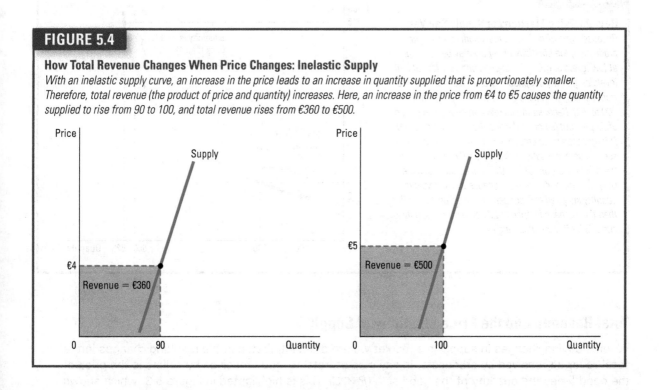

If supply is elastic, then a similar increase in price brings about a much larger than proportionate increase in supply. In Figure 5.5, we assume a price of €4 and a supply of 90 with total revenue of €360. Now a price increase from €4 to €5 leads to a much greater than proportionate increase in supply from 90 to 150 with total revenue rising to €750.

FIGURE 5.5

How Total Revenue Changes When Price Changes: Elastic Supply

With an elastic supply curve, an increase in price leads to an increase in quantity supplied that is proportionately larger. Therefore, total revenue (the product of price and quantity) increases. Here, an increase in the price from €4 to €5 causes the quantity supplied to rise from 90 to 150, and total revenue rises from €360 to €750.

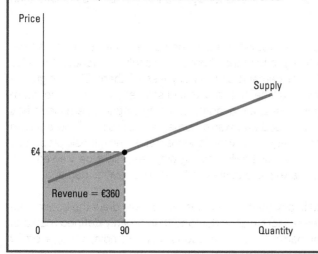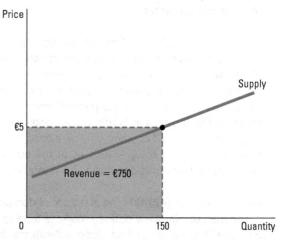

THE PRICE ELASTICITY OF DEMAND

Businesses cannot directly control demand. They can seek to influence demand (and do) by utilizing a variety of strategies and tactics, but ultimately the consumer decides whether to buy a product or not. One important way in which consumer behaviour can be influenced is through a firm changing the prices of its goods (many firms do have some control over the price they can charge although as we have seen, in perfectly competitive markets this is not the case as the firm is a price taker). An understanding of the price elasticity of demand is important in anticipating the likely effects of changes in price on demand.

The Price Elasticity of Demand and Its Determinants

The law of demand states that a fall in the price of a good raises the quantity demanded. The **price elasticity of demand** measures how much the quantity demanded responds to a change in price. Demand for a good is said to be *elastic* or *price sensitive* if the quantity demanded responds substantially to changes in the price. Demand is said to be *inelastic* or *price insensitive* if the quantity demanded responds only slightly to changes in the price.

> **price elasticity of demand** a measure of how much the quantity demanded of a good responds to a change in the price of that good, computed as the percentage change in quantity demanded divided by the percentage change in price

The price elasticity of demand for any good measures how willing consumers are to move to or away from a good as its price changes. Thus the elasticity reflects the many economic, social and psychological forces that influence consumer tastes. Based on experience, however, we can state some general rules about what determines the price elasticity of demand.

Availability of Close Substitutes Goods with close substitutes tend to have a more elastic demand, because it is easier for consumers to switch from that good to others. For example, butter and spread are easily substitutable. A small increase in the price of butter, assuming the price of spread is held fixed, causes the quantity of butter sold to fall by a relatively large amount. As a rule, the closer the substitute the more elastic the good is because it is easier for consumers to switch from one to the other. By contrast, because eggs are a food without a close substitute, the demand for eggs is likely to be less elastic than the demand for butter.

Necessities Versus Luxuries Necessities tend to have relatively inelastic demands, whereas luxuries have relatively elastic demands. People use gas and electricity to heat their homes and cook their food. If the price of gas and electricity rose together, people would not demand dramatically less of them. They might try and be more energy-efficient and reduce their demand a little, but they would still need hot food and warm homes. By contrast, when the price of sailing dinghies rises, the quantity of sailing dinghies demanded falls substantially. The reason is that most people view hot food and warm homes as necessities and a sailing dinghy as a luxury. Of course, whether a good is a necessity or a luxury depends not on the intrinsic properties of the good but on the preferences of the buyer. For an avid sailor, sailing dinghies might be viewed as a necessity with inelastic demand and hot food and a warm place to sleep a luxury with elastic demand.

Definition of the Market The elasticity of demand in any market depends on how we draw the boundaries of the market. Narrowly defined markets tend to have more elastic demand than broadly defined markets, because it is easier to find close substitutes for narrowly defined goods. For example, food, a broad category, has a fairly price inelastic demand because there are no good substitutes for food. Ice cream, a narrower category, has a more price elastic demand because it is easy to substitute other desserts for ice cream. Vanilla ice cream, a very narrow category, has a very price elastic demand, because other flavours of ice cream are good substitutes for vanilla.

Proportion of Income Devoted to the Product Some products have a relatively high price and take a larger proportion of income than others. Buying a new suite of furniture for a lounge, for example, tends to take up a large amount of income, whereas buying an ice cream might account for only a tiny proportion of income. If the price of a three-piece suite rises by 10 per cent, therefore, this is likely to have a greater effect on demand for this furniture than a similar 10 per cent increase in the price of an ice cream. The higher the proportion of income devoted to the product the greater the price elasticity is likely to be.

Time Horizon Goods tend to have more elastic demand over longer time horizons. When the price of petrol rises, the quantity of petrol demanded falls only slightly in the first few months. Over time, however, people buy more fuel-efficient cars, switch to public transport or perhaps to electric vehicles and move closer to where they work. Within several years, the quantity of petrol demanded falls more substantially. Similarly, if the price of a unit of electricity rises much above an equivalent energy unit of gas, demand may fall only slightly in the short run because many people already have electric cookers or electric heating appliances installed in their homes and cannot easily switch. If the price difference persists over several years, however, people may find it worth their while to replace their old electric heating and cooking appliances with new gas appliances and the demand for electricity will fall.

Computing the Price Elasticity of Demand

The principles for computing price elasticity of demand are similar to those discussed when we looked at price elasticity of supply. The price elasticity of demand is computed as the percentage change in the quantity demanded divided by the percentage change in the price. That is:

$$\text{Price elasticity of demand} = \frac{\text{Percentage change in quantity demanded}}{\text{Percentage change in price}}$$

Suppose that a 10 per cent increase in the price of a packet of breakfast cereal causes the amount bought to fall by 20 per cent. Because the quantity demanded of a good is negatively related to its price, the percentage change in quantity will always have the opposite sign to the percentage change in price. In this example, the percentage change in price is a *positive* 10 per cent (reflecting an increase), and the percentage change in quantity demanded is a *negative* 20 per cent (reflecting a decrease). For this reason, price elasticities of demand are sometimes reported as negative numbers. In this book, we follow the common practice of dropping the minus sign and reporting all price elasticities as positive numbers. (Mathematicians call this the *absolute value*.) With this convention, a larger price elasticity implies a greater responsiveness of quantity demanded to price. Using this convention, we calculate the elasticity of demand as:

$$\text{Price elasticity of demand} = \frac{20\%}{10\%} = 2$$

In this example, the price elasticity is 2, reflecting that the change in the quantity demanded is proportionately twice as large as the change in the price.

PITFALL PREVENTION We have mentioned the use of the term 'relative' earlier and here is a good example to illustrate the importance of this term. Remember that elasticity can be any value greater than or equal to 0. We can look at two goods, both of which are classed as 'inelastic' but where one is more inelastic than the other. If we are comparing good X, which has an elasticity of 0.2, and good Y, which has an elasticity of 0.5, then both are inelastic, but good Y is *relatively* elastic by comparison. As with so much of economics, careful use of terminology is important in conveying a clear understanding.

Using the Midpoint Method

As with the price elasticity of supply, we use the midpoint method to calculate price elasticity of demand. We can express the midpoint method with the following formula for the price elasticity of demand between two points, denoted (Q_1, P_1) and (Q_2, P_2):

$$\text{Price elasticity of demand} = \frac{(Q_2 - Q_1)/([Q_2 + Q_1]/2)}{(P_2 - P_1)/([P_2 + P_1]/2)}$$

The numerator is the proportionate change in quantity, and the denominator is the proportionate change in price, both computed using the midpoint method.

The Variety of Demand Curves

Economists classify demand curves according to their elasticity. Demand is *elastic* when the elasticity is greater than 1, so that quantity changes proportionately more than the price. Demand is *inelastic* when the elasticity is less than 1, so that quantity moves proportionately less than the price. If the elasticity is exactly 1, so that quantity moves the same amount proportionately as price, demand is said to have *unit elasticity*.

Because the price elasticity of demand measures how much quantity demanded responds to changes in the price, it is closely related to the slope of the demand curve. The following heuristic (rule of thumb), again assuming we are using comparable scales on the axes, is a useful guide: the flatter the demand curve that passes through a given point, the greater the price elasticity of demand. The steeper the demand curve that passes through a given point, the lower the price elasticity of demand.

Figure 5.6 shows five cases, each of which uses the same scale on each axis. This is important to remember, because simply looking at a graph and the shape of the curve without recognizing the scale can result in incorrect conclusions about elasticity. In the extreme case of a zero elasticity shown in panel (a), demand is *perfectly inelastic*, and the demand curve is vertical. In this case, regardless of the price, the quantity demanded stays the same. As the elasticity rises, the demand curve gets flatter and flatter, as shown in panels (b), (c) and (d). At the opposite extreme shown in panel (e), demand is *perfectly elastic*. This occurs as the price elasticity of demand approaches infinity and the demand curve becomes horizontal, reflecting the fact that very small changes in the price lead to huge changes in the quantity demanded.

FIGURE 5.6

The Price Elasticity of Demand

The steepness of the demand curve indicates the price elasticity of demand (assuming the scale used on the axes are the same). Note that all percentage changes are calculated using the midpoint method.

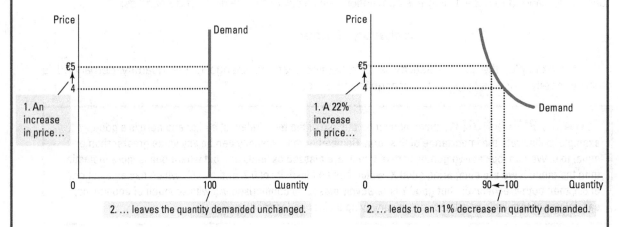

(a) Perfectly inelastic demand: Elasticity equals 0

1. An increase in price...

2. ... leaves the quantity demanded unchanged.

(b) Inelastic demand: Elasticity is less than 1

1. A 22% increase in price...

2. ... leads to an 11% decrease in quantity demanded.

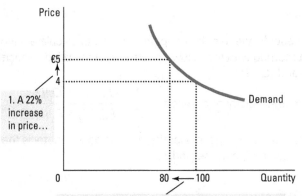

(c) Unit elastic demand: Elasticity equals 1

1. A 22% increase in price...

2. ... leads to a 22% decrease in quantity demanded.

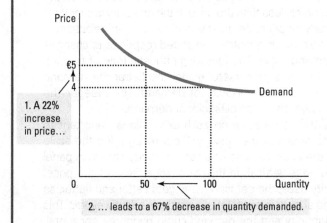

(d) Elastic demand: Elasticity is greater than 1

1. A 22% increase in price...

2. ... leads to a 67% decrease in quantity demanded.

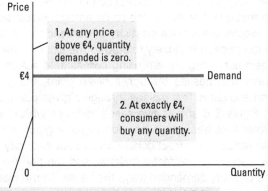

(e) Perfectly elastic demand: Elasticity equals infinity

1. At any price above €4, quantity demanded is zero.

2. At exactly €4, consumers will buy any quantity.

3. At a price below €4, quantity demanded is infinite.

Total Expenditure, Total Revenue and the Price Elasticity of Demand

When studying changes in demand in a market, we are interested in the amount paid by buyers of the good, which will in turn represent the total revenue that sellers receive. **Total expenditure** is given by the total amount bought multiplied by the price paid. We can show total expenditure graphically, as in Figure 5.7. The height of the box under the demand curve is P, and the width is Q. The area of this box, $P \times Q$, equals the total expenditure in this market. In Figure 5.7, where $P = €4$ and $Q = 100$, total expenditure is €4 × 100 = €400.

> **total expenditure** the amount paid by buyers, computed as the price of the good times the quantity purchased

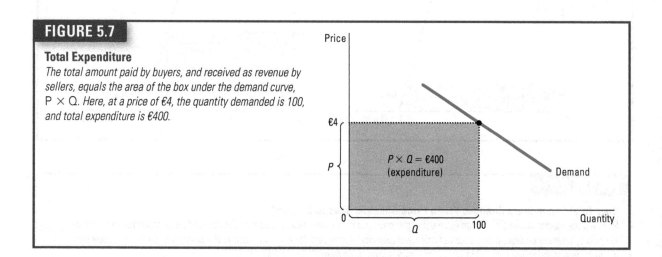

FIGURE 5.7

Total Expenditure
The total amount paid by buyers, and received as revenue by sellers, equals the area of the box under the demand curve, P × Q. Here, at a price of €4, the quantity demanded is 100, and total expenditure is €400.

For businesses, having some understanding of the price elasticity of demand is important in decision making. If a firm is thinking of changing price, how will the demand for its product react? The firm knows that there is an inverse relationship between price and demand, but the effect on its revenue will be dependent on the price elasticity of demand. It is entirely possible that a firm could reduce its price and increase total revenue. Equally, a firm could raise price and find its total revenue falling. At first glance this might sound counter-intuitive, but it all depends on the price elasticity of demand for the product.

If demand is price inelastic, as in Figure 5.8, then an increase in the price causes an increase in total expenditure. Here an increase in price from €1 to €3 causes the quantity demanded to fall only from 100 to 80, and so total expenditure rises from €100 to €240. An increase in price raises $P \times Q$ because the fall in Q is proportionately smaller than the rise in P.

We obtain the opposite result if demand is price elastic: an increase in the price causes a decrease in total expenditure. In Figure 5.9, for instance, when the price rises from €4 to €5, the quantity demanded falls from 50 to 20, and so total expenditure falls from €200 to €100. Because demand is price elastic, the reduction in the quantity demanded is so great that it more than offsets the increase in the price. That is, an increase in price reduces $P \times Q$ because the fall in Q is proportionately greater than the rise in P.

Although the examples in these two figures are extreme, they illustrate a general rule:

- When demand is price inelastic (a price elasticity less than 1), price and total expenditure move in the same direction.
- When demand is price elastic (a price elasticity greater than 1), price and total expenditure move in opposite directions.
- If demand is unit price elastic (a price elasticity exactly equal to 1), total expenditure remains constant when price changes.

FIGURE 5.8

How Total Expenditure Changes When Price Changes: Inelastic Demand
With an inelastic demand curve, an increase in the price leads to a decrease in quantity demanded that is proportionately smaller. Therefore, total expenditure (the product of price and quantity) increases. Here, an increase in the price from €1 to €3 causes the quantity demanded to fall from 100 to 80, and total expenditure rises from €100 to €240.

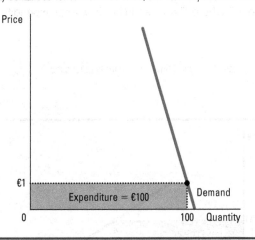 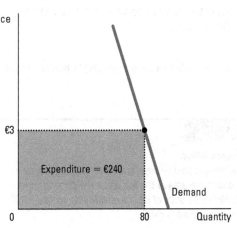

FIGURE 5.9

How Total Expenditure Changes When Price Changes: Elastic Demand
With a price elastic demand curve, an increase in the price leads to a decrease in quantity demanded that is proportionately larger. Therefore, total expenditure (the product of price and quantity) decreases. Here, an increase in the price from €4 to €5 causes the quantity demanded to fall from 50 to 20, so total expenditure falls from €200 to €100.

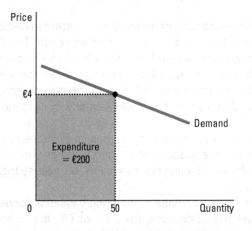 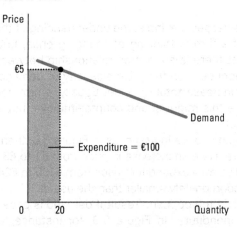

? **WHAT IF...** a high street clothes retailer is planning its summer sales campaign and wants to cut prices to help it get rid of stock, increase footfall (the number of customers entering its premises) and increase revenue. It knows of the concept of price elasticity of demand, but how does it set about estimating the price elasticity of demand for its products so that it can more accurately set price cuts which will achieve its aims?

Elasticity and Total Expenditure Along a Linear Demand Curve

Look at the straight line demand curve shown in Figure 5.10. A linear demand curve has a constant slope. The slope is defined as the ratio of the change in price ('rise') to the change in quantity ('run'). This particular demand curve's slope is constant because each €1 increase in price causes the same 2-unit decrease in the quantity demanded.

FIGURE 5.10

Elasticity of a Linear Demand Curve
The slope of a linear demand curve is constant, but its elasticity is not. The demand schedule in the table was used to calculate the price elasticity of demand by the midpoint method. At points with a low price and high quantity, the demand curve is price inelastic. At points with a high price and low quantity, the demand curve is price elastic.

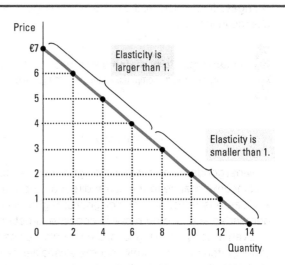

Price (€)	Quantity	Total revenue (Price × Quantity)	% change in price	% change in quantity	Price elasticity	Quantity description
7	0	0	15	200	13.0	Elastic
6	2	12	18	67	3.7	Elastic
5	4	20	22	40	1.8	Elastic
4	6	24	29	29	1.0	Unit elastic
3	8	24	40	22	0.6	Inelastic
2	10	20	67	18	0.3	Inelastic
1	12	12	200	15	0.1	Inelastic
0	14	0				

Even though the slope of a linear demand curve is constant, the elasticity is not. The reason is that the slope is the ratio of *changes* in the two variables, whereas the elasticity is the ratio of *percentage changes* in the two variables. You can see this by looking at the table in Figure 5.10, which shows the demand schedule for the linear demand curve in the graph. The table uses the midpoint method to calculate the price elasticity of demand. At points with a low price and high quantity, the demand curve is price inelastic. At points with a high price and low quantity, the demand curve is price elastic.

The table also presents total revenue at each point on the demand curve. These numbers illustrate the relationship between total revenue and price elasticity. When the price is €1, for instance, demand is price inelastic and a price increase to €2 raises total revenue. When the price is €5, demand is price elastic and a price increase to €6 reduces total revenue. Between €3 and €4, demand is exactly unit price elastic and total revenue is the same at these two prices.

In analysing markets, we will use both demand and supply curves on the same diagram. We will refer to changes in total revenue when looking at the effects of changes in equilibrium conditions, but remember that revenue for sellers represents the same identity as expenditure for buyers.

OTHER DEMAND ELASTICITIES

In addition to the price elasticity of demand, economists also use other elasticities to describe the behaviour of buyers in a market.

The Income Elasticity of Demand

The **income elasticity of demand** measures how the quantity demanded changes as consumer income changes. It is calculated as the percentage change in quantity demanded divided by the percentage change in income.

> **income elasticity of demand** a measure of how much the quantity demanded of a good responds to a change in consumers' income, computed as the percentage change in quantity demanded divided by the percentage change in income

$$\text{Income elasticity of demand} = \frac{\text{Percentage change in quantity demanded}}{\text{Percentage change in income}}$$

Most goods are *normal goods*: higher income increases quantity demanded. Because quantity demanded and income change in the same direction, normal goods have positive income elasticities. A few goods, such as bus rides, are *inferior goods*: higher income lowers the quantity demanded. Because quantity demanded and income move in opposite directions, inferior goods have negative income elasticities.

Even among normal goods, income elasticities vary substantially in size. Necessities, such as food and clothing, tend to have small income elasticities because consumers, regardless of how low their incomes, choose to buy some of these goods. Luxuries, such as caviar and diamonds, tend to have high income elasticities because consumers feel that they can do without these goods altogether if their income is too low.

The Cross-Price Elasticity of Demand

The **cross-price elasticity of demand** measures how the quantity demanded of one good changes as the price of another good changes. It is calculated as the percentage change in quantity demanded of good 1 divided by the percentage change in the price of good 2.

> **cross-price elasticity of demand** a measure of how much the quantity demanded of one good responds to a change in the price of another good, computed as the percentage change in quantity demanded of the first good divided by the percentage change in the price of the second good

$$\text{Cross-price elasticity of demand} = \frac{\text{Percentage change in quantity demanded of good 1}}{\text{Percentage change in the price of good 2}}$$

Whether the cross-price elasticity is a positive or negative number depends on whether the two goods are substitutes or complements. Substitutes are goods that are typically used in place of one another, such as broccoli and cabbage. An increase in the price of broccoli induces people to eat cabbage instead. Because the price of broccoli and the quantity of cabbage demanded move in the same direction, the cross-price elasticity is positive. Conversely, complements are goods that are typically used together, such as computers and software. In this case, the cross-price elasticity is negative, indicating that an increase in the price of computers reduces the quantity of software demanded. As with price elasticity of demand, cross-price elasticity may increase over time: a change in the price of electricity will have little effect on demand for gas in the short run but much stronger effects over several years.

FYI

The Mathematics of Elasticity

We present this section for those who require some introduction to the maths behind elasticity. For those who do not need such a technical explanation, this section can be safely skipped without affecting your overall understanding of the concept of elasticity.

Point Elasticity of Demand

Figure 5.10 showed that the value for elasticity can vary at every point along a straight line demand curve. Point elasticity of demand (*ped*) allows us to be able to be more specific about the elasticity at different points. In the formula repeated below, the numerator (the top half of the fraction) describes the change in quantity in relation to the base quantity and the denominator the change in price in relation to the base price.

$$ped = \frac{\left(\dfrac{Q_2 - Q_1}{(Q_2 + Q_1)/2}\right) \times 100}{\left(\dfrac{P_2 - P_1}{(P_2 + P_1)/2}\right) \times 100}$$

If we cancel out the 100s in the above equation and rewrite it a little more elegantly (using the Greek letter delta (Δ) to mean 'change in') we get:

$$ped = \frac{\dfrac{\Delta Q}{Q}}{\dfrac{\Delta P}{P}}$$

Here the $\Delta Q = Q_2 - Q_1$ and $\Delta P = P_2 - P_1$. Rearranging the above we get:

$$ped = \frac{\Delta Q}{Q} \times \frac{P}{\Delta P}$$

There is no set order required to this equation so it can be rewritten as:

$$ped = \frac{\Delta Q}{\Delta P} \times \frac{P}{Q}$$

The eagle eyed among you will notice that the expression $\Delta Q / \Delta P$ is the inverse of the slope of a linear demand curve. Look at the example in Figure 5.11. Here we have two demand curves, D_1 and D_2, given by the equations:

$$P = 20 - 5Q$$

And:

$$Q = 5 - 0.25P$$

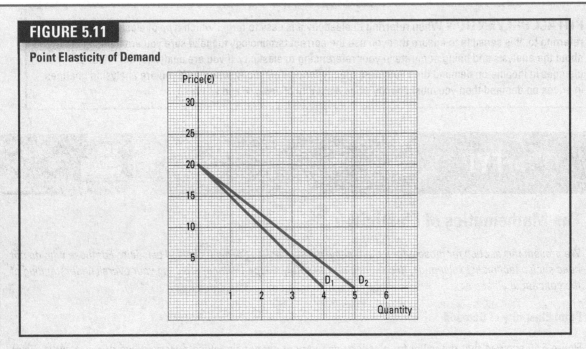

FIGURE 5.11

Point Elasticity of Demand

For demand curve D_1, the vertical intercept is 20 and the horizontal intercept is 4 and so the slope of the line D_1 is −5.

For demand curve D_2, the vertical intercept is 20 and the horizontal intercept is 5, the slope of the line D_2 is −4. To verify this let us take demand curve D_1; if price were 10 then we could find the quantity from $10 = 20 − 5Q$. Rearranging gives $5Q = 20 − 10, 5Q = 10$, so $Q = 2$. Looking at demand curve D_2 if price were 10, then the quantity would be $5 − (0.25 \times 10) = 2.5$.

Now let us assume that price falls from 10 to 5 in each case. The quantity demanded for D_1 would now be $5 = 20 − 5Q, 5Q = 15, Q = 3$ and for $D_2, 5 − (0.25 \times 5) = 3.75$.

Representing this graphically for demand curve D_1, we get the result shown in Figure 5.12.

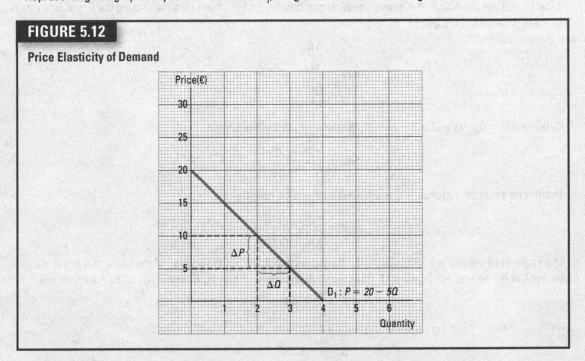

FIGURE 5.12

Price Elasticity of Demand

The slope of the line as drawn is:

$$\frac{\Delta P}{\Delta Q} = \frac{-5}{1} = -5$$

The slope is the same at all points along a linear demand curve. The ratio of P/Q at different points on the demand curve, however, will differ because of the price which we start with prior to a change. Using demand curve D_1, the ratio of P/Q at the initial price of 10 is $10/2 = 5$. At a price of 5, the ratio of P/Q given by the demand curve D_1 would be $5/3 = 1.67$.

Going back to our formula:

$$ped = \frac{\Delta Q}{\Delta P} \times \frac{P}{Q}$$

The first part of the equation ($\Delta Q/\Delta P$) is the inverse slope of the demand curve and the second part of the equation P/Q gives us a specific point on the demand curve relating to a particular price and quantity combination. Multiplying these two terms gives us the price elasticity of demand at a particular point, and so is referred to as *point elasticity of demand*. The price elasticity of demand when price changes from 10 to 5 in demand curve D_1 above, would be:

$$ped = \frac{\Delta Q}{\Delta P} \times \frac{P}{Q}$$

$$ped = \frac{1}{5} \times \frac{10}{2}$$

$$ped = 1$$

If we were looking at a fall in price from 15 to 10 we would get:

$$ped = \frac{\Delta Q}{\Delta P} \times \frac{P}{Q}$$

$$ped = \frac{1}{5} \times \frac{15}{1}$$

$$ped = 3$$

If looking at a price fall from 5 to 2.5 then we would get:

$$ped = \frac{\Delta Q}{\Delta P} \times \frac{P}{Q}$$

$$ped = \frac{0.5}{2.5} \times \frac{5}{3}$$

$$ped = 0.33$$

Calculus

The demand curve is often depicted as a linear curve, but there is no reason why it should be linear and it can be curvilinear. To measure elasticity accurately in this case, economists use calculus.

If you are following a quantitative methods course, you will probably cover differentiation and integration, the two key elements of calculus. Differentiation is used to calculate rates of change through finding a derivative. A derivative tells you the slope of a curve at a particular point. The slope of a curve is given by $\frac{\Delta y}{\Delta x}$ or $\frac{rise}{run}$. The derivative is rise over run per run, or the rate of change in one variable as a result of a very small or infinitesimal change in another variable. Given a basic function $y = ax + b$, the derivative is found using the linear function rule $\frac{dy}{dx} = a$. If the function is of the form $y = x^n$, the derivative $\frac{dy}{dx}$ is found using the power function rule: $\frac{dy}{dx} = nx^{n-1}$.

(*Continued*)

The rules of calculus applied to a demand curve give a far more accurate measurement of *ped* at a particular point.

For a linear demand function, the approximation to the point elasticity at the initial price and quantity is given by:

$$\frac{(Q_2 - Q_1)}{(P_1 - P_1)} \times \frac{P_1}{Q_1}$$

which gives the same result as the point elasticity which is defined in terms of calculus and is given by:

$$\frac{dQ}{dP} \times \frac{P}{Q}$$

Point elasticity defined in terms of calculus gives a precise answer; all the other formulae are approximations of some sort. The formula looks similar, but it must be remembered that what we are talking about in this instance is an infinitesimally small change in quantity following an infinitesimally small change in price expressed by the formula: $\frac{dQ}{dP}$, where $\frac{dQ}{dP}$ is the derivative of a linear function.

Given our basic linear equation of the form: $Q = a - bP$, the linear function rule gives $\frac{dQ}{dP}$ as the coefficient of P, which is $-b$.

Take the following demand equation:

$$Q = 60 - 3P$$

To find the price elasticity of demand when price = 15, first, we need to find Q.

$$Q = 60 - 3P$$

$$Q = 60 - 3(15)$$

$$Q = 15$$

We calculate $\frac{dQ}{dP}$ as -3. Substitute this into the formula to get:

$$ped = -3\left(\frac{15}{15}\right)$$

$$ped = -3$$

It is useful to remember that given an elasticity figure we can calculate the expected change in demand as a result of a change in price. For example, if the *ped* is given as 0.6 then an increase in price of 5 per cent will result in a fall in quantity demanded of 3 per cent.

By using the inverse of the elasticity equation, for any given value of *ped* we can calculate how much of a price change is required to bring about a desired change in quantity demanded. Suppose that a government wanted to reduce the demand for motor vehicles as part of a policy to reduce congestion and pollution. What sort of price change might be required to bring about a 10 per cent fall in demand?

Assume that the *ped* for motor vehicles is 0.8. The inverse of the basic elasticity formula is:

$$\frac{1}{ped} = \frac{\%\Delta P}{\%\Delta Q}$$

Substituting our known values into the formula we get:

$$\frac{1}{0.8} = \frac{\%\Delta P}{10}$$

$$1.25 = \frac{\%\Delta P}{10}$$

$$\%\Delta P = 12.5$$

To bring about a reduction in demand of 10 per cent, the price of motor vehicles would have to rise by 12.5 per cent.

Other Elasticities

Income and cross-elasticity of demand are all treated in the same way as the analysis of price elasticity of demand above.

Income elasticity of demand (*yed*) would be:

$$yed = \frac{\Delta Q}{\Delta Y} \times \frac{Y}{Q}$$

Using calculus:

$$yed = \frac{dQ}{dY} \times \frac{Y}{Q}$$

For cross-elasticity (*xed*) the formulae would be:

$$xed = \frac{\Delta Q_a}{\Delta P_b} \times \frac{P_b}{Q_a}$$

Using calculus:

$$xed = \frac{dQ_a}{dP_b} \times \frac{P_b}{Q_a}$$

Where Q_a is the quantity demanded of one good, *a*, and P_b is the price of a related good, *b* (either a substitute or a complement).

Demand can be expressed as a multivariate function where demand is dependent on a range of variables which include price, incomes, tastes and so on. It is possible to calculate the elasticities of all these other factors using the same principles as those outlined above. In each case, it is usual to calculate the elasticity with respect to a change in one of the variables while holding the others constant.

For example, take the demand equation $Q = 1,400 - 4P + 0.04Y$. This equation tells us that demand is dependent on the price and the level of income. From this equation, we can calculate the *ped* and *yed*. In this example, we will use calculus to find both elasticities assuming $P = 50$ and $Y = 8,000$. Given these values:

$$Q = 1,400 - 4(50) + 0.04(8,000)$$
$$Q = 1,400 - 200 + 320$$
$$Q = 1,520$$

With:

$$\frac{dQ}{dp} = -4$$

$$ped = -4\left(\frac{50}{1,520}\right)$$

$$ped = -0.132$$

Given:

$$\frac{dQ}{dY} = 0.04$$

$$yed = 0.04\left(\frac{8,000}{1,520}\right)$$

$$yed = 0.21$$

Now look at this demand equation:

$$Q_a = 100 - 8P_a - 6P_b + 4P_c + 0.015Y$$

This equation gives the relationship between demand and the prices of other goods labelled a, b and c respectively. We can use this to find the respective cross-elasticities. Assume that the price of good a is 20, the price of good b, 40, the price of good c, 80, and $Y = 20,000$. Substituting these into our formula gives:

$$Q_a = 100 - 8(20) - 6(40) + 4(80) + 0.015(20,000)$$
$$Q_a = 100 - 160 - 240 + 320 + 300$$
$$Q_a = 320$$

The change in demand of good a with respect to changes in the price of good *b* is given by:

$$\frac{dQ_a}{dp_b} = -6$$

$$xed = -6\left(\frac{40}{320}\right)$$

$$xed = -6(0.125)$$

$$xed = -0.75$$

The relationship between good a and b is that they are complements. A rise in the price of good b will lead to a fall in the quantity demanded of good a.

The change in the price of good a with respect to changes in the price of good c is given by:

$$\frac{dQ_a}{dp_c} = 4$$

$$xed = 4\left(\frac{80}{320}\right)$$

$$xed = 4(0.25)$$

$$xed = 1$$

In this case the relationship between the two goods is that they are substitutes: a rise in the price of good c would lead to a rise in the quantity demanded of good a.

Price Elasticity of Supply

Many of the principles outlined above apply also to the price elasticity of supply. The formula for the price elasticity of supply (*pes*) using the point method is:

$$pes = \frac{\Delta Q_s}{\Delta P} \times \frac{P}{Q_s}$$

Using calculus:

$$pes = \frac{dQ_s}{dP} \times \frac{P}{Q_s}$$

However, we need to note a particular issue with *pes* which relates to the graphical representation of supply curves. This is summarized in the following:

- A straight line supply curve intersecting the *y*-axis at a positive value has a *pes* > 1.
- A straight line supply curve passing through the origin has a *pes* = 1.
- A straight line supply curve intersecting the *x*-axis at a positive value has a *pes* < 1.

To see why any straight line supply curve passing through the origin has a *pes* of 1 we can use some basic knowledge of geometry and similar triangles. Figure 5.13 shows a straight line supply curve S_1 passing through the origin. The slope of the supply curve is given by $\frac{\Delta P}{\Delta Q_s}$. We have highlighted a triangle shaded orange with the ratio $\frac{\Delta P}{\Delta Q_s}$ relating to a change in price of 7.5 and a change in quantity supplied of 1. The larger triangle formed by taking a price of 22.5 and a quantity supplied of 3 shows the ratio of the price and quantity at this point $\left(\frac{P}{Q}\right)$. The two triangles formed by these are both classed as similar triangles. They have different lengths to their three sides but the internal angles are all the same. The ratio of the sides must therefore be equal as shown by:

$$\frac{\Delta P}{\Delta Q_s} = \frac{P}{Q_s} \qquad (1)$$

Given our definition of point elasticity of supply, if we substitute equation (1) into the formula and rearrange we get:

$$pes = \frac{\Delta Q_s}{\Delta P} \times \frac{P}{Q_s}$$

Therefore:

$$pes = 1$$

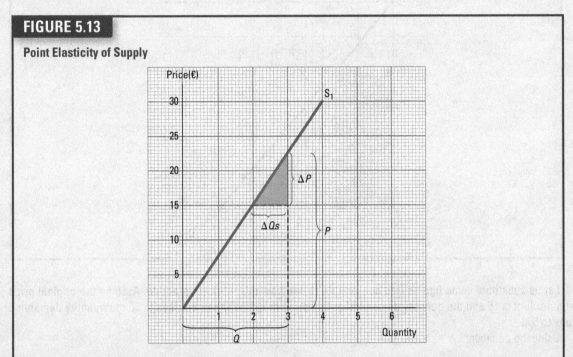

FIGURE 5.13

Point Elasticity of Supply

Elasticity and Total Expenditure/Revenue

We have used the term 'total expenditure' in relation to the demand curve to accurately reflect the fact that demand is related to buyers and when buyers pay for products this represents expenditure. Many books use the term expenditure and revenue interchangeably, and in this short section we are going to refer to revenue. Total revenue is found by multiplying the quantity purchased by the average price paid. This is shown by the formula:

$$TR = P \times Q$$

Total revenue can change if either price or quantity, or both, change. This can be seen in Figure 5.14, where a rise in the price of a good from P_0 to P_1 has resulted in a fall in quantity demanded from Q_0 to Q_1.

We can represent the change in price as ΔP. The new price is $(P + \Delta P)$. The change in quantity is ΔQ and the new quantity will be $(Q + \Delta Q)$. TR can be represented thus:

$$TR = (P + \Delta P)(Q + \Delta Q)$$

If we multiply out this expression as shown, then we get:

$$TR = PQ + P\Delta Q + \Delta PQ + \Delta P\Delta Q$$

In Figure 5.14, this can be seen graphically.

As a result of the change in price there is an additional amount of revenue shown by the purple rectangle (ΔPQ). However, this is offset by the reduction in revenue caused by the fall in quantity caused by the increase in price shown by the blue rectangle ($P\Delta Q$). There is also an area indicated by the yellow rectangle which is equal to $\Delta P\Delta Q$. This leaves us with a formula for the change in TR as:

$$\Delta TR = \Delta PQ + P\Delta Q + \Delta P\Delta Q$$

(Continued)

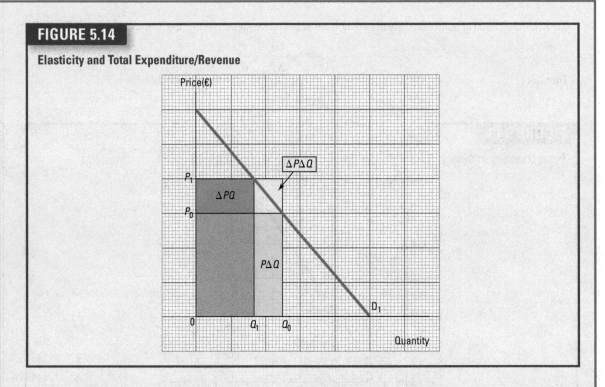

FIGURE 5.14

Elasticity and Total Expenditure/Revenue

Let us substitute some figures into our formula to see how this works in practice. Assume the original price of a product is 15 and the quantity demanded at this price is 750. When price rises to 20 the quantity demanded falls to 500.

Using the equation:

$$TR = PQ + P\Delta Q + \Delta PQ + \Delta P\Delta Q$$

TR is now:

$$TR = 15(750) + 15(-250) + 5(750) + 5(-250)$$
$$TR = 10,000$$

The change in *TR* is:

$$\Delta TR = \Delta PQ + P\Delta Q + \Delta P\Delta Q$$
$$\Delta TR = 5(750) + 15(-250) + 5(-250)$$
$$\Delta TR = 3,750 - 3,750 - 1,250$$
$$\Delta TR = -1,250$$

In this example the effect of the change in price has been negative on *TR*. We know from our analysis of price elasticity of demand that this means the percentage change in quantity demand was greater than the percentage change in price. In other words, *ped* must be price elastic at this point (>1). For the change in *TR* to be positive, therefore, the *ped* must be <1.

We can express the relationship between the change in *TR* and *ped* as an inequality as follows:

$$ped = \frac{\Delta Q}{\Delta P} \times \frac{P}{Q} > 1$$

When price increases, revenue decreases if *ped* meets this inequality. Equally, for a price increase to result in a rise in revenue *ped* must meet the inequality:

$$ped = \frac{\Delta Q}{\Delta P} \times \frac{P}{Q} < 1$$

JEOPARDY PROBLEM A business selling plumbing equipment to the trade (i.e. professional plumbers only) increases the price of copper piping by 4 per cent and reduces the price of radiators by 5 per cent. A year later the company analyses its sales figures and finds that revenue for copper piping rose in the first three months after the price rise but then fell dramatically thereafter, while the revenue for sales of radiators also fell throughout the period.

Explain what might have happened to bring about this situation. Illustrate your answer with diagrams where appropriate.

CASE STUDY Energy prices and Price Elasticity of Demand

The latter part of 2022 saw significant concern around energy prices. Between 2018–19 and the summer of 2021, the average household bill for gas and electricity was around the £1,000 mark but this increased to almost £2,000 by summer 2022 and was forecast to rise to almost £4,500 by the third quarter of 2023. If that figure had been realized, the increase in average energy prices would have been around 350 per cent. If we take gas in particular, the energy industry regulator, Ofgem, reported that the price per therm for gas in

December 2018 was around 63p. The price fell to around 13p per therm by June 2020 but then saw a rapid increase largely due to increased demand post-pandemic and the uncertainties over supply caused by the conflict in Ukraine. By November 2021 the price was 201p per therm and rose to a high of 313.57p in March 2022 before falling back to almost 150p per therm in June 2022.

We know that when prices rise demand falls, so what happened to energy consumption in response to the increase in prices? According to government figures, total demand for gas in 2018 was 79,324 cubic metres (m^3). This fell to 78,430 m^3 in 2019 and to 73,837 m^3 in 2020. Demand for gas was 77,676 m^3 in 2021 and 71,556 m^3 in 2022.

How consumers and businesses respond to rising energy prices can have an effect on the extent to which the demand for energy changes in the short and long-run.

Questions

1 Use the data provided in the case study to calculate the price elasticity of demand for gas. In calculating the elasticity, state any assumptions you have made and what data you have used. You may wish to calculate elasticity by year or across the years, depending on which data you use. Comment on the results of your calculations.

2 Given your calculation in 1 above, what would you predict would have happened to the demand for gas into 2023 assuming the price rise was as forecast? Justify your reasoning.

3 How do you explain the fact that despite the price of gas increasing in 2021, demand rose compared to 2020?

4 What would you expect to happen to the demand for gas in the next ten years if prices continue to rise and remain at relatively high levels? Explain the relevance of the price elasticity of demand and supply as part of your answer.

References: www.cornwall-insight.com/price-cap-forecasts-for-january-rise-to-over-4200-as-wholesale-prices-surge-again-and-ofgem-revises-cap-methodology/ (accessed 15 May 2023).
https://assets.publishing.service.gov.uk/government/uploads/system/uploads/attachment_data/file/1093649/ET_4.1_JUL_22.xlsx (accessed 15 May 2023).
www.ofgem.gov.uk/information-consumers/energy-advice-households/check-if-energy-price-cap-affects-you (accessed 15 May 2023).

APPLICATIONS OF SUPPLY AND DEMAND ELASTICITY

Here we apply the versatile tools of supply, demand and elasticity to answer two questions.

Why Are Improvements in Agricultural Technologies Not Always Good News for Farmers?

Since the 1970s, the technology used in agriculture has increased dramatically. It might seem at first sight that this would be good news for farmers. We can analyse the effect to see if it is good news for farmers by using the three steps we introduced in Chapter 4. Improvements in technology have led to increases in productivity and increases in supply of agricultural products. This shifts the supply curve for agricultural products to the right and lowers the market price of food.

The demand curve remains the same because consumers' desire to buy agricultural products at any given price is not affected by the fact that technology has increased supply. Moreover, the demand for food is relatively price inelastic. Figure 5.15 shows an example of such a change. When the supply curve shifts from S_1 to S_2, the quantity of agricultural products sold increases from 500,000 tonnes to 550,000 tonnes, and the price falls from €200 per tonne to €80 per tonne. The improvement in technology allows farmers to produce more products (Q rises), but now each tonne sells for less (P falls).

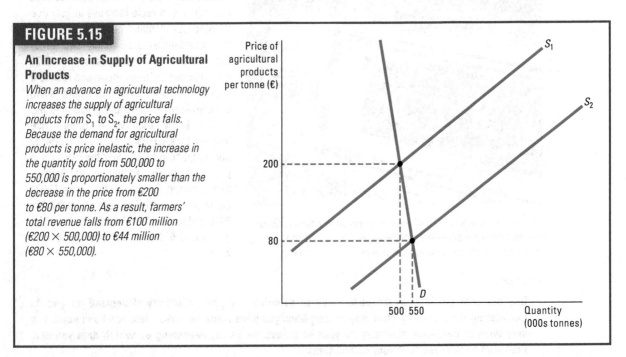

FIGURE 5.15

An Increase in Supply of Agricultural Products
When an advance in agricultural technology increases the supply of agricultural products from S_1 to S_2, the price falls. Because the demand for agricultural products is price inelastic, the increase in the quantity sold from 500,000 to 550,000 is proportionately smaller than the decrease in the price from €200 to €80 per tonne. As a result, farmers' total revenue falls from €100 million (€200 × 500,000) to €44 million (€80 × 550,000).

Because the demand for agricultural products is assumed to be relatively price inelastic, the decrease in price causes total revenue for farmers to fall from €100 million (200 × 500,000) to €44 million. Thus, technological developments lower the total revenue that farmers receive for the sale of their products. This partly explains why governments step in to provide income support for farmers in the form of subsidies.

If farmers are made worse off by the developments in new technology, why do they adopt it? The answer to this question goes to the heart of how competitive markets work. If each farmer is a small part of the market for agricultural products, they take the price as given. For any given price, it is better to use the new technology to produce and sell more products. Yet, when all farmers do this, the supply rises, the price falls and farmers are worse off. You might expect that increases in technology over time go hand in hand with the general increase in living standards in society. People are generally better off today than they were in the 1970s. Would demand for agricultural products not increase as incomes increase? Research has shown that the income elasticity of demand for food is income inelastic, meaning that as incomes increase, demand for food increases by a proportionately smaller amount. Even if the demand curve for agricultural products shifts to the right as a result of this rise in incomes, it does not shift far enough to the right to compensate for the price reduction caused by the increase in supply and so farmers still see a fall in revenue.

When analyzing the effects of technology, it is important to keep in mind that what is bad for farmers is not necessarily bad for society as a whole. Improvements in technology can be bad for some famers who find it difficult to survive, but it represents good news for consumers of agricultural products who see the price of food falling.

Why Do Prices of Ski Holidays Differ So Much at Different Times of the Season?

For many people, winter provides the opportunity to take a snow sports holiday. There are considerable variations in the prices they pay for their holiday, which is highly dependent on when they are able to travel. For example, a quick check of a ski company website for the 2023–24 season revealed the prices shown in Table 5.1 for seven-night ski trips per person to Austria, leaving from London.

There is a considerable variation in the prices that holidaymakers must pay, €700 being the greatest difference. Prices are particularly high leaving on 29 December and 11 and 18 February. Why? The reason is that at this time of the season the demand for ski holidays increases substantially because they coincide with annual holiday periods: 29 December is part of the Christmas/New Year holiday and when schoolchildren are also on holiday; 11 and 18 February are the start dates of a week's school holiday for many UK children.

TABLE 5.1 **Prices for 7-night Ski Holidays in Austria, from London**

Departure date	Price per person (€)
29 December 2023	1,300
7 January 2024	850
14 January 2024	800
21 January 2024	900
28 January 2024	850
4 February 2024	850
11 February 2024	1,300
18 February 2024	1,500
25 February 2024	1,000

The supply of ski holidays does have a limit. There will be a finite number of accommodation places and passes for ski-lifts, and so the elasticity of supply is relatively inelastic (Figure 5.16). It is difficult for tour operators to increase supply of accommodation or ski-passes easily in the short run to meet rising demand at these times. The result is that the increase in demand for ski holidays at these peak times means prices rise significantly to choke off the excess demand, as highlighted in Figure 5.16. If holidaymakers can be flexible about when they take their holidays, then they will be able to benefit from lower prices for the same holiday. Away from these peak periods the demand for ski holidays is lower, and so tour operators have spare capacity. The supply curve out of peak times is more elastic in the very short run. If there was a sudden increase in demand in mid-January, for example, then tour operators would have the capacity to accommodate that demand, so prices would not rise as much as when that capacity is strictly limited.

Cases for which supply is very price inelastic in the short run but more price elastic in the long run may see different prices exist in the market. Air and rail travel and the use of electricity may all be examples where prices differ markedly at peak times compared with off-peak times because of supply constraints and the ability of firms to be able to discriminate between customers at these times.

SELF TEST How might a drought that destroys half of all farm crops be good for farmers? If such a drought is good for farmers, why do farmers not destroy their own crops in the absence of a drought?

FIGURE 5.16

The Supply of Ski Holidays in Europe
The supply curve for ski holidays is relatively price inelastic in the short run. An increase in demand from D_1 to D_2 at peak times leads to a relatively large increase in price per person.

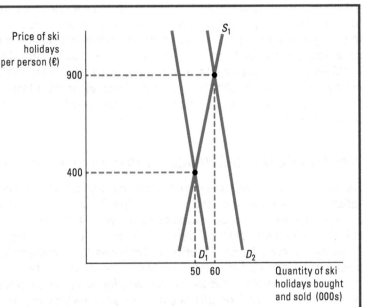

FYI

Estimates of Elasticities

We have discussed the concept of elasticity in general terms, but there is empirical evidence on elasticity of products in the real world. We present some examples of estimates of price elasticity of supply and demand for a range of products in Table 5.2 and Table 5.3. It must be remembered that the following are estimates, and you may find other data where the elasticities differ from those given here.

TABLE 5.2 — Estimates of Price Elasticity of Supply

Good	PES estimate
Public transport in Sweden	0.44 to 0.64
Labour in South Africa	0.35 to 1.75
Beef:	
• Zimbabwe	2.0
• Brazil	0.11 to 0.56
• Argentina	0.67 to 0.96
Corn (short run in US)	0.96
Housing, long run in selected US cities:	Dallas: 38.6
	San Francisco: 2.4
	New Orleans: 0.9
	St. Louis: 8.1
Uranium	2.3 to 3.3
Recycled aluminium	0.5
Oysters	1.64 to 2.00
Retail store space	3.2
Natural gas (short-run)	0.5

Source: signsofchaos.blogspot.co.uk/2005_11_01_archive.html

TABLE 5.3	**Estimates of Price Elasticity of Demand**	
	Good	**PED estimate**
	Tobacco	0.4
	Milk	0.3
	Wine	0.6
	Shoes	0.7
	Cars	1.9
	Particular brand of car	4.0
	Movies	0.9
	Entertainment	1.4
	Furniture	3.04
	Fuel	0.4
	Bread	0.25

SUMMARY

- The price elasticity of supply measures how much the quantity supplied responds to changes in the price. This elasticity often depends on the time horizon under consideration. In most markets, supply is more price elastic in the long run than in the short run.

- The price elasticity of supply is calculated as the percentage change in quantity supplied divided by the percentage change in price. If the price elasticity is less than 1, so that quantity supplied moves proportionately less than the price, supply is said to be price inelastic. If the elasticity is greater than 1, so that quantity supplied moves proportionately more than the price, supply is said to be price elastic.

- The price elasticity of demand measures how much the quantity demanded responds to changes in the price. Demand tends to be more price elastic if close substitutes are available, if the good is a luxury rather than a necessity, if the market is narrowly defined or if buyers have substantial time to react to a price change.

- The price elasticity of demand is calculated as the percentage change in quantity demanded divided by the percentage change in price. If the elasticity is less than 1, so that quantity demanded moves proportionately less than the price, demand is said to be price inelastic. If the elasticity is greater than 1, so that quantity demanded moves proportionately more than the price, demand is said to be price elastic.

- Total revenue, the total amount received by sellers for a good, equals the price of the good times the quantity sold. For price inelastic demand curves, total revenue rises as price rises. For price elastic demand curves, total revenue falls as price rises.

- The income elasticity of demand measures how much the quantity demanded responds to changes in consumers' income. The cross-price elasticity of demand measures how much the quantity demanded of one good responds to changes in the price of another good.

- The tools of supply and demand can be applied in many different kinds of markets. This chapter uses them to analyse the market for agricultural products and for ski holidays.

IN THE NEWS

The Supply and Demand of Chemical Fertilizers

One of the key inputs for agricultural and horticultural production is fertilizer. Between 2018 and 2020, fertilizer prices on global markets hovered around $400 per tonne (€388pt) but since then, prices have risen sharply. In early 2022, the price rose to almost $1,300 per tonne (€1,260pt) before falling back a little to around $800 per tonne (€776pt)

(*Continued*)

in mid-2022. One of the reasons for this sudden increase in price was the conflict in Ukraine which escalated towards the end of February 2022. Russia accounted for around 20 per cent of nitrogen fertilizers and its neighbour, Belarus, for around 40 per cent of potassium, both vital elements in successful and productive growing. According to World-Grain.com, the supply of fertilizer in 2022 could have fallen by around 17 per cent and global demand by around 5 per cent. As the conflict escalated, sanctions imposed reduced supplies flowing through to the rest of the world and issues around exporting from ports in Ukraine also hampered supply. Another reason for the increase in the price of fertilizer is the use of gas in the production process of nitrogen. The higher price of gas (refer to the Case Study in this chapter) contributed to the problems of producing fertilizers. When the constraints on supply are combined with increasing demand as a result of the post-pandemic global economy, the effect has been to increase prices.

The price increases have caused concern that food producers, in particular, will be affected with some farmers finding it difficult to afford to buy fertilizers with the resulting effect that crop yields will fall. Some of the most vulnerable nations of the world, and some of the most vulnerable populations, will be affected by what some called a 'global food crisis'. Ukraine is an important crop producer and there were reports that in 2022, only around 70–80 per cent of its normal land area was able to be sown and those areas that were, had been affected by the reduction in the availability of fertilizer.

One of the challenges facing the agriculture and horticulture industry is the reliance on Russia and its allies on supplies of fertilizer. Thoughts have turned to how this reliance can be reduced. One solution is to develop other types of fertilizers rather than the chemical-based ones typically used such as nitrogen, phosphorous and potassium. One such option is

Fertilizer costs have increased rapidly as a result of external influences, putting pressure on farmers' costs of production and ultimately, consumer prices.

to develop manure-based fertilizers. Manure-based fertilizers would make use of animal waste produced by cattle, poultry, goats and pigs. Not only would development of these types of fertilizer help reduce the reliance on Russian supplies but would also, it is argued, be of benefit in reducing carbon footprints which are associated with the use of gas, for example, in the production of nitrogen fertilizers. The use of animal manure would also represent a move to the concept of the 'circular economy' in agriculture and horticulture. The European Parliament give a definition of the circular economy as 'a model of production and consumption, which involves sharing, leasing, reusing, repairing, refurbishing and recycling existing materials and products as long as possible. In this way, the life cycle of products is extended.'

Questions

1. Using your knowledge of the price elasticity of supply and demand and the data provided in the article, estimate the possible price elasticity of supply and demand for chemical-based fertilizers in agriculture and horticulture.
2. What do you think are the most important factors determining the price elasticity of supply and demand for chemical-based fertilizers?
3. Consider the impact on total expenditure and total revenue of fertilizer producers and consumers of the rise in the price of fertilizers as outlined in the article. Use appropriate supply and demand diagrams to help illustrate your answer.
4. What relevance do the concepts of income elasticity and cross-price elasticity of demand have in the context of the fertilizer market?
5. How would the development of manure-based fertilizers affect the price elasticity of supply and demand for chemical-based fertilizers? What would determine the extent of the effect of this development on the price elasticity of supply and demand for chemical-based fertilizers?

References: www.foodnavigator.com/Article/2022/06/22/Fertilizer-crisis-Can-Europe-reduce-its-dependence-on-Russia (accessed 15 May 2023). www.bloomberg.com/news/articles/2022-08-02/europe-may-turn-to-manure-in-switch-away-from-russian-fertilizer (accessed 15 May 2023). www.nationalgeographic.com/environment/article/global-food-crisis-looms-as-fertilizer-supplies-dwindle (accessed 15 May 2023). www.europarl.europa.eu/news/en/headlines/economy/20151201STO05603/circular-economy-definition-importance-and-benefits (accessed 15 May 2023). www.cnbc.com/2022/04/06/a-fertilizer-shortage-worsened-by-war-in-ukraine-is-driving-up-global-food-prices-and-scarcity.html (accessed 15 May 2023). www.world-grain.com/articles/18653-global-fertilizer-market-remains-unstable (accessed 15 May 2023).

QUESTIONS FOR REVIEW

1 How is the price elasticity of supply calculated? Explain what the calculation measures.

2 Is the price elasticity of supply usually larger in the short run or the long run? Why?

3 What are the main factors that affect the price elasticity of supply? Think of some examples to use to illustrate the factors you cover.

4 Define the price elasticity of demand and the income elasticity of demand.

5 List and explain some of the determinants of the price elasticity of demand. Think of some examples to use to illustrate the factors you cover.

6 If the price elasticity of demand is greater than 1, is demand price elastic or price inelastic? If the price elasticity equals 0, is demand perfectly price elastic or perfectly price inelastic? Explain.

7 Draw a supply and demand diagram with the demand curve more price inelastic than the supply curve. Show the equilibrium price, equilibrium quantity and the total revenue received by producers. Use your diagram to show under what circumstances producers see a rise in total revenue.

8 If demand is price elastic, how will an increase in price change total revenue? Explain.

9 What do we call a good whose income elasticity is less than 0?

10 Outline some of the factors that will affect the elasticity of supply and demand for houses for private purchase in the short run and the long run.

PROBLEMS AND APPLICATIONS

1 Seafront properties along the promenade at Brighton on the south coast of England have a price inelastic supply, and cars have a price elastic supply. Suppose that a rise in population doubles the demand for both products (that is, the quantity demanded at each price is twice what it was).

   a. What happens to the equilibrium price and quantity in each market?
   b. Which product experiences a larger change in price?
   c. Which product experiences a larger change in quantity?
   d. What happens to total consumer spending on each product?

2 Because better weather makes farmland more productive, farmland in regions with good weather conditions is more expensive than farmland in regions with bad weather conditions. Over time, however, as advances in technology have made all farmland more productive, the price of farmland (adjusted for overall inflation) has fallen. Use the concept of price elasticity to explain why productivity and farmland prices are positively related across space but negatively related over time.

3 For each of the following pairs of goods, which good would you expect to have a more price elastic demand and why?

   a. Required textbooks or mystery novels.
   b. Beethoven recordings or classical music recordings in general.
   c. Heating oil during the next six months or heating oil during the next five years.
   d. Lemonade or water.

4 Suppose that business travellers and holidaymakers have the following demand for airline tickets from Birmingham to Naples:

Price (€)	Quantity demanded (business travellers)	Quantity demanded (holidaymakers)
150	2,100	1,000
200	2,000	800
250	1,900	600
300	1,800	400

   a. As the price of tickets rises from €200 to €250, what is the price elasticity of demand for (i) business travellers and (ii) holidaymakers? (Use the midpoint method in your calculations.)
   b. Why might holidaymakers have a different price elasticity from business travellers?

5 Suppose that your demand schedule for streamed films is as follows:

Price (€)	Quantity demanded (income = €10,000)	Quantity demanded (income = €12,000)
8	40	50
10	32	45
12	24	30
14	16	20
16	8	12

   a. Use the midpoint method to calculate your price elasticity of demand as the price of streamed films increases from €8 to €10 per film if (i) your income is €10,000, and (ii) your income is €12,000.

   b. Calculate your income elasticity of demand as your income increases from €10,000 to €12,000 if (i) the price is €12, and (ii) the price is €16 per streamed film.

6 Two drivers, Jan and Lou, each drive up to a petrol station. Before looking at the price, each places an order. Jan says, 'I'd like 30 litres of petrol.' Lou says, 'I'd like €30-worth of petrol.' What is each driver's price elasticity of demand?

7 Consider public policy aimed at smoking.

   a. Studies indicate that the price elasticity of demand for cigarettes is about 0.4. If a packet of 20 cigarettes in the UK is currently priced at £12.00 and the government wants to reduce smoking by 20 per cent, by how much should it increase the price?

   b. If the government permanently increases the price of cigarettes, will the policy have a larger effect on smoking one year from now or five years from now? Explain.

   c. Studies also find that teenagers have a higher price elasticity of demand for cigarettes than do adults. Why might this be true?

8 Pharmaceutical drugs have a price inelastic demand, and computers have a price elastic demand. Suppose that technological advance doubles the supply of both products (that is, the quantity supplied at each price is twice what it was).

   a. What happens to the equilibrium price and quantity in each market?

   b. Which product experiences a larger change in price?

   c. Which product experiences a larger change in quantity?

   d. What happens to total consumer spending on each product?

9 Suppose that there is severe flooding in a region in which there is a high concentration of wheat farmers.

   a. Farmers whose crops were destroyed by the floods were much worse off, but farmers whose crops were not destroyed benefited from the floods. Why?

   b. What information would you need about the market for wheat to assess whether farmers as a group were hurt or helped by the floods?

10 Explain why the following might be true: a drought around the world raises the total revenue that farmers receive from the sale of grain, but a drought only in France reduces the total revenue that French farmers receive.

6 TAXES AND SUBSIDIES

LEARNING OUTCOMES

After reading this chapter you should be able to:

- Distinguish between direct and indirect taxes and give examples of each.
- Distinguish between tax avoidance and tax evasion.
- Explain the difference between a specific tax and an *ad valorem* tax
- Draw diagrams to show the incidence of both a specific and an *ad valorem* tax and comment on the market outcomes as a result.
- Comment on the effect of the price elasticity of demand and supply on the incidence of taxation.
- Explain the meaning of the term 'subsidy'.
- Draw a diagram to show the effect of a subsidy and the resulting market outcomes.

INTRODUCTION

In the last two chapters, we reviewed the theory of markets using the model of demand and supply. The model looks at how the demand for goods and services and the supply of goods and services allocates resources via the price mechanism. Under the assumptions of the model, the resource allocation is efficient in maximizing consumer and producer surplus. In most countries, the market mechanism is influenced by taxes and subsidies. Taxes are imposed on businesses and individuals by governments, partly to raise money to spend on the provision of public goods such as roads, schools and national defence and partly to influence behaviour in some way. Subsidies are the opposite of taxes; they are imposed on the provision of goods and services to influence the allocation of resources in some desired way. In many European countries, public transport systems are heavily subsidized, as is agriculture.

Taxes and subsidies distort market outcomes. The use of the word 'distortion' should not be presumed to be negative; the imposition of taxes and subsidies may be for reasons of equity, and it may also be the case that market outcomes with taxes and subsidies results in a different kind of efficient outcome.

TAXATION AND BUSINESS

Businesses in most countries face considerable tax burdens, whether it is administering income tax payments to national revenue services, paying value added or sales taxes, paying taxes on profits, excise duties and other taxes such as religious taxes (in countries like Saudi Arabia and Germany, for example) or taxes related to employment referred to as payroll taxes. According to Eurostat and the Organisation for Economic Cooperation and Development (OECD) data, tax revenue accounted for around 41.1 per cent of gross domestic product (GDP) in the European Union (EU) 27 in 2020. This is relatively high in comparison to other developed countries. In the United States, for example, tax revenue accounted for around 26.6 per cent of GDP in 2020, it was around 33.2 per cent in Japan, 28.5 per cent in Australia and 33.2 per cent in Canada.

Within the EU there are variations in the percentage of GDP accounted for by tax revenue. Countries like Denmark, France and Belgium had relatively high percentages between 42 and 46.9 per cent in 2021, whereas in Bulgaria, Romania and Ireland the percentages are between 21.1 and 30.3 per cent.

Taxes can be either direct or indirect. **Direct taxes** are levied on income and wealth and, the responsibility for payment is on the individual or organization on which the tax is levied. Income taxes for employees and corporation taxes on business profits are two examples of direct taxes. **Indirect taxes** tend to be imposed on goods and services, and while businesses are invariably ultimately responsible for the payment of the tax to the tax authorities, some or all of the tax can be passed on to a consumer. Value Added Tax (VAT) and excise duty are examples of indirect taxes. The balance between revenue from direct taxes and indirect taxes also varies across countries. Some 62.7 per cent of tax revenue in Denmark comes from direct taxes, whereas in the Netherlands, Ireland, Norway and Sweden, the percentage is between 35 and 50 per cent. Invariably it is income taxes which account for most of the revenue from direct taxation. In the UK, for example, total tax receipts for the fiscal year 2022/23 was £1,017 billion and of that figure, 24.5 per cent was raised through income tax and 17.5 per cent was through National Insurance Contributions. VAT accounted for 15.7 per cent. The amount of revenue generated from indirect taxes across the EU has increased since around 2009, with the average tax rate on consumption rising from just under 16 per cent in 2009 to just over 17 per cent in 2020. VAT rates across the EU27 vary from 17 per cent in Luxembourg to 27 per cent in Hungary. The standard rate of VAT across the EU27 cannot be less than 15 per cent.

> **direct tax** taxes levied on income and wealth with the responsibility for payment lying with the individual or organization
> **indirect tax** tax levied on consumption and invariably paid by businesses to tax authorities, but where some or all of the tax can be passed on to a consumer

The collection, administration and payment of taxes and subsidies imposes considerable costs on businesses. In the UK, for example, businesses which employ workers administer the payment of income taxes and National Insurance Contributions (NICs) to His Majesty's Revenue and Customs, the UK tax authority which collects tax on behalf of the government. While the individual worker is ultimately responsible for the amount of income tax they pay, businesses are very much in the front line of the administration of the so-called pay-as-you-earn (PAYE) tax systems. Businesses are responsible for paying taxes on profits, on capital gains on the sale of assets, and many charities have certain tax exemptions which they can claim. In addition, businesses are responsible for paying indirect taxes such as VAT, excise duties and rates to tax authorities. Some or all of this tax can be passed on to consumers, or it can be claimed back to reduce the amount payable in the case of VAT.

In most countries, the tax system is complex. Businesses must understand what taxes have to be paid and when, how they are to be paid, what tax allowances can be claimed and what thresholds exist before tax has to be paid, among other things. Many businesses, large and small, will employ accountants with expertise in the tax system to help them comply with the law and avoid paying taxes when not necessary. In recent years, there has been strong criticism of some larger global firms who use tax laws in various countries to avoid paying tax. **Tax avoidance** is not illegal, it is using the tax system to benefit the business. **Tax evasion** is illegal. It is the deliberate non-payment of tax due. While many large firms can legally avoid tax, the morality of so doing has been questioned.

> **tax avoidance** the legal use of the tax system to minimize the amount of tax paid
> **tax evasion** the deliberate and illegal activity by an individual or organization not to pay the required statutory tax due

A Formal Analysis of Taxes and Subsidies

In analysing the impact of taxes on market outcomes, we will look at indirect taxes and assume that the tax is levied on businesses. Businesses can pass on some of the taxation to consumers, and our analysis will look at the burden or incidence of taxation. Economists use the term **tax incidence** to refer to the distribution of a tax burden.

tax incidence the way the burden of a tax is shared among participants in a market

With indirect taxes, it is possible that both consumers and businesses will face some of the burden of taxation. We can analyze the incidence of tax by using the tools of supply and demand.

How Taxes on Sellers Affect Market Outcomes

Consider a tax levied on sellers of a good. Suppose the government imposes a tax on sellers of nail varnish remover of €0.50 per bottle. We can analyze the effect of this tax using three steps.

Step One The immediate impact of the tax is on the sellers of nail varnish remover. The quantity of nail varnish remover demanded at any given price is the same; thus, the demand curve does not change. By contrast, the tax on sellers makes the nail varnish remover business less profitable at any given price, so it shifts the supply curve.

Step Two Because the tax on sellers raises the cost of producing and selling nail varnish remover, it reduces the quantity supplied at every price. The supply curve shifts upwards to the left.

We can be precise about the magnitude of the shift. For any market price of nail varnish remover, the effective price to sellers (the amount they get to keep after paying the tax) is €0.50 lower. For example, if the market price of a bottle is €3.00, the effective price received by sellers would be €2.50. To induce sellers to supply any given quantity, the market price must now be €0.50 higher to compensate for the effect of the tax. Thus, as shown in Figure 6.1, the supply curve shifts *upward* from S_1 to S_2 by exactly the size of the tax (€0.50). The vertical distance between the two supply curves is the amount of the tax.

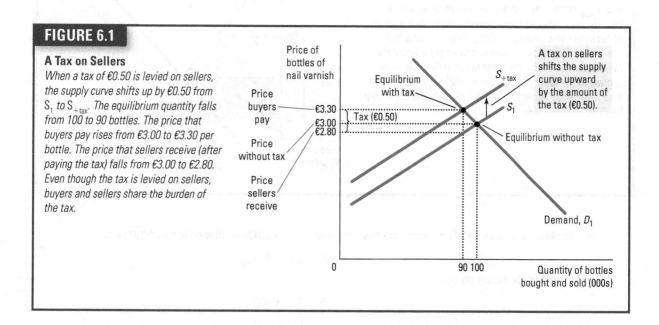

FIGURE 6.1

A Tax on Sellers
When a tax of €0.50 is levied on sellers, the supply curve shifts up by €0.50 from S_1 to S_{+tax}. The equilibrium quantity falls from 100 to 90 bottles. The price that buyers pay rises from €3.00 to €3.30 per bottle. The price that sellers receive (after paying the tax) falls from €3.00 to €2.80. Even though the tax is levied on sellers, buyers and sellers share the burden of the tax.

Step Three Having determined how the supply curve shifts, we can now compare the initial and the new equilibrium. The figure shows that the equilibrium price of nail varnish remover rises from €3.00 to €3.30, and the equilibrium quantity bought and sold falls from 100,000 to 90,000 bottles per time period. The tax reduces the size of the nail varnish remover market, and buyers and sellers share the burden of the tax. Because the market price rises, buyers pay €0.30 more for each bottle of nail varnish remover than they did before the tax was enacted. Sellers receive a higher price than they did without the tax, but the effective price (after paying the tax) falls from €3.00 to €2.80.

Implications A tax on sellers places a wedge between the price that buyers pay and the price that sellers receive. The wedge between the buyers' price and the sellers' price is the same, and would be the same regardless of whether the tax is levied on buyers or sellers. In reality, most governments levy taxes on sellers rather than on buyers, however. The wedge shifts the relative position of the supply and demand curves. In the new equilibrium, buyers and sellers share the burden of the tax.

The total amount of tax paid by buyers and sellers can also be determined from Figure 6.1. Buyers pay an additional €0.30 per bottle times the number of bottles purchased (90,000) and so the total tax paid by buyers is €27,000. The burden of the tax on sellers is €0.20 per bottle and they sell 90,000 bottles so sellers contribute €18,000 to the tax authorities. The total tax revenue is the vertical distance between the two supply curves multiplied by the amount bought and sold. In this example, the total tax raised is €0.50 × 90,000 = €45,000.

A Specific Tax on Sellers We can identify a general principle highlighted in Figure 6.2. The original equilibrium price before the tax is Pe and the original equilibrium quantity is Qe. The levying of a specific tax shifts the supply curve to the left to S_{+tax}. The new equilibrium price is Pe_1 and the new equilibrium quantity is Qe_1. The amount of the tax is the vertical distance between the two supply curves at the new equilibrium (AC). Buyers now pay a price of Pe_1 compared to Pe and so pay $Pe_1Pe × Qe_1$ in tax, shown by the lighter shaded rectangle Pe_1ABPe. Sellers now receive D whereas they received Pe before the tax was levied. As a result, the burden of the tax for sellers is the amount $DPe × Qe_1$. The total amount paid by sellers is given by the darker shaded area $PeBCD$. The total tax revenue due to the tax authorities is the area Pe_1ACD.

FIGURE 6.2

Determining the Incidence (Burden) of Taxation

A specific tax of AC per unit shifts the supply curve from S to S_{+tax}. Consumers now pay a higher price Pe$_1$ and buy Qe$_1$. The tax burden on the consumer is shown by the value of the lighter shaded area Pe$_1$ABPe. Sellers now receive the amount D for each unit sold compared to Pe before the tax was levied. The burden of the tax on sellers, therefore, is given by the value of the darker shaded area PeBCD. The total tax revenue raised and due to the authorities is the area Pe$_1$ACD.

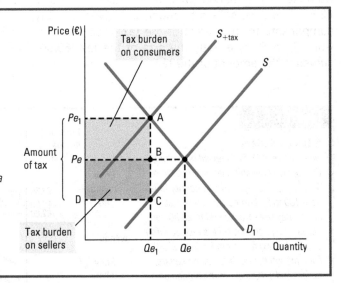

The Algebra of a Specific Tax Assume that the demand function is given by the equation:

$$P = 30 - 1.5Q_D$$

and the supply equation by:

$$P = 6 + 0.5Q_S$$

A specific tax levied on the seller of t would make the supply function:

$$P = 6 + 0.5Q_S + t$$

In equilibrium, therefore:

$$6 + 0.5Q_S + t = 30 - 1.5Q_D$$
$$0.5Q_S + 1.5Q_D = 30 - 6 - t$$
$$2Q = 24 - t$$
$$Q = 12 - 0.5t$$

If no tax was levied, then the quantity would be 12. If the tax t was levied at a rate of €6 per unit then the quantity would be 9, and if the tax was levied at a rate of €8 per unit, $Q = 8$.

We can substitute $Q = 12 - 0.5t$ into the demand equation and determine the effect on price of the tax. The demand equation would thus be:

$$P = 30 - 1.5(12 - 0.5t)$$

If $t = 5$ then the price would be:

$$P = 30 - 1.5(12 - 0.5(5))$$
$$P = 30 - 14.25$$
$$P = 15.75$$

If $t = 8$ then the price would be:

$$P = 30 - 1.5(12 - 4)$$
$$P = 30 - 12$$
$$P = 18$$

An *Ad Valorem* Tax on Sellers The basic principle that the buyer and seller both share the burden of the tax is the same as that for a specific tax, but there is a subtle difference in the way the supply curve shifts. Imagine the market for training shoes where the government announces that it is going to impose a sales tax of 20 per cent. Again, we use our three-step method to analyze the effect.

Step One The initial impact of the tax is again on the sellers. The quantity of training shoes demanded at any given price is the same; thus the demand curve does not change. The seller faces an increase in the cost of production but this time the effective increase in cost varies at each price. If the tax was 20 per cent and training shoes cost €20 to produce, the seller would have to give €4 to the government in tax (20 per cent of €20); if training shoes cost €50 to produce, the seller would have to give €10 to the government, and if training shoes cost €75 to produce the seller would have to give €15 to the government. The supply curve shifts to the left but it is not a parallel shift.

Step Two The tax on sellers raises the cost of producing and selling trainers as for a specific tax, but the amount that sellers must give to the government is lower at low prices than at high prices, because 20 per cent of a small amount is a different value than 20 per cent of a higher amount. The supply curve pivots upwards and to the left of the original supply curve as shown in Figure 6.3. At lower prices the seller must pay a smaller amount of tax per pair than at higher prices. The vertical distance between the supply curves at every price is 20 per cent of the price without the tax.

For any market price of training shoes, the effective price to sellers (the amount they get to keep after paying the tax) is lower, because the selling price is 120 per cent of the cost.

For example, if the market price of trainers happened to be €20 per pair, the effective price received by sellers would be €16.67. Whatever the market price, sellers will supply a quantity of trainers as if the price were 16.67 per cent (1/6) lower than it is. To induce sellers to supply any given quantity, the market price must now be 20 per cent higher to compensate for the effect of the tax. Thus, as shown in Figure 6.3, the supply curve shifts *upward* from S_1 to S_2 by 20 per cent at each price.

Step Three Having determined how the supply curve shifts, we can now compare the initial and the new equilibrium. Panel (a) of Figure 6.3 shows that the equilibrium price of training shoes rises from €20 to €23, and the equilibrium quantity falls from 100,000 pairs to 85,000 pairs. The tax reduces the size of the training shoe market, and buyers and sellers share the burden of the tax. Because the market price rises, buyers pay €3 more for each pair of trainers than they did before the tax was imposed. Sellers receive a higher price than they did without the tax, but the effective price (after paying the tax) falls from €20 to €19 per pair.

In panel (b) of Figure 6.3 the initial equilibrium price before the tax is €50 and the amount of training shoes bought and sold is 150,000 pairs. A 20 per cent tax will mean that sellers must pay the tax authorities €10 on each pair sold. Panel (b) of Figure 6.3 shows the equilibrium price has risen to €55, so buyers must pay €5 more per pair of trainers and the price that sellers receive falls from €50 before the tax to €45 afterwards. In this example, the burden of the tax is shared equally between the buyer and seller.

FIGURE 6.3

An *Ad Valorem* Tax on Sellers

When a tax of 20 per cent is levied on sellers, the supply curve shifts to the left from S_1 to S_2. At low prices, the amount of the tax paid is relatively low, but 20 per cent of higher prices has to be given to the government. The shift in the supply curve is, therefore, not parallel. The market outcome will vary depending on the demand for trainers and the original market price. If market price were €20, as shown in panel (a), the equilibrium quantity falls from 100,000 to 85,000 pairs. The price that buyers pay rises from €20 to €23 per pair. The price that sellers receive (after paying the tax) falls from €20 to €19. Even though the tax is levied on sellers, buyers and sellers share the burden of the tax.

In panel (b) the equilibrium price before the tax is €50 per pair and the equilibrium quantity bought and sold is 150,000 pairs of trainers. The tax of 20 per cent means that the vertical distance between the two supply curves is now €10 at this quantity, which is how much the supplier must give to the tax authorities for every pair sold. The buyer now faces a price of €55 per pair, and the price the seller receives (after paying the tax) falls from €50 to €45.

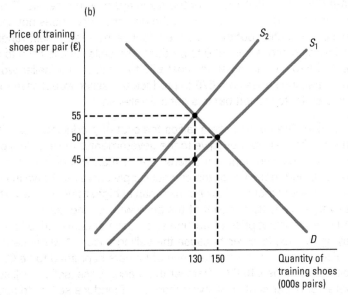

Elasticity and Tax Incidence

When a good is taxed, buyers and sellers of the good share the burden of the tax. Rarely, however, will the burden be shared equally. The burden of the tax is determined by the price elasticity. Consider the impact of taxation in the two markets in Figure 6.4. In both cases, the figure shows the initial demand curve, the initial supply curve and a new supply curve that reflects the tax imposed on sellers. The difference in the two panels is the relative elasticity of supply and demand. Panel (a) of Figure 6.4 shows a tax in a market with very elastic supply and relatively inelastic demand. That is, sellers are very responsive to changes in the price of the good (so the supply curve is relatively flat), whereas buyers are not very responsive (so the demand curve is relatively steep). When a tax is imposed on a market with these elasticities, the price received by sellers does not fall much, so sellers bear only a small burden. By contrast, the price paid by buyers rises substantially, indicating that buyers bear most of the burden of the tax. If the price elasticity of demand is low (represented in panel (a) by a steep curve) then demand will fall proportionately less in response to a rise in price, because buyers are not very price sensitive. The seller can shift the burden of the tax onto the buyer, safe in the knowledge that demand will only fall by a relatively small amount.

Panel (b) of Figure 6.4 shows a tax in a market with relatively price inelastic supply and very price elastic demand (represented by a flatter curve). In this case, sellers are not very responsive to changes in the price (so the supply curve is steeper), while buyers are very responsive. The figure shows that when a tax is imposed, the price paid by buyers does not rise much, while the price received by sellers falls substantially. Thus sellers bear most of the burden of the tax. In this case, sellers know that if they try to pass on the tax to buyers that demand will fall by a relatively large amount.

FIGURE 6.4

How the Burden of a Tax is Divided

In panel (a), the supply curve is price elastic and the demand curve is price inelastic. In this case, the price received by sellers falls only slightly, while the price paid by buyers rises substantially. Thus buyers bear most of the burden of the tax. In panel (b), the supply curve is price inelastic and the demand curve is price elastic. In this case, the price received by sellers falls substantially, while the price paid by buyers rises only slightly. Thus, sellers bear most of the burden of the tax.

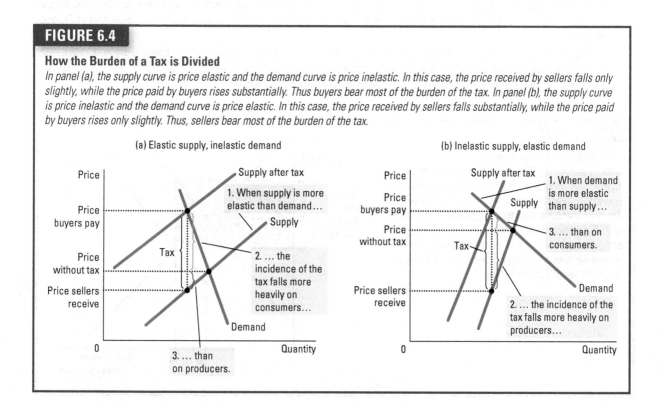

The two panels of Figure 6.4 show a general lesson about how the burden of a tax is divided: a tax burden falls more heavily on the side of the market that is less price elastic. Why is this the case? In essence, the price elasticity measures the willingness of buyers or sellers to leave the market when conditions become unfavourable. If demand is price inelastic, it means that buyers do not have good alternatives to consuming this particular good. If supply is price inelastic, it means that sellers do not have good alternatives to producing this particular good. When the good is taxed, the side of the market with fewer good alternatives cannot easily leave the market and must, therefore, bear more of the burden of the tax.

SELF TEST In a supply and demand diagram, show how a tax on car sellers of €1,000 per car affects the quantity of cars sold and the price of cars. In your diagram, show the change in the price paid by car buyers and the change in price received by car sellers.

How Subsidies Affect Market Outcomes

A **subsidy** is the opposite of a tax. Subsidies are levied when governments want to encourage the consumption of a good which they deem is currently under produced. Subsidies are generally given to sellers and have the effect of reducing the cost of production, as opposed to a tax which increases the cost of production. Subsidies exist in a variety of different areas including education, transport, agriculture, regional development, housing and employment.

> **subsidy** a payment to buyers and sellers to supplement income or lower costs and which thus encourages consumption or provides an advantage to the recipient

Subsidies in education help to make the cost of attending higher education lower than it would otherwise be. Most European countries provide subsidies for transport systems, and the Common Agricultural Policy in the EU oversees subsidies to farmers. In Switzerland some €2.5 billion is spent on subsidies for rail transport, in Germany the figure is nearer to €9 billion, while in the UK subsidies account for around €3 billion and in France, €6.8 billion.

Figure 6.5 shows how a subsidy works using the rail system as an example. In the absence of a subsidy the equilibrium number of journeys bought and sold is Q_e and the equilibrium train ticket for each journey is price €75. We again use a three-step approach to analyze the effect.

FIGURE 6.5

A Subsidy on Rail Transport

When a subsidy of €30 per journey is given to sellers, the supply curve shifts to the right by €30 from S_1 to S_2. The equilibrium quantity rises from Q_e to Q_1 journeys per year. The price that buyers pay for a journey falls from €75 to €60. The subsidy results in lower prices for passengers and an increased number of journeys available. Even though the subsidy is given to sellers, buyers and sellers share the benefits of the subsidy.

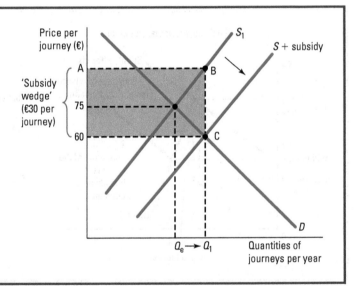

Step One If the government gives a subsidy of €30 per (average) ticket to train operators, it is the supply curve for journeys which is affected; the demand curve is not affected because the number of train journeys demanded at each price stays the same. The subsidy to train operators reduces the cost of providing a train journey by €30 and so the supply curve will shift.

Step Two Because the subsidy reduces the cost to the train operators, the supply curve shifts downwards to the right by the amount of the subsidy from S_1 to $S_{+subsidy}$. To provide the number of train journeys shown by Q_1, the actual cost to train operators is A, but they get a subsidy shown by the distance BC, which is €30 per ticket sold.

Step Three Comparing the initial and the new equilibrium, we can see that the equilibrium price of each train journey is now lower at €60 and the equilibrium number of journeys travelled increases to Q_1. Passengers and train operators both benefit from the subsidy as passengers can obtain train tickets at a lower price than before the subsidy and have more journeys available, and sellers receive more revenue than they did before the subsidy, allowing them the potential to invest in the service they provide. The total cost of providing the subsidy is the amount of the subsidy (€30 per ticket in this case) multiplied by the number of tickets bought and sold (Q_e), shown by the shaded area ABC60. The precise division of the benefits between buyers and sellers will depend on the relative price elasticities of demand and supply.

Implications There is considerable debate surrounding the value of subsidies. We have seen from the example how price and quantity can be affected following the imposition of a subsidy. In the case of transport, it may have the effect of altering the incentives for people to travel on the train rather than on the roads, and so have the benefit of reducing congestion on the roads and the pollution that is associated with road use. There are also costs associated with subsidies; the subsidy must be financed, and this generally falls on the taxpayer. In many cases with subsidies, not all taxpayers will be part of the market being subsidized. For example, one argument for not subsidizing higher education fees for students is that many taxpayers will not have had a university education, but are expected to contribute towards students' fees. The benefit to the student is from higher potential earnings over their lifetime. Why then, it is argued, should 'ordinary' taxpayers pay a contribution when they are not seeing any direct benefit?

Subsidies may also encourage firms to overproduce, which has a wider effect on the market. Subsidies on commodities such as cotton, bananas and sugar distort the workings of the market and change global comparative advantage. Overproduction leads to excess supply on world markets and drives down prices, as well as diverting trade to rich countries who can support producers through subsidies at the expense of poor countries, whose producers cannot compete because prices are lower than the free market price.

 WHAT IF... a government imposed a subsidy on a product with a highly price inelastic demand curve and a very price elastic supply curve. What do you think would be the effects in both the short term and the long term for consumers and businesses in this market?

CONCLUSION

Taxes and subsidies are interventions in the market mechanism which have implications for market outcomes. In the next chapter, we will look at how taxes and subsidies can be used to create what policy makers would argue are more desirable market outcomes. We have looked at the market mechanism as a way of allocating resources efficiently using the principles of consumer and producer surplus. Such a definition, however, does not necessarily mean that the outcome is equitable or desirable, as we shall see in Chapter 7.

SUMMARY

- Taxes and subsidies are levied on businesses and individuals and affect market outcomes.
- Direct taxes are levied on income and wealth, whereas indirect taxes tend to be levied on consumption.
- Tax avoidance involves reducing the amount of tax paid by utilizing the tax laws and tax system. Tax evasion is the deliberate attempt to not pay taxes which are legally due.
- A tax on sellers shifts the supply curve upwards to the left and results in higher prices and lower equilibrium quantities bought and sold. The precise effect is dependent on the price elasticities of demand and supply for the goods in question.
- A specific tax is a per unit tax whereas an *ad valorem* tax is a percentage tax.
- The incidence or burden of taxation refers to who pays the tax. The incidence of tax is determined by the elasticity of demand and supply of the goods and services on which the tax is levied.
- Subsidies are designed to encourage production of goods and services and help reduce the price to consumers.

CASE STUDY   The Common Agricultural Policy

The Common Agricultural Policy (CAP) is one of the most widely debated and controversial policies of the EU. There are around 500 million people in the EU who need access to food. Providing this food are around 22 million farmers on 10 million farms who are part of a food industry which employs around 40 million people. The export industry in food from the EU is worth some €130 billion. These facts help put into context the importance of agriculture to the EU, but it is also an industry which has inherent challenges, not least with external factors such as the weather, pests and diseases.

Because of the importance and potential instability in agriculture, the CAP has been developed with three main objectives in mind. First, the CAP seeks to help support farmers to mitigate against wide fluctuations in incomes from one year to the next. However, it is not simply helping farmers maintain incomes; the products that farmers choose to produce must be products which consumers want to buy and which are produced ethically, sustainably and safely. Second, the CAP seeks to help stabilize markets so that consumers also do not face large swings in prices in response to changes in supply conditions in the industry. Third, the CAP aims to promote rural development and the protection of the rural landscape. In recent years there have been discussions on revamping the CAP and in December 2021, an agreement on reform of the CAP was adopted and came into force in January 2023. The new CAP places more of an emphasis on protecting the environment and on improving competitiveness and fairness. There are ten key objectives identified, which include climate change, the food value chain, generational renewal, environmental care and landscapes.

The new CAP will have a budget of around €387 billion for the period 2021–2027. One of the criticisms of CAP subsidies is that a disproportionate amount of subsidy payments goes to wealthy landowners. It is argued that the policy has tended to promote the development of bigger industrial-scale farming, driving out small farmers and encouraging farming practices which are not as environmentally friendly as they could be. In 2017, for example, the pressure group Greenpeace said that farming interests run by Sir James Dyson received £1.6 million (€1.8m) in subsidy payments, and that 20 of the top 100 companies and landowners who received subsidies were on the Sunday Times Rich List. The effect of subsidies, it is argued, has been to distort the workings of the market rather than achieve diversity and protection for smaller farmers.

Supporters of subsidies point to measures to improve transparency within the EU on who gets payments and how much. Data on farm payments is published in considerable detail by the EU. Supporters of subsidies argue that the price paid by taxpayers to support agriculture is outweighed by the benefits that accrue in terms of the supply of food and more stable prices. Many farmers would go out of business if they did not receive EU payments, but that in itself is an issue. If farmers had to rely on their own business acumen and performance, it is argued that agriculture would be more efficient and not subject to the distortions that exist because of the CAP. This is one of the reasons for the reform of the CAP to try to help make farming more sustainable (in all the definitions of that word) and to ensure future generations of farmers have an industry to work in that is commercially viable.

The CAP aims to help support farmers and make supplies of food widely available to everyone.

(Continued)

IN THE NEWS

Corporate Taxes

One of the main taxes that businesses must pay is a tax on profits that it makes. Business profits are the equivalent of the income of an individual, and corporate taxes are a direct tax. In principle, this sounds simple enough. Calculate the profit a firm makes, multiply this by the corporate tax rate and that is the tax a business should pay. For example, a company making a profit of €100,000 when the corporate tax is 20 per cent would be liable to pay €20,000 in tax.

In practice, it is not nearly so simple and straight forward. Particularly for large enterprises, there are considerable complexities. There has been a debate about the amount of corporate taxes paid by a number of high profile global businesses. Google, Apple, Starbucks, Ikea, GAP and Microsoft have all been the subject of news stories where they are accused of not paying their 'fair share of tax'.

Amazon has also been the subject of criticism. Amazon has business interests around the globe, but is ultimately a US business. One of its businesses, Amazon Europe, is based in Luxembourg, but the business operates across a wide range of European counties, each with different corporate tax laws and rates. In the UK, for example, Corporation Tax is 19 per cent at the time of writing, in Ireland it is 13 per cent, in Germany 15 per cent, 19 per cent in Luxembourg, 33 per cent in France and in Guernsey, 0 per cent for some business activities. How does a company operating across so many different tax jurisdictions pay its due taxes? In 2020 Amazon reported that it generated €44 billion in revenues on its European business but reported a €1.2 billion loss and as a result did not have to pay any tax. It was reported that Amazon received incomes of £19.5 billion from UK sales in 2020 and paid £293 million in tax in 2019.

Critics argued that Amazon ought to be paying more tax given its massive turnover, and that the company was using its size and complex organization to 'play the system' and avoid paying tax. It is argued that companies like Amazon are able to use the tax laws and systems in different countries, as well as accounting rules, to define the way it carries out its business and minimize its tax liabilities, not least through routing some of its business activities through 'tax havens' where tax rates might be much lower or even zero. In the case of Amazon, different parts of the business provide services to other parts of the business for a fee, reducing the profits liable to tax in certain jurisdictions. Even though the revenues for the warehouse and logistics part of the business grew from €1.04 billion in 2015 to €1.6 billion during the financial year 2016, Amazon reported that despite this increase in revenue, its profit on the warehouse and logistics business fell by half, hence the explanation of a lower tax liability.

Tax evasion is illegal, but tax avoidance is not. Although it is not illegal, many people feel firms have a moral duty not to seek to avoid paying their fair share of tax.

(Continued)

Amazon defended itself by noting that it pays 'all taxes that are required in every country where we operate'. It also pointed out that it had invested €20 billion into its European business and employs around 65,000 people across the continent.

Some economists would argue that corporate taxes might sound a 'good thing' because they are levied on some entity as opposed to an individual. However, in reality, entities are made up of individuals and if you increase the tax on corporations, individuals ultimately have to pay it, and this can affect jobs and investment. Critics of companies like Amazon and others mentioned above note that while they are not breaking the law, they have a moral duty to pay their 'fair share of tax', and that tax avoidance breaches such moral duties. The only way to tackle the problem, they argue, is to institute new tax laws which apply across a range of countries so that different tax systems cannot be (legally) exploited to avoid paying tax. Getting agreement on the reform of tax systems across countries is extremely difficult.

Questions

1 Why is a tax on corporate profits a 'direct tax'?
2 To what extent do you think companies like Google, Amazon, Ikea and Starbucks have a moral duty to pay more tax than they do?
3 Comment on the following argument: 'The benefits to Europe of the economic activity generated by businesses like Amazon outweighs the relatively small amounts of tax they seem to pay.'
4 To what extent do you agree that it is not the fault of businesses that tax systems and tax laws are so complex, or that they can use systems to legally avoid paying tax?
5 Is reform of tax systems across Europe and indeed the globe the real answer to reducing tax avoidance?

QUESTIONS FOR REVIEW

1 Explain the difference between direct and indirect taxes using appropriate examples to illustrate your answer.
2 What is the difference between tax avoidance and tax evasion?
3 Explain the difference between a specific tax and an *ad valorem* tax.
4 Use a demand and supply diagram to show the effect on market outcomes if businesses producing wine had a duty of €0.75 imposed per bottle.
5 What is meant by the 'incidence or burden' of a tax?
6 In the UK, VAT is at zero rate on the sale of children's nappies. Use a demand and supply diagram to show the effect on market outcomes for children's nappies of a decision to levy VAT at 15 per cent on the product.
7 How does a tax imposed on a good with a high price elasticity of demand affect the market equilibrium? Who bears most of the burden of the tax in this instance?
8 How does a tax imposed on a good with a low price elasticity of demand affect the market equilibrium? Who bears most of the burden of the tax in this instance?
9 Using an appropriate diagram, show how the burden of changes in ad valorem taxes alters depending on the elasticity of supply.
10 How does a subsidy on a good affect the price paid by buyers, the price received by sellers and the quantity bought and sold?

PROBLEMS AND APPLICATIONS

1 Do you agree with the following statements? Why or why not?

a. 'Taxes are an unnecessary distortion to the workings of the market system.'
b. 'It is preferable to levy indirect taxes rather than direct taxes because indirect taxes are fairer.'
c. 'More and more people are growing their own in their gardens. Governments should seek to tax the value of output of fruit and vegetables produced by domestic growers.'

2 Assume a business takes a decision to register its headquarters in Guernsey and sets up a small office in which some members of the senior management team are located. The business has no other business operations in Guernsey, but has other business activities across Europe. In doing this, it does not incur any liability for corporation tax. Comment on this business decision.

3 A government decides to influence the market outcomes of sales of petrol and diesel by imposing a duty of €0.60 per litre on diesel and €0.20 per litre on petrol. What might the effects of such a policy be:

    a. in the immediate short term
    b. in the medium term
    c. in the long term?

   Use supply and demand diagrams to help illustrate your answer.

4 'It does not matter whether a tax is imposed on a seller or a buyer, the effect will be the same.' Comment on this statement.

5 'A fine is a tax for doing something wrong. A tax is a fine for doing something right.' Discuss.

6 An *ad valorem* tax is levied on producers of insecticide used by households in their gardens. The insecticide contains a chemical which, while generally safe, the government would rather people did not use.

    a. Use a supply and demand diagram to show the effect of the tax on the price and quantity bought and sold of this product. In thinking about your answer, consider the possible price elasticities of the demand and supply curves and how this might affect market outcomes.
    b. Given your answer to a, what is the incidence of the tax and what is the total tax revenue to the government?
    c. Why do you think the government might have chosen to tax this particular product rather than ban it outright?
    d. What other measures might a government use to shift consumption away from a product like insecticides which may not be desirable?

7 'An increase in corporate taxes is a tax on jobs and incentives for businesses to expand'. Comment on this view.

8 In the UK, there has been strong criticism of the 5 per cent VAT on ladies' sanitary products. Do you think such criticism is justified? What sort of products do you think should be zero rated for VAT and why?

9 Subsidies have been a policy option for a number of governments seeking to boost the growth of renewable energy sources such as wind and solar power. To what extent do you think that such policies are justified?

10 Why might it be tempting for governments to impose ever higher taxes on businesses producing goods which are deemed to be damaging to public health such as tobacco and alcohol? Is it simply a case of reducing consumption?

PART 3
MICROECONOMICS: THE LIMITATIONS OF MARKETS

7 MARKET FAILURE

LEARNING OUTCOMES

After reading this chapter you should be able to:

- See how decision making and transactions can often ignore social costs and benefits leading to externalities.
- Define market failure and give examples of how it arises.
- Explain the difference between private and social costs.
- Draw diagrams to show consumer and producer surplus and identify changes in both as a result of changes in price.
- Use diagrams to explain how both negative and positive externalities arise and show the welfare costs of inefficient resource allocation.
- Discuss different government-led solutions to market failure including regulation, taxes and subsidies.
- Analyze the use of tradable permits.
- Evaluate the arguments surrounding the economic analysis of pollution.
- Consider some of the issues relating to social and ethical responsibility of firms.
- Analyze the use of property rights as a means of correcting externalities.

INTRODUCTION

We have looked at markets and how firms operate in those markets. Efficiency has been a recurring feature of the discussion of markets and firms but we must be careful how we define efficiency. Efficiency is about getting the most we can from scarce resources. More specifically we can define efficiency in relation to business in four ways:

- Technical efficiency: a business can improve its technical efficiency if it can find a way of using its existing resources to produce more. It may be that it could use machinery instead of people to do the same job much faster without having to take a break!

- Productive efficiency: a business can improve productive efficiency by producing output at the lowest cost possible. If it can find a way of sourcing cheaper raw materials, for example, which allows it to reduce costs, then it can improve its productive efficiency.
- Allocative efficiency: this looks at efficiency from the perspective of consumers. Are the products being produced by businesses wanted and valued by consumers (both individual consumers and business consumers)? Efficiency occurs where the goods and services being produced match the demand by consumers. Allocative efficiency occurs where the cost of resources used to produce the products is equal to the value placed on the product by consumers, represented by the price they are willing to pay.
- Social efficiency: when businesses produce products they incur costs, raw materials, wages, rents, interest payments, insurance, plant and equipment and so on. These are the private costs. However, there are also costs which businesses may not consider, such as the pollution they generate in production. These are costs borne by society. Social efficiency occurs where the private and social cost of production is equal to the private and social benefits derived from their consumption.

In recent years, there has been a greater awareness of the effects that a firm's operations have on its wider stakeholders and the importance of considering the perspective of social efficiency. We know, for example, that cigarette and alcohol manufacturers produce products which can result in serious health issues for users and problems for society as a whole: a case of overproduction and overconsumption. We know that there is a way to reduce the instances of sexually transmitted diseases, including the very serious problem of HIV and AIDS, through wider use of condoms, but this is a product which is underused.

Market theory in its purest sense assumes that markets work efficiently and that when they do, resources are allocated efficiently. The reality is much more complex than this, partly because of the definition of efficiency that is used. Market failure occurs where the market does not allocate resources efficiently.

Sources of Market Failure

There are a number of sources of market failure which can be summarized as follows:

- In many cases, there is imperfect knowledge of and between buyers and sellers. This might arise because consumers do not have adequate technical knowledge, or where advertising can mislead or misinform. Producers are likely to be unaware of all the opportunities open to them and cannot always accurately measure productivity. For both consumers and producers, decisions are often based not on rational assessment of the costs and benefits but on a wide range of rules of thumb (called heuristics).
- Goods are not homogeneous; they are differentiated through branding, technology, labelling and product information, among other methods.
- Firms cannot always substitute or move factors of production from one use to another easily. Labour can be both geographically and occupationally immobile, some capital items have limited uses (for example, what else could the Channel Tunnel be used for?) and land cannot be moved to where it might be needed nor exploited if it is not suitable.
- In some markets there are not large numbers of sellers, but the market may be dominated by a relatively small number of very large firms which have some element of monopoly power. Firms with monopoly power might indulge in collusion, price fixing, rigging of markets and the erection of barriers to entry.
- There are some products which cannot be provided in sufficient quantity by the market, for example merit goods and public goods.
- Inequality exists in factor or income endowment, for example through unequal wealth distribution, the location of resources (for example, oil and mineral reserves), where poverty exists and through discrimination.
- Decisions may be made which do not take into account all costs and benefits. Decision makers may consider just the private costs and benefits but not the social costs and benefits, and so resources are not allocated efficiently.

The market failures examined in this chapter fall under a general category called *externalities*. An externality arises when an individual or business engages in an activity that influences the well-being of a bystander (a third party) who neither pays nor receives any compensation for that effect. If the impact on the bystander is adverse, it is called a *negative externality*; if it is beneficial, it is called a *positive externality*.

Private and Social Costs

When making decisions, businesses and individuals are likely to consider the private costs and private benefits. In deciding to publish a textbook, for example, a publishing business incurs various private costs such as the cost of paper, printing, marketing, editorial work, paying author royalties and various overheads such as administration. The publisher will consider a number of private benefits which include the share of profits to owners or shareholders, and the employment of individuals within the business. However, in making the decision to publish the book, the business may not take into consideration the cost (or benefit) to society that is imposed because of that decision. Distribution of textbooks contributes to congestion, and road wear and tear; there are the emissions that the vehicles give off, the noise pollution and the increased risk of accident which may cause injury or even death to a third party. Firms that make and sell paper, which is used in the production of books, also create a by-product of the manufacturing process, a chemical called dioxin. Scientists believe that once dioxin enters the environment it raises the population's risk of cancer, birth defects and other health problems. There may also be some social benefits of the decision; knowledge development is improved because of the book being available, employees of the firm will spend the money they earn on goods and services in the local area and workers at paper mills will have jobs.

These social costs and benefits are not necessarily taken into consideration by the business when making the decision to publish the book. The internal costs and benefits may be far more important in the firm's decision making. The social costs and benefits are borne by a third party. The cost of repairing damaged roads, the cost of dealing with accident and injury, delays caused because of congestion, the effects and costs of dealing with pollution and so on, all must be borne by others, often the taxpayer. Equally, any social benefits arising from the decision are gained by those not party to the initial decision without them having to pay for the benefit derived.

In the presence of externalities, society's interest in a market outcome extends beyond the well-being of buyers and sellers who participate in the market; it also includes the well-being of bystanders who are affected indirectly. For a business, this might be its wider stakeholders. Because buyers and sellers neglect the external effects of their actions when deciding how much to demand or supply, the market equilibrium is not efficient when there are externalities. That is, the equilibrium fails to maximize the total benefit to society. The release of dioxin into the environment, for instance, is a negative externality. Self-interested paper firms will not consider the full cost of the pollution they create and, therefore, will emit too much pollution unless the government prevents or discourages them from doing so.

Externalities come in many varieties, as do the policy responses that try to deal with the market failure. Here are some examples:

- The exhaust from cars is a negative externality because it creates smog that other people breathe. Drivers do not take into consideration this externality and so tend to drive too much thus increasing pollution. The government attempts to solve this problem by setting emissions standards for cars. It also taxes fuel to reduce the amount that people drive. These policy remedies have effects on business costs and behaviour which might ultimately have to be passed onto the consumer in the form of higher prices. The benefits might be that more research and development (R&D) into efficient cars is carried out by firms looking to gain some competitive advantage in the market, something that might benefit both firms and consumers.
- Airports create negative externalities because people who live near the airport or on the flight path are disturbed by noise. Airports and airlines do not bear the full cost of the noise and, therefore, may be less inclined to spend money on noise reduction technologies. The government may address this problem by regulating the times that airlines can take-off and land at an airport, or by providing subsidies to help local homeowners invest in triple glazing and other sound proofing measures for homes on the flight path.
- Research into new technologies provides a positive externality because it creates knowledge that other people can use. Because inventors and business R&D units cannot capture the full benefits of their

inventions, they tend to devote too few resources to research. The government addresses this problem partially through the patent and intellectual property system, which gives inventors and businesses an exclusive use over their inventions or right to exploit intellectual property for a period, and through the provision of subsidies to encourage firms to invest in R&D.

● The provision of public transport brings benefits to many people not only because it helps them get around more easily but it also helps relieve congestion thus benefiting other road users. Governments are often prepared to subsidize public transport because there are positive benefits to society as a whole.

● Immunization programmes against communicable diseases and infections such as flu and Covid-19 are often provided free of charge by a country's health service. The benefits not only accrue to the individuals who receive the inoculations but in far wider circles. Those who are inoculated are less likely to pass on infection to others, in particular, the more vulnerable members of society. Days of lost work are reduced, which in turn helps businesses operate more effectively. Data published by the Office for National Statistics in the UK for 2022 suggest that around 185.6 million working days were lost due to illness and injury. Each working day lost represents a financial cost to the economy as a whole in lost production. If an immunization system contributes to a reduction in the instances of employee absence, this can have significant effects on businesses and the economy.

In each of these cases, some decision maker fails to take account of the external effects of their behaviour. The government responds by trying to influence this behaviour to protect the interests of bystanders.

EXTERNALITIES

Welfare Economics: An Overview

Firms rely on consumers. Consumers buy products from firms, but their behaviour will depend on a variety of factors, not least their willingness to pay for a product. Whenever you go into a shop or choose a product online, you are making complex neural calculations. There will be a price which you are prepared to pay to acquire a product, and there will be a slightly higher price which for some reason you are not prepared to pay. The maximum price is the **willingness to pay**, and it measures how much a buyer values a product. Buyers are invariably happy to buy products at prices less than their willingness to pay, but would refuse to buy at a price more than their willingness to pay. We can also assume that the buyer would be indifferent about buying a good at a price exactly equal to their willingness to pay.

> **willingness to pay** a measure of how much a buyer values a good by the amount they are prepared to pay to acquire the good

When buying a good, a consumer can expect to derive some benefit. The willingness to pay reflects the value of the benefit that the buyer expects to receive. This is why firms spend large sums of money trying to understand how consumers value products and what affects their behaviour. If a consumer buys a product for €10 but would have been prepared to pay €20 we say that the buyer receives *consumer surplus* of €10. **Consumer surplus** is the amount a buyer is willing to pay for a good minus the amount the buyer pays for it. We refer to 'getting a bargain' regularly in everyday language. In economics, a bargain means paying much less for something than we expected or anticipated. As a result, we get a greater degree of consumer surplus than expected. Consumer surplus measures the benefit to buyers of participating in a market.

> **consumer surplus** the amount a buyer is willing to pay for a good minus the amount the buyer pays for it

USING THE DEMAND CURVE TO MEASURE CONSUMER SURPLUS

Consumer surplus is closely related to the demand curve for a product. The market demand curve represents the willingness and ability to pay of all consumers in the market. Because buyers always want to pay less for the goods they buy, lower prices make buyers of a good better off. How much does buyers' well-being rise in response to a lower price? We can use the concept of consumer surplus to answer this question precisely.

Figure 7.1 shows a demand schedule for a market. Let us assume that it is the market for tickets for a music festival. If the festival organizers set the price at P_1, Q_1 consumers will want to buy a ticket. The marginal buyer represented by the point Q_1 has a willingness to pay of just P_1; at any price above P_1, this festival goer is not willing to pay. However, all the buyers represented by the amount 0–Q_1 were willing to pay a price higher than P_1 to get tickets. All these buyers gained some degree of consumer surplus shown by the area above the price and below the demand curve. In panel (a) of Figure 7.1, consumer surplus at a price of P_1 is the area of triangle ABC. Now suppose that the price set by the festival organizers was set at P_2 rather than P_1, as shown in panel (b). The consumer surplus now equals area ADF. The increase in consumer surplus attributable to the lower price is the area BCFD.

This increase in consumer surplus is composed of two parts. First, those buyers who would have bought Q_1 of the good at the higher price P_1 are better off because they now pay less. The increase in consumer surplus of existing buyers is the reduction in the amount they are now being asked to pay; it equals the area of the rectangle BCED. Second, some new buyers enter the market because they are now willing and able to buy tickets at the lower price. The quantity demanded for festival tickets would be Q_2 rather than Q_1. The consumer surplus these newcomers receive is the area of the triangle CEF.

FIGURE 7.1

How the Price Affects Consumer Surplus
In panel (a) the price is P_1, the quantity of festival tickets demanded is Q_1 and consumer surplus equals the area of the triangle ABC. If the ticket price is set at P_2 rather than P_1, as in panel (b), the quantity demanded would be Q_2 rather than Q_1, and the consumer surplus rises to the area of the triangle ADF. The increase in consumer surplus (area BCFD) occurs in part because existing consumers now pay less (area BCED) and in part because new consumers enter the market at the lower price (area CEF).

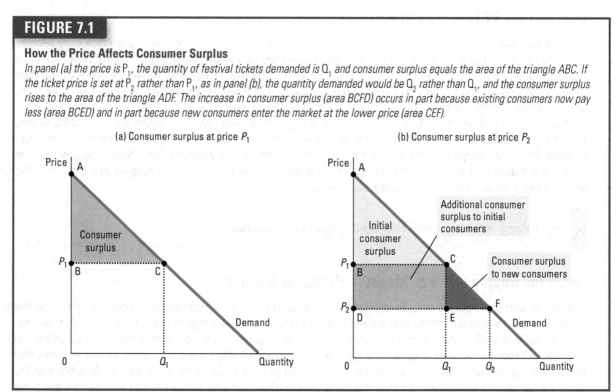

The lesson from this example holds for all demand curves: the area below the demand curve and above the price measures the consumer surplus in a market. The reason is that the height of the demand curve measures the value buyers place on the good, as measured by their willingness to pay for it. The difference between this willingness to pay and the market price is each buyer's consumer surplus. Thus, the total area below the demand curve and above the price is the sum of the consumer surplus of all buyers in the market for a good or service.

What Does Consumer Surplus Measure?

Our goal in developing the concept of consumer surplus is to make normative judgements about the desirability of market outcomes. Firms can also use the concept of consumer surplus in designing branding, advertising and promotion campaigns and deciding on pricing strategies.

Because consumer surplus measures the benefit that buyers receive from a good *as the buyers themselves perceive it*, it is a good measure of economic well-being if businesses want to respect and possibly exploit the preferences of buyers. A key assumption of consumer surplus is that consumers are the best judges of how much benefit they receive from the goods they buy. This may not always be the case.

> **SELF TEST** Draw a demand curve for streamed box sets. In your diagram, show a price of streamed box sets and the consumer surplus that results from that price. Explain in words what this consumer surplus measures.

PRODUCER SURPLUS

We now turn to the other side of the market and consider the benefits sellers receive from participating in a market. The analysis of sellers' welfare is like our analysis of buyers' welfare.

Cost and the Willingness to Sell

As with our analysis of the buyer side, sellers are willing to offer goods for sale if the price they receive exceeds the cost. Here the term cost should be interpreted as the producer's opportunity cost. Cost is a measure of a firm's willingness to sell their product. Each producer in a market would be eager to sell their products at a price greater than their cost, would refuse to sell their products at a price less than their cost, and would be indifferent about selling their products at a price exactly equal to cost.

If a producer can sell a product at a price that is higher than the lowest amount they would be willing to sell that product for, then they will receive some benefit. We say that the producer receives *producer surplus*. **Producer surplus** is the amount a seller is paid minus the cost of production. Producer surplus measures the benefit to sellers of participating in a market. The total producer surplus in a market is the value of the sum of all the individual producer surplus.

 producer surplus the amount a seller is paid minus the cost of production

Using the Supply Curve to Measure Producer Surplus

Just as consumer surplus is closely related to the demand curve, producer surplus is closely related to the supply curve. It is not surprising that sellers always want to receive a higher price for the goods they sell. How far sellers' well-being will rise in response to a higher price can be calculated precisely by using the concept of producer surplus. Figure 7.2 shows a typical upward sloping supply curve. Let us assume that this is the supply curve for firms providing online rental access to films per time period. At a price of P_1, firms can expect to sell Q_1 rentals over the time period. The producer surplus is the area below the price and above the supply curve. In panel (a) of Figure 7.2, at the price of P_1 the producer surplus is the area of triangle ABC.

Panel (b) shows what happens if the price of online film rentals rises from P_1 to P_2. Producer surplus now equals area ADF. This increase in producer surplus has two parts. First, those sellers who were already selling Q_1 of the good at the lower price P_1 are better off because they now get more for what they sell. The increase in producer surplus for existing sellers equals the area of the rectangle BCED.

Second, some new sellers enter the market because they are now willing to produce the good at the higher price, resulting in an increase in the quantity supplied from Q_1 to Q_2. The producer surplus of these newcomers is the area of the triangle CEF.

FIGURE 7.2

How the Price Affects Producer Surplus

In panel (a) the price is P_1, the quantity demanded is Q_1 and producer surplus equals the area of the triangle ABC. When the price rises from P_1 to P_2, as in panel (b), the quantity supplied rises from Q_1 to Q_2 and the producer surplus rises to the area of the triangle ADF. The increase in producer surplus (area BCFD) occurs in part because existing producers now receive more (area BCED) and in part because new producers enter the market at the higher price (area CEF).

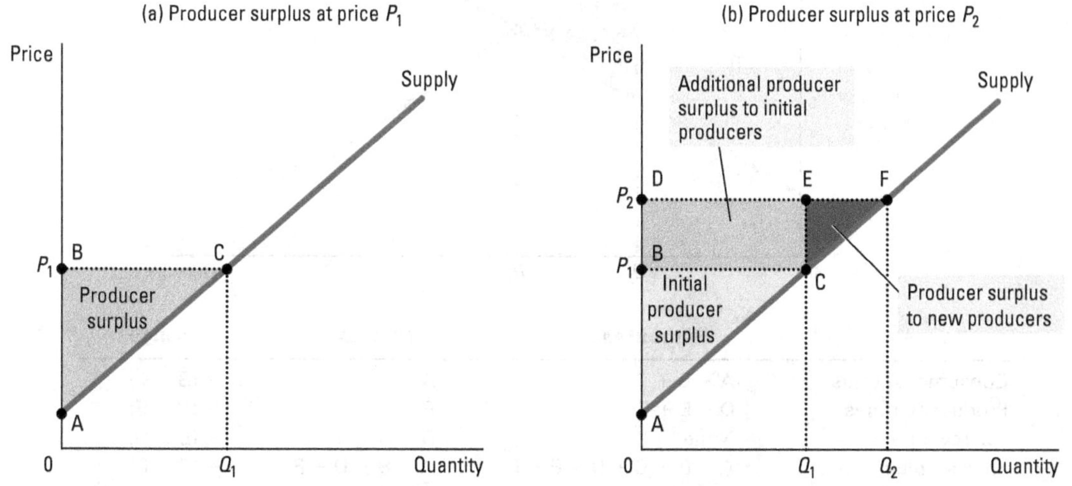

As this analysis shows, we use producer surplus to measure the well-being of sellers in much the same way as we use consumer surplus to measure the well-being of buyers. Because these two measures of economic welfare are so similar, we can use them together to analyze market inefficiencies.

These inefficiencies and changes in welfare can be estimated by referring to the **deadweight loss**. The deadweight loss is the fall in total surplus that results when a tax (or some other policy) distorts a market outcome. This can be considered by calculating the changes in both producer and consumer surplus because of the tax or policy change minus the benefits (which may be the tax revenue accruing to the government, for example). Figure 7.3 summarizes the effects of a tax by comparing welfare before and after the tax is imposed. The third column in the table in Figure 7.3 shows the changes. The tax causes consumer surplus to fall by the area B + C and producer surplus to fall by the area D + E. Tax revenue rises by the area B + D. Not surprisingly, the tax makes buyers and sellers worse off and the government better off.

> **deadweight loss** the fall in total surplus that results from a market distortion, such as a tax

The change in total welfare includes the change in consumer surplus (which is negative), the change in producer surplus (which is also negative), and the change in tax revenue (which is positive). When we add these three pieces together, we find that total surplus in the market falls by the area C + E. Thus the losses to buyers and sellers from a tax exceed the revenue raised by the government. The area C + E measures the size of the deadweight loss as the fall in total surplus.

FIGURE 7.3

How a Tax Affects Welfare

A tax on a good reduces consumer surplus (by the area B + C) and producer surplus (by the area D + E). Because the fall in producer and consumer surplus exceeds tax revenue (area B + D), the tax is said to impose a deadweight loss (area C + E).

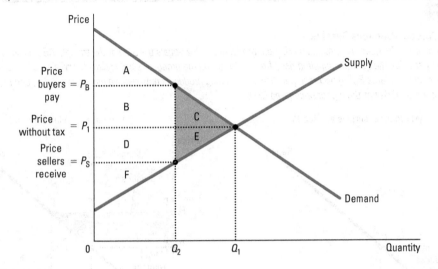

	Without tax	With tax	Change
Consumer surplus	A + B + C	A	− (B + C)
Producer surplus	D + E + F	F	− (D + E)
Tax revenue	None	B + D	+ (B + D)
Total surplus	A + B + C + D + E + F	A + B + D + F	− (C + E)

The area C + E shows the fall in total surplus and is the deadweight loss of the tax.

SELF TEST Draw a supply curve for streamed box sets. In your diagram show a price of streamed box sets and the producer surplus that results from that price. Explain in words what this producer surplus measures.

Market Inefficiencies

To make our analysis concrete, we will consider a specific market, the market for aluminium. Figure 7.4 shows the supply and demand curves in the market for aluminium.

Remember that supply and demand curves contain important information about costs and benefits. The demand curve for aluminium reflects the value of aluminium to consumers, as measured by the prices they are willing to pay. At any given quantity, the height of the demand curve shows the willingness to pay of the marginal buyer. In other words, it shows the value to the consumer of the last unit of aluminium bought. In this case, the consumer may be a business which uses aluminium in its production process. Similarly, the supply curve reflects the costs of producing aluminium. At any given quantity, the height of the supply curve shows the cost of the marginal seller. In other words, it shows the cost to the producer of aluminium of the last unit sold.

In the absence of government intervention, the price adjusts to balance the supply and demand for aluminium. The quantity produced and consumed in the market equilibrium, shown as Q_{MARKET} in Figure 7.4, is efficient in the sense that it maximizes the sum of producer and consumer surplus. That is, the market allocates resources in a way that maximizes the total value to the consumers who buy and use aluminium minus the total costs to the producers who make and sell aluminium.

FIGURE 7.4

The Market for Aluminium

The demand curve reflects the value to buyers, and the supply curve reflects the costs of sellers. The equilibrium quantity, Q$_{MARKET}$, maximizes the total value to buyers minus the total costs of sellers. In the absence of externalities, therefore, the market equilibrium is efficient.

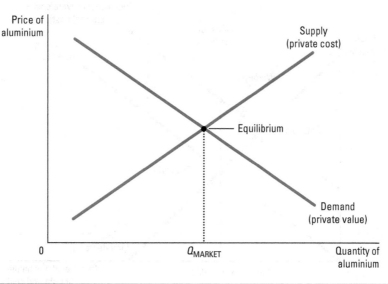

Negative Externalities

Now let us suppose that aluminium factories emit pollution: for each unit of aluminium produced, a certain amount of a pollutant enters the atmosphere. This pollutant may pose a health risk for those who breathe the air; it is a negative externality. There is a cost involved in dealing with the effects of the pollutant, which may be the health care that those affected must receive. This cost may not be taken into consideration by producers of aluminium, who may only consider the private costs of production. How does this externality affect the efficiency of the market outcome?

Because of the externality, the cost to *society* of producing aluminium is larger than the cost to the aluminium producers. For each unit of aluminium produced, the *social* (or *external*) *cost* includes the private costs of the aluminium producers plus the costs to those bystanders affected adversely by the pollution. Figure 7.5 shows the social cost of producing aluminium. The social cost curve is above the supply curve because it considers the external costs imposed on society by aluminium producers. At every price the social cost is higher than the private cost, and we can say that the social cost curve is the sum of the private costs and the social or external cost. The difference between these two curves reflects the social or external cost of the pollution emitted.

What quantity of aluminium should be produced? To answer this question, we can refer to our analysis of consumer and producer surplus. The ideal would be to maximize the total surplus derived from the market, the value to consumers of aluminium minus the cost of producing aluminium with the proviso that the cost of producing aluminium includes the external costs of the pollution.

This ideal would be the level of aluminium production at which the demand curve crosses the social cost curve. This intersection determines the optimal amount of aluminium from the standpoint of society as a whole. As a general principle, the socially efficient output occurs where the marginal social cost equals the marginal social benefit at a particular output. Below this level of production, the value of the aluminium to consumers (as measured by the height of the demand curve) exceeds the social cost of producing it (as measured by the height of the social cost curve). Producing any more than this level means the social cost of producing additional aluminium exceeds the value to consumers.

FIGURE 7.5

Pollution and the Social Optimum

In the presence of a negative externality, such as pollution, the social cost of the good exceeds the private cost. The optimal quantity, $Q_{OPTIMUM}$, is therefore lower than the equilibrium quantity, Q_{MARKET}.

Price of aluminium

Social cost (private cost + external cost)

Cost of pollution

Supply (private cost)

Welfare loss

Optimum

Equilibrium

Demand (private value)

$Q_{OPTIMUM}$ Q_{MARKET}

Quantity of aluminium bought and sold

Note that the equilibrium quantity of aluminium, Q_{MARKET}, is larger than the socially optimal quantity, $Q_{OPTIMUM}$. The reason for this inefficiency is that the market equilibrium reflects only the private costs of production. In the market equilibrium, the marginal consumer values aluminium at less than the social cost of producing it. That is, at Q_{MARKET} the demand curve lies below the social cost curve. Thus, reducing aluminium production and consumption below the market equilibrium level raises total economic well-being. We can measure changes in well-being by the welfare loss associated with different market outcomes. We measure the difference in the value placed on each marginal unit of production of aluminium between $Q_{OPTIMUM}$ and Q_{MARKET} by consumers as shown by the shaded triangle in Figure 7.5.

How can society hope to achieve the optimal outcome? The answer is to somehow force the decision maker to take into consideration some or all of the social costs of the decision. In our example, one way to do this would be to tax aluminium producers for each tonne of aluminium sold. The tax would shift the supply curve for aluminium upward by the size of the tax. If the tax accurately reflected the social cost of the pollution released into the atmosphere, the new supply curve would coincide with the social cost curve. In the new market equilibrium, aluminium producers would produce the socially optimal quantity of aluminium.

The use of such a tax is called **internalizing an externality** because it gives buyers and sellers in the market an incentive to take account of the external effects of their actions. Aluminium producers would take the costs of pollution into account when deciding how much aluminium to supply because the tax would make them pay for these external costs.

 internalizing an externality altering incentives so that people take account of the external effects of their actions

Positive Externalities

Although some activities impose costs on third parties, others yield benefits. Education, for example, yields positive externalities because a more educated population means firms can employ more flexible and productive employees, which helps improve productive and technical efficiency and increases the potential for economic growth, which benefits everyone. Notice that the productivity benefit of education is not necessarily an externality: the consumer of education (the student) reaps most of the benefit in the form of higher wages. If some of the productivity benefits of education spill over and benefit other people, as is the case if economic growth is stimulated, then this effect would count as a positive externality as well.

The analysis of positive externalities is similar to the analysis of negative externalities. As Figure 7.6 shows, the demand curve does not reflect the value to society of the good. The value placed on an activity such as education is valued less by consumers than the total value to society. Because the social value (or external benefit) is greater than the private value, the social value curve lies above the demand curve. The social value curve is the private value plus the external benefit to society at each price. At every price the benefit to society is greater than the private benefit, hence the social value curve (or social benefit curve) lies to the right of the private benefit curve. The optimal quantity is found where the social value curve and the supply curve (which represents costs) intersect. Hence, the socially optimal quantity is greater than the quantity determined by the private market.

Once again, the government can correct the market failure by inducing market participants to internalize the externality. The appropriate response in the case of positive externalities is exactly the opposite to the case of negative externalities. To move the market equilibrium closer to the social optimum, a positive externality requires a subsidy. In fact, that is exactly the policy many governments follow by heavily subsidizing education.

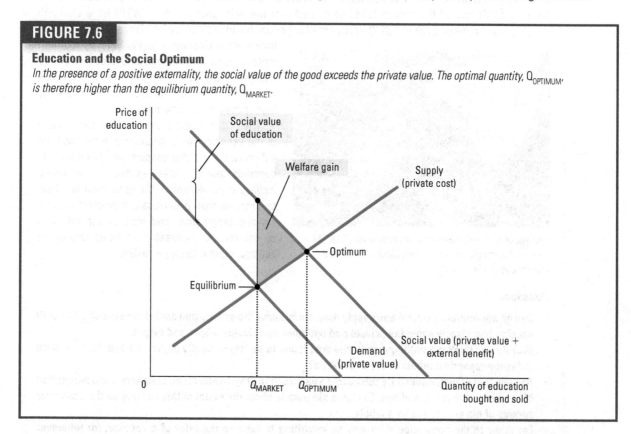

FIGURE 7.6

Education and the Social Optimum

In the presence of a positive externality, the social value of the good exceeds the private value. The optimal quantity, $Q_{OPTIMUM}$, is therefore higher than the equilibrium quantity, Q_{MARKET}.

To summarize: negative externalities lead markets to produce a larger quantity than is socially desirable. Positive externalities lead markets to produce a smaller quantity than is socially desirable. To remedy the problem, the government can internalize the externality by taxing goods that have negative externalities and subsidizing goods that have positive externalities.

JEOPARDY PROBLEM From a social efficiency perspective, consider the situation where an orbital motorway around a busy major city is highly congested during the day but is largely deserted between the hours of 11.00 pm and 5.30 am. What steps might be taken to improve the efficiency of such a road system?

CASE STUDY   Valuing the Benefits of Covid-19 Vaccines

One of the principal messages that was given at the start of the pandemic was the importance of developing effective and safe vaccines. This was completed in a relatively short space of time and the number of people who submitted themselves for vaccination in many countries when it became available was significant. Vaccines offering protection against Covid-19 provided benefits in two ways. First, the vaccine offered some increased protection against the risk of catching the virus, helping the body to cope with its effects and reducing the chances of serious complications from the virus. This represented an individual benefit to those who accepted the vaccine. Second, it increased the 'herd immunity' of the population at large and thus helped reduce not only transmission rates but also the worst effects of the virus and so reduced hospitalizations, absences from work and so on. Vaccinations, therefore, also conferred wider social benefits.

Take up of the Covid-19 vaccine was an important factor in the extent to which both these benefits played out. The willingness to take up the offer of a vaccine did, however, depend on individual circumstances. Some people argued that the vaccine was a device for some sinister government purpose, others questioned its safety, but the vast majority of the population of most countries were seemingly supportive of its development and implementation. Research led by Joan Costa-Font at the London School of Economics (LSE) estimated that the willingness to pay (WTP) for a Covid-19 vaccine was between $100 and $200 across the four countries in their study (the United States, Spain,

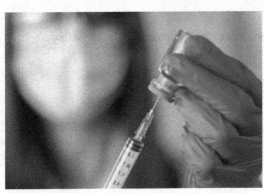

The successful development of a vaccine for Covid-19 helped shorten the disruption providing widespread private and social benefits.

Italy and the UK) with a higher WTP by younger, more affluent individuals, and those who had children. They also found that the WTP in those who had contracted the virus was significantly higher than those who had not.

Their findings suggested that the social value of the vaccine was considerably larger than the individual price of the vaccine, which led them to conclude that vaccines resulted in 'significant' welfare improvements. This conclusion led them to propose that government subsidization of a vaccine programme, and possibly the provision of incentives to increase the take-up rate of the vaccine, were entirely justifiable.

Questions

1 Use an appropriate demand and supply diagram to show the private and social benefits of a Covid-19 vaccine and clearly show the private and optimum equilibrium prices and output.

2 Why do you think the willingness to pay was found to be 'significantly higher' among younger more affluent people than others in the population?

3 Assume that a government fully subsidizes a vaccination programme for all members of the population of a country over the age of five. Sketch a diagram to show the effect of this subsidy on the consumer surplus of the population as a whole.

4 For those in the population who may be unwilling to take up the offer of a vaccine, for whatever reason, what sort of incentives might the government introduce to encourage take-up of the vaccine for this group?

Reference: Costa-Font, J., Rudisill, C., Harrison, S. and Salmasi, L. (2021) Social vs market value: How much is a COVID-19 vaccine worth? London School of Economics, London. Available from https://blogs.lse.ac.uk/businessreview/2021/06/28/social-vs-market-value-how-much-is-a-covid-19-vaccine-worth/ (accessed 7 June 2023).

GOVERNMENT, BUSINESS AND EXTERNALITIES

It is widely acknowledged by firms that their activities result in both positive and negative externalities, and that market failure means that resources are not allocated as efficiently as they might be. In virtually every country, governments step in to try to influence business behaviour to counter market failure, and provide incentives to change behaviour to generate an outcome which is seen as benefiting society as a whole.

There are two main ways in which governments intervene in business: *command-and-control policies* regulate behaviour directly. *Market-based policies* provide incentives for private decision makers to behave differently and resolve the perceived problem.

Regulation

The government can remedy an externality by making certain behaviours either required or forbidden. For example, it is a crime in any European country for firms to dump poisonous chemicals into the water supply. In this case, the external costs to society far exceed the benefits to the polluter. The government therefore institutes a command-and-control policy that prohibits this act altogether.

In most cases of pollution, however, the situation is not this simple. Despite the stated goals of some environmentalists, it would be impossible to prohibit all polluting activity. For example, virtually all forms of transport, even the horse, produce some undesirable polluting by-products. It would not be sensible for the government to ban all transport. Instead of trying to eradicate pollution altogether, society must weigh the costs and benefits to decide the kinds and quantities of pollution it will allow.

Environmental regulations can take many forms. Sometimes the government may dictate a maximum level of pollution that a factory may emit, or set permitted noise levels for an airline. At other times the government requires that firms adopt a particular technology to reduce emissions, or will only grant a licence to operate if certain criteria are met. In all cases, to design good rules, government regulators need to know the details about specific industries and about the alternative technologies that could be adopted. This information is often difficult for government regulators to obtain.

Market-Based Policies: Pigouvian Taxes and Subsidies

Instead of regulating behaviour in response to an externality, the government can use market-based policies to align private incentives with social efficiency. For instance, as we saw earlier, the government can internalize the externality by taxing activities that have negative externalities, and subsidizing activities that have positive externalities. Taxes enacted to correct the effects of negative externalities are called **Pigouvian taxes**, after the English economist Arthur Pigou (1877–1959), an early advocate of their use.

 Pigouvian tax a tax enacted to correct the effects of a negative externality

Pigouvian taxes to deal with pollution can have benefits over regulations, because such taxes can reduce pollution at a lower cost to society. To see why, let us consider an example.

Suppose that two factories, a paper mill and a steel mill, are each dumping 500 tonnes of effluent into a river each year. The government decides that it wants to reduce the amount of pollution. It considers two solutions:

- Regulation. The government could tell each factory to reduce its pollution to 300 tonnes of effluent per year.
- Pigouvian tax. The government could levy a tax on each factory of €50,000 for each tonne of effluent it emits.

The regulation would dictate a level of pollution, whereas the tax would give factory owners an economic incentive to reduce pollution.

Proponents of a tax would first point out that a tax is just as effective as regulation in reducing the overall level of pollution. The government can achieve whatever level of pollution it wants by setting the tax at the appropriate level. The higher the tax, the larger the reduction in pollution. Indeed, if the tax is high enough, the factories will close down altogether, reducing pollution to zero.

Regulation, on the other hand, requires each factory to reduce pollution by the same amount, but an equal reduction is not necessarily the least expensive way to clean up the water. It is possible that the paper mill can reduce pollution at lower cost than the steel mill. If so, the paper mill would respond to the tax by reducing pollution substantially to avoid the tax, whereas the steel mill would respond by reducing pollution less and paying the tax.

The Pigouvian tax places a price on the right to pollute. Just as markets allocate goods to those buyers who value them most highly, a Pigouvian tax allocates pollution to those factories that face the highest cost of reducing it. Whatever the level of pollution the government chooses, it can achieve this goal at the lowest total cost using a tax.

Pigouvian taxes can also be better for the environment. Under the command-and-control policy of regulation, the factories have no reason to reduce emissions further once they have reached the target of 300 tonnes of effluent. By contrast, the tax gives the factories an incentive to develop cleaner technologies, because a cleaner technology would reduce the amount of tax the factory must pay.

Pigouvian taxes are unlike most other taxes. Many taxes distort incentives and move the allocation of resources away from the social optimum. The reduction in economic well-being, that is, in consumer and producer surplus, exceeds the amount of revenue the government raises, resulting in a deadweight loss. By contrast, when externalities are present, society also cares about the well-being of the bystanders who are affected. Pigouvian taxes correct incentives for the presence of externalities and thereby move the allocation of resources closer to the social optimum. Thus, while Pigouvian taxes raise revenue for the government, they can also enhance economic efficiency.

Tradable Pollution Permits

Returning to our example of the paper mill and the steel mill, let us suppose that the government adopts regulation and requires each factory to reduce its pollution to 300 tonnes of effluent per year. Then one day, after the regulation is in place and both mills have complied, the two firms go to the government with a proposal. The steel mill wants to increase its emission of effluent by 100 tonnes. The paper mill has agreed to reduce its emission by the same amount if the steel mill pays it €5 million. Should the government allow the two factories to make this deal?

From the standpoint of economic efficiency, allowing the deal is good policy. The deal must make the owners of the two factories better off, because they are voluntarily agreeing to it. Moreover, the deal does not have any external effects because the total amount of pollution remains the same. Thus, social welfare is enhanced by allowing the paper mill to sell its right to pollute to the steel mill.

The same logic applies to any voluntary transfer of the right to pollute from one firm to another. If the government allows firms to make these deals, it will have created a new scarce resource: pollution permits. A market to trade these permits governed by the forces of supply and demand will help allocate the right to pollute. The firms that can reduce pollution only at high cost will be willing to pay the most for the pollution permits. The firms that can reduce pollution at low cost will prefer to sell whatever permits they have.

One advantage of allowing a market for pollution permits, sometimes referred to as a 'cap and trade' system, is that the initial allocation of pollution permits among firms does not matter from the standpoint of economic efficiency. Those firms that can reduce pollution most easily would be willing to sell whatever permits they get, and those firms that can reduce pollution only at high cost would be willing to buy whatever permits they need. If there is a free market for the pollution rights (an important assumption), the final allocation will be efficient whatever the initial allocation.

Although reducing pollution using permits may seem quite different from using Pigouvian taxes, in fact the two policies have much in common. In both cases, firms pay for their pollution. With Pigouvian taxes, polluting firms must pay a tax to the government. With pollution permits, polluting firms must pay to buy the permit. Even firms that already own permits must pay to pollute: the opportunity cost of polluting is what they could have received by selling their permits on the open market. Both Pigouvian taxes and pollution permits internalize the externality of pollution by making it costly for firms to pollute.

The similarity of the two policies can be seen by considering the market for pollution. Both panels in Figure 7.7 show the demand curve for the right to pollute. This curve shows that the lower the price of polluting, the more firms will choose to pollute. In panel (a) the government uses a Pigouvian tax to set a price for pollution. In this case, the supply curve for pollution rights is perfectly elastic (because firms can pollute as much as they want by paying the tax), and the position of the demand curve determines the quantity of pollution. In panel (b) the government sets a quantity of pollution by issuing pollution permits. In this case, the supply curve for pollution rights is perfectly inelastic (because the quantity of pollution is fixed by the number of permits), and the position of the demand curve determines the price of pollution. Hence, for any given demand curve for pollution, the government can achieve any point on the demand curve either by setting a price with a Pigouvian tax or by setting a quantity with pollution permits.

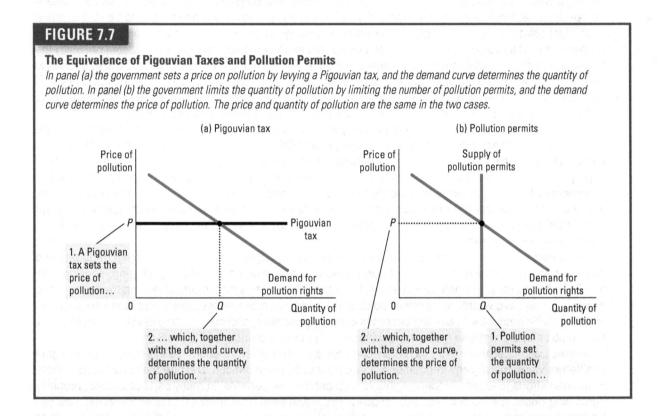

FIGURE 7.7

The Equivalence of Pigouvian Taxes and Pollution Permits
In panel (a) the government sets a price on pollution by levying a Pigouvian tax, and the demand curve determines the quantity of pollution. In panel (b) the government limits the quantity of pollution by limiting the number of pollution permits, and the demand curve determines the price of pollution. The price and quantity of pollution are the same in the two cases.

In some circumstances, however, selling pollution permits may be better than levying a Pigouvian tax. Suppose the government wants no more than 700 tonnes of effluent to be dumped into the river. The government may not know the demand curve for pollution, and so is not sure what size tax would achieve its goal. In this case, it can auction off 700 one tonne pollution permits. The auction price would yield the appropriate size of the Pigouvian tax.

A number of governments around the world have used such a system as a way to control pollution. In 2002, EU environment ministers unanimously agreed to set up a market to trade pollution permits for carbon dioxide (CO_2), the main greenhouse gas of concern. Pollution permits, like Pigouvian taxes, are increasingly being viewed as a cost-effective way to keep the environment clean.

Property Rights

In some cases, private solutions to externalities can occur, but need some form of legal back-up to be able to work. One such example is the establishment of property rights. For any economy to work efficiently, a system of property rights has to be established and understood. The principle behind property rights is this: if an individual decided to throw a brick through the window of someone else's house, the house owner would have the right to expect legal redress. Assuming the individual who caused the damage can be identified and there was proof that it was they who caused the damage, the property owner can expect compensation, under the law, to put right the damage. This may include replacing the window pane and for any emotional trauma experienced by the house owner.

With rivers, streams, land and air, it is less easy to establish who the legal owners are. If some system could be devised whereby the ownership of property could be established, then those who cause damage to that property can be brought to book. Extending property rights, therefore, might be one area where externalities can be internalized. For example, if property rights over the air that we breathe can be extended, then any firm polluting that air (in whatever way, noise, smell, smoke, etc.) could face prosecution for doing so. The threat of prosecution is sufficient to act as an incentive to change behaviour.

Extension of property rights also means that the owner of the property (which can be intellectual as well as physical) can also exercise the right to sell or share that property if they so wish at some mutually agreeable price. Extending property rights allows individuals, groups and organizations to be able to arrive at efficient solutions. If, for example, an individual was assigned property rights for the air 1 km above their property, then if a nearby factory wanted to pollute that air they would have to enter negotiations with the house owner to do so at some mutually agreeable price. The resulting right to pollute could also be sold to another party. A more developed system of property rights can, therefore, improve well-being. It has also been identified as playing a crucial role in good governance, particularly relevant for developing countries to be able to attract the sort of inward investment that will help their economies to grow.

There are problems with extending property rights, however. How do we apportion rights to such things as air, the seas, rivers and land? The cost of establishing property rights and getting international agreement on what they entail is considerable, and may counteract the social benefits provided. If property rights were extended to the volume of air 1 km above a person's property, imagine the complexity of the negotiations that would have to be carried out with any business nearby, or airlines and the military for the right to share that air. Property owners may also have insufficient knowledge about their rights and exactly what they mean; it is also not a costless exercise to prove that property rights have been violated.

In the music and film industry the complexities of property rights have been the subject of debate and countless lawsuits in recent years. It not only relates to the issues of file sharing, pirating, copying CDs and DVDs for personal use and downloading, but also to the artists/actors themselves and the rights to the music that they have written and performed on stage and screen. Similar issues are also being experienced in the publishing industry as pirating becomes a growing problem, and the resulting development of digital technologies as a substitute mean the traditional printed book is under some pressure.

Intellectual property law is an incredibly complex area, and different countries interpret property rights in different ways, making any international agreement even more difficult. Despite the complexities, there have been efforts to extend property rights to help bring social benefits. In many parts of Europe, property rights over public spaces such as national parks, rivers and seas have meant that environmental laws can be established and enforced, and this has led to an improvement in well-being for millions who are able to use these spaces, enjoy cleaner rivers and exploit the resources of the sea.

Objections to the Economic Analysis of Pollution

Some environmentalists argue that it is in some sense morally wrong to allow anyone to pollute the environment in return for paying a fee. Clean air and clean water, they argue, are fundamental human rights that should not be debased by considering them in economic terms. How can you put a price on clean air and clean water? The environment is so important, they claim, that we should protect it as much as possible, regardless of the cost.

Critics of this view note that people face trade-offs. Certainly, clean air and clean water have value. But their value must be compared to their opportunity cost, that is, to what one must give up to obtain them. Eliminating all pollution is impossible. Trying to eliminate all pollution would reverse many of the technological advances that allow us to enjoy a high standard of living. Few people would be willing to accept poor nutrition, inadequate medical care or shoddy housing to make the environment as clean as possible.

A clean environment is a normal good. It has a positive income elasticity: higher income countries can afford a cleaner environment than lower income ones and, therefore, usually have more rigorous environmental protection. In addition, like most other goods, clean air and water obey the law of demand: the lower the price of environmental protection, the more the public will want. The economic approach of using pollution permits and Pigouvian taxes reduces the cost of environmental protection and should, therefore, increase the public's demand for a clean environment.

> **SELF TEST** A glue factory and a steel mill emit smoke containing a chemical that is harmful if inhaled in large amounts. Describe three ways the local authority might respond to this externality. What are the pros and cons of each solution?

Social and Ethical Responsibility

Many firms complain about government interference in business and about the taxes they have to pay. Some will also argue that the subsidy system is fundamentally flawed because it is unfair (not unsurprisingly, the ones who are most vociferous in this condemnation of subsidies are the ones who do not receive any). There is an argument that government could reduce its involvement in markets if firms behaved more responsibly. Unfortunately, firms do not always behave responsibly (even if we could accurately define what the term 'responsible' meant in this context).

Social responsibility refers to the responsibility a firm has for the impact of their product and activities on society. **Ethical responsibility** refers to the moral basis for business activity and whether what the business does is 'right' and is underpinned by some moral purpose, doing what is 'right'.

> **social responsibility** the responsibility a firm has for the impact of their product and activities on society
> **ethical responsibility** the moral basis for business activity and whether what the business does 'is right' and is underpinned by some moral purpose, doing what is 'right'

The problem arises when asking 'Doing what is right for whom?' A private sector firm is primarily responsible to its shareholders, the owners of the business, who in turn will wish to see the firm grow, expanding sales and profits. In so doing there may be a conflict with the responsibility a firm has for the health and welfare of its customers. Drug companies have a responsibility to develop new products, market them and generate profits for their shareholders. In so doing, to what extent should they compromise the health and safety of those who consume their products?

Many businesses will claim to have a socially responsible code of practice that they adhere to, as well as an ethical stance to their activities, but such claims are sometimes refuted and criticized by opponents. It is all very well claiming to have no artificial colouring and preservative in food products, for example, but this might be disingenuous at the very least if the product is high in salt and sugars which can contribute to obesity, heart disease and high blood pressure if consumed in too high a quantity.

Part of the policy response by governments could be passing legislation that forces businesses to give clearer information on packaging to help consumers make more informed choices about what they buy. Such legislation would impose additional costs on businesses, and ultimately would put up the price of the product to the consumer, reducing consumer surplus. Are consumers willing to pay such a price for the extra information? If firms do engage in activities that increase levels of responsibility and ethical standards, this comes at a cost. Many European consumers enjoy low prices for clothing while some firms in the Far East who manufacture these products receive very low prices for their efforts. Would consumers in Europe be willing to pay higher prices for their clothes in order that Far East manufacturers get higher prices and so can improve wages and conditions for employees? It is not at all clear that such a philanthropic approach would be embraced by consumers.

The issues therefore are complex and open to subjective interpretation. The solution may be to try to arrive at some form of balance between the rights of people to choose their own lifestyle, be informed about the consequences of that lifestyle and to be protected from the unknown by the government. Where that balance lies though is not at all clear.

CONCLUSION

The invisible hand is powerful but not omnipotent. In theory, a market's equilibrium maximizes the sum of producer and consumer surplus. When buyers and sellers in the market are the only interested parties, this outcome is efficient from the standpoint of society. But when there are external effects, such as pollution, evaluating a market outcome requires considering the well-being of third parties as well. In this case, the invisible hand of the marketplace may fail to allocate resources efficiently.

Because of the problem of externalities, the government often steps in to try to rectify market failure. When government does intervene in the market, firms are affected either because they must pay taxes, or receive subsidies or through the regulations that are imposed. These interventions invariably impose costs on businesses and in many countries, there are complaints from business representatives of the burden of taxes and regulation.

Society must make a judgement about the extent to which such government interference confers benefits on society as a whole which are greater than the costs of that intervention. It can be argued that firms should take more responsibility for their actions, but getting agreement on what that responsibility should be and whether consumers are prepared to pay for increased social and ethical responsibility in the form of higher prices will always be difficult.

Yet, even now, it can be argued that society should not abandon market forces entirely. Rather, the government could address the problem by requiring decision makers to bear the full costs of their actions. Pigouvian taxes on emissions and pollution permits, for instance, are designed to internalize the externality of pollution. Increasingly, they are perceived as effective policies for those interested in protecting the environment. Market forces, properly redirected, can be an effective remedy for market failure.

SUMMARY

- Market failure occurs when resources are not allocated efficiently.

- Typically, market failure occurs because of a lack of perfect information between firms and buyers, or because firms have some element of market power.

- When a transaction between a buyer and seller directly affects a third party, the effect is called an externality. Negative externalities, such as pollution, cause the socially optimal quantity in a market to be less than the equilibrium quantity. Positive externalities, such as the broad benefits that arise from developments in technology, cause the socially optimal quantity to be greater than the equilibrium quantity.

- Those affected by externalities can sometimes solve the problem privately. For instance, when one business confers an externality on another business, the two businesses can internalize the externality by merging.

- When private parties cannot adequately deal with external effects, such as pollution, the government often steps in. Sometimes the government prevents socially inefficient activity by regulating behaviour. At other times, it internalizes an externality using Pigouvian taxes. Another public policy is to issue permits. For instance, the government could protect the environment by issuing a limited number of pollution permits. The result of this policy is largely the same as imposing Pigouvian taxes on polluters.

IN THE NEWS

Tradable Pollution Permits

Tradable pollution permits have been touted as one of the most effective ways of controlling carbon emissions and a number of countries have set up these schemes or are considering doing so. However, one of the issues that have been noted in relation to these schemes is how they are designed and operated. It could be argued that as these schemes are relatively new, they are going to be subject to continued refinement and redesign as new learning comes to light. In the UK a cap-and-trade scheme operates with the intention of reducing carbon emissions through the 'polluter pays' principle. One industry that is subject to this scheme is the airline industry. Airlines are cited as being a key contributor to carbon emissions. According to the Air Transport Action Group (ATAG), the global airline industry is responsible for around 914 million tonnes of CO_2, or around 2.1 per cent of human induced CO_2 emissions each year.

(*Continued*)

The UK Emissions Trading Scheme (UK ETS) includes an aim to reduce carbon emissions by the aviation industry. The idea behind the scheme is to issue permits for carbon emissions which set a cap on the total amount of emissions but which also provides airlines with the option of trading any excess permits they have with others who may not be able to meet their targets. However, one concern with the scheme is that airlines might find a way around the cap. The scheme covers routes within the UK, between the UK and Gibraltar, and flights from the UK to the European Economic Area. Airlines based in the UK, for example, can find themselves at a competitive disadvantage compared to airlines based outside the scope of the UK ETS, and some non-UK airlines that operate outside the UK but on routes covered by the scheme might decide to move their operations to areas not covered by the scheme. The effect of this is called carbon leakage. To help reduce the risk of carbon leakage, the UK government provides allowances which are effectively permits given to the airlines without

Air travel contributes to the emission of carbon. Could tradeable permits improve the social efficiency?

charge so they do not have to pay for the carbon emissions they produce. One criticism of this policy is that the government is giving out too many of these 'free' permits, around 4.4 million of them with an estimated value of £242 million in 2021, compared to an estimated 3.4 million permits that the airlines had to buy to allow them to emit carbon. The surplus permits can be sold back to the ETS market or retained for future years. Critics argue that this policy dilutes the effect of the scheme and point to research evidence that suggests the size of carbon leakage is relatively small and does not warrant the number of permit allowances issued.

Questions

1 Draw a supply and demand diagram to show the aviation market in the UK, the price of flights, and number of flights bought and sold in a time period. Use the diagram to show the market outcome. Now add in the social cost and show the socially optimal outcome. Explain why the two outcomes are different.
2 Show how the setting of a pollution cap on carbon emissions by airlines could result in a reduction in the amount of carbon emissions from the market outcome to the socially optimal outcome you identified in question 1.
3 If the government issues more 'free' carbon permit allowances than airlines actually need, what effect does this have on the policy to reduce carbon emissions by airlines?
4 Critics of the allowances scheme argue that the size of the carbon leakage problem in the aviation industry is relatively small. What factors do you think might influence the size of this leakage?
5 How does the article illustrate the complexities of introducing a cap-and-trade system such as the UK ETS? How might policymakers seek to avoid some of the challenges involved to create a more efficient and effective market?

References: www.transportenvironment.org/discover/secret-subsidies-how-the-gov-is-gifting-free-money-to-airlines/ (accessed 7 June 2023).
www.atag.org/facts-figures/ (accessed 7 June 2023).
www.gov.uk/government/publications/participating-in-the-uk-ets/participating-in-the-uk-ets#free-allocation-for-aircraft-operators (accessed 7 June 2023).
https://assets.publishing.service.gov.uk/government/uploads/system/uploads/attachment_data/file/763260/carbon-leakage-report.pdf (accessed 7 June 2023).

QUESTIONS FOR REVIEW

1 Identify, using examples, three sources of market failure.
2 Using an appropriate example, explain the difference between a private cost and a social cost and a private benefit and a social benefit.
3 Give an example of a negative externality and an example of a positive externality.
4 Use a supply and demand diagram to explain the effect of a negative externality in production.

5 In a supply and demand diagram, show producer and consumer surplus in the market equilibrium.

6 A government imposes a specific tax on energy companies which use fossil fuels to generate energy. Use a supply and demand diagram and show the effect of the tax on consumer and producer surplus and comment on the incidence of the tax on consumers of energy and producers of energy.

7 What is meant by the term 'deadweight loss'?

8 In what way does the patent system help society solve an externality problem?

9 List some of the ways that the problems caused by externalities can be solved without government intervention.

10 What are Pigouvian taxes? Why do some economists prefer them over regulations as a way to protect the environment from pollution?

PROBLEMS AND APPLICATIONS

1 Do you agree with the following statements? Why or why not?

a. 'The benefits of Pigouvian taxes to reduce pollution have to be weighed against the deadweight losses that these taxes cause.'

b. 'When deciding whether to levy a Pigouvian tax on consumers or producers, the government should be careful to levy the tax on the side of the market generating the externality.'

2 Consider the market for fire extinguishers.

a. Why might fire extinguishers exhibit positive externalities?

b. Draw a graph of the market for fire extinguishers, labelling the demand curve, the social value curve, the supply curve and the social cost curve.

c. Indicate the market equilibrium level of output and the efficient level of output. Give an intuitive explanation for why these quantities differ.

d. If the external benefit is €10 per extinguisher, describe a government policy that would result in the efficient outcome.

3 The cost of producing Blu-ray DVD players has fallen over the past few years. Let us consider some implications of this fact.

a. Use a supply and demand diagram to show the effect of falling production costs on the price and quantity of Blu-ray DVD players sold.

b. In your diagram, show what happens to consumer surplus and producer surplus.

c. Suppose the supply of Blu-ray DVD players is very price elastic. Who benefits most from falling production costs? Consumers or producers of Blu-ray DVD players?

4 The government decides to reduce air pollution by reducing the use of petrol. It imposes €0.50 tax for each litre of petrol sold.

a. Should it impose this tax on petrol companies or motorists? Explain, using a supply and demand diagram.

b. If the demand for petrol were more price elastic, would this tax be more effective or less effective in reducing the quantity of petrol consumed? Explain with both words and a diagram.

c. Are consumers of petrol helped or hurt by this tax? Why?

d. Are workers in the oil industry helped or hurt by this tax? Why?

5 Many observers believe that the levels of pollution in our economy are too high.

a. If society wishes to reduce overall pollution by a certain amount, why is it efficient to have different amounts of reduction at different firms?

b. Command-and-control approaches often rely on uniform reductions among firms. Why are these approaches generally unable to target the firms that should undertake bigger reductions?

c. Economists argue that appropriate Pigouvian taxes or tradable pollution rights will result in efficient pollution reduction. How do these approaches target the firms that should undertake bigger reductions?

6 The Pristine River has two polluting firms on its banks. European Industrial and Creative Chemicals each dump 100 tonnes of effluent into the river each year. The cost of reducing effluent emissions per tonne equals €10 for European Industrial and €100 for Creative. The government wants to reduce overall pollution from 200 tonnes to 50 tonnes per year.

   a. If the government knew the cost of reduction for each firm, what reductions would it impose to reach its overall goal? What would be the cost to each firm and the total cost to the firms together?
   b. In a more typical situation, the government would not know the cost of pollution reduction at each firm. If the government decided to reach its overall goal by imposing uniform reductions on the firms, calculate the reduction made by each firm, the cost to each firm and the total cost to the firms together.
   c. Compare the total cost of pollution reduction in parts a and b. If the government does not know the cost of reduction for each firm, is there still some way for it to reduce pollution to 50 tonnes at the total cost you calculated in part a? Explain.

7 Some people object to market-based policies to reduce pollution, claiming that they place a monetary value on cleaning our air and water. Critics reply that society implicitly places a monetary value on environmental clean-up even under command-and-control policies. Discuss why this is true.

8 There are three industrial firms in Eurovia.

Firm	Initial pollution level (units)	Cost of reducing pollution by 1 unit (€)
A	70	20
B	80	25
C	50	10

The government wants to reduce total pollution to 120 units. It gives each firm 40 tradable pollution permits.

   a. Who sells permits and how many do they sell? Who buys permits and how many do they buy? Briefly explain why the sellers and buyers are each willing to do so. What is the total cost of pollution reduction in this situation?
   b. How much higher would the costs of pollution reduction be if the permits could not be traded?

9 Use a supply and demand diagram to show the welfare effects of a decision by the government to fund universal inoculation for a strain of meningitis for all teenagers aged 18, who leave school to either go into the workplace or into further or higher education. Why might the government have taken such a decision? (Hint: think about the socially efficient optimum and positive externalities.)

10 In the UK, some political parties and pressure groups have argued for the legalization of cannabis. Part of the argument is based around the idea of internalizing externalities, and part is based around using a regulated market to achieve a more efficient outcome. Use your knowledge of welfare economics, property rights and externalities to consider the economic argument for such a policy. What arguments might opponents of any legalization put forward to such a policy?

8 THE CONSUMER AND CONSUMER BEHAVIOUR

INTRODUCTION

Business activity requires a producer and a consumer or businesses cannot survive without some individual, group or other business buying their output. It makes sense, therefore, for businesses to understand how consumers think and behave. How do consumers make decisions about purchases? What makes a consumer choose one product repeatedly over the many others that are available? How are they influenced by advertising (if at all) and how important are brands in influencing consumer behaviour? We are going to look at these issues in this chapter.

First we present a classical theory of consumer behaviour based on an assumption of rational behaviour which is referred to as the *standard economic model*. The model presented can explain some consumer behaviour in some situations, but as with all models it has its limitations. Since the early 1990s more research has been done into how consumers make purchasing decisions. Technology such as functional magnetic resonance imaging (fMRI) and positive emission tomography (PET) has allowed researchers to analyze how the brain responds to different stimuli, and what parts of the brain become active when purchasing decisions are made or when individuals are exposed to stimuli such as advertising.

This research, along with that of psychologists and anthropologists among other disciplines, has led to the development of different, sometimes competing, sometimes complementary, theories of consumer behaviour. We look at some of these theories.

Consumers come in many forms. Some are individuals, some are large organizations such as other businesses, government or its agents and some are small businesses. These are not all going to behave the same and so an understanding of those upon whom you rely is going to be of some importance in a successful business.

The Standard Economic Model

When you walk into a shop, you are invariably confronted by a wide range of goods. Most people have limited financial resources and cannot buy everything they want. How are purchasing choices made?

One assumption might be that you consider the constraint that is your income, the prices of the various goods being offered for sale and the value they represent (more of this shortly) and choose to buy a bundle of goods that, given your resources, best suits your needs and desires and maximizes value. This is a constrained optimization problem that forms the basis of many classical economic theories.

We can summarize some key assumptions of the standard economic model as:

- Buyers (or economic agents as they are sometimes referred to) are rational meaning they do the best they can, given their circumstances.
- More is preferred to less.
- Buyers seek to maximize their utility.
- Consumers act in self-interest and do not consider the utility of others.

Value

A key concept in consumer behaviour is value. Value is a subjective term. What one person or business thinks represents value is often different from the view of some other individual or business. **Value** is the worth to an individual of owning an item represented by the satisfaction derived from its consumption. Classical economists used the term **utility** to refer to the satisfaction derived from consumption. Utility is an ordinal concept; we can use some measure of utility to represent consumer choices in some order, but that order tells us nothing about the differences in the values we use. For example, if a group of five people were asked to rank different brands of cola in order of preference using a 10-point scale (with each point referred to as a *util*) we might be able to conclude that brand X was the most popular, followed by brand Y and brand Z. If person 1 ranked brand X at 10 utils while person 2 ranked the same brand as 5 utils we cannot say that person 1 values brand X twice as much as person 2, only that they place it higher in their preferences.

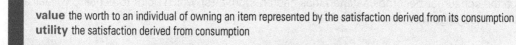

value the worth to an individual of owning an item represented by the satisfaction derived from its consumption
utility the satisfaction derived from consumption

One way in which we can measure value is the amount consumers are prepared to pay. It is highly likely that at some point in your life you will have said something like, 'I wouldn't have that if you paid me'. How much of our limited income we are prepared to pay reflects the value we put on acquiring a good. It might not tell us much about the satisfaction from consuming the good (the buyer might not be the final consumer) but it does give some idea of value. For example, two friends, Alexa and Monique, are in a store looking at shoes. Alexa picks up a pair priced at €100. Monique looks at Alexa and asks why on earth she is thinking of buying them? No way would Monique pay that sort of money for those shoes. A discussion ensues about the shoes; clearly there is a difference of opinion on them and thus how much they are 'worth'. If Alexa buys the shoes, then the value to her must be at least €100 because that is what she must give up in money terms to acquire it. It may be that Alexa would have been prepared to pay much more than €100 for the shoes, in which case she is getting consumer surplus. Monique leaves the store baffled at Alexa's purchasing decision. Monique clearly feels that giving up €100 to buy those shoes was a 'waste of money'.

The amount buyers are prepared to pay for a good, therefore, tells us something about the value they place on it. It is not just the amount of money we hand over that reflects value but what that amount of money could have bought, that is, the opportunity cost. We could make a reasonable assumption that Monique believed there was a way in which she could allocate €100 to get more value. In other words, the alternative that €100 could buy (whatever that might be) represented greater value than acquiring the particular pair of shoes Alexa chose.

Total and Marginal Utility

Given that utility can be used as a word to represent satisfaction derived from consumption, we can look at what happens to utility as consumption increases. Given our assumption that consumers prefer more to less, intuition might tell us that total utility increases as consumption increases. This may be true up to a point. To understand this let us use an example.

You have spent two hours in the gym working very hard. You are hot, sweaty and very thirsty. After your shower, you go to the nearest café and order a glass of orange juice. If you were asked to rate the satisfaction derived from consuming the orange juice out of 10 (utils) at that time, you might rate it at 10. You order a second glass as you are still thirsty; the second glass still brings some satisfaction, but if asked to rate it you might give it 8. Total utility is now 18 utils, and the second glass has increased total utility. However, you did not rate the second glass quite as high as the first because some of your thirst has been quenched. **Marginal utility** measures the addition to total utility because of the consumption of an extra unit. The marginal utility of the first glass was 10 but for the second glass the marginal utility was 8.

> **marginal utility** the addition to total utility because of one extra unit of consumption

If you now ordered a third glass you might rate this at 5. Total utility is now 23 but the marginal utility of the third glass is 5. By the time you get to the fifth or sixth glass the marginal utility is likely to be very low and at some point could even be negative. For example, if you have already had 8 glasses of orange juice your stomach might be telling you that it really does not need another one. Having the ninth glass might make you physically sick, and so the marginal utility of the ninth glass would be negative. It follows that total utility will start to decline at this point.

This example illustrates a general principle called the law of **diminishing marginal utility**. This states that the more a consumer has of a given commodity the smaller the satisfaction gained from consuming each extra unit. As consumption of a good rises, total utility will rise at first, but at a slower rate until some point at which the consumer becomes satiated (has had enough) after which point total utility will fall and marginal utility will be negative.

> **diminishing marginal utility** a 'law' that states that marginal utility will fall as consumption increases

This principle is important in considering the relationship between price and the demand curve. Diminishing marginal utility implies that we value successive units of consumption less than the previous and so it makes sense that consumers are not prepared to pay as much for successive units of consumption. To encourage consumers to buy more, sellers must reduce prices, which partly explains why the demand curve slopes downwards from left to right.

Many firms will be acutely aware that they have rivals competing for consumers, and that consumers have a choice. Switching between one good and another is a feature of business. The marginal rate of substitution (MRS) measures how much of one good a consumer requires to be compensated for a one unit reduction in consumption of another good. The MRS between two goods depends on their marginal utilities. For example, if the marginal utility of good X is twice the marginal utility of good Y, then a person would need 2 units of good Y to compensate for losing 1 unit of good X, and the MRS equals 2. More generally, the MRS of substitution equals the marginal utility of one good divided by the marginal utility of the other good.

What Consumers Can Afford

Most people would like to increase the quantity or quality of the goods they consume, to take longer holidays, drive fancier cars or eat at better restaurants. People consume less than they desire because their spending is *constrained*, or limited, by their income. To keep things simple, we use a model which examines the decisions facing a consumer who buys only two goods: cola and pizza. Of course, real people buy thousands of different kinds of goods. Yet using this model greatly simplifies the problem without altering the basic insights about consumer choice.

Suppose that the consumer has an income of €1,000 per month and that they spend their entire income each month on cola and pizza. The price of a litre of cola is €2 and the price of a pizza is €10. The table in Figure 8.1 shows some of the many combinations of cola and pizza that the consumer can buy. The first line in the table shows that if the consumer spends all their income on pizza, they can eat 100 pizzas during the month, but they would not be able to buy any cola at all. The second line shows another possible consumption bundle: 90 pizzas and 50 litres of cola. And so on. Each consumption bundle in the table costs exactly €1,000.

The graph in Figure 8.1 illustrates these consumption bundles that the consumer can choose. The vertical axis measures the number of litres of cola, and the horizontal axis measures the number of pizzas. Three points are marked on this Figure. At point A, the consumer buys no cola and consumes 100 pizzas. At point B, the consumer buys no pizza and consumes 500 litres of cola. At point C, the consumer buys 50 pizzas and 250 litres of cola. Point C, which is exactly at the middle of the line from A to B, is the point at which the consumer spends an equal amount (€500) on cola and pizza. Of course, these are only three of the different combinations of cola and pizza that the consumer can choose shown by the line from A to B. This line, called the **budget constraint**, shows the consumption bundles that the consumer can afford. In this case, it shows the trade-off between cola and pizza that the consumer faces.

> **budget constraint** the limit on the consumption bundles that a consumer can afford

FIGURE 8.1

The Consumer's Budget Constraint
The budget constraint shows the various bundles of goods that the consumer can afford for a given income. Here the consumer buys bundles of cola and pizza. The table and graph show what the consumer can afford if their income is €1,000, the price of cola is €2 and the price of pizza is €10.

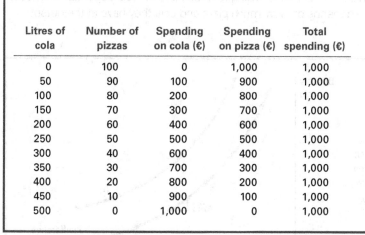

Litres of cola	Number of pizzas	Spending on cola (€)	Spending on pizza (€)	Total spending (€)
0	100	0	1,000	1,000
50	90	100	900	1,000
100	80	200	800	1,000
150	70	300	700	1,000
200	60	400	600	1,000
250	50	500	500	1,000
300	40	600	400	1,000
350	30	700	300	1,000
400	20	800	200	1,000
450	10	900	100	1,000
500	0	1,000	0	1,000

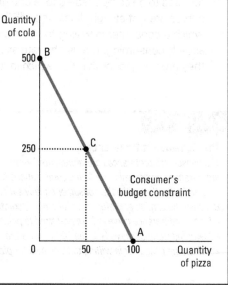

The slope of the budget constraint measures the rate at which the consumer can trade one good for the other. The slope between two points is calculated as the change in the vertical distance divided by the change in the horizontal distance ('rise over run'). From point A to point B, the vertical distance is 500 litres, and the horizontal distance is 100 pizzas. Because the budget constraint slopes downward, the slope is a negative number. This reflects the fact that to get one extra pizza, the consumer must *reduce* their consumption of cola by five litres. In fact, the slope of the budget constraint (ignoring the minus sign) equals the *relative price* of the two goods, the price of one good compared to the price of the other. A pizza costs five times as much as a litre of cola, so the opportunity cost of a pizza is 5 litres of cola. The budget constraint's slope of 5 reflects the trade-off the market is offering the consumer: 1 pizza for 5 litres of cola.

> **SELF TEST** Draw the budget constraint for a person with income of €1,000 if the price of cola is €5 per litre and the price of pizza is €10. What is the slope of this budget constraint?

Preferences: What the Consumer Wants

The consumer's preferences allow them to choose between different bundles of cola and pizza. If you offer the consumer two different bundles, they choose the bundle that best suits their tastes. If the two bundles suit their tastes equally well, we say that the consumer is *indifferent* between the two bundles.

Just as we have represented the consumer's budget constraint graphically, we can also represent their preferences graphically. We do this with indifference curves. An **indifference curve** shows the bundles of consumption that make the consumer equally happy or which give equal utility. In this case, the indifference curves show the combinations of cola and pizza with which the consumer is equally satisfied.

> **indifference curve** a curve that shows consumption bundles that give the consumer the same level of satisfaction

Figure 8.2 shows two of the consumer's many indifference curves. The consumer is indifferent between combinations A, B and C, because they are all on the same curve. Not surprisingly, if the consumer's consumption of pizza is reduced, say from point A to point B, consumption of cola must increase to keep them equally happy. If consumption of pizza is reduced again, from point B to point C, the amount of cola consumed must increase yet again.

The slope at any point on an indifference curve equals the rate at which the consumer is willing to substitute one good for the other. This is the MRS. In this case, the MRS measures how much pizza the consumer requires to be compensated for a one unit reduction in cola consumption. Notice that because the indifference curves are not straight lines, the MRS is not the same at all points on a given indifference curve. The rate at which a consumer is willing to trade one good for the other depends on the amounts of the goods they are already consuming. That is, the rate at which a consumer is willing to trade pizza for cola depends on whether they are hungrier or thirstier, which in turn depends on how much pizza and cola they have at the outset.

FIGURE 8.2

The Consumer's Preferences

The consumer's preferences are represented with indifference curves, which show the combinations of cola and pizza that make the consumer equally satisfied. Because the consumer prefers more of a good, points on a higher indifference curve (I₂) are preferred to points on a lower indifference curve (I₁). The MRS shows the rate at which the consumer is willing to trade cola for pizza.

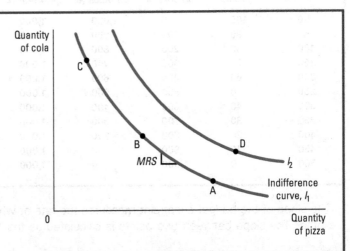

The consumer is equally happy at all points on any given indifference curve, but they prefer some indifference curves to others. We assume that consumers would rather have more of a good than less of it. Because they prefer more consumption to less, higher indifference curves are preferred to lower ones. The idea that buyers can rank preferences from best to worst (or vice versa) is captured by **expected utility theory**. In Figure 8.2, any point on curve I_2 is preferred to any point on curve I_1.

> **expected utility theory** the idea that buyers can rank preferences from best to worst (or vice versa)

A consumer's set of indifference curves gives a complete ranking of the consumer's preferences. That is, we can use indifference curves to rank any two bundles of goods. For example, the indifference curves in Figure 8.2 tell us that point D is preferred to point A because point D is on a higher indifference curve than point A. This may be obvious because point D offers the consumer both more pizza and more cola. However, point D is also preferred to point C because point D is on a higher indifference curve. Point D has less cola than point C, but it has more than enough extra pizza to make the consumer prefer it. By seeing which point is on the higher indifference curve, we can use the set of indifference curves to rank any combinations of cola and pizza.

> **PITFALL PREVENTION** Remember that an indifference curve shows bundles of goods which give equal utility so that consumers have no preference between them: they are equally preferred. However, it is assumed that consumers always prefer more to less so would prefer to be on the highest indifference curve possible.

Optimization: What the Consumer Chooses

We have the two pieces necessary to consider the consumer's decision about what to buy. Remembering the assumptions we set out earlier in the chapter, we can state that the consumer would like to end up with the best possible combination of cola and pizza. That is, the combination on the highest possible indifference curve. The consumer can only make choices under the constraint of their budget, which measures the total resources available to them.

Figure 8.3 shows the consumer's budget constraint and three of their many indifference curves. The highest indifference curve that the consumer can reach (I_2 in the figure) is the one that just barely touches the budget constraint. The point at which this indifference curve and the budget constraint touch is called the *optimum*. The consumer would prefer point A, but cannot afford that point because it lies above their budget constraint. The consumer can afford point B, but that point is on a lower indifference curve and provides the consumer less satisfaction. The optimum represents the best combination of consumption of cola and pizza available to the consumer given their budget constraint.

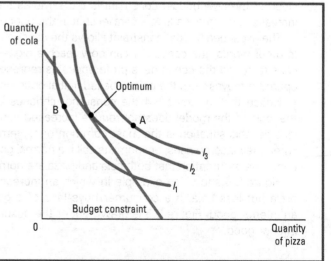

FIGURE 8.3

The Consumer's Optimum
The consumer chooses the point on their budget constraint that lies on the highest indifference curve. At this point, called the optimum, the MRS equals the relative price of the two goods. Here the highest indifference curve the consumer can reach is I_2. The consumer prefers point A, which lies on indifference curve I_3, but the consumer cannot afford this bundle of cola and pizza. In contrast, point B is affordable, but because it lies on a lower indifference curve, the consumer does not prefer it.

At the optimum, the slope of the indifference curve equals the slope of the budget constraint, so the indifference curve is *tangential* to the budget constraint. The slope of the indifference curve is the MRS between cola and pizza, and the slope of the budget constraint is the relative price of cola and pizza. The consumer chooses consumption of the two goods so that the MRS equals the relative price. That is:

$$MRS = \frac{P_x}{P_y}$$

Because the marginal rate of substitution equals the ratio of marginal utilities, we can write this condition for optimization as:

$$\frac{MU_x}{MU_y} = \frac{P_x}{P_y}$$

Now rearrange this expression to become:

$$\frac{MU_x}{P_x} = \frac{MU_y}{P_y}$$

This equation has a simple interpretation: at the optimum, the marginal utility per euro spent on good X equals the marginal utility per euro spent on good Y. Why? If this equality did not hold, the consumer could increase utility by changing behaviour, switching spending from the good that provided lower marginal utility per euro to spend more on the good that provided higher marginal utility per euro. This would be the rational thing to do.

This analysis of consumer choice shows how market prices reflect the marginal value that consumers place on goods. In making consumption choices, the consumer takes as given the relative price of the two goods and then chooses an optimum at which their MRS equals this relative price. The relative price is the rate at which the *market* is willing to trade one good for the other, whereas the MRS is the rate at which the *consumer* is willing to trade one good for the other. At the consumer's optimum, the consumer's valuation of the two goods (as measured by the MRS) equals the market's valuation (as measured by the relative price). As a result of this consumer optimization, market prices of different goods reflect the value that consumers place on those goods.

How Changes in Income Affect the Consumer's Choices

Now that we have seen how the consumer makes the consumption decision, let us examine how consumption responds to changes in income. To be specific, suppose that income increases. With higher income, the consumer can afford more of both goods. The increase in income, therefore, shifts the budget constraint outward, as in Figure 8.4. Because the relative price of the two goods has not changed, the slope of the new budget constraint is the same as the slope of the initial budget constraint. That is, an increase in income leads to a parallel shift in the budget constraint.

The expanded budget constraint allows the consumer to choose a better combination of cola and pizza. In other words, the consumer can now reach a higher indifference curve. Given the shift in the budget constraint and the consumer's preferences as represented by their indifference curves, the consumer's optimum moves from the point labelled 'initial optimum' to the point labelled 'new optimum'.

Notice that in Figure 8.4 the consumer chooses to consume more cola and more pizza. Although the logic of the model does not require increased consumption of both goods in response to increased income, this situation is the most common one. Remember that if a consumer wants more of a good when their income rises, economists call it a normal good. The indifference curves in Figure 8.4 are drawn under the assumption that both cola and pizza are normal goods.

Figure 8.5 shows an example in which an increase in income induces the consumer to buy more pizza but less cola. If a consumer buys less of a good when their income rises, economists call it an inferior good. Figure 8.5 is drawn under the assumption that pizza is a normal good and cola is an inferior good.

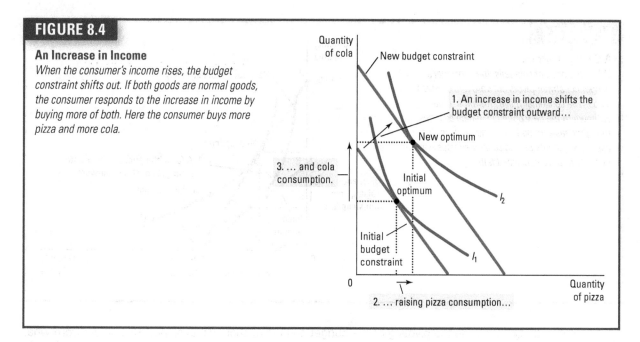

FIGURE 8.4

An Increase in Income

When the consumer's income rises, the budget constraint shifts out. If both goods are normal goods, the consumer responds to the increase in income by buying more of both. Here the consumer buys more pizza and more cola.

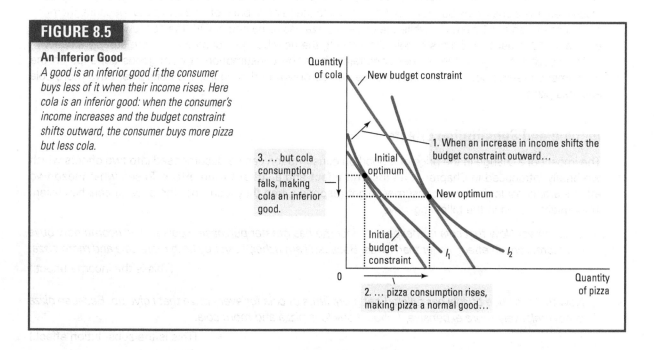

FIGURE 8.5

An Inferior Good

A good is an inferior good if the consumer buys less of it when their income rises. Here cola is an inferior good: when the consumer's income increases and the budget constraint shifts outward, the consumer buys more pizza but less cola.

How Changes in Prices Affect the Consumer's Choices

Let's now use this model of consumer choice to consider how a change in the price of one of the goods alters the consumer's choices. Suppose that the price of cola falls from €2 to €1 a litre. It is no surprise that the lower price expands the consumer's set of buying opportunities. In other words, a fall in the price of any good causes the budget constraint to pivot. With their available income of €1,000 the consumer can now buy twice as many litres of cola than before, but the same amount of pizza. Figure 8.6 shows that point A in the figure stays the same (100 pizzas). If the consumer spends their entire income of €1,000 on cola, they can now buy 1,000 rather than only 500 litres. Thus the end point of the budget constraint pivots outwards from point B to point D.

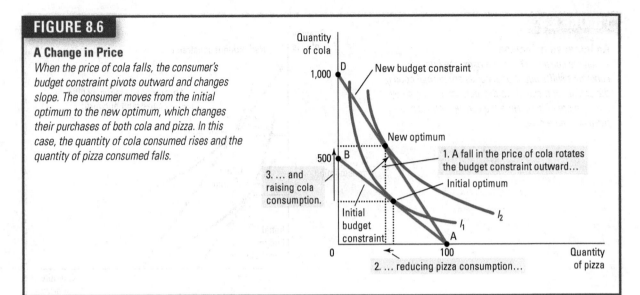

FIGURE 8.6

A Change in Price
When the price of cola falls, the consumer's budget constraint pivots outward and changes slope. The consumer moves from the initial optimum to the new optimum, which changes their purchases of both cola and pizza. In this case, the quantity of cola consumed rises and the quantity of pizza consumed falls.

Notice that in this case the pivoting of the budget constraint changes its slope. (This differs from what happened previously when prices stayed the same but the consumer's income changed.) As we have discussed, the slope of the budget constraint reflects the relative price of cola and pizza. Because the price of cola has fallen to €1 from €2, while the price of pizza has remained at €10, the consumer can now trade a pizza for 10 rather than 5 litres of cola. As a result, the new budget constraint is more steeply sloped.

How such a change in the budget constraint alters the consumption of both goods depends on the consumer's preferences. For the indifference curves drawn in this figure, the consumer buys more cola and less pizza.

Income and Substitution Effects

The impact of a change in the price of a good on consumption can be decomposed into two effects which we briefly introduced in Chapter 4: an **income effect** and a **substitution effect**. To see what these two effects are, consider how our consumer might respond when they learn that the price of cola has fallen. They might reason in the following ways:

Great news! Now that cola is cheaper, my income has greater purchasing power. My income now buys me more. I am, in effect, richer than I was. Because I am richer, I can buy both more cola and more pizza.

(This is the income effect.)

Now that the price of cola has fallen, I get more litres of cola for every pizza that I give up. Because pizza is now relatively more expensive, I should buy less pizza and more cola.

(This is the substitution effect.)

> **income effect** the change in consumption that results when a price change moves the consumer to a higher or lower indifference curve
> **substitution effect** the change in consumption that results when a price change moves the consumer along a given indifference curve to a point with a new marginal rate of substitution

The decrease in the price of cola makes the consumer better off. If cola and pizza are both normal goods, the consumer will want to spread this improvement in their purchasing power over both goods. This income effect tends to make the consumer buy more pizza and more cola. Yet, at the same time, consumption of cola has become less expensive relative to consumption of pizza. This substitution effect tends to make the consumer choose more cola and less pizza.

Now consider the result of these two effects. The consumer certainly buys more cola, because the income and substitution effects both act to raise purchases of cola. But it is ambiguous whether the consumer buys more pizza, because the income and substitution effects work in opposite directions. This conclusion is summarized in Table 8.1.

TABLE 8.1	Income and Substitution Effects When the Price of Cola Falls		
Good	**Income effect**	**Substitution effect**	**Total effect**
Cola	Consumers are richer, so they buy more cola.	Cola is relatively cheap, so consumers buy more cola.	Income and substitution effects act in the same direction, so consumers buy more cola.
Pizza	Consumers are richer, so they buy more pizza.	Pizza is relatively more expensive, so consumers buy less pizza.	Income and substitution effects act in opposite directions, so the total effect on pizza consumption is ambiguous.

We can interpret the income and substitution effects using indifference curves. The income effect is the change in consumption that results from the movement to a higher indifference curve. The substitution effect is the change in consumption that results from being at a point on an indifference curve with a different MRS.

Figure 8.7 shows graphically how to decompose the change in the consumer's decision into the income effect and the substitution effect. When the price of cola falls, the consumer moves from the initial optimum, point A, to the new optimum, point C. We can view this change as occurring in two steps. First, the consumer moves *along* the initial indifference curve I_1 from point A to point B. The consumer is equally happy at these two points, but at point B the marginal rate of substitution reflects the new relative price. (The dashed line through point B reflects the new relative price by being parallel to the new budget constraint.) Next, the consumer *shifts* to the higher indifference curve I_2 by moving from point B to point C. Even though points B and C are on different indifference curves, they have the same marginal rate of substitution. That is, the slope of the indifference curve I_1 at point B equals the slope of the indifference curve I_2 at point C.

Although the consumer never actually chooses point B, this hypothetical point is useful to clarify the two effects that determine the consumer's decision. Notice that the change from point A to point B represents a pure change in the MRS without any change in the consumer's welfare. Similarly, the change from point B to point C represents a pure change in welfare without any change in the MRS. Thus the movement from A to B shows the substitution effect, and the movement from B to C shows the income effect.

FIGURE 8.7

Income and Substitution Effects
The effect of a change in price can be broken down into an income effect and a substitution effect. The substitution effect, the movement along an indifference curve to a point with a different marginal rate of substitution, is shown here as the change from point A to point B along indifference curve I_1. The income effect, the shift to a higher indifference curve, is shown here as the change from point B on indifference curve I_1 to point C on indifference curve I_2.

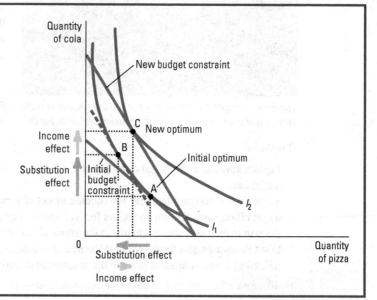

> **?** **WHAT IF...** a rise in prices takes place at the same time as a fall in incomes? How would this affect consumer optimum?

CASE STUDY   Rising Interest Rates

Following the Financial Crisis of 2007–09, many developed nations' economies experienced very low interest rates. In the UK, for example, the Bank of England had kept interest rates at below 1 per cent for 13 years. The Bank of England then set the Bank rate at a record low of 0.1 per cent as Covid-19 took hold. As economies came out of the pandemic, supply constraints led to prices rising at faster rates and central banks began to respond by pushing up interest rates. The conflict in Ukraine increased the pressures on prices and further interest rate rises were seen throughout 2022. In December 2021, for example, the Bank rate in the UK stood at 0.1 per cent. The Bank of England began introducing quarter point rises throughout the first half of 2022 and then larger increases. By December 2022, the Bank rate stood at 3 per cent and by July 2023 had risen to 5 per cent.

Increases in interest rates affect both consumers and savers. Many people will have experienced an increase in their mortgage rate following the increase in interest rates in 2022/23 but savers also saw a better rate of return on their savings compared to the previous 13 years of low rates. How changes in the interest rate feed through to the economy as a whole depends to some extent on income and substitution effects. The effect on consumer spending will be influenced in part by the size of the income effect, on the one hand. Higher rates of interest would be expected to reduce consumption because of the substitution effect. Consuming goods becomes more expensive because the opportunity cost of saving rises. Every pound or euro devoted to consumption now costs the individual more in foregone interest returns. On the other hand, higher interest rates can result in increased consumption through the income effect. Those with savings should receive a better return on their savings which can be used on increased consumption. The net effect on consumption will depend on the relative strength of the income and substitution effects and, of course, the size of the increase in interest rates. A rise of a quarter of 1 per cent may not make that much difference to the savings of households, even assuming banks do pass on the rate rise to savers (which is not always the case). If interest rates continue to increase, and this is not unexpected given the pressure on prices, we might expect to see the strength of the income and substitution effects changing. Many economists generally take it that higher interest rates will reduce net consumption, because the positive income effect is outweighed by the negative substitution effect.

The Bank of England is the central bank of the UK and sets the structure of interest rates across the banking system in the UK.

Questions

1 Explain how a rise in interest rates can affect the decisions consumers might make around purchasing decisions.
2 Sketch out a diagram to show the income effect of a rise in interest rates for savers and how this might affect consumption decisions for two notional goods labelled X and Y. (Hint: think about how the rise in interest rates might affect the slope of the budget constraint.)
3 What factors do you think would influence the relative size of the income and substitution effects following a rise in interest rates of the magnitude described in the case study?

Reference: www.bankofengland.co.uk/knowledgebank/what-are-interest-rates (accessed 7 June 2023).

BEHAVIOURAL ECONOMICS

The standard economic model described above has some merits, but the key assumption that consumers behave rationally in making purchasing decisions does have some limitations. Why, for example, do consumers complain about a €0.10 increase in a litre of fuel but are happy to spend €5 on a lottery ticket where the chances of winning are considerably less than being struck by lightning? Why do people make pledges to get fitter, eat more healthily or quit habits like smoking, but fail in their efforts very quickly? Why do employees get angry if they find out that a colleague is getting a higher pay rise than them? Why do people give up a considerable amount of time to queue (often in very inclement weather) to grab a 'bargain' at the sales when they could have used the time queuing to earn more than they 'save' getting the bargain? Why do people queue for hours to get their hands on the latest technology device from Apple, or the latest version of a video game or to watch a new release of a cult movie?

Many of the things we do in life and the decisions we make cannot be explained as those of rational beings. (Rational beings are sometimes referred to by economists as *homoeconomicus*.) Although in some ways humans reflect the rational, calculating people assumed in economic theory, in reality they are far more complex. They can be forgetful, impulsive, confused, emotional and short-sighted. Economists have suggested that humans are only 'near rational' or that they exhibit 'bounded rationality'. **Bounded rationality** is the idea that humans make decisions under the constraints of limited, and sometimes unreliable, information, that they face limits to the amount of information they can process and that they face time constraints in making decisions.

> **bounded rationality** the idea that humans make decisions under the constraints of limited, and sometimes unreliable, information that they are unable to fully process

Studies of human decision making, primarily in the field of psychology but now widely adopted by economics, have tried to detect systematic mistakes that people make. We outline some of the key findings below.

People Are Overconfident Imagine that you were asked some numerical questions, such as the number of African countries in the United Nations, the height of the tallest mountain in Europe and so on. Instead of being asked for a single estimate, however, you could be asked to give a 90 per cent confidence interval, a range such that you were 90 per cent confident the true number falls within it. When psychologists run experiments like this, they find that most people give ranges that are too small: the true number falls within their intervals far less than 90 per cent of the time. That is, most people are too sure of their own abilities.

People Give Too Much Weight to a Small Number of Vivid Observations Imagine that you are thinking about buying a new smartphone by company X. To learn about its reliability, you read *Consumer Reports*, which has surveyed 1,000 owners of the particular smartphone that you are looking at. Then you run into a friend who owns such a phone and they tell you that they are unhappy with the phone. How do you treat your friend's observation? If you think rationally, you will realize that they have only increased your sample size from 1,000 to 1,001, which does not provide much new information. Placing a reliance on your friend's opinion should be of little importance, but people do place a disproportionate degree of importance on such information.

In addition, a process called the *reticular activation system* (RAS) works to bring your attention to instances of this smartphone: you will suddenly start to notice more of them. The RAS is an automatic mechanism in the brain that brings relevant information to our attention. This effect may also exert an influence on decision making which has little to do with rationality: simply noticing more of the smartphones does not change their reliability.

People Are Reluctant to Change Their Mind People tend to interpret evidence to confirm beliefs they already hold. In one study, subjects were asked to read and evaluate a research report on whether capital punishment deters crime. After reading the report, those who initially favoured the death penalty said they were more sure in their view, and those who initially opposed the death penalty also said they were more sure in their view. The two groups interpreted the same evidence in exactly opposite ways.

People Have a Natural Tendency to Look for Examples Which Confirm Their Existing View or Hypothesis Nassim Nicholas Taleb, the author of the book *The Black Swan* (Penguin, 2010), calls this 'naïve empiricism'. People identify, select or observe limited examples of past instances and quote them as evidence for a viewpoint or hypothesis. For example, extreme weather events can be selected as evidence of climate change or a rise in the price of petrol of 10 per cent is quoted as being symptomatic of a broader increase in prices of all goods.

People Use Rules of Thumb (Heuristics) The standard economic model implies that to act rationally buyers will consider all available information in making purchasing decisions and weigh up this information to maximize utility subject to a budget constraint. It is likely that many consumers will (a) not have access to sufficient information to be able to make a fully rational choice and (b) even if they did they would not be able to process this information fully, partly due to a lack of mental facility (not everyone can do arithmetic quickly in their head or make statistical calculations on which to base their choices). Instead, when making decisions many people will use shortcuts that help simplify the decision making process. These shortcuts are referred to as **heuristics** or *rules of thumb*. Some of these heuristics can be deep-seated and firms can take advantage of them to influence consumer behaviour.

heuristics rules of thumb or shortcuts used in decision making

There are a number of different types of heuristics:

Anchoring Heuristics This refers to the tendency for people to start with something they are familiar with or know and make decisions or adjustments based on this anchor. For example, a consumer may base the price they expect to pay for a restaurant meal on the last two prices they paid when eating out. If the price at the next restaurant is higher than this anchor price, it may be that the consumer thinks the restaurant is 'expensive' or 'not good value for money' and may choose not to go again, whereas if the price they pay is lower than the anchor price they might see the restaurant as being good value for money and choose to return. Often these anchors are biased and so the adjustment or decision is flawed in some way.

Availability Heuristics These refer to cases where decisions are made based on an assessment of the risks of the likelihood of something happening. If examples readily come to mind because of excessive media coverage, for example, decisions may be taken with a skewed assessment of the risks. If a consumer brings to mind the idea that the last couple of winters have been particularly bad, then they might be more likely to buy equipment to help them combat adverse weather for the next winter. Consumers who use commuter trains are more likely to give negative feedback about the service they have received if their recent experience has been of some delays or cancellations even if the overall level of punctuality of the train operator has been very high.

Representative Heuristics People tend to make judgements by comparing how representative something is to an image or stereotype that they hold. For example, people may be more prepared to pay money to buy a lottery ticket if a close friend has just won a reasonable amount of money on the lottery or make an association that if Bose headphones are good quality (for example) then its home theatre systems are also going to be good quality.

Persuasion Heuristics These are various attributes that a consumer attaches to a product or a brand. For example, it has been shown that size does matter to consumers and so marketers can exploit this by making more exaggerated claims in adverts or using facts and figures to make the product more compelling in the mind of the consumer. The more that the marketers can highlight the positive attributes of their product (and the negative ones of their rivals) the more likely consumers are to make choices in favour of their product. In addition, consumers are also persuaded by people they like and respect. This may be utilized by firms through the people they use in adverts and celebrity endorsements, but may also be important in terms of the people a firm employs to represent them in a sales or marketing capacity. It may also be relevant in cases where friends or colleagues discuss products and is one of the reasons why firms are keen to build a better understanding of how social media can be exploited. Finally, persuasion heuristics can manifest themselves in the 'bandwagon' effect. If many people go and see a film and rave about it then there is even more incentive for others to go and see it as well. Firms may look to try and create a bandwagon effect to utilize this persuasion heuristic in their marketing.

Simulation Heuristics These occur when people use mental processes to establish the likely outcome of something. The easier it is to simulate or visualize that outcome the more likely the individual is to make a decision based on it. For example, if it is easy to imagine a product which makes you look good, then you are more likely to buy it. Pharmaceutical firms know that consumers are more likely to buy and take medicines that deal with known and experienced symptoms (things like headaches, strained muscles, sore throats and runny noses) which are easy to visualize and imagine, than taking regular medicines for something like high cholesterol, because it is hard to build a mental process for the effects of high cholesterol.

Expected Utility Theory and Framing Effects In our discussion of the standard economic model we referred to expected utility theory, the idea that preferences can and will be ranked by buyers. Expected utility theory is important in that every day we must make decisions based on ranking preferences. Imagine you are faced with buying your first car. You have limited income and have to go to second-hand dealers. You are wary of the potential problems inherent in buying a second-hand car. You know that if the car develops a mechanical fault it often costs more to repair than to replace, so you go to the dealers with this in mind. You find two cars that you like. One is priced at €500 and its age suggests that it has a 50 per cent chance of breaking down in the first year. The second car is €900 but has a 20 per cent chance of breaking down in the first year. Which do you choose? Expected utility theory says that consumers can rank the preference between these two options. We assume that if the car breaks down it is more expensive to repair than to replace so our calculations are based on replacing the car rather than repairing it (we are talking rational human beings after all here).

The expected replacement cost of the first car would be the price we paid (€500) multiplied by the probability of it breaking down (50 per cent) which works out as €500 × 0.50 = €250. The expected replacement cost of the second car is 0.2 × 900 = €180. The rational choice, therefore, would be to purchase the more expensive car. The problem is that the way in which such choices are presented can affect our judgements and the rational decision is violated.

Research into this area is extensive and persuasive. Essentially, choices can be affected by the way in which they are framed. In our example above, if you were faced with the choice of buying a car which has an 80 per cent chance of losing €720 in a year's time, or another car which has a 50 per cent chance of losing €250 after a year, which would you now choose? In this second case the two options are presented differently but are essentially the same as the first set of choices. The risks now appear different.

Firms are careful to frame the way they present products and information to consumers to influence purchasing decisions and exploit these differences in perception. For example, firms selling insurance know that people make judgements about the extent to which they are exposed to risk in deciding whether to take out insurance and how much cover they need. Adverts and marketing, therefore, may be framed to give the impression to consumers that they face increased risk.

ASYMMETRIC INFORMATION

'I know something you don't know.' This statement is a common taunt among children, but it also conveys a deep truth about how people sometimes interact with one another. Many times in life, one person knows more about what is going on than another. A difference in access to relevant knowledge is called an *information asymmetry*.

Examples abound. A worker knows more than their employer about how much effort they put into their job. A seller of a used car knows more than the buyer about the car's condition. The first is an example of a *hidden action*, whereas the second is an example of a *hidden characteristic*. In each case, the party in the dark (the employer, the car buyer) would like to know the relevant information, but the informed party (the worker, the car seller) may have an incentive to conceal it.

Because asymmetric information is so prevalent, economists have devoted much effort in recent decades to studying its effects. And, indeed, the 2001 Nobel Prize in economics was awarded to three economists (George Akerlof, Michael Spence and Joseph Stiglitz) for their pioneering work on this topic. Let us discuss some of the insights that this research has revealed.

Hidden Actions: Principals, Agents and Moral Hazard

Moral hazard is a problem that arises when one person, called the **agent**, is performing some task on behalf of another person, called the **principal**. If the principal cannot perfectly monitor the agent's behaviour, the agent tends to undertake less effort than the principal considers desirable and is not fully responsible for the consequences of their actions. The phrase *moral hazard* refers to the risk, or 'hazard', of inappropriate or otherwise 'immoral' behaviour by the agent.

> **moral hazard** the tendency of a person who is imperfectly monitored to engage in dishonest or otherwise undesirable behaviour
>
> **agent** a person who is performing an act for another person, called the principal
>
> **principal** a person for whom another person, called the agent, is performing some act

In addition to moral hazard, **adverse selection** can also result from asymmetric information. Adverse selection is a feature of banking, finance and insurance industries. A bank, for example, sets rules and regulations for its accounts which may lead to some customers, who are not very profitable to the bank, adversely selecting the bank: customers the bank would rather not have. In insurance, the person seeking insurance cover has more information about their situation than the insurer. A person who knows they are high risk will look to buy insurance but not necessarily divulge the extent of the risk they pose to the insurance company. How does the insurance company distinguish between its high-risk and low-risk customers? The insurance company would rather take on the low-risk customers than the high-risk ones, but high-risk customers adversely select the insurance company. In finance, some investment banks have been accused of putting very risky assets into financial products and clients buying these products do not know the full extent of the risk they are buying. These clients would have been better off not dealing with those suppliers. In such a situation, the principal tries various ways to encourage the agent to act more responsibly (such as pricing insurance for high risk customers higher than for low risk ones). Adverse selection tends to arise before a contractor or agreement is made (i.e. ex-ante), whereas moral hazard tends to arise after a contract or agreement is made (i.e. ex-post).

> **adverse selection** the tendency for the mix of unobserved attributes to become undesirable from the standpoint of an uninformed party

> **?** **WHAT IF...** governments believed that the market is the best regulator of banks and sought to increase competition in the banking industry. Would this reduce moral hazard?

The employment relationship is the classic example. The employer (business) is the principal, and the worker is the agent. The moral hazard problem is the temptation of imperfectly monitored workers to shirk their responsibilities. How do firms respond to this problem?

- Better monitoring. Human resources departments in larger firms develop processes to improve the monitoring of workers and to also put in place performance management systems to help provide incentives for employees to meet their employment responsibilities.
- High wages. According to *efficiency wages theories*, some employers may choose to pay their workers a wage above the level that equilibrates supply and demand in the labour market. A worker who earns an above-equilibrium wage is less likely to shirk, because if they are caught and fired, they might not be able to find another high-paying job.

- Delayed payment. Firms can delay part of a worker's compensation, so if the worker is caught shirking and is fired, they suffer a larger penalty. One example of delayed compensation is the year-end bonus. Similarly, a firm may choose to pay its workers more later in their lives. Thus the wage rises that workers receive as they age may reflect not just the benefits of experience but also a response to moral hazard.

These various mechanisms to reduce the problem of moral hazard need not be used alone. Employers can use a combination of them.

Beyond the workplace, there are many other examples of moral hazard that affect businesses. Individuals with insurance cover, be it fire, motor vehicle or medical insurance, may behave differently as a result of having that cover. A motorist, for example, might drive more recklessly in the knowledge that in the event of an accident the cost will be met primarily by the insurance company. Similarly, families choosing to live near a river may benefit from the scenic views, but the increased risk of flooding imposes a cost to the insurance company and the government in the event of a serious flood. The Financial Crisis of 2007–09 raised the issue of bankers' bonuses. One argument put forward was that banks were acting recklessly in giving large bonuses to workers which encouraged inappropriate and risky investment. Such behaviour was encouraged because bankers 'knew' that governments would step in to prevent banks from failing.

Many regulations are aimed at addressing the problem: an insurance company may require homeowners to buy smoke detectors or pay higher premiums if there is a history of reckless driving (or even refuse to provide insurance cover to the individual), the government may prohibit building homes on land with high risk of flooding and new regulations may be introduced to curb the behaviour of banks. The insurance company does not have perfect information about how cautious homeowners are, the government does not have perfect information about the risk that families undertake when choosing where to live and regulators do not know fully the risks that bankers take in investment decisions. As a result, the problem of moral hazard persists.

Signalling to Convey Private Information

Markets respond to problems of asymmetric information in many ways. One of them is **signalling**, which refers to actions taken by an informed party for the sole purpose of credibly revealing their private information.

 signalling an action taken by an informed party to reveal private information to an uninformed party

We have seen examples of signalling earlier in this chapter: firms may spend money on advertising to signal to potential customers that they have high quality products. The intention is that the informed party is using a signal to convince the uninformed party that the informed party is offering something of high quality.

What does it take for an action to be an effective signal? Obviously, it must be costly. If a signal were free, everyone would use it, and it would convey no information. For the same reason, there is another requirement: the signal must be less costly, or more beneficial, to the person with the higher quality product. Otherwise, everyone would have the same incentive to use the signal and it would reveal nothing.

Screening to Induce Information Revelation

When an informed party takes actions to reveal their private information, the phenomenon is called signalling. When an uninformed party takes actions to induce the informed party to reveal private information, the phenomenon is called **screening**.

 screening an action taken by an uninformed party to induce an informed party to reveal information

Some screening is common sense. A person buying a used car may ask that it be checked by a car mechanic or a trade association before the sale. A seller who refuses this request reveals their private information that the car is not of high quality. The buyer may decide to offer a lower price or to look for another car.

Other examples of screening are more subtle. For example, consider a firm that sells car insurance. The firm would like to charge a low premium to safe drivers and a high premium to risky drivers. How can it tell them apart? Drivers know whether they are safe or risky, but the risky ones will not admit to it. A driver's history is one piece of information (which insurance companies in fact use), but because of the intrinsic randomness of car accidents, history is an imperfect indicator of future risks.

The insurance company might be able to sort out the two kinds of drivers by offering different insurance policies that would induce them to separate themselves. One policy would have a high premium and cover the full cost of any accidents that occur. Another policy would have low premiums but would have, say, a €1,000 excess (the driver would be responsible for the first €1,000 of damage, and the insurance company would cover the remaining risk). Notice that the excess is more of a burden for risky drivers because they are more likely to have an accident. Thus a low premium policy with a relatively large excess would attract the safe drivers, while the high premium policy with a low excess would attract the risky drivers. Faced with these two policies, the two kinds of drivers would reveal their private information by choosing different insurance policies.

> **SELF TEST** A person who buys a life insurance policy pays a certain amount per year and receives for their family a much larger payment in the event of their death. Would you expect buyers of life insurance to have higher or lower death rates than the average person? How might this be an example of moral hazard? Of adverse selection? How might a life insurance company deal with these problems?

CONCLUSION

This chapter has examined different but complementary models of consumer behaviour. The standard economic model relies on a set of assumptions with rational human beings at its heart. Economists are always looking to refine their models. The influence of other disciplines has led to theories of consumer behaviour which go some way to helping understand the imperfections in the standard economic model. Firms are increasingly using these insights to help develop marketing strategies to influence consumer behaviour and increase sales. Advertising and branding are two of these areas which are used by firms to influence consumer behaviour. They are features of imperfect competition and we will look at these in more detail later in the book. Finally, we looked at issues which arise from asymmetric information. The very fact that most businesses know more about their product than do consumers gives rise to potential problems, and we looked in particular at moral hazard and adverse selection and how it affects the financial industry.

If there is a unifying theme to these topics, it is that life is messy. Information is imperfect, government is imperfect and people are imperfect. Of course, you knew this long before you started studying economics, but economists need to understand these imperfections as precisely as they can if they are to explain, and perhaps even improve, the world around them.

SUMMARY

- The standard economic model assumes humans behave rationally and seek to maximize utility subject to the constraint of limited income.
- Increased consumption raises total utility up to a point, but marginal utility falls as consumption increases and is called the 'law of diminishing marginal utility'.
- A consumer's budget constraint shows the possible combinations of different goods they can buy given their income and the prices of the goods. The slope of the budget constraint equals the relative price of the goods.
- The consumer's indifference curves represent their preferences. An indifference curve shows the various bundles of goods that make the consumer equally happy. Points on higher indifference curves are preferred to points on lower indifference curves. The slope of an indifference curve at any point is the consumer's MRS, the rate at which the consumer is willing to trade one good for the other.
- The consumer optimizes by choosing the point on their budget constraint that lies on the highest indifference curve. At this point, the slope of the indifference curve (the MRS between the goods) equals the slope of the budget constraint (the relative price of the goods).

- When the price of a good falls, the impact on the consumer's choices can be broken down into an income effect and a substitution effect. The income effect is the change in consumption that arises because a lower price makes the consumer better off. The substitution effect is the change in consumption that arises because a price change encourages greater consumption of the good that has become relatively cheaper. The income effect is reflected in the movement from a lower to a higher indifference curve, whereas the substitution effect is reflected by a movement along an indifference curve to a point with a different slope.

- The study of psychology and economics reveals that human decision making is more complex than is assumed in conventional economic theory. People are not always rational, they use rules of thumb (heuristics) and are influenced by the way in which information is presented (framing effects) which may alter outcomes.

- In many economic transactions, information is asymmetric. When there are hidden actions, principals may be concerned that agents suffer from the problem of moral hazard. When there are hidden characteristics, buyers may be concerned about the problem of adverse selection among the sellers. Private markets sometimes deal with asymmetric information with signalling and screening.

IN THE NEWS

Consumer Behaviour

As countries came out of lockdown restrictions, it became clear that supply chains had been badly disrupted by lockdowns and Covid-19 restrictions. Demand increased across a range of goods and suppliers struggled to keep up with the rise in demand. In February 2022, conflict broke out in Ukraine which further disrupted supply chains and especially energy supplies. The result was an acceleration in inflation. In March 2021, for example, inflation in the UK was recorded by the Office for National Statistics (ONS) at 1.0 per cent. It accelerated quickly and in October 2022, the ONS reported inflation at 9.6 per cent. Forecasts predicted that inflation would reach double digit figures into 2023 before easing back. Accelerating inflation was also seen in other countries around the world.

Consumer behaviour is not always rational as panic buying highlights.

Increases in the cost of living affect everyone but not to the same degree. Those on the lowest incomes may be faced with having to make different choices about what they spend their money on. Middle income families may also make different choices but for different reasons, while those on higher incomes may notice prices rising but not be affected by them in any significant way. In managing rising costs of production, businesses also face difficult choices. Warren Ackerman, writing in *The Grocer*, noted in November 2022 that manufacturers of fast moving consumer goods (FMCGs) were facing considerable cost pressures but recognized that pushing prices up too far risked losing customers. These types of producers monitor consumer spending patterns and Ackerman comments on how such patterns were beginning to show through. The number of times people chose to eat out had fallen; when people did shop at supermarkets, the amount they bought tended to be lower. Because prices are higher, people may spend the same amount of money when they go out or when they shop at a supermarket, but that same amount of money buys fewer goods. Ackerman noted that shoppers may turn to so-called discount retailers like Adli and Lidl where they feel they get better value for money. The change in consumer behaviour also has some upsides with spending on eating at home rising as people substitute eating out.

In response to the changes in consumer behaviour, firms are also changing their ways of working and their processes. Given that they may find it difficult to pass on higher costs to consumers in the form of higher prices, it may

(*Continued*)

be the case that they cut costs by reducing the product range available, focusing on the goods that generate revenue (the 80:20 rule is highly relevant here) and cutting back on marketing spending. With these types of responses, we can identify effects around changes in consumer behaviour but from a different perspective. If, for example, supermarkets focus on well-known branded products and cut back on offering a wider range of products, then the suppliers of these less popular products will suffer because their consumer (the retailer) is cutting back on its spending on those products. This highlights the importance of focusing on who the customer is and what their needs and behaviour are in relation to changing external conditions.

Questions

1 Comment on how inflation changes consumers' perceptions of value. Select and use appropriate examples to illustrate your answer.

2 Select two goods of your choice to use in a consumer choice model. Assume that the price of one good rises at a faster rate than the other as a result of inflationary pressures in the economy. Using your model, show how the consumer optimum might change as a result of the changes in the prices of these two goods.

3 Using the model from question 2, split out the income and substitution effects on consumption of both goods and comment on the relative size of these effects and the final outcome. Clearly state the assumptions you have made in your analysis.

4 'Inflation is getting terrible. Everything is going up – only last week I noticed that the price of bread has risen to £2.25 a loaf when earlier this year it was only £1.45. Everything is becoming less affordable now and I am going to have to cut back my spending.' Analyze and evaluate this statement from the perspective of the standard economic model and behavioural explanations of consumer behaviour.

5 Why is it important for businesses to clearly define who their customers are when making decisions in response to external changes such as those outlined in the article.

References: www.thegrocer.co.uk/second-opinion/how-inflation-is-changing-consumer-behaviour-and-whats-next/673149.article (accessed 7 June 2023).
www.ons.gov.uk/economy/inflationandpriceindices (accessed 7 June 2023).

QUESTIONS FOR REVIEW

1 A consumer goes into a coffee shop and has four cups of coffee. Explain what we might observe about the total utility and marginal utility of the individual. How does your explanation illustrate the law of diminishing returns?

2 A consumer has income of €3,000. Bread is priced at €3 a loaf and potatoes priced at €6 a kilo.

a. Draw the consumer's budget constraint. What is the slope of this budget constraint?
b. Draw a consumer's indifference curves for bread and potatoes. Pick a point on an indifference curve for bread and potatoes and show the marginal rate of substitution. What does the MRS tell us?
c. Show the optimal consumption choice. What is the MRS at this optimum?

3 The price of potatoes rises from €6 to €10 a kilo, while the price of bread remains at €3 a loaf. For a consumer with a constant income of €3,000, show what happens to consumption of bread and potatoes. Decompose the change into income and substitution effects.

4 To what extent does the concept of bounded rationality render the assumptions of the standard model redundant?

5 Explain and give an example of the following heuristics:

a. representative heuristics
b. availability heuristics
c. simulation heuristics
d. adjustment heuristics

6 What is moral hazard? List three things an employer might do to reduce the severity of this problem.

7 What is adverse selection? Give an example of a market in which adverse selection might be a problem.

8 Why is framing important in influencing consumer behaviour? Illustrate your answer with an example.

9 Define *signalling* and *screening,* and give an example of each.

PROBLEMS AND APPLICATIONS

1 Jacqueline divides her income between coffee and croissants (both of which are normal goods). A pest damages the coffee crop in Brazil and causes a large increase in the price of coffee.

  a. Show how the effect of this pest on the crop might affect Jacqueline's budget constraint.
  b. Show how the effect of this pest on the crop might affect Jacqueline's optimal consumption bundle assuming that the substitution effect outweighs the income effect for croissants.
  c. Show how the effect of this pest on the crop might affect Jacqueline's optimal consumption bundle assuming that the income effect outweighs the substitution effect for croissants.

2 Surette buys only orange juice and yoghurt.

  a. In 2024, Surette earns €50,000, orange juice is priced at €2 a carton and yoghurt is priced at €4 a tub. Draw Surette's budget constraint.
  b. Now suppose that all prices increase by 10 per cent in 2025 and that Surette's salary increases by 10 per cent as well. Draw Surette's new budget constraint. How would Surette's optimal combination of orange juice and yoghurt in 2025 compare to her optimal combination in 2024?

3 Economist George Stigler once wrote that, according to consumer theory, 'If consumers do not buy less of a commodity when their incomes rise, they will surely buy less when the price of the commodity rises.' Explain this statement using the concepts of income and substitution effects.

4 Choose three products you purchased recently. Think about the reasons that you made the particular purchase decision in each case in relation to the various heuristics.

5 Look at the following two statements:

  ● Which would you prefer, a 50 per cent chance of winning €150 or a 50 per cent chance of winning €100? Why?
  ● Would you prefer a decision that guarantees a €100 loss or would you rather take a gamble where the chance of winning €50 was rated at 50 per cent but the chance of losing €200 was also rated at 50 per cent? Why?

  What is the difference between these two types of statements and how do they illustrate the concept of framing?

6 Each of the following situations involves moral hazard. In each case, identify the principal and the agent, and explain why there is asymmetric information. How does the action described reduce the problem of moral hazard?

  a. Landlords require tenants to pay security deposits.
  b. Firms compensate top executives with options to buy company shares at a given price in the future.
  c. Car insurance companies offer discounts to customers who install anti-theft devices in their cars.

7 Some AIDS activists believe that health insurance companies should not be allowed to ask applicants if they are infected with the HIV virus that causes AIDS. Would this rule help or hurt those who are HIV-positive? Would it help or hurt those who are not HIV-positive? Would it exacerbate or mitigate the problem of adverse selection in the market for health insurance? Do you think it would increase or decrease the number of people without health insurance? In your opinion, would this be a good policy?

8 In what way can asymmetric information lead to consumer outcomes which are different from those predicted by the standard economic model?

9 Consider ways in which employers can screen employees to weed out those who may not be productive in their jobs. How can employees signal their potential value to a potential employer?

10 The government is considering two ways to help the needy: giving them cash, or giving them free meals at soup kitchens. Give an argument for giving cash. Give an argument, based on asymmetric information, for why the soup kitchen may be better than the cash handout.

PART 4
MICROECONOMICS: THE ECONOMICS OF FIRMS IN MARKETS

9 COSTS AND REVENUES IN PRODUCTION

LEARNING OUTCOMES

After reading this chapter you should be able to:

- Define and calculate total revenue, total cost, average cost, average revenue, marginal cost, marginal revenue and profit.
- Explain why the marginal cost curve must intersect the average total cost curve at the minimum point of the average total cost curve.
- Explain why a production function might exhibit increasing marginal product at low levels of output and decreasing marginal product at high levels of output.
- Explain why, as a firm expands its scale of operation, it tends to first exhibit economies of scale, then constant returns to scale, then diseconomies of scale.
- Use examples to show how economies of scale arise.
- Explain the difference between internal and external economies of scale.

THE COSTS OF PRODUCTION

The economy is made up of thousands of firms that produce the goods and services we enjoy every day: Mercedes Benz produces cars, Miele produces kitchen appliances and Nestlé produces food and drink. Some firms, such as these three, are large; they employ thousands of workers and have thousands of shareholders who share in the firms' profits. Other firms, such as the local hairdresser's salon or restaurant, are small; they employ only a few workers and may be owned by a single person or family.

As we examine firm behaviour in more detail you will gain a better understanding of what decisions lie behind the supply curve in a market which we introduced in Chapter 4. In addition, it will introduce you to a part of economics called *industrial organization,* the study of how firms' decisions regarding prices and quantities depend on the market conditions they face. The town in which you live, for instance, may have several restaurants, but only one water supply company. How does this difference in the number of firms affect the prices in these markets and the efficiency of the market outcomes? The field of industrial organization addresses exactly this question.

Before we turn to these issues, however, we need to discuss the costs of production. All firms, regardless of size, incur costs as they make the goods and services that they sell. A firm's costs are a key determinant of its production and pricing decisions. In this chapter, we define some of the variables that economists use to measure a firm's costs, and we consider the relationships among them.

WHAT ARE COSTS?

We begin our discussion of costs at Flavio's Pizza Factory. By examining some of the issues that Flavio faces in his business, we can learn some lessons about costs that apply to all firms in the economy.

Total Revenue, Total Cost and Profit

The amount of pizzas Flavio sells multiplied by the price he sells the pizzas at is the total revenue the firm receives. If Flavio sells 500,000 pizzas a year and the average price of each pizza sold is €5 the total revenue will be €5 × 500,000 = €2.5 million.

To produce those 500,000 pizzas, Flavio will have had to employ labour, buy machinery and equipment, run and maintain that equipment, buy the raw materials to make the pizzas (flour, cheese, tomatoes and so on), pay rent or a mortgage on the factory, pay off loans he may have secured (both the sum borrowed and any interest charged), pay for market research, marketing costs such as advertising and promotion, administration costs (such as managing the firm's payroll, monitoring the finances, processing sales and purchase invoices), and many other everyday payments down to the cost of using the telephone, energy, postage, maintaining the buildings and so on. These represent Flavio's **total cost**.

> **total cost** the market value of the inputs a firm uses in production

If Flavio subtracts all the costs over the year from the revenues received in the same year, he will either have a surplus (i.e. his revenue will be greater than his costs) or possibly have spent more on costs than received in revenues. Profit is the reward for the risk taken in carrying out production and is calculated as follows:

Profit = Total revenue − Total cost

We can express this in the formula:

$$\pi = TR - TC$$

where the Greek letter pi (π) represents profit.

Let us assume for the moment that Flavio's objective is to make his firm's profit as large as possible, in other words, he wants to maximize profit. Flavio needs to be able to measure his total revenue and his total costs. We know how to calculate total revenue. In many cases that is a relatively easy thing to do, but the measurement of a firm's total cost is more subtle and open to different interpretations.

> **PITFALL PREVENTION** It is important to understand the distinction between profit and cash flow. The latter is the money flowing into and out of a business over a period of time, whereas profit takes into consideration the total revenue and total cost. A firm could be profitable but have cash flow problems, which could force it out of business.

Costs as Opportunity Costs

When measuring costs at Flavio's Pizza Factory, or any other firm, it is important to keep in mind that the cost of something is what you give up to get it. Recall that the *opportunity cost* of an item refers to the sacrifice of the benefits of the next best alternative. To calculate opportunity cost we divide the sacrifice (the numerator) by the gain (the denominator):

$$\text{Opportunity cost of } X = \frac{\text{Sacrifice in } Y}{\text{Gain in } X}$$

When economists speak of a firm's cost of production, they include the opportunity costs of making its output of goods and services.

A firm's opportunity costs of production are sometimes obvious but sometimes less so. When Flavio pays €1,000 for a stock of flour, he can no longer use that €1,000 to buy something else; he must sacrifice what else that €1,000 could have purchased. Because these costs require the firm to pay out some money, they are called **explicit costs**. By contrast, some of a firm's opportunity costs, called **implicit costs**, do not require a cash outlay. Imagine that Flavio is skilled with computers and could earn €100 per hour working as a programmer. For every hour that Flavio works at his pizza factory, he gives up €100 in income, and this foregone income is also classed as part of his costs by an economist.

> **explicit costs** input costs that require an outlay of money by the firm
> **implicit costs** input costs that do not require an outlay of money by the firm

This distinction between explicit and implicit costs highlights an important difference between how economists and accountants analyze a business. Economists are interested in studying how firms make production and pricing decisions. Because these decisions are based on both explicit and implicit costs, economists include both when measuring a firm's costs. By contrast, accountants have the job of keeping track of the money that flows into and out of firms. As a result, they measure the explicit costs, but often ignore the implicit costs.

The difference between economists and accountants is easy to see in the case of Flavio's Pizza Factory. When Flavio gives up the opportunity to earn money as a computer programmer, his accountant will not count this as a cost of his pizza business. Because no money flows out of the business to pay for this cost, it never shows up on the business's financial statements. An economist, however, will count the foregone income as a cost because it will affect the decisions that Flavio makes in his pizza business. This is an important part of thinking like an economist. If the wage as a computer programmer rose from €100 to €500 per hour, the opportunity cost of running the business in terms of what Flavio is sacrificing in foregone income has risen. Flavio might decide he could earn more by closing the business and switching to computer programming.

The Cost of Capital as an Opportunity Cost An important implicit cost of almost every firm is the opportunity cost of the financial capital that has been invested in the business. Suppose, for instance, that Flavio used €300,000 of his savings to buy his pizza factory from the previous owner. If Flavio had instead left this money deposited in a savings account that pays an interest rate of 5 per cent, he would have earned €15,000 per year (assuming simple interest). To own his pizza factory, therefore, Flavio has given up €15,000 a year in interest income. This foregone €15,000 is an implicit opportunity cost of Flavio's business. An economist views the €15,000 in interest income that Flavio gives up every year as a cost of his business, even though it is an implicit cost. Flavio's accountant, however, will not show this €15,000 as a cost, because no money flows out of the business to pay for it.

To explore further the difference between economists and accountants, let us change the example slightly. Suppose now that Flavio did not have the entire €300,000 to buy the factory but, instead, used €100,000 of his own savings and borrowed €200,000 from a bank at an interest rate of 5 per cent. Flavio's accountant, who only measures explicit costs, will now count the €10,000 interest paid on the bank loan every year as a cost because this amount of money now flows out of the pizza business. By contrast, according to an economist, the opportunity cost of owning the business is still €15,000. The opportunity cost equals the interest on the bank loan (an explicit cost of €10,000) plus the foregone interest on savings (an implicit cost of €5,000).

Economic Profit Versus Accounting Profit

Now let us return to the firm's objective: profit. Because economists and accountants measure costs differently, they also measure profit differently. An economist measures a firm's **economic profit** as the firm's total revenue minus all the opportunity costs (explicit and implicit) of producing the goods and services sold. An accountant measures the firm's **accounting profit** as the firm's total revenue minus only the firm's explicit costs.

> **economic profit** total revenue minus total cost, including both explicit and implicit costs
> **accounting profit** total revenue minus total explicit cost

Figure 9.1 summarizes this difference. Notice that because the accountant ignores the implicit costs, accounting profit is usually larger than economic profit. For a business to be profitable from an economist's standpoint, total revenue must cover all the opportunity costs, both explicit and implicit.

> **SELF TEST** Richard Collishaw is a dairy farmer who is also a skilled metal worker. He makes unique garden sculptures that could earn him €40 an hour. One day, he spends 10 hours working with his dairy herd. The cost of operating the machinery and plant used in the milking process is €200. What opportunity cost has he incurred? What cost would his accountant measure? If the milk produced will yield €400 in revenue, does Richard earn an accounting profit? Does he earn an economic profit? Would you advise Richard to continue as a farmer or switch to metal working?

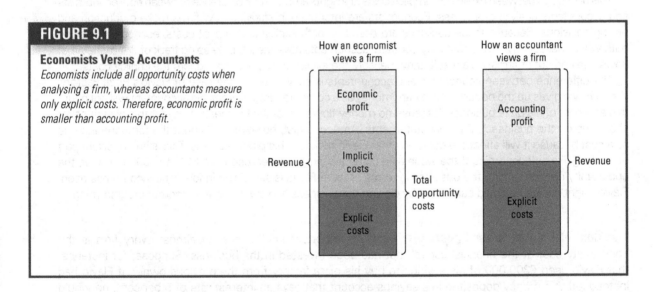

FIGURE 9.1

Economists Versus Accountants
Economists include all opportunity costs when analysing a firm, whereas accountants measure only explicit costs. Therefore, economic profit is smaller than accounting profit.

PRODUCTION AND COSTS

We have seen how the transformation process is characterized by firms buying inputs to carry out production. There is a relationship between the amount of inputs used, the cost of production and the amount produced. In this section, we examine the link between a firm's production process and its total cost using Flavio's Pizza Factory as an example.

The Production Function

The relationship between factor inputs can be expressed as a mathematical relationship called a production function. The **production function** shows the amount of output which can be produced given different combinations of factor inputs, land, labour and capital. If Flavio increases the number of people working in his factory, then the amount of pizzas produced would be likely to rise. However, it could also be possible that Flavio might decide to cut the number of workers he employs and buy a machine which can do their job and still increase the amount of pizzas produced.

> **production function** the relationship between the quantities of inputs used to make a good and the quantity of output of that good

In reality, firms face complex decisions over how to organize production and a whole discipline has grown up around this called operations management, which in turn is closely linked to organizational behaviour and organizational design. Some firms rely on large amounts of labour compared to other factors for production and are referred to as *labour intensive*, whereas other firms have relatively small amounts of labour but very large amounts of capital and are referred to as *capital intensive*.

Let us assume there are two factor inputs, labour (*L*) and capital (*K*). The production function can be expressed as follows:

$$Q = f(L_1, K_1)$$

This states that the level of output (*Q*) is dependent upon the amount of labour and capital employed. More complex production functions are developed which include more specific dependent variables which can have different values. For example, we can specify a particular amount of labour, a particular amount of capital, as well as a certain quantity of land. Using this as a model, we can then vary some factor inputs while holding the others constant and analyze the effect on the level of output.

Obviously, this is a very simple introduction to the production function and as we will see later, changing the amount of factor inputs can have different consequences.

 WHAT IF... Flavio's factory had a total floor area of 2,000 square metres, three-quarters of which was taken up with machinery. Flavio employs 50 workers. If he employs a further ten workers, will output of pizzas increase? If he employs another ten will output continue to increase? What do you think would happen to output if Flavio continued to increase the number of workers he employs?

The Short Run and the Long Run

In business, the distinction between the short run and the long run is of considerable importance. The **short run** is defined as the period of time in which some factors of production cannot be altered. The **long run** is that period of time when all factors of production can be altered. The distinction is really conceptual rather than specific. Many businesses will not be able to calculate the short run or the long run, but they will know that the distinction will be an important consideration in their decision making. The long run for a market trader in a local street market may be weeks or months, but for an energy supply company could be 20 years.

> **short run** the period of time in which some factors of production cannot be changed
> **long run** the period of time in which all factors of production can be altered

In the short run, let us assume that the size of Flavio's factory is fixed (a not unreasonable assumption) but that Flavio can vary the quantity of pizzas produced by changing the number of workers.

Table 9.1 shows how the quantity of pizzas Flavio's factory produces per hour depends on the number of workers. As you see in the first two columns, if there are no workers in the factory Flavio produces no pizzas. When there is one worker he produces 50 pizzas. When there are two workers he produces 90 pizzas, and so on.

TABLE 9.1	A Production Function and Total Cost: Flavio's Pizza Factory				
Number of workers	Output (quantity of pizzas produced per hour)	Marginal product of labour (per hour)	Cost of factory (€)	Cost of workers (€)	Total cost of inputs (cost of factory + cost of workers) (€)
0	0	50	30	0	30
1	50	40	30	10	40
2	90	30	30	20	50
3	120	20	30	30	60
4	140	10	30	40	70
5	150		30	50	80

Figure 9.2 (panel (a)) presents a graph of these two columns of numbers. The number of workers is on the horizontal axis, and the number of pizzas produced is on the vertical axis. This is a graph of the production function.

FIGURE 9.2

Flavio's Production Function

The production function in panel (a) shows the relationship between the number of workers hired and the quantity of output produced. Here the number of workers employed (on the horizontal axis) is from the first column in Table 9.1, and the quantity of output produced (on the vertical axis) is from the second column. The production function gets flatter as the number of workers increases, which reflects diminishing marginal product. The total cost curve in panel (b) shows the relationship between the quantity of output produced and total cost of production. Here the quantity of output produced (on the horizontal axis) is from the second column in Table 9.1, and the total cost (on the vertical axis) is from the sixth column. The total cost curve gets steeper as the quantity of output increases because of diminishing marginal product.

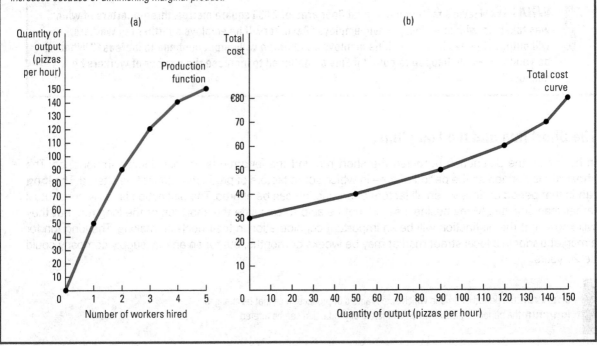

If Flavio can estimate his production function, how would such information help him in his decision making? This is what we are trying to model. Remember that a model is a representation of reality. No one is suggesting that every firm or business person sits down, works out production functions and graphs them (although there are plenty of examples of very sophisticated analysis of this sort which does take place), but the important thing from our perspective is the conceptualization of the decision making process.

Decision making may involve Flavio thinking at the margin. If you were Flavio you might want to have some understanding of the effect on the amount of pizzas produced of employing an extra worker. You might also want to compare this outcome with how much you had to pay the extra worker. To help make these decisions, the third column in Table 9.1 gives the marginal product of a worker. The **marginal product** of any input in the production process is the increase in the quantity of output obtained from one additional unit of that input. Employing the first worker adds 50 pizzas per hour to total production. Hiring the second worker increases pizza production from 50 to 90, so the marginal product of this second worker is 40 pizzas. Notice that as the number of workers increases, the marginal product of each successive worker declines. The second worker has a marginal product of 40 pizzas, the third, 30 pizzas and the fourth, 20 pizzas. This property of the production function is called **diminishing marginal product**. At first, when only a few workers are hired, they have easy access to Flavio's kitchen equipment. As the number of workers increases, additional workers have to share equipment and work in more crowded conditions. Hence, as more and more workers are hired, each additional worker contributes less to the production of pizzas.

> **marginal product** the increase in output that arises from an additional unit of input
> **diminishing marginal product** the property whereby the marginal product of an input declines as the quantity of the input increases

Diminishing marginal product is also apparent in Figure 9.2 (panel (a)). The production function's slope ('rise over run') tells us the change in Flavio's output of pizzas ('rise') for each additional input of labour ('run'). That is, the slope of the production function measures the marginal product of a worker. As the number of workers increases, the marginal product declines and the production function becomes flatter.

From the Production Function to the Total Cost Curve

The last three columns of Table 9.1 are reproduced as a graph in Figure 9.2 (panel (b)) to show Flavio's cost of producing pizzas. In this example, the cost of operating the factory is €30 per hour and the cost of a worker is €10 per hour. If Flavio hires 1 worker, his total cost is €40. If he hires 2 workers, his total cost is €50, and so on. With this information, the table now shows how the number of workers Flavio hires is related to the quantity of pizzas he produces and to his total cost of production.

We are interested in studying firms' production and pricing decisions. For this purpose, the most important relationship in Table 9.1 is between quantity produced (in the second column) and total costs (in the sixth column). Panel (b) of Figure 9.2 graphs these two columns of data with the quantity produced on the horizontal axis and total cost on the vertical axis. This graph is called the *total cost curve*.

Now compare the total cost curve in panel (b) of Figure 9.2 with the production function in panel (a). These two curves are opposite sides of the same coin. The total cost curve gets steeper as the amount produced rises, whereas the production function gets flatter as production rises. These changes in slope occur for the same reason. High production of pizzas means that Flavio's kitchen is crowded with many workers. Because the kitchen is crowded, each additional worker adds less to production, reflecting diminishing marginal product. Therefore, the production function is relatively flat. Now turn this logic around: when the kitchen is crowded, producing an additional pizza requires a lot of additional labour and is thus very costly. Therefore, when the quantity produced is large, the total cost curve is relatively steep.

> **SELF TEST** If Farmer Schmidt plants no seeds on his farm, he gets no harvest. If he plants 1 bag of seeds he gets 3 tonnes of wheat. If he plants 2 bags he gets 5 tonnes. If he plants 3 bags he gets 6 tonnes. A bag of seeds is priced at €100, and seeds are his only cost. Use these data to graph the farmer's production function and total cost curve. Explain their shapes.

THE VARIOUS MEASURES OF COST

Our analysis of Flavio's Pizza Factory demonstrated how a firm's total cost reflects its production function. From data on a firm's total cost we can derive several related measures of cost. To see how these related measures are derived, we consider the example in Table 9.2. Workers at Flavio's factory regularly use Lia's Coffee Bar.

TABLE 9.2   **The Various Measures of Cost: Lia's Coffee Bar**

Quantity of coffee (cups per hour)	Total cost (€)	Fixed cost (€)	Variable cost (€)	Average fixed cost (€)	Average variable cost (€)	Average total cost (€)	Marginal cost (€)
0	3.00	3.00	0.00	–	–	–	
							0.30
1	3.30	3.00	0.30	3.00	0.30	3.30	
							0.50
2	3.80	3.00	0.80	1.50	0.40	1.90	
							0.70
3	4.50	3.00	1.50	1.00	0.50	1.50	
							0.90
4	5.40	3.00	2.40	0.75	0.60	1.35	
							1.10
5	6.50	3.00	3.50	0.60	0.70	1.30	
							1.30
6	7.80	3.00	4.80	0.50	0.80	1.30	
							1.50
7	9.30	3.00	6.30	0.43	0.90	1.33	
							1.70
8	11.00	3.00	8.00	0.38	1.00	1.38	
							1.90
9	12.90	3.00	9.90	0.33	1.10	1.43	
							2.10
10	15.00	3.00	12.00	0.30	1.20	1.50	

The first column of the table shows the number of cups of coffee that Lia might produce, ranging from 0 to 10 cups per hour. The second column shows Lia's total cost of producing coffee. Figure 9.3 plots Lia's total cost curve. The quantity of coffee (from the first column) is on the horizontal axis, and total cost (from the second column) is on the vertical axis. Lia's total cost curve has a shape similar to Flavio's. In particular, it becomes steeper as the quantity produced rises, which (as we have discussed) reflects diminishing marginal product.

FIGURE 9.3

Lia's Total Cost Curve
Here the quantity of output produced (on the horizontal axis) is from the first column in Table 9.2, and the total cost (on the vertical axis) is from the second column. As in Figure 9.2, the total cost curve gets steeper as the quantity of output increases because of diminishing marginal product.

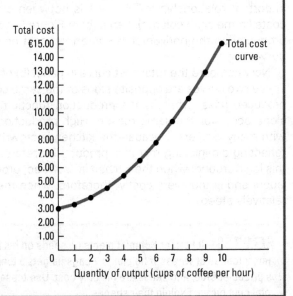

Fixed and Variable Costs

Lia's total cost can be divided into two types. Some costs, called **fixed costs**, are not determined by the amount of output produced; they can change but not as a result of changes in the amount produced. They are incurred even if the firm produces nothing at all. Lia's fixed costs include any rent she pays because this cost is the same regardless of how much coffee Lia produces. Similarly, if Lia needs to hire staff to serve the drinks, regardless of the quantity of coffee sold, the worker's salary is a fixed cost. The third column in Table 9.2 shows Lia's fixed cost, which in this example is €3.00.

> **fixed costs** costs that are not determined by the quantity of output produced

Some of the firm's costs, called **variable costs**, change as the firm alters the quantity of output produced. Lia's variable costs include the cost of coffee beans, water, milk, sugar and paper cups: the more coffee Lia makes, the more of these items she needs to buy. Similarly, if Lia pays her workers overtime to make more coffee, the wages of these workers are variable costs. The fourth column of the table shows Lia's variable cost. The variable cost is 0 if she produces nothing, €0.30 if she produces one cup of coffee, €0.80 if she produces two cups and so on.

> **variable costs** costs that are dependent on the quantity of output produced

A firm's total cost is the sum of fixed and variable costs. In Table 9.2 total cost in the second column equals fixed cost in the third column plus variable cost in the fourth column.

Average and Marginal Cost

As the owner of her firm, Lia has to decide how much to produce. A key part of this decision is how her costs will vary as she changes the level of production. In making this decision, Lia might ask two questions about the cost of producing coffee:

- How much does it cost to make the typical cup of coffee?
- How much does it cost to increase production of coffee by one cup?

Although at first these two questions might seem to have the same answer, they do not. Both answers will turn out to be important for understanding how firms make production decisions.

To find the cost of the typical unit produced, we would divide the firm's total costs by the quantity of output it produces. For example, if the firm produces 2 cups per hour, its total cost is €3.80, and the cost of the typical cup is €3.80/2, or €1.90. Total cost divided by the quantity of output is called **average total cost**. Because total cost is just the sum of fixed and variable costs, average total cost can be expressed as the sum of average fixed cost and average variable cost. **Average fixed cost** is the fixed cost divided by the quantity of output, and **average variable cost** is the variable cost divided by the quantity of output.

> **average total cost** total cost divided by the quantity of output
> **average fixed cost** fixed costs divided by the quantity of output
> **average variable cost** total variable cost divided by the quantity of output

Although average total cost tells us the cost of the typical unit, it does not tell us how much total cost will change as the firm alters its level of production. The last column in Table 9.2 shows the amount that total cost rises when the firm increases production by one unit of output. This number is called **marginal cost**. For example, if Lia increases production from 2 to 3 cups, total cost rises from €3.80 to €4.50, so the marginal cost of the third cup of coffee is €4.50 minus €3.80, or €0.70.

> **marginal cost** the increase in total cost that arises from an extra unit of production

It may be helpful to express these definitions mathematically:

Average total cost = Total cost/Quantity

$$ATC = \frac{TC}{Q}$$

and:

Marginal cost = Change in total cost/Change in quantity

$$MC = \Delta TC / \Delta Q$$

Here the Greek letter delta Δ represents 'the change' in a variable. These equations show how average total cost and marginal cost are derived from total cost. Average total cost tells us the cost of a typical unit of output if total cost is divided evenly over all the units produced. Marginal cost tells us the increase in total cost that arises from producing an additional unit of output.

> **PITFALL PREVENTION** Confusion over the relationship between average and marginal concepts is a source of problems in understanding. It is often useful to think of the relationship using something concrete from your own life such as the relationship between the average number of goals/points you score in a hockey, rugby, netball or football match (or whatever sport you take part in) and what happens to your average and marginal points/goal tally as you play additional games.

CASE STUDY   The Zero Marginal Cost Economy

In the analysis presented in this chapter so far, it is implied that firms have fixed costs, which will include the cost of setting up the business, and variable costs which are directly dependent on the amount produced. Variable costs and marginal costs are the same. As the business grows, it is possible for marginal costs to decline as firms increase productivity and efficiency. This allows the firm to be more competitive and to increase its margins.

This model of business costs is changing. Take the example of a taxi firm. Many taxi firms have a fleet of vehicles which they purchase. These vehicles may be subject to some sort of tax (in the UK, for example, vehicles are subject to excise duty), have to be insured and have other associated operating costs. Drivers must be hired and as a result the marginal cost of an additional taxi journey is likely to be positive. It might take many fares to cover the cost of the vehicle and its associated costs.

Compare this model to that of Uber. Uber provides the same sort of service as traditional taxi firms, but owns no vehicles and employs a relatively small number of people. If it wants to expand into a new area, it advertises for new drivers via its website and can, as a result, increase output at virtually no marginal cost to the business. This model is based on existing car owners 'sharing' their cars, all of which is based on communications developments provided by the internet.

Other products and services are beginning to grow in the same way. Software is increasingly being shared across development communities, 'hotel' accommodation is expanding in towns and cities through Airbnb, 'crowd funding' or 'crowd banking' is enabling businesses to secure investment at much lower cost than traditional banking, students can enrol for courses on MOOCs (massive online open courses), and the humble textbook is facing increasing competition from open source content.

As these types of developments take hold, the traditional model of marginal cost analysis becomes less relevant.

Is the way in which businesses are changing also resulting in near-zero marginal costs?

(Continued)

The idea of using the internet as a means of putting the demand for goods and services in touch with those who are willing and able to supply goods and services could result in significant changes to the way we understand business activity. Jeremy Rifkin has attempted to explore the consequences of the so called 'internet of things' and greater collaboration in his 2015 book *The Zero Marginal Cost Society*. Rifkin notes that developments in technology are helping to push marginal costs to almost zero, and the traditional analysis of markets becomes increasingly redundant. This is because the demand and supply of goods and services is not dependent on traditional market forces; Uber is not a 'traditional' taxi firm but still provides the means for people to get from A to B; Airbnb is not a traditional hotel but allows people to find and utilize relatively low priced accommodation. Goods and services which traditionally have had value in exchange now have value in sharing.

Questions

1 Take the example of a taxi firm which purchases a fleet of vehicles and hires drivers to operate the service it provides. Consider the fixed and variable costs that the firm incurs as part of its operations. Having considered these costs, what factors might the firm take into account in setting its price for passengers per mile travelled?

2 Compare the business model of the taxi firm in question 1 to the business model operated by ride-hailing services like Uber. Given the differences in the two models, how does a 'traditional' family taxi firm compete with the likes of Uber?

3 To what extent do you agree with Rifkin's view that marginal costs in many industries are being pushed to near zero and that traditional analysis of markets is becoming increasingly redundant?

FYI

The Mathematics of Margins

The concept of the margin refers to small changes in variables such as revenue and costs. We know that total revenue is a function of (is dependent upon) the price and the number of units sold. Total cost is a function of the factor inputs used in production given by the sum of the fixed and variable costs. Given that both total revenue and total cost are functions we can use calculus to derive the respective marginal revenue and marginal costs.

Consider the following inverse demand function (the demand function here is described as 'inverse' because price is expressed as the dependent variable and quantity as the independent variable):

$$P = 200 - 4Q$$

We know that $TR = P \times Q$

Substituting the demand function into the *TR* formula we get:

$$P = (200 - 4Q)\, Q$$

$$P = 200Q - 4Q^2$$

Using the power function rule outlined in Chapter 5, we can derive marginal revenue (*MR*) by:

$$MR = \frac{d(TR)}{dQ}$$

MR in the example above is:

$$\frac{d(TR)}{dQ} = 200 - 8Q$$

If demand was 10 pizzas, MR would be 200 − 8(10) = 120. If demand rose by one unit to 11 then total revenue would rise by 200 − 8(11) = 112.

We can apply a similar approach to deriving the marginal cost. Take the *TC* function:

$$TC = Q^2 + 14Q + 20$$

We can look at the expression $Q^2 + 14Q$ and conclude that this part of the function is where the value of Q is dependent on some factor and will vary. As a result, this is the variable cost component. The last term in the function, denoted by the value 20, is not dependent on Q and so is the fixed cost element. We know that when differentiating this term the result is zero. We would expect this to be the case because, by definition, fixed costs are not affected by changes in output. Marginal cost, therefore, relates to changes in the variable costs of production.

To derive the marginal cost, we use:

$$MC = \frac{d(TC)}{dQ}$$

Differentiating our *TC* function gives:

$$MC = \frac{d(TC)}{dQ} = 2Q + 14$$

If output is 15, then $MC = 2(15) + 14 = 44$
If output rises to 16 then $MC = 2(16) + 14 = 46$

Cost Curves and Their Shapes

Just as in previous chapters we found graphs of supply and demand useful when analysing the behaviour of markets, we will find graphs of average and marginal cost useful when analysing the behaviour of firms. Figure 9.4 graphs Lia's costs using the data from Table 9.2. The horizontal axis measures the quantity the firm produces, and the vertical axis measures marginal and average costs. The graph shows four curves: average total cost (*ATC*), average fixed cost (*AFC*), average variable cost (*AVC*) and marginal cost (*MC*).

FIGURE 9.4

Lia's Average Cost and Marginal Cost Curves
This figure shows the average total cost (ATC), average fixed cost (AFC), average variable cost (AVC) and marginal cost (MC) for Lia's Coffee Bar. All of these curves are obtained by graphing the data in Table 9.2. These cost curves show three features that are typical of many firms: (1) MC rises with the quantity of output. (2) The ATC curve is U-shaped. (3) The MC curve crosses the ATC curve at the minimum of ATC.

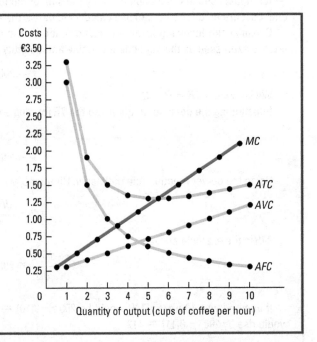

The cost curves shown here for Lia's Coffee Bar have some features that are common to the cost curves of many firms in the economy. Let us examine three features in particular: the shape of MC, the shape of ATC and the relationship between marginal and ATC.

Rising Marginal Cost Lia's MC rises with the quantity of output produced. This reflects the property of diminishing marginal product. When Lia is producing a small quantity of coffee she has few workers and much of her equipment is not being used. Because she can easily put these idle resources to use, the marginal product of an extra worker is large, and the MC of an extra cup of coffee is small. By contrast, when Lia is producing a large quantity of coffee, her bar is crowded with workers and most of her equipment is fully utilized. Lia can produce more coffee by adding workers, but these new workers have to work in crowded conditions and may have to wait to use the equipment. Therefore, when the quantity of coffee being produced is already high, the marginal product of an extra worker is low, and the MC of an extra cup of coffee is large.

U-Shaped Average Total Cost Lia's ATC curve takes on a U-shape. To understand why this is so, remember that ATC is the sum of AFC and AVC. AFC always declines as output rises because the fixed cost does not change as output rises and so gets spread over a larger number of units. AVC typically rises as output increases because of diminishing marginal product. ATC reflects the shapes of both AFC and AVC. As shown in Figure 9.4 at very low levels of output, such as 1 or 2 cups per hour, ATC is high because the fixed cost is spread over only a few units. ATC then declines as output increases until the firm's output reaches five cups of coffee per hour, when ATC falls to €1.30 per cup. When the firm produces more than six cups, ATC starts rising again because AVC rises substantially. If further units of output were produced the ATC curve would continue to slope upwards giving the typical U-shape referred to.

The bottom of the U-shape occurs at the quantity that minimizes ATC. This quantity is sometimes called the **efficient scale** of the firm. For Lia, the efficient scale is five or six cups of coffee. If she produces more or less than this amount, her ATC rises above the minimum of €1.30.

> **efficient scale** the quantity of output that minimizes ATC

The Relationship between Marginal Cost and Average Total Cost If you look at Figure 9.4 (or back at Table 9.2) you will see that whenever MC is less than ATC, ATC is falling. Whenever MC is greater than ATC, ATC is rising. This feature of Lia's cost curves is not a coincidence from the particular numbers used in the example: it is true for all firms and is a basic mathematical relationship.

To see why, think about averages and consider what happens to average cost as output goes up by one unit. If the cost of the extra unit is above the average cost of units produced up to that point, then it will tend to pull up the new average cost of a unit. If the new unit actually costs less than the average cost of a unit up to that point, it will tend to drag the new average down. The price of an extra unit is what economists call MC, so what we have just asserted is tantamount to saying that if MC is less than average cost, average cost will be falling; and if MC is above average cost, average cost will be rising.

This relationship between ATC and MC has an important corollary: the MC curve crosses the ATC curve at its minimum. Why? At low levels of output, MC is below ATC, so ATC is falling. After the two curves cross, MC rises above ATC. For the reason we have just outlined, ATC must start to rise at this level of output. Hence, at this point of intersection the cost of an additional unit is the same as the average and so the average does not change and the point is the minimum of ATC.

Typical Cost Curves

In the examples we have studied so far, the firms exhibit diminishing marginal product and, therefore, rising MC at all levels of output. Yet actual firms are often a bit more complicated than this. The principle of diminishing marginal product in the short run does hold, but when it occurs will vary depending on the type of firm and the nature of the production process. In many firms, diminishing marginal product does not start to occur until significant numbers of workers are hired. The particular features of the production process might mean that marginal product rises as additional workers are hired because a team of workers can divide tasks and work more productively than individual workers. Firms do analyze their cost structures and make decisions on changes based on how factor inputs can be better organized to increase productivity, and the principle of diminishing marginal product, while explained simply in our example, still holds and informs decision making even in complex business operations.

The table in Figure 9.5 shows the cost data for a firm, called Berit's Bagel Bin. These data are used in the graphs. Panel (a) shows how total cost (*TC*) depends on the quantity produced, and panel (b) shows average total cost (*ATC*), average fixed cost (*AFC*), average variable cost (*AVC*) and marginal cost (*MC*). In the range of output up to four bagels per hour, the firm experiences increasing marginal product, and the MC curve falls. After five bagels per hour, the firm starts to experience diminishing marginal product, and the marginal cost curve starts to rise. This combination of increasing then diminishing marginal product also makes the AVC curve U-shaped.

FIGURE 9.5

Berit's Cost Curves

Many firms, like Berit's Bagel Bin, experience increasing marginal product before diminishing marginal product and, therefore, have cost curves shaped like those in this Figure. Panel (a) shows how total cost (TC) depends on the quantity produced. Panel (b) shows how average total cost (ATC), average fixed cost (AFC), average variable cost (AVC) and marginal cost (MC) depend on the quantity produced. These curves are derived by graphing the data from the table. Notice that MC and AVC fall for a while before starting to rise.

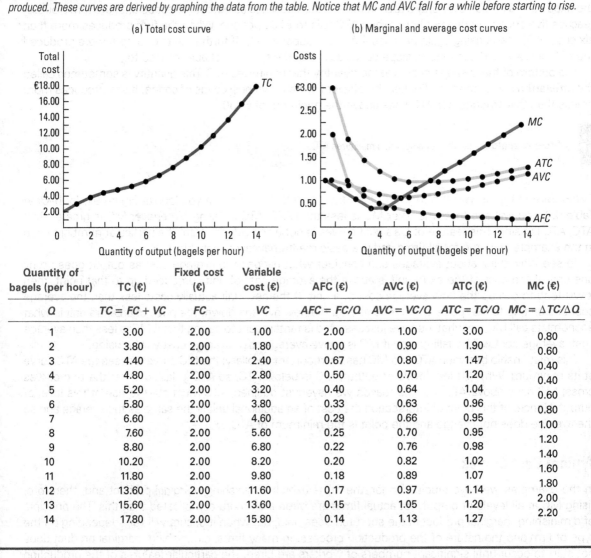

Quantity of bagels (per hour)	TC (€)	Fixed cost (€)	Variable cost (€)	AFC (€)	AVC (€)	ATC (€)	MC (€)
Q	TC = FC + VC	FC	VC	AFC = FC/Q	AVC = VC/Q	ATC = TC/Q	MC = ΔTC/ΔQ
1	3.00	2.00	1.00	2.00	1.00	3.00	
							0.80
2	3.80	2.00	1.80	1.00	0.90	1.90	
							0.60
3	4.40	2.00	2.40	0.67	0.80	1.47	
							0.40
4	4.80	2.00	2.80	0.50	0.70	1.20	
							0.40
5	5.20	2.00	3.20	0.40	0.64	1.04	
							0.60
6	5.80	2.00	3.80	0.33	0.63	0.96	
							0.80
7	6.60	2.00	4.60	0.29	0.66	0.95	
							1.00
8	7.60	2.00	5.60	0.25	0.70	0.95	
							1.20
9	8.80	2.00	6.80	0.22	0.76	0.98	
							1.40
10	10.20	2.00	8.20	0.20	0.82	1.02	
							1.60
11	11.80	2.00	9.80	0.18	0.89	1.07	
							1.80
12	13.60	2.00	11.60	0.17	0.97	1.14	
							2.00
13	15.60	2.00	13.60	0.15	1.05	1.20	
							2.20
14	17.80	2.00	15.80	0.14	1.13	1.27	

Despite these differences from our previous example, Berit's cost curves share the three properties that are most important to remember:

- MC eventually rises with the quantity of output.
- The ATC curve is U-shaped.
- The MC curve crosses the ATC curve at the minimum of ATC.

SELF TEST Suppose BMW's TC of producing four cars is €60,000 and its TC of producing five cars is €85,000. What is the ATC of producing five cars? What is the MC of the fifth car? Draw the MC curve and the ATC curve for a typical firm, and explain why these curves cross where they do.

COSTS IN THE SHORT RUN AND IN THE LONG RUN: ECONOMIES OF SCALE

Earlier in the chapter we noted the distinction between the short run and long run. We are now going to look in more detail at the relationship between the short and long run.

The Relationship Between Short Run and Long Run Average Total Cost

For many firms, the division of total costs between fixed and variable costs depends on the time horizon. Consider, for instance, a car manufacturer, such as Renault. Over a period of only a few months, Renault cannot adjust the number or sizes of its car factories. To increase output, it could try to make use of its existing plant and maybe hire more workers at the factories it already has. The cost of these factories is, therefore, a fixed cost in the short run. The investment in these factories represents sunk costs; Renault will have paid to set up these factories and these costs cannot be recovered or avoided. One of the features of sunk costs is that they should not influence future decision making. This is important when considering exiting a market. There might be a temptation to continue trying to produce a product for which the market no longer exists in the numbers needed to make it viable. If that is the case, it is more sensible to exit that market. Some businesses might attempt to continue because they feel that past investment spending, the sunk costs, must be justified in some way. It may be the case that continuing to pour money into a failing venture represents poor economic decision making. Making a decision to continue investing in a failing product or a declining market will not allow sunk costs to be recovered or to avoid these costs, hence these costs should not be a factor in decision making about future production.

Over a period of several years, Renault can expand the size of its factories, build new factories or close old ones. Thus, the cost of its factories is a variable cost in the long run. Because many input factors are fixed in the short run but variable in the long run, a firm's long run cost curves differ from its short run cost curves. Figure 9.6 shows an example. The figure presents three short run average total cost curves representing the cost structures for a small, medium and large factory. It also presents the long run average total cost curve. As the firm adjusts the size of the factory to the quantity of production, it moves along the long run curve, and it is adjusting the size of the factory to the quantity of production.

This graph shows how short run and long run costs are related. The long run average total cost curve is a much flatter U-shape than the short run average total cost curve. In addition, all the short run curves lie on or above the long run curve. These properties arise because firms have greater flexibility in the long run. In essence, in the long run, the firm chooses which short run curve it wants to use. But in the short run, it must use whatever short run curve it chose in the past.

The figure shows an example of how a change in production alters costs over different time horizons. When Renault wants to increase production from 1,000 to 1,200 cars per day, it has little choice in the short run but to hire more workers at its existing medium-sized factory. Because of diminishing marginal product, average total cost rises from €10,000 to €12,000 per car. In the long run, however, Renault can expand both the size of the factory and its workforce, and average total cost returns to €10,000.

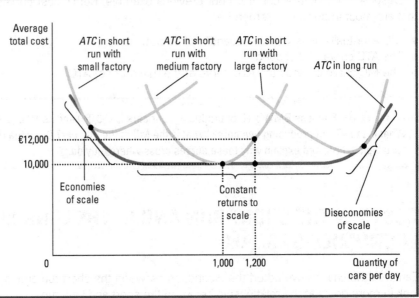

FIGURE 9.6

Average Total Cost in the Short and Long Runs
Because fixed costs are variable in the long run, the average total cost curve in the short run differs from the average total cost curve in the long run.

ECONOMIES AND DISECONOMIES OF SCALE

One of the consistent features in the development of businesses since the 1920s has been the tendency for firms to grow and become bigger, and to operate on a much bigger scale. One of the main reasons behind the growth of firms and the growth in the scale at which firms operate is because there are cost advantages. One thing to note at the outset is that it is clear that a firm operating at a large scale incurs higher total costs. Economies and diseconomies of scale, however, focus on the average or unit cost of production. A simple example serves to illustrate the principle. Assume there are two firms which employ a certain number of factor inputs, as shown in Table 9.3.

TABLE 9.3   Economies of Scale

	Capital	Land	Labour	Output	TC (€)	AC (€)
Firm A	5	3	4	100	57	0.57
Firm B	10	6	8	500	164	0.33

   Firm A employs 5 units of capital, 3 units of land and 4 units of labour and uses these factor inputs to produce 100 units of output. Firm B operates at a different scale. It employs double the number of factor inputs of capital, land and labour and uses these factor inputs to produce 500 units of output per time period.

   Let us assume that the cost of each unit of capital is €5, of land is €8 and labour €2 per unit per time period. The total cost of production for Firm A is €57 per time period and its average cost of production is thus €0.57 per unit. Firm B has a much higher total cost as might be expected given it employs more factor inputs. Its total costs are around 2.9 times that of Firm A. However, B is able to use those factor inputs to produce 5 times the output and as a result its unit costs are €0.33 per unit. By operating on a bigger scale, Firm B gains benefits of lower unit costs.

   A lower average or unit cost might give a firm an advantage both in terms of the margins it can make on each sale and the price it can charge to consumers. If it can charge a lower price, it might be better placed to capture market share and new business. **Economies of scale** are the advantages of large scale production that result in lower cost per unit produced. There are essentially two types of economies of scale: internal and external.

Internal Economies of Scale

Internal economies of scale arise from the growth of the firm. They are the cost advantages a firm can gain as it expands and finds more efficient and effective ways of producing. There are a number of sources of internal economies of scale.

> **economies of scale** the advantages of large scale production that result in lower cost per unit produced
> **internal economies of scale** the advantages of large scale production that arise through the growth of the firm

Technical Economies of Scale The basis of technical economies of scale is that machinery and other factor inputs can be utilized at bigger scales to bring down the unit cost of production. They can arise through different ways:

The Principle of Increased Dimensions The growth in carrying capacity of road, rail, sea and air freight has largely been driven by what is called the principle of increased dimensions. Assume that the dimensions of the trailer on a lorry are 10 metres in length, 2 metres wide and 4 metres high and that the trailer carries packages one metre cubed. The carrying capacity of the trailer is 80 cubic metres and so can carry 80 packages. If the dimensions of the trailer were doubled, the carrying capacity would now be $20 \times 4 \times 8 = 640m^3$. The carrying capacity has increased by 8 times and 640 packages could now be carried on each journey. The cost of producing the larger trailer would be higher as a result of doubling its dimensions, but it is unlikely that the cost would double. It is also unlikely that the cost of operating the lorry would double. Provided total costs increase by a smaller proportion than the increase in the carrying capacity, the unit cost will fall. The principle of increased dimensions is relevant to transport, freight, distribution and warehousing. Let us take another example using the transport industry. A single decker bus might cost €75,000 to buy and over the course of a year, cost €100,000 to operate. In that time, it carries 100,000 passengers. The total cost is, therefore, €175,000 for the year and the average cost of carrying each passenger is €1.75. If the firm were to use a double decker bus, the cost of buying such a vehicle might be €85,000 and the operating costs might also be higher at €110,000. The total cost, therefore, would be €195,000. However, if we assume that the double decker bus can carry twice the number of passengers, then the average cost of carrying each passenger becomes €0.975.

The Principle of Multiples The principle of multiples is based on the idea that firms operating at larger scales can make use of capital equipment more efficiently than small firms and reduce the unit cost as a result. For example, assume two firms are in the business of producing up-market soft drinks and that there are four core processes each driven by capital equipment which operates at different capacities as shown in Table 9.4.

TABLE 9.4   **The Principle of Multiples**

Machine A Bottling of drink	Machine B Capping of bottles	Machine C Labelling bottles	Machine D Packing bottles
Capacity = 1,000 per hour Cost = €1,000 per machine	Capacity = 2,000 per hour Cost = €500 per machine	Capacity = 1,500 per hour Cost = €1,500 per machine	Capacity = 3,000 per hour Cost = €2,000 per machine

Firm A is a small firm and is only able to afford to purchase one of each machine needed for the process. The maximum capacity it can operate at is 1,000 units per hour because it is constrained by the capacity of Machine A. To produce 1,000 units per hour incurs a total cost of €5,000. Its average cost per unit is therefore €5.

Firm B is a much larger firm and it can afford to employ multiple quantities of each machine to maximize efficiency. It can employ six of machine A, 3 of B, 4 of C and 2 of Machine D. As a result, its capacity is 6,000 units per hour. Notice that in this example, Firm A is using the lowest common multiple to maximize efficiency. In operating multiple machines, its total cost is €17,500 but as it produces 6,000 units, its average cost per unit is ≈ €2.92. Because Firm B can operate on a much larger scale, it can secure advantages in competing with Firm A in the market.

Indivisibility of Plant Many industries will see a mix of large scale operators and small scale ones and it is possible for each to be efficient. For example, in the manufacture of kitchens, there are some large scale, mass producers who make standardized units which can be mixed and matched for customers to create individual kitchens, and these mass producers can operate efficiently. There is also the space in the market for bespoke manufacturers who design kitchens for individual customers and focus on quality and the element of individualism as their competitive strategy. These smaller firms can also operate efficiently. There are some industries, however, which can only operate efficiently at large scale. One of the reasons is due to the indivisibility of plant. In the chemical industry, for example, the processes necessary for producing products on a commercial basis require large investment in capital equipment and it is not possible to produce commercially on a small scale. The capital equipment necessary for production cannot be broken down into smaller units.

Specialization Firms can gain unit cost advantages by employing specialists, which leads to increased efficiency. In many industries, few workers are responsible for the complete production process and many workers never see the end product to which their skills and effort have contributed. The production process is typically broken down into smaller processes with specialists employed at each stage. Such processes lend themselves to mass production and the spreading of costs across a large range of output. The proportionate increase in output from this division of labour is greater than the increase in costs and so unit costs decrease.

Commercial Economies of Scale Commercial economies of scale refers to the ability of firms operating at scale to be able to negotiate lower prices for supplies and other factor inputs. This is sometimes referred to as 'buying in bulk'. Supermarkets, for example, enter into agreements with farmers to purchase almost all of their output. For the farmer, the guarantee of selling all their product can be beneficial even if each unit sells for a lower price. If left entirely to the market, some farmers could be left with unsold output. If the output is perishable, then this would not only represent lost revenue but also some cost for disposal. Many firms operating at large scale will enter into agreements with suppliers to provide raw materials, component parts and so on, again providing benefits for both the supplier and the buyer. Car manufacturers, for example, might agree to buy sound systems from another firm for installation in its vehicles in large quantities. The individual price for each unit can be lower because of the volume of purchase and of better quality than the car firm could design and manufacture itself because of the specialism of the supplier.

Financial Economies of Scale Acquiring finance is a key element of most firms' operations. Typically, the smaller the firm the more risk associated with it from the lenders' perspective. Firms operating at scale tend to be more secure. As a result, firms operating at scale may be in a position to negotiate cheaper finance deals and also have access to a wider range of finance options. For example, larger firms can issue bonds which can be bought and sold on the fixed income market, but issuing bonds is not something that small firms such as sole proprietorships (which outnumber large firms many times in most economies) can do. Large firms are also able to make use of specialists in corporate finance and employ specialist accountants in their finance teams, which can optimize the access to and use of finance to improve the efficiency of the firm and reduce its unit costs.

Managerial Economies of Scale As an extension to the idea of division of labour, large firms are able to employ specialists in different areas of the business with expertise that can help the business become more efficient. This might include specialists in human resources management, finance and accounting, marketing, sales, operations management and so on. While larger firms clearly spend more on recruiting these specialists compared to smaller firms, if the proportionate increase in output that results is greater than the additional cost, unit costs will fall. In many smaller firms, in contrast, some individuals might have to devote attention to many aspects of the business: ensuring the business pays the correct amount of tax, complying with laws and regulations, carrying out recruitment and so on, and this might not be as efficient as having specialists employed for each role.

Risk Bearing Economies of Scale Smaller firms tend to be associated with a greater risk of failure. Larger firms can mitigate against these risks through being in a position to diversify into different product areas so that they are not reliant on one product for their survival. If demand for one product were to fall, the firm could rely on other products to maintain their profitability and efficiency. Larger firms will also have operations across regions, countries and continents, and this can also help in managing swings in business activity. A downturn in the Latin American market, for example, might be offset by an upturn in a firm's Asian markets. Firms operating at scale can also invest in research and development (R&D) and on extending product ranges, which helps reduce risk further.

External Economies of Scale

External economies of scale are the advantages of large scale production that arise because of the growth of the industry as a whole. External economies of scale might be accessible to businesses because of the concentration of firms in an industry in a particular area or region. For example, the City of London has a concentration of financial firms in banking, accounting, insurance and finance. This concentration of firms provides benefits through the supply of skilled labour, the access to expertise, the benefits which derive from reputation, training facilities, infrastructure, and local knowledge and skills. The growth of certain ports has brought with it considerable investment in infrastructure in roads and rail which help improve the efficiency with which goods can be transported across countries. Information exchange across some industries can be highly developed with trade journals, R&D, market information and forecasting being shared across different firms. In agriculture, for example, farmers can access high quality information about prices, market supply forecasts and scientific developments which can help them to plan more efficiently and to maximize output and minimize inputs. In the north of England, there is a concentration of chemical plants around the River Tees. Chemical firms on Teesside can benefit from expertise in the emergency services who have been specifically trained to deal with fires or safety incidents involving chemicals. Firms may also be able to take advantage of local infrastructure or expertise in waste disposal, which makes it cheaper per unit compared to having to pay for these costs individually.

A Graphical Representation of Economies of Scale

We can use our knowledge of costs to look at how economies of scale can be represented graphically. In the short run, firms face at least some fixed factors of production and the average cost curve will be drawn under the assumption of these fixed factors. Firms operating at different scales will have different average cost curves, although the shape of the average cost curve (under the assumptions of the model) will still be a U-shaped curve. As firms change their scale of production, there can be benefits which reduce the average cost of production and we can identify a long run average cost (LRAC) curve. There will be some point at which further increases in the scale of production will not yield any significant unit cost benefits, referred to as the **minimum efficient scale**. Equally, we can refer to the **minimum efficient plant size**, which is the point where increasing the scale of production of an individual plant in an industry further yields no significant unit cost benefits.

When long run average total cost declines as output increases, there are said to be economies of scale. When long run average total cost rises as output increases, there are said to be **diseconomies of scale**. When long run average total cost does not vary with the level of output, there are said to be **constant returns to scale**. In the example of Figure 9.6, Renault has economies of scale at low levels of output, constant returns to scale at intermediate levels of output and diseconomies of scale at high levels of output.

> **minimum efficient scale** the point at which further increases in the scale of production will not yield any significant unit cost benefits
> **minimum efficient plant size** the point where increasing the scale of production of an individual plant in an industry further yields no significant unit cost benefits
> **diseconomies of scale** the property whereby long run average total cost rises as the quantity of output increases
> **constant returns to scale** the property whereby long run average total cost stays the same as the quantity of output changes

The Causes of Diseconomies of Scale Diseconomies of scale can arise because of *coordination problems* that are inherent in any large organization. Referring back to our example of Renault, the more cars Renault produces, the more stretched the management team becomes, and the less effective the managers become at keeping costs down. Communication between workers and management and between different functional areas become more difficult. This can result in decisions taking longer to implement, reduced flexibility in responding to customer and market changes, and rising unit costs.

In larger firms, worker motivation may be affected as they are more removed from the 'big picture' than may be the case in smaller firms. Some workers only ever see a small part of the whole production process and it becomes more difficult for them to feel part of the business and have any influence in the way the business develops and operates. This can result in lower productivity and alienation and, again, in rising unit costs.

Larger firms may also suffer from the problems of asymmetric information. When operations are on a large scale and scattered across many different countries, the actions of individuals employed by the firm become more difficult to control and monitor. Firms may have to put in place systems to monitor activity to try to encourage efficiency and effective decision making, but this can be expensive. Even with such monitoring systems, firms may still not be sure that individuals in key positions in the business will make decisions based on what is best for the business. Some individuals may make decisions based on their own self-interest or make decisions which are misguided and not beneficial to the business. For example, how do firms know that the recruitment process across all a business's global operations is carried out fairly and with improving productivity in mind, rather than any other personal reasons of the individuals involved? Is it necessary, for example, to increase the number of workers employed to improve productivity and efficiency, or is it more a case of some individuals seeking to boost their own status and power base?

> **?** **WHAT IF...** some senior managers in a firm abided by the rules of the firm's travel and expenses guide which says that for flights longer than six hours, they can book business class, but if business class is not available, first class flights can be taken. The managers have realized that if they delay making a booking for a flight, it is possible that all business class seats will be filled, which means they must travel first class. Is this an example of diseconomies of scale?

In 1966, Harvey Leibenstein coined the term 'X-efficiency' in a paper published in the *American Economic Review*. Leibenstein posited that some large firms may not be able, or have the incentive, to control costs as closely as traditional theory might suggest, which in turn results in higher unit cost. He used the term **X-inefficiency** to refer to this lack of incentive. The lack of incentive to control costs might be particularly prevalent in firms where competitive pressures are not so high and where firms might have a considerable degree of market power. X-efficiency might result, for example, from firms having excess labour, which lowers productivity; having marketing, entertainment, and travel and expenses costs which are not subject to close control; failing to seek out cheaper or better quality supplies; having poorer customer service; and lacking innovation and dynamism in a business in product development. If firms could operate at more efficient levels they are said to be experiencing X-inefficiency.

 X-inefficiency the failure of a firm to operate at maximum efficiency due to a lack of competitive pressure and reduced incentives to control costs

This analysis shows why long run average total cost curves are often U-shaped. At low levels of production, the firm benefits from increased size because it can take advantage of greater specialization. Coordination problems, meanwhile, are not yet acute. By contrast, at high levels of production, the benefits of specialization have already been realized, and coordination problems become more severe as the firm grows larger. Thus, long run average total cost is falling at low levels of production because of increasing specialization and rising at high levels of production because of increasing coordination problems.

The Implications of Economies of Scale

Imagine a firm which makes bricks. The firm's existing plant has a maximum capacity of 100,000 bricks per week and the total costs are €30,000 per week. The average cost for each brick, assuming the plant operates at full capacity, is therefore €0.30. The firm sets a price of €0.40 per brick giving it a profit margin of €0.10 per brick. If it sells all 100,000 bricks it produces each week, the total revenue per week will be €40,000.

Now imagine that in the long run the firm expands. It doubles the size of its plant. The total costs, obviously, increase – they are now using more land and putting up more buildings, as well as hiring extra labour and buying more equipment and raw materials. All this expansion will increase the total cost, but this doubling of capacity will not lead to a doubling of the cost.

Following this expansion, assume TC is now €50,000 per week. The expansion of the plant means that the firm can double its output so its capacity is now 200,000 bricks per week. The percentage increase in the total costs is less than the percentage increase in output. Total costs have risen by €20,000 or 66 per cent and total output by 100 per cent, which means that the average cost per brick is now €0.25.

The firm now faces two scenarios. In scenario 1, the firm could maintain its price at €0.40 and increase its profit margin on each brick sold from €0.10 to €0.15. Assuming it sells all the bricks it produces its revenue would increase to €80,000 per week. In scenario 2, the firm might choose to reduce its price to improve its competitiveness against its rivals. It could maintain its former profit margin of €0.10 and reduce the price to €0.35 improving the chances of increasing its competitiveness. In this case, if it sells all it produces, its revenue would be €70,000 per week.

What the firm chooses to do would be dependent on its competitive position. If it played a dominant role in the market it might be able to increase its price and still sell all it produces. If it was in a more competitive market it might not have sold all its capacity in the first place, so being able to reduce its price might mean that it can now increase sales against its rivals and increase its total revenue.

Economies of scale, therefore, occur where the proportionate rise in output as a result of the expansion or growth of the firm, as defined by a rise in all the factor inputs, is greater than the proportionate rise in costs as a result of the expansion.

SELF TEST If Airbus produces 9 jets per month, its long run total cost is €9.0 million per month. If it produces 10 jets per month, its long run total cost is €9.5 million per month. Does Airbus exhibit economies or diseconomies of scale?

CONCLUSION

The purpose of this chapter has been to develop some tools that we can use to study how firms make production and pricing decisions. You should now understand what economists mean by the term *costs* and how costs vary with the quantity of output a firm produces. To refresh your memory, Table 9.5 summarizes some of the definitions we have encountered. By themselves, of course, a firm's cost curves do not tell us what decisions the firm will make. But they are an important component of that decision.

TABLE 9.5   **The Many Types of Cost: A Summary**

Term	Definition	Mathematical description
Explicit costs	Costs that require an outlay of money by the firm	–
Implicit costs	Costs that do not require an outlay of money by the firm	–
Fixed costs	Costs that do not vary with the quantity of output produced	FC
Variable costs	Costs that do vary with the quantity of output produced	VC
Total cost	The market value of all the inputs that a firm uses in production	$TC = FC + VC$
Average fixed cost	Fixed costs divided by the quantity of output	$AFC = FC/Q$
Average variable cost	Variable costs divided by the quantity of output	$AVC = VC/Q$
Average total cost	TC divided by the quantity of output	$ATC = TC/Q$
Marginal cost	The increase in TC that arises from an extra unit of production	$\dfrac{d(TC)}{dQ}\ \Delta TC/\Delta Q$

SUMMARY

- Profit equals total revenue minus total cost.

- When analysing a firm's behaviour, it is important to include all the opportunity costs of production. Some of the opportunity costs, such as the wages a firm pays its workers, are explicit. Other opportunity costs, such as the wages the firm owner gives up by working in the firm rather than taking another job, are implicit.

- A firm's costs reflect its production process. A typical firm's production function gets flatter as the quantity of an input increases, displaying the property of diminishing marginal product. As a result, a firm's TC curve gets steeper as the quantity produced rises.

- A firm's TCs can be divided between fixed costs and variable costs. Fixed costs are costs that are not determined by the quantity of output produced. Variable costs are costs that directly relate to the amount produced and so change when the firm alters the quantity of output produced.

- From a firm's TC, two related measures of cost are derived. ATC is TC divided by the quantity of output. MC is the amount by which TC changes if output increases (or decreases) by one unit.

- When analysing firm behaviour, it is often useful to graph ATC and MC. For a typical firm, MC rises with the quantity of output. ATC first falls as output increases and then rises as output increases further. The MC curve always crosses the ATC curve at the minimum of ATC.

- As a firm grows in size and changes its scale of operations, it can benefit from economies of scale. If a firm's costs rise by a smaller proportion than an increase in output when it changes its scale of production, average or unit costs can fall.

- Economies of scale can be internal or external. Internal economies of scale arise from the growth of the firm, while external economies of scale arise from the growth of the industry.

- As firms grow in size, they can become unwieldy, difficult to coordinate and manage and communication can break down. This can lead to diseconomies of scale where unit costs rise as the scale of operations grow.

IN THE NEWS

Electric Vertical Takeoff and Landing Aircraft (eVTOLs)

The car revolutionized travel for millions of people around the world but its popularity has brought its own issues, not least the challenges motor vehicles provide with regard to pollution. In many towns and cities, roads are very busy and sometimes gridlocked. Many drivers stuck in traffic must have looked to the skies and wished they could fly to their destination. That wish may be within reach for some. Companies are developing electric vertical takeoff and landing aircraft (eVTOLs) that are powered by electricity and have the capacity to take off and land in relatively small areas. It has been reported that a number of airlines are exploring and investing in eVTOLs. In October 2022,

Could eVTOLs be the transport of the future?

US airline Delta announced it was partnering with an eVTOL manufacturer Joby, to develop a city to airport service initially targeting New York and Los Angeles. The service is designed to make what can be a stressful trip from home to the airport, stress free, by exploiting the technology to provide short-range journeys to and from the airport.

The cost of developing this type of technology is significant and there are also a number of challenges that exist before this type of service becomes a reality, but commentators note that this could become a reality before 2030 and that we

(*Continued*)

might expect to see this sort of technology used more extensively into the 2030s, maybe even becoming more widely utilized to begin to replace car journeys. The infrastructure requirements are going to be one of the major challenges, but equally, to make this type of technology viable, economies of scale, both internal and external, are going to be crucial. Such services would have to operate on a large scale to bring down the unit costs and thus allow operators to charge affordable prices to customers. The idea might sound like science fiction but at one stage in the human past, so did the idea of a motor vehicle and an aeroplane!

Questions

1 Consider the plan to provide a short-range travel service using eVTOLs from major city centres to airports as planned by the Delta/Joby partnership. Comment on the type of fixed costs incurred in such a project. How important do you think that the fixed costs are likely to be in whether the planned service becomes a reality?

2 Assume that the plan to offer eVTOL services from home to airport becomes a reality. Comment on the importance of understanding marginal costs in operating such a service.

3 Economies of scale are likely to be important in whether the idea of this type of service ever becomes a reality. What sort of internal economies of scale might a company developing this type of transport look to exploit in achieving reductions in unit costs?

4 What sort of external economies of scale would be important in helping this type of service to become a reality and why do you think that Delta has initially chosen New York and Los Angeles as its two target cities to run this service?

5 'Economies of scale are pivotal in helping this type of idea become a reality.' Comment on this statement and on some of the other factors firms like Delta and Joby would need to consider in ensuring this type of development does not remain just a dream.

References: www.cnbc.com/2022/12/03/how-electric-air-taxis-could-shake-up-the-airline-industry.html (accessed 7 June 2023). https://news.delta.com/delta-joby-aviation-partner-pioneer-home-airport-transportation-customers (accessed 7 June 2023).

QUESTIONS FOR REVIEW

1 What is the relationship between a firm's total revenue, total cost and profit?

2 What is the difference between 'economic profit' and 'accounting profit'?

3 Draw a production function that exhibits diminishing marginal product of labour. Draw the associated total cost curve. (In both cases, be sure to label the axes.) Explain the shapes of the two curves you have drawn.

4 Define total cost, average total cost and marginal cost. How are they related?

5 Draw the marginal cost and average total cost curves for a typical firm. Explain why the curves have the shapes that they do and why they cross where they do.

6 How and why does a firm's average total cost curve differ in the short run and in the long run?

7 Explain why the marginal cost curve must cut the average cost curve at its lowest point.

8 What is the difference between internal and external economies of scale?

9 In what ways can economies of scale be of benefit to firms?

10 What are diseconomies of scale and how and why do they typically arise?

PROBLEMS AND APPLICATIONS

1 This chapter discusses many types of costs: opportunity cost, total cost, fixed cost, variable cost, average total cost and marginal cost. Fill in the type of cost that best completes each phrase below.

a. The true cost of taking some action is its _____.
b. _____ is falling when MC is below it, and rising when MC is above it.
c. A cost that does not depend on the quantity produced is a _____.
d. In the breakfast cereal industry in the short run, _____ includes the cost of cereals such as wheat and corn and sugar, but not the cost of the factory.
e. Profits equal total revenue minus _____.
f. The cost of producing an extra unit of output is the _____.

2 Patrice is thinking about opening a café. He estimates that it would cost €500,000 per year to rent the premises, buy the equipment to make hot drinks and snacks and to buy in the ingredients. In addition, he would have to leave his €50,000 per year job as an accountant.

a. Define opportunity cost.
b. What is Patrice's opportunity cost of running the café for a year? If Patrice thought he could sell €510,000 worth of coffee and snacks in a year, should he open the café? Explain your answer.

3 A commercial fisher notices the following relationship between hours spent fishing and the quantity of fish caught:

Hours	Quantity of fish (in kg)
0	0
1	10
2	18
3	24
4	28
5	30

a. What is the marginal product of each hour spent fishing?
b. Use these data to graph the fisher's production function. Explain its shape.
c. The fisher has a fixed cost of €10 (their fishing rod). The opportunity cost of their time is €5 per hour. Graph the fisher's total cost curve. Explain its shape.

4 Clean Sweep is a company that makes brooms and then sells them door-to-door. Here is the relationship between the number of workers and Clean Sweep's output in a given day:

Workers	Output	Marginal product	Average total cost	Marginal cost
0	0			
1	20			
2	50			
3	90			
4	120			
5	140			
6	150			
7	155			

a. Fill in the column of marginal product. What pattern do you see? How might you explain it?
b. A worker costs €100 a day, and the firm has fixed costs of €200. Use this information to calculate TC at each level of output.
c. Fill in the column for ATC. (Recall that $ATC = TC/Q$.) What pattern do you see?
d. Now fill in the column for MC. (Recall that $MC = \Delta TC/\Delta Q$.) What pattern do you see?
e. Compare the column for marginal product and the column for MC. Explain the relationship.
f. Compare the column for ATC and the column for MC. Explain the relationship.

5 Consider the following cost information for a pizzeria:

Q (dozens)	Total cost (€)	Variable cost (€)
0	300	0
1	350	50
2	390	90
3	420	120
4	450	150
5	490	190
6	540	240

a. What is the pizzeria's fixed cost?

b. Construct a table in which you calculate the MC per dozen pizzas using the information on TC. Also calculate the MC per dozen pizzas using the information on variable cost. What is the relationship between these sets of numbers? Comment.

6 Healthy Harry's Juice Bar has the following cost schedules:

Q (vats)	Variable cost (€)	Total cost (€)
0	0	30
1	10	40
2	25	55
3	45	75
4	70	100
5	100	130
6	135	165

a. Calculate AVC, ATC and MC for each quantity.

b. Graph all three curves. What is the relationship between the MC curve and the ATC curve? Between the MC curve and the AVC curve? Explain your answer.

7 Consider the following inverse demand function:

$$P = 60 - 0.5Q_D$$

Use this function to derive the MR and state what MR for the firm would be if demand increased from 100 to 101 units.

8 Consider the following TC function:

$$TC = 4Q^2 + 6$$

a. What are the fixed costs of this firm?

b. Derive the MC function.

c. What is the MC if output rises from 2,000 to 2,001 units?

9 One of the biggest challenges facing firms as they expand their operations is the possibility of diseconomies of scale setting in. What do you think are the main diseconomies of scale and how might a firm seek to reduce their impact? Use a specific example as part of your answer.

10 Consider an industry which has expanded rapidly in recent years and where the benefits of economies of scale have led to a substantial reduction in unit costs.

a. What would you expect to happen to the number of firms in this industry over this time period?

b. Given your answer to a., does this suggest that economies of scale are not always beneficial to the economy as a whole? Explain your answer.

c. As the industry continues to expand, what might be the effects on competition in the industry and the effect on consumers as a result?

10 BUSINESS GOALS AND BEHAVIOUR

THE GOALS OF FIRMS

It might seem obvious that businesses exist to make profits and, indeed, for many that is a key requirement. However, it is too simplistic to analyze business just based on that assumption. Changes since the early 1990s have led to businesses in the private sector having to balance a wider range of objectives along with making a profit. As noted in Chapter 1, for some businesses, other aims take priority and in the public sector, simply covering cost may be an aim as part of the overall priority of providing products which benefit society. We have also seen that a market mechanism can allocate products efficiently, but when imperfections exist the market may not work as effectively in allocating scarce resources. In some cases, the government steps in to regulate or influence market outcomes. There are some products which have characteristics which make it very difficult for the market to work at all. In those cases, the government may have to provide for the needs of its citizens. We can identify different types of products by looking at two characteristics:

- Is the good **excludable**? Can people who do not pay for the use of a good be prevented from using the good or gaining benefit from it?
- Is the good **rival**? Does one person's use of the good diminish another person's ability to use it?

> **excludable** the property of a good whereby a person can be prevented from using it or gaining benefit when they do not pay for it
> **rival** the property of a good whereby one person's use diminishes other people's use

Using these two characteristics, we can further categorize goods in four ways:

1. **Private goods** are both excludable and rival. Consider a chocolate bar, for example. A chocolate bar is excludable because it is possible to prevent someone else from eating it. You just don't give it to them. A chocolate bar is rival because if one person eats it, another person cannot eat the same bar.
2. **Public goods** are neither excludable nor rival. That is, people cannot be prevented from using a public good, and one person's use of a public good does not reduce another person's ability to use it. For example, a country's national defence system protects all the country's citizens equally. The fact that one person is being defended does not affect whether or not another citizen is defended.
3. **Common resources** are rival but not excludable. For example, fish in the ocean are a rival good: when one person catches fish, there are fewer fish for the next person to catch. Yet these fish are not an excludable good because, given the vast size of an ocean, it is difficult to stop fishers from taking fish out of it when, for example, they have not paid for a licence to do so.
4. When goods are excludable but not rival, they are examples of a *natural monopoly* and are also referred to as **club goods**. For instance, consider fire protection in a small town. It is easy to exclude people from using this good: the fire service can just let their house burn down. Yet fire protection is not rival. Firefighters spend much of their time waiting for a fire, so protecting an extra house is unlikely to reduce the protection available to others. In other words, once a town has paid for the fire service, the additional cost of protecting one more house is small. Other club goods include fibre and wireless internet provision, cinemas and toll roads.

In this chapter, we are going to look at the wide range of factors that might drive business activity primarily through the provision of private goods.

> **private goods** goods that are both excludable and rival
> **public goods** goods that are neither excludable nor rival
> **common resources** goods that are rival but not excludable
> **club goods** goods that are excludable but non-rival

Aims and Objectives

As a general rule, **aims** are the long-term goals of the business. These aims are often captured in the business mission and vision statement. **Objectives** are the means by which a business will seek to achieve its aims. They are invariably measurable targets, set to help the business identify the extent to which it is on target to meet its aims.

> **aims** the long-term goals of a business
> **objectives** the means by which a business will be able to achieve its aims

Many firms will summarize their overall goals through a mission or vision statement. If you look at the mission statements of large businesses, it is likely that you will not find many instances where profit is specifically referred to. Instead it is likely that there will be references, in one form or another, to customers, environmental and social responsibility, quality, shareholder value, stakeholder well-being and to employees.

This highlights the complex web of stakeholder responsibilities which now guide many firms' long-term goals. Many of these goals are interlinked. References to 'economic success' or 'profitability', for example, are linked to shareholder value; quality may not only be associated with customer satisfaction but, depending on the definition, with social and environmental responsibility.

Strategies and Tactics

A **strategy** is generally regarded as being to do with the long term: where the business wants to be at some point in the future. A **tactic**, on the other hand, is seen more as a short-term framework for decision making. Tactics are the 'how' to the question posed by strategy, the 'where'. To get to where you want to be in the future (the strategy) requires certain steps to be put in place to enable the business to progress towards that place (the tactics).

> **strategy** a series of actions, decisions and obligations that lead to the firm gaining a competitive advantage and exploiting the firm's core competencies
>
> **tactic** short-term framework for decision making

The length of the time period which defines 'the future' is more difficult to identify and there is much debate about the use of the term. For example, we often hear sports managers talking of the 'strategy they devised for the game'. In this case is the 'future' the time period until the game has finished? If the 'strategy' is to win a particularly difficult game against fierce rivals, then in the context of decision making this could be seen as being 'long term'. The team manager will then employ tactics to use in the game to achieve the desired goal of winning the match. These tactics will be the 'how' in terms of what formation is put out, which players will play where, who marks whom, whether to focus on defence or attack, which particular opposition players to target to limit their influence on the game and the sort of 'plays', set piece moves, etc. that will be used at certain times in the game.

Others would argue that winning the game is not an example of strategy because it is not the long term. The long term would be where the team wants to be at the end of the season, what financial position it wants to be in, or where it wants to be in five years' time.

Because there is so much debate on these points we cannot come to any definitive conclusion and this should be borne in mind as you read this book and others; you are likely to see many different interpretations. For the purposes of this book we will use the definitions of strategy and tactics given above. We will also refer more generally to a firm having 'goals', which is a more generic term which can be understood by all and which does not embroil us in the debate over semantics. This is not meant to detract from the seriousness of the debate, however. Having a clear understanding of what is being done in a business, what decisions are being made, when and why, are all vitally important for business success. Equally it is very important to clearly define what we mean by the term 'success'. How is this success defined and what does it look like? Having a clear definition gives us a benchmark against which to judge the extent to which the goals have been achieved.

Despite the varying goals that exist, private sector firms must make a profit if they are to survive in the long run. Rarely will any business activity be able to continue if costs are consistently greater than revenues. Some private sector businesses whose primary aim is to provide some sort of social benefit will still have to at least cover their costs in the long run. These businesses may not refer to 'profit' but to 'surpluses' and seek to ensure that any surplus is reinvested back in to the business to help better achieve the social aim rather than be distributed among owners of the business.

There is, however, a theoretical point at which a firm can maximize its profit and this may be something that influences a wide range of business decision making, including how much to produce, what price to charge and how to monitor and control costs. In balancing out the other objectives a firm has, there will be an inevitable impact on profits. For example, if a firm expresses a goal to reduce its environmental impact then this is likely to have an impact on its costs, and this may mean that profit will be less than the maximum that could be made if this focus was not part of its decision making.

The Public Sector and the Private Sector

In Chapter 1 we introduced the distinction between the public sector and the private sector. Public sector provision of products might be through some sort of public corporation which is ultimately responsible to a national parliament, but which operates as an independent entity in a similar way to many private sector businesses. Day-to-day decisions are made by managers, but the overall finance for the business comes from a mixture of government funding and charges for products. The goals of such organizations may be to provide high quality services to customers at reasonable prices so that the operation can at least cover its costs. Any profit (or surplus) is used for reinvesting to improve the quality of the customer provision. These products are sometimes provided free at the point of use. In other cases consumers must pay a price, although the price might be much lower than would be the case if the product were provided by a private sector firm. Business activity in the public sector may take place because it is difficult to charge people for the products concerned because they are not excludable or rival, or people may not be able to afford to pay for them and so access to these products may be lower than is deemed desirable. Table 10.1 shows some typical examples of business activity which is carried out in the public sector across the Europe, Middle East and Africa (EMEA) territories. It is clear from this table that some of the goods provided are obviously public goods, while there are other examples where the goods are private goods but the public sector may choose to also provide them. This may be because some goods can be classed as merit goods. A **merit good** is one which could be provided by the private sector, but which may also be offered by the public sector because it is believed that a less than optimal amount would be available to the public if resource allocation was left entirely to the private sector. This may be because people either would not be able to afford them or because they do not see such purchases as a priority. For example, some people may choose not to take out private health insurance because they think that they will not get ill, or would rather spend their money on something that gives more immediate gratification. It is not until they get ill or have an accident and face health cost bills that they realize they may have made an unwise decision.

> **merit good** a good which could be provided by the private sector, but which may also be offered by the public sector because it is believed that a less than optimal amount would be available to the public if resource allocation was left entirely to the private sector

TABLE 10.1 **Business Activity in the Private and Public Sector**

Type of good	Public good or both public and private
Health care	Both
Dental care	Both
Pension provision	Both
Street lighting	Public
Roads	Both
Public parks	Public
Beaches	Both
Justice	Public
Police	Public
Refuse collection	Both
Education	Both

The examples given in Table 10.1 highlight how some goods can be both public and private goods, or obviously public goods. For example, street lighting is a public good because it is almost impossible for a private business to be able to provide this good and charge individuals for its use. Beaches, on the other hand, can be both a private good and a public good. Users can be charged for use if a business has bought a stretch of beach and can allow only certain people to use it following payment.

Many beaches are provided by the state for the benefit of all. Both private and public beaches have a cost of provision as they must be kept clean and have lifeguards and other safety features. In the case of public provision, the taxpayer will ultimately fund the cost, while if the beach was owned by a private firm the cost would be covered by the payments members make to access the beach.

In many countries, the public sector accounts for a significant proportion of business activity, as highlighted in Table 10.2 which shows government expenditures as a percentage of GDP in 2022 for a selection of countries.

TABLE 10.2	Government Expenditures as a Percentage of GDP (Selected Countries), 2022	

Country	Government expenditure as a percentage of GDP
Austria	51.6
Denmark	51.3
Germany	46.7
Greece	52.3
Iceland	45.9
Ireland	25.9
Italy	51.4
Kuwait	56.6
Netherlands	42.7
Norway	51.8
Poland	44.0
South Africa	32.6
Turkey	34.7
United Kingdom	42.3
United States	38.9

Source: www.heritage.org/index/explore?view=by-variables

Private sector businesses can be small firms owned by just one person, or large multinational businesses that operate around the world (globally). In the case of large businesses, there might be many thousands of owners involved. Few firms in the private sector can afford to take their eye off financial performance even if profit is not the major goal. We are going to split business goals into two sections, financial and non-financial objectives. It is important to remember there may be very close links between the two.

FINANCIAL OBJECTIVES

A key assumption of a competitive firm is that it seeks to maximize profits and does so at the output level where marginal cost equals marginal revenue. We will explore this idea in more detail later in the book. As we look at some other financial objectives of business, it is important to bear in mind some of the models being presented here are simply that: models. They will help to conceptualize what we mean by certain principles and to enable us to understand why businesses make some decisions. These models help explain a principle and so help us understand why, for example, a rail company might charge a different price for the same journey at different times of the day, or why an airline or holiday company will slash prices of seats or package holidays at the last minute, or why sometimes it is better to think about reducing output rather than constantly looking to increase it.

BREAK-EVEN ANALYSIS

When a new business starts up, or if an existing business decides to develop a new product, one initial goal may be to achieve break-even. Break-even refers to the output level at which the total costs of production are equal to the total revenue generated from selling that output. Many firms will look at break-even analysis as part of their planning tools. They can look at the variables involved and how different figures plugged into these variables can affect decision making.

Figure 10.1 shows how we can represent break-even graphically. The vertical axis shows both costs and revenues and the horizontal axis shows output and sales. A firm faces fixed costs which must be paid regardless of whether it produces any output. The fixed cost curve, FC, is represented as a horizontal line at a cost of C. Variable costs (VC) are zero when the firm produces no output but rise as output rises.

FIGURE 10.1

Break-Even Analysis

A break-even chart shows a firm's total cost, made up of FC and VC and its TR. The output level where TR = TC is the break-even point shown by output Q_{BE}. Any output level below Q_{BE} would mean that the firm was producing at a loss, the amount of the loss indicated by triangle A, because TC would be greater than TR, but any output above Q_{BE} would mean the firm was operating at a profit. At output level Q_1, the amount of profit is indicated by the shaded triangle B. The distance between Q_{BE} and Q_1 is called the margin of safety and denotes how far sales could fall before the firm starts to make losses.

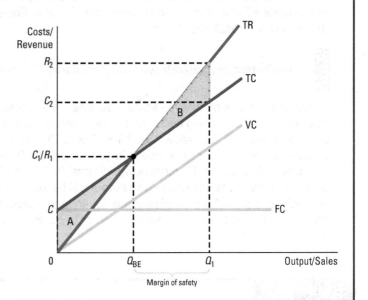

The *VC* curve shows these costs rising in direct proportion to output. Total cost is the sum of variable costs and fixed cost (*TC = VC + FC*) and so the *TC* curve has a vertical intercept equal to the level of fixed costs (*C*) and then rises as output rises. The vertical distance between the *TC* and *VC* curve is constant because of the proportional relationship between output and VC assumed above.

The *TR* curve is dependent on the price that the firm chooses to charge for its product. The higher the price charged the steeper the *TR* curve. The break-even level of output in Figure 10.1 is the amount where *TC = TR*, which is depicted as Q_{BE}. At this output level the *TC* are C_1 and the *TR* the same at R_1 shown by C_1/R_1 in Figure 10.1. At any output level below Q_{BE} the firm will find that its *TC* is greater than *TR* and so it will make a loss on that output. The range of output in which a loss is made is represented by the area shown by the shaded triangle A.

At output levels above Q_{BE}, for example Q_1, the firm's *TR*, shown by R_2, is greater than its *TC*, shown by C_2 and as a result it makes profits on this output equal to the value represented by the distance $R_2 - C_2$. The total amount of profit made at output Q_1 is represented by the shaded triangle B. If the firm did operate at Q_1 then it could experience a fall in sales and still be generating a profit, provided sales did not fall below the break-even output Q_{BE}. The distance between the break-even output and current production where *TR* is greater than *TC* is called the **margin of safety**.

> **margin of safety** the distance between the break-even output and current production where total revenue is greater than total cost

We can also look at the break-even point in a more mathematical way. A firm needs to aim to sell its output at a price greater than the variable cost of production.

Imagine a firm producing chocolate bars. The ingredient costs are €0.30 per bar and the direct labour costs are estimated at €0.10 per bar. Total VC are therefore €0.40 per bar. If the selling price of the chocolate bar is €0.60 then every bar sold covers the VC of production and leaves €0.20 which can be used to help pay off the fixed costs which also must be paid. This sum is called the **contribution**. The contribution is the difference between the selling price and the variable cost per unit. Knowing the contribution per unit, the break-even output can be given by:

$$\text{Break-even} = \frac{\text{Fixed costs}}{\text{Contribution per unit}}$$

The break-even point can be affected by the costs of production. Any change in fixed costs, for example, will shift the FC line up or down and thus the TC curve. Equally, changes in raw materials costs can affect the VC and as a result the TC curve.

> **contribution** the difference between the selling price and the variable cost per unit

The firm can use break-even analysis to assess the impact of the changes in costs and make decisions as a result. These planning decisions can be extended to analyze the possible effects of changes in prices and hence revenue. We know that $TR = P \times Q$. If a firm changes its price the shape of the TR curve will alter. If a firm chooses to increase its price, then the TR curve will pivot and become steeper, as shown in Figure 10.2. With the TR curve now indicated as TR_1, the firm will not have to sell as many products to cover its costs and so the break-even output will be lower at Q_{BE2}. A firm might choose to reduce its price, in which case the TR curve will become flatter. In this case, the TR curve will now be represented as TR_2 and the firm must sell more products in order to cover its costs, and so the break-even output would rise to Q_{BE3}.

FIGURE 10.2

The Effect on Break-Even Output of Changes in Price

Total revenue is found by multiplying price times the quantity sold. If the price is increased the TR curve will become steeper as shown by the curve TR$_1$. As a result, the firm would now only need to produce output Q$_{BE2}$ in order to break-even. If price was reduced the TR curve becomes flatter indicated by curve TR$_2$ and the firm would have to sell a higher output level Q$_{BE3}$ to break-even.

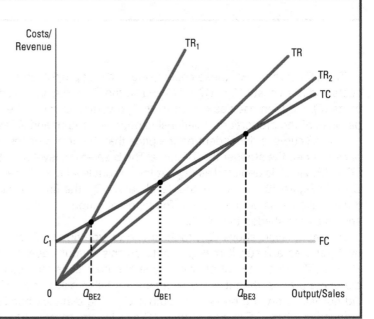

Limitations of Break-Even Analysis

As mentioned above, break-even is best seen as a planning tool and the outline given here is a simplistic one. There are a number of limitations with break-even analysis. First, there is an assumption that all output is sold. This is not the case for many firms where production takes place but products are not immediately sold and as such firms have stock (inventory).

Second, the shape of the TR and TC curves is unlikely to be smooth, as not every additional product a firm sells can be sold at the same price. Equally, given the dynamic nature of markets, any estimation of costs or revenues is not likely to be relevant for very long.

Third, we know that if a firm changes price, demand will be affected. Break-even analysis says nothing about what the effect of a price change on actual sales will be, nor how long it will take a firm to sell the output level to break-even. The effect on sales of a change in price will be dependent on the price elasticity of demand.

CASE STUDY   Break-even at the Box Office

The DC franchise is based on the production of films and television series about superhero characters from DC Comics. The films and television series are produced by DC Studios but distributed by Warner Bros. *Black Adam* starring Dwayne Johnson as a character given superhuman powers by Egyptian gods around 5,000 years ago and released from prison to bring justice to the modern world, was released in 2022. According to information provided by Collider, an entertainment news source, films like this need to generate revenue approximately twice their production and marketing budgets to break-even. Reports put the break-even revenue at around $600 million although other estimates put it lower at $400 million. According to Collider, in early December 2022 the film had generated around $387 million in global revenue and there were questions

The production costs of films can be massive and box-office receipts do not always meet expectations.

about whether the film would break-even. Even if it does, the film would be likely to be classed as a 'failure' in not generating the sort of revenues that were expected by the producers of the film. Its release in the latter part of October 2022 across around 4,400 US cinemas generated an average of almost $19,000 per cinema in the first week, but the numbers started to fall fairly rapidly after that as interest in the film waned. By late November, the number of cinemas carrying the film fell to around 2,600 with each cinema generating only around $1,400. The film did suffer from competition from other major releases that came out around the same time.

Questions

1   Assume an average price of a ticket to a cinema is $8. Further assume that the total production cost for *Black Adam* was $500 million. Using this information, calculate the break-even number of tickets that need to be sold to achieve break-even.

2   What assumptions might the film's producers have made prior to the decision to go ahead with the production of the film and how might these assumptions vary in reality?

3   If the film fails to reach its break-even revenue, how does this affect the producers of the film and how does it impact their decision making for future films?

4   What are the limitations of using break-even analysis in planning for the production of a product such as a film?

References: https://collider.com/black-adam-box-office-loss/ (accessed 7 June 2023).
www.the-numbers.com/movie/Black-Adam#tab=box-office (accessed 7 June 2023).

Revenue Maximization

In recent years, there has been criticism of some executives in businesses because their reward packages seem to have grown disproportionately in comparison to the performance of the business. One of the problems with this is understanding the definition of 'performance'. Executives might be persuaded to focus on goals which may give an impression of the business doing well, such as targeting sales. Other things being equal, a rise in sales is a 'good' thing, although of course this might not say anything about the cost involved in achieving any such increase in sales.

We know that total revenue is price multiplied by quantity sold. The goal of revenue maximization may also be referred to as *sales revenue maximization*. The principle is straightforward. There are three ways to increase sales: do something with price, do something to influence how much is sold, or do a combination of the two. We have seen how both reducing and increasing price can increase total revenue depending on the price elasticity of demand for the product. There are a number of pricing strategies that can be employed and we will look at these in more detail later in the book. Equally, firms will use a number of tactics to try to increase sales which will include other elements of the marketing mix apart from price:

- the product itself
- how consumers are able to access the product (place)
- how consumers are made aware of the product (promotion)
- the processes involved which include things like customer service commitments and the information customers can access
- a focus on the people who are involved in the business (the employees and physical evidence)
- how the firm is viewed in the eyes of its customers, and the extent to which the view conforms with prior assumptions. For example, going into a car showroom and seeing new cars which are dirty and poorly presented in a shabby environment would not be an image most car dealers would want to present.

Graphical Representation of Sales Revenue Maximization

We know from our look at the theory of demand that to increase demand, a firm needs to reduce its price. We also know that along a straight line demand curve the elasticity ranges from elastic through to inelastic.

The price elasticity of demand (*ped*) varies at every point along a straight line demand curve. The higher up the demand curve (towards the vertical axis) where price is relatively high but quantity demanded relatively low, *ped* will be elastic, whereas at the lower end of the demand curve (towards the horizontal axis) the price is relatively low but quantity demanded relatively high and as a result *ped* will be inelastic. There will also be a point midway between these two ranges where the *ped* is of unit elasticity.

This knowledge is important when looking at market structure and imperfect competition such as oligopoly and monopoly where the firm does not face a horizontal demand curve where $P = AR = MR$. In markets where firms are not operating under the assumptions of perfect competition, they will face a downward sloping demand curve. Given that the demand curve slopes down from left to right, in order to sell an additional unit, the producer must offer it at a lower price than previous units and so the MR will always be lower than the average revenue. Graphically, the MR curve lies below the demand curve (the AR curve), as shown in Figure 10.3. MR is the addition to total revenue as a result of selling one more (or one fewer) unit of production. When the addition to total revenue does not change because of the sale of one extra unit of production, the MR is zero. The definition of unit elasticity is that the percentage change in quantity demanded is equal to the percentage change in price and so there will be no change in total revenue. It follows that the MR curve cuts the horizontal axis where the $ped = 1$. This is summarized in Figure 10.3.

FIGURE 10.3

Changing Price Elasticity of Demand Along a Demand Curve and Marginal Revenue

If the firm faces a downward sloping demand curve, then the slope of the curve is constant but the price elasticity of demand is not. To sell additional quantities, the firm must reduce price, so the addition to total revenue (MR) will be less than the price (AR). The MR curve will lie below the demand curve. At the point where ped = unity (1), the addition to TR will be zero and so this represents the horizontal intercept of the MR curve. At points where the ped is less than unity (ped = inelastic), the MR is negative as the addition to TR is falling.

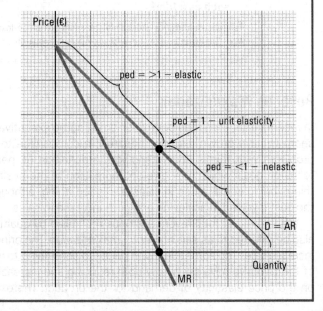

What this tells us is that the total revenue curve will be positive when the price elasticity of the demand curve is elastic, at its maximum when price elasticity is equal to 1 and begins to decline when the price elasticity of the demand curve is inelastic.

The total revenue curve can be graphed as in Figure 10.4 showing the relationship between sales revenue on the vertical axis in euros, and the volume of sales on the horizontal axis. Panel (a) shows the *TR* for a price taking firm in competitive conditions where $P = AR = MR$. In this situation, the *TR* curve will be a positive curve rising in direct proportion to sales. Panel (b) shows the situation for a firm facing a downward sloping demand curve. The *TR* curve begins as a positive function of sales rising as more sales are achieved, reaching a maximum at a volume of sales of Q_1 and then declining thereafter. This is because the firm must reduce prices in order to sell more output, and is linked to the explanation given of the shape of the *MR* and demand curve in Figure 10.3.

FIGURE 10.4

The Total Revenue Curve

Panel (a) shows the TR *curve for a firm in a competitive market. If the firm is a price taker, then* P $=$ AR $=$ MR *and the demand curve it faces will be horizontal. The* TR *curve will be a positive curve rising in direct proportion to sales. Panel (b) shows the* TR *curve for a firm facing a downward sloping demand curve. As sales increase* TR *starts to rise, but the rate of growth in* TR *will gradually slow, reaching a maximum and then beginning to decline.*

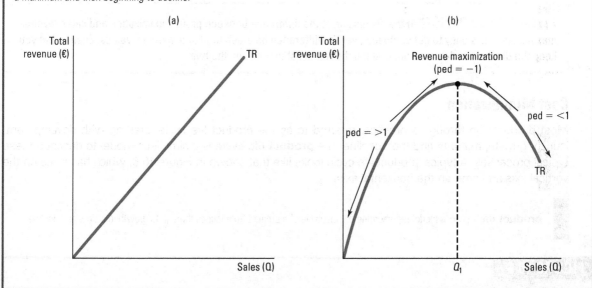

We have seen how a firm can achieve profit maximization at the point where $MR = MC$. At this point the gap between the total revenue curve and the total cost curve is at a maximum. We can superimpose the *TC* curve onto the *TR* curve shown in panel (b) of Figure 10.4 to get the situation depicted in Figure 10.5. From this we can see that the point of profit maximization occurs when sales volumes are at Q_{PM}. At this point the distance between the *TR* and *TC* curves is at its maximum. However, the point of sales revenue maximization occurs where sales volume is Q_{SM} to the right of the profit maximizing sales level. This implies that if sales revenue maximization is pursued as a goal by a firm, it may be that it achieves this goal at lower profits, and this is likely to be because the cost of generating additional sales rises faster than the increase in revenue generated. This could be due to very expensive marketing campaigns, for example, or aggressive pricing tactics which drive out rivals but at very reduced margins.

Figure 10.5 also shows a sales volume of Q_L. At this level of sales, *TC* is greater than *TR* and the firm is making a loss. Despite generating much higher sales, this is being achieved at greater and greater cost. If this continued the firm would continue to make increasing losses.

FIGURE 10.5

Profit Maximization and Revenue Maximization

This figure superimposes a TC curve onto the TR curve for a firm facing a downward sloping demand curve. The point of profit maximization occurs where the distance between the TR and TC curves is at a maximum at a sales level of Q_{PM}. This is not the sales revenue maximizing position, which is achieved where sales are Q_{SM} and the TR curve is at its maximum. If the firm continued to try to increase sales beyond this point the TR would start to decline. At a sales level of Q_L, the firm makes a loss as TC is greater than TR at that sales level.

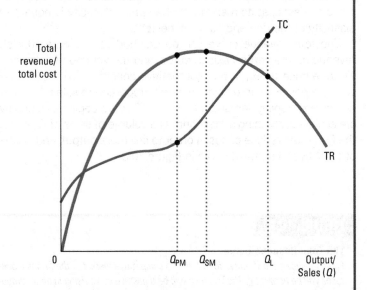

PITFALL PREVENTION In the discussion of the difference between profit maximization and sales revenue maximization, it is easy to get confused over the difference between total and marginal values. Ensure that you keep the distinction clear and understand the relationship between the two.

Cost Minimization

Most products go through a process, referred to as the product life cycle, starting with development, launch, growth, maturity and then decline. The **product life cycle** is a simplistic model to describe these typical processes. A typical product life cycle looks like that shown in Figure 10.6, which has sales on the vertical axis and time on the horizontal axis.

 product life cycle a model representing the life cycle of a product from launch through to growth, maturity and decline

FIGURE 10.6

The Product Life Cycle

The product life cycle can be represented by a graph which shows sales on the vertical axis and time on the horizontal axis. At the introduction stage sales begin to rise slowly and then may pick up speed. Sales will continue to grow until the market matures, after which time sales will start to decline.

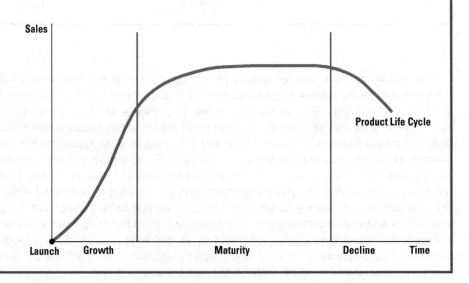

Sales are clearly zero during the development stage and so at the point of launch the vertical and horizontal intercept will be 0. As the product gains traction in the market, sales will start to rise, often picking up speed as a firm's marketing campaigns take effect. At some point, sales will start to slow and at this point the market is either saturated because of new firms entering to take advantage of profits that exist and which have been highlighted by the product concerned, or tastes have changed and the market begins to mature and stagnate. After a certain point, the market will start to decline and sales will gradually taper off. This is the decline stage of the product life cycle.

The reason why we have introduced the product life cycle is that there are links between the position of a product and the goal of minimizing cost. It can be assumed that every firm might want to keep costs to a minimum, but as a specific strategy this might be particularly relevant in a mature market, where the product faces little prospect of significant sales growth from year to year although the firm wishes to stay in the market. By sales growth we mean year-on-year increases in sales. For example, assume that unit sales in year X_1 are 1 million. If in year X_2 sales rise to 1.2 million then sales growth will have been 20 per cent. If in year X_3 sales are 1.25 million, then sales growth will have been 4.16 per cent. However, if in year X_4 sales remain at 1.25 million then sales growth will be zero. The firm might still wish to stay in the market because sales are deemed healthy at this level. The firm may see relatively stable revenues from such sales levels being generated for the foreseeable future although there is little prospect of growing sales in the future.

In such a market, how does the firm increase profit? It knows it can do little to increase revenue given the maturity of the market, so the other option is to focus on costs. This could mean looking at making its human resource management more efficient by not only looking at whether it has the optimal number of staff to carry out its operations effectively, but whether those staff are in the right positions, whether talent is being exploited and whether the business can be reorganized to bring about a more optimal structure which allows it to continue meeting customer expectations but at the same time cut costs, both total and unit.

Productivity Increasing productivity can be a way in which firms control or cut costs. Productivity is a measure of output per factor of production per unit of time. It can be summarized in the following formula:

$$\text{Productivity} = \frac{\text{Total output}}{\text{Units of the factor}}$$

If, for example, a cutlery manufacturer produced 20,000 sets of cutlery per month and employed 200 workers, then output per worker (productivity) would be 100 sets per month. Increasing productivity is an important goal for firms because of the contribution it makes to reducing unit costs.

To see how productivity can help a focus on controlling costs, assume that our cutlery manufacturer sells each set for €75 and that the current unit cost of production is €50, so the margin on unit sales is €25. If the firm sells all 20,000 units a month it generates revenues of €1.5 million and costs will be €1 million.

Now assume that the firm makes some organizational changes which include reducing the tiers of management and streamlining the sales function. In addition, new machinery in its factory helps workers to operate more efficiently and, because of these changes, productivity per worker rises to 120 units per month. Clearly there will have been some costs involved in making these changes, but if the proportionate increase in costs is less than the proportionate increase in productivity then the firm's unit costs can fall, improving its margins.

If workers are paid an average of €2,500 per month with a productivity level of 100 units per month then we can work out that the unit labour costs to produce the cutlery sets is €25. If wages stay the same but the new changes increase productivity to 120 units per month, the unit labour costs are now only €20.83 per set. Other things being equal, the firm can now increase its margin from €25 to €29.17. Assuming it continues to sell all 20,000 units per month its profit increases by €83,400 per month.

It is also possible that the firm, in recognition of the changes the workforce are having to adjust to, could even pay the workers a higher wage and still see an increase in profit provided the increase in wages was more than offset by the rise in productivity.

Shareholder Value

Shareholder value refers to the way in which shareholders receive reward for the risk they have taken in investing in the business. This risk is rewarded through either an increase in the share price of the business or in the value of the dividends paid to shareholders, or both.

Shareholders are the part owners of a business. Owning a share in a business represents a claim to the future earnings of that business. Those earnings will be dependent, in part, on the way in which the business is led and managed. The decisions of the executives and managers in a firm will affect the ability of the firm to generate revenues, to control costs and therefore make profits over time. The profits will be partly distributed to shareholders in the form of dividends. Investors may also buy shares in the hope that the price will rise and, as a result, the shares can be sold at a personal profit to the investor.

Fundamental to shareholder value is the idea that if a CEO focuses attention on improving the performance of the company through various measures, then the stock price will invariably follow if it is assumed that stock prices accurately reflect fundamental values (something that was called into question in the years following the Financial Crisis of 2007–09).

The definition of performance, however, is where there is lots of debate. Should performance include just measures of profit? Do increases in the rate of growth of sales revenue over time signify good performance? Some would suggest firms focus on what is termed **free cash flow**. Free cash flow is the cash generated from the firm's operations minus that spent on capital assets. What this figure represents is the ability of the business to generate cash over and above that necessary to carry out its operations, service its assets and expand those assets. Cash generation is necessary to enable any firm to be able to expand over time and to develop new products and thus maintain its competitiveness.

free cash flow the cash generated from the firm's operations minus that spent on capital assets

NON-FINANCIAL OBJECTIVES

The following represents a summary of what can be called non-financial objectives. Non-financial objectives are often hard to disentangle, partly because, as mentioned earlier, decisions that affect one part of a business are also likely to affect another part. A decision to expand market share, for example, can lead to increases in revenue and profit and thus improve shareholder value.

Satisficing

The theory of satisficing was developed by Carnegie Tech Nobel-laureate, Herbert Simon in 1956. Simon argued that human beings do not act as rational automatons and are unable to compute optimized outcomes with mathematical precision. For example, CEOs may not have either the time nor the brain capacity to sit and calculate the profit-maximizing output. Instead they tend to behave using a mix of satisfying and sufficing, termed satisficing. CEOs, for example, must satisfy shareholder demands and make healthy profits, but not necessarily by maximizing profit. The profit level must be sufficient to satisfy shareholder demands.

As a result, the assumption of profit maximizing or any other sort of maximizing or minimizing might not hold in the real world where uncertainty, the complexity of organizations and the vagaries of human behaviour mean that decisions are regularly made which are sub-optimal.

Linked to this is so-called **agency theory**, whereby managers in a firm are viewed as being agents of shareholders, and may pursue their own self-interest rather than the interests of the shareholders. If the interests of shareholders and managers diverge then there can be an agency problem. Measures may need to be put into place to more closely align the interests of owners and managers.

agency theory where managers act as the agents of shareholders, resulting in a divorce between ownership and control such that managers pursue their own self-interests rather than the interests of shareholders

Market Power

Market power might include a number of different characteristics. It can involve firms seeking growth through acquisition (merger or takeover), both within their core market and outside it. The latter is referred to as conglomerate acquisition and leads to firms having interests across a range of diverse and often totally unrelated markets. The Indian Tata Group, for example, owns businesses involved with information technology and communications, engineering, automotive, chemicals, energy, and consumer products such as beverages and ceramics.

Expanding power can give a firm considerable influence over its market and enable it to have some influence over price or on output. We will look in more detail at the effects on firm behaviour in markets where the assumptions of highly competitive firms are dropped, in later chapters. Part of the drive to expand market power might also involve a desire to increase market share. **Market share** refers to the proportion of total sales in a market accounted for by an individual firm.

In the UK grocery market in May 2023, for example, Tesco was the market leader with around 27.1 per cent of the market in the 12 weeks to 14th May 2023. Sainsbury's accounted for 14.8 per cent, Asda for 13.96 per cent, Morrisons for 8.7 per cent, Aldi for 10.1 per cent, the Co-op for 5.8 per cent, Waitrose for 4.6 per cent, Lidl for 7.7 per cent, Iceland for 2.3 per cent and Ocado for 1.7 per cent (source of data, Kantar Worldpanel).

market share the proportion of total sales accounted for by a product/business in a market

Many CEOs will want to monitor market share, partly because it gives some indication of the market power of the firm, but also because there may be personal gratification in expanding market share ahead of rivals; the CEO network can often be very close and highly competitive.

Market share can be expanded through sub-optimal tactics such as cutting prices. The aim is to encourage consumers to switch, and once they have been won over to then retain them. We saw in Chapter 2 how acquiring and retaining customers have different costs. The tactic of cutting prices to win over customers can be an expensive one in terms of the effect on margins and profits; prices might be cut to the point where the firm is selling products at below cost to win market share. In the longer term, such a tactic is not sustainable, but in the short term it may well be sufficient to win a significant number of new or returning customers.

Social, Ethical and Environmental Objectives

Few large firms will neglect the concern among their wider stakeholders of the social, ethical and environmental impact of a firm's operations. The vast majority have incorporated some sort of social and environmental responsibility reporting into their operations in addition to the annual report of financial accounts. Critics have argued that some firms use social and environmental issues as a cynical marketing tool. This may be true in some cases, but regardless of the reasons for introducing such policies, many firms have changed the way they run their operations to improve levels of social and environmental responsibility.

Examples of the sort of things that have been introduced include:

- a greater awareness of the effects of pollution in all its forms
- measures to reduce pollution through increasing efficiency in the use of resources
- developing operations to utilize cleaner technologies to reduce the environmental impact
- sourcing raw materials from renewable sources
- looking at options to recycle, including making products that are almost fully recyclable
- reducing energy and water use.

Such measures are not only beneficial to the environment but also to businesses. Initial investment costs, for example in cleaner energy systems, can be high but the longer-term effects can be significant in terms of reduced unit costs. The social and environmental movement has forced businesses to take a long hard look at themselves and their operations, and to make changes to the way they operate.

This can be no bad thing for any business looking to find ways of improving, however the definition of 'improving' is framed.

In addition to environmental objectives, firms have increasingly developed social and ethical responsibilities in recognition of the wider stakeholders they interact with. These include:

- local sponsorship programmes
- being involved in charity work
- monitoring closely the way workers are treated, especially if the firm outsources part of its operations
- basing decision making not simply on profitability, but on what is perceived to be 'right and proper'
- doing work with the local community including getting employees to work with local projects
- developing closer relationships with suppliers
- promoting diversity and inclusivity.

Ethical decision making involves conducting operations which conform to accepted moral codes, doing things the 'right' way. Such decision making includes the way in which a business manages and reports its financial affairs to help reduce the instances of fraud, bribery and corruption. Other aspects of ethical decision making include giving workers freedom of speech (a particularly relevant point given the increasing use of social media as a means of communicating), paying taxes fairly, producing products which are safe (but which may be more costly to produce), and making decisions about who to trade with, who to recruit as suppliers and why those decisions are made. For example, a firm may choose not to engage in trade with the government of a country which it sees as being repressive, even if such trade could be lucrative.

> **?** **WHAT IF...** a firm has been making significant losses for five years, which is pushing it to the brink of insolvency. It is offered the prospect of entering a lucrative trade deal with a very corrupt government, which would enable it to not only reverse the losses but also safeguard the jobs of its workers. What should the business do?

Putting into place social, ethical and environmental policies can be expensive and invariably requires considerable changes in a corporate culture and the way the business operates. Many businesses will look at such changes as being long term in their ultimate effects and benefits, and part of the process involves convincing shareholders that these benefits will outweigh the initial costs. If carefully considered and developed, some of these policies can be sources of competitive advantage which can be distinctive and defensible, and therefore make very good business sense, having an impact on the firm's reputation and credibility.

It must be remembered that moves to improve social, ethical and environmental responsibility and the incorporation of policies as part of the goals of a firm do not happen everywhere. The vast majority of businesses are small and medium sized, and it may be impractical for these businesses to have such goals. In addition, the geographical spread of business means that efforts to promote such policies as business goals may be confined to parts of developed Western economies. Problems in securing deals on reducing carbon emissions, for example, highlight the tensions that exist between emerging economies and mature economies.

Brand Recognition

A brand is a means of creating awareness and identity in a product or range of products such that consumers come to recognize it when making purchasing decisions. A brand does not have to be associated with high value, high price or quality. A brand might clearly reflect to the consumer what the association and personality is, what it means. Brands such as Dolce and Gabbana, for example, have associations with high quality fashion, whereas a brand such as Netto or Poundland have an association with low prices and value for money. If a shopper goes to Netto, they do not expect (nor want) expensively laid out and equipped stores; they expect to be able to buy a range of goods at competitive prices.

Building a brand and subsequent brand recognition may be a goal of business activity. Many firms spend significant sums of money on building brand recognition over time and it should come as no surprise that guarding that hard-earned recognition is something firms are keen to protect. Laws in many countries recognize such efforts, and attempts by other firms to imitate a brand can be challenged in the courts.

Ultimately, the goal of brand recognition is to influence consumer behaviour. When an individual goes into a fuel station, for example, the array of chocolate bars by the pay station is designed to encourage impulse buying. Brand recognition may be an important factor and is why consumers, almost without thinking, go for a chocolate bar they are aware of and recognize as satisfying their needs. Creating a situation when consumers default to the purchase of one brand ahead of rivals would be the ultimate goal of many businesses in this area, and the developments in neuroscience are beginning to reveal more about how brand association and recognition work in influencing purchasing decisions.

Reputation and Image

Linked with social, ethical and environmental responsibility and branding is a goal to develop reputation and image. This might be a reputation for high levels of customer service, quality, reliability, value for money, technically sophisticated products, social awareness, design, style, anything that the firm thinks will help it to gain a competitive edge and which it can exploit.

Social Enterprise

Social enterprises are a combination of charity and business activity. The concept developed in Italy in the 1980s and is a growing feature of business activity throughout Europe. Social enterprises generate surpluses to survive in the long term, but these surpluses are invested into some social or community-based project rather than being shared between the owners through dividends. These sorts of businesses are referred to as being part of the *not-for-profit* or *third sector* activity.

The goals of the business in such cases might be to generate surpluses to help communities access water supplies in less developed countries, promote recycling or fair trade, provide affordable homes, help young people to take a more active role in society and so on.

> **SELF TEST** Are the different business goals outlined above mutually exclusive? Is it possible to be a socially and environmentally responsible business while at the same time minimizing cost and maximizing profit?

SUMMARY

- We have looked at a range of business goals. Some of these can be classified as aims and others, objectives.

- The 'traditional' (classical) assumption of profit maximization is one example of a financial objective or goal, but increasingly other goals are becoming just as important.

- Brand recognition or a well-developed set of policies to minimize the environmental impact of a business's operations, for example, could be seen as being routes to generate increased sales and thus contribute to higher profits. The aim could still be profit maximization, the objective to help achieve this through promoting brand recognition or environmental responsibility.

- Others might argue that brand recognition or social and environmental awareness is a long-term aim in itself.

- Rather than be overly concerned with such distinctions, it is important to recognize that business goals are varied and dependent in part on the type of business and the type of business organization.

- All these goals are interrelated and are parts of a jigsaw. Ultimately, businesses in the private sector need to generate profits. They must close down if the businesses' activities are unsustainable.

- Of concern to the business economist, therefore, are the ways in which the stakeholder demands on business can be reconciled.
- It is safe to say that it is unlikely that all stakeholder demands can be met, so business owners must balance these competing demands and find a way of carrying out business which maximizes overall benefits at minimum cost.
- It is important to recognize that there will always be some cost involved in carrying out business, so regardless of the environmental, social and ethical claims of a firm, there will be some areas of operation where criticism can be levelled at the business's activities. How these criticisms are managed is often a crucial part of the role of CEOs and managers.

IN THE NEWS

Shareholder Value

There is a debate surrounding the goals of firms. Economists have used the idea of profit maximization as the basis for analysis of firm behaviour for many years. In some respects, this has manifested itself in the idea of maximizing shareholder value. The idea of shareholder value is often attributed to the economist Milton Friedman. In a 1970 article published in the *New York Times*, Friedman noted that a firm's executives were the employees of the owners of the business and that their responsibility was to fulfil the owners' desires. Friedman made an assumption that the desire of the owners was to see profits. It follows, therefore, that maximizing profit should be the primary objective of firms. This has been seen as the origins of the idea of maximizing shareholder value, whereby the aim of the business is to increase the share price and hence the market value of the firm, and the way to achieve this is through continually increasing profits.

In his original article, Friedman does note that the 'responsibility is to conduct the Business in accordance with their desires, which will generally be to make as much money as possible while conforming to the basic rules of the society, both those embodied in law and those embodied in ethical custom'. This reference to the law and 'ethical custom' has been interpreted as suggesting the firm should focus on profit maximization within the law and whatever ethical guidelines exist, both those which stem from government and those which may exist in society in general.

Is shareholder value about increasing the size of the pie for everyone?

A paper published by Oliver Hart of Harvard University and Luigi Zingales from the University of Chicago in July 2017 questions Friedman's article and promotes the idea of 'shareholder welfare'. Hart and Zingales note that shareholders may not necessarily be motivated by profit, but have other desires which include social and ethical considerations. If this is the case, and there is no reason to doubt this, then executives of firms should be carrying out business to reflect these broader stakeholder objectives, which may conflict with the idea of maximizing profit. Hart and Zingales note that Friedman's approach implies that the firm should concentrate on profit and government should deal with any of the externalities that arise so that firm's behaviour is regulated appropriately.

(Continued)

There is an implied assumption here, which is the question of whether maximizing profit should ever be carried out ethically, in other words, are the two things inseparable? Hart and Zingales argue that there is a difference between shareholder value and shareholder welfare, and that the latter should be the focus of business objectives. They argue that to better reflect shareholder welfare, owners who will have many different views and perspectives on why they own a business above simply earning income, should vote on the broad outlines of corporate policy. The outcome might reflect different objectives partly because separating out making profit from other objectives can be very difficult and, therefore, cannot be dealt with by government alone.

Questions

1 What do you think is the difference between shareholder value and shareholder welfare?
2 Would you agree that maximizing profits should be the sole objective of firms and any externalities from business production should be the responsibility of government?
3 Can the idea of maximizing shareholder value or welfare apply to businesses which are not publicly quoted?
4 Is it possible to separate out 'money-making activities' from ethical activities for a firm? Hart and Zingales use the example of the US supermarket, Walmart, selling 'high capacity ammunition magazines' for firearms. Would shareholders be willing to forego profit for a ban on the selling of these goods in Walmart stores?
5 To what extent would a voting system such as that suggested by Hart and Zingales succeed in changing firm behaviour from shareholder value to shareholder welfare?

Reference: Hart, O. and Zingales, L. (2017). Companies should maximize shareholder welfare not market value. Chicago Booth Stigler Center, New Working Paper Series No. 12. research.chicagobooth.edu/~/media/A51FEA9DBBF7409E84C381919F4925F6.pdf (accessed 17 July 2023).

QUESTIONS FOR REVIEW

1 Using an example, explain the difference between aims and objectives.
2 Give a definition of public goods, private goods, common resources, merit goods and club goods and give two examples of each.
3 Explain why, at the point of maximum TR, the price elasticity of demand for a good is -1.
4 What is meant by the terms 'break-even point' and 'margin of safety'?
5 What is the meaning of the term 'productivity'?
6 How can increases in factor productivity help a firm to achieve cost minimization?
7 Why might a firm have a goal of increasing market share?
8 Using examples, explain the difference between social and environmental objectives.
9 Explain how an objective to base decisions on strong ethical principles can lead to stakeholder conflict.
10 What is a social enterprise?

PROBLEMS AND APPLICATIONS

1 Why can it be difficult to distinguish between aims and objectives and strategies and tactics?
2 Merit goods can be provided by the market but are often provided by the state. Consider the costs and benefits of both sources of provision and suggest how society might decide on the most appropriate method of provision which benefits the most people.

3   A firm faces the following cost and revenue schedules:

Output (Q)	TR	TC
0	0	3
1	6	5
2	12	8
3	18	12
4	24	17
5	30	23
6	36	30
7	42	38
8	48	47

Calculate the profit, marginal revenue and marginal cost, and state what the profit maximizing output will be for the firm under the assumption that it seeks to maximize profit.

4   A firm has the following information available to its managers:

- Fixed costs are €1,500, price is €8 and the variable costs are €0.50 per unit.
- What is the break-even output for this firm?

5   Assume the firm in Question 4 is operating at its break-even output. A discussion is being held about deciding to change price with the aim of increasing profit. It is operating at 98 per cent capacity. The sales director wants to reduce price, but the operations manager wants to increase price. Which of these two options would you recommend the firm take and why?

6   If a firm faces a downward sloping demand curve, why does total revenue not continue rising as a firm sells more of its output?

7   Workers in a firm have petitioned the management for a 5 per cent pay increase. How might the firm's management approach negotiations on the pay claim? (Hint: the management may be interested in raising the issue of productivity.)

8   Which of the following do you think is the most important element of shareholder value: the dividend to shareholders, the firm's share price or free cash flow? Explain your answer.

9   How might an energy firm such as BP or Shell claim that they can maximize shareholder value, but at the same time emphasize their environmental and social credentials?

10 A firm is operating in a market in which the good it sells is in the maturity stage of its life cycle. How does knowledge of this shape its decisions about what its goals for that product might be? How might these decisions be influenced if the firm had a new product in development which it believed could take significant market share in the future?

11 BUSINESS ORGANIZATION

TYPES OF BUSINESS ORGANIZATION

Anyone can start a business. You need an idea about having something to sell which a sufficient number of other people are interested in and are willing to pay to acquire with the result being that the amount of money generated from sales is at least sufficient to cover costs. Indeed, the vast majority of businesses in most countries are small businesses. Some of these small businesses will grow and become more complex and, as they do, the way they are organized and the legal requirements they have to adhere to will change. In this section we will look at some of main types of business organization.

Sole Traders

A sole trader is the simplest form of business organization. It consists of just one person who has full control of the business. The individual owns all the assets, takes responsibility for decision making and for the profit or losses generated by the business. A sole trader (also termed sole proprietor) is classed as being self-employed and is responsible for paying any taxes in the country in which they operate. In the UK, for example, if the turnover (sales revenue) is above £85,000 a year, then the sole trader would have to register for paying value added tax (VAT). There are few legal requirements in setting up a sole proprietorship, but owners are expected to keep a record of their accounts and to follow certain guidelines around the name of the business. For example, it is not permitted to use a business name that might be interpreted as offensive or which suggests some link to the government in some way without prior permission being sought. A sole trader can employ other people but these people play no role in the ownership of the business. Across the EU, there are around 23 million enterprises of which around 93 per cent employ fewer than 10 people. The percentage of enterprises which have no employees is similar to that in the UK with around three-quarters of businesses not having any employees.

An important characteristic of sole proprietorships is unlimited liability. **Unlimited liability** means that the owner is personally responsible and liable for all the debts of the business. If a sole trader had to cease trading then any debts owed to creditors, such as suppliers, landlords, the tax authorities and so on, are the personal responsibility of the owner. In some cases this can mean that a sole trader has to sell personal assets to raise the funds to settle these debts. If this means having to sell the house, car, prized antique or any other personal possession, then this has to be done. Ultimately if the sole trader cannot settle these debts then they are declared bankrupt. Note that while the term 'bankrupt' is often used in a generic way to describe any business failure, in legal terms it has a specific meaning. An individual can become bankrupt, a business becomes insolvent. The lack of legal separation between business and owner as a sole trader means that if the 'business' fails the sole proprietor can declare bankruptcy.

 unlimited liability a situation where the owner of a business is legally responsible for all the debts of the business

Partnerships

A partnership is a business organization that consists of two or more people. A partnership has unlimited liability and so has no legal status separating the partners from the business. Individuals considering entering a partnership would normally draw up some sort of partnership agreement which clarified roles, responsibilities and liabilities. If, for example, five people entered a partnership but one put in 50 per cent of the capital of the business, then the agreement might state that this individual would be entitled to 50 per cent of the profits generated by the business. As is the case for a sole trader, partners have to register as self-employed with the tax authorities.

Limited Liability Partnerships

In recent years, changes to company law in the UK have permitted the setting up of limited liability partnerships (LLPs). **Limited liability** is an important principle in business organization and refers to a situation where the owner's liability for the debts of a company is limited to the amount of capital they have agreed to subscribe. Owners with limited liability cannot be forced to sell off personal possessions to settle the debts of a business should it become insolvent. There are similarities to a traditional partnership but in addition similarities to the setting up of limited companies. However, non-profit making charities cannot form an LLP. The main reason for setting up an LLP is that the partners (of which there must be at least two) can limit their liability to the debts of the business.

 limited liability a legal principle where an owner's liability for the debts of a company are limited to the amount they have agreed to subscribe

The rights and responsibilities of each partner are laid out in a deed of partnership, which is a legally binding agreement which will include the personal details of the partners, how much capital each has put into the business, details of how the partnership would be terminated if one of the partners left or died, as well as the roles and responsibilities of each partner. The designate partner must also contact the tax authorities to file a partnership statement along with the LLP's tax return which provides details of how any profits made in the business have been divided up among the partners. An LLP must have at least two designated members. A designated member has the same duties in an LLP as a member but in addition is responsible for appointing auditors, signing and delivering accounts, notifying the Registrar of Companies of changes to the business, such as change of address or name, preparing other documents that the Registrar of Companies may require and acting on behalf of the business if it is wound up. An LLP can choose its own name but there are certain restrictions over this. Using the same name as a company already registered would not be allowed, neither would a name which implies that the business is a government agency, is deemed offensive or where its use would constitute some sort of criminal offence. For example, names which use the words Authority, European, Charter, Registered, Association, Benevolent, Trade Union, Trust, Foundation, National and British might have to have approval from the Secretary of State. This is because the use of these and other words may mislead the public into thinking the business is something it is not.

SELF TEST Explain the difference between limited and unlimited liability.

Private Limited Companies

Private limited company status is an important and popular form of business organization because it confers the benefits of limited liability on owners. A private limited company (abbreviated to Ltd) is a distinct legal entity. This means that the business is the entity that can sue or be sued rather than any of the individuals that may own the business. It is this legal status that makes a limited company attractive. If the business fails then the owners risk losing the money they have invested in the company. However, creditors cannot seek to claim recovery of what they are owed by forcing owners to sell their personal possessions to settle these debts. This is an advantage to the company owner but not to the company that may be dealing with it. This is why some smaller limited companies have greater problems accessing credit and supply agreements compared to non-limited companies.

A limited company can issue shares as a means of raising capital; however, these shares cannot be sold to, or traded by, the public. There are normally two or more people involved as shareholders although there are cases of single member companies, limited by shares or guarantee, consisting of one member. Such cases usually arise when a limited company is reduced to one member due to the death of a shareholder or some other circumstance.

There are three types of private limited company.

Private Company Limited by Shares The business is owned by the shareholders whose liability is limited to the amount they have agreed to invest in the business. Assume a member holds 10,000 shares with a nominal value of £1 each. If the business has to close then the shareholder risks losing all or part of this sum. If the business closed but was able to pay back £2,000 to the shareholder from the remaining assets of the business, then the amount unpaid that the owner would be liable for would be £8,000. However, the shareholder would not be liable for any of the debts of the company in excess of the £10,000 they have originally invested.

Private Company Limited by Guarantee This type of company is used in cases such as social enterprises, sports associations and non-governmental organizations (NGOs) where the members, who are referred to as guarantors and not shareholders, wish to specify the liability they have to the business. In this case the business does not have share capital and so guarantors do not contribute to the capital of the business and do not, as a consequence, purchase shares. The members agree to a nominal sum, which may be £1, in the event of the business being wound up.

Private Unlimited Company A private unlimited company is one in which members may contribute share capital and be shareholders or guarantors, the difference being that the liability of the members is unlimited. The trade-off for this lack of protection is that the amount of information that the members have to disclose is less than the other types of limited company. The rules surrounding limited companies in the UK have changed in recent years as a result of the Companies Act 2006. Much of the change relates to the documentation that has to be submitted and the way in which the company is organized and run. Two key documents are (1) the Memorandum of Association – a document which specifies basic details of the business, and (2) the Articles of Association – which sets out the rules for the running and regulation of the company's internal affairs.

Public Limited Companies (PLCs)

Public Limited Company status tends to be associated with larger business organizations (although not exclusively). PLCs must follow clear guidelines and regulations as well as the legislation. The main reason for this is the way that these organizations are financed. PLCs are able to sell shares to members of the general public and, as such, safeguards have to be put in place to protect those who do choose to invest in these organizations.

In the UK, PLCs cannot commence trading until they have fulfilled a number of requirements and received a Trading Certificate from Companies House. PLCs are subject to many of the same rules as private companies in respect of the number of members (at least two) and to have at least two company directors. There are a number of provisions in the 2006 Act outlined above that do not apply to PLCs. For example, these organizations have to submit accounts within six months of its accounting reference period to Companies House and failure to meet such a deadline incurs a penalty charge. The major benefit of setting up a PLC is that the access to capital is much wider than in other forms of business organization because a PLC can issue shares to the public. These shares can be freely traded through a stock exchange. If it needs additional capital, adverts can be placed inviting the public to take up more of its shares.

Business Organization Outside the UK

In other countries, the principles of limited liability are similarly enshrined in law. In Germany, owners of a business are called Gesellschafter (members) and the wording after a business name GmbH (Gesellschaft mit beschränkter Haftung) signifies that these members have limited liability. Such companies must have a minimum starting capital of €25,000 and are run by a managing director who acts on behalf of the company unless the business employs more than 500 workers. In this case the company has to be run by a supervisory board (Aufsichtsrat).

German company law has a number of features that increase bureaucracy. For example, stock issues, share transfers or any changes to articles of association have to involve the services of a specialist lawyer called a notary, which can increase both the time taken and the cost. In addition, members can place significant limitations on the actions of directors through the issuance of bonding orders to which they must adhere. The procedures in Germany can be more time consuming than in other European countries, with the exception of Spain where the procedures can be even more onerous.

Other forms of business organization in Germany include the Aktiengesellschaft (AG). This used to be the more popular type of business organization but was replaced by the GmbH primarily because of the complexity of the AG. The AG consists of a supervisory board controlled by shareholders and possibly employees, who provide the overall policy for the company that is managed. This form of business organization does have similarities with structures in other countries such as the Aktiebolag (AB) in Sweden, the Societate pe Actiuni (SA) in Romania and Aktieselskab (AS) in Denmark. There are also a number of countries that use the suffix SA after the company name. These are similar to public limited companies in the UK. The initials SA stand for Société Anonyme, which translates into English as 'anonymous society'. The wide variation in the detail of company law throughout the EU and the different regulatory structures under which countries operate can present problems to companies either operating in different European countries or who are seeking to consolidate through acquisition. As a result, Europe-wide legislation has been passed to help companies overcome some of these difficulties.

The Council Regulation on the Statute for a European Company of the EU became law in 2001 and applied to all EU states in 2004. It allows companies to become a Societas Europaea (SE) and also enables the setting up of European Co-operative Societies. An SE can be set up in four main ways: through conversion from a national company, through the creation of a subsidiary to the main company, by acquisition of companies originating from different EU nations or through the creation of a joint venture between companies from different European nations. The SE must have a minimum share capital to the value of €120,000 and have a registered office in a location where it carries out its main administration – its headquarters, in other words. The running of the SE combines elements of the single-tier administrative board system with the two-tier system outlined in the AG above. The management board is appointed by the supervisory board and carries out the day-to-day operations of the company. No member can be on the supervisory and management board. If running as a single-tier company, the administrative board runs the business. Regardless of the system, each of these boards has responsibilities for authorizing different actions including raising finance, acquisitions or disposal of assets, the signing of large scale contracts relating to supply or performance and certain investment projects. As with PLCs, an annual statement of accounts must be drawn up and made public. The SE is liable for tax in relation to wherever the administrative offices are located.

Co-operatives

The International Co-operative Alliance is an organization that represents co-operative organizations around the world. It defines a co-operative as:

> *people-centred enterprises jointly owned and democratically controlled by and for their members to realise their common economic, social and cultural needs and aspirations. As enterprises based on values and principles, they put fairness and equality first allowing people to create sustainable enterprises that generate long-term jobs and prosperity. Managed by producers, users or workers, cooperatives are run according to the 'one member, one vote' rule.*

(Source: www.ica.coop/en).

The roots of this type of organization go back to the North West of the UK in 1844 when workers in the cotton mills of Rochdale formed the Rochdale Equitable Pioneers Society. The basic idea was to try to find a way to gain some benefits of economies of scale by pooling their resources together to bulk purchase basic foodstuffs such as sugar, butter, flour and oatmeal. In so doing they aimed to get lower prices on these goods and then share the benefits between the members. Members had an equal say in the running of the co-operative and shared in any profits that were made. The success of the so-called Rochdale Pioneers led to the expansion of the movement around the world. While the modern co-operative movement has adapted to changing times the basic principles have been retained. There have been a number of different types of co-operative organization relating to wholesale, retail, manufacturing, employee, banking and savings, and agricultural and fishing activities, among other things. While these activities vary, the basis of the movement is similar.

A number of key principles underpin every co-operative movement. These include:

- Equality of opportunity for anyone to be a member of the organization regardless of gender, race, religion, etc.
- Co-operatives are voluntary organizations.
- Most organizations are democratic with all members having the right to vote on policy and decisions. Elected representatives are responsible to the membership.
- Members mostly pay a nominal sum to become a member and receive a share in the organization. No one member is able to build up share allocations. The share capital invariably becomes the common property of all the members who have control over this capital.
- In some cases, any profits (regarded as 'surpluses') are either divided equally among all members or are allocated to specific purposes such as reinvestment into the organization or a nominated NGO agreed by the members.
- Co-operatives are independent and autonomous. Any agreement with external organizations must be made with the agreement of the membership.
- In keeping with the co-operative and self-help ideal, organizations promote the benefits of education and training as means to improve the welfare of all.
- Active co-operation between co-operative movements is encouraged as a means of strengthening the organization as a whole.
- Co-operatives have a concern for sustainable development of communities at a local, national and international level.
- Co-operatives emphasize a concern for ethical trading and business operation.

Social Enterprises

One major development in the type of business organization in this field has been the growth of social enterprises. Social enterprises are a mix of business activity and charity. The idea of social enterprises originated in Italy in the early 1980s. The primary objective of a social enterprise is to focus on investing any surpluses (profits) into some community, social objective or business activity or issue rather than dividing the profit up between the owners of the business. As such they have been described as a 'third sector' – the private not-for-profit sector. As these enterprises have developed, there has been increasing interest from government in how social enterprises can be utilized to provide products and services that might have traditionally been seen as being within the remit of the public sector. Governments may be prepared to provide some financial support and assistance to such enterprises (for example, by speeding up planning applications) as a means of providing public sector services more efficiently.

Social enterprises are becoming an increasingly important sector. In the UK, it has been estimated that there are over 60,000 social enterprises with a combined turnover of £27 billion accounting for some 5 per cent of businesses with employees. In other countries social enterprises have developed in different ways. The following is a short summary of social enterprise activity in other European states.

Belgium: There are only a small number of social enterprise organizations in Belgium. In 1996 the legal framework was amended to include the concept of a 'social purpose company'. The administration associated with setting up a social enterprise in Belgium is more onerous than in other countries and may explain the limited development of this form of organization.

Denmark: The concept is beginning to take hold in Denmark; there are four key areas of activity seeing a rise in social enterprise which include voluntary support groups such as self-help groups for those who have contemplated suicide, going through divorce, suffering from domestic abuse etc., co-operatives in retail, insurance and farming, education and training groups such as the 'work-integration social enterprises' (WISE) and various urban development projects.

France: In 2002 French law was amended to allow for the creation of a 'collective interest co-operative society' – SCIC (société coopérative d'intérêt collectif). This type of organization allows a wide range of stakeholders such as voluntary workers, local government and other partners to develop local projects. As in other European countries the idea of social enterprises is gathering momentum and moving on from projects designed to support greater integration of disadvantaged persons into the labour force, which had been the primary focus of WISE organization in the 1990s.

Germany: Given the country's political background, the idea of a social enterprise is not seen as being distinct from the idea of a social market economy which dominates German political thinking. There are what might be recognized as social enterprises in Germany, but many of these do not see themselves as being distinct in the same way that may be the case in the UK, for example. Such organizations include welfare organizations, volunteer services, co-operatives, local community and trading groups and women's movements. There are not, however, separate legal structures for these types of organizations as yet.

Italy: Italy is the home of social enterprise primarily in the form of social co-operatives. However, the concept has expanded beyond these types of organization and legislation passed in 2005 has now clarified the legal and organizational structure of social enterprises. There are a number of key areas where social enterprises can develop including education and training, social tourism, culture and heritage, welfare, health and environment.

Sweden: The development of the social enterprise concept in Sweden is closely linked with the provision of public sector services which have increased in demand since the 1980s. Government has been unable to keep up with the demand and social enterprise has filled some of the gap. Childcare services are a good example of this; some 10 per cent of provision is through social co-operatives.

ORGANIZATIONAL DESIGN AND STRUCTURE

Any organization consists of a collection of individuals who make it up; it will have some stated purpose which defines why it exists and what it is trying to achieve. There will be some way of measuring the extent to which the organization succeeds in achieving its purpose. Its goals will be defined and, most likely, reviewed on a regular basis. The organization will consist of large numbers of relationships and interactions both internally and externally. There will be relationships between individuals in teams, between departments or functions, between managers and subordinates, and between regional organizations among others. There will also be relationships with a wide range of external stakeholders: customers, suppliers, banks, tax authorities, regulators, legislative bodies, community groups, trades unions and so on. All these relationships will have different types or information flows, both formal and informal. They will involve problems, challenges, external influences, power games and conflict.

How all these are determined and dealt with are guided by the way the organization is designed and structured. **Organization design** refers to the alignment between the purposes and aims of the organization and how its people and resources are structured to help achieve its goals. The structure specifies how the people that make it up relate to each other, the authority invested in those people, and the rights and responsibilities of each person and group. The establishment of roles in an organization is an important step in helping to make sure that appropriate resources are identified and put in place to allow for the achievement of organizational aims and objectives. Clarification of roles will enable the organization to meet its goals and should be designed to make sure that everyone is aware of what those goals are.

> **organization design** the alignment between the purposes and aims of the organization and how its people and resources are structured to help achieve its goals

The type of organizational structure may be partly dependent on size. Small organizations may have relatively simply structures; small to medium sized organizations may have the capacity to introduce a greater degree of specialization into their structure with particular functions being grouped together. The bigger the organization, the more diverse the range of roles and responsibilities is likely to be and the more complex the structure will be as a result. Larger organizations may have different operations in different parts of the country and in different countries of the world. Despite this the overall goals of the organization will remain the same. The challenge is to ensure that the goals are communicated effectively and to get everyone working in the organization to be able to understand their roles and responsibilities and the processes required to move towards achieving those goals. Organizational structure defines much of what the organization is. It helps identify the communication routes within the organization and for those outside that do business with it. The structure will also clarify the web of relationships that have to exist between those in the organization. This may reflect the type of culture within the organization – its collection of shared attitudes, practices, values and goals. For example, an individual may have the title 'executive vice president' while another has the title 'managing supervisor'. The organization structure will state what relationship (if any) the one position has with the other and help to clarify what that relationship should be. Is it one of superior (higher than another in rank or authority) and subordinate? If so, to what extent is the relationship hierarchical and how many rungs of the ladder exist between them? The structure will then enable those working in it to know who to go to and who they are answerable to when seeking or making decisions. The structure will also clarify the extent of formality and informality of relationships. For example, do staff who have 'superior' positions expect to be called by their first names or addressed as Ms, Mr, Mrs, etc? To what extent do individuals in an organization have the responsibility and authority to make decisions? Who are they accountable to and for what?

> **SELF TEST** What is the difference between organizational design and organizational structure?

Types of Organizational Structure

In deciding upon an organizational structure, a number of factors have to be taken into consideration. Organizational structures have people at their heart. Unlike other resources, humans respond to change and structure in different ways. The organization must consider what human resources it possesses, how these can be organized to maximize efficiency and keep costs under control but also increase the chances that the organizational goals of the business will be achieved. Any organization may have a different structure with each having advantages and disadvantages. The outcomes of different structures may not be immediately apparent and the organization may find that its new structure does not work. It is important to remember, therefore, that structures will need to be reviewed and there may be a need for restructuring on a regular basis as the workforce changes, as markets change and as the business environment changes.

The design will include decisions about the basis for the structure. Will it focus on function, division, geographical region or product? Whatever structure is set up, decisions will have to be made about the roles within the structure, the relative importance of these roles, the relationships between roles and where these roles will be located. The latter point is obviously important for organizations with multinational operations. Having decided on the roles, decisions will then have to be taken about the extent of the authority and responsibility each is invested with and how the performance of the roles will be monitored and managed in relation to the overall goals. We must remember that the roles created must enable decisions to be made throughout the business which allow operations to be carried out efficiently. Organizations must be aware of the potential disadvantages arising from a particular structure and, if an existing structure is being changed, how it will manage the change. An organization that has had a structure in place for many years with individuals in roles that have become highly familiar may be affected considerably by proposed changes with a subsequent impact on motivation, self-esteem and productivity.

Each type of structure outlined below has its advantages and disadvantages and there is no one right approach. Each business is different, even those operating in the same industry. No two sets of employees are going to be alike and so what may work for one business may not work for another. For this reason it is not advisable for any business leader to assume that a successful structure in one business can simply be transplanted to another and work.

The main organizational structures that exist can be represented in diagrammatic form. These diagrams highlight the main relationships between different individuals and groups within the business.

Hierarchical Structure A hierarchical structure will show the superior/subordinate relationships throughout the organization. Figure 11.1 outlines this traditional form of organizational structure and one which increasingly is being revised in the light of the changing internal and external business environment.

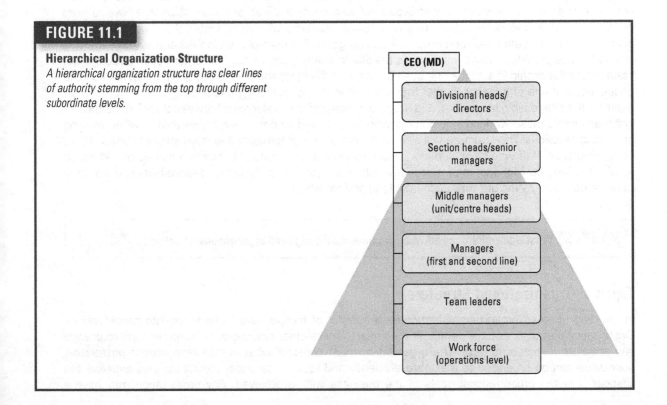

FIGURE 11.1

Hierarchical Organization Structure
A hierarchical organization structure has clear lines of authority stemming from the top through different subordinate levels.

CEO (MD)

Divisional heads/ directors

Section heads/senior managers

Middle managers (unit/centre heads)

Managers (first and second line)

Team leaders

Work force (operations level)

The lines of authority extend upwards in the organization with those at the lowest levels having less authority than those higher up. Tall hierarchical structures have many layers of responsibility throughout the business. Such structures also tend to reflect the different functions in the business – marketing, sales, administration, production and so on, and the relationships between them and the staff who work in each department.

Functional Structure Functional structures may also be hierarchical but not necessarily. Within this structure, people who do similar work (sharing a profession or specialism) are grouped together by expertise. It is a structure that focuses on the way work is done. Figure 11.2 outlines how this type of business structure is based around the functions that exist within it and allows individuals to exercise their particular specialism. For example, those in the marketing function may have experience and qualifications in marketing and in working in marketing departments in other businesses, while those in accounting and finance will have a specialism in that area. Functional structures tend to be appropriate where the business only produces a limited range of products. Where a business has a wide product portfolio, especially across different markets, the problems of managing the business effectively might mean that other forms of structure are more suitable. With wider product portfolios the expertise of staff in each function may be insufficient to cover the full range of products.

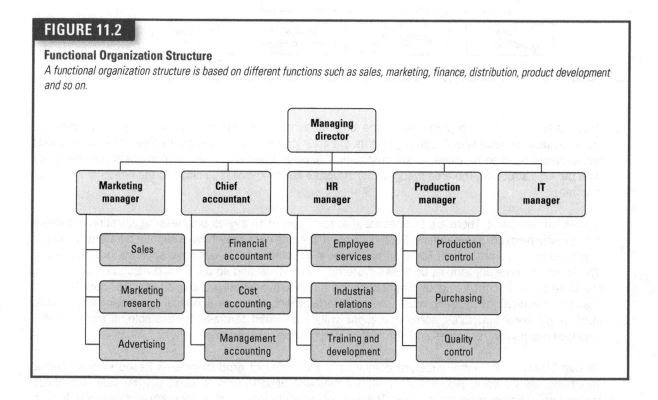

FIGURE 11.2

Functional Organization Structure

A functional organization structure is based on different functions such as sales, marketing, finance, distribution, product development and so on.

Product Based Structure Here the organization is based around the range of products that the business produces. Within this structure, people are grouped according to the product(s) they work on. This structure focuses on the outputs of the transformational process; refer to Figure 11.3. Such an organization is suitable for a business that has a wide product portfolio or where production facilities may be based in different locations – both nationally and internationally. Each product line may in turn have its own functional departments that serve the product. This type of structure enables a business to be able to offer a wide range of products but with the support network of functional areas. Each section of the business is able to specialize in its own area. One potential disadvantage, however, can be in making sure that each product section is coordinated with the others and that each throws its weight behind the overall corporate goals. There can develop a 'balkanization' or 'siloed' approach with each area taking on its own identity and failing to integrate fully with the whole business strategy.

FIGURE 11.3

Product Based Structure

A product based organization structure is based on different product areas. Each area may have its own structure which, again, could be hierarchical.

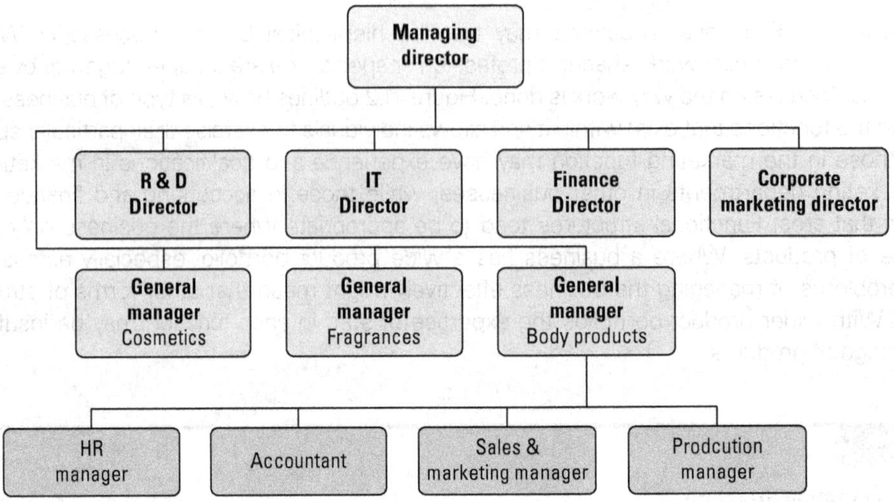

Area Based Structure In some cases the organization may be structured according to geographical areas. Aside from area knowledge arguments the area structure may offer cost efficiencies when goods and services need to be close to the customer. Delivery, repair and maintenance costs may be lower with the area structure. The area (geographic) structure keeps knowledge close to the needs of individual countries.

Divisional Structure There are businesses that form part of an overall business organization but which are in many respects independent. Each division of the business may have a slightly different focus but may have some common link. For example, some electronics companies have separate business areas that focus on home appliances, business systems, audio visual and so on. Each division of the business therefore is a profit centre in its own right but contributes to the overall group business financials. Sony, for example, has divisions covering music, home entertainment, computers, optical equipment and movies. In some divisional structures, some operations will be provided centrally; for example, in some smaller organizations human resources and financial control may be overseen centrally.

Matrix Structure A matrix structure combines the benefits of product or area based with functional structures, as shown in Figure 11.4. It allows specialist departments to exist side by side with those focused on particular products or areas. The lines of authority exist both horizontally and vertically. In such a structure groups of workers might belong to a functional area, for example marketing, but its members may be assigned to different projects to lend their expertise. The individual is thus answerable both to their functional head and also to the project head. Such structures provide the element of progression for careers and flexibility for the business to utilize expertise across the organization but at the same time can create tension and confusion among staff who may be working for a number of different people across the business. This can create conflict between the managers of the function and the various projects as well as issues of coordination and control.

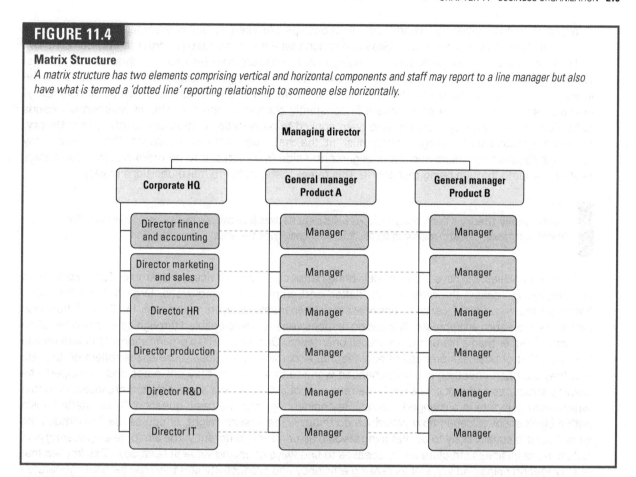

FIGURE 11.4

Matrix Structure

A matrix structure has two elements comprising vertical and horizontal components and staff may report to a line manager but also have what is termed a 'dotted line' reporting relationship to someone else horizontally.

? ■ **WHAT IF...** a business leader decides to restructure their organization, removing several layers of management. What might the reasons be for this change in structure and what challenges might exist in the execution of this change?

CHANGES IN ORGANIZATIONAL STRUCTURES

The stylized diagrammatic representations that are given above tend to oversimplify the way in which many organizations are set up. The complexity of organizations does require some element of structure, but different structures may be appropriate for different parts of an organization. Many organizations now have local, regional, national and international presence. Such divisions tend to focus on North America, the emerging economies and EMEA (Europe, Middle East and Africa). The organizational structure adopted in one area is not always relevant or appropriate to another.

As a result many organizations have looked at developing more flexible structures that are designed to change with the way in which the business environment changes over time. The emphasis on hierarchy is gradually diminishing and extended layers of management be seen as being too rigid and bureaucratic for a world that changes almost every day. In addition, these hierarchical structures tend to be seen as not being conducive to innovation, a key element in maintaining and generating competitive advantage. The emphasis on organizational structure therefore tends to be more on so-called organic structures. These are characterized by fewer rules and regulations, more informal links between departments and functions, a greater emphasis on team work and co-operation and the exchange of information and ideas. The management culture in such an organization is less authoritative and places an emphasis not on difference of approach but on similarity, where good relationships are seen as being essential to generating the communication and vibrancy of new ideas and action that a business needs in order to stay competitive.

However, there is no single best way of doing things and there is widespread acceptance that the best way to organize is based upon (is contingent on) the situation. Strategic 'fit' (alignment) is about matching the internal resources, capabilities and transformational activities with the needs and demands of the external environment. If the external environment is constantly changing, then the internal environment needs to be flexible. Contingency theories have been applied to organizational structure. **Contingency theory**, therefore, suggests that the organization must 'fit' the challenges of the environment. Organizations may vary their structure to ensure such fit or alignment. Aside from a desire to be more creative, companies seek to compete through being responsive. This refers to the ability to make decisions quickly.

> **contingency theory** a theory of organizations which suggests there is no one way to organize a business but that leaders and managers need to respond to situations (or contingencies) as they arise

Many companies will have a goal of delivering better customer service, for example. Such goals might be achieved by making the organization 'flatter' and empowering employees. Organizations are made flatter by the removal of certain ('unnecessary') management layers. Advances in ICT and business systems enable such an approach. A focus on responsiveness is also enabled through a process orientation (horizontal) rather than a hierarchical (vertical) orientation. One approach to organizational structure design has been that of business process re-engineering. According to this idea, businesses reflect on the fact that they are often operating in a very changed world to that in which they originated and developed. The existing structures and processes might be reflective of a different era and a different organization to that which must compete in a changed market. Re-engineering asks the basic question: 'If we started again with a blank sheet of paper, how would we do things?' The answer might, of course, be 'Very much the same,' but it is equally likely to be that things would be done very differently. The aim of re-engineering is to redesign the business structure and processes to find ways of adding value at least cost. This implies that re-engineering helps find ways of increasing efficiency and productivity and this may be partly generated through changes to the organizational structure.

For almost a century scholars have been writing about the environment and its impact upon business; environmental determinism theory states that: 'internal organizational responses are wholly or mainly shaped, influenced or determined by external environmental factors'. Back in the 1960s, Alfred Chandler (source: Chandler, A.D. (1969) *Strategy and Structure: Chapters in the History of the American Industrial Enterprise*. Cambridge, MA: MIT Press) famously argued that 'structure-follows-strategy' (and strategy must fit the external environment). The work of Pugh (source: Pugh, D.S. (1984) *Organization Theory*, 2nd edition. London: Penguin) and others was instrumental in shaping theories about internal context (internal environment) and organizational form. Externally, the contemporary turbulent environment calls for flexible, adaptable and responsive structures; historically, a more predictable environment favoured the bureaucratic/hierarchical approach.

ORGANIZATONAL CULTURE AND ETHICS

How should people in an organization behave? How should they address and speak to each other? What sort of values should people who work for an organization have and to what extent should these values be shared? What are the social norms that exist in a business? These are all questions which are bound up in the culture and ethics of an organization. **Organizational culture** refers to the shared beliefs, values, behaviours and actions that exist within an organization. Closely linked to organizational culture is organizational ethics. Ethics are the moral principles that govern behaviour. It is often noted that ethics is about 'doing the right thing' but equally could also be said to be being aware of when something is not right. The problem with this definition is that there is often no agreement on what the word 'right' means. In many cases, firms provide guidance on what is deemed 'right' and 'wrong' through their policies and procedures, which may be written down and communicated to staff and emphasized in induction and ongoing training. Such policies can include how employees should use social media in relation to work and in referring to their work. Guidelines will be in place on what is considered acceptable and unacceptable behaviours relating to recruitment, bullying, sexual and physical harassment, diversity and inclusivity.

> **organizational culture** the shared beliefs, values, behaviours and actions that exist within an organization

Some ethical behaviour is also clarified in law, which of course firms have to abide by. For example, many countries have passed anti-bribery legislation which makes it illegal to seek to reward someone financially or otherwise in return for carrying out acts or performing improper functions. This may, for example, cover instances where some financial reward is offered to a decision maker on the awarding of a contract.

The way culture and ethical values are framed in an organization can be through different ways. Symbols, slogans, signs and public facing statements might be used to convey the values, beliefs and expected behaviours in an organization. This might even be something as simple as the way offices are designed and the furniture which is used. Some organizations might want to emphasize their tradition and history through the buildings they occupy. Others might choose ultra-modern businesses which reflect wealth, luxury or status. Signs and symbols are one thing, but organizations are made up of people and the behaviour of these people, how they treat each other and the social norms are all displayed and individuals are expected to adhere to these. How and who makes decisions and how accountable they are for the consequences of those decisions are all also important elements of organizational culture which are also bound up with ethical principles. The social norms, what is deemed acceptable and what is not acceptable, and the shared beliefs of an organization will also be reflected in the ethical values of the organization. This may influence all aspects of an organization right down to the sort of people the business hires. There is increasing social pressure, for example, for businesses to reflect a greater degree of diversity and inclusivity in the workplace.

Some organizations will want to give the impression that they have 'one culture' which all its employees share and exhibit and to communicate this with its external stakeholders. In reality, most firms will have not just one but many different cultures, especially if it operates on a global scale. Even if an organization only operates in one country, it is likely that there will be a number of sub-cultures existing. These might be associated with particular functions in an organization, or develop because of the location of the business, or there may be generational sub-cultures, or local leadership and management can create different sub-cultures. The existence of sub-cultures is not in itself a negative thing, but if conflict arises between them they can become corrosive and the organization can operate sub-optimally.

CASE STUDY   Organizational Culture

Goldman Sachs is a famous and successful investment bank. Securing a job at Goldman is often seen as being highly prestigious and the route to a successful career and, for some of those in this industry, the source of a significant income. In February 2021, a group of 13 employees of Goldman based in the United States communicated some concerns and complaints they had about their conditions of work to line managers. The total workforce employed by Goldman is around 34,000. It was well into March before this communication became public and the Goldman CEO, David Solomon, commented on it.

More firms are aware of the impact on productivity of a poor work-life balance.

(Continued)

The group in the United States complained of excessive workload and expectations from managers, long working hours – up to 95 hours a week was being quoted – and the extremely high expectations that are placed on staff. The communication from the 13 members of staff included emotive words such as 'inhumane' and 'abuse' and highlighted problems of micromanagement, poor work–life balance, unrealistic deadlines and the impact on their physical and mental health.

Solomon was reported to have welcomed the communication and said that the leadership treated the comments very seriously. He also said that Goldman was facing extremely high demand for its services and was quoted as saying: 'Just remember: if we all go an extra mile for our client, even when we feel that we're reaching our limit, it can really make a difference in our performance.'

Questions

1 What sort of culture do you think exists at a firm like Goldman Sachs?
2 Comment on the quote in the case study by the Goldman CEO. Do you think that ethically, he was right to make such a comment?
3 Does the fact that 13 of the analysts took a stand to complain show that power relationships in a firm like Goldman extend throughout an organization and not exist simply at the top?

Reference: www.bbc.co.uk/news/business-56495463 (accessed 9 June 2023).

JEOPARDY PROBLEM A clothing retailer has a clear value statement that emphasizes its commitment to treating people fairly and to sustainability. A whistleblower from inside the organization conducts an interview with a news outlet about how workers in supplier firms earn less than a dollar a day and how senior leaders in the firm plan for clothes to be viewed as 'disposable' items so that sales growth is maintained. How does this individual's report reflect the culture and ethics of this organization in relation to its stated values?

POWER RELATIONSHIPS AND THEIR INFLUENCE ON DECISION MAKING

Organizational politics is something that everyone who works in an organization experiences at some time. The word 'politics' means power. Its origin comes from the Greek philosopher Aristotle who wrote about it in his book *Politika*. The book concerned affairs of state, about decision making, who makes decisions, why and with what consequences. Organizations are full of people who make decisions and so the power to make decisions is an important determinant on how and why those decisions are made.

When we looked at types of organization structure, we saw how relationships between people, groups, functions, divisions and so on were structured. These structures help define who has power and how decisions are made. These decisions should be designed to help the organization achieve its purpose more effectively. Sometimes they will be made after careful analysis and deliberation, but at other times decisions may have to be made quickly in response to changes or made with the intention of influencing others' behaviour in some way. Organizational politics is about how individuals and groups ensure compliance with decisions made and how they overcome resistance.

The origins of the power invested in different people vary. Sometimes it comes from the position they hold in the organization; a chief executive officer may hold more power than a director of marketing, for example. In other cases the power comes from the level of expertise that an individual has, from their personality, from their ability to confer rewards or impose punishments, from the way individuals form relationships and networks, and can also be through a more darker side where threats or coercion are used. Power can be used for negative purposes but also for positive ones. The culture and ethical values of an organization can influence the way in which power is used, but equally, the way an organization is structured is also important. Flatter organizational structures can help remove layers of hierarchy that may stifle decision making and innovation. Empowering those lower down an organization's structure can not only help speed up decision making but it can also influence the culture of an organization making it more egalitarian and flexible. These can all be influenced by the power relationships that exist and how people choose to use the power they have. Even those at the very lowest levels of an organization have some power in that workers can choose how much time and effort they put into their jobs. In recent years, the idea of 'quiet quitting' has emerged where people do just the bare minimum that they are contracted to do and nothing more. Those who choose this approach may do so for many reasons, but one may be due to the fact that they do not feel part of the organization, do not feel they belong and do not identify with the organization they work for.

The political structure of an organization is critical to its culture and its ethical values. The way that power is distributed and how it is used is a factor which determines behaviours in an organization. These behaviours can become the social norm and become institutionalized, where behaviours, practices, actions and so on become widely accepted throughout the organization. Sometimes this institutionalized behaviour is corrosive; in other cases it can be a driver for growth and improvement. This is where the idea of culture as a set of shared beliefs can come from. Employees may acquire, or have determined, ways of working together which become accepted practice. This may include how people dress, how they speak to each other, how they interact with stakeholders and so on. These could be formal and laid down in policies, or informal. Either way, the culture becomes embedded; employees know what is acceptable and not acceptable behaviour in the organization and how these behaviours are enforced or implemented.

Ultimately, we have to keep in mind that the structure of an organization and how power is distributed need to be aligned with the purpose of the organization.

> **SELF TEST** Select an example of a business leader with whom you are familiar. Describe the type of power that they exercise in their organization and comment on the source of their power.

SUMMARY

- There are five main types of business organization: sole traders, partnerships, private limited companies, public limited companies and co-operatives.

- Organizational design and structure are important factors in the way in which businesses might align themselves with their purpose.

- Typical structures used by businesses include hierarchical, product-based, functional, divisional, area or regional based structures, and matrix structures. Each has advantages and disadvantages and there may be elements of each type utilized in some (larger) organizations.

- Many firms have sought to review their structures in recent years in response to the changing external environment with flatter structures becoming more common to help boost flexibility and the ability to respond to changes.

- An organization's success is often closely linked to the culture it has and the ethical values it espouses. An organization's culture can be communicated through physical means and through the behaviours of its leaders and workers.

- Culture and ethics can also be influenced by the power structures and relationships that exist in an organization, the way in which people relate to other and how decisions are made.

IN THE NEWS

Private Sector Businesses in the UK

Figures released by the Department for Business Energy and Industrial Strategy showed that the total number of private sector businesses at the start of 2022 was 5.5 million. Of this number, 5.47 million were small businesses employing between 0 and 49 people. Some 35,900 were classed as medium sized employing between 50 and 249 employees, and 7,700 businesses were large employing upwards of 250 people. At the start of the millennium, the number of business enterprises was 3.5 million, so the figure for 2022 represents a 57 per cent increase over the period. However, the number was down on 2020 when the number stood at 6.0 million.

The figures for the start of 2022 show a 1.5 per cent fall in the number of businesses compared to the start of 2021 – 82,000. Sole proprietorships with no employees account for 74 per cent, and the total number of small businesses employing under 50 people represents 99.2 per cent of the business population. This number of businesses employs almost 13 million people and has a combined turnover of £1.4 trillion (€1.6 trillion). The total number of enterprises

with no employees was around 4.4 million. The number of businesses employing more than 250 employees was around 7,700 employing around 10.6 million people with a combined turnover of just over £2 trillion (€2.25 trillion). There were 3.1 million sole proprietorships representing 56 per cent of the total, of which 2.1 million were actively trading. There were 353,000 ordinary partnerships representing 6 per cent of the total population. There were just over 2 million limited liability companies. The biggest concentration of businesses was in London and the South East at around 1.8 million and accounting for 34 per cent of the total. The North East had the fewest number of businesses at 155,000. Scotland had 341,000, Wales 219,000 and Northern Ireland 128,000.

Private sector businesses are important in maintaining and growing employment levels but many small firms have no employees.

Questions

1. Looking at the figures for the types of business in the UK. Why do you think that partnerships represent such a small proportion of the total number of businesses?
2. Comment on the relative importance of different business types to the economy as a whole.
3. What do you think might have been the reasons for the increase in the number of businesses since 2000 and why do you think the number of businesses fell from 2020?
4. Why is an analysis of the number and type of businesses important in framing government policy on business and industrial strategy?
5. Consider the risks involved in setting up a small business as a sole proprietorship or ordinary partnership. How might governments help provide support for these types of businesses to help them manage the risk more effectively and what would be the longer-term benefits to the UK economy as a result?

Reference: www.gov.uk/government/statistics/business-population-estimates-2022/business-population-estimates-for-the-uk-and-regions-2022-statistical-release-html (accessed 9 June 2023).

QUESTIONS FOR REVIEW

1 Use an appropriate example to explain the difference between limited and unlimited liability.

2 What are the main differences between a sole trader and a partnership as forms of business organization?

3 Outline the main differences and similarities between private and public limited companies.

4 What are the main features of a co-operative and why are co-operatives typically associated with more socially conscious enterprises?

5 Distinguish between organization design and organization structure.

6 How might the design of an organization help or hinder its function or purpose?

7 Explain the main differences between functional and divisional structures.

8 What is meant by 'contingency theory' as applied to organizational structure?

9 How can an organization's culture and ethics contribute to it more effectively achieving its purpose?

10 Why are power relationships so important in an organization to help it better achieve its purpose?

PROBLEMS AND APPLICATIONS

1 An individual is thinking of setting up their own business. They have spoken with the bank who is prepared to lend some money to help start the business but have asked the individual to offer their house as collateral (security) for the loan. Do some research to find out the success/failure rates of sole trader type businesses and comment on the risks that the individual is taking in planning to set up their own business. Is it worth it?

2 Assume that an individual set up a business as a painter and decorator ten years ago and has managed to build the business up to be relatively successful. They now employ three people and are finding that demand has increased to the extent that they have bookings for jobs for the next eight months. The owner wants to expand and bring new capital into the business and is trying to decide whether to expand as a partnership or as a private limited company. Using your knowledge of both types of business organization, what advice would you give this individual about the direction they should go in?

3 Why do you think that public limited companies are subject to so many rules and regulations around setting them up when the shareholders have limited liability?

4 In traditional models of the firm, it is assumed that they are profit-maximizing entities. Given the popularity of co-operatives and social enterprises, to what extent do you think this assumption is too limiting in explaining firm behaviour?

5 Are organizations entities in themselves or are they something else?

6 Do some research on a well-known business of your choice and discuss what type of organizational structure the business has.

7 A five-star Michelin restaurant and a fast food restaurant both have the same business purpose – to provide customers with food. Why are they likely to be organized so differently and have a different culture?

8 To what extent do you think Covid-19 has affected the organizational structure and culture of firms?

9 A manufacturing firm has faced a number of difficulties in recent years which have put its survival at risk. It currently employs 300 people in three sites across Germany. The senior leaders have been negotiating with a government which has a very poor reputation for human rights but are on the brink of signing a contract to supply products which would guarantee the survival of the firm for the next ten years. Should it sign the contract? Explain in relation to the concepts of culture and ethics.

10 Consider the department in the school of the university in which you are studying. What are the power relationships that exist in the department and what are the sources of power of people in the department?

12 MARKET STRUCTURES: PERFECT COMPETITION

COMPETITION AND COMPETITIVE MARKETS

Where more than one firm offers the same or a similar product in a market, there is competition. However, there are different degrees of competition ranging from highly competitive markets through to markets where supply may be from a small number of very large firms, or in some cases just one firm. The more competitive the market, the smaller each firm is in comparison to the size of the market. Where firms can influence the market price of the good they sell through being able to differentiate its product offering in some way, they will have some element of *market power*.

Our analysis of competitive firms starts with the model of perfect competition. The perfectly competitive market model is based on the assumption that each firm is small in relation to the overall size of the market and thus are price takers. There is freedom of entry and exit and firms produce homogenous products.

Few markets have all the characteristics of perfectly competitive markets. Milk production is an example of one that does have a number of characteristics of a perfectly competitive market. There are many thousands of small firms that produce milk. Each has limited control over the price because many other sellers are offering a homogeneous product; milk from one farm is essentially identical to that from other farms. It is assumed that because each seller is small they can sell all they want at the going price. There is little reason to charge less, and if a higher price is charged, buyers will go elsewhere.

Entry into the dairy industry is relatively easy. Anyone can decide to start a dairy farm and for existing dairy farmers it is relatively easy to leave the industry. It should be noted that much of the analysis of competitive firms does not rely on the assumption of free entry and exit because this condition is not necessary for firms to be price takers. Entry and exit are often powerful forces shaping the long run outcome in competitive markets.

While on the sellers' side, the market for milk exhibits many characteristics of perfect competition, it is not the case that there are many thousands of individual buyers. The vast majority of individuals buy and use milk, but we buy from retailers who have processed and packaged the product, not from farmers. Farmers may have to sell their milk to large firms who manage this processing and distribution to retailers. These firms may seek to exploit market power. However, for the purposes of analysis, we are going to assume that no single buyer of milk can influence the price of milk, because each buyer purchases a small amount relative to the size of the market.

The Marginal Cost Curve and the Firm's Supply Decision

It is assumed that firms in perfect competition seek to maximize profits. The point of profit maximization is the output level where marginal cost equals marginal revenue ($MC = MR$). Consider the profit-maximizing position for a competitive firm as shown in Figure 12.1. The figure shows a horizontal line at the market price (P). The price line is horizontal because the firm is a price taker: the price of the firm's output is the same, regardless of the quantity that the firm decides to produce. For a perfectly competitive firm, the firm's price equals both its average revenue (AR) and its MR. The firm can sell all it wants at the reigning market price (bear in mind that the firm is small in relation to the total market and as a result output levels will be relatively small). If the firm is currently selling 100 units and the market price is €2 per unit then the $AR = TR/Q$ and will be 200/100 = €2. If it now sells an additional unit at €2, its AR will be 202/101 = €2 and the MR will also be €2. Therefore, under these highly competitive conditions, $P = AR = MR$.

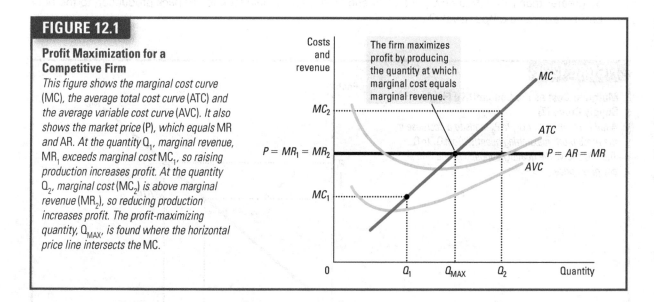

FIGURE 12.1

Profit Maximization for a Competitive Firm

This figure shows the marginal cost curve (MC), the average total cost curve (ATC) and the average variable cost curve (AVC). It also shows the market price (P), which equals MR and AR. At the quantity Q_1, marginal revenue, MR_1 exceeds marginal cost MC_1, so raising production increases profit. At the quantity Q_2, marginal cost (MC_2) is above marginal revenue (MR_2), so reducing production increases profit. The profit-maximizing quantity, Q_{MAX}, is found where the horizontal price line intersects the MC.

Figure 12.2 shows how a competitive firm responds to an increase in the price which may have been caused by a change in global market conditions. Remember that competitive firms are price takers and must accept the market price for their product. Prices of commodities such as grain, sugar, cotton, coffee, pork and so on are set by organized international markets, and so the individual firm has limited power to influence price. When the price is P_1, the firm produces quantity Q_1, the quantity that equates marginal cost to the price (which, remember, is the same as MR). Assume that an outbreak of bovine tuberculosis results in the need to slaughter a large proportion of dairy cattle leading to a shortage of milk on the market. When the price rises to P_2, the individual firm finds that MR is now higher than marginal cost at the previous level of output, so the firm will seek to increase production (assuming it is not one of the firms whose dairy herd has been wiped out). The new profit-maximizing quantity is Q_2, at which marginal cost equals the new higher price. Because the firm's MC determines the quantity of the good the firm is willing to supply at any price, it is the competitive firm's supply curve.

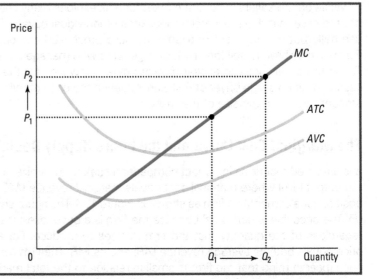

FIGURE 12.2

Marginal Cost as the Competitive Firm's Supply Curve (1)

An increase in the price from P_1 to P_2 leads to an increase in the firm's profit-maximizing quantity from Q_1 to Q_2. Because the MC shows the quantity supplied by the firm at any given price, it is the competitive firm's supply curve.

A similar, but reversed, situation would occur if the price fell for some reason as shown in Figure 12.3. In this situation, the firm would find that at the initial equilibrium output level, Q_1, marginal cost would be greater than MR with a new price of P_2 and so the firm would look to cut back production to the new profit-maximizing output level Q_2.

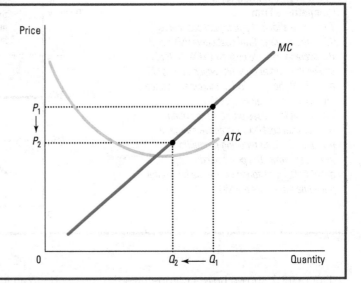

FIGURE 12.3

Marginal Cost as the Competitive Firm's Supply Curve (2)

A fall in the price from P_1 to P_2 leads to a decrease in the firm's profit-maximizing quantity from Q_1 to Q_2. The MC shows the quantity supplied by the firm at any given price.

The Firm's Short Run Decision to Shut Down

Clearly, in reality, the profit-maximizing output might be hard to identify because it relies on the firm being able to identify all its costs and revenues accurately over a period of time. It also needs to have the capacity to expand and contract quickly in response to changing market conditions. We also know that firms make losses; sometimes very big losses. If we assume that a firm exists to make a profit, do we conclude that if it makes a loss it will shut down its operations? This is obviously not the case in some situations, although at some point a decision to cease operating will be taken. How does the firm make that sort of decision?

We can distinguish between a temporary shutdown of a firm and the permanent exit of a firm from the market. A *shutdown* refers to a short run decision not to produce anything during a specific period of time because of current market conditions. This is different from a complete cessation of operations, referred to as exit. *Exit* is a long run decision to leave the market. The short run and long run decisions differ because most firms cannot avoid their fixed costs in the short run, but can do so in the long run. A firm that shuts down temporarily must still pay its fixed costs, whereas a firm that exits the market saves both its fixed and its variable costs.

For example, consider the production decision that a milk producer faces. The cost of the land and the capital equipment, such as tractors, milking parlours and sheds, form part of the farmer's fixed costs. If the firm decides to suspend the supply of milk, the cost of the land and capital cannot be recovered. When making the short run decision whether to shut down production for a period, the fixed cost of land and capital is a *sunk cost*. By contrast, if the dairy farmer decides to leave the industry altogether, they can sell the land and some of the capital equipment. When making the long run decision whether to exit the market, the cost of land and capital is not sunk.

Now let us consider what determines a firm's shutdown decision in the short run. If the firm shuts down, it loses all revenue from the sale of the products it is not now producing and which could be sold. At the same time, it does not have to pay the variable costs of making its product (but must still pay the fixed costs). Common sense would tell us that a firm shuts down if the revenue that it would get from producing is less than its variable costs of production: it is simply not worth producing a product which costs more to produce than the revenue generated by its sale. Doing so would reduce profit or make any existing losses even greater.

If *TR* stands for total revenue and *VC* stands for variable costs, then the firm's decision can be written as:

$$\text{Shut down if } TR < VC$$

The firm shuts down if TR is less than variable cost. By dividing both sides of this inequality by the quantity *Q*, we can write it as:

$$\text{Shut down if } TR/Q < VC/Q$$

Notice that this can be further simplified. *TR/Q* is total revenue divided by quantity, which is AR. For a competitive firm, AR is the good's price *P*. Similarly, *VC/Q* is average variable cost, *AVC*. Therefore, the firm's shutdown criterion is:

$$\text{Shut down if } P < AVC$$

That is, a firm chooses to shut down if the price of the good is less than the AVC of production. This is our common sense interpretation: when choosing to produce, the firm compares the price it receives for the typical unit to the AVC that it must incur to produce the typical unit. If the price does not cover the AVC, the firm is better off stopping production altogether. The firm can reopen in the future if conditions change such that price exceeds AVC.

 WHAT IF... the price the firm received was equal to AVC in the long run. Would the firm still be able to continue in production indefinitely?

We now have a full description of a competitive firm's profit-maximizing strategy. If the firm produces anything, it produces the quantity at which MC equals the price of the product. If the price is less than AVC at that quantity, the firm is better off shutting down and not producing anything. These results are illustrated in Figure 12.4. The competitive firm's short run supply curve is the portion of its MC that lies above AVC.

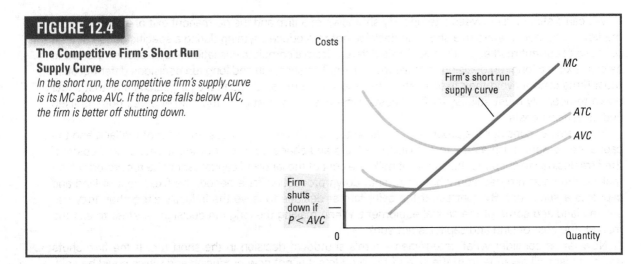

FIGURE 12.4

The Competitive Firm's Short Run Supply Curve
In the short run, the competitive firm's supply curve is its MC above AVC. If the price falls below AVC, the firm is better off shutting down.

Economists say that a cost is a **sunk cost** when it has already been committed and cannot be recovered. In a sense, a sunk cost is the opposite of an opportunity cost: an opportunity cost is what you must give up if you choose to do one thing instead of another, whereas a sunk cost cannot be avoided, regardless of the choices you make. Because nothing can be done about sunk costs, you can ignore them when making decisions about various aspects of life, including business strategy.

sunk cost a cost that has already been committed and cannot be recovered

Our analysis of the firm's shutdown decision is one example of the importance of recognizing sunk costs. We assume that the firm cannot recover its fixed costs by temporarily stopping production. As a result, the firm's fixed costs are sunk in the short run, and the firm can ignore these costs when deciding how much to produce. The firm's short run supply curve is the part of the MC that lies above AVC, and the size of the fixed cost does not matter for this supply decision.

The Firm's Long Run Decision to Exit or Enter a Market

The firm's long run decision to exit the market is similar to its short run decision in some respects. If the firm exits, it again will lose all revenue from the sale of its product, but now it saves on both fixed and variable costs of production. Thus, the firm exits the market if the revenue it would get from producing is less than its total costs. We can again make this criterion more useful by writing it mathematically. If *TR* stands for total revenue and *TC* stands for total cost, then the firm's criterion can be written as:

$$\text{Exit if } TR < TC$$

The firm exits if TR is less than TC in the long run. By dividing both sides of this inequality by quantity *Q*, we can write it as:

$$\text{Exit if } TR/Q < TC/Q$$

We can simplify this further by noting that *TR/Q* is AR, which, for a competitive firm is the same as the price *P,* and that *TC/Q* is average total cost *ATC.* Therefore, the firm's exit criterion is:

$$\text{Exit if } P < ATC$$

That is, a firm chooses to exit if the price of the good is less than the ATC of production.

One of the financial objectives for new firms starting up is to make profit. The entry criterion where some profit will be made is:

$$\text{Enter if } P > ATC$$

The criterion for entry is the opposite of the criterion for exit.

We can now describe a competitive firm's long run profit-maximizing strategy. If the firm is in the market, it aims to produce at the quantity at which marginal cost equals the price of the good. Yet if the price is less than ATC at that quantity, the firm chooses to exit (or not enter) the market. These results are illustrated in Figure 12.5. The competitive firm's long run supply curve is the portion of its MC that lies above ATC.

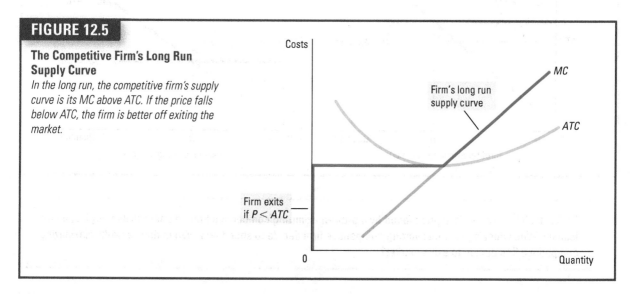

FIGURE 12.5

The Competitive Firm's Long Run Supply Curve

In the long run, the competitive firm's supply curve is its MC above ATC. If the price falls below ATC, the firm is better off exiting the market.

Measuring Profit in Our Graph for the Competitive Firm

As we analyze exit and entry, it is useful to be able to analyze the firm's profit in more detail. Recall that profit (π) equals TR minus total cost (TC):

$$\pi = TR - TC$$

We can rewrite this definition by multiplying and dividing the right-hand side by Q:

$$\pi = [(TR/Q) - (TC/Q)] \times Q$$

Note that TR/Q is AR, which is the price P, and TC/Q is average total cost ATC. Therefore:

$$\pi = (P - ATC) \times Q$$

This way of expressing the firm's profit allows us to measure profit in our graphs. Panel (a) of Figure 12.6 shows a firm earning positive profit (this is also referred to as 'economic' or 'abnormal' profit and in some instances, 'supernormal profit'). As we have already discussed, the firm maximizes profit by producing the quantity at which price equals marginal cost. Now look at the shaded rectangle. The height of the rectangle is $P - ATC$. The width of the rectangle is Q, the quantity produced. Therefore, the area of the rectangle is $(P - ATC) \times Q$, which is the firm's profit.

Similarly, panel (b) of this figure shows a firm with losses (negative or subnormal profit). In this case, maximizing profit means minimizing losses, a task accomplished once again by producing the quantity at which price equals marginal cost. Now consider the shaded rectangle. The height of the rectangle is $ATC - P$, and the width is Q. The area is $(ATC - P) \times Q$, which is the firm's loss. Because a firm in this situation is not making enough revenue to cover its ATC, the firm would choose to exit the market.

FIGURE 12.6

Profit as the Area Between Price and ATC

The area of the shaded box between price and ATC represents the firm's profit or loss. The height of this box is the difference between price and average total cost, and the width of the box is the quantity of output (Q). In panel (a), price is above ATC, and the height of the box is (P − ATC), so the firm has positive profit. In panel (b), price is less than ATC, and the height of the box is (ATC − P), so the firm has losses.

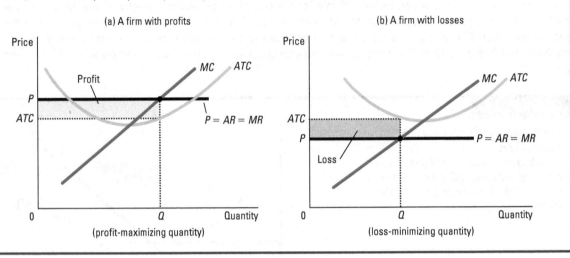

(a) A firm with profits   (b) A firm with losses

SELF TEST How does the price faced by a profit-maximizing competitive firm compare to its marginal cost? Explain. When does a profit-maximizing competitive firm decide to shut down? When does a profit-maximizing competitive firm decide to exit a market?

THE SUPPLY CURVE IN A COMPETITIVE MARKET

Now that we have examined the supply decision of a single firm, we can discuss the supply curve for a market. There are two cases to consider. First, we examine a market with a fixed number of firms. Second, we examine a market in which the number of firms can change as old firms exit the market and new firms enter. Both cases are important, for each applies over a specific time horizon. Over short periods of time it is often difficult for firms to enter and exit, so the assumption of a fixed number of firms is appropriate. But over long periods of time, the number of firms can adjust to changing market conditions.

The Short Run: Market Supply with a Fixed Number of Firms

Consider first a market with 1,000 identical firms. For any given price, each firm supplies a quantity of output so that its marginal cost equals the price, as shown in panel (a) of Figure 12.7. That is, as long as price is above AVC, each firm's MC is its supply curve. The quantity of output supplied to the market equals the sum of the quantities supplied by each of the 1,000 individual firms. Thus to derive the market supply curve, we add the quantity supplied by each firm in the market. As panel (b) of Figure 12.7 shows, because the firms are identical, the quantity supplied to the market is 1,000 times the quantity supplied by each firm.

The Long Run: Market Supply with Entry and Exit

Now consider what happens if firms are able to enter or exit the market. Let us suppose that everyone has access to the same technology for producing the good and access to the same markets to buy the inputs into production. Therefore, all firms and all potential firms have the same cost curves.

FIGURE 12.7

Market Supply with a Fixed Number of Firms

When the number of firms in the market is fixed, the market supply curve, shown in panel (b), reflects the individual firms' MCs, shown in panel (a). Here, in a market of 1,000 firms, the quantity of output supplied to the market is 1,000 times the quantity supplied by each firm.

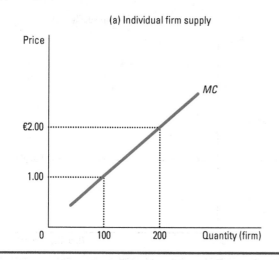

(a) Individual firm supply

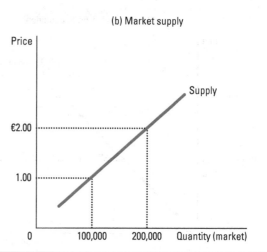

(b) Market supply

Decisions about entry and exit in a market of this type depend on the incentives facing the owners of existing firms and the entrepreneurs who could start new firms. If firms already in the market are profitable, then new firms will have an incentive to enter the market. This entry will expand the number of firms, increase the quantity of the good supplied and drive down prices and profits. Conversely, if firms in the market are making losses, then some existing firms will exit the market. Their exit will reduce the number of firms, decrease the quantity of the good supplied and drive up prices and profits. At the end of this process of entry and exit, firms that remain in the market must be making zero economic profit, or normal profit.

> **PITFALL PREVENTION** When talking about zero economic profit, it is important to remember the distinction between economic profit and accounting profit. When economists talk of zero profit they are referring to economic profit.

Recall that we can write a firm's profits as:

$$\pi = (P - ATC) \times Q$$

This equation shows that an operating firm has zero profit if, and only if, the price of the good equals the ATC of producing that good. If price is above ATC, profit is positive, which encourages new firms to enter. If price is less than ATC, profit is negative, that is, firms have made a loss, which encourages some firms to exit. The process of entry and exit ends only when price and ATC are driven to equality.

This analysis has a surprising implication. We noted earlier in the chapter that competitive firms produce so that price equals marginal cost. We just noted that free entry and exit forces price to equal ATC. If price is to equal both marginal cost and ATC, these two measures of cost must equal each other. Marginal cost and ATC are equal, however, only when the firm is operating at the minimum of ATC. Recall that the level of production with lowest ATC is called the firm's efficient scale. Therefore, the long run equilibrium of a competitive market with free entry and exit must have firms operating at their efficient scale.

Panel (a) of Figure 12.8 shows a firm in such a long run equilibrium. In this figure, price *P* equals marginal cost *MC*, so the firm is profit-maximizing. Price also equals average total cost *ATC*, so profits are zero. New firms have no incentive to enter the market, and existing firms have no incentive to leave the market.

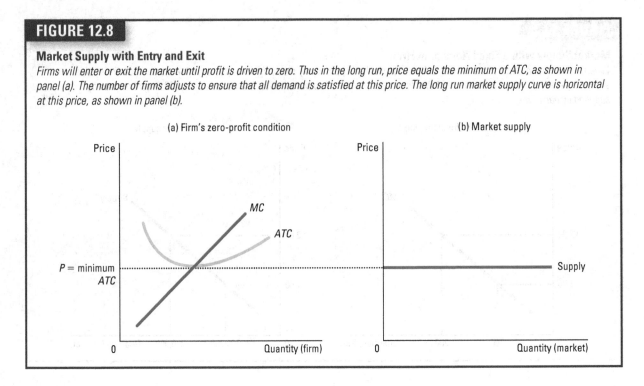

FIGURE 12.8

Market Supply with Entry and Exit

Firms will enter or exit the market until profit is driven to zero. Thus in the long run, price equals the minimum of ATC, as shown in panel (a). The number of firms adjusts to ensure that all demand is satisfied at this price. The long run market supply curve is horizontal at this price, as shown in panel (b).

From this analysis of firm behaviour, we can determine the long run supply curve for the perfectly competitive market. In a market with free entry and exit, there is only one price consistent with zero profit, the minimum of ATC. As a result, the long run market supply curve must be horizontal at this price, as in panel (b) of Figure 12.8. Any price above this level would generate profit, leading to entry and an increase in the total quantity supplied. Any price below this level would generate losses, leading to exit and a decrease in the total quantity supplied. Eventually, the number of firms in the market adjusts so that price equals the minimum of ATC, and there are enough firms to satisfy all the demand at this price.

Why Do Competitive Firms Stay in Business if They Make Zero Profit?

At first, it might seem odd that competitive firms earn zero profit in the long run. After all, people start businesses to make a profit. If entry eventually drives profit to zero, there might seem to be little reason to stay in business.

To understand the zero profit condition more fully, recall that profit equals TR minus TC, and that TC includes all the opportunity costs of the firm. In particular, TC includes the opportunity cost of the time and money that the firm's owners devote to the business. In the zero profit equilibrium, the firm's revenue must compensate the owners for the time and money that they expend to keep their business going.

Consider an example. Suppose that a farmer had to invest €1 million to open their farm, which otherwise could have been deposited in a bank to earn €50,000 a year in interest. In addition, the farmer had to give up another job that would have paid them €30,000 a year. Then the farmer's opportunity cost of farming includes both the interest they could have earned and the foregone wages, a total of €80,000. This sum must be calculated as part of the farmer's TCs. Zero profit is also referred to as **normal profit**, the minimum amount required to keep factor inputs in their current use. Even if profit is driven to zero, the revenue from farming compensates them for these opportunity costs.

normal profit the minimum amount required to keep factors of production in their current use

Keep in mind that accountants and economists measure costs differently; accountants keep track of explicit costs but usually do not consider implicit costs. As a result, in the zero profit equilibrium, economic profit is zero, but accounting profit is positive. Our farmer's accountant, for instance, would conclude that the farmer earned an accounting profit of €80,000, which is enough to keep the farmer in business. In the short run as we shall see, profit can be above zero or normal profit, which is referred to as **abnormal profit**.

abnormal profit the profit over and above normal profit

 WHAT IF... a firm earned profit which was only 1 per cent less than zero profit. Would it still be worthwhile continuing in production?

A Shift in Demand in the Short Run and Long Run

Because firms can enter and exit a market in the long run but not in the short run, the response of a market to a change in demand depends on the time horizon. To see this, let us trace the effects of a shift in demand. This analysis will show how a market responds over time, and it will show how entry and exit drive a market to its long run equilibrium.

Suppose the market for milk begins in long run equilibrium. Firms are earning zero profit, so price equals the minimum of ATC. Panel (a) of Figure 12.9 shows the situation. The long run equilibrium is point A, the quantity sold in the market is Q_1 and the price is P_1.

Now suppose scientists discover that milk has miraculous health benefits. The demand curve for milk shifts outward from D_1 to D_2, as in panel (b). The short run equilibrium moves from point A to point B; as a result, the quantity rises from Q_1 to Q_2 and the price rises from P_1 to P_2. All the existing firms respond to the higher price by raising the amount produced. Because each firm's supply curve reflects its MC, how much they each increase production is determined by the MC. In the new short run equilibrium, the price of milk exceeds ATC, so the firms are making positive or abnormal profit.

Over time, the profit in this market encourages new firms to enter. Some farmers may switch to milk production from other farm products, for example. As the number of firms grows, the short run supply curve shifts to the right from S_1 to S_2, as in panel (c), and this shift causes the price of milk to fall. Eventually, the price is driven back down to the minimum of ATC, profits are zero and firms stop entering. Thus, the market reaches a new long run equilibrium, point C. The price of milk has returned to P_1, but the quantity produced has risen to Q_3. Each firm is again producing at its efficient scale, but because more firms are in the dairy business, the quantity of milk produced and sold is higher.

The Effect of a Fall in Demand in the Short Run and Long Run   In the event that there was a fall in demand for a product in a perfectly competitive market the reverse process would occur. Assume that it is discovered that milk and milk products have a direct link to an increase in diabetes. The demand for milk would fall and price would consequently fall. Firms in the industry would now be making subnormal profits with price less than ATC. This would result in some firms leaving the industry, and the industry or market supply curve shifting to the left. This would push the price back up to a new long run equilibrium where all firms are once again making zero or normal profit but the output of the industry as a whole would be lower.

FIGURE 12.9

An Increase in Demand in the Short Run and Long Run

The market starts in a long run equilibrium, shown as point A in panel (a). In this equilibrium, each firm makes zero profit, and the price equals the minimum ATC. Panel (b) shows what happens in the short run when demand rises from D_1 to D_2. The equilibrium goes from point A to point B, price rises from P_1 to P_2, and the quantity sold in the market rises from Q_1 to Q_2. Because price now exceeds ATC, firms make profits, which over time encourage new firms to enter the market. This entry shifts the short run supply curve to the right from S_1 to S_2 as shown in panel (c). In the new long run equilibrium, point C, price has returned to P_1 but the quantity sold has increased to Q_3. Profits are again zero, price is back to the minimum of ATC, but the market has more firms to satisfy the greater demand.

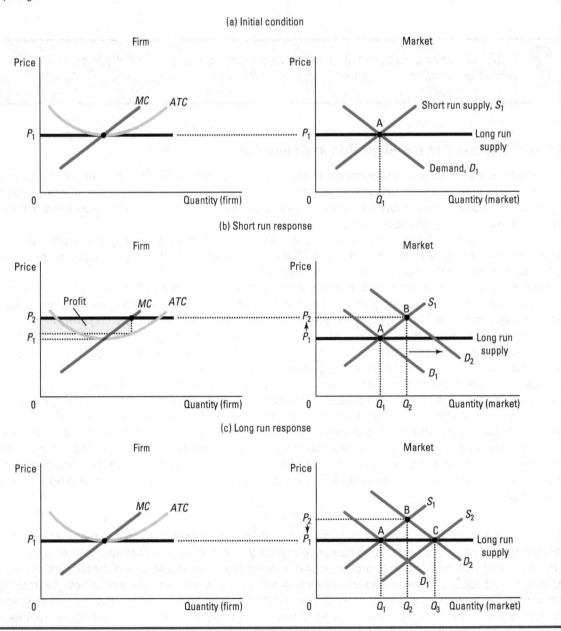

Why the Long Run Supply Curve Might Slope Upwards

We have seen that entry and exit can cause the long run market supply curve to be horizontal. The essence of our analysis is that there are a large number of potential entrants, each of which faces the same costs. As a result, the long run market supply curve is horizontal at the minimum of ATC. When the demand for the good increases, the long run result is an increase in the number of firms and in the total quantity supplied, without any change in the price.

The reality is that the assumptions we have made in our model do not hold in all cases. There are two reasons that the long run market supply curve might slope upward. The first is that some resources used in production may be available only in limited quantities. For example, consider the market for farm products. Anyone can choose to buy land and start a farm, but the quantity and quality of land is limited. As more people become farmers, the price of farmland is bid up, which raises the costs of all farmers in the market. Thus an increase in demand for farm products cannot induce an increase in quantity supplied without also inducing a rise in farmers' costs, which in turn means a rise in price. The result is a long run market supply curve that is upwards sloping, even with free entry into farming.

A second reason for an upwards sloping supply curve is that firms may have different costs. For example, consider the market for painters. Anyone can enter the market for painting services, but not everyone has the same costs. Costs vary in part because some people work faster than others, use different materials and equipment, and because some people have better alternative uses of their time than others. For any given price, those with lower costs are more likely to enter than those with higher costs. To increase the quantity of painting services supplied, additional entrants must be encouraged to enter the market. Because these new entrants have higher costs, the price must rise to make entry profitable for them. Thus, the market supply curve for painting services slopes upwards even with free entry into the market.

Notice that if firms have different costs, some firms earn profit even in the long run. In this case, the price in the market reflects the ATC of the *marginal firm,* the firm that would exit the market if the price were any lower. This firm earns zero profit, but firms with lower costs earn positive profit. Entry does not eliminate this profit because would be entrants have higher costs than firms already in the market. Higher-cost firms will enter only if the price rises, making the market profitable for them.

Thus for these two reasons, the long run supply curve in a market may be upwards sloping rather than horizontal, indicating that a higher price is necessary to induce a larger quantity supplied. Nevertheless, the basic lesson about entry and exit remains true. Because firms can enter and exit more easily in the long run than in the short run in a perfectly competitive market, the long run supply curve is typically more elastic than the short run supply curve.

SELF TEST In the long run with free entry and exit, is the price in a market equal to marginal cost, ATC, both or neither? Explain with a diagram.

CASE STUDY   **Friedrich Hayek and the Model of Perfect Competition**

Friedrich Hayek (1899–1992) was a noted political economist who was awarded the Nobel Prize for Economics in 1974. He was part of the Austrian school of economics which placed an emphasis in its analysis on the lack of perfect information. Perfect information on the part of buyers and sellers is one of the assumptions of the perfectly competitive market model.

Hayek argued that one of the issues with the theory of perfect competition is that its long run conclusions of equilibrium are effectively determined by the assumptions that are made. In other words, economists have assumed equilibrium will be the desirable and appropriate outcome, and looked for the conditions that would have to exist to allow for this outcome to occur. In many respects, that is the way in which many theories of economics developed in the nineteenth century. Economists of that era were dealing with and observing different problems in a different economic setting than the one that exists today.

Hayek's main observations on the perfectly competitive model were originally developed in the late 1940s and are based around the information that buyers and sellers possess; that sellers, for example, know the

(Continued)

most efficient combination of resources to produce at lowest cost (and by implication, that regulators also can identify this point). Equally, the information that consumers possess is such that they are able to identify the price they are willing to pay based on their knowledge of the product in question and the substitutes that are available. Moreover, Hayek argued that the very elements of what can be understood as 'competition', branding, advertising, differentiating, improving products, improving customer service and so on, are redundant in the model of 'perfect competition'. Hayek suggested that we should not be worried about how closely a market matches the model of perfect competition in regulating and legislating, but whether there is any competition at all. Hayek argued that competition is a dynamic process and the model of perfect competition assumes away the dynamic process because its assumptions are based on static analysis: the process by which equilibrium is reached, where the outcome is 'static' and at rest.

Perfectly competitive markets are meant to result in increased choice and low prices for consumers but is the theory valid?

Questions

1. **Consider the long run outcomes of the model of perfect competition. Do you think that the outcomes are both desirable and appropriate as the basis for judging real world markets? Justify your answer.**
2. **Hayek argued that competition is a dynamic process, but that the model of perfect competition is based on static analysis. To what extent can it be argued that the model does have a dynamic element and that there is an incentive for sellers to 'compete'?**
3. **Can sellers and regulators ever 'know' what the most efficient allocation of resources is, i.e. where the point of minimum ATC lies in their industry?**
4. **'There is little value and relevance in the model of perfect competition, and as a consequence it should be removed from undergraduate economics curricula.' To what extent do you agree with this statement?**

BEHIND THE SUPPLY CURVE

We have been discussing the behaviour of competitive profit-maximizing firms. Marginal analysis has given us a theory of the supply curve in a competitive market and a deeper understanding of market outcomes.

We have learned that given the assumptions of this model of the competitive market, consumers buying goods from a firm in a competitive market are paying a price close to the cost of producing that good. In particular, if firms are competitive and profit-maximizing, the price of a good equals the marginal cost of making that good. If firms can freely enter and exit the market, the price also equals the lowest possible ATC of production.

The Relevance of the Perfectly Competitive Model

The perfectly competitive market model has been criticized as being unrealistic and unhelpful in predicting firm behaviour. This is primarily because all the assumptions of the perfectly competitive model rarely hold in reality. Why then, is the model still taught in schools and universities if it is not reflective of the real world?

In the perfectly competitive market model, the long run equilibrium has firms producing where price equals marginal cost and making zero or normal profit. Because each firm is small in relation to the total market, they cannot wield market power. Because the products are homogeneous, there is no need to 'waste' resources in advertising. As each firm produces where price equals marginal cost and at the minimum point of ATC in the long run, the market exhibits both productive and allocative efficiency. Allocative efficiency refers to the situation where the marginal cost to firms is equal to the marginal benefit to consumers of the output being produced. Productive efficiency is a situation where firms are producing maximum output at minimum cost and there is no other way of producing that output, *ceteris paribus* (other things equal) using fewer resources. In long run equilibrium, therefore, consumer and producer surplus is maximized, as is economic welfare.

The model provides us with a benchmark as to the costs and benefits of markets that do operate in the real world. For example, in the UK, one of the reasons why the energy supply industry was privatized in the 1980s was to create a market which was more competitive and would benefit consumers and encourage efficiency. No one would claim that the energy supply industry is remotely like the economists' model, but it is possible for regulators and governments to look at the extent to which the industry differs from that which would exist if the market were more competitive and make decisions as a consequence. How far is price above marginal cost? How far are firms producing away from minimum ATC? What is the extent of consumer surplus in the market? How easy is it for firms to enter and exit the industry? To what extent have consumers got good information about the activities of firms to enable them to make appropriate choices? These are all questions which can be assessed and recommendations made about how the industry should operate. In making these recommendations, regulators and governments might be in a position to improve market outcomes.

We have used examples in this chapter of farms and farming. One of the reasons for this is that the agricultural industry does reflect the perfectly competitive market model to a degree. Commodities such as tea, coffee, wheat, corn, soya beans, rape, barley, milk and so on are relatively homogeneous, are produced by many firms which are small in relation to the total market (which is global in some cases) and where firms are price takers. There are also relatively low barriers to entry. The model can be used to analyze these markets, make predictions about how firms might behave and how far the market delivers both allocative and productive efficiency.

As with any model it is important to recognize that it is not a perfect representation of the real world; neither is it meant to be. It helps thinking about real world markets, about what we might want to see in terms of firm behaviour and market outcomes, and in turn helps decision makers both in the industry and outside to devise policies and make decisions which seek to improve welfare and the benefit to consumers and society.

SUMMARY

- Because a competitive firm is a price taker, its revenue is proportional to the amount of output it produces. The price of the good equals both the firm's AR and its MR.

- To maximize profit, a firm chooses a quantity of output such that MR equals MC. Because MR for a competitive firm equals the market price, the firm chooses quantity so that price equals MC. Thus, the firm's MC is its supply curve.

- In the short run when a firm cannot recover its fixed costs, the firm will choose to shut down temporarily if the price of the good is less than AVC. In the long run when the firm can recover both fixed and variable costs, it will choose to exit if the price is less than ATC.

- In a market with free entry and exit, profits are driven to zero in the long run. In this long run equilibrium, all firms produce at the efficient scale, price equals the minimum of ATC, and the number of firms adjusts to satisfy the quantity demanded at this price.

- Changes in demand have different effects over different time horizons. In the short run, an increase in demand raises prices and leads to profits, and a decrease in demand lowers prices and leads to losses. If firms can freely enter and exit the market, then in the long run the number of firms adjusts to drive the market back to the zero profit equilibrium.

IN THE NEWS

Pig Farming

For some years now, pig farmers in the UK have been warning of a crisis in the industry. Low prices, rising costs and competition from abroad have all been putting pressure on farmers. According to figures produced by the UK Department for the Environment, Food and Rural Affairs (Defra), the number of farms focusing on pig production has fallen from around 12,100 in 2007 to just over 10,000 in 2022. The National Pig Association (NPA) reported that the full economic cost of production was around 237p per kilogram in October 2022 but the standard pig price (SPP) stood at around 200p per kilogram. The cost of producing pigs is partly driven by higher feed prices caused by supply chain problems resulting from the conflict in Ukraine and an increase in energy

The pig farming industry faces considerable pressures but to what extent is it perfectly competitive?

costs. Cheaper imports from the EU have also resulted in UK pig farmers struggling to compete.

Some pig farmers have complained that meat processors, a key buyer of pigs from farms, have been exerting a downwards pressure on price. One of the complaints was that the increase in the cost of living in the UK was forcing retailers to try to keep prices lower to retain customers and, as a result, pig farmers were being squeezed. One of the largest processors of pigs, Woodheads-Morrisons, which processes around 30,000 pigs each week, pushed prices down to around 167p per kilogram in the latter part of 2022. Woodheads-Morrisons is owned by the Morrisons supermarket group. Some pig farmers have argued that while prices paid by supermarkets to farmers has fallen, the profits supermarkets are making have increased. They argue that they understand the need to keep prices to consumers under control, but they believe that supermarkets need to take some responsibility for ensuring that suppliers are also treated fairly and that, maybe, some supermarkets need to accept lower profits as a result.

Questions

1. To what extent is the pig farming industry reflective of the perfectly competitive market model discussed in this chapter?
2. Considering the cost of production of pigs given in the article and the price that pig farmers are receiving, use an appropriate diagram to show the profit or loss that pig farmers are making and explain what predictions you would make about the number of pig farmers in the UK industry.
3. If the price pig farmers receive is lower than the cost of production, should pig farmers leave the industry?
4. One of the competitive pressures facing pig farmers is cheaper imports coming from the EU. Does the model of perfect competition allow for this sort of competitive pressure?
5. One pig farmer in the UK was quoted as saying: 'We don't want people to pay more for [pork products], but if the supermarkets can't change that percentage profit margin, if they won't do that, then they're showing responsibilities towards consumers, [and] I would argue that a large corporation like that should also show a moral responsibility towards their suppliers.' To what extent do you agree with this viewpoint and how does it reflect one of the weaknesses in the model of perfect competition?

References: https://ahdb.org.uk/pork/uk-pig-numbers-and-holdings (accessed 7 June 2023).
www.npa-uk.org.uk/Pig_industry_crisis-NPA_blog_January_6_2022_SPP_up_Tesco_highlights_pig_harvest_issues.html (accessed 7 June 2023).
www.farminguk.com/news/big-reduction-takes-pig-prices-below-2-per-kg-mark_61716.html (accessed 7 June 2023).
www.morrisons-farming.com/where-we-work/woodheads/ (accessed 7 June 2023).

QUESTIONS FOR REVIEW

1 What is meant by a 'competitive firm'?

2 Draw the cost curves for a typical firm in a perfectly competitive market. For a given price, explain how the firm chooses the level of output that maximizes profit.

3 Under what conditions will a firm shut down temporarily? Explain.

4 Under what conditions will a firm exit a market? Explain.

5 Under what conditions will a firm enter a market? Explain.

6 Does a firm's price equal marginal cost in the short run, in the long run, or both? Explain.

7 Does a firm's price equal the minimum of ATC in the short run, in the long run, or both? Explain.

8 Explain why a firm will continue in production even if it makes zero profit.

9 If a firm is making abnormal profit in the short run, what will happen to these profits in the long run assuming the conditions for a highly competitive market exist?

10 Are market supply curves typically more elastic in the short run or in the long run? Explain.

PROBLEMS AND APPLICATIONS

1 What are the characteristics of a competitive market? Which of the following drinks do you think is best described by these characteristics? Why are the others not?

    a. tap water
    b. bottled water
    c. cola
    d. beer

2 Your flatmate's long hours in the chemistry lab finally paid off. They discovered a secret formula that lets people do an hour's worth of studying in 5 minutes. So far, they have sold 200 doses, and face the following ATC schedule:

Q	ATC (€)
199	199
200	200
201	201

If a new customer offers to pay your flatmate €300 for one dose, should they make one more? Explain.

3 Farming is often cited as an example of an industry which adheres closely to the perfectly competitive market model.

    a. In what ways do you think farms and farming match the assumptions of the model and in what ways does the industry differ from the model?
    b. There are many farmers producing milk across the UK and Europe. Is milk a homogenous product? In what ways might farmers try and differentiate their milk?

4 T42 is a small firm which produces tea leaves and faces costs of production as follows:

Quantity (tonnes)	Total fixed costs (€)	Total variable costs (€)
0	1,000	0
100	1,000	500
200	1,000	700
300	1,000	900
400	1,000	1,400
500	1,000	2,000
600	1,000	3,600

a. Calculate the firm's average fixed costs, AVCs, ATCs and marginal costs at each level of production.
b. The market price of tea is €500 per tonne. Seeing that it cannot make a profit, the farmer decides to shut down operations. What are the firm's profits/losses? Was this a wise decision? Explain.
c. Vaguely remembering her introductory business economics course, the farmer's daughter tells her father it is better to produce 100 tonnes of tea, because MR equals MC at that quantity. What are the firm's profits/losses at that level of production? Was this the best decision? Explain.

5 'High prices traditionally cause expansion in an industry, eventually bringing an end to high prices and manufacturers' prosperity.' Explain, using appropriate diagrams.

6 Suppose the book printing industry is competitive and begins in long run equilibrium.

a. Draw a diagram describing the typical firm in the industry.
b. Hi-Tech Printing Company invents a new process that significantly reduces the cost of printing books. What happens to Hi-Tech's profits and the price of books in the short run when Hi-Tech's patent prevents other firms from using the new technology?
c. What happens in the long run when the patent expires and other firms are free to use the technology?

7 Many small boats are made of fibreglass, which is derived from crude oil. Suppose that the price of oil rises.

a. Using diagrams, show what happens to the cost curves of an individual boat-making firm and to the market supply curve.
b. What happens to the profits of boat-makers in the short run? What happens to the number of boat-makers in the long run?

8 Suppose that the EU textile industry is competitive, and there is no international trade in textiles. In long run equilibrium, the price per unit of cloth is €30.

a. Describe the equilibrium using graphs for the entire market and for an individual producer.

Now suppose that textile producers in non-EU countries are willing to sell large quantities of cloth in the EU for only €25 per unit.

b. Assuming that EU textile producers have large fixed costs, what is the short run effect of these imports on the quantity produced by an individual producer? What is the short run effect on profits? Illustrate your answer with a graph.
c. What is the long run effect on the number of EU firms in the industry?

9 Assume that the soya milk industry is competitive.

a. Illustrate a long run equilibrium using diagrams for the soya milk market and for a representative soya producer.
b. Suppose that an increase in the number of people choosing a vegan lifestyle induces a surge in the demand for soya milk. Using your diagrams from part a., show what happens in the short run to the soya market and to each existing soya producer.
c. If the demand for soya milk remains high, what would happen to the price over time? Specifically, would the new long run equilibrium price be above, below or equal to the short run equilibrium price in part (b)? Is it possible for the new long run equilibrium price to be above the original long run equilibrium price? Explain.

10 The liquorice industry is competitive. Each firm produces 2 million liquorice bootlaces per year. The bootlaces have an ATC of €0.20 each and they sell for €0.30.

a. What is the marginal cost of a liquorice bootlace?
b. Is this industry in long run equilibrium? Why or why not?

13 MARKET STRUCTURES: MONOPOLY

LEARNING OUTCOMES

After reading this chapter you should be able to:

- List three sources of monopoly power.
- Use a monopolist's cost curves and the demand curve they face to show the profit earned by a monopolist.
- Show the deadweight loss from a monopolist's production decision.
- Show why forcing a natural monopoly to set its selling price equal to its marginal cost of production creates losses for the monopolist.
- Demonstrate the result that price discrimination by a monopolist can raise economic welfare above that generated by standard monopoly pricing.

INTRODUCTION

If you own a personal computer, it probably uses some version of Windows, the operating system sold by the US company, Microsoft Corporation. When Microsoft first designed Windows many years ago, it applied for and received a copyright, first from the US government and then from many of the governments of the world. The copyright gives Microsoft the exclusive right to make and sell copies of the Windows operating system. If a person wants to buy a copy of Windows, they have little choice but to give Microsoft the price that the firm has decided to charge for its product. One version or another of Windows is the operating system used by around 90 per cent of the desktop PCs in the world. Microsoft is said to have a *monopoly* in the market for operating systems.

If you use a PC or laptop, there is a very high chance that when you use a search engine it will be Google, which dominates the search engine market with a market share of around 92.6 per cent, as reported by StatCounter in June 2023.

In most countries, the option for consumers to purchase utilities like gas, water and electricity is limited to a very small number of firms. In some cases, there might only be one supplier.

The business decisions of Microsoft, Google and utility firms are not well described by the model of a competitive market. A firm such as Microsoft has few close competitors and such a dominant market share that it can influence the market price of its product: it has market power. When a firm has some element of market power its behaviour is different from that under the assumptions which characterized a highly competitive market.

> **PITFALL PREVENTION** Care is needed when using the word 'competitive' in economic analysis. In everyday usage, we use competitive to describe the degree of rivalry between groups or individuals. In economics, a firm in a competitive market is one which operates under the assumptions of a competitive market structure. Once we relax those assumptions we are interested in how a firm's behaviour changes. Competition between firms in market structures where there is considerable market power is certainly intense, but the options available to firms and their behaviours are different from those firms operating under more perfectly competitive conditions.

An imperfectly competitive market is one where the assumptions of perfect competition do not hold. At the extreme of imperfect competition is monopoly, which is a single supplier of a good with no competitors. Just as the extreme model of perfect competition does not exist in its purest form, there are few examples of a perfect monopoly. However, what we can identify are certain characteristics in particular markets where firms behave as if they are a monopoly supplier. A firm with a 90 per cent market share such as Microsoft in the operating system market is not a pure monopoly. There are other operating systems such as Apple's Mac OS, and Linux, for example, but the market power that Microsoft can wield is considerable.

Where a firm has some element of market power it can alter the relationship between a firm's costs and the price at which it sells its product to the market. A competitive firm takes the price of its output given by the market, then chooses the quantity it will supply so that price equals marginal cost. By contrast, the price charged by firms with market power exceeds marginal cost. This result is clearly true in the case of Microsoft's Windows. The marginal cost of Windows, the extra cost that Microsoft would incur by making one more copy of the program available, is only a few euros. The market price of Windows is many times marginal cost.

It is perhaps not surprising that firms with considerable market power can charge relatively high prices for their products. Customers of monopolies might seem to have little choice but to pay whatever the monopoly charges. If so, why is a copy of Windows priced at about €120 and not €1,200? Or €12,000? The reason is that if Microsoft set the price that high, fewer people would buy the product. People would buy fewer computers, switch to other operating systems or make illegal copies. Monopolies cannot achieve any level of profit they want, because high prices reduce the amount that their customers buy. Although monopolies can control the prices of their goods, their profits are not unlimited. In other words, under conditions of imperfect competition firms do not face a horizontal demand curve, which would suggest they can sell any amount they offer at the going market price. Instead, firms face a downward sloping demand curve, which means that if they want to sell more products they must accept lower prices. If this is the case, then price does not equal average revenue and marginal revenue is lower. This is partly what leads to changed behaviour.

A **monopoly** is a firm which is the sole supplier of a product in a market. In reality we describe firms as monopolies even though there are other suppliers, as we have seen in the case of operating systems. Because there are concerns about the effect of market power on consumers and suppliers, most national competition policy defines monopolies in a much stricter way. A firm might be able to exercise some monopoly power if it has 25 per cent or more of the market. However, for the purposes of our analysis let us assume that there is only one supplier in the market.

 monopoly a firm that is the sole seller of a product without close substitutes

As we examine the production and pricing decisions of monopolies, we also consider the implications of monopoly for society as a whole. We base our analysis of monopoly firms, like competitive firms, on the assumption that they aim to maximize profit. Because monopoly firms face different market conditions, the outcome in a market with a monopoly is not always in the best interests of society. It is these market imperfections that form the basis for so much government policy.

THE SOURCES OF MONOPOLY POWER

The fundamental cause of monopoly is *barriers to entry*: a monopoly remains the only seller in its market because other firms cannot enter the market and compete with it. Barriers to entry, in turn, have four main sources.

Monopoly Resources

The simplest way for a monopoly to arise is for a single firm to own a key resource. For example, consider the market for water in a small town on a remote Scottish island not served by the water company from the mainland. If there is only one well in town and it is impossible to get water from anywhere else, then the owner of the well has a monopoly on water. Not surprisingly, the monopolist has much greater market power than any single firm in a competitive market. In the case of a necessity like water, the monopolist could command quite a high price, even if the marginal cost is low.

Although exclusive ownership of a key resource is a potential cause of monopoly, in practice monopolies rarely arise for this reason. Actual economies are large, and resources are owned by many people. Indeed, because many goods are traded internationally, the natural scope of their markets is often worldwide. There are, therefore, few examples of firms that own a resource for which there are no close substitutes.

Government-Created Monopolies

In many cases, monopolies arise because the government has given one person or firm the exclusive right to sell some good or service. European kings, for example, once granted exclusive business licences to their friends and allies in order to raise money. A highly prized monopoly was the exclusive right to sell and distribute salt in a particular region of Europe. Even today, governments sometimes grant a monopoly (perhaps even to itself) because doing so is viewed to be in the public interest. In Sweden, the retailing of alcoholic beverages is carried out under a state-owned monopoly known as the Systembolaget, because the Swedish government deems it to be in the interests of public health to be able to directly control the sale of alcohol.

The patent and copyright laws are two important examples of how the government creates a monopoly to serve the public interest. When a pharmaceutical company discovers a new drug, it can apply to the government for a **patent**. If the government deems the drug to be truly original, it approves the patent, which gives the company the exclusive right to manufacture and sell the drug for a fixed number of years, often 20. Similarly, when a novelist finishes a book, they can copyright it. The copyright is a government guarantee that no one can print and sell the work without the author's permission. The copyright makes the novelist a monopolist in the sale of their novel.

> **patent** the exclusive right to manufacture and sell a product for a fixed number of years

The effects of patent and copyright laws are easy to see. Because these laws give one producer a monopoly, they lead to higher prices than would occur under competition. By allowing these monopoly producers to charge higher prices and earn higher profits, the laws encourage some desirable behaviour. Drug companies are allowed to be monopolists in the drugs they discover in order to encourage research. Authors are allowed to be monopolists in the sale of their books to encourage them to write more and better books.

Thus, the laws governing patents and copyrights have benefits and costs. The benefits of the patent and copyright laws are the increased incentive for creative activity. These benefits are offset, to some extent, by the costs of monopoly pricing, which we examine fully later in this chapter.

Natural Monopolies

An industry is a **natural monopoly** when a single firm can supply a good or service to an entire market at a lower cost than could two or more firms. A natural monopoly arises when there are economies of scale over the relevant range of output. Figure 13.1 shows the average total costs of a firm with economies of scale. In this case, a single firm can produce any amount of output at least cost. That is, for any given amount of output, a larger number of firms leads to less output per firm and higher average total cost.

> **natural monopoly** a monopoly that arises because a single firm can supply a good or service to an entire market at a smaller cost than could two or more firms

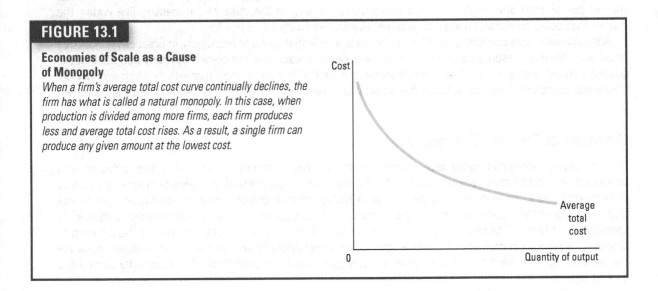

FIGURE 13.1

Economies of Scale as a Cause of Monopoly
When a firm's average total cost curve continually declines, the firm has what is called a natural monopoly. In this case, when production is divided among more firms, each firm produces less and average total cost rises. As a result, a single firm can produce any given amount at the lowest cost.

An example of a natural monopoly is the distribution of water. To provide water to residents of a town, a firm must build a network of pipes throughout the town. If two or more firms were to compete in the provision of this service, each firm would have to pay the fixed cost of building a network. Thus, the average total cost of water is lowest if a single firm serves the entire market.

When a firm is a natural monopoly, it is less concerned about new entrants eroding its monopoly power. Normally, a firm has trouble maintaining a monopoly position without ownership of a key resource or protection from the government. The monopolist's profit attracts entrants into the market, and these entrants make the market more competitive. By contrast, entering a market in which another firm has a natural monopoly is unattractive. Would be entrants know that they cannot achieve the same low costs that the monopolist enjoys because, after entry, each firm would have a smaller piece of the market.

External Growth

Many of the largest firms in the world have grown partly through acquisition, merger or takeover of other firms. As they do so, the industry becomes more concentrated; there are fewer firms in the industry. The so-called 'Big Four' accounting firms are an example where smaller accounting firms have merged or been taken over, resulting in a number of large firms dominating the industry. One effect of this type of growth is that a firm might be able to develop monopoly power over its rivals and erect barriers to entry to make it harder for new firms to enter. It is for this reason that governments monitor such acquisitions to see if there are implications for competition.

SELF TEST Identify three examples of firms with monopoly power, and explain the primary reason for the source of the monopoly power of each.

HOW MONOPOLIES MAKE PRODUCTION AND PRICING DECISIONS

Now that we know how monopolies arise, we can consider how a monopoly firm decides how much of its product to make and what price to charge for it. The analysis of monopoly behaviour in this section is the starting point for evaluating whether monopolies are desirable and what policies the government might pursue in monopoly markets.

Monopoly Versus Competition

The key difference between a competitive firm and a monopoly is the monopoly's ability to influence the price of its output. A monopoly is the sole producer in its market, therefore it can alter the price of its good by adjusting the quantity it supplies to the market.

Because a monopoly is the sole producer in its market, its demand curve is the market demand curve. Thus the monopolist's demand curve slopes downward for all the usual reasons, as in panel (b) of Figure 13.2. If the monopolist raises the price of its good, consumers buy less of it. Looked at another way, if the monopolist reduces the quantity of output it sells, the price of its output increases.

FIGURE 13.2

Demand Curves for Competitive and Monopoly Firms
Because competitive firms are price takers, they in effect face horizontal demand curves, as in panel (a). Because a monopoly firm is the sole producer in its market, it faces the downward sloping market demand curve, as in panel (b). As a result, the monopoly has to accept a lower price if it wants to sell more output.

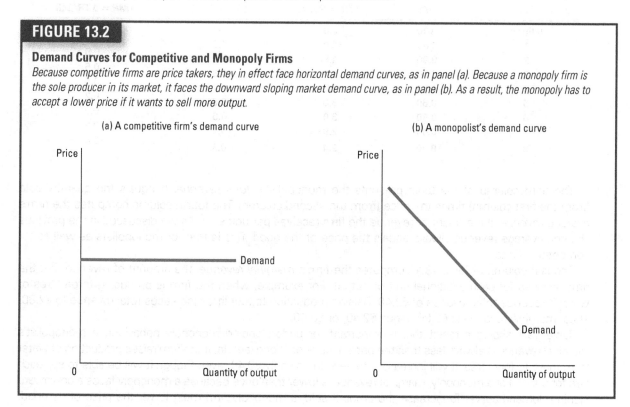

PITFALL PREVENTION Because a monopolist faces a downwards sloping demand curve it can either set price and accept the level of demand to determine its sales or it can fix output at a certain level and allow the market to determine the price it can charge. It cannot do both, i.e. it cannot fix price *and* output together.

The market demand curve provides a constraint on a monopoly's ability to profit from its market power. A monopolist would prefer, if it were possible, to charge a high price and sell a large quantity at that high price. The market demand curve makes that outcome impossible. In particular, the market demand curve describes the combinations of price and quantity that are available to a monopoly firm. By adjusting the quantity produced (or, equivalently, the price charged), the monopolist can choose any point on the demand curve, but it cannot choose a point off the demand curve.

What point on the demand curve will the monopolist choose? As with competitive firms, we assume that the monopolist's goal is to maximize profit. Because the firm's profit is total revenue minus total costs, our next task in explaining monopoly behaviour is to examine a monopolist's revenue.

A Monopoly's Revenue

Consider a town with a single producer of water. Table 13.1 shows how the monopoly's revenue might depend on the amount of water produced.

The first two columns show the monopolist's demand schedule. If the monopolist produces just one litre of water, it can sell that litre for €1. If it produces two litres, it must lower the price to €0.90 to sell both litres. If it produces three litres, it must lower the price to €0.80, and so on. If you graphed these two columns of numbers, you would get a typical downward sloping demand curve.

TABLE 13.1 A Monopoly's Total, Average and Marginal Revenue

Quantity of water	Price (€)	Total revenue (€)	Average revenue (€)	Marginal revenue (€)
(Q)	(P)	(TR = P × Q)	(AR = TR/Q)	(MR = ΔTR/ΔQ)
0 litres	1.10	0.0	–	
				1.0
1	1.00	1.0	1.0	
				0.8
2	0.90	1.8	0.9	
				0.6
3	0.80	2.4	0.8	
				0.4
4	0.70	2.8	0.7	
				0.2
5	0.60	3.0	0.6	
				0.0
6	0.50	3.0	0.5	
				-0.2
7	0.40	2.8	0.4	
				-0.4
8	0.30	2.4	0.3	

The third column of the table presents the monopolist's *total revenue*. It equals the quantity sold (from the first column) times the price (from the second column). The fourth column computes the firm's *average revenue*, the amount of revenue the firm receives per unit sold. As we discussed in the previous chapter, average revenue always equals the price of the good. This is true for monopolists as well as for competitive firms.

The last column of Table 13.1 computes the firm's *marginal revenue*, the amount of revenue that the firm receives for each additional unit of output. For example, when the firm is producing three litres of water it receives total revenue of €2.40. Raising production to four litres increases total revenue to €2.80. Thus, marginal revenue is €2.80 minus €2.40, or €0.40.

Table 13.1 shows a result that is important for understanding monopoly behaviour: a monopolist's marginal revenue is always less than the price of its good. For example, if the firm raises production of water from three to four litres, it will increase total revenue by only €0.40, even though it will be able to sell each litre for €0.70. For a monopoly, marginal revenue is lower than price because a monopoly faces a downward sloping demand curve. To increase the amount sold, a monopoly firm must lower the price of its good. Hence, to sell the fourth litre of water, the monopolist must get less revenue for each of the first three litres.

Marginal revenue for monopolies is very different from marginal revenue for competitive firms. When a monopoly increases the amount it sells, it has two effects on total revenue ($P \times Q$):

- *The output effect.* More output is sold, so Q is higher, which tends to increase total revenue.
- *The price effect.* The price falls, so P is lower, which tends to decrease total revenue.

When a monopoly increases production by 1 unit, it must reduce the price it charges for every unit it sells, and this cut in price reduces revenue on the units it was already selling. As a result, a monopoly's marginal revenue is less than its price.

Figure 13.3 graphs the demand curve and the marginal revenue curve for a monopoly firm. (Because the firm's price equals its average revenue, the demand curve is also the average revenue curve.) These two curves always start at the same point on the vertical axis because the marginal revenue of the first unit sold equals the price of the good. But thereafter, for the reason we just discussed, the monopolist's marginal revenue is less than the price of the good. Thus, a monopoly's marginal revenue curve lies below its demand curve and the slope of the marginal revenue curve is twice that of the average revenue or demand curve.

You can determine from Figure 13.3 (as well as in Table 13.1) that marginal revenue can even become negative. Marginal revenue is negative when the price effect on revenue is greater than the output effect. In this case, when the firm produces an extra unit of output, the price falls by enough to cause the firm's total revenue to decline, even though the firm is selling more units.

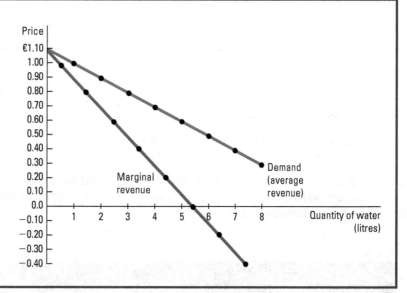

FIGURE 13.3

Demand and Marginal Revenue Curves for a Monopoly

The demand curve shows how the quantity affects the price of the good. The marginal revenue curve shows how the firm's revenue changes when the quantity increases by one unit. Because the price of all units sold must fall if the monopoly increases production, marginal revenue is always less than the price.

Profit Maximization

Now that we have considered the revenue of a monopoly firm, we are ready to examine how such a firm maximizes profit. We apply the logic of marginal analysis to the monopolist's decision about how much to produce.

Figure 13.4 graphs the demand curve, the marginal revenue curve and the cost curves for a monopoly firm.

Suppose, first, that the firm is producing at a low level of output, such as Q_1. In this case, marginal cost is less than marginal revenue. If the firm increased production by one unit, the additional revenue would exceed the additional costs, and profit would rise. Thus when marginal cost is less than marginal revenue, the firm can increase profit by producing more units.

A similar argument applies at high levels of output, such as Q_2. In this case, marginal cost is greater than marginal revenue. If the firm reduced production by one unit, the costs saved would exceed the revenue lost. Thus if marginal cost is greater than marginal revenue, the firm can raise profit by reducing production.

In the end, the firm adjusts its level of production until the quantity reaches Q_{MAX}, at which marginal revenue equals marginal cost. Thus the monopolist's profit-maximizing quantity of output is determined by the intersection of the marginal revenue curve and the marginal cost curve. In Figure 13.4, this intersection occurs at point A.

FIGURE 13.4

Profit Maximization for a Monopoly
A monopoly maximizes profit by choosing the quantity at which marginal revenue equals marginal cost (point A). It then uses the demand curve to find the price that will induce consumers to buy that quantity (point B).

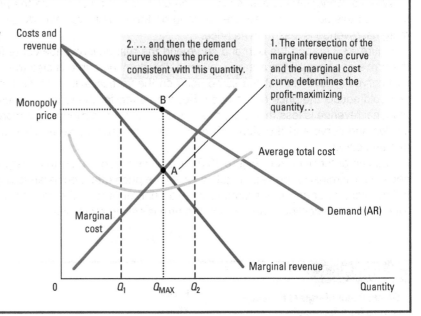

There is an important difference between competitive firms and monopolies: the marginal revenue of a competitive firm equals its price, whereas the marginal revenue of a monopoly is less than its price. That is:

● For a competitive firm: $P = (MR = MC)$
● For a monopoly firm: $P > (MR = MC)$

Assuming profit maximization, the decision to produce at a point where marginal revenue and marginal cost are equal is the same for both types of firm. What differs is the relationship of the price to marginal revenue and marginal cost.

FYI

Why a Monopoly Does Not Have a Supply Curve

You may have noticed that we have analyzed the price in a monopoly market using the market demand curve and the firm's cost curves. We have not made any mention of the market supply curve. By contrast, when we analyzed prices in competitive markets, the two most important words were always *supply* and *demand*.

What happened to the supply curve? Although monopoly firms make decisions about what quantity to supply, a monopoly does not have a supply curve. A supply curve tells us the quantity that firms choose to supply at any given price. This concept makes sense when we are analysing price-taking competitive firms. A monopoly firm is a price maker, not a price taker. It is not meaningful to ask what such a firm would produce at any price, because the firm sets the price at the same time it chooses the quantity to supply.

Indeed, the monopolist's decision about how much to supply is impossible to separate from the demand curve it faces. The shape of the demand curve determines the shape of the marginal revenue curve, which in turn determines the monopolist's profit-maximizing quantity. In a competitive market, supply decisions can be analyzed without knowing the demand curve, but that is not true in a monopoly market. Therefore, we never talk about a monopoly's supply curve.

How does the monopoly find the profit-maximizing price for its product? The demand curve answers this question because the demand curve relates the amount that customers are willing to pay to the quantity sold. Thus, after the monopoly firm chooses the quantity of output that equates marginal revenue and marginal cost, it uses the demand curve to find the price consistent with that quantity. In Figure 13.4, the profit-maximizing price is found at point B.

We can now see a key difference between markets with competitive firms and markets with a monopoly firm: in competitive markets, price *equals* marginal cost. In monopolized markets, price *exceeds* marginal cost. As we will see in a moment, this finding is crucial to understanding the social cost of monopoly.

A Monopoly's Profit

To see the monopoly's profit, recall that the profit equation can be written:

$$\text{Profit} = (P - ATC) \times Q$$

Consider the shaded box in Figure 13.5. The height of the box (the distance BC) is price minus average total cost, $P - ATC$, which is the profit on the typical unit sold.

The width of the box (the distance DC) is the quantity sold Q_{MAX}. Therefore, the area of this box is the monopoly firm's total profit.

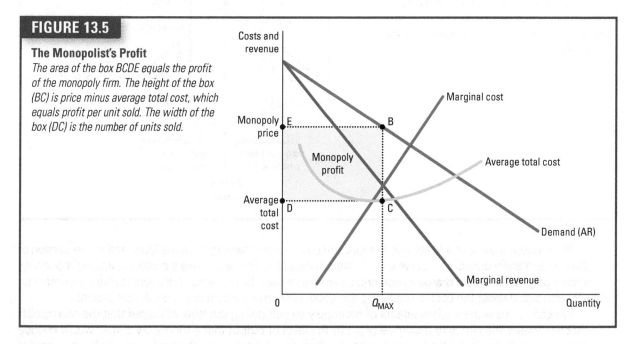

FIGURE 13.5

The Monopolist's Profit
The area of the box BCDE equals the profit of the monopoly firm. The height of the box (BC) is price minus average total cost, which equals profit per unit sold. The width of the box (DC) is the number of units sold.

THE WELFARE COST OF MONOPOLY

We have seen that a monopoly, in contrast to a competitive firm, charges a price above marginal cost. From the standpoint of consumers, this high price makes monopoly undesirable. At the same time, however, the monopoly is earning profit from charging this high price. From the standpoint of the owners of the firm, the high price makes monopoly very desirable. Is it possible that the benefits to the firm's owners exceed the costs imposed on consumers, making monopoly desirable from the standpoint of society as a whole?

We can answer this question using the concepts of consumer and producer surplus as our measure of economic well-being.

The Deadweight Loss

We begin by considering what the monopoly firm would do if it were run not only for the profit earned by the firm's owners but also for the benefits received by the firm's consumers. The monopoly owners try to maximize total surplus, which equals producer surplus (profit) plus consumer surplus. Keep in mind that total surplus equals the value of the good to consumers minus the costs of making the good incurred by the monopoly producer.

Figure 13.6 analyzes what level of output the monopoly owners would choose. The demand curve reflects the value of the good to consumers, as measured by their willingness to pay for it. The marginal cost curve reflects the costs of the monopolist. Thus, the socially efficient quantity is found where the demand curve and the marginal cost curve intersect. Below this quantity, the value to consumers exceeds the marginal cost of providing the good, so increasing output would raise total surplus. Above this quantity, the marginal cost exceeds the value to consumers, so decreasing output would raise total surplus.

FIGURE 13.6

The Efficient Level of Output

A monopoly owner who wanted to maximize total surplus in the market would choose the level of output where the demand curve and marginal cost curve intersect. Below this level, the value of the good to the marginal buyer (as reflected in the demand curve) exceeds the marginal cost of making the good. Above this level, the value to the marginal buyer is less than marginal cost.

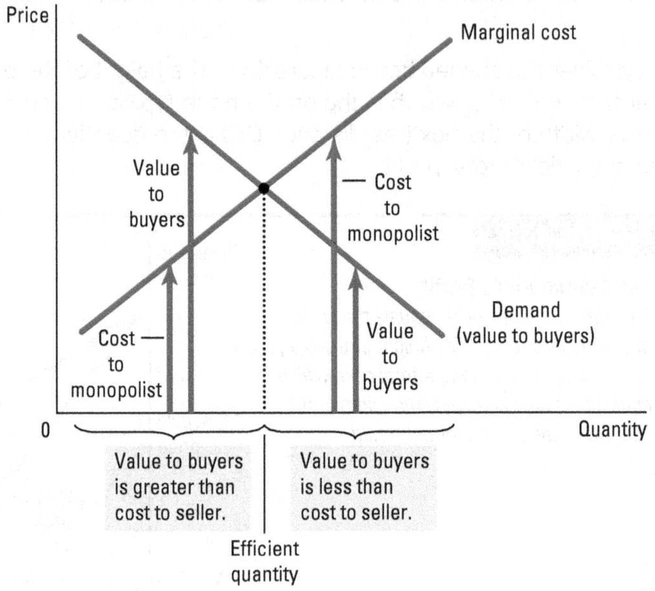

The monopoly owner could achieve this efficient outcome by charging the price found at the intersection of the demand and marginal cost curves. Thus, like a competitive firm and unlike a profit-maximizing monopoly, a monopoly owner would charge a price equal to marginal cost. Because this price would give consumers an accurate signal about the cost of producing the good, consumers would buy the efficient quantity.

We can evaluate the welfare effects of monopoly by comparing the level of output that the monopolist chooses where the aim is to maximize profit to the level of output that a monopoly owner would choose if its aim was to maximize total surplus in the market. As we have seen, the profit-maximizing monopolist chooses to produce and sell the quantity of output at which the marginal revenue and marginal cost curves intersect, as opposed to the quantity at which the demand and marginal cost curves intersect, which an owner would choose if maximizing total surplus. Figure 13.7 shows the comparison. The profit-maximizing monopolist produces less than the socially efficient quantity of output.

We can also view the inefficiency of monopoly in terms of the monopolist's price. Because the market demand curve describes a negative relationship between the price and quantity of the good, a quantity that is inefficiently low is equivalent to a price that is inefficiently high. When a monopolist charges a price above marginal cost, some potential consumers value the good at more than its marginal cost but less than the monopolist's price. These consumers do not end up buying the good. Because the value these consumers place on the good is greater than the cost of providing it to them, this result is inefficient. Thus, monopoly pricing prevents some mutually beneficial trades from taking place.

The inefficiency of monopoly can be measured in Figure 13.7, which shows the deadweight loss. Recall that the demand curve reflects the value to consumers and the marginal cost curve reflects the costs to the monopoly producer. Thus, the area of the deadweight loss triangle between the demand curve and the marginal cost curve equals the total surplus lost because of monopoly pricing.

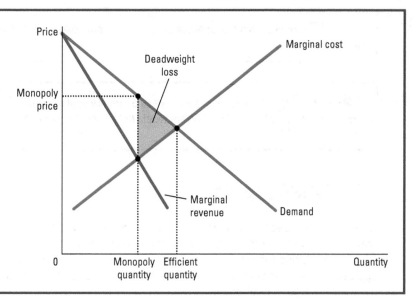

FIGURE 13.7

The Inefficiency of Monopoly
Because a profit-maximizing monopoly charges a price above marginal cost, not all consumers who value the good at more than its cost buy it. Thus, the quantity produced and sold by this monopoly producer is below the socially efficient level. The deadweight loss is represented by the area of the triangle between the demand curve (which reflects the value of the good to consumers) and the marginal cost curve (which reflects the costs of the monopoly producer).

The deadweight loss is caused because a monopoly exerts its market power by charging a price above marginal cost, creating a wedge. The wedge causes the quantity sold to fall short of the social optimum. In this situation, a private firm gets the monopoly profit.

> **JEOPARDY PROBLEM** How might a government granting monopoly rights to a TV company to provide national TV broadcasting of certain sporting events lead to an overall increase in welfare in society?

The Monopoly's Profit: A Social Cost?

It is tempting to decry monopolies for 'profiteering' at the expense of the public. Indeed, a monopoly firm does earn a higher profit by virtue of its market power. According to the economic analysis of monopoly, however, the firm's profit is not in itself necessarily a problem for society.

Welfare in a monopolized market, like all markets, includes the welfare of both consumers and producers. Whenever a consumer pays an extra euro to a producer because of a monopoly price, the consumer is worse off by a euro, and the producer is better off by the same amount. This transfer from the consumers of the good to the owners of the monopoly does not affect the market's total surplus, the sum of consumer and producer surplus. In other words, the monopoly profit itself does not represent a shrinkage in the size of the economic pie; it merely represents a bigger slice for producers and a smaller slice for consumers. Unless consumers are for some reason more deserving than producers, a judgement that goes beyond the realm of economic efficiency, the monopoly profit is not a social problem.

The problem in a monopolized market arises because the firm produces and sells a quantity of output below the level that maximizes total surplus. The deadweight loss measures how much the economic pie shrinks as a result. This inefficiency is connected to the monopoly's high price: consumers buy fewer units when the firm raises its price above marginal cost. Keep in mind that the profit earned on the units that continue to be sold is not the problem. The problem stems from the inefficiently low quantity of output. Put differently, if the high monopoly price did not discourage some consumers from buying the good, it would raise producer surplus by exactly the amount it reduced consumer surplus, leaving total surplus the same as could be achieved by a monopoly owner aiming to maximize total surplus.

There is, however, a possible exception to this conclusion. Suppose that a monopoly firm has to incur additional costs to maintain its monopoly position. For example, a firm with a government-created monopoly might need to hire lobbyists to convince lawmakers to continue its monopoly. In this case, the monopoly may use up some of its monopoly profits paying for these additional costs. If so, the social loss from monopoly includes both these costs and the deadweight loss resulting from a price above marginal cost.

SELF TEST How does a monopolist's quantity of output compare to the quantity of output that maximizes total surplus?

WHAT IF... a monopolist did not have a primary goal of maximizing profit (i.e. where the aim was based on profit satisficing). What would determine the size of the welfare loss?

PRICE DISCRIMINATION

So far we have been assuming that the monopoly firm charges the same price to all customers. Yet in many cases firms try to sell the same good to different customers for different prices, even though the costs of producing for the two customers are the same. This practice is called **price discrimination**. Firms operating under perfect competition are not able to price discriminate. For a firm to price discriminate it must have some market power.

> **price discrimination** the business practice of selling the same good at different prices to different customers

A Parable About Pricing

To understand why a monopolist would want to price discriminate, let us consider a simple example. Imagine that you are the chief executive officer of Readalot Publishing Company. Readalot's best-selling author has just written their latest novel. To keep things simple, let us imagine that you pay the author a flat €2 million for the exclusive rights to publish the book. Let us also assume, for simplicity, that the cost of printing the book is zero. Readalot's profit, therefore, is the revenue it gets from selling the book minus the €2 million it has paid to the author. Given these assumptions, how would you, as Readalot's CEO, decide what price to charge for the book?

Your first step in setting the price is to estimate what the demand for the book is likely to be. Readalot's marketing department tells you that the book will attract two types of readers. The book will appeal to the author's 100,000 diehard fans. These fans will be willing to pay as much as €30 for the book. In addition, the book will appeal to about 400,000 less enthusiastic readers who will be willing to pay up to €5 for the book.

What price maximizes Readalot's profit? There are two natural prices to consider: €30 is the highest price Readalot can charge and still get the 100,000 diehard fans, and €5 is the highest price it can charge and still get the entire market of 500,000 potential readers. At a price of €30, Readalot can sell 100,000 copies, achieve revenue of €3 million, and make a profit of €1 million. At a price of €5, it sells 500,000 copies, has revenue of €2.5 million, and makes a profit of €500,000. Thus, Readalot maximizes profit by charging €30 and foregoing the opportunity to sell to the 400,000 less enthusiastic readers.

Notice that Readalot's decision causes a deadweight loss. There are 400,000 readers willing to pay €5 for the book, and the marginal cost of providing it to them is zero. Thus, €2 million of total surplus is lost when Readalot charges the higher price. This deadweight loss is the usual inefficiency that arises whenever a monopolist charges a price above marginal cost.

Now suppose that Readalot's marketing department makes an important discovery: these two groups of readers are in separate markets. All the diehard fans live in Switzerland and all the other readers live in Turkey. Moreover, it is difficult for readers in one country to buy books in the other. How does this discovery affect Readalot's marketing strategy?

In this case, the company can make even more profit. To the 100,000 Swiss readers, it can charge €30 for the book. To the 400,000 Turkish readers, it can charge €5 for the book (or the Turkish lira equivalent).

In this case, revenue is €3 million in Switzerland and €2 million in Turkey, for a total of €5 million. Profit is then €3 million, which is substantially greater than the €1 million the company could earn charging the same €30 price to all customers. Not surprisingly, Readalot chooses to follow this strategy of price discrimination.

Although the story of Readalot Publishing is hypothetical, it describes accurately the business practice of many publishing companies. New novels are often initially released as an expensive hardcover edition and later released in a cheaper paperback edition. The difference in price between these two editions far exceeds the difference in printing costs. The publisher's goal is just as in our example. By selling the hardcover to diehard fans (and libraries) who must have the book as soon as it is published and the paperback to less enthusiastic readers who do not mind waiting, the publisher price discriminates and raises its profit.

 WHAT IF... the price elasticity of demand does not vary widely between different markets. Would a monopolist still be able to practise price discrimination?

The Moral of the Story

The story of Readalot Publishing provides three lessons about price discrimination. The first is that price discrimination is a rational strategy for a profit-maximizing monopolist. In other words, by charging different prices to different customers, a monopolist can increase its profit. In essence, a price-discriminating monopolist charges each customer a price closer to their willingness to pay than is possible with a single price.

The second lesson is that price discrimination requires the ability to separate customers according to their willingness to pay. In our example, customers were separated geographically. Sometimes monopolists choose other differences, such as age or income, to distinguish among customers. Energy companies are able to discriminate through setting different prices at different times of the day with off-peak usage priced lower than peak time. Similarly, rail companies charge different prices to passengers at certain times of the day with peak travel attracting a much higher price than off-peak travel. Where there is a difference in the price elasticity of demand, the monopolist can exploit this and practise price discrimination. Between the hours of 6.00 a.m. and 9.30 a.m. on weekday mornings, for example, the price elasticity of demand for rail travel is relatively low, whereas between 9.30 a.m. and 4.00 p.m. it tends to be relatively high. A higher price can be charged at the peak time, but during the off-peak period the firm may benefit from charging a lower price and encouraging more passengers to travel; the cost of running the train is largely fixed and the marginal cost of carrying an additional passenger is almost zero. Lowering the price, therefore, is a way of utilizing the capacity on the train and adding to profit.

A corollary to this second lesson is that certain market forces can prevent firms from price discriminating. In particular, one such force is *arbitrage*, the process of buying a good in one market at a low price and selling it in another market at a higher price in order to profit from the price difference. In our example, suppose that Swiss bookshops could buy the book in Turkey for €5 and resell it to Swiss readers at a price well below €30. This arbitrage would prevent Readalot from price discriminating, because no Swiss resident would buy the book at the higher price. In fact, the increased use of the internet for buying books and other goods through companies like Amazon and eBay is likely to affect the ability of companies to price discriminate internationally. Where firms can enforce the division of the market, as in the case of rail fares, they can practise price discrimination. A passenger buying a ticket at off-peak rates is not allowed to travel on a train running during peak periods, and hence arbitrage is circumvented.

The third lesson from our parable is that price discrimination can raise economic welfare. Recall that a deadweight loss arises when Readalot charges a single €30 price, because the 400,000 less enthusiastic readers do not end up with the book, even though they value it at more than its marginal cost of production. By contrast, when Readalot price discriminates, all readers end up with the book, and the outcome is efficient. Thus price discrimination can eliminate the inefficiency inherent in monopoly pricing.

Note that the increase in welfare from price discrimination shows up as higher producer surplus rather than higher consumer surplus. In our example, consumers are no better off for having bought the book: the price they pay exactly equals the value they place on the book, so they receive no consumer surplus. The entire increase in total surplus from price discrimination accrues to Readalot Publishing in the form of higher profit.

The Analytics of Price Discrimination

Let us consider a little more formally how price discrimination affects economic welfare. We begin by assuming that the monopolist can price discriminate perfectly. *Perfect price discrimination* describes a situation in which the monopolist knows exactly the willingness to pay of each customer and can charge each customer a different price. In this case, the monopolist charges each customer exactly their willingness to pay, and the monopolist gets the entire surplus in every transaction.

Figure 13.8 shows producer and consumer surplus with and without price discrimination. Without price discrimination, the firm charges a single price above marginal cost, as shown in panel (a). Because some potential customers who value the good at more than marginal cost do not buy it at this high price, the monopoly causes a deadweight loss. Yet when a firm can perfectly price discriminate, as shown in panel (b), each customer who values the good at more than marginal cost buys the good and is charged their willingness to pay. All mutually beneficial trades take place, there is no deadweight loss, and the entire surplus derived from the market goes to the monopoly producer in the form of profit.

FIGURE 13.8

Welfare With and Without Price Discrimination

Panel (a) shows a monopolist that charges the same price to all customers. Total surplus in this market equals the sum of profit (producer surplus) and consumer surplus. Panel (b) shows a monopolist that can perfectly price discriminate. Because consumer surplus equals zero, total surplus now equals the firm's profit. Comparing these two panels, you can see that perfect price discrimination raises profit, raises total surplus and lowers consumer surplus.

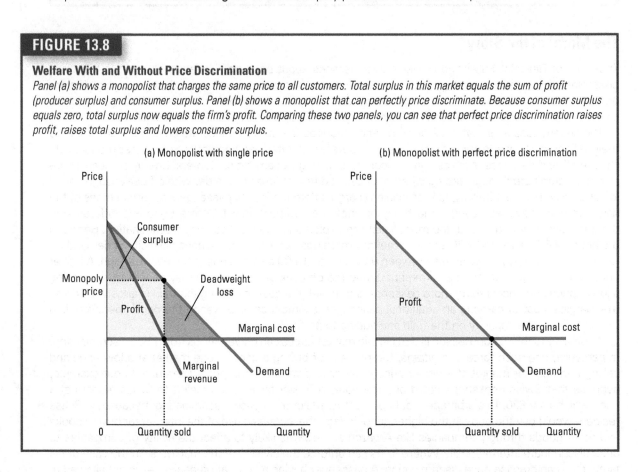

In reality, of course, price discrimination is not perfect. Customers do not walk into shops with signs displaying their willingness to pay. Instead, firms price discriminate by dividing customers into groups: young versus old, weekday versus weekend shoppers, Germans versus British and so on. Unlike those in our parable of Readalot Publishing, customers within each group differ in their willingness to pay for the product, making perfect price discrimination impossible.

How does this imperfect price discrimination affect welfare? The analysis of these pricing schemes is quite complicated, and it turns out that there is no general answer to this question. Compared to the monopoly outcome with a single price, imperfect price discrimination can raise, lower or leave unchanged total surplus in a market. The only certain conclusion is that price discrimination raises the monopoly's profit, otherwise the firm would choose to charge all customers the same price.

Examples of Price Discrimination

Firms use various business strategies aimed at charging different prices to different customers. Now that we understand the economics of price discrimination, let us consider some examples.

Cinema Tickets Many cinemas charge a lower price for children and senior citizens than for other patrons. This fact is hard to explain in a competitive market. In a competitive market, price equals marginal cost, and the marginal cost of providing a seat for a child or senior citizen is the same as the marginal cost of providing a seat for anyone else. Yet this fact is easily explained if cinemas have some local monopoly power and if children and senior citizens have a lower willingness to pay for a ticket. In this case, cinemas raise their profit by price discriminating.

Airline Prices Seats on aeroplanes are sold at many different prices. Most airlines charge a lower price for a round-trip ticket between two cities if the traveller stays over for Saturday night. At first this seems odd. Why should it matter to the airline whether a passenger stays on Saturday night? The reason is that this rule provides a way to separate business travellers and personal travellers. A passenger on a business trip has a high willingness to pay and, most likely, does not want to stay over on a Saturday night. By contrast, a passenger travelling for personal reasons has a lower willingness to pay and is more likely to be willing to stay away on a Saturday night. Thus, the airlines can successfully price discriminate by charging a lower price for passengers who stay over on Saturday night.

Quantity Discounts So far in our examples of price discrimination the monopolist charges different prices to different customers. Sometimes, however, monopolists price discriminate by charging different prices to the same customer for different units that the customer buys. Traditionally, English bakers would give you an extra loaf for nothing if you bought 12. While the quaint custom of the 'baker's dozen' (i.e. 13 for the price of 12) is largely a thing of the past, many firms offer lower prices to customers who buy large quantities. This is a form of price discrimination, because the customer effectively pays a higher price for the first unit bought than for the last. Quantity discounts are often a successful way of price discriminating because a customer's willingness to pay for an additional unit declines as the customer buys more units.

CASE STUDY **Price Discrimination**

To practise price discrimination, firms need information about their customers, about their buying behaviours and their willingness to pay. Customers may not walk into shops with labels attached to them providing this information but the growth of online retailing and developments in point of sales

The increasing use of technology in making purchase allows firms to gather valuable information on consumer purchasing behaviour.

technologies allow many more firms to gather useful information which can be analyzed and used to help firms price discriminate more effectively. The term 'price discrimination' has somewhat negative connotations and 'dynamic pricing' has tended to replace it. The idea behind dynamic pricing is that firms can use information on buyers' behaviours and willingness to pay and provide them with prices that can be changed instantly when a buyer searches for a good or service. This is one of the reasons why two people could be searching for the same product on the same website but be faced with different prices. In the world of dynamic pricing, prices do not fluctuate according to changes in supply and demand but on the particular buying habits and behaviours of individual customers.

(*Continued*)

Questions

1 **To what extent do you think that the principle of dynamic pricing as it has evolved in recent years has allowed firms to more closely achieve perfect price discrimination?**

2 **If a firm is able to monitor buyer behaviour and better target their customers with prices that reflect their willingness to pay, what happens to consumer and producer surplus in such instances?**

3 **Should we be concerned that increasingly in the online retailing world, prices are not set by supply and demand but by algorithms based on improved information about buyer behaviour?**

Reference: www.theguardian.com/lifeandstyle/2022/dec/12/prices-that-change-by-the-second-why-shopping-around-for-deals-online-isnt-always-worth-it (accessed 10 June 2023).

PUBLIC POLICY TOWARDS MONOPOLIES

We have seen that monopolies, in contrast to competitive markets, fail to allocate resources efficiently. Monopolies produce less than the socially desirable quantity of output and, as a result, charge prices above marginal cost. Policy makers in the government can respond to the problem of monopoly in one of four ways, by:

- trying to make monopolized industries more competitive
- regulating the behaviour of the monopolies
- turning some private monopolies into public enterprises
- doing nothing at all.

Monitoring Competition

All industrialized countries have some sort of process for legally prohibiting mergers that are against the public interest.

The earliest moves towards using legal remedies to monopoly power were taken in the United States in the late nineteenth and early twentieth centuries, forming the basis of legislation that has become known in the United States as the anti-trust laws (in the UK and the rest of Europe, anti-trust law and anti-trust policy are more commonly referred to as competition law and competition policy, although usage of both terms is becoming widespread). These laws cover proposed mergers between two companies that already have substantial market share. These proposals are closely examined by the authorities, who might well decide that the merger would make the industry in question substantially less competitive and, as a result, would reduce the economic well-being of the country or region as a whole.

In Europe, each country has a competition authority. In the UK, it is the Competition and Markets Authority (CMA); in Germany it is the Federal Cartel Office (*Bundeskartellamt*); in 2009 the French Competition Authority (*Autorité de la Concurrence*) began discharging its regulatory powers following reform of competition regulation; and in Italy the Anti-trust Authority (*Autorità Garante della Concorrenza e del Mercato*) oversees competition issues. National competition authorities such as these co-operate with each other and with the EU Competition Commission through the European Competition Network (ECN). The aim of the network is to coordinate activities and share information to help enforce EU competition law in member states where the opportunities for cross-border business have increased as the EU has developed and expanded.

While each national country can enforce its own competition legislation, these laws must be in line with overall EU competition legislation. UK competition laws continue to apply to competition and trade within the UK and EU rules still apply to EU countries following Brexit. The Brexit agreement provides an understanding that both the UK and the EU will still apply competition rules which existed prior to Brexit, so the position has not changed to any great extent following Brexit.

There are well-defined criteria for deciding whether a proposed merger of companies belonging to more than one EU country is subject to reference exclusively to the European Commission rather than to national authorities, such as the size of the worldwide or European turnover of the companies in question.

Competition legislation covers three main areas:

- Acting against cartels (where a small number of firms act together) and cases where businesses engage in restrictive business practices which prevent free trade.
- Banning pricing strategies which are anti-competitive such as price fixing, predatory pricing, price gouging and so on, and through behaviour which might lead to a restriction in competition such as the sharing of information or carving up of markets between different firms, rigging bids in tender processes or deliberately restricting production to reduce competition.
- Monitoring and supervising acquisitions and joint ventures.

The legislation allows competition authorities the right to fine firms who are found guilty of restricting competition, ordering firms to change behaviour and banning proposed acquisitions. Investigations will consider whether the acquisition, regardless of what size company it produces, is in the public interest. This is in recognition of the fact that companies sometimes merge not to reduce competition, but to lower costs through more efficient joint production. These benefits from mergers are referred to as *synergies*.

Clearly, governments must be able to determine which mergers are desirable and which are not. That is, it must be able to measure and compare the social benefit from synergies to the social costs of reduced competition.

Regulation

Another way in which the government deals with the problem of monopoly is by regulating the behaviour of monopolists. This solution is common in the case of natural monopolies, for instance utility companies supplying water, gas and electricity. These companies are not allowed to charge any price they want. Instead, government agencies regulate their prices.

What price should the government set for a natural monopoly? This question is not as easy as it might at first appear. We might conclude that the price should equal the monopolist's marginal cost. If price equals marginal cost, customers will buy the quantity of the monopolist's output that maximizes total surplus, and the allocation of resources will be efficient.

There are, however, two practical problems with marginal cost pricing as a regulatory system. The first is illustrated in Figure 13.9. Natural monopolies, by definition, have declining average total cost.

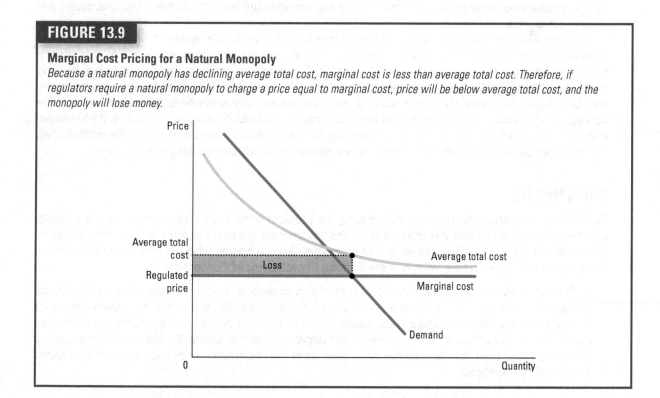

FIGURE 13.9

Marginal Cost Pricing for a Natural Monopoly
Because a natural monopoly has declining average total cost, marginal cost is less than average total cost. Therefore, if regulators require a natural monopoly to charge a price equal to marginal cost, price will be below average total cost, and the monopoly will lose money.

When average total cost is declining, marginal cost is less than average total cost. If regulators are to set price equal to marginal cost, that price will be less than the firm's average total cost, and the firm will lose money. Instead of charging such a low price, the monopoly firm would just exit the industry.

Regulators can respond to this problem in various ways, none of which is perfect. One way is to subsidize the monopolist. In essence, the government picks up the losses inherent in marginal cost pricing. Yet to pay for the subsidy, the government needs to raise money through taxation, which involves its own deadweight losses. Alternatively, the regulators can allow the monopolist to charge a price higher than marginal cost. If the regulated price equals average total cost, the monopolist earns exactly zero economic profit. Yet average cost pricing leads to deadweight losses, because the monopolist's price no longer reflects the marginal cost of producing the good. Average cost pricing is like a tax on the good the monopolist is selling.

The second problem with marginal cost pricing as a regulatory system (and with average cost pricing as well) is that it gives the monopolist no incentive to reduce costs. Each firm in a competitive market tries to reduce its costs, because lower costs mean higher profits. If a regulated monopolist knows that regulators will reduce prices whenever costs fall, the monopolist will not benefit from lower costs. In practice, regulators deal with this problem by allowing monopolists to keep some of the benefits from lower costs in the form of higher profit, a practice that requires some departure from marginal cost pricing.

For example, in the UK, utility companies have often been subject to price caps whereby the regulator determines that the real price of the company's product (a kilowatt hour of electricity, for example) should fall by a given number of percentage points each year, reflecting productivity rises. Say, for example, this is 2 per cent. The company would then be allowed to raise its prices each year by the inflation rate *minus* 2 per cent. If the company increases its productivity by, say, 4 per cent each year, however (in other words it can produce the same amount of output with 4 per cent fewer inputs), then in real terms its profits will go up each year. In this way, the system of price caps aims to give natural monopolies the motivation to improve efficiency and productivity that would be supplied by the invisible hand in a competitive market.

Public Ownership

The third policy used by the government to deal with monopoly is public ownership. That is, rather than regulating a natural monopoly that is run by a private firm, the government can run the monopoly itself. An industry owned by the government is called a nationalized industry. This solution is common in many European countries, where the government owns and operates utilities such as the telephone, water and electric companies.

Whether private or public ownership of natural monopolies is preferable will be dependent on how the ownership of the firm affects the costs of production. Private owners have an incentive to minimize costs if they reap part of the benefit in the form of higher profit. If the firm's managers are doing a bad job of keeping costs down, the firm's owners will fire them. By contrast, if the government bureaucrats who run a monopoly do a bad job, the losers are the customers and taxpayers, whose only recourse is the political system. The bureaucrats may become a special interest group and attempt to block cost-reducing reforms. If you believe that the voting booth is a less reliable way of ensuring firms are well run when compared to the profit motive, then this may determine whether you prefer to see private or publicly owned natural monopolies.

Doing Nothing

Each of the foregoing policies aimed at reducing the problem of monopoly has drawbacks. As a result, some economists argue that it is often best for the government not to try to remedy the inefficiencies of monopoly pricing. Here is the assessment of economist George Stigler, who won the Nobel Prize for his work in industrial organization, writing in the *Fortune Encyclopedia of Economics*:

A famous theorem in economics states that a competitive enterprise economy will produce the largest possible income from a given stock of resources. No real economy meets the exact conditions of the theorem, and all real economies will fall short of the ideal economy – a difference called 'market failure'. In my view, however, the degree of 'market failure' for the American economy is much smaller than the 'political failure' arising from the imperfections of economic policies found in real political systems.

As this quotation makes clear, determining the proper role of the government in the economy requires judgements about politics as well as economics.

> **SELF TEST** Describe the ways policy makers can respond to the inefficiencies caused by monopolies. List a potential problem with each of these policy responses.

CONCLUSION: THE PREVALENCE OF MONOPOLY

This chapter has discussed the behaviour of firms that have control over the prices they charge. We have seen that these firms behave very differently from the competitive firms studied in the previous chapter.

From the standpoint of public policy, a crucial result is that monopolists produce less than the socially efficient quantity and charge prices above marginal cost. As a result, they cause deadweight losses. In some cases, these inefficiencies can be mitigated through price discrimination by the monopolist, but at other times they call for policy makers to take an active role.

How prevalent are the problems of monopoly? There are two answers to this question.

In one sense, monopolies are common. Most firms have some control over the prices they charge. They are not forced to charge the market price for their goods, because their goods are not exactly the same as those offered by other firms. A Honda Accord is not the same as a Volkswagen Passat. Ben & Jerry's ice cream is not the same as Wall's. Each of these goods has a downward sloping demand curve, which gives each producer some degree of monopoly power.

Yet firms with substantial monopoly power are quite rare. Few goods are truly unique. Most have substitutes that, even if not exactly the same, are very similar. Ben & Jerry's can raise the price of its ice cream a little without losing all its sales; but if it raises it very much, sales will fall substantially.

In the end, monopoly power is a matter of degree. It is true that many firms have some monopoly power but it is also true that their monopoly power is usually limited in some way.

SUMMARY

- Imperfect competition is where the assumptions of perfect competition are dropped and firms have some degree of market power.

- Having market power means firms' behaviour may be different from that which operates under competitive conditions.

- At the extreme of imperfect competition is monopoly.

- A monopoly is a firm that is the sole seller in its market. A monopoly arises when a single firm owns a key resource, when the government gives a firm the exclusive right to produce a good, or when a single firm can supply the entire market at a smaller cost than many firms could.

- Because a monopoly is the sole producer in its market, it faces a downward sloping demand curve for its product. When a monopoly increases production by one unit, it causes the price of its good to fall, which reduces the amount of revenue earned on all units produced. As a result, a monopoly's marginal revenue is always below the price of its good.

- Like a competitive firm, a monopoly firm maximizes profit by producing the quantity at which marginal revenue equals marginal cost. The monopoly then chooses the price at which that quantity is demanded. Unlike a competitive firm, a monopoly firm's price exceeds its marginal revenue, so its price exceeds marginal cost.

- A monopolist's profit-maximizing level of output is below the level that maximizes the sum of consumer and producer surplus. That is, when the monopoly charges a price above marginal cost, some consumers who value the good more than its cost of production do not buy it. As a result, monopoly causes deadweight losses.

- Policy makers can respond to the inefficiency of monopoly behaviour in four ways. They can use competition law to try to make the industry more competitive. They can regulate the prices that the monopoly charges. They can turn the monopolist into a government-run enterprise. Or, if the market failure is deemed small compared to the inevitable imperfections of policies, they can do nothing at all.

- Monopolists can often raise their profits by charging different prices for the same good based on a buyer's willingness to pay. This practice of price discrimination can raise economic welfare by getting the good to some consumers who otherwise would not buy it. In the extreme case of perfect price discrimination, the deadweight losses of monopoly are completely eliminated. More generally, when price discrimination is imperfect, it can either raise or lower welfare compared to the outcome with a single monopoly price.

IN THE NEWS

Concert Tickets

If you want to buy a concert ticket for a major artist's performance, the chances are that you will utilize the services provided by Ticketmaster. In 2010, two companies, Live Nation and Ticketmaster merged to become Live Nation Entertainment and the firm dominates the live entertainment industry. Critics of the merger argued that it would lead to higher ticket prices and less choice for customers. In 2022, Live Nation reported its third quarter revenues were up 63 per cent compared to the same period in 2019, to $6.2 billion (€5.88 billion). Year to date figures quoted by Live Nation in October 2022 showed that 89 million customers attended 31,000 events.

Many people enjoy music concerts but few enjoy the challenge of securing fair-priced tickets.

In November 2022, Live Nation oversaw the pre-sale and sale of tickets for the newly announced tour by Taylor Swift. Fans of the singer are referred to as 'Swifties'. Many had pre-registered for the pre-sale, an approach used to try to prevent tickets falling into the hands of re-sellers. On the day pre-sale tickets became available, 15 November, thousands of fans faced lengthy online queues, many complained of being thrown off the site after hours of waiting, and thousands were left disappointed at not being able to access tickets. The planned sale of tickets to the general public was cancelled with Live Nation reporting that unprecedented demand had forced it to cease sales. One Live Nation spokesperson commented that the company could have sold millions more tickets, but that stadium capacity was limited, and some fans were always going to be disappointed. One of the problems the company faced was attacks from bots, software programs designed to carry out repetitive tasks, in this case searching out and buying tickets, which resulted in tickets not going to fans but to re-sellers. On the same day that fans were seeking to purchase tickets through Live Nation, re-seller sites were offering tickets at many times the face value.

The problem experienced by 'Swifties' is not unique; other fans have complained about long wait times, high fees, limited choice and poor service. The problems are ones that critics of the merger in 2010 had warned about and it seems that the experience of 'Swifties' prompted the US Department of Justice to investigate the monopoly position of Live Nation. A number of news sites were reporting that senior politicians in the US Senate were voicing concerns about Live Nation and expressing support for a review into the company's monopoly position. Live Nation itself strongly rejected accusations that it was anti-competitive. In a statement provided to Pitchfork, an online music publication site, the company noted:

As we have stated many times in the past, Live Nation takes its responsibilities under the antitrust laws seriously and does not engage in behaviours that could justify antitrust litigation, let alone orders that would require it to alter fundamental business practices.

(Continued)

The concert promotion business is highly competitive, with artist management in control of selecting their promoting team. The demand for live entertainment continues to grow, and there are more promoters than ever working with artists to help them connect with fans through live shows. The US Department of Justice itself recognized the competitive nature of the concert promotion business at the time of the Live Nation–Ticketmaster merger. That dynamic has not changed.

Questions

1 It is reported that Live Nation controls around 70 per cent of the live entertainment industry in the United States. Comment on the source of Live Nation's monopoly power.

2 Referring to the information provided in the section on how monopolies make production and pricing decisions, explain how Live Nation might decide on pricing and output (ticket sales) for an event like the Taylor Swift Eras tour.

3 Re-seller sites are able to sell tickets for many times their face value. Explain why this is so and use the concepts of the price elasticity of demand and supply to illustrate your answer.

4 Live Nation's financial figures show a considerable increase in sales of tickets for concerts across world. Assuming that Live Nation generates a considerable profit from its activities, to what extent would you argue that this profit represents a social cost?

5 Look at the statement provided to Pitchfork by Live Nation where it defends its activities and position. In the example of the sales of tickets for Taylor Swift, the company argued that demand simply outstripped available supply by a considerable amount. To what extent do you think Live Nation's defence is justified, that it does not abuse its monopoly position, and that any anti-competitive investigations into its activities are unjustified?

References: www.livenationentertainment.com/2022/11/live-nation-entertainment-reports-third-quarter-2022-results/ (accessed 10 June 2023).
www.rollingstone.com/music/music-features/taylor-swift-ticketmaster-live-nation-monopoly-antitrust-commentary-1234635257/ (accessed 10 June 2023).
https://pitchfork.com/news/justice-department-to-investigate-live-nation-entertainment-for-potential-abuse-of-power/ (accessed 10 June 2023).

QUESTIONS FOR REVIEW

1 Explain the difference between a perfectly competitive market and an imperfectly competitive market.

2 Do firms which operate in a market where there is a dominant firm not face competition? Explain.

3 Give an example of a government-created monopoly. Is creating this monopoly necessarily bad public policy? Explain.

4 Define natural monopoly. What does the size of a market have to do with whether an industry is a natural monopoly?

5 Why is a monopolist's marginal revenue less than the price of its good? Can marginal revenue ever be negative? Explain.

6 Draw the demand, marginal revenue and marginal cost curves for a monopolist. Show the profit-maximizing level of output. Show the profit-maximizing price.

7 In your diagram from the previous question, show the level of output that maximizes total surplus. Show the deadweight loss from the monopoly. Explain your answer.

8 What gives the government the power to regulate mergers between firms? From the standpoint of the welfare of society, give a good reason and a bad reason that two firms might want to merge.

9 Describe the two problems that arise when regulators tell a natural monopoly that it must set a price equal to marginal cost.

10 Give two examples of price discrimination. In each case, explain why the monopolist chooses to follow this business strategy.

PROBLEMS AND APPLICATIONS

1 A publisher faces the following demand schedule for the next novel of one of its popular authors:

Price (€)	Quantity demanded
100	0
90	100,000
80	200,000
70	300,000
60	400,000
50	500,000
40	600,000
30	700,000
20	800,000
10	900,000
0	1,000,000

The author is paid €2 million to write the book, and the marginal cost of publishing the book is a constant €10 per book.

a. Compute total revenue, total cost and profit at each quantity. What quantity would a profit-maximizing publisher choose? What price would it charge?

b. Compute marginal revenue. (Recall that $MR = \Delta TR/\Delta Q$.) How does marginal revenue compare to the price? Explain.

c. Graph the marginal revenue, marginal cost and demand curves. At what quantity do the marginal revenue and marginal cost curves cross? What does this signify?

d. In your graph, shade in the deadweight loss. Explain in words what this means.

e. If the author was paid €3 million instead of €2 million to write the book, how would this affect the publisher's decision regarding the price to charge? Explain.

f. Suppose the publisher was not profit maximizing but was concerned with maximizing economic efficiency. What price would it charge for the book? How much profit would it make at this price?

2 Suppose that a natural monopolist was required by law to charge average total cost. On a diagram, label the price charged and the deadweight loss to society relative to marginal cost pricing.

3 Consider the delivery of mail. In general, what is the shape of the average total cost curve? How might the shape differ between isolated rural areas and densely populated urban areas? How might the shape have changed over time? Explain.

4 Suppose the Eau de Jeunesse Water Company has a monopoly on bottled water sales in France. If the price of tap water increases, what is the change in Eau de Jeunesse's profit-maximizing levels of output, price and profit? Explain in words and with a graph.

5 The Wise Economists, a top rock band, have just finished recording their latest music album. Their record company's marketing department determines that the demand for streams for the album is as follows:

Price (€)	Number of downloads
24	10,000
22	20,000
20	30,000
18	40,000
16	50,000
14	60,000

The company can produce the album with no fixed cost and a variable cost of €5 per stream:

a. Find total revenue for quantity equal to 10,000, 20,000 and so on. What is the marginal revenue for each 10,000 increase in the quantity sold?

b. What quantity of streams would maximize profit? What would the price be? What would the profit be?

c. If you were The Wise Economists' agent, what recording fee would you advise them to demand from the record company? Why?

6 A company is considering building a bridge across a river. The bridge would cost €2 million to build and nothing to maintain. The following table shows the company's anticipated demand over the lifetime of the bridge:

Price per crossing (€)	Number of crossings (000s)
8	0
7	100
6	200
5	300
4	400
3	500
2	600
1	700
0	800

a. If the company were to build the bridge, what would be its profit-maximizing price? Would that be the efficient level of output? Why or why not?

b. If the company is interested in maximizing profit, should it build the bridge? What would be its profit or loss?

c. If the government were to build the bridge, what price should it charge for passengers and vehicles to use the bridge? Explain your answer.

d. Should the government build the bridge? Explain.

7 The Placebo Drug Company holds a patent on one of its discoveries.

a. Assuming that the production of the drug involves rising marginal cost, draw a diagram to illustrate Placebo's profit-maximizing price and quantity. Also show Placebo's profits.

b. Now suppose that the government imposes a tax on each bottle of the drug produced. On a new diagram, illustrate Placebo's new price and quantity. How does each compare to your answer in part (a)?

c. Although it is not easy to see in your diagrams, the tax reduces Placebo's profit. Explain why this must be true.

d. Instead of the tax per bottle, suppose that the government imposes a tax on Placebo of €110,000 regardless of how many bottles are produced. How does this tax affect Placebo's price, quantity and profits? Explain.

8 Pablo, Dirk and Franz run the only bar in town. Pablo wants to sell as many drinks as possible without losing money. Dirk wants the bar to bring in as much revenue as possible. Franz wants to make the largest possible profits. Using a single diagram of the bar's demand curve and its cost curves, show the price and quantity combinations favoured by each of the three partners. Explain.

9 The Best Computer Company just developed a new computer chip, on which it immediately acquires a patent.

a. Draw a diagram that shows the consumer surplus, producer surplus and total surplus in the market for this new chip.

b. What happens to these three measures of surplus if the firm can perfectly price discriminate? What is the change in deadweight loss? What transfers occur?

10 Many schemes for price discriminating involve some cost. For example, discount offers take up time and resources from both the buyer and the seller. This question considers the implications of costly price discrimination. To keep things simple, let us assume that our monopolist's production costs are simply proportional to output, so that average total cost and marginal cost are constant and equal to each other.

a. Draw the cost, demand and marginal revenue curves for the monopolist. Show the price the monopolist would charge without price discrimination.

b. In your diagram, mark the area equal to the monopolist's profit and call it X. Mark the area equal to consumer surplus and call it Y. Mark the area equal to the deadweight loss and call it Z.

c. Now suppose that the monopolist can perfectly price discriminate. What is the monopolist's profit? (Give your answer in terms of X, Y and Z.)

d. What is the change in the monopolist's profit from price discrimination? What is the change in total surplus from price discrimination? Which change is larger? Explain. (Give your answer in terms of X, Y and Z.)

e. Now suppose that there is some cost of price discrimination. To model this cost, let us assume that the monopolist must pay a fixed cost C in order to price discriminate. How would a monopolist make the decision whether to pay this fixed cost? (Give your answer in terms of X, Y, Z and C.)

f. How would a monopoly owner, who cares about total surplus, decide whether the monopolist should price discriminate? (Give your answer in terms of X, Y, Z and C.)

g. Compare your answers to parts e and f. How does the monopolist's incentive to price discriminate differ from the monopoly owner interested in maximizing total surplus? Is it possible that the monopolist will price discriminate even though it is not socially desirable?

14

MARKET STRUCTURES: IMPERFECT OR MONOPOLISTIC COMPETITION

LEARNING OUTCOMES

After reading this chapter you should be able to:

- Show the long run adjustment that takes place in a monopolistically competitive market when a firm generates economic profits.
- Show why monopolistically competitive firms produce at less-than-efficient scale in the long run.
- Discuss the inefficiencies of monopolistically competitive markets.
- Consider the arguments for and against advertising and branding.
- State the key characteristics of contestable markets.

THE NATURE OF MONOPOLISTIC COMPETITION

In most markets, we do not see the extremes described in perfect competition or monopoly, instead there are often many firms competing with each other, but some are much larger than others. The competition between firms might be very localized. A number of restaurants in a typical city centre, for example, might compete on differences in price, differences in the product, the quality of the service provided, through exploiting human psychology to make it appear there is a difference between competing products or by finding some way to encourage customer loyalty.

These things and more are all characteristic of imperfect competition. In conditions of imperfect competition, products are not homogeneous. There might be many substitutes for a product in the market, but in some way or another the firm tries to make their product different from rivals so that the degree of substitutability is reduced. In differentiating products, the firm is able to have some control over the price that they charge. The sellers in this market are price makers rather than price takers, and price will be above marginal cost.

Because these markets have some features of competition and some features of monopoly it is called **monopolistic competition**.

 monopolistic competition a market structure in which many firms sell products that are similar but not identical

Monopolistic competition describes a market with the following attributes:

- *Many sellers*. There are many firms competing for the same group of customers with each firm being small compared to the market as a whole.
- *Product differentiation*. Each firm produces a product that is at least slightly different from those of other firms. The firm is able to have some control over the extent to which it can differentiate its product from its rivals, thus reducing the degree of substitutability and garnering an element of customer or brand loyalty. Therefore, rather than being a price taker, each firm faces a downward sloping demand curve.
- *Free entry*. Firms can enter (or exit) the market without restriction. Thus, the number of firms in the market adjusts until economic profits are driven to zero.

Table 14.1 lists examples of the types of market with these attributes.

TABLE 14.1	Examples of Markets Which Have Characteristics of Monopolistic Competition

Architects	Vets
Restaurants	Hotel accommodation
Conference organizers	Air conditioning systems
Wedding planners	Pest control
Plumbing	Removal services
Coach hire	Beauty consultants
Funeral directors	Shop fitters
Fabric manufacturers	Waste disposal
Tailors	Dentists
Music teachers	Children's entertainers
Tyre fitters	Gas engineers
Garden centres	Steel fabricators
Landscape architects	Driving schools
Environmental consultants	Opticians
Furniture manufacturers	Chimney sweeps

Competition with Differentiated Products

To understand monopolistically competitive markets, we first consider the decisions facing an individual firm. We then examine what happens in the long run as firms enter and exit the industry. Next, we compare the equilibrium under monopolistic competition to the equilibrium under perfect competition. Finally, we consider whether the outcome in a monopolistically competitive market is desirable from the standpoint of society as a whole.

The Monopolistically Competitive Firm in the Short Run

Each firm in a monopolistically competitive market is, in many ways, like a monopoly. Because its product is different from those offered by other firms, it faces a downward sloping demand curve. If we assume that a monopolistically competitive firm aims for profit maximization, it chooses the quantity at which marginal revenue equals marginal cost and then uses its demand curve to find the price consistent with that quantity.

Figure 14.1 shows the cost, demand and marginal revenue curves for two typical firms, each in a different monopolistically competitive industry. In both panels of this figure, the profit-maximizing quantity is found at the intersection of the marginal revenue and marginal cost curves. The two panels in this figure show different outcomes for the firm's profit. In panel (a), price exceeds average total cost, so the firm makes a profit. In panel (b), price is below average total cost. In this case, the firm is unable to make a positive profit, so the best the firm can do is to minimize its losses.

All this should seem familiar. A monopolistically competitive firm chooses its quantity and price just as a monopoly does. In the short run, these two types of market structure are similar.

FIGURE 14.1

Monopolistic Competitors in the Short Run
Monopolistic competitors maximize profit by producing the quantity at which marginal revenue equals marginal cost. The firm in panel (a) makes a profit because, at this quantity, price is above average total cost. The firm in panel (b) makes losses because, at this quantity, price is less than average total cost.

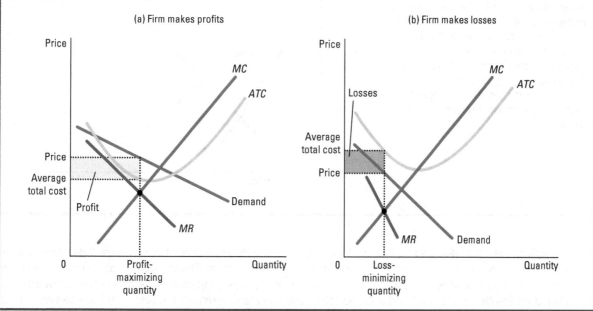

The Long Run Equilibrium

The situations depicted in Figure 14.1 prompt changes in behaviour which result in a different outcome in the long run. When firms are making profits, as in panel (a), new firms have an incentive to enter the market. This entry means that more firms are now offering products for sale in the industry. The increase in supply causes the price received by all firms in the industry to fall. If an existing firm wishes to sell more, it must reduce its price. There are now more substitutes available in the market, and the effect is that there is an increase in the number of products from which customers can choose, which reduces the demand faced by each firm already in the market. In other words, profit encourages entry and entry shifts the demand curves faced by the incumbent firms to the left. As the demand for incumbent firms' products falls, these firms experience declining profit.

Conversely, when firms are making losses, as in panel (b), firms in the market have an incentive to exit. As firms exit, the supply will fall and price will rise. There are now fewer substitutes and so customers have fewer products from which to choose. This decrease in the number of firms effectively expands the demand faced by those firms that stay in the market. In other words, losses encourage exit, which has the effect of shifting the demand curves of the remaining firms to the right. As the demand for the remaining firms' products rises, these firms experience rising profit (that is, declining losses).

This process of entry and exit continues until the firms in the market are making exactly zero economic profit. Figure 14.2 depicts the long run equilibrium. Once the market reaches this equilibrium, new firms have no incentive to enter, and existing firms have no incentive to exit.

 WHAT IF... a firm operating in a very localized market making short run abnormal profit could erect some sort of barrier to entry. Would it still be able to make abnormal profits in the long run?

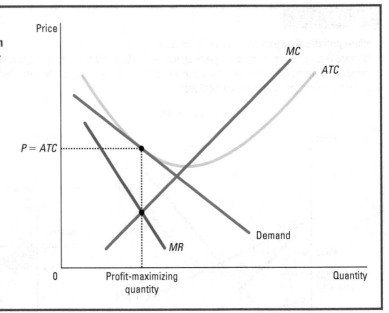

FIGURE 14.2

Monopolistic Competition in the Long Run
In a monopolistically competitive market, if firms are making abnormal profit, new firms enter and the demand curves for the incumbent firms shift to the left. Similarly, if firms are making losses (subnormal profit), some of these firms exit and the demand curves of the remaining firms shift to the right. Because of these shifts in demand, a monopolistically competitive firm eventually finds itself in the long run equilibrium shown here. In this long run equilibrium, price equals average total cost, and the firm earns zero (normal) profit.

Notice that the demand curve in this figure just barely touches the average total cost curve. Mathematically, we say the two curves are *tangential* to each other. These two curves must be tangential once entry and exit have driven profit to zero. Because profit per unit sold is the difference between price (found on the demand curve) and average total cost, the maximum profit is zero only if these two curves touch each other without crossing.

To sum up, two characteristics describe the long run equilibrium in a monopolistically competitive market:

● As in a monopoly market, price exceeds marginal cost. This conclusion arises because profit maximization requires marginal revenue to equal marginal cost, and because the downward sloping demand curve makes marginal revenue less than the price.
● As in a competitive market, price equals average total cost. This conclusion arises because free entry and exit drive economic profit to zero.

The second characteristic shows how monopolistic competition differs from monopoly. Because a monopoly is the sole seller of a product without close substitutes, it can earn abnormal profit, even in the long run. By contrast, because there is free entry into a monopolistically competitive market, the economic profit of a firm in this type of market is driven to zero.

Monopolistic Versus Perfect Competition

Figure 14.3 compares the long run equilibrium under monopolistic competition to the long run equilibrium under perfect competition. There are two noteworthy differences between monopolistic and perfect competition: excess capacity and the mark-up.

Excess Capacity Entry and exit drive each firm in a monopolistically competitive market to a point of tangency between its demand and average total cost curves. Panel (a) of Figure 14.3 shows that the quantity of output at this point is smaller than the quantity that minimizes average total cost. Thus under monopolistic competition, firms produce on the downward sloping portion of their average total cost curves. In this way, monopolistic competition contrasts starkly with perfect competition. As panel (b) of Figure 14.3 shows, free entry in competitive markets drives firms to produce at the minimum of average total cost.

The quantity that minimizes average total cost is called the *efficient scale* of the firm. In the long run, perfectly competitive firms produce at the efficient scale, whereas monopolistically competitive firms produce below this level. Firms are said to have *excess capacity* under monopolistic competition.

In other words, a monopolistically competitive firm, unlike a perfectly competitive firm, could increase the quantity it produces and lower the average total cost of production.

FIGURE 14.3

Monopolistic Versus Perfect Competition

Panel (a) shows the long run equilibrium in a monopolistically competitive market, and panel (b) shows the long run equilibrium in a perfectly competitive market. Two differences are notable. (1) The perfectly competitive firm produces at the efficient scale, where average total cost is minimized. By contrast, the monopolistically competitive firm produces at less than the efficient scale. (2) Price equals marginal cost under perfect competition, but price is above marginal cost under monopolistic competition.

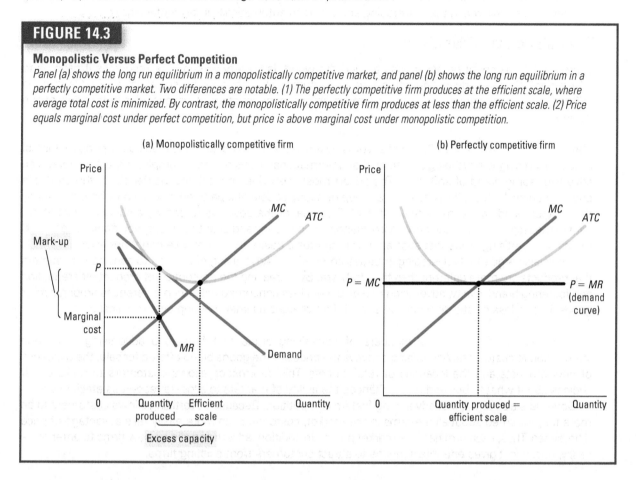

Mark-Up Over Marginal Cost A second difference between perfect competition and monopolistic competition is the relationship between price and marginal cost. For a competitive firm, such as that shown in panel (b) of Figure 14.3, price equals marginal cost. For a monopolistically competitive firm, such as that shown in panel (a), price exceeds marginal cost, because the firm always has some market power.

How is this mark-up over marginal cost consistent with free entry and zero profit? The zero profit condition ensures only that price equals average total cost. It does *not* ensure that price equals marginal cost. Indeed, in the long run equilibrium, monopolistically competitive firms operate on the declining portion of their average total cost curves, so marginal cost is below average total cost. Thus, for price to equal average total cost, price must be above marginal cost. Because of this a monopolistically competitive firm is always eager to get another customer. Because its price exceeds marginal cost, an extra unit sold at the posted price means more profit.

One characteristic of monopolistic competition is the use of advertising and establishment of brand names. Advertising and branding are important in understanding the behaviour of firms in imperfect competition.

ADVERTISING AND BRANDING

The fact that firms in monopolistic competitive markets seek to differentiate their products means they are incentivized to find ways in which these differences can be cemented in the minds of consumers, so consumers can become aware of the characteristic features of their product. Advertising and branding are ways in which firms seek to highlight and emphasize the way in which their products are differentiated.

In theory, advertising and branding are redundant in perfectly competitive markets because products are homogenous. We have seen that the model of perfect competition is associated with maximizing efficiency. Does this mean that advertising and branding automatically imply inefficiency?

The Debate Over Advertising

There are billions spent on advertising around the world. Is society wasting the resources it devotes to advertising? Or does advertising serve a valuable purpose? Assessing the social value of advertising is difficult and often generates heated argument among economists. Let us consider both sides of the debate.

The Critique of Advertising Critics of advertising argue that firms advertise to manipulate people's tastes. Much advertising is psychological rather than informational. Consider, for example, the typical television advert for some brand of soft drink. The advert most likely does not tell the viewer about the product's price or quality. Instead, it might show a group of happy people at a party on a beach on a beautiful sunny day. In their hands are cans of the soft drink. The goal of the advert is to convey a subconscious (if not subtle) message: 'You too can have many friends and be happy and beautiful, if only you drink our product.' Critics of advertising argue that such an advert creates a desire that otherwise might not exist.

Critics also argue that advertising impedes competition. Advertising often tries to convince consumers that products are more different than they truly are. By increasing the perception of product differentiation and fostering brand loyalty, advertising makes buyers less concerned with price differences among similar goods. With a less elastic demand curve, each firm charges a larger mark-up over marginal cost.

The Defence of Advertising Defenders of advertising argue that firms use advertising to provide information to customers. Advertising conveys the prices of the goods being offered for sale, the existence of new products and the locations of retail outlets. This information allows customers to make better choices about what to buy and thus enhances the ability of markets to allocate resources efficiently.

Defenders also argue that advertising fosters competition. Because advertising allows customers to be more fully informed about all the firms in the market, customers can more easily take advantage of price differences. Thus, each firm has less market power. In addition, advertising allows new firms to enter more easily, because it gives entrants a means to attract customers from existing firms.

Advertising as a Signal of Quality

Many types of advertising contain little apparent information about the product being advertised. Consider a firm advertising its latest coffee machine. It might use the services of a well-known actor in a jovial and comedic setting. How much information does the advertisement really provide?

The answer is: more than you might think. Defenders of advertising argue that even advertising that appears to contain little hard information may in fact tell consumers something about product quality. The willingness of the firm to spend a large amount of money on advertising can itself be a *signal* to consumers about the quality of the product being offered.

Consider a hypothetical problem facing two firms: Nestlé and Kellogg's. Each company has just come up with a recipe for a new breakfast cereal, which it plans to sell for €3 a box. To keep things simple, let us assume that the €3 is all profit. Each company knows that if it spends €10 million on advertising, it will get 1 million consumers to try its new cereal. And each company knows that if consumers like the cereal, they will buy it not once but many times.

Let us consider Nestlé's decision. Based on market research, Nestlé knows that its cereal is only mediocre. Although advertising would sell one box to each of 1 million consumers, the consumers would quickly learn that the cereal is not very good and stop buying it. Nestlé decides it is not worth paying €10 million in advertising to get only €3 million in sales, so it does not bother to advertise. It sends its cooks back to the drawing board to find another recipe.

Kellogg's, on the other hand, knows that its cereal is great. Each person who tries it will buy a box a month for the next year. Thus, the €10 million in advertising will bring in €36 million in sales. Advertising is profitable here because Kellogg's has a good product that consumers will buy repeatedly. Thus Kellogg's chooses to advertise.

Now that we have considered the behaviour of the two firms, let us consider the behaviour of consumers. We began by asserting that consumers are inclined to try a new cereal that they see advertised. But is this behaviour rational? Should a consumer try a new cereal just because the seller has chosen to advertise it?

In fact, it may be completely rational for consumers to try new products that they see advertised. In our story, consumers decide to try Kellogg's new cereal because Kellogg's advertises. Kellogg's chooses to advertise because it knows that its cereal is quite good, while Nestlé chooses not to advertise because it knows that its cereal is only mediocre. By its willingness to spend money on advertising, Kellogg's signals to consumers the quality of its cereal. Each consumer thinks, quite sensibly, 'Wow, if the Kellogg Company is willing to spend so much money advertising this new cereal, it must be really good.'

What is most surprising about this theory of advertising is that the content of the advertisement is irrelevant. Kellogg's signals the quality of its product by its willingness to spend money on advertising. (This example is used for illustrative purposes only and is not meant to infer that Nestlé produces inferior products!) What the advertisements say is not as important as the fact that consumers know adverts are expensive. By contrast, cheap advertising cannot be effective at signalling quality to consumers. In our example, if an advertising campaign costs less than €3 million, both Nestlé and Kellogg's would use it to market their new cereals. Because both good and mediocre cereals would be advertised, consumers could not infer the quality of a new cereal from the fact that it is advertised. Over time, consumers would learn to ignore such cheap advertising.

This theory can explain why firms pay celebrities large amounts of money to make advertisements that, on the surface, appear to convey no information at all. The information is not in the advertisement's content, but simply in its existence and expense.

CASE STUDY   Can Anyone Escape Advertising?

Advertising is far more prevalent than we often appreciate. Imagine taking a trip to town to meet your friend for lunch. You pick up the junk mail at the front door putting it to one side to look at later and set off to catch the bus. Two delivery vehicles pass by, each promoting their business on the side and back of the vehicles. At the bus stop a man is carrying two bags in supermarket colours, slogan and logos. He is with his son who is wearing clothes clearly identifying several well-known clothing companies. There are other people waiting for the bus with items of clothing bearing a range of brand logos. One has just finished her Costa coffee. As you look up into the sky, a plane trailing a banner promoting a furniture store sale passes by.

An interesting thought experiment might be estimating how much you would have spent if you had bought a product from each 'advert' you witnessed on your relatively short journey! The chances are, though, that you will not respond to every advert you see. So what is the purpose of advertising?

Sometimes, it is not easy to escape the reach of advertisers!

We might filter information received from adverts, but some advertising does raise awareness and might lead to individuals making more informed choices.

It has long been recognized that psychology has a lot to do with advertising. Sutherland (2020) argues that advertising influences the order in which we evoke or notice the alternatives we consider, rather than persuade us to buy. The primary aim of advertising, Sutherland argues, is to generate a series of small effects, which ultimately influence our behaviour and may cause us to view

(*Continued*)

differently the products or the brands that we choose, especially in a crowded marketplace with a large amount of competition.

Exactly how adverts work, therefore, is not easy to quantify. Sutherland suggests that many involved in the advertising industry do not really understand why some adverts seem to work and others do not work anything like as well.

Questions

1 **Take an advert of your choice and describe the advert. Analyze the advert and consider what information it provides the consumer (if any) and what you think the purpose of the advert is.**

2 **Why do you think that some adverts 'work' and so do not? Use appropriate examples to illustrate your answer.**

3 **Comment on Sutherland's assertion that most adverts are designed to generate a series of small effects designed to influence behaviour over the longer term.**

4 **Given what you know about advertising, do you think firms should be subject to more or less regulation in the way they advertise their products?**

References: Sutherland, M. (2020) *Advertising and the Mind of the Consumer: What Works, What Doesn't and Why,* Revised 3rd International Edition. Abingdon: Routledge.

BRAND NAMES

Advertising is closely related to **branding**. In many markets, there are two types of firms. Some firms sell products with widely recognized brand names, while other firms sell generic substitutes. For example, in a typical supermarket, you can find Pepsi next to less familiar colas, or Kellogg's cornflakes next to the supermarket's own brand of cornflakes, made for it by an unknown firm. Most often, the firm with the famous brand name spends more on advertising and charges a higher price for its product. Branding is designed to give a product or a firm an identity which consumers can relate to and which differentiates it from its rivals. Just as there is disagreement about the economics of advertising, there is disagreement about the economics of brand names and branding. Let us consider both sides of the debate.

 branding the means by which a business creates an identity for itself and highlights the way in which it differs from its rivals

Critics of brand names argue that branding causes consumers to perceive differences that do not really exist. In many cases, the generic good is almost indistinguishable from the brand name good. Consumers' willingness to pay more for the brand name good, these critics assert, is a form of irrationality fostered by advertising. Economist Edward Chamberlin, one of the early developers of the theory of monopolistic competition, concluded from this argument that brand names were bad for the economy. Chamberlin proposed that the government discourage their use by refusing to enforce the exclusive trademarks that companies use to identify their products.

More recently, economists have defended brand names as a useful way for consumers to ensure that the goods they buy are of high quality. There are two related arguments. First, brand names provide consumers with *information* which cannot be easily judged in advance of purchase. Second, brand names give firms an *incentive* to meet the needs of consumers, because firms have a financial stake in maintaining the reputation of their brand names. Note that branding does not always equate to high quality. Some firms will happily admit their goods are 'cheap and cheerful', but point out that they provide consumers with value for money. Firms such as Aldi, Lidl, Poundstretcher and Poundland are just as interested in developing their brand names as much as Armani and Ralph Lauren. Consumers can associate the brand name with value for money.

To see how these arguments work in practice, consider a famous brand name: Ibis hotels. Imagine that you are driving through an unfamiliar town and you need somewhere to stay for the night. You see a Hotel Ibis and a local hotel next door to it. Which do you choose? The local hotel may in fact offer better accommodation at lower prices, but you have no way of knowing that. In contrast, Hotel Ibis offers a consistent product across many European cities. Its brand name is useful to you as a way of judging the quality of what you are about to buy.

The Ibis brand name also ensures that the company has an incentive to maintain quality. For example, if some customers were to become very ill from bad food served at breakfast at a Hotel Ibis, the news would be disastrous for the company. Ibis would lose much of the valuable reputation that it has built up over the years and, as a result, it would lose sales and profit, not just in the hotel that served the bad food but in its many hotels across Europe. By contrast, if some customers were to become ill from bad food served at breakfast in a local hotel, that restaurant might have to close down, but the lost profits would be much smaller. Ibis has a greater incentive to ensure that its breakfast food is safe.

The debate over brand names centres on the question of whether consumers are rational in preferring brand names over generic substitutes. Critics of brand names argue that brand names are the result of an irrational consumer response to advertising. Defenders of brand names argue that consumers have good reason to use brand name products, because they can be more confident in the quality and consistency of message of these products.

SELF TEST How might advertising make markets less competitive? How might it make markets more competitive? Give the arguments for and against brand names.

JEOPARDY PROBLEM A firm manufacturing batteries in a market with a number of competitors spends a large amount of money over a three-year period both advertising its product and building its brand image. It finds, in the following years, that if it increases its price its revenue increases. Its internal research suggests this is contrary to what would have happened prior to the advertising campaign. What has changed in the intervening years to lead to this outcome?

CONTESTABLE MARKETS

The theory of contestable markets was developed by William J. Baumol, John Panzar and Robert Willig in 1982. The key characteristic of a perfectly contestable market (the benchmark to explain firms' behaviours) is that firms are influenced by the threat of new entrants into a market. The more highly contestable a market is, the lower the barriers to entry. We have seen how, in monopolistically competitive markets, despite the fact that each firm has some monopoly control over its product, the ease of entry and exit means that in the long run, profits can be competed away as new firms enter the market. This threat of new entrants may make firms behave in a way that departs from what was assumed to be the traditional goal of firms: to maximize profits. The suggestion by Baumol and colleagues was that firms may deliberately limit profits made to discourage new entrants. Profits might be limited by what is termed **entry limit pricing**. This refers to a situation where a firm will keep prices lower than they could be in order to deter new entrants. Similarly, firms may also practise **predatory or destroyer pricing** whereby the price is held below average cost for a period to try to force out competitors or prevent new firms from entering the market. Incumbent firms may be in a position to do this because they may have been able to gain some advantages of economies of scale which new entrants may not be able to exploit.

entry limit pricing a situation where a firm will keep prices lower than they could be in order to deter new entrants
predatory or destroyer pricing a situation where firms hold price below average cost for a period to try and force out competitors or prevent new firms from entering the market

In a contestable market firms may also erect other artificial barriers to prevent entry into the industry by new firms. Such barriers might include operating at over-capacity, which provides the opportunity to flood the market and drive down price in the event of a threat of entry. Firms will also carry out aggressive marketing and branding strategies to 'tighten' up the market or find ways of reducing costs and increasing efficiency to gain competitive advantage. Searching out sources of competitive advantage is a topic written on extensively by Michael Porter, who defined **competitive advantage** as being the advantages firms can gain over another which are both distinctive and defensible. These sources are not simply to be found in terms of new product development, but through close investigation and analysis of the supply chain, where little changes might make a difference to the cost base of a firm which it can then exploit to its advantage.

Hit-and-run tactics might be evident in a contestable market where firms enter the industry, take the profit and get out quickly (possible because of the freedom of entry and exit). In other cases, firms may indulge in what is termed **cream-skimming**, identifying parts of the market that are high in value added and exploiting those markets.

> **competitive advantage** the advantages firms can gain over another which have the characteristics of being both distinctive and defensible
> **cream-skimming** a situation where a firm identifies parts of a market that are high in value added and seeks to exploit those markets

The theory of contestable markets has been widely adopted as a beneficial addition to the theory of the firm and there has been extensive research into its application.

There are numerous examples of markets exhibiting contestability characteristics including financial services; airlines, especially flights on domestic routes; the IT industry and in particular, internet service providers (ISPs), software and web developers; energy suppliers; and the postal service. The key to analysing market structures, therefore, could be argued to be the focus on the degree of freedom of entry and exit. If policy makers can keep barriers to entry as low as possible, that is, try to ensure a high degree of contestability, then there is more likelihood that market outcomes will be efficient.

MONOPOLISTIC COMPETITION AND THE WELFARE OF SOCIETY

Is the outcome in a monopolistically competitive market desirable from the standpoint of society as a whole? Can policy makers improve on the market outcome? There are no simple answers to these questions.

One source of inefficiency is the mark-up of price over marginal cost. Because of the mark-up, some consumers who value the good at more than the marginal cost of production (but less than the price) will be deterred from buying it. Thus a monopolistically competitive market has the normal deadweight loss of monopoly pricing.

Although this outcome is clearly undesirable compared to the best outcome of price equal to marginal cost, there is no easy way for policy makers to fix the problem. To enforce marginal cost pricing, policy makers would need to regulate all firms that produce differentiated products. Because such products are so common in the economy, the administrative burden of such regulation would be overwhelming.

Moreover, regulating monopolistic competitors would entail all the problems of regulating natural monopolies. In particular, because monopolistic competitors are making zero profits already, requiring them to lower their prices to equal marginal cost would cause them to make losses. To keep these firms in business, the government would need to help them cover these losses. Rather than raising taxes to pay for these subsidies, policy makers may decide it is better to live with the inefficiency of monopolistic pricing.

Another way in which monopolistic competition may be socially inefficient is that the number of firms in the market may not be the 'ideal' one. That is, there may be too much or too little entry. One way to think about this problem is in terms of the externalities associated with entry. Whenever a new firm considers entering the market with a new product, it considers only the profit it would make. Yet its entry would also have two external effects:

- *The product-variety externality.* Because consumers get some consumer surplus from the introduction of a new product, entry of a new firm conveys a positive externality on consumers.
- *The business-stealing externality.* Because other firms lose customers and profits from the entry of a new competitor, entry of a new firm imposes a negative externality on existing firms.

Thus in a monopolistically competitive market, there are both positive and negative externalities associated with the entry of new firms. Depending on which externality is larger, a monopolistically competitive market could have either too few or too many products.

Both of these externalities are closely related to the conditions for monopolistic competition. The product-variety externality arises because a new firm would offer a product different from those of the existing firms. The business-stealing externality arises because firms post a price above marginal cost and, therefore, are always eager to sell additional units. Conversely, because perfectly competitive firms produce identical goods and charge a price equal to marginal cost, neither of these externalities exists under perfect competition.

In the end, we can conclude only that monopolistically competitive markets do not have all the welfare properties of perfectly competitive markets. That is, total surplus is not maximized under monopolistic competition. Yet because the inefficiencies are subtle, hard to measure and hard to fix, there is no easy way for public policy to improve the market outcome.

SELF TEST List the three key attributes of monopolistic competition. Draw and explain a diagram to show the long run equilibrium in a monopolistically competitive market. How does this equilibrium differ from that in a perfectly competitive market?

SUMMARY

- A monopolistically competitive market is characterized by three attributes: many firms, differentiated products and free entry.

- The equilibrium in a monopolistically competitive market differs from that in a perfectly competitive market in two related ways. First, each firm in a monopolistically competitive market has excess capacity. That is, it operates on the downward sloping portion of the average total cost curve. Second, each firm charges a price above marginal cost.

- Monopolistic competition does not have all the properties of perfect competition. There is the standard deadweight loss of monopoly caused by the mark-up of price over marginal cost. In addition, the number of firms (and thus the variety of products) can be too large or too small. In practice, the ability of policy makers to correct these inefficiencies is limited.

- The product differentiation inherent in imperfectly competitive markets leads to the use of advertising and brand names. Critics of advertising and brand names argue that firms use them to take advantage of consumer irrationality and to reduce competition. Defenders of advertising and brand names argue that firms use them to inform consumers and to compete more vigorously on price and product quality.

- The model of contestable markets suggests that firms may fear the threat of new entrants into the market because of low barriers to entry. As a result, they may not necessarily seek to maximize profits but adopt different pricing tactics to discourage entry from rivals.

- Firms in contestable markets may seek ways in which they can generate competitive advantage where such advantages are both distinctive and defensible.

IN THE NEWS

Predatory Pricing

Toypa Magazacilik Ticaret AŞ (Toypa) is a Turkish company founded in 2001 involved in the retailing of toys, games, hobby and craft kits. In February 2022, Turkish competition authorities reported on an investigation into Toypa over allegations that the company had abused its market position in the Turkish retail toy market and engaged in predatory pricing. The allegation was instigated by one of Toypa's rivals, Armağan Oyuncak Sanayi ve Ticaret AŞ (Armağan). The two firms compete in the bricks-and-mortar retail space with both companies having outlets in similar shopping areas. Armağan argued that Toypa began applying discounts up to 20 per cent on a number of branded products in its shops in May 2018. Because the products concerned had a high market share and

The toy industry could be classified as monopolistically competitive but firms could seek to exploit their market power.

low margins, Armağan said that it had been forced to offer similar discounts and that this action caused it to suffer losses. Armağan argued that without following suit in offering the discounts it would not have been able to compete with Toypa. The company also argued that Toypa's behaviour restricted entry into the market thus further reducing competition. In itself, competing through offering price discounts is not predatory pricing but Armağan argued that these discounts were only applied in Toypa's stores in areas where Armağan also had stores and did not apply in stores where Armağan was not in close proximity.

In a preliminary investigation, the Turkish Competition Board (TCB) found no evidence of barriers to entry into the market, and also dismissed the accusations of predatory pricing, partly on the basis that there was no evidence that Toypa had incurred losses consistent with below-cost pricing. Armağan appealed this initial judgement and a second investigation was conducted. In this second investigation, the TCB explored whether Toypa's position in the market could be classed as 'dominant' in terms of the broader definition of the 'retail toy sales market'. It also sought to establish the revenue generation of both companies through sales of the branded products which had been the subject of discounts. On both of these counts, the TCB found no evidence to incriminate Toypa and concluded that a full investigation was not required.

Questions

1 Using an appropriate cost and revenue diagram, show how a monopolistically competitive firm might seek to outcompete a rival by applying significant discounts on its products.
2 To what extent do you think a decision to discount prices in stores near to rivals is evidence of predatory pricing?
3 The TCB sought to explore the nature of the retail toy sales market to establish whether Toypa could be argued to be dominant in the market, and thus in a position to exploit its market power. What factors do you think the TCB might have had to consider in establishing the nature of this market, and thus Toypa's position in it?
4 One of the argument that Armağan put forward in its statement to the TCB was that Toypa's behaviour amounted to a barrier to entry into the industry. Comment on how Toypa's alleged behaviour might have resulted in barriers to entry being erected into the retail toy sales market. How strong do you think these alleged barriers to entry were likely to have been?
5 Consider the judgement by the TCB and discuss the issues that it sought to consider in arriving at its judgement on the allegations against Toypa made by Armağan.

Reference: www.lexology.com/commentary/competition-antitrust/turkey/elig-gurkaynak-attorneys-at-law/reassessment-by-turkish-competition-board-after-administrative-courts-annulment-decision-in-predatory-pricing-case (accessed 7 June 2023).

QUESTIONS FOR REVIEW

1 Describe the three attributes of monopolistic competition. How is monopolistic competition like monopoly? How is it like perfect competition?

2 Draw a diagram depicting a firm in a monopolistically competitive market that is making profits in the short run.

   a. Now show what happens to this firm as new firms enter the industry.

   b. Now draw the diagram of the long run equilibrium in a monopolistically competitive market. How is price related to average total cost? How is price related to marginal cost?

3 Does a monopolistic competitor produce too much or too little output compared to the most efficient level? What practical considerations make it difficult for policy makers to solve this problem?

4 What effect does the existence of mark-up have on efficiency in monopolistically competitive markets?

5 Provide two arguments in favour of advertising and two arguments against advertising.

6 Does branding represent a waste of resources?

7 What is meant by the term 'competitive advantage' and why is it important for any advantages to be 'distinctive' and 'defensible' for competitive advantage to be beneficial?

8 How might advertising with no apparent informational content in fact convey information to consumers?

9 What are the principal features of contestable markets?

10 Explain how monopolistic competition may result in social inefficiencies and what regulators or governments could do to reduce any such inefficiencies.

PROBLEMS AND APPLICATIONS

1 Classify the following markets as perfectly competitive, monopolistic or monopolistically competitive, and explain your answers:

   a. wooden HB pencils

   b. bottled water

   c. copper

   d. local telephone service

   e. strawberry jam

   f. lipstick.

2 Sparkle is one firm of many in the market for toothpaste, which is in long run equilibrium.

   a. Draw a diagram showing Sparkle's demand curve, marginal revenue curve, average total cost curve and marginal cost curve. Label Sparkle's profit-maximizing output and price.

   b. What is Sparkle's profit? Explain.

   c. On your diagram, show the consumer surplus derived from the purchase of Sparkle toothpaste. Also show the deadweight loss relative to the efficient level of output.

   d. If the government forced Sparkle to produce the efficient level of output, what would happen to the firm? What would happen to Sparkle's customers?

3 If you were thinking of entering the ice cream business, would you try to make ice cream that is just like one of the existing (successful) brands? Explain your decision using the ideas of this chapter.

4 Using the example of an optician, explore ways in which the firm might seek to differentiate itself from its rivals. What would you expect the short run outcome to be of a successful differentiation and what would the long run outcome be? Using the concept of competitive advantage, what would the long run outcome depend upon?

5 The theory of contestable markets suggests that firms do not always pursue the aim of profit maximization. To what extent do you think this is a far more realistic and reasonable assumption about the way firms behave 'in the real world'?

6 To maximize profit, a firm must target an output level where marginal cost equals marginal revenue. To what extent is mark-up pricing consistent with this 'rule'?

7 A ban on cigarette advertising on television, which many countries imposed in the 1970s, actually led to increased profits for cigarette companies. Explain, using the ideas in this chapter, why this might have arisen. Could the ban still be good public policy? Explain your answer.

8 Describe three adverts that you have seen on TV. In what ways, if any, were each of these adverts socially useful? In what ways were they socially wasteful? Did the adverts affect the likelihood of you buying the product? Why or why not?

9 For each of the following pairs of firms, explain which firm would be more likely to engage in advertising:

  a. a family-owned farm or a family-owned restaurant
  b. a manufacturer of forklift trucks or a manufacturer of cars
  c. a company that invented a very reliable watch or a company that invented a less reliable watch that costs the same amount to make.

10 The text suggests that the internet service provider (ISP) market is an example of a contestable market. Research into this market and discuss the extent to which you think the market is characteristic of a contestable market.

15 MARKET STRUCTURES: OLIGOPOLY

LEARNING OUTCOMES

After reading this chapter you should be able to:

- Use the idea of concentration ratios to describe oligopolistic market structures.
- Describe the characteristics of oligopoly.
- Explain the equilibrium conditions for an oligopoly.
- Explain and apply the idea of the prisoners' dilemma to explain interdependency in oligopolistic market structures.
- Show why the outcome of the prisoners' dilemma may change if the game is repeated.
- Show why some business practices that appear to reduce competition may have a legitimate business purpose.

OLIGOPOLY

The Europeans love chocolate. The average German eats about 180 62-gram bars of chocolate a year. The Belgians are not far behind at 177 bars, the Swiss around 173 and the British eat around 164 bars per year. There are many firms producing chocolate in Europe including Anthon Berg in Denmark, Camille Bloch, Lindt and Favarger in Switzerland, Guylian and Godiva in Belgium, and Hachez in Germany. However, Europeans are likely to find that what they are eating has probably been made by one of three companies: Cadbury now (owned by Mondelēz International), Mars or Nestlé. These firms dominate the chocolate industry in the EU. Being so large and dominant they are able to influence the quantity of chocolate bars produced and, given the market demand curve, the price at which chocolate bars are sold.

The European market for chocolate bars fits a model of imperfect competition called **oligopoly**, literally competition among the few. The essence of an oligopolistic market is that there are a few sellers which dominate the market and where the products they sell are identical or near identical. In this situation, competition between these large firms might be focused on strategic interactions among them. As a result, the actions of any one seller in the market can have a large impact on the profits of all the other sellers. That is, oligopolistic firms are interdependent in a way that competitive firms are not.

> **oligopoly** competition among the few, a market structure in which only a few sellers offer similar or identical products and dominate the market

There is no magic number that defines 'few' from 'many' when counting the number of firms. Do the approximately dozen companies that now sell cars in Europe make this market an oligopoly or a more competitive market structure? The answer is open to debate. Similarly, there is no sure way to determine when products are differentiated and when they are identical. Are different brands of milk really the same? Again, the answer is debatable. When analysing actual markets, economists must keep in mind the lessons learned from studying all types of market structure and then apply each lesson as it seems appropriate.

Our goal is to see how the interdependence that characterizes oligopolistic markets shapes the firms' behaviour and what problems it raises for public policy.

Markets With Only a Few Dominant Sellers

If a market is dominated by a relatively small number of sellers it is said to be *concentrated*. The **concentration ratio** refers to the proportion of the total market share accounted for by the top x number of firms in the industry. For example, a five-firm concentration ratio of 80 per cent means that five firms account for 80 per cent of market share; a three-firm concentration ratio of 72 per cent would indicate that three firms account for 72 per cent of total market sales and so on.

concentration ratio the proportion of total sales in an industry accounted for by a given number of firms

There are a number of examples of oligopolistic market structures including brewing, banking, mobile phone networks, the chemical and oil industries, the grocery/supermarket industry, detergents and entertainment. Note that in each of these industries there might be many sellers in the industry (there are thousands of small independent breweries across Europe, for example) but sales are dominated by a relatively small number of firms. In brewing, the industry is dominated by A-BInBev, Heineken, Carlsberg and SABMiller. These four firms account for around 60 per cent of total global beer sales.

A key feature of oligopoly is the tension that exists between firms of cooperation and self-interest. The group of oligopolists is best off cooperating and acting like a monopolist, producing a smaller quantity of output and charging a price above marginal cost. Yet because each oligopolist cares about only its own profit, there are powerful incentives at work that hinder a group of firms from maintaining the monopoly outcome.

A Duopoly Example

To understand the behaviour of oligopolies, let us consider an oligopoly with only two members, called a *duopoly*. Duopoly is the simplest type of oligopoly. Oligopolies with three or more members face the same problems as oligopolies with only two members, so we do not lose much by starting with the case of duopoly.

Imagine a town in which only two residents, Ishaq and Coralie, own wells that produce water safe for drinking. Each Saturday, Ishaq and Coralie decide how many litres of water to pump, bring the water to town, and sell it for whatever price the market will bear. To keep things simple, suppose that the marginal cost of water equals zero.

Table 15.1 shows the town's demand schedule for water. The first column shows the total quantity demanded, and the second column shows the price. If the two well owners sell a total of 10 litres of water, water is priced at €1.10 a litre. If they sell a total of 20 litres, the price falls to €1.00 a litre, and so on. If you graphed these two columns of numbers, you would get a standard downward sloping demand curve.

The last column in Table 15.1 shows the total revenue from the sale of water. It equals the quantity sold times the price. Because there is no cost to pumping water, the total revenue of the two producers equals their total profit. Let's now consider how the organization of the town's water industry affects the price of water and the quantity of water sold.

Competition, Monopolies and Cartels

Consider what would happen if the market for water were perfectly competitive. In a competitive market, the production decisions of each firm drive price equal to marginal cost. In the market for water, marginal cost is zero. Thus, under competition, the equilibrium price of water would be zero, and the equilibrium quantity would be 120 litres. The price of water would reflect the cost of producing it, and the efficient quantity of water would be produced and consumed.

TABLE 15.1	The Demand Schedule for Water

Quantity (in litres)	Price per litre (€)	Total revenue (and total profit) €
0	1.20	0
10	1.10	11.00
20	1.00	20.00
30	0.90	27.00
40	0.80	32.00
50	0.70	35.00
60	0.60	36.00
70	0.50	35.00
80	0.40	32.00
90	0.30	27.00
100	0.20	20.00
110	0.10	11.00
120	0	0

Now consider how a monopoly would behave. Table 15.1 shows that total profit is maximized at a quantity of 60 litres and a price of €0.60 a litre. A profit-maximizing monopolist, therefore, would produce this quantity and charge this price. As is standard for monopolies, price would exceed marginal cost. The result would be inefficient, for the quantity of water produced and consumed would fall short of the socially efficient level of 120 litres.

What outcome should we expect from our duopolists? One possibility is that Ishaq and Coralie get together and agree on the quantity of water to produce and the price to charge for it. Such an agreement among firms over production and price is called **collusion**, and the group of firms acting in unison is called a **cartel**. Once a cartel is formed, the market is in effect served by a monopoly, and we can apply our analysis from Chapter 13. If Ishaq and Coralie were to collude, they would agree on the monopoly outcome, because that outcome maximizes the total profit that the producers can get from the market. Our two producers would produce a total of 60 litres, which would be sold at a price of €0.60 a litre. Once again, price exceeds marginal cost and the outcome is socially inefficient.

> **collusion** an agreement among firms in a market about quantities to produce or prices to charge
> **cartel** a group of firms acting in unison

A cartel must agree not only on the total level of production but also on the amount produced by each member. In our case, Ishaq and Coralie must agree how to split between themselves the monopoly production of 60 litres. Each member of the cartel will want a larger share of the market, because a larger market share means larger profit. If Ishaq and Coralie agreed to split the market equally, each would produce 30 litres, the price would be €0.60 a litre and each would get a profit of €18.

 WHAT IF... one of the firms entering into a cartel had much more market power than the other firms in the agreement. Would this mean the cartel is more likely to succeed or not?

The Equilibrium for an Oligopoly

Although oligopolists would like to form cartels and earn monopoly profits, often that is not possible. Competition laws prohibit explicit agreements among oligopolists as a matter of public policy. In addition, squabbling among cartel members over how to divide the profit in the market sometimes makes agreement among them impossible. Let us therefore consider what happens if Ishaq and Coralie decide separately how much water to produce.

At first, you might expect Ishaq and Coralie to reach the monopoly outcome on their own, for this outcome maximizes their joint profit. In the absence of a binding agreement, however, the monopoly outcome is unlikely. To see why, imagine that Ishaq expects Coralie to produce only 30 litres (half of the monopoly quantity). Ishaq might reason as follows:

I could produce 30 litres as well. In this case, a total of 60 litres of water would be sold at a price of €0.60 a litre. My profit would be €18 (30 litres × €0.60 a litre). Alternatively, I could produce 40 litres. In this case, a total of 70 litres of water would be sold at a price of €0.50 a litre. My profit would be €20 (40 litres × €0.50 a litre). Even though total profit in the market would fall, my profit would be higher, because I would have a larger share of the market.

Of course, Coralie might reason the same way. If so, Ishaq and Coralie would each bring 40 litres to town. Total sales would be 80 litres, and the price would fall to €0.40. Thus if the duopolists individually pursue their own self-interest when deciding how much to produce, they produce a total quantity greater than the monopoly quantity, charge a price lower than the monopoly price and earn total profit less than the monopoly profit.

Although the logic of self-interest increases the duopoly's output above the monopoly level, it does not push the duopolists to reach the competitive allocation. Consider what happens when each duopolist is producing 40 litres. The price is €0.40, and each duopolist makes a profit of €16. In this case, Ishaq's self-interested logic leads to a different conclusion:

Right now my profit is €16. Suppose I increase my production to 50 litres. In this case, a total of 90 litres of water would be sold, and the price would be €0.30 a litre. Then my profit would be only €15. Rather than increasing production and driving down the price, I am better off keeping my production at 40 litres.

The outcome in which Ishaq and Coralie each produce 40 litres looks like some sort of equilibrium. In fact, this outcome is called a **Nash equilibrium** (named after economic theorist John Nash, whose life was portrayed in the book, *A Beautiful Mind*, and the film of the same name). A Nash equilibrium is a situation in which economic actors interacting with one another each choose their best strategy given the strategies the others have chosen. In this case, given that Coralie is producing 40 litres, the best strategy for Ishaq is to produce 40 litres. Similarly, given that Ishaq is producing 40 litres, the best strategy for Coralie is to produce 40 litres. Once they reach this Nash equilibrium, neither Ishaq nor Coralie has an incentive to make a different decision.

> **Nash equilibrium** a situation in which economic actors interacting with one another each choose their best strategy given the strategies that all the other actors have chosen

This example illustrates the tension between cooperation and self-interest. Oligopolists would be better off cooperating and reaching the monopoly outcome. Yet because they pursue their own self-interest, they do not end up reaching the monopoly outcome and maximizing their joint profit. Each oligopolist is tempted to raise production and capture a larger share of the market. As each of them tries to do this, total production rises and the price falls.

At the same time, self-interest does not drive the market all the way to the competitive outcome. Like monopolists, oligopolists are aware that increases in the amount they produce reduce the price of their product. Therefore they stop short of following the competitive firm's rule of producing up to the point where price equals marginal cost.

In summary, when firms in an oligopoly individually choose production to maximize profit, they produce a quantity of output greater than the level produced by monopoly and less than the level produced by competition. The oligopoly price is less than the monopoly price but greater than the competitive price (which equals marginal cost).

> **JEOPARDY PROBLEM** An oligopolistic market consists of a four-firm concentration ratio of 80 per cent. An economist does some research on this market and finds that prices have remained stable in the market for the last five years. What might the explanation be for this behaviour?

How the Size of an Oligopoly Affects the Market Outcome

We can use the insights from this analysis of duopoly to discuss how the size of an oligopoly is likely to affect the outcome in a market. Suppose, for instance, that Jean and Patrice suddenly discover water sources on their property and join Ishaq and Coralie in the water oligopoly. The demand schedule in Table 15.1 remains the same, but now more producers are available to satisfy this demand. How would an increase in the number of sellers from two to four affect the price and quantity of water in the town?

If the sellers of water could form a cartel, they would once again try to maximize total profit by producing the monopoly quantity and charging the monopoly price. Just as when there were only two sellers, the members of the cartel would need to agree on production levels for each member and find some way to enforce the agreement. As the cartel grows larger, however, this outcome is less likely. Reaching and enforcing an agreement becomes more difficult as the size of the group increases.

If the oligopolists do not form a cartel, perhaps because competition laws prohibit it, they must each decide on their own how much water to produce. To see how the increase in the number of sellers affects the outcome, consider the decision facing each seller. At any time, each well owner has the option to raise production by one litre. In making this decision, the well owner weighs two effects:

- *The output effect.* Because price is above marginal cost, selling one more litre of water at the going price will raise profit.
- *The price effect.* Raising production will increase the total amount sold, which will lower the price of water and lower the profit on all the other litres sold.

If the output effect is larger than the price effect, the well owner will increase production. If the price effect is larger than the output effect, the owner will not raise production. (In fact, in this case, it is profitable to reduce production.) Each oligopolist continues to increase production until these two marginal effects exactly balance, taking the other firms' production as given.

Now consider how the number of firms in the industry affects the marginal analysis of each oligopolist. The larger the number of sellers, the less concerned each seller is about its own impact on the market price. That is, as the oligopoly grows in size, the magnitude of the price effect falls. When the oligopoly grows very large, the price effect disappears altogether, leaving only the output effect. In this extreme case, each firm in the oligopoly increases production as long as price is above marginal cost.

We can now see that a large oligopoly is essentially a group of competitive firms. A competitive firm considers only the output effect when deciding how much to produce: because a competitive firm is a price taker, the price effect is absent. Thus, as the number of sellers in an oligopoly grows larger, an oligopolistic market looks more and more like a competitive market. The price approaches marginal cost, and the quantity produced approaches the socially efficient level.

> **PITFALL PREVENTION** Remember that in an oligopolistic market structure there can be many hundreds and, in some cases, thousands of firms. The crucial thing to remember is that the market is dominated by a small number of very large firms.

This analysis of oligopoly offers a new perspective on the effects of international trade. Imagine that Toyota and Honda are the only car manufacturers in Japan, Volkswagen and BMW are the only car manufacturers in Germany, and Citroën and Peugeot are the only car manufacturers in France. If these nations prohibited international trade in cars, each would have a car manufacturing oligopoly with only two members, and the market outcome would likely depart substantially from the competitive ideal. With international trade, however, the car market is a world market, and the oligopoly in this example has six members. Allowing free trade increases the number of producers from whom each consumer can choose, and this increased competition keeps prices closer to marginal cost. Thus, the theory of oligopoly provides another reason why all countries can benefit from free trade.

> **SELF TEST** If the members of an oligopoly could agree on a total quantity to produce, what quantity would they choose? If the oligopolists do not act together but instead make production decisions individually, do they produce a total quantity more or less than in your answer to the previous question? Why?

INTERDEPENDENCE, GAME THEORY AND THE ECONOMICS OF COMPETITION

As we have seen, oligopolies would like to reach the monopoly outcome, but doing so requires co-operation, which at times is difficult to maintain. In this section, we look more closely at the problems people face when cooperation is desirable but difficult. To analyze the economics of cooperation, we need to learn a little about **game theory**.

Game theory is the study of how people behave in strategic situations. By 'strategic' we mean a situation in which each person, when deciding what actions to take, must consider how others might respond to that action. One of the main features of oligopolistic markets is interdependence. Because the number of firms in an oligopolistic market is small, each firm must act strategically. Each firm knows that its decisions will be monitored and studied by its rivals and that its rivals will react to its decisions. If one firm is contemplating increasing price it must consider whether its rivals will also increase their price, keep their prices the same or possibly lower prices. If one firm is planning on introducing a new variation of its product, a new distribution system which gives it some supply chain cost advantages, or is planning a major marketing campaign to boost sales of its products, it must consider what its rivals will do in response. Does the firm seek to introduce new products or systems to a market quickly and gain the benefits of what are referred to as 'first mover advantage'? If it introduces a new product or system, how quickly and closely will rivals seek to copy? Will rivals wait to see what mistakes the first mover in the market makes and learn from those mistakes before introducing competitive products/ systems? Should a firm seek to enter into some agreement with its rivals and if it does so what risks does it undertake? The risks might include a lack of trust in the agreement and the potential for the rival to renege on any agreement and the possible legal ramifications of entering into a collusive agreement. Each firm knows that its profit depends not only on how much it produces but also on how much the other firms produce. The interdependence between firms in an oligopoly means that the study of how individuals and groups behave in strategic situations takes on an importance for understanding the behaviour of oligopolies.

A particularly important 'game' is called the **prisoners' dilemma**. This game provides insight into the difficulty of maintaining cooperation. Many times in life, people fail to cooperate with one another even when cooperation would make them all better off. An oligopoly is just one example. The story of the prisoners' dilemma contains a general lesson that applies to any group trying to maintain cooperation among its members.

> **game theory** the study of how people behave in strategic situations
> **prisoners' dilemma** a particular 'game' between two prisoners that illustrates why cooperation is difficult to maintain even when it is mutually beneficial

The Prisoners' Dilemma

The prisoners' dilemma is a story about two criminals who have been captured by the police. Let us call them Mr Green and Mr Blue. The police have enough evidence to convict Mr Green and Mr Blue of a relatively minor crime, possessing stolen property, so that each would spend a year in prison. The police suspect that the two criminals have committed an armed jewellery robbery together, but they lack hard evidence to convict them of this major crime. The police question Mr Green and Mr Blue in separate rooms, and they offer each of them the following deal:

> *With the evidence we have, we can lock you up for one year. If you confess to the jewellery robbery and implicate your partner, however, we will give you immunity and you can go free. Your partner will get 20 years in prison. If you both confess to the crime, we won't need your testimony and we can avoid the cost of a trial, so you will each get an intermediate sentence of eight years.*

If Mr Green and Mr Blue, heartless criminals that they are, care only about their own sentences, what would you expect them to do? Would they confess or remain silent? Figure 15.1 shows their choices. Each prisoner has two strategies: confess or remain silent. The sentence each prisoner gets depends on the strategy he chooses and the strategy chosen by his partner in crime.

Consider first Mr Green's decision. He reasons as follows:

I don't know what Mr Blue is going to do. If he remains silent, my best strategy is to confess, since then I'll go free rather than spending a year in prison. If he confesses, my best strategy is still to confess, since then I'll spend eight years in prison rather than 20. So, regardless of what Mr Blue does, I am better off confessing.

In the language of game theory, a strategy is called a **dominant strategy** if it is the best strategy for a player to follow regardless of the strategies pursued by other players. In this case, confessing is a dominant strategy for Mr Green. He spends less time in prison if he confesses, regardless of whether Mr Blue confesses or remains silent.

dominant strategy a strategy that is best for a player in a game regardless of the strategies chosen by the other players

---

FIGURE 15.1

The Prisoners' Dilemma

In this game between two criminals suspected of committing a crime, the sentence that each receives depends both on their decision whether to confess or remain silent and on the decision made by the other. Mr Blue and Mr Green each have the choice of confessing or remaining silent. If Mr Blue chooses to confess but Mr Green also confesses, each gets eight years in prison as indicated by the top left quadrant. If Mr Blue chooses to remain silent but Mr Green confesses, Mr Blue will get 20 years in prison but Mr Green will go free as shown in the bottom left quadrant.

Mr Green's decision

	Confess	Remain silent
Confess	Mr Green gets 8 years Mr Blue gets 8 years	Mr Green gets 20 years Mr Blue goes free
Remain silent	Mr Green goes free Mr Blue gets 20 years	Mr Green gets 1 year Mr Blue gets 1 year

Mr Blue's decision

Now consider Mr Blue's decision. He faces exactly the same choices as Mr Green, and he reasons in much the same way. Regardless of what Mr Green does, Mr Blue can reduce his time in jail by confessing. In other words, confessing is also a dominant strategy for Mr Blue.

In the end, both Mr Green and Mr Blue confess, and both spend eight years in prison. Yet, from their standpoint, this is a terrible outcome. If they had *both* remained silent, both of them would have been better off, spending only one year in prison on the possession charge. By each pursuing his own interests, the two prisoners together reach an outcome that is worse for each of them.

To see how difficult it is to maintain cooperation, imagine that, before the police captured Mr Green and Mr Blue, the two criminals had made a pact not to confess. Clearly, this agreement would make them both better off *if* they both lived up to it, because they would each spend only one year in prison. Would the two criminals in fact remain silent, simply because they had agreed to? Once they are being questioned separately, the logic of self-interest takes over and leads them to confess. Cooperation between the two prisoners is difficult to maintain, because cooperation is individually irrational.

Oligopolies as a Prisoners' Dilemma

The game oligopolists play in trying to reach the monopoly outcome is similar to the game that the two prisoners play in the prisoners' dilemma.

Consider an oligopoly with two firms, BP and Shell, in a hypothetical situation. Both firms refine crude oil. After prolonged negotiation, the two firms agree to keep refined oil production low to keep the world price of refined oil high. After they agree on production levels, each firm must decide whether to cooperate and live up to this agreement or to ignore it and produce at a higher level. Figure 15.2 shows how the profits of the two firms depend on the strategies they choose.

FIGURE 15.2

An Oligopoly Game

In this game between members of an oligopoly, the profit that each earns depends on both its production decision and the production decision of the other oligopolist.

	BP's decision	
	High production	**Low production**
Shell's decision — **High production**	BP gets $4 billion Shell gets $4 billion	BP gets $3 billion Shell gets $6 billion
Shell's decision — **Low production**	BP gets $6 billion Shell gets $3 billion	BP gets $5 billion Shell gets $5 billion

---

Suppose you are the CEO of BP. You might reason as follows:

If Shell keeps to its agreement and limits production, we both earn $5 billion in profit. If I can trust Shell to keep its side of the deal, I could raise production and sell more refined oil on world markets. In this scenario, my firm earns profit of $6 billion and so I am better off with high production. If I cannot trust Shell to live up to the agreement and it produces at a high level but I stick to low production, then my firm earns $3 billion but Shell earns $6 billion. In this case I am better off also opting for high production and earning $4 billion. So, regardless of what Shell chooses to do, my firm is better off reneging on our agreement and producing at a high level.

Producing at a high level is a dominant strategy for BP. Of course, Shell reasons in exactly the same way, and so both firms produce at a high level. The result is the inferior outcome (from BP and Shell's standpoint) with lower profits for each firm compared to them both sticking to their original agreement of keeping production low.

This example illustrates why oligopolies have trouble maintaining monopoly profits. The monopoly outcome is jointly rational for the oligopoly, but each oligopolist has an incentive to cheat. Just as self-interest drives the prisoners in the prisoners' dilemma to confess, self-interest makes it difficult for the oligopoly to maintain the co-operative outcome with low production, high prices and monopoly profits.

Other Examples of the Prisoners' Dilemma

We have seen how the prisoners' dilemma can be used to understand the problem facing oligopolies. The same logic applies to many other situations as well. Here we consider two examples in which self-interest prevents cooperation and leads to an inferior outcome for the parties involved.

Advertising When two firms advertise to attract the same customers, they face a problem similar to the prisoners' dilemma. For example, consider the hypothetical decisions facing two games console manufacturers, Sony and Microsoft, which is represented in Figure 15.3. If neither company advertises, the two companies split the market and earn €4 billion in profit each. If both advertise, they again split the market, but profits are lower at €3 billion each, since each company must bear the cost of advertising. Yet if one company advertises while the other does not, the one that advertises attracts customers from the other. If Sony advertise but Microsoft do not, Sony earns €5 billion in profit while Microsoft earns just €2 billion. Figure 15.3 shows that advertising is a dominant strategy for each firm. Thus, both firms choose to advertise, even though both firms would be better off if neither firm advertised.

FIGURE 15.3

An Advertising Game

In this game between firms selling similar products, the profit that each earns depends on both its own advertising decision and the advertising decision of the other firm.

	Microsoft's decision	
	Advertise	**Don't advertise**
Sony's decision — Advertise	Microsoft gets €3 billion / Sony gets €3 billion	Microsoft gets €2 billion / Sony gets €5 billion
Sony's decision — Don't advertise	Microsoft gets €5 billion / Sony gets €2 billion	Microsoft gets €4 billion / Sony gets €4 billion

Common Resources Common resources tend to be subject to overuse because they are rival in consumption but not excludable, for example fish in the sea. We can view this problem as an example of the prisoners' dilemma.

Imagine that two mining companies, Kazakhmys and Vedanta, own adjacent copper mines. The mines have a common pool of copper worth €12 million. The decision matrix for each company is shown in Figure 15.4. Drilling a shaft to mine the copper costs €1 million. If each company drills one shaft, each will get half of the copper and earn a €5 million profit as indicated by the bottom right quadrant (€6 million in revenue minus €1 million in costs).

Because the pool of copper is a common resource, the companies will not use it efficiently. Suppose that either company could drill a second shaft. If one company has two of the three shafts, that company gets two-thirds of the copper, which yields a profit of €6 million. If Vedanta drills two wells but Kazakhmys only drills one well, Vedanta faces costs of €2 million and gains profits of €6 million. Kazakhmys has €1 million in costs and takes profit of €3 million. This outcome is shown in the bottom left quadrant. Yet if each company drills a second shaft, the two companies again split the copper. In this case, each bears the cost of a second shaft, so profit is only €4 million for each company. Drilling two wells is a dominant strategy for each company. Once again, the self-interest of the two players leads them to an inferior outcome.

FIGURE 15.4

A Common Resources Game

In this game between firms mining copper from a common pool, the profit that each earns depends on both the number of shafts it drills and the number of shafts drilled by the other firm.

	Vedanta's decision	
	Drill two shafts	**Drill one shaft**
Kazakhmys' decision — Drill two shafts	Vedanta gets €4 million profit / Kazakhmys gets €4 million profit	Vedanta gets €3 million profit / Kazakhmys gets €6 million profit
Kazakhmys' decision — Drill one shaft	Vedanta gets €6 million profit / Kazakhmys gets €3 million profit	Vedanta gets €5 million profit / Kazakhmys gets €5 million profit

Why Firms Sometimes Cooperate

The prisoners' dilemma shows that cooperation is difficult. But is it impossible? Not all prisoners, when questioned by the police, decide to turn in their partners in crime. Cartels sometimes do manage to maintain collusive arrangements, despite the incentive for individual members to defect. Very often, the reason that players can solve the prisoners' dilemma is that they play the game not once but many times.

To see why cooperation is easier to enforce in repeated games, let us return to our duopolists, Ishaq and Coralie. Recall that Ishaq and Coralie would like to maintain the monopoly outcome in which each produces 30 litres, but self-interest drives them to an equilibrium in which each produces 40 litres. Figure 15.5 shows the game they play. Producing 40 litres is a dominant strategy for each player in this game.

FIGURE 15.5

Ishaq and Coralie's Oligopoly Game

In this game between Ishaq and Coralie, the profit that each earns from selling water depends on both the quantity he or she chooses to sell and the quantity the other chooses to sell.

		Ishaq's decision	
		Sell 40 litres	Sell 30 litres
Coralie's decision	Sell 40 litres	Ishaq gets €16 profit / Coralie gets €16 profit	Ishaq gets €15 profit / Coralie gets €20 profit
	Sell 30 litres	Ishaq gets €20 profit / Coralie gets €15 profit	Ishaq gets €18 profit / Coralie gets €18 profit

Imagine that Ishaq and Coralie try to form a cartel. To maximize total profit, they would agree to the co-operative outcome in which each produces and sells 30 litres. If Ishaq and Coralie are to play this game only once, neither has any incentive to live up to this agreement. Self-interest drives each of them to renege and produce and sell 40 litres.

Now suppose that Ishaq and Coralie know that they will play the same game every week. When they make their initial agreement to keep production low, they can also specify what happens if one party reneges. They might agree, for instance, that once one of them reneges and produces 40 litres, both of them will produce 40 litres forever after. This penalty is easy to enforce, for if one party is producing at a high level, the other has every reason to do the same.

The threat of this penalty may be all that is needed to maintain cooperation. Each person knows that defecting would raise their profit from €18 to €20. This benefit would last for only one week. Thereafter, profit would fall to €16 and stay there. As long as the players care enough about future profits, they will choose to forego the one-time gain from defection. Thus, in a game of repeated prisoners' dilemma, the two players may well be able to reach the co-operative outcome.

SELF TEST What does the prisoners' dilemma teach us about the idea of interdependence in oligopolistic markets?

PUBLIC POLICIES TOWARD OLIGOPOLIES

Cooperation among oligopolists is undesirable from the standpoint of society as a whole, because it leads to production that is too low and prices that are too high. To move the allocation of resources closer to the social optimum, policy makers try to induce firms in an oligopoly to compete rather than cooperate. Let us consider how policy makers do this and then examine the controversies that arise in this area of public policy.

Restraint of Trade and Competition Law

One way that policy discourages cooperation is through the common law. Normally, freedom of contract is an essential part of a market economy. Businesses and households use contracts to arrange mutually advantageous trades. In doing this, they rely on the court system to enforce contracts. Yet, for many centuries, courts in Europe and North America have deemed agreements among competitors to reduce quantities and raise prices to be contrary to the public interest. They have therefore refused to enforce such agreements.

Given the long experience of many European countries in tackling abuses of market power, it is perhaps not surprising that competition law is one of the few areas in which the EU has been able to agree on a common policy. The European Commission can refer directly to the Treaty of Rome to prohibit price fixing and other restrictive practices such as production limitation, and is especially likely to do so where a restrictive practice affects trade between EU member countries. The EU Competition Commission sets out its role as follows:

European anti-trust policy is developed from two central rules set out in the Treaty on the Functioning of the European Union:

- *Article 101 of the Treaty prohibits agreements between two or more independent market operators which restrict competition. This provision covers both horizontal agreements (between actual or potential competitors operating at the same level of the supply chain) and vertical agreements (between firms operating at different levels, i.e. an agreement between a manufacturer and its distributor). Only limited exceptions are provided for in the general prohibition. The most flagrant example of illegal conduct infringing Article 101 is the creation of a cartel between competitors, which may involve price-fixing and/or market sharing.*

- *Article 102 of the Treaty prohibits firms that hold a dominant position on a given market to abuse that position, for example by charging unfair prices, by limiting production, or by refusing to innovate to the prejudice of consumers.*

The Commission is empowered by the Treaty to apply these rules and has a number of investigative powers to that end (e.g. inspections at business and non-business premises, written requests for information, etc.). The Commission may also impose fines on undertakings which violate the EU anti-trust rules. The main rules on procedures are set out in Council Regulation (EC) 1/2003.

National Competition Authorities (NCAs) are empowered to apply Articles 101 and 102 of the Treaty fully, to ensure that competition is not distorted or restricted. National courts may also apply these provisions to protect the individual rights conferred on citizens by the Treaty.

ec.europa.eu/competition/antitrust/overview_en.html

Controversies Over Competition Policy

Over time, much controversy has centred on the question of what kinds of behaviour competition law should prohibit. Most commentators agree that price fixing agreements among competing firms should be illegal. Yet competition law has been used to condemn some business practices whose effects are not obvious. Here we consider three examples.

Resale Price Maintenance One example of a controversial business practice is *resale price maintenance*, also called *fair trade*. Imagine that Superduper Electronics sells smart Blu-ray DVD players to retail stores for €100. If Superduper requires the retailers to charge customers €150, it is said to engage in resale price maintenance. Any retailer that charged less than €150 would have violated its contract with Superduper.

At first, resale price maintenance might seem anti-competitive and, therefore, detrimental to society. Like an agreement among members of a cartel, it prevents the retailers from competing on price. For this reason, the courts have often viewed resale price maintenance as a violation of competition law.

Yet some economists defend resale price maintenance on two grounds. Firstly, they deny that it is aimed at reducing competition. To the extent that Superduper Electronics has any market power, it can exert that power through the wholesale price, rather than through resale price maintenance. Moreover, Superduper has no incentive to discourage competition among its retailers. Indeed, because a cartel of retailers sells less than a group of competitive retailers, Superduper would be worse off if its retailers were a cartel.

Secondly, some economists believe that resale price maintenance has a legitimate goal. Superduper may want its retailers to provide customers with a pleasant showroom and a knowledgeable salesforce. Yet, without resale price maintenance, some customers would take advantage of one store's service to learn about the smart Blu-ray DVD player's special features and then buy the item at a discount retailer that does not provide this service. To some extent, good service is a public good among the retailers that sell Superduper's products. We know that when one person provides a public good, others are able to enjoy it without paying for it. In this case, discount retailers would free ride on the service provided by other retailers, leading to less service than is desirable. Resale price maintenance is one way for Superduper to solve this free-rider problem.

The example of resale price maintenance illustrates an important principle: business practices that appear to reduce competition may in fact have legitimate purposes. This principle makes the application of competition law all the more difficult. The competition authorities in each EU nation under the European Competition Network are in charge of enforcing these laws and must determine what kinds of behaviour public policy should prohibit as impeding competition and reducing economic well-being. Often that job is not easy.

Predatory Pricing Firms with market power normally raise prices above the competitive level. Should policy makers ever be concerned that firms with market power might charge prices that are too low? This question is at the heart of a second debate over competition policy.

Imagine that a large airline, call it National Airlines, has a monopoly on some route. Then Fly Express enters and takes 20 per cent of the market, leaving National with 80 per cent. In response to this competition, National starts slashing its fares. Some anti-trust analysts argue that National's move could be anti-competitive: the price cuts may be intended to drive Fly Express out of the market so National can recapture its monopoly and raise prices again. Such behaviour is called *predatory pricing*.

Although it is common for companies to complain to the relevant authorities that a competitor is pursuing predatory pricing, some economists are sceptical of this argument and believe that predatory pricing is rarely, and perhaps never, a profitable business strategy. Why? For a price war to drive out a rival, prices must be driven below cost. Yet if National starts selling cheap tickets at a loss, it had better be ready to fly more planes, because low fares will attract more customers. Fly Express, meanwhile, can respond to National's predatory move by cutting back on flights. As a result, National ends up bearing more than 80 per cent of the losses, putting Fly Express in a good position to survive the price war. In such cases, the predator can suffer more than the prey.

Economists continue to debate whether predatory pricing should be a concern for competition policy makers. Various questions remain unresolved. Is predatory pricing ever a profitable business strategy? If so, when? Are the authorities capable of telling which price cuts are competitive and thus good for consumers and which are predatory? There are no simple answers.

Tying A third example of a controversial business practice is *tying*. Suppose that Makemoney Movies produces two new films, *Spiderman* and *Hamlet*. If Makemoney offers cinemas the two films together at a single price, rather than separately, the studio is said to be tying its two products.

Some economists have argued that the practice of tying should be banned. Their reasoning is as follows: imagine that *Spiderman* is a blockbuster, whereas *Hamlet* is an unprofitable art film. The studio could use the high demand for *Spiderman* to force cinemas to buy *Hamlet*. It seems that the studio could use tying as a mechanism for expanding its market power.

Other economists are sceptical of this argument. Imagine that cinemas are willing to pay €20,000 for *Spiderman* and nothing for *Hamlet*. Then the most that a cinema would pay for the two films together is €20,000, the same as it would pay for *Spiderman* by itself. Forcing the cinema to accept a worthless film as part of the deal does not increase the cinema's willingness to pay. Makemoney cannot increase its market power simply by bundling the two films together.

Why, then, does tying exist? One possibility is that it is a form of price discrimination. Suppose there are two cinemas. City Cinema is willing to pay €15,000 for *Spiderman* and €5,000 for *Hamlet*. Country Cinema is just the opposite: it is willing to pay €5,000 for *Spiderman* and €15,000 for *Hamlet*. If Makemoney charges separate prices for the two films, its best strategy is to charge €15,000 for each film, and each cinema chooses to show only one film. Yet if Makemoney offers the two films as a bundle, it can charge each cinema €20,000 for the films. Thus, if different cinemas value the films differently, tying may allow the studio to increase profit by charging a combined price closer to the buyers' total willingness to pay.

The argument that tying allows a firm to extend its market power to other goods is not well founded, at least in its simplest form. Yet economists have proposed more elaborate theories for how tying can impede competition. Given our current economic knowledge, it is unclear whether tying has adverse effects for society as a whole.

All the analysis is based on an assumption that rivals may have sufficient information to be able to make a decision and that the decision will be a rational one based on this information. In reality, firms do not have perfect information and do not behave rationally. Most firms in oligopolistic markets work very hard to protect sensitive information and only give out what they have to by law. Some information may be given to deliberately obfuscate the situation and hide what their true motives/strategies/tactics are. Economists have tried to include these imperfections into theories. Behavioural economics has offered some greater insights into the observed behaviour of the real world which often does not conform to the assumptions implied by the assumption of rationality.

CASE STUDY   The Petroleum Refining Industry in the UK

In the first six months of 2022, motorists saw fuel prices rising sharply on the forecourts. The conflict in Ukraine, global supply chain issues, the post-pandemic upturn and the consequences of Brexit were all cited as being contributory factors. One of the common complaints against the fuel industry is that fuel prices seem very quick to respond to upward cost pressures in the supply chain but not so quick to respond when those pressures ease. The petroleum refining industry in the UK consists of 15 firms with a total market size of £49 billion. There are six refineries operating in the UK.

In June 2022, concern over whether firms in the refining industry were exploiting their market power to increase profits led to the UK Secretary of State for Business, Energy and Industrial Strategy to ask the Competition and Markets Authority (CMA) to conduct an urgent review of the industry. The review found that there was considerable volatility in the market and that retail prices for fuel had reached 'historic peaks'. It also found that there were widening gaps between the price of oil entering refineries and the price at which the refined product left. There was, according to the CMA, no clear evidence that retailers of fuel were benefitting from wider spreads between their purchase price and selling price. Since the urgent investigation was completed, fuel prices on the forecourts have fallen. While refining spreads appeared to be increasing again, the CMA found no major evidence that over the medium term, firms were making profits that would give cause for concern. Part of the consideration here was the fact that many had suffered losses during the pandemic and lockdown and while profits in 2022 were 'higher than usual' taking into account the previous five years, profit levels were not 'excessive'.

A final report into the market was published in July 2023. The report raised concerns about competition in the industry, that retail margins had widened and competition was weaker.

(Continued)

The fuel industry faced significant challenges post-pandemic and as a result of the conflict in Ukraine as many motorists found to their cost.

Questions

1 Given the information in the case study, do you think the petroleum refining industry in the UK can be classed as oligopolistic?

2 If the spread between purchase prices and selling prices widens, does this imply that firms are exploiting their market power and seeking to generate excess profits?

3 According to the UK Petroleum Industry Association (UKPIA), there are around 8,400 petrol stations in the UK. Of these, 51 per cent are operated by four firms: Esso, BP, Shell and Texaco. How relevant do you think that the information provided by game theory is to the behaviour of these four firms as they conduct their business?

References: https://assets.publishing.service.gov.uk/media/638e16808fa8f569f3571ab4/Executive_Summary.pdf (accessed 9 June 2023).
www.ibisworld.com/united-kingdom/market-research-reports/petroleum-refining-industry/ (accessed 9 June 2023).
www.ukpia.com/downstream-policy/uk-downstream/marketing-and-forecourts/ (accessed 9 June 2023).

CONCLUSION

Oligopolies would like to act like monopolies, but self-interest drives them closer to competition. Thus oligopolies can end up looking either more like monopolies or more like competitive markets, depending on the number of firms in the oligopoly and how cooperative the firms are. The story of the prisoners' dilemma shows why oligopolies can fail to maintain co-operation, even when cooperation is in their best interest.

Policy makers regulate the behaviour of oligopolists through competition law. The proper scope of these laws is the subject of ongoing controversy. Although price fixing among competing firms clearly reduces economic welfare and most countries pass legislation to prevent this, some business practices that appear to reduce competition may have legitimate if subtle purposes. As a result, policy makers need to be careful when they use the substantial powers of competition law to place limits on firm behaviour.

SUMMARY

- A market structure that is defined as an oligopoly is one where there might be many firms, but the market is dominated by a relatively small number of large firms.

- A characteristic feature of oligopoly is the degree of interdependence between the small number of large firms. This means that each takes note of what the other is doing in making decisions.

- Oligopolists can maximize their total profits by forming a cartel and acting like a monopolist. Yet, if oligopolists make decisions about production levels individually, the result is a greater quantity and a lower price than under the monopoly outcome. The larger the number of firms in the oligopoly, the closer the quantity and price will be to the levels that would prevail under competition.

- The prisoners' dilemma shows that self-interest can prevent people from maintaining cooperation, even when cooperation is in their mutual interest.
- Policy makers use competition law to prevent oligopolies from engaging in behaviour that reduces competition. The application of these laws can be controversial, because some behaviour that may seem to reduce competition may in fact have legitimate business purposes.

IN THE NEWS

The DRAM Industry

Samsung, SK Hynix and Micron represent a three-firm concentration ratio of 95 per cent in the dynamic random access memory (DRAM) chip business. DRAM chips are used in personal computers, servers and workstations. These three firms clearly dominate the DRAM industry and this is an excellent example of an oligopolistic market structure. Micron has around 20 per cent of the total market, SK Hynix around 30 per cent and Samsung around 45 per cent. Looking at our model of oligopoly, it might be assumed that the sensible strategy for the three firms would be to cooperate in order to exploit a monopoly outcome which would increase price above marginal cost and maximize profits.

Should firms in an oligopoly collude to improve their profits?

In reality, the three firms appear to have engaged in a price war which has been somewhat destructive. Between 2014 and 2016, the price of DRAM chips fell sharply as the three firms expanded output which resulted in excess supply. We have seen that firms can either choose to set price and allow the demand curve to determine the quantity sold (and thus the level of output) or they can set output and allow the demand curve to set the price. Regardless of the route, with prices falling, Micron and SK Hynix saw their share prices fall. From 2016 onwards, the three companies were more conservative in their supply of chips, at the same time as there was an increase in demand, so the price of DRAM chips began to increase. In 2017, average prices rose by more than 10 per cent and prices peaked around the end of 2017 and early 2018 before falling back sharply. In January 2018, for example, the price of DDR4 8Gb DRAM was around $9.48 whereas in October 2022, the price was quoted at $2.39. The changes in market conditions have led to the three firms being able to generate much higher revenues.

Questions

1 With reference to the DRAM market, to what extent does the concentration ratio determine the competitiveness of such a market?
2 Why would it make sense for the three firms in the DRAM market to cooperate (ignore the fact that such cooperation could be considered illegal).
3 How easy is it for regulators to prove that firms in an oligopolistic market structure might engage in anti-competitive co-operative behaviour?
4 Why do you think that firms such as those in the article might engage in a price war? Can there ever be a winner in a price war?
5 Given the change in prices in the DRAM market between 2017 and 2022 what can you conclude about the relationship between supply and demand in the market for DRAM chips?

References: https://www.dramexchange.com/ (accessed 9 June 2023).
www.mordorintelligence.com/industry-reports/dynamic-random-access-memory-market (accessed 9 June 2023).

QUESTIONS FOR REVIEW

1 Is it the case that an oligopoly market structure only consists of a small number of large firms? Explain.

2 What is meant by the term 'concentration ratio'. What does a 'four-firm concentration ratio of 76 per cent' indicate?

3 In an oligopoly, there is a high degree of interdependence between firms. What does this mean?

4 How does the number of firms in an oligopoly affect the outcome in its market?

5 What is the prisoners' dilemma, and what does it have to do with oligopoly?

6 Give two examples other than oligopoly to show how the prisoners' dilemma helps to explain behaviour.

7 Why might an oligopolist's behaviour depend on the number of times a 'game' is played?

8 What kinds of behaviour do competition laws prohibit?

9 What is resale price maintenance, and why is it controversial?

10 Why might predatory pricing not be a useful tactic for an oligopolistic firm to pursue?

PROBLEMS AND APPLICATIONS

1 A large share of the world supply of diamonds comes from Russia and South Africa. Suppose that the marginal cost of mining diamonds is constant at €1,000 per diamond, and the demand for diamonds is described by the following schedule:

Price (€)	Quantity
8,000	5,000
7,000	6,000
6,000	7,000
5,000	8,000
4,000	9,000
3,000	10,000
2,000	11,000
1,000	12,000

a. If there were many suppliers of diamonds, what would be the price and quantity?

b. If there was only one supplier of diamonds, what would be the price and quantity?

c. If Russia and South Africa formed a cartel, what would be the price and quantity? If the countries split the market evenly, what would be South Africa's production and profit? What would happen to South Africa's profit if it increased its production by 1,000 while Russia stuck to the cartel agreement?

d. Use your answer to part c. to explain why cartel agreements are often not successful.

2 This chapter discusses companies that are oligopolists in the market for the goods they sell. Many of the same ideas apply to companies that are oligopolists in the market for the inputs they buy. If sellers who are oligopolists try to increase the price of goods they sell, what is the goal of buyers who are oligopolists?

3 Assume that two airline companies decide to engage in collusive behaviour.

Let us analyze the game between two such companies. Suppose that each company can charge either a high price for tickets or a low price. If one company charges €100, it earns low profits if the other company charges €100 also, and high profits if the other company charges €200. On the other hand, if the company charges €200, it earns very low profits if the other company charges €100, and medium profits if the other company charges €200 also.

● Draw the decision box for this game.
● What is the Nash equilibrium in this game? Explain.
● Is there an outcome that would be better than the Nash equilibrium for both airlines? How could it be achieved? Who would lose if it were achieved?

4 Farmer Collishaw and Farmer Scott graze their cattle on the same field. If there are 20 cows grazing in the field, each cow produces €4,000 of milk over its lifetime. If there are more cows in the field, then each cow can eat less grass, and

its milk production falls. With 30 cows on the field, each produces €3,000 of milk; with 40 cows, each produces €2,000 of milk. Cows are priced at €1,000 apiece.

- Assume that Farmer Collishaw and Farmer Scott can each purchase either 10 or 20 cows, but that neither knows how many the other is buying when they make their purchase. Calculate the payoffs of each outcome.
- What is the likely outcome of this game? What would be the best outcome? Explain.
- There used to be more common fields than there are today. Why?

5 Little Kona is a small coffee company that is considering entering a market dominated by Big Brew. Each company's profit depends on whether Little Kona enters and whether Big Brew sets a high price or a low price as highlighted in the decision box in Figure 15.6. Big Brew threatens Little Kona by saying, 'If you enter, we are going to set a low price, so you had better stay out'. Do you think Little Kona should believe the threat? Why or why not? What do you think Little Kona should do?

FIGURE 15.6

		Big Brew	
		High price	Low price
Little Kona	Enter	Big Brew makes €3 million / Little Kona makes €2 million	Big Brew makes €1 million / Little Kona loses €1 million
	Don't enter	Big Brew makes €7 million / Little Kona makes zero	Big Brew makes €2 million / Little Kona makes zero

6 Suppose that you and a fellow student are assigned a project on which you will receive one combined grade. You each want to receive a good grade (which means you have to work), but you also want to do as little work as possible (which means you shirk). In particular, here is the situation:

- If both of you work hard, you both get an A, which gives each of you 40 units of happiness.
- If only one of you works hard, you both get a B, which gives each of you 30 units of happiness.
- If neither of you works hard, you both get a D, which gives each of you 10 units of happiness.

a. Fill in the payoffs in the following matrix in Figure 15.7:

FIGURE 15.7

		Your decision	
		Work	Shirk
Classmate's decision	Work	You: / Classmate:	You: / Classmate:
	Shirk	You: / Classmate:	You: / Classmate:

b. What is the likely outcome? Explain your answer.
c. If you get this person as your partner on a series of projects throughout the year, rather than only once, how might that change the outcome you predicted in part b?
d. Another person on your course cares more about good grades. They get 50 units of happiness for a B and 80 units of happiness for an A. If this person was your partner (but your preferences were unchanged), how would your answers to parts a. and b. change? Which of the two partners would you prefer? Would they also want you as a partner?

7 Synergy and Dynaco are the only two firms in a specific hi-tech industry. They face the following payoff matrix in Figure 15.8 as they decide upon the size of their research budget.

FIGURE 15.8

		Synergy's decision	
		Large budget	Small budget
Dynaco's decision	Large budget	Synergy gains €20 million Dynaco gains €30 million	Synergy gains zero Dynaco gains €70 million
	Small budget	Synergy gains €30 million Dynaco gains zero	Synergy gains €40 million Dynaco gains €50 million

a. Does Synergy have a dominant strategy? Explain.
b. Does Dynaco have a dominant strategy? Explain.
c. Is there a Nash equilibrium for this scenario? Explain.

8 Assume that 30 years ago, the brewing industry in a country consisted of many hundreds of small regional brewers. Over time three of the larger firms began acquiring smaller rivals and now there is a three-firm concentration ratio of 85 per cent.

a. What would you expect to have happened to the nature of the products sold in the industry over that time period?
b. What would you have expected to have happened to the price of beers consumers face in this market as it becomes more consolidated?
c. Should regulators have been concerned for the effect on efficiency and consumers in such an industry? Explain.

9 Consider an oligopoly with four firms who decide to engage in a price war. Can there be any winners in this war?

10 Describe several activities in your life in which game theory could be useful. What is the common link among these activities?

16 CORPORATE STRATEGY AND PRICING POLICY

INTRODUCTION

In this chapter, we will be looking at aspects of corporate strategy and pricing policy. Strategy is a subject with many different points of view, but we will present an outline of the key issues. We are going to start by looking at the idea of corporate strategy and then at some of the principal pricing strategies that firms in imperfectly competitive markets can adopt. Pricing strategies are not relevant in perfect competition, because firms are price takers and have no control over the price they charge.

BUSINESS STRATEGY

There are many books written on strategy and there are intense debates between academics, between business leaders and between academics and business leaders about exactly what it means. What follows is an outline of the main schools of thought. Strategy can be individual to particular firms and industries, and is highly complex, differing from organization to organization.

What is Strategy?

To take a broad definition, strategy can be seen as a series of actions, decisions and obligations which lead to the firm gaining a competitive advantage and exploiting the firm's core competencies. This definition implies the future, so we can reframe the definition to say that strategy is about where the business wants to be at some point in the future and what steps it needs to take to get there. It is, therefore, about setting the overall direction of the business. In times of change, much of this direction will happen in an environment of uncertainty.

The Strategic Hierarchy

Typically, we might expect the strategic direction of the firm to be formulated at the highest levels of the business. This strategy then informs decisions and behaviour lower down the organization. This may be the case in many firms but we must also be aware that organizations now recognize that the senior team does not always have all the answers. Increasingly, strategy is formulated at lower levels of the organization. Such strategic formulation and management is likely to be carried out in the context of the firm's overall strategy, but that overall strategy may be formulated around a series of strategic intents rather than being anything specific. **Strategic intent** was picked up by Max Boisot in 1995 following the development of the idea by Gary Hamel and C.K. Prahalad in an article in the *Harvard Business Review* in 1989.

Strategic intent refers to establishing and sharing a vision of where a business wants to be at some point in the future and encouraging all those involved in the business to understand and work towards achieving this vision. Strategic intent can be thought of as a framework for decision making in an uncertain environment where detailed plans can be very quickly blown off course. Whenever key decisions need to be made, the decision maker/s need to refer back to the strategic intent and ask themselves the question: what decision would help to allow the firm to operate at a higher level in line with the intent or the vision?

strategic intent a framework for establishing and sharing a vision of where a business wants to be at some point in the future and encouraging all those involved in the business to understand and work towards achieving this vision

Strategic Planning

If a firm is able to articulate where it wants to be in the future, then it needs to put something in place to help it achieve that goal. This might be a plan of some description. Strategic planning aims to put in place a system for decision making which is designed to help the business achieve its long-term goals. Such a plan may include four elements: establishing the purpose, objectives, strategies and tactics, commonly referred to by the acronym POST.

In order to develop the plan, there needs to be a clear understanding of the organization and where it stands in relation to its external environment. Such an awareness building exercise might start with an analysis of the firm and its market, its place within that market and to understand the market itself. Typically, strategic analysis might involve assessing the firm's external and internal environment. The external environment might include factors over which the firm has no direct control. An assessment of the internal environment focuses on the firm's resources and skills – the things over which it has more direct control.

The analysis might be carried out by various means such as a **SWOT analysis** (an analysis of the firm's strengths, weaknesses, opportunities and threats), through using a model such as Porter's five forces or Barney's VRIO framework (value, rarity, imitability and organization), PESTLE analysis (political, economic, social, technological, legal and environmental) or analysing its product portfolio using the Boston Consulting Group's matrix. This matrix classifies the firm's products in four ways as: cash cows, rising stars, problem children or dogs. Each of these classifications relates to the extent to which the product is part of a growing market and the proportion of market share the product has.

SWOT analysis an analysis of the firm's strengths, weaknesses, opportunities and threats

A cash cow will be a product that is in a mature market. The market is not growing but the product has a high market share, so it does not require significant expenditure to maintain sales. A problem child will be a product which has a low market share in a growing market. There might be something that is preventing the product from capturing more of the market, and the firm may have to invest more money if the product is to make any progress. It may even have to decide to withdraw it from the market, something which would be sensible if the cost of supporting it was much higher than the revenues it was projected to bring in. A rising star is a product which is part of a growing market and whose market share is also rising. This type of product may be a future cash cow. A dog is a product in a market which is declining and it may also have a low market share. This is a product which is a candidate for withdrawal from the market. These different categories can be represented in a matrix as shown in Figure 16.1.

FIGURE 16.1

The Boston Consulting Group Matrix

The Boston Consulting Group Matrix classifies products in relation to market share (horizontal axis) and the extent to which it is a part of a growing market (vertical axis). The matrix then groups products into four classifications: stars, dogs, cash cows and problem children.

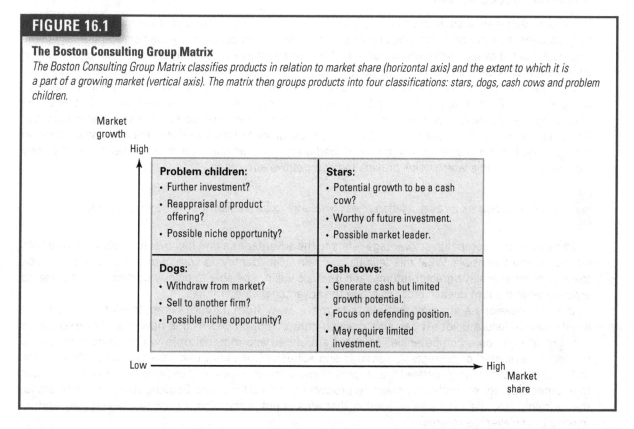

Many larger firms have large product portfolios, so using the Boston Matrix may be one way in which they can analyze this portfolio. The firms can make decisions about supporting products, whether new product development needs to be carried out (which may be the case if they have a number of cash cows), and their overall market presence. It is a framework, therefore, for making decisions and reflects the firm's obligations and where it wants to be in the future.

Porter's five forces model was developed by Michael Porter in the 1980s and is cited extensively in literature relating to strategy. The five forces framework allows a firm to analyze its own competitive strength set in the context of external factors. This includes the existing competitive rivalry between suppliers in the market, the potential threat posed by new entrants, how much bargaining power buyers and suppliers in the market have, and what threat is provided by substitute products.

The five forces model has been, and remains, extremely influential in business strategy. It is not, however, without its limitations. In particular, the movement of businesses to build collaboration through things such as joint ventures, supplier agreements, buyer agreements, research and development collaboration, and cost sharing all mean that buyer and supplier power might be moderated and not simply be seen as a threat. It is also important that a business recognizes the importance and role of its internal culture, and the quality of its human resources in influencing its competitive strategy and some of these can be analyzed using the VRIO framework.

Regardless of the model used, the firm needs to have a clear understanding of its position in the market and that of its competitors to be able to formulate actions that will enable it to be where it wants to be in the future. Some element of planning will be essential, but the dynamic nature of business means that plans must be flexible and subject to constant amendment if they are to be of any longer-term benefit. Few firms would create a plan and then stick rigidly to it.

The strategic plan may be a way in which the firm outlines its strategy but how does it choose this strategy in the first place? There are a number of different approaches which have been suggested. The following provides a brief outline of each.

Resource-Based Model

Every firm uses resources. It could be argued that each firm has a unique set of resources and it can use this uniqueness as the basis for choosing its strategy. Resources could be unique because the firm owns a particular set of assets which few other firms have, or employs a particularly brilliant team of production designers; it could be the location of the business that is unique, or the way in which the firm has designed and organized its production operations. These resources can be analyzed to find, identify and isolate **core competencies**. Core competencies are the things a business does which are the source of competitive advantage over its rivals. Firms can be in the same industry and have access to similar resources, but for some reason one firm might better utilize these resources to achieve returns that are above others in the industry. The firm's strategy can be developed once these unique features have been identified and exploited, and it is this which helps provide the competitive advantage.

 core competencies the things a business does which are the source of competitive advantage over its rivals

Remember that competitive advantage refers to the advantages a firm has over its rivals which are both distinctive and defensible. What this tells us is if a firm can identify its core competencies it can exploit these in order to achieve greater returns, and its rivals will not be able to quickly or cheaply find a way to emulate what the firm does in order to erode the advantage/s the firm has.

If a firm develops a strategy that starts to move away from its core competencies, then there is a potential for failure unless it can also develop core competencies in this new area. For example, a firm like 3M has core competencies in substrates (the base material onto which something will be printed or laminated or protected), coatings and adhesives. It might use its expertise in these areas to formulate a strategy which seeks to exploit these competencies. If it decides that it will branch out to another area, for example into cleaning products to complement its Scotchguard protection brand, then it might find the expertise needed in that area is not something it possesses, and may end up making below average returns.

There are plenty of examples of firms that have tried to branch out into new areas outside their expertise and have failed. Harley Davidson, for example, attempted to move into the perfume market. Bic, the ball point pen manufacturer, tried the lingerie market, and the magazine, *Cosmopolitan*, attempted to launch a range of yoghurts. In each case the moves were unsuccessful, partly because consumers failed to understand the association between what were established brands and a new departure, but also because the new ideas did not represent the core competencies of each firm.

Emergent Strategy

The dynamic and often chaotic nature of the business environment means that whatever plans a business has are likely to be outdated almost as soon as they are written, or overtaken by events which occur and which are outside the control of the business. The model of emergent strategy recognizes this reality.

A firm might start off with an intended (sometimes referred to as deliberate) strategy which is planned and focused on achieving stated long-term goals. However, it is highly likely that some part of this intended strategy will not be realized, and as situations and circumstances change the firm will have to make decisions. These decisions are made with the overall intended strategy in mind, but adjusted to take account of the changed circumstances.

Over time this decision making forms a pattern which becomes emergent strategy. This implies that firms may adopt broad policies of intent rather than detailed plans, so that they can respond to changed circumstances and learn as they go along.

Logical Incrementalism

The term *logical incrementalism* was used by James Brian Quinn, a professor of management at Amos Tuck School, Dartmouth, Colorado. Quinn suggests that managers might be seen to be making various incremental decisions in response to events which may not seem to have any coherent structure. However, these responses may have some rational basis whereby the firm has an overall strategy, but local managers respond to local situations. The overall strategy can be realized, but incrementally. Such incremental decisions may be affected by resource constraints at a local level, which mean that trade-offs and compromises must be made in order to adjust to these local conditions.

Market-Based Strategy

Market-based strategy turns the focus onto the business environment in which the firm operates and strategy is chosen based on an understanding of the competitive environment. Analysis of the competitive environment is focused on two key areas: the firm's cost structure and how it differentiates itself from its rivals.

It is often assumed that a firm can adopt pricing strategies regardless of other factors in an attempt to win market share or expand sales, but as will be noted later in this chapter, flexibility on the choice of pricing strategy is partly dependent on whether a firm can afford to adopt a pricing strategy. For example, it is only possible to adopt prices that are lower in comparison to rivals if the firm's cost base allows it to do so.

Value Chain Analysis One of the first things a business has to do is to look at its value chain and examine every aspect to determine where inefficiencies may exist and where cost benefits can be gained. The term **value chain** refers to how value is added at each stage in the activities and operations which a firm carries out. If the value created is greater than the cost of making the good or service available to the consumer, then the firm will generate profit. It makes sense, therefore, to focus on these value stages and extract maximum value at minimum cost as the basis of creating sustainable competitive advantage.

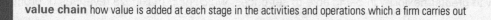

value chain how value is added at each stage in the activities and operations which a firm carries out

Crucially, value chain analysis can focus on aspects of the business which may have been seen as being unimportant but necessary. For example, publishers have warehouses where stock is processed prior to delivery to customers, whoever those customers may be: book shops, university campuses, online retailers and so on. Time spent looking at ways in which orders can be processed and shipped in the minimum time possible and at minimum cost could help create competitive advantage. If such efficient processes can be developed, it can not only help manage costs within the business and improve productivity, but the reputation of the firm can be enhanced, which may result in additional sales in the market when competition is strong. Two Business Economics textbooks may be as good as each other, but if one publisher can guarantee order-shipment-delivery times weeks ahead of the other, and with 99.99 per cent reliability, then this may be the reason why a customer (a book shop, for example) chooses one book over another.

Porter outlined a number of key value chain activities:

- Inbound logistics includes goods inwards, warehousing and stock control.
- Operations relates to the processes that transform inputs into outputs.
- Outbound logistics focuses on fulfilling orders, shipping and distribution, marketing and sales, which deals with making consumers aware of the product and ensuring that products get to consumers at the right time, at the right place, at the right price and in sufficient quantities.
- Service, which is associated with the functions that help build product value and reputation and includes customer relations, customer service and maintenance and repair (or lack of it).

By exploiting value chain analysis a firm can identify ways of reducing its costs below that of its competitors and thus gain competitive advantage, which is distinctive and defensible. This is the essence of **cost leadership**. A firm might be able to identify particular efficiencies as described above, or exploit possible economies of scale to gain the advantage over its rivals. As the firm progresses through these processes it can also benefit from the *learning curve* (sometimes also referred to as the *experience curve*). As tasks and processes are repeated, the firm will become more efficient and effective at carrying out those tasks, and in a cumulative way, build in further improvements and efficiencies as time progresses.

 cost leadership a strategy to gain competitive advantage through reducing costs below competitors

Cost leadership may be beneficial in markets where price competition is fierce, where there is a limit to the degree of differentiation of the product possible, where the needs of consumers are similar and where consumers can relatively easily substitute one rival product for another. In other words, they incur low switching costs.

> **SELF TEST** Why might a firm want to reduce maintenance and repair to a bare minimum as a means of increasing value?

A detailed analysis of every aspect of the firm's value chain can reveal small but possibly important activities where efficiencies can be improved to generate added value and reduce cost. Ensuring that the various functions and activities are coordinated can also help generate competitive advantage.

Travelling around many countries these days, you might notice extremely large distribution centres located near to major arterial roads, airports, ports or railways. The development of these massive distribution centres has come through value chain analysis. A number of retail chain stores have a system where the distribution centre acts as a hub receiving supplies and distributing them along 'spokes'. Such systems have helped give firms cost advantages, as well as improving their reputation for efficient delivery and order processing. Hub-and-spoke systems are also used by airlines to help simplify routes and keep costs under control, as well as get passengers to their destinations as efficiently as possible.

If a firm is able to generate cost advantages through value chain analysis it can gain a position of being a cost leader, with greater flexibility in being able to set prices, which help maximize revenues or profit.

Differentiation The second focus of market-based strategies is on differentiation. **Differentiation** is the way in which a firm seeks to portray or present itself as being different or unique in some way. This can be physical in the form of the actual product itself, or mental and emotional through the way in which the business is able to develop its brands, advertise and promote itself and create emotional attachments to its products. Firms attempting to differentiate themselves do need to be aware of the importance of taking into account changing tastes and fashions. What differentiates a firm one year might become a burden the next, and the perception of the business may become difficult to change as time moves on.

 differentiation the way in which a firm seeks to portray or present itself as being different or unique in some way

Apple has been very successful at differentiating itself from its rivals both in terms of the functionality and design of its products, and in the way it creates a loyal following of customers who are keen to snap up its products whenever they are released. Similarly, firms like Bose and Bang & Olufsen have created a reputation for high-quality sound systems and enviable design, which sets them apart from their rivals. Food manufacturers like Heinz increasingly place an emphasis on quality, on the use of natural ingredients and low fat and sodium as a means of differentiating themselves. Hotel chains such as Holiday Inn place an emphasis on consistency, so that wherever a guest stays, in whatever country it may be, there are certain features that are familiar and comforting so that guests do not experience any shocks.

Niche Strategies A **market niche** is an (often) small segment of an existing market with specific wants and needs which are not currently being met by the market. Focusing on a niche might allow a business to identify some very specific customer requirements which it can meet profitably. Imagine a firm which develops flip-flops which have a built-in supportive arch. It is unlikely that 'everyone' will buy this product, but for those people who suffer from foot problems, such as fallen arches or flat feet, the product might be extremely useful, so that they might be prepared to pay a premium price for the comfort they bring.

> **market niche** a small segment of an existing market with specific wants and needs which are not currently being met by the market

The niche market in this case is a small section of the overall market for summer footwear comprising people who have foot problems.

Niche strategies are often beneficial to small firms which have developed specialized products, but are certainly not unique to these types of business. Small businesses may not have the resources to compete in terms of cost. If producing a mass market product, they may have problems in differentiating themselves from their bigger rivals. In such cases, niche marketing may be an appropriate strategy to follow.

Larger firms may also target niche markets by creating trademarks, brands or securing patents. In such cases, firms may be able to not only target a wider market, but also specific niches within it. In our flip-flop example the Dr Scholl footwear brand might patent the design of foot support flip-flops and secure the niche market as a result.

> **SELF TEST** What are the key features of a market niche? Give three examples of niche products with which you are familiar.

Strategic Implementation

Having analyzed the firm and the market and then decided on some strategy, the next phase is to implement the strategy. This is invariably the most challenging part of strategic management. Implementation involves the plans and direction actually being put into practice, and a firm taking decisions to translate words into action.

The senior leaders and managers in a business who have created the strategy must communicate it to a range of stakeholders (not just the employees). They must then make sure that the structures, design, people and operations are in place to deliver the strategy. In addition, the senior team will have to put in place systems to monitor the progress of the strategy. This is not to suggest that the whole process is simply a top-down approach; as noted earlier, an increasing number of firms recognize that strategy must be a focus at all levels of the business, and that individuals and groups lower down the hierarchy have to have the flexibility and freedom to make choices and decisions. All these choices and decisions must be made with the overall strategy in mind.

One framework which has been suggested for managing strategic implementation is the FAIR framework. This stands for Focus, Alignment, Integration and Review. In the focus phase, senior managers identify shorter-term objectives in conjunction with departmental or functional heads, in line with the overall strategic goals. These shorter-term objectives then have to be aligned throughout the functional and departmental areas of the organization, with resourcing and practical implications considered and worked through. These plans are then integrated into the day-to-day operational processes and workflows, but management of these processes has to be reviewed periodically to see the extent to which the strategy is being implemented and what the results are.

Summary

This brief overview of a very complex topic has outlined some of the issues and thinking on strategy. There are many excellent books and articles on strategy and strategic management, many of which go into much greater detail about the debates and differing perspectives that characterize the field. Ultimately, however, a firm has to have some understanding of itself and its market, identify and articulate a clear vision about where it wants to be in the future and find ways of implementing the strategic choices it has made.

CASE STUDY   Red Oceans and Blue Oceans

Strategy can focus on seeking to find ways of doing something different in your existing market but the chances of securing competitive advantage may be illusory. Chan Kim and Renée Mauborgne characterize markets where rival firms seek to outcompete each other only to find that the market becomes saturated and profits and growth for all in the industry are reduced to 'red oceans', so-called because competition is 'cut throat'. They contrast this with blue ocean strategies in which a firm seeks to differentiate itself and find new, uncontested market space. Rattan Chadha and Michael Levie faced this situation when thinking about hotels. They could have made the beds bigger, make the toiletries in the bathrooms more luxurious, improved the food and dining experience for guests in some way, and various other approaches. However, the chances are they would involve additional cost and not succeed in developing a competitive advantage because competitors can simply do the same and erode any short-term advantage.

Instead, Chadha and Levie analyzed the industry to identify the key factors that influenced customer behaviour. In particular they were interested in why frequent travellers, their target market, made the decision to trade up from a three-star hotel to a five-star one. They noted that a three-star hotel would typically offer three-fifths of what a five-star hotel would offer. The target market, frequent travellers travelling for both business and pleasure, were termed 'mobile citizens'. The two entrepreneurs' analysis identified certain characteristics of these customers which they grouped into three areas: the sense of luxury in their surroundings, the sleeping environment and the location. It was these factors which determined whether these customers would choose to trade up from a three-star to a five-star hotel.

The two then applied their analysis to an ERRC grid which stands for eliminate, raise, reduce and create. Their research found that things like front desks, concierge services, full-service restaurants, room service and bellhops were not valued and so could be eliminated. What needed to be raised was the sleeping environment and location, streaming services, super-fast internet access and simple things like plenty of plug sockets and plugs for gadgets. The sizes of rooms were not a critical factor but the quality of the beds and linen and bathroom facilities were, so this allowed Chadha and Levie to reduce the size of the rooms, meaning more rooms per given area, but also allowed them to reduce the price compared to traditional

five-star hotels. Finally, they created self-check-in kiosks and developed what they called a 'communal living environment' with bars open 24/7 and access to technology such as iMacs. Front desk staff were replaced with 'ambassadors' who could multi-task and address a whole range of potential customer concerns and needs.

The result of this analysis and innovation is that CitizenM hotels have high occupancy rates compared to many of their traditional rivals, secure very high customer feedback ratings and show a 50 per cent reduction in staffing costs compared to the industry average.

Re-thinking the hotel industry can result in the creation of a 'blue ocean'.

Questions

1 **Does the existence of red oceans imply that any strategy development by a firm is likely to be futile? Explain.**
2 **Why can attempts to differentiate often not result in competitive advantage?**
3 **What might be the limitations associated with the idea of blue ocean strategic thinking?**
4 **Comment on the strategy adopted by Chadha and Levie and assess the extent to which their approach will result in sustained competitive advantage.**

References: www.blueoceanstrategy.com/what-is-blue-ocean-strategy/ (accessed 10 June 2023).
www.blueoceanstrategy.com/blog/blue-ocean-strategy-in-the-hotel-industry/ (accessed 10 June 2023).

PRICING STRATEGIES

One of the key decisions any firm operating in an imperfectly competitive market has to make is on the price to charge for its products. There are a number of pricing strategies (some argue they should properly be called tactics). The purpose of a pricing strategy is to influence sales in some way, or to reflect something about the product that the firm wishes to communicate to its customers and potential customers. At its simplest, there are only a few things a firm can do: either set a price lower than its rivals, set a price higher in order to reflect a standard or some suggestion of quality, or seek to set a price at a similar level to that of its rivals.

Of course, the ability of the firm to use price as a means of influencing sales depends to a large extent on its costs. The difference between the cost of production and price is called a **margin**, the amount of profit a firm makes on each sale. Of course, this definition does depend on how 'cost of production' is calculated. However, for our purposes, looking at margins as the profit a firm makes from each sale is sufficient for our analysis. A firm operating at a higher cost base than its rivals will struggle in the long term to match the low prices its rivals may be able to charge because they have a lower average cost.

 margin the amount of profit a firm makes on each sale

Cost-Plus Pricing

This is perhaps the simplest form of pricing. The firm calculates the cost of production per unit and then sets price above this cost. The price can therefore reflect the margin or mark-up that the firm desires. For this reason, cost-plus pricing is also referred to as *mark-up pricing* or *full-cost pricing*. Let us take an example. Assume that a hairdresser calculates the average cost of a styling, including the cost of the stylist's time, the chemicals used during the styling, and the fixed costs attributed to each customer (for example, the cost of heating and lighting, rent on the premises, rates, insurance, drinks and magazines given to customers, performing rights fees for music played in the salon and so on) at €30. If the salon owner desired a profit margin of 10 per cent then they should charge a price of €33, but if a mark-up of 50 per cent was required then the customer will be charged €45. The formula for calculating price given a desired mark-up percentage is:

Selling price = Total cost per unit × (1 + percentage mark-up, expressed as a decimal)

If our salon owner calculated the total cost per customer of a simple wash, cut and blow-dry at €12, and the desired mark-up was 25 per cent, then the price charged would be:

$$12 \times (1 + 0.25) = 12 \times 1.25 = €15$$

One of the benefits of cost-plus pricing is that the firm can see very easily what overall profit it is likely to make if it sells the desired number of units. It is also possible to set different prices with the same mark-up. The total cost per unit of doing a simple wash, cut and blow-dry is not the same as someone having a completely new style with highlights, but by using this formula the salon owner could be sure that the different prices charged generate the same percentage mark-up.

One of the problems is that basing price simply on a desired mark-up does not take into account market demand and the competition. In reality, many firms will take these factors into consideration and adjust the size of the mark-up accordingly. Assume that our salon owner knows that there is another salon in town that charges €14 for a wash, cut and blow-dry and that the owner wants to undercut the rival. They set the price at €13. What is the mark-up now?

To calculate the mark-up in this case we use the formula:

$$\text{Mark-up (per cent)} = \left(\frac{\text{Selling price} - \text{Total cost per unit}}{\text{Total cost per unit}} \right) \times 100$$

The mark-up percentage, therefore, will be:

$$\frac{13 - 12}{12} \times 100 = 8.33\%$$

The mark-up is not the same as the margin. In the example above the margin is the difference between the selling price and total cost per unit, which is €1. This margin is then expressed as a percentage of the selling price and so would be:

$$\frac{1}{13} \times 100 = 7.69\%$$

It is possible that the salon owner might have a desired margin level (let us say it is 20 per cent) in which case this can be used to determine the selling price using the formula:

$$\text{Selling price} = \frac{\text{Total cost per unit}}{(1 - \text{Margin})}$$

In our example the selling price will now be:

$$\frac{12}{(1 - 0.20)} = \frac{12}{0.8} = €15$$

> **SELF TEST** Using examples, explain the difference between mark-up and margin.

Contribution or Absorption Cost Pricing

This is related to cost-plus pricing and is based on the same principles, but instead of attempting to calculate the total cost per unit the firm will estimate the variable cost only, and then add some mark-up to determine the selling price. The difference between the variable cost per unit and the selling price is called the contribution. This sum represents a contribution to the fixed costs which must also be paid. As the firm sells more and more units the contribution eventually covers the fixed costs and, for all subsequent sales, the contribution will add to profit. The contribution is an important element, as we saw in our discussion of break-even analysis.

Contribution pricing may be useful if it is difficult for the firm to ascribe fixed costs to output easily, which may be the case in some service industries.

Psychological Pricing

The basis of psychological pricing is that humans respond to different prices in different ways by behaving differently or having a different emotional response. The classic example of psychological pricing is that of a firm charging €5.99 for a product rather than €6.00. This is partly due to the way we view things. Many people may look at the first figure in a price and pay little attention to the last two digits (called the *left-digit effect*). If the firm believes that customers would see the number '5' as being 'reasonable' but '6' as being too expensive, then setting the price at €5.99 might encourage consumers to purchase believing they are getting some sort of discount.

Psychological pricing is based on a fundamental assumption that consumers do not behave rationally. If they did, then why would they be willing to buy something at €15.49 but not at €15.50? It could also be argued that psychological pricing treats consumers as if they are not very bright and cannot see through the tactic. We can only conclude that the prevalence of use of this tactic would suggest that it does work.

Penetration Pricing

As the name suggests, penetration pricing is a tactic that is used to gain some penetration in a market. The firm sets its price at the lowest possible level in order to capture sales and market share. This is a tactic that may be used when a firm launches a new product onto the market and wants to capture market share. Once that market share has been captured and some element of brand loyalty built up, the firm may start to push up the price. If this is the longer-term aim, then there could be a problem with consumers getting used to low prices and being put off when prices begin to rise. At this point, the price elasticity of demand is crucial to the longer-term success of the product. If consumers are sensitive about price, then increases might lead to a switch to substitutes or the consumer leaving the market altogether.

Penetration pricing assumes that firms will operate at low margins while pursuing such a tactic, but if successful and sales volumes are high, total profit could still be relatively high. Penetration pricing implies that a firm needs to have considerable control over its costs to enable it to operate at low margins.

> **SELF TEST** Why does penetration pricing tend to be a tactic that is associated with high-volume products?

Market Skimming

Market or price skimming is a tactic that can be used to exploit some advantage a firm has which allows it to sell its products at a high price. The term 'skimming' refers to the fact that the firm is trying to 'skim' profits while market conditions prevail by setting price as high as demand will allow.

Such a situation can arise when a firm launches a new product onto the market which has been anticipated for some time. Companies like Apple are very good at building such anticipation (some would call it hype) so that when the product does finally launch, the market price can be set relatively high. It may be that some months later the price of the product starts to fall, partly because of the need to persuade consumers who are marginal buyers, i.e. those that are not devoted to the product and would only consider buying at lower prices, or because the competition has reacted and launched substitutes.

The high initial prices imply that the firm is able to generate relatively high margins in the early stages of the product. These may be used to help offset the development costs which, in the case of technology products like smartphones, tablets and gaming consoles (where market skimming is not unusual as a pricing tactic), can be relatively high.

Destroyer or Predatory Pricing

This is a tactic designed to drive out competition. A firm uses its dominance in the market and its cost advantages to set price below a level its competitors are able to match. The intention is that some rivals will be forced from the market and so competition is reduced. Ultimately the firm which instigated the strategy is able to operate with greater monopoly power. This tactic is illegal in many countries and comes under anti-competitive laws; however, it is often difficult to prove.

Loss Leader

The use of loss leaders is a tactic that is often seen in larger businesses and especially in supermarkets. A loss leader is a product deliberately sold below cost and therefore at a loss to encourage sales of other products. At holiday times, for example, many supermarkets will sell alcohol at prices below cost. They advertise this in the hope that consumers will come into the store, buy the products which are on offer, but also buy other things as well. The other items that are bought generate a profit, and this profit offsets the losses made on the loss leader.

The type of product chosen to be the loss leader can be important. Often a firm will choose something that it thinks consumers will have a good understanding of in terms of value and original price. By doing this it hopes that the 'incredible' offer it is making will be noticed more obviously by the consumer and thus encourage the consumer to take advantage.

Products which are complements may also be the target of such a tactic. For example, selling a smart Blu-ray DVD player at a loss may encourage consumers to buy smart Blu-ray DVDs; or a firm sells wet shavers at low prices but consumers find that replacement blades tend to be sold at relatively high prices (and often packaged in large quantities so that not just one new blade can be purchased). Potential drawbacks could occur if the consumer is highly disciplined and only buys the goods on offer, but evidence suggests this is relatively unusual.

> **SELF TEST** How might a firm calculate whether a loss leader has been a successful tactic?

Premium or Value Pricing

The type of market a firm operates in can be a determinant of the pricing strategy it adopts. On the one hand, fast selling consumer goods at a price which is competitive might generate large volume sales for firms but yields low margins (such as chocolate bars, newspapers and ball point pens). At the other end of the scale, a firm might deliberately set its price high to reflect the quality or exclusivity of the product. It knows that sales volumes will be low, but the margins are high and as a result profits can still be high on low sales.

Premium pricing may be a feature of certain types of technology-based products, luxury yachts, some motor cars, jewellery, designer fashion items, hotels, perfumes and first class travel. In each of these cases the firm may deliberately set prices high or restrict output so that price rises relative to demand.

Competition Pricing

Competition pricing occurs where a firm will note the prices charged by its rivals and either set its own price at the same level or below, to capture sales. One of the problems with this is that firms must have a very clear understanding of their competitors. For example, if a rival firm was charging a particular price for a product because it benefited from economies of scale and had lower average costs, then a new firm coming into the market and looking to compete on price might find that it cannot do so because it does not have the cost advantages. It could also be the case that a rival has set a price based on established brand loyalty, and simply setting a price at or below this in an attempt to capture sales may not work, because the price difference is insufficient to break the loyalty that consumers have for the branded product.

In markets where competition is limited, 'going rate' pricing may be applicable. Each firm charges similar prices to that of its rivals, and in each case price may be well above marginal cost. Such a situation might be applicable to the banking sector, petrol and fuel, supermarkets and some electrical goods where prices tend to be very similar across different sellers.

Price Leadership

In some markets, a firm may be dominant and can act as a price leader. In such cases, rivals have difficulty in competing on price; if they charge too high a price they risk losing market share. Reducing prices could result in the price leader matching price and forcing smaller rivals out of the market. The other option, therefore, is to act as a follower, taking the pricing leads of rivals, especially where those rivals have a clear dominance of market share.

 WHAT IF... a firm which is seen as a price leader, increases prices by 10 per cent, but its rivals who are classed as followers decide not to raise price in this case?

Marginal Cost Pricing

This typically occurs when a firm faces a situation where the marginal cost of producing an extra unit is very low and the bulk of the costs are fixed costs. In such a situation, the cost of selling an additional unit is either very low or non-existent and the firm is able to be flexible about the prices it can charge.

An example occurs in the transport industry on airlines and trains. If an airline operates a scheduled flight with 300 seats available from Amsterdam to Riyadh, then the bulk of the costs will be incurred regardless of how many seats are sold. Let us assume that five days prior to departure only half of the seats have been sold, and it does not look as if demand is going to rise in the time leading up to the flight departing. If the firm calculates that the cost of taking an extra passenger is €5 (the additional cost of fuel, food and processing) then it makes sense for the firm to accept any price above €5 in the time leading up to departure.

If the standard ticket was priced at €300, but demand is weak, then it is clear that the airline ought to reduce price. It could conceivably keep reducing prices down to €5 in order to fill all the seats, because every additional €1 above this amount would contribute to the fixed costs and thus make it worthwhile for the airline.

> **PITFALL PREVENTION** We have covered a range of pricing strategies in this section. It is important to remember that firms do not make pricing decisions in isolation. If a firm decides to adopt a price skimming strategy, for example, it will not do this without taking into account many other factors including what its competitors are charging, what type of product they are selling and so on, all of which may be factors that are characteristic of decision making in other pricing strategies.

BUSINESS FORECASTING

Identifying Patterns

In developing strategies and tactics, businesses have to look to the future and that means they have to make forecasts. By its very nature, forecasting relies heavily on historical trends and patterns which the business identifies using different types of analysis. Some patterns and trends can start to happen quickly, while others might develop over a longer period of time. One of the challenges facing a business is deciding when to use trend in its forecasting. Changes might be a blip, and sales settle down soon after. The change might be due to seasonal variation, or an anomaly in customer behaviours.

To anticipate sales trends, businesses will look to identify patterns in data collected from different sources. Some of this will be from market research, some will be from customer data held by the firm and some will be from secondary sources such as market data reports. Secondary research of this type is often highly detailed and complex.

The main difficulties facing any business are knowing when a pattern is emerging, and the extent to which events that they observe are correlated. Just because two things are changing together, whether positively or negatively, does not mean that there is necessarily any causal relationship between the two, however intuitive that the correlation might appear to be. There are a number of techniques that are commonly used to analyze trends.

Methods of Analysing Trends

Common ways of analysing cost and sales data are to look at nominal and real growth rates, averages such as the mean, median and mode, and measures of dispersion including the range and standard deviation. Businesses will also use methods to analyze relationships between sets of data to determine whether there is any statistical relationship between the two, the strength of the relationship and whether the relationship, if any, occurs by chance or if there is a cause and effect relationship.

Growth Rates It is often not enough to know that sales growth is occurring; the rate at which growth is occurring can give valuable information about trends. Calculating the rate of growth makes it easier to compare similar products and is often more meaningful to the observer than numbers alone. For example, take the two products in Table 16.1.

TABLE 16.1 **Product Sales for Two Businesses, 2024 and 2025**

	Sales 2024 (€m)	Sales 2025 (€m)
Product A	240	300
Product B	15	25

In terms of sales growth, Product A has seen sales increase by 60 million over the year whereas Product B has only seen sales rise by 10 million in comparison. It might be concluded that Product A is performing far better than Product B. We can draw another comparison by looking at the rate of growth of the two products. We do this by taking the difference between the sales in the current year (2025) and the original year (2024) and divide by the original year. This can be summarized in the general formula:

$$\text{Percentage growth rate} = (V_{present} - V_{past})/V_{past} \times 100$$

Using this formula, we find that the growth rate of Product A is 25 per cent while the growth rate of Product B is 66.6 per cent. Sales of Product B are rising much faster than those of Product A. If such a trend were to continue into subsequent years, it might suggest that this was a product with a bright future. However, two years' worth of figures does not tell us a great deal, and it is only over a period of time that a picture can emerge about the overall growth trend of a product. Figure 16.2 shows sales growth over a period for Product X. The visual presentation of the data allows us to see that from the starting point of 2018, sales grew at a steady rate for the next four years, then began to level off from 2023 but maintained total sales at around €450 million for the next two years.

FIGURE 16.2

Sales Growth of Product X from 2012–2019
The chart shows the growth in sales of a product over a period of 8 years. For the first four years sales grow at an increasing rate but thereafter, levels off and the rate of growth remains flat between 2024 and 2025.

	Sales (€m)
2025	452
2024	450
2023	440
2022	410
2021	380
2020	350
2019	300
2018	240

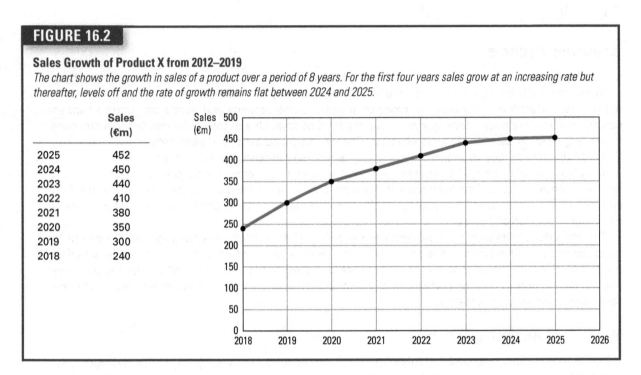

It is important to place the growth in context. Is growth occurring in a new market, a mature market or a declining market? If the sales figures for Product X in Figure 16.2 were in a declining market, then it may be a sign to the business that there might be hard decisions to make in the near future about the longer-term prospects for this product, and whether it would be economically viable to invest further money in supporting or promoting this product.

Real and Nominal Figures When looking at growth figures it is important to compare like with like to help remove distortions of the data. For example, assume the supermarket Carrefour reports a rise in sales of 7 per cent over the last year. Do these data include sales from new stores that might have opened in the last year? If it does, then it is not comparing like with like. The sales of 250 stores are likely to be lower than the sales of 260 stores. Like-for-like sales figures remove the effects of new store openings or closures, or where there might be differences in the types of products offered.

Another way in which data can be distorted is through the effect of inflation. Sales data are often calculated by multiplying number sold by price. Inflation has to be accounted for when looking at a range of data that can be affected by rising prices. If the effects of inflation have been taken into consideration in the data calculation, then it is expressed as 'real' data as opposed to nominal data. **Real variables** refers to data measured in physical units whereas **nominal variables** is data measured in monetary units.

real variables variables measure in physical units
nominal variables variables measured in monetary units

Measures of Central Tendency

There are three commonly used measures of central tendency, each describing a different indication of the typical or central value in a data series: the mean, median and mode.

The Mean The mean is found by taking the sum of items in the series and dividing it by the number of items in the series. For example, assume we were given the following sales figures for a business for the first seven months, as shown in Table 16.2.

TABLE 16.2	7-Month Sales Figures for a Business						
	January	February	March	April	May	June	July
Sales (000s)	600	340	560	460	520	460	530

The average monthly sales would be found by taking the sum of the seven sales figures (the series) and dividing by the number of items in the series, seven in this case. The mean number of sales over this period would be 3,470/7 = 495.7 or a mean sales level of 495,714 per month.

The Median The median is the middle number of the series. To find the median, arrange the data in numerical order and find the middle item. In Table 16.2, the median would be 520. If there are an even number of items in the series, then take the sum of the two values in the middle and divide them by 2 (this is, of course, finding the mean of the two values).

The Mode The mode is the most frequently occurring value in a data series. In Table 16.2, the number 460 occurs twice and so is the mode.

Limitations of Averages

The fact that we have three different interpretations of the average in the data above highlights one of the limitations of using averages. In more complex data, the average can hide a number of statistical quirks. There are sophisticated techniques available to try to take account of these quirks and make the data more accurate.

The average is essentially a representative figure of the data set being worked on. In some cases that figure can be relatively accurate, and in others not so, because of the nature of the data set being used. Some items in the series might be wildly out of character with the rest of the items in that series and so will skew the data. For example, if we were trying to find the average profits of a group of companies, but one of the companies had exceptional profits, the inclusion of that company would skew the average: it would be an 'outlier'. As with any statistical data, care must be taken in its use and interpretation. Analysts can use techniques like moving averages to analyze time-series data. The technique allows the analyst to smooth out short-term fluctuations, and in so doing highlight longer-term trends and patterns. Even using more sophisticated techniques like moving averages, decision makers must be mindful of the limitations of using methods of dispersal. Placing reliance solely on statistics is rarely done in business decision making without some recourse to qualitative data.

Measures of Dispersion

To help make interpretation of averages more accurate, measures of dispersion are used. The range is used to show the difference between the highest and the lowest items in the data series. This is important to get some idea of the breadth of data in the sample. The standard deviation is used to measure the variance of the data set from the mean. It can help highlight how reliable the mean is as representative of the data set.

Looking for Patterns in Data Collections

In preparing forecasts, analysts will look at historical data to see if there are patterns in the data which may help in forecasting. A simple example illustrates this point. Commodity prices such as the price of oil tend to be relatively volatile, with daily and weekly changes showing periods of rising and falling prices. However, while there are short-term fluctuations in price, there can be an obvious pattern; price may be rising over time, falling or be flat.

Much of the data used in business are what is called 'time-series' data. Time-series data refers to variables that change over a period of time. Such data might include economic growth, sales data, stock levels, share prices and so on. Analysts might be interested in developing hypotheses about the behaviour of these variables and any patterns that might exist. Such hypotheses can then be used to assess relationships between variables, contributing to strategic planning and decision making, including what price to set.

Of course, not all data exhibit clear patterns or trends, and in any event analysts must take into consideration that just because a set of data exhibits a pattern does not mean the pattern will be repeated in the future. Ultimately, a trend is going to be one of three things: a rising trend, a falling one or a stable trend. In each case, it is important to identify the degree of rise, fall or stability.

To help identify patterns in data, analysts may look at the frequency and reliability of trends. How often does the trend occur? Does it occur with any sort of regularity? These might be some of the things to ask when observing patterns in data. Analysts might also need to be aware of the impact of external factors, for example seasonal variations, random events and cyclical trends. Many larger businesses will make use of sophisticated statistical techniques in analysing data. These advanced statistical techniques will take into account the fact that, in some cases, patterns of volatility are difficult to identify. This is called heteroskedasticity.

Correlation

Correlation refers to the degree to which there is a relationship between two or more random variables, and if there is a relationship, how significant it is. Correlation does not identify whether the relationship is causal or not. For example, a retailer might want to assess the effect of changes in its pricing policies over time on sales. Reducing price for something like Black Friday might lead to an increase in sales, but can the firm be sure that this is the case? Could the rise in sales have just been a coincidence? Could there be other factors that have led to the rise in sales, and if so how significant are those other factors compared to the change in price?

If a relationship can be identified, then the closer the relationship, the higher the degree of correlation. The letter 'r' is used to denote the correlation; a perfect correlation would be where $r = 1$. The following example highlights how correlation might be used.

A small business in a town sells fruit and vegetables. Two years ago, a new supermarket was opened on the outskirts of the town. The owner has noticed a steady decline in sales since the opening of the supermarket. The owner puts the decline in sales down to the fact that their former customers are shopping at the supermarket rather than their shop.

On the face of it, the link between the decline in sales and the opening of the supermarket seems overwhelming; it is logical and entirely intuitive to see a direct causal relationship between the two. However, there might be other factors that could have caused the drop in sales. There might be other competition that exists, the quality of the service offered, or the products themselves might have been poor. All of these factors could have led to a decline in sales even if the supermarket had not opened. While cause and effect relationships appear to be strong, it must always be asked whether what is being observed has arisen by chance and whether there are other factors that need to be considered in explaining the observations. If other factors can be identified, how significant are these factors in explaining any relationship?

Time-Series Analysis

Time-series analysis is used to analyze movements of a variable over a time period, usually years, quarters, months and so on. Such analysis helps to assess the importance of trends, the effect of seasonality, key moments in any change in trend (sometimes referred to as 'tipping points') and the magnitude of changes. The use of time-series data has a number of advantages:

- Data from several years can sometimes give an accurate guide to future performance and is therefore useful in forecasting.
- Statistical techniques can make the data informative and useful as well as relatively accurate.

However, the accuracy and reliability of the analysis of such data depends on the quality of the data and the accuracy of the techniques used to analyze it. Data may not always be reliable or accurate. Analysts often work with historical data, showing events that have already happened. Depending on the source of the data, it might be several months before accurate data can be gathered that can be used; by this time, it might be out of date. Such data is sometimes referred to as a *lagging indicator*. It must also be remembered that what happened in the past is not always a reliable indicator of what might happen in the future.

Artificial Intelligence and Forecasting

Traditional methods of forecasting have their limitations and in many businesses, the quantity of data collected, the complexity of this data and the range of key performance indicators (KPIs) businesses use mean that these limitations are brought into even sharper focus. The developments in artificial intelligence and machine learning mean that the opportunity to bring together vast quantities of data and identify patterns that can be used to help develop more accurate forecasts is being more widely adopted. AI can use algorithms (lists of 'rules' to follow to solve a problem or task) to help identify large numbers of factors that might influence the forecast, far more so than many traditional approaches. As a result, they provide a far richer set of forecasts which can help improve decision making.

SALES FORECASTING

A common way of forecasting sales involves the use of extrapolation.

Extrapolation

If a set of data is being used to analyze past trends, then the data might be capable of being subject to extrapolation. This is a technique that enables the user to construct new data outside the existing data set. The new data is based on prior knowledge. There are, again, statistical techniques to get relatively accurate extrapolated data. At its simplest, extrapolation involves extending an existing trend. Extrapolation can be effective as a means of analysing possible future trends in markets and in sales forecasting, but relies on the knowledge used being reliable and showing a stable trend over a period of time. To show the basic idea behind this technique, refer to the data in Table 16.3 and the graph of the data produced in Figure 16.3.

TABLE 16.3	Company X Sales Figures, 2021–25

Year	Sales (€m)
2021	3.0
2022	3.6
2023	4.2
2024	4.8
2025	5.4

We can see from the graph that sales are rising at a constant rate between 2021 and 2025. Given this history, it would be reasonable to assume that we could extrapolate the projected sales figures for 2026 by extending the line shown in red in Figure 16.4. This would be a simple example of extrapolation.

Of course, for many businesses, sales data are rarely this neat and tidy, but the principle still holds: historical data can be used as a guide to future trends. The more volatile the data, the harder it is to extrapolate with any degree of certainty. How data are extrapolated will depend on the purpose of the data. A more optimistic extrapolation might be relevant if the data are being used to make a pitch either to senior managers within the company or to other businesses which the company is dealing with. It will be for the intended audience to decide, and often question, the reason why the extrapolation has been made, and on what evidence the forecast is based upon.

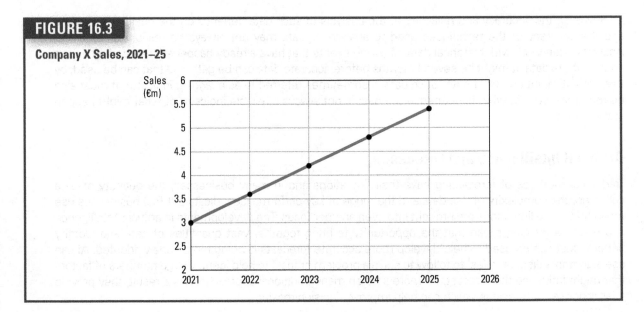

FIGURE 16.3

Company X Sales, 2021–25

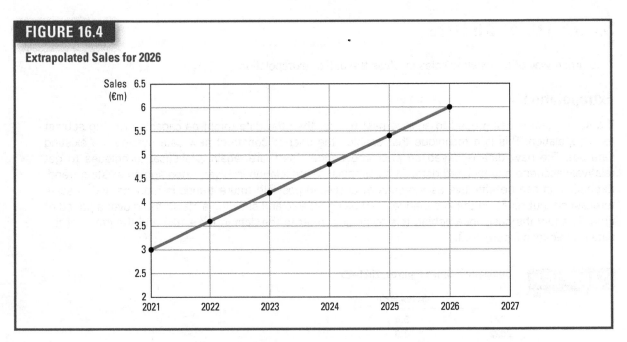

FIGURE 16.4

Extrapolated Sales for 2026

QUALITATIVE DATA

Forecasting does not just rely on quantitative data. Businesses will also make use of a range of qualitative data to help inform decision making. Qualitative data will tell a business more than just how many items will (or will not) be bought; it tells them why customers would buy a product, how many times, how frequently, what they like or dislike about a product, and so on. Qualitative data can be gathered by the following methods:

- Focus groups: a group of individuals selected and assembled by researchers to discuss and comment on, from personal experience, a topic, issue or product.
- User groups: similar to focus groups but consisting of those who have experience in the use of a product, system, service, etc.
- Panel surveys: repeated measurements from the same sample of people over a period of time.
- Delphi method: a technique which calls upon the expertise and insights of a panel of experts to help with forecasting. Experts answer a series of at least two questionnaires. The results of the questionnaires

from each round are then summarized anonymously by a facilitator. The process leads to a consensus of views and opinions which can make the resulting analysis more reliable than data analysis only. Participants in this process could be drawn together from around the world, as there is no need to have people together at the same time.

- In-house judgements: this makes use of the expertise and judgements of those involved in the business itself in aiding and making judgements.

The Use of Information Technology in Analysing Markets

The ever increasing sophistication of market analysis requires ever greater use of technology to help with the building, sorting and analysing of such data. We have already mentioned how software packages help with detailed statistical analysis, but IT is increasingly used in other ways. This includes the use of technologies developed under 'Industry 4.0', for example the analysis of big data, and the use of algorithms which can provide information to analysts about patterns, trends, behaviours and so on, which can provide more accurate and sophisticated data on which decisions can be based.

Customer Relationship Management (CRM) The development of digital technology has enabled businesses, especially large businesses that can afford IT systems, to access and build large databases of customer information. CRM looks at the methods used by a business to organize its business activities around specifically defined market segments. CRM will utilize technology to identify and profile customers through their interaction with the business. This interaction may be through a website or through the use of data-tracking devices such as loyalty cards or guarantee registrations. The use of loyalty cards, for example, enables a business to capture details about when a customer uses its products and services, how often, what they buy, when they buy it and how much they spend. This all helps to build a profile of the customer and provides the business with valuable information.

Businesses will also enter into partnerships and register with agencies that specialize in matching possible customer profiles with particular products. If a customer buys a dishwasher, for example, the guarantee registration card also asks for a variety of other information, such as whether the purchaser has a car, when the insurance is due, whether they are a homeowner, what their hobbies and interests are, and so on. This information can, within the confines of data protection legislation, be shared with other businesses that are then able to target promotion and advertising at those customers. Around the time that a car owner's insurance comes up for renewal, they can expect to receive contact from motor insurance companies offering details of their products.

All this information needs to be managed, handled, stored and sorted so it can be used extensively. Businesses increasingly use ways of mining information it has in the databases to generate a range of different types of information which can be used for forecasting and developing strategy. This is referred to as 'big data'. Many larger businesses are investing heavily in exploring how to make sense of the massive quantities of data that a firm captures through its systems on a regular basis.

SUMMARY

- Strategy looks at where a firm wants to be in the future.
- Strategy involves an analysis of the firm and its market, making strategic choices and then implementing those choices.
- Firms have to consider a wide range of factors prior to adopting any strategy, not least the sort of market structure they operate in, what rivals might do in response, how consumers value the product, what the cost structures are and how these compare to rivals, the extent to which brand loyalty affects demand, and the price elasticity of demand.
- There is considerable debate over strategy. Ultimately we might conclude that if it was easy then everyone would do it well and be successful!
- There are a range of pricing strategies (or tactics).
- Price is only one aspect of positioning a product, i.e. where the product sits in relation to the market.
- Any decision on price will be one part of the overall strategy of the firm.
- Businesses use a variety of quantitative and qualitative techniques to produce forecasts and help in strategic decision making.

IN THE NEWS

Dynamic Pricing Strategies in the Restaurant Industry

Many restaurants will find that customers have an annoying habit of booking a table between the times of 7 p.m. to 8 p.m. At those times customers flood into the restaurant all expecting to be waited on and served immediately and expecting that their food orders will arrive soon after they have placed them. In the kitchens, meanwhile, staff are rushed off their feet trying to juggle the flow of orders arriving all at the same time. If only some of these customers chose to eat at 6 p.m. or 9 p.m., life would be so much easier. Many businesses find that they face swings in demand not just during the day but during the week and months. In the case of restaurants, they may find that at certain times of the day or week, they are virtually empty whereas at other times they are extremely busy. Is the willingness to pay of the customer the same at 7 p.m. as it is at 4 p.m? Probably not. In this case, firms can utilize something called dynamic pricing.

Dynamic pricing is simply the practice of charging consumers different prices for the same goods. It is subtly different from price discrimination in that it is not necessarily about separating consumers in different markets, but exploiting different levels of demand to have multiple price points and as a result expand revenues. Dynamic pricing is being used across a range of industries including cinemas, hotels, airlines and transport services such as ride-hailing apps. There is now evidence that the restaurant industry is exploring this approach to pricing. In November 2022, a conference of members of the restaurant industry held in Las Vegas, discussed members' experiences with dynamic pricing. One immediate response to the idea is that if you charged those who want to eat at 7 p.m. 15 per cent more for the privilege, would they simply look elsewhere and thus the restaurant would see its revenue fall? Possibly, but not necessarily. Conference representatives noted that as customers, especially those in younger age brackets,

became more used to the idea of dynamic pricing that acceptance was increasing. Dynamic pricing in restaurants was also noted as not simply being a case of increasing prices in busy times but using data to set prices that seek to generate customer interest. For example, one conference attendee commented: 'Rather than increasing prices blanketly across the board, the next time costs rise maybe they only increase prices on particular days of the week or particular hours of the day. So you can still offer lower price points that drive consumers in, but still take great care of your margins.' Other adopters noted that despite initial fears, customer pushback against the pricing policy was not as strong as many might fear, but care in adopting the policy was needed.

How easy is it for restaurants to charge different prices for the same goods to different consumers?

Questions

1. Use a simple demand diagram and your knowledge of total expenditure (total revenue for a firm) to show how a restaurant could exploit different price points to increase revenues.
2. Dynamic pricing is also sometimes given the more derogatory term 'price gouging'. Do you think that such a pricing strategy is fair?
3. To what extent do you think that a customer's willingness to pay for a restaurant meal at 7 p.m. is significantly different from that at (say) 4 p.m?

(Continued)

4   One aspect of implementing dynamic pricing in the restaurant industry is understanding customer needs and gathering appropriate data on which to base prices. 'The keys to successful implementation are integration with point-of-sale technology and ensuring the customer experience isn't compromised.' Comment on this statement in relation to the successful implementation of such a pricing strategy.

5   The restaurant industry has suffered in recent years from the Covid-19 pandemic, rising costs including energy and raw materials, and labour shortages. How might the idea of raising (or lowering) prices at certain times of the day or week to 'drive customers in and take care of margins' be a successful and appropriate pricing strategy in the light of the cost and resource challenges facing restaurants?

Reference: www.nrn.com/technology/why-restaurants-are-finally-adopting-dynamic-pricing-strategies (accessed 10 June 2023).

QUESTIONS FOR REVIEW

1   Give a definition of the term 'strategy'.

2   Explain how the idea of 'strategic intent' helps a firm provide a framework for strategic decision making.

3   Outline two frameworks which a business might use in strategic analysis.

4   Give a bullet point list to outline the main features of the:

   a. resource-based model
   b. emergent strategy
   c. logical incrementalism.

5   How can value chain analysis help a firm establish an appropriate pricing policy?

6   Why might niche market strategies be beneficial to small and medium-sized firms?

7   Outline three challenges facing a business in implementing strategy.

8   Outline two advantages and two disadvantages to a firm of using cost-based pricing policies.

9   Explain the difference between market skimming and price penetration strategies.

10 Describe two methods a firm could use to forecast its costs in the next two years.

PROBLEMS AND APPLICATIONS

1   A chemical firm believes it has a core competency in identifying and exploiting particular chemical processes in intermediate products (i.e. chemical products which will be used to help make other chemical products/drugs etc.). How might this core competency lead to competitive advantage?

2   'The thicker the strategic plan the less relevant it will be.' (Quotation adapted from Davies, B. and Ellison, L. 1999, *Strategic Direction and Development of the School*, London: Routledge.) To what extent do you agree with this view? Explain your reasoning.

3   Consider the models of emergent strategy and logical incrementalism. To what extent would you agree with the view that they are effectively describing the reality of decision making in an uncertain environment?

4   Using an appropriate example, explain how value chain analysis can be a source of cost leadership and competitive advantage.

5   Choose a product with which you are familiar. Explain how the firm producing that product tries to differentiate it from rivals.

6 A firm producing fancy dress costumes estimates the fixed costs per costume at €20 and the variable costs at €5.

   a. Using this information, calculate the price if:
   - The desired profit margin is 75 per cent.
   - The desired mark-up is 45 per cent.

   b. The firm knows that its rivals charge €50 per costume and it wants to undercut its rivals by 10 per cent. Calculate the price, the profit margin and the mark-up.

7 Two firms operate in different markets and introduce a new product into their respective markets. One uses a price penetration strategy and the other a market skimming strategy. At the end of the first year they both make the same amount of profit. Explain how this situation could arise.

8 Explain why predatory pricing is illegal in many countries. Do you agree that it should be illegal, or is this pricing strategy just an inevitable consequence of competition? Explain your reasoning.

9 The tactic of using loss leaders is sometimes referred to as the 'razor strategy', because firms who sell wet razors do so below cost but then charge high prices for replacement blades. What sort of razors do you think this sort of tactic would work with? (Hint: think of the difference between a product such as the Gillette Fusion and disposable razors such as those produced by Bic.) How does a firm prevent consumers treating the razors used as loss leaders as disposable?

10 What factors does a firm have to have in place in order to adopt a premium pricing strategy?

17 SUPPLY CHAINS

THE IMPORTANCE AND ROLE OF SUPPLY CHAINS

In many cases we take the goods we consume for granted and rarely stop to think about how they were produced or got to us. Many will have gone through many different processes and stages and in some cases will have crisscrossed the globe before we consume them. A **supply chain** is a network of firms that facilitates the production and distribution of a good or service to consumers. These firms can include suppliers of raw materials and inputs, manufacturers, warehousing, transport and distribution firms, and retailers.

supply chain a network of firms that facilitate the production and distribution of a good or service to consumers

It is often useful to visualize supply chains through the use of a diagram and an example. Figure 17.1 presents a simplified representation of a supply chain. In many cases, the supply chain for products will be much more complex than this but the principle remains the same. Most goods and services rely on an extensive network of other firms to ensure that the consumer gets the product they have produced.

Figure 17.1 shows a stylized representation of a simple supply chain. Inputs into the process are provided by different suppliers and firms will have to negotiate with these suppliers to ensure that the inputs they need are supplied at the right price, in the right quantities, at the right time, to the right place and at the right quality. This is sometimes referred to as the '5-Rs of procurement'. As supplies of inputs and raw materials are received, they may need to be stored and organized for use in the production process. In some cases, firms will arrange for supplies to be received and then used in the process very quickly. This is referred to as **just-in time management**. The aim of this strategy is to minimize stock (inventory) holding and processing costs and to increase the rate at which inventory is turned over. Having inputs stored in warehouses for any length of time means firms have laid out costs to buy those supplies but are not generating any revenue from them, which represents inefficiency.

FIGURE 17.1

A Visual Representation of a Supply Chain

Supply chain management can be divided into three core sections: procurement, which involves the purchase of inputs to the production process; operations management, which deals with the manufacturing and distribution process; and finally the consumer.

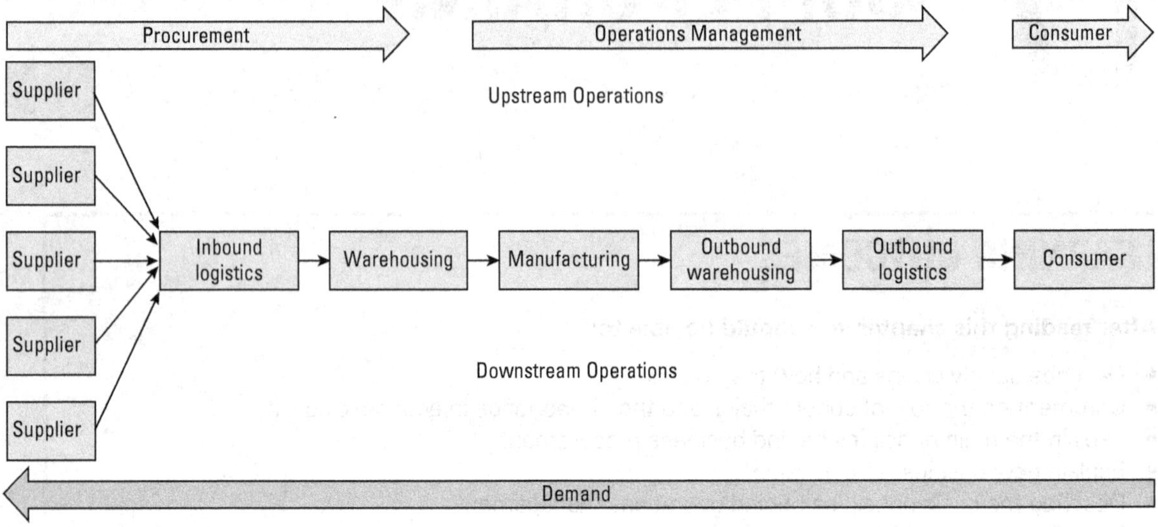

---

just-in-time management an approach to inventory management which seeks to ensure inputs arrive at a firm only when they are needed

---

Once the inputs have gone through the manufacturing process they are then prepared for shipment. In some cases, the finished products will be stored in warehouses or sent directly to firms who specialize in warehousing and distribution in preparation for shipping to the consumer. Of course, some firms may be selling their 'finished' products to other firms for further processing. If the manufacturer is selling goods that are destined for the final consumer, i.e. those that will actually buy and use the products, then the outbound logistics will be involved with how to get the goods to different retailers or to the onward distribution sites associated with online retailing. The process from supplier to consumer is referred to as 'upstream' activities. However, all this activity is determined by demand from the consumer. Without that demand there would be no reason to produce anything. The level of demand, therefore, determines the downstream activities.

This is a simplified representation of a supply chain and, in many cases, the networks and processes will be far more complex than this. The Case Study in Chapter 3 highlighted the complex transformation process of silicon chips used in many devices.

This example serves to highlight how complex the web of networks can be that are associated with getting goods and services to the consumer. The degree of complexity depends on the nature of the industry and the product concerned, but supply chains have become more and more complex as firms have sought ways to benefit from economies of scale and become more efficient. Many of the brands we use are produced by the same company. Smeg and Beko, for example, produce their own white goods (electrical appliances such as fridges, freezes, washing machines and dishwashers) but also produce appliances for other companies. The efficient and effective movement around Europe of goods is essential to supporting supply chains. To help with this, the EU has adopted a policy called the Trans-European Network (TEN-T) which seeks to promote the development of rail, road, inland waterways, shipping routes, airports, ports and rail terminals across Europe. The aim is to facilitate the smooth running of distribution networks and to remove bottlenecks from supply chains.

This type of coordinated investment in infrastructure serves to highlight its importance in improving the efficiency of supply chains and in responding to the increasingly complex needs of businesses. Supply chains have become more integrated over time, a process where different parts of the chain develop closer relationships with the aim of reducing response times, improving delivery times for just-in-time manufacturing, reducing cost and waste. While the supply chains of most firms rely on a network of different, independent firms, part of the goal of supply chain integration is to try to get to the stage where the supply chain becomes almost like one company. This can be achieved in part by merger or acquisition of elements of the supply chain but also through close partnerships between different firms. This can lead to increased efficiency and reduced costs but also makes supply chains more vulnerable to external shocks. The importance and complexity of supply chains has been highlighted when events cause them to be disrupted.

> **SELF TEST** Take a product that you use every day and try to map out the supply chain for this product.

The Effect of External Events on Supply Chains

External events can have serious implications for supply chains and result in effects on consumers. Quite simply, if supply chains are disrupted then goods and services are not available in the quantities required by consumers. This has been highlighted by the effect of the Covid-19 pandemic and the conflict in Ukraine. However, it is not just these events that have had an impact. Other events have also caused major problems. For example, in 2011, there was an earthquake in the region of Fukushima in Japan. The resulting tsunami and damage caused by the earthquake caused significant disruption to the production of key Japanese manufacturing facilities, which in turn affected production across the world as component parts were unable to be shipped in the numbers required. In February 2021, another earthquake in the region, not as powerful as the one in 2011, caused further disruption; Toyota, for example, reported that 14 production lines at nine plants across the country had been affected by the disruption to component supplies caused by this second earthquake. Other events that have caused supply chain disruptions include Brexit, extreme weather events and the blockage of a major waterway in Egypt (refer to the case study in this chapter).

The pandemic resulted in many countries imposing lockdowns and shutting down non-essential businesses. In addition, the suspension of travel caused major disruption to production processes across the world. Even when restrictions began to be eased and business resumed, the consequences on production and supply were significant and have taken many months to begin to return to 'normal'. Production of semiconductors, for example, was drastically reduced as lockdowns closed production facilities. The demand for technology to enable business to continue in some form or another during lockdown, such as video meeting technologies, meant demand for semiconductors increased. As lockdowns eased, demand for products using semiconductors expanded rapidly and supply could not keep pace, resulting in a global shortage of semiconductors which affected many businesses. Car manufacture, for example, relies on the use of semiconductors and many car manufacturers simply could not meet demand. Waiting times for new cars were reported by some manufacturers to be in excess of six months. Car production in Germany, for example, fell from 4.66 million per year in 2019 to 3.1 million in 2021.

At the same time, the fall-out from Brexit caused labour supply problems in the UK with haulage firms reporting widespread shortages of personnel. In January 2022, the conflict in Ukraine escalated and the supply of a number of key agricultural products such as wheat and sunflower oil were disrupted. In addition, energy supplies were also affected and all of these combined to form a 'perfect storm' which continues to impact on supply chains.

PROCUREMENT POLICIES

Figure 17.1 outlined the key elements of supply chains. One of these was procurement. **Procurement** is often referred to as the purchasing of goods and services from other firms to facilitate production and distribution. For example, a farm producing potatoes will need to buy seed potatoes and fertilizers as part of the production of the crop but may also purchase harvesting machinery services provided by specialists and will also need to negotiate contracts for collection and distribution of potatoes to wholesalers and retailers who are purchasing the products.

However, procurement can also be seen in more broader terms than simply purchasing. It also encompasses all the activities associated with obtaining the necessary support for its business. For example, the potato farm used in the example above will not simply go out and buy seed potatoes and fertilizer without conducting research into the firms it will buy from. Which firms offer the best quality seed potatoes? Which firms are the most competitive in terms of price and reliability of supply? What type of agreements can be secured with these firms and how long should the agreements be for? When the seed potatoes arrive, they will need to be inspected and records will need to be kept at every stage in the process to ensure traceability in the supply chain. Such activities, therefore, involve a much wider range of skills than simply purchasing, and different firms will be in different positions to be able to manage these with some in a position to employ specialists in the field whereas others may not. This can affect how efficient the firm is in managing its procurement and how competitive it can be in the market place.

 procurement a process that encompasses all the activities associated with obtaining the necessary support for its business

Types of Procurement

Procurement can be viewed in two main ways: direct and indirect procurement. Most obviously, firms will need supplies of raw materials, component parts and physical inputs into the production process and this characterizes direct procurement. Typically, direct procurement can be associated with securing supplies to enable the firm to produce its end product and so contributes to variable costs and impacts directly on a firm's profits. However, firms must also purchase other physical products like equipment and machinery, IT equipment, software licences, office supplies, desks and furniture. Some of these will be classed as overheads or fixed costs and the costs can be spread across output. If the purchase involves physical goods it can be referred to as goods procurement. Firms will also need to purchase services such as insurance, maintenance contracts, consultancy, legal services and advertising. These might be classed as services procurement, but again they are associated with fixed costs or overheads, the costs of which are spread across output.

The 5-Rs of Procurement

We mentioned earlier that there are five rights of procurement – the 5-Rs. Purchases of any item or service needs to be of the right quality, at the right price, in the right quantity, delivered to the right place, at the right time. These can be viewed as being the underlying principles of procurement, but there are also a number of elements tied up with these basic principles. One of the main ones is the legal environment around which firms undertake procurement. Many countries will have legislation in place to govern intellectual property, to establish the fundamentals around contracts, and to protect individuals such as laws around modern slavery, bribery and corruption laws, and so on.

In addition to adhering to legal obligations, many businesses will be conscious of a need to meet basic **corporate social responsibility (CSR)** requirements and their responsibilities to the environment. The responsibilities to the environment are sometimes referred to as the 3-Ps or the 'triple bottom line' – people, planet and profit. When engaging with potential suppliers a firm may vet them to ensure that they comply with the basic principles adopted by the firm. This might include an assessment of the extent to which overseas suppliers pay their workers a fair and decent living wage, and how workers are treated by suppliers. It is important to recognize that the financial health of suppliers is essential to the firm's continued survival which, in turn, is bound up in the financial health of the purchasing firm. A firm might also want to know how suppliers take account of their environmental responsibilities and the extent to which suppliers meet legal requirements. These might all be factors which are considered in establishing business relationships with a supplier.

corporate social responsibility (CSR) a business philosophy that recognizes combining the need to generate profit with the wider responsibilities to the environment, communities, ethical considerations, and society in general.

> **?** **WHAT IF...** a business is seeking to source critical component parts for its production process and the only current source is from a manufacturer that has a reputation for poor worker welfare and employing children on low wages. If the business does not acquire these components it risks becoming insolvent and jeopardizing 150 jobs. What should it do?

The Procurement Process

While the process differs across different firms and is often dependent on the degree of specialization adopted in relation to the purchaser, there are a number of accepted steps that a firm would generally undertake in the procurement process. The most obvious is to clearly identify and detail what products or services need to be purchased. This may include the necessary technical specifications that have to be adhered to, base standards of quality, consistency and so on. Some companies will have more formal processes which involve issuing requisition orders which may have to be signed off by senior managers. Having identified the product or service the firm then needs to identify potential suppliers and assess them from the point of view of the needs of the purchaser. This may include the vetting process outlined above. Negotiations with potential suppliers would typically include gathering information about pricing, quality, reliability and so on, and also the terms and conditions under which an agreement would be based. This may include establishing and agreeing service level agreements with potential suppliers which specify what happens if the terms and conditions are not met for some reason. For example, if a supplier cannot meet its obligations, would there be a financial penalty to pay and, if so, under what circumstances would such a penalty kick in?

In many cases, firms will sign a formal agreement or contract with suppliers which cover the details of the relationship. Once signed the supply process takes place and firms will have systems in place to receive shipments, check them to make sure they are correct and of the requisite standard and quality, match invoicing to the delivery and trigger a process payment. Both firms in such an arrangement would want to keep careful records to track delivery, supplies and payment. Traceability is becoming an increasingly important part of the procurement process and in managing supply chains effectively. Firms are also increasingly using sophisticated techniques to monitor the efficiency and effectiveness of the procurement process. Data analysis tools might utilize simple ratios such as the supplier defect rate, which is the ratio of the number of defective parts received to the total number of parts received from the supplier. The fulfilment accuracy ratio shows the ratio of the number of accurate orders received to the total number of orders received. However, increasingly firms are making more use of big data and technologies such as blockchain as ways of monitoring and analysing the procurement process.

> **PITFALL PREVENTION** Remember that procurement is not simply about buying in raw materials and components but covers a broad range of activities associated with all aspects of a business's operations.

ADDING VALUE

Earlier in the book we introduced the idea of added value. It was defined as the difference between the cost of factor inputs into production and the amount that consumers are prepared to pay for the product. Some commentators equate supply chains with value chains as there are opportunities throughout the supply chain for a firm to find ways to add value. The concept of value, as we have noted, is highly subjective, but firms must find ways to understand their consumers and increase their willingness to pay. We can see an example of value added through looking at three types of pizza that many supermarkets sell. One is wrapped in simple cellophane packaging and has a basic label which tells you it is a cheese and tomato pizza. It retails at €1.60. The second is also a pizza but it is not only wrapped in cellophane to keep it fresh but is also housed in a box. The box includes a picture of the product inside and instead of it being called a 'cheese and tomato pizza', it is called a 'Margherita'. It does have more cheese than the 'cheese and tomato pizza' and is described as being 'stone baked'. It retails at €3.50. The third pizza is also housed in a box but with a clear plastic window so consumers can see the product itself. It has a label on the box in stylish writing alerting the customer that this is part of the 'finest' range. It is also described as a 'Buffalo Mozzarella and Sun-dried Tomato Pizza'. It also has swirls of ground basil decorating the pizza. It retails at €4.50.

In essence, each product is a circle of dough with a tomato sauce spread on it garnished with cheese. However, the firm has differentiated each product in a slightly different way which communicates a different message to the consumer. The 'finest' product is clearly the most expensive at €4.50, but the way the product is packaged and described clearly tells the consumer this price is justified by the additional ingredients and the more luxurious packaging seeks to emphasize this message.

Looking at these three products you might ask does the buffalo mozzarella pizza cost an additional €2.90 per unit? Almost certainly not. Is the buffalo mozzarella pizza 2.8 times better than the cheese and tomato pizza? Is it almost 1.3 times better than the stone baked pizza? That is a difficult question to answer because different consumers will have different views on this. Some would answer 'yes' others 'no'. The key for the producer is do enough people think paying 2.8 times more for the buffalo mozzarella pizza and 1.3 times more than the stone baked pizza is worth it to make the product commercially viable?

The way the firm packed and presented the product and the information provided might be a way in which the consumer is persuaded to buy it above other options and other competitor products. Of course, the product itself does have to be better quality in some way or customers would very quickly discover it was not, and not repeat purchase.

This simple example highlights some of the ways in which firms seek to add value. What follows are some of the other ways in which firms seek to add value.

Creating Value

The idea of adding value is to create a product at a price that consumers are willing to pay for and that is higher than the input cost of producing it. This means that firms need to understand their consumers. Understanding consumers is vital to ensure that the internal decisions that are made are suitably targeted to ensure that the end result is added value. This implies that there are simple ways to add value, some of which we referred to in the example of the pizza. These could include the design of the product, improving the quality, the packaging or finding some way of making the product distinct or different from competitors in some way.

There are, however, a number of other ways firms use to add value. These can include influencing the perceptions of consumers in some way. The idea is to encourage the consumer to perceive that your product is somehow different or better even if in reality it may not be. The way the buffalo mozzarella pizza is packaged, the information provided on the packaging, the font used for the written information, the colour palette and so on are all ways in which perceptions can be influenced. In addition, firms can use branding to create an identity for the product so that consumers will associate certain characteristics, features, qualities or emotions to the product and be encouraged to choose that product over others. This reduces the degree of substitutability of the product. Reliability and the quality of after-sales service can also be an important feature in not only recruiting new customers but in retaining them and encouraging repeat purchase. This may also be achieved through ensuring the design of the product makes it both easy to use and convenient. Smartphones and computers used to be quite complex to set up, but firms have worked hard on automating the setup of new devices to make it as easy as possible and to encourage consumers to switch to newer, improved models without undue inconvenience.

Firms can also use the understanding of their customers to target particular characteristics or demographics. This is termed **market segmentation** and involves separating out a firm's customers into sub-groups based on their shared characteristics or behaviours. This could be through geographical location, age, gender, income, educational background, social class, values, hobbies, purchasing habits and so on.

> **market segmentation** the separating out of a group of customers according to particular needs, attitudes, behaviours or shared characteristics

One example of how market segmentation can work in adding value can be seen through the increased popularity of cycling in recent years. Firms have identified this popularity and clothing firms have produced a range of cycling clothing which specifically targets the needs and interests of this group of consumers. Shorts and trousers, jerseys and tops, gloves and eye wear might all be products that can be designed to target this group and add value. In essence, a tee-shirt and a cycling top can be very similar, but using a different material for the cycling top, making the colour more vibrant and adding on logos could all allow the clothing manufacturer to charge a higher price than a standard tee-shirt without the same proportional increase in costs.

> **SELF TEST** Choose two products that you are familiar with and think about how these products seek to add value.

The Value Proposition The **value proposition** is the reason why consumers should buy your product and not those of a rival. It is associated with the extent to which the product successfully resolves customer needs and problems. In considering the value proposition firms will need to understand and communicate what the promise of the benefits of ownership and consumption of the product might be and how this promise is delivered.

> **value proposition** the reason why consumers should buy a product rather than those of a rival or competitor

The value proposition typically has four elements. The first is to assess the customer's perspective. What problems do customers need solving and/or what are their needs (including identifying needs that customers do not necessarily know they need!). Secondly, the firm needs to show what the product can do for the consumer, what are the benefits that the product will confer, how does the product solve their problems and meet their needs, and why should the consumer care about the product? Then the firm needs to consider how it can make the product distinctive and different from competitors in a way that matters to the target market. Finally, the firm needs to find a way of proving to the consumer that the promises made are real, that the consumer can trust the promises made and believe in the company. Part of this process will be finding ways in which the benefits to the consumer can be quantified in some way. This might be something as simple as telling consumers that eight out of ten customers would recommend the product.

OPERATIONS MANAGEMENT

Earlier in the book we provided different definitions of the term efficiency. Productive efficiency referred to producing a given output at lowest cost, technical efficiency as producing an output using the fewest number of factor inputs, allocative efficiency as generating an output that is wanted and valued by consumers, and finally social efficiency which refers to producing an output that maximizes both private and social benefits at minimum private and social cost. Operations management is focused on how firms manage their operations and the production process at all stages through the supply chain to achieve greater efficiency. It follows that, if seeking to manage operations to improve efficiency, a firm needs to be clear about how it defines efficiency. In reality it may be that firms must balance the different approaches to efficiency we have outlined and find its own definition.

As we have seen, the supply chain outlines all the processes that take place from acquiring factor inputs, through processing and eventually distribution to the consumer. At each of these stages there will be opportunities to achieve efficiencies, and operations management is all about how these efficiencies can be identified and acted upon. To do this, firms must have an understanding of their product and the market they operate in, to have processes in place for forecasting and planning, to have some system to identify and monitor quality, and to understand and analyze the logistics around the distribution of the product.

The planning process can be complex. In simple terms, the firm must plan to ensure that the output it produces meets the demand for the product. To have some understanding of demand, the firm will need to employ different forecasting and we looked at some of these techniques in an earlier chapter. The different elements of the supply chain must be clearly understood and the relationships between the network of firms involved must be developed, nurtured and improved to ensure the smooth running of the supply chain. The firm will need to understand what quality means with regard to its product and what is the most effective way it can employ to monitor quality. This is not only important to ensure the consumer gets the product that they expect but to reduce wastage. Firms can use two main approaches to quality – quality control and quality assurance. **Quality control** typically involves a team which carries out checks on products at different stages of the production process to determine whether the output being produced meets required standards. Some of these standards will be internal to the firm but some will also be legal requirements, for example in relation to food production to ensure food is safe to eat. Quality control has the advantage that the team is focused on quality and can be objective in their assessment but can cause disconnects in the firm as they tend to be a separate group from those involved in production. If quality is not checked until the final stages of the process then problems downstream may not be picked up and can result in wastage.

> **quality control** a process where checks are carried out on products at different stages of the production process to determine whether the output being produced meets required standards

Quality assurance is a more holistic approach to quality and is the responsibility of everyone in the organization. At any stage in the production process, workers are encouraged to raise concerns around quality and are empowered to make decisions at a local level. This can have the benefit that problems can be identified much earlier in the process but relies on each individual taking quality seriously and understanding the parameters that exist around the quality of the product.

> **quality assurance** a holistic approach to quality where ensuring appropriate standards is the responsibility of everyone in the organization

Operations management is a complex area and deserving of a whole book on its own. Increasingly, developments in technology are being utilized to help improve operations management. Artificial intelligence, machine learning, blockchain, the internet of things and big data are all being used as ways of improving operations management. One simple example is the use of digital twins. A digital twin is a virtual model of a physical object, which could be a key piece of machinery used in the production process, for example. The digital twin is equipped with technology to enable it to monitor the performance of the machine. The data collected can be analyzed and assessed and used to run simulations on the digital twin to help improve performance, identify potential problems and alert managers to maintenance requirements before problems arise. The use of this technology can result in the machine being operated at a greater capacity with less downtime and fewer problems, all of which can improve efficiency.

CASE STUDY   *Ever Given*

On 23 March 2021, a container ship called *Ever Given* entered the 193 kilometre (120 mile) long Suez Canal as part of its journey from Malaysia to Rotterdam in the Netherlands. The almost 200,000 tonne container ship is capable of carrying around 20,000 containers. On this trip it was carrying around 18,300 containers each costing around €10,000 to send at this time. Instead of a smooth passage through the canal lasting around 11–16 hours, *Ever Given* got stuck and blocked the waterway. It was not refloated until 29 March. There are around 52 ships that pass through the canal every day and with the route blocked, a backlog of ships began to build up. By Sunday 28 March, it was estimated that there were almost 370 ships being held up by the blocked canal. Other shipping operators had re-routed their ships around South Africa, which typically adds around eight days to the journey.

The blocking of the Suez Canal caused widespread global disruption.

Estimates put the cost of the disruption to global trade at around $60 billion (€56 billion or £50 billion). Tens of thousands of businesses around the world were affected by the incident. The grounding of *Ever Given* emphasized how fragile global supply chains are and how dependent tens of thousands of businesses are on the transport of raw materials, semi-finished products and finished goods. Sylvain Gauden, Chief Underwriting Officer for Marine and Energy Reinsurance at SCOR, a global reinsurance company, perhaps summed it up best when they noted: 'The grounding of the giant Ever Given has shown the world the hidden reality of our economic system'.

Questions

1   It was reported that some of the goods in the containers stuck on *Ever Given* included IKEA furniture, bikes and bicycle equipment and spare parts, microchips, bedding, foodstuffs, barbecues, swimwear, toys and car parts. Using your knowledge of supply chains, explain how the delays caused by *Ever Given* would affect businesses waiting for delivery of the goods on board.

2   Comment on the quote by Sylvain Gauden. Should we be worried about this 'hidden reality of our economic system'?

3   *Ever Given* was launched in 2018 and is part of a new fleet of container ships that are getting ever bigger. These, so-called ultra-large container vessels (ULCVs) may generate economies of scale, but observers have noted that there also needs to be the physical infrastructure to handle them. Consider the arguments for and against countries investing in 'deeper harbours, bigger cranes and wider gantries' to enable these types of ships to be handled and to make supply chains more resilient.

References: www.bbc.co.uk/news/business-56559073 (accessed 9 June 2023).
www.scor.com/en/expert-views/lessons-ever-given (accessed 9 June 2023).
www.wired.co.uk/article/ever-given-global-supply-chain (accessed 9 June 2023).

SUPPLY CHAIN RESILIENCE

The problems faced by firms in recent years as a result of supply chain disruptions have resulted in a greater focus on supply chain resilience. This refers to ways in which supply chains can be made more durable to better withstand the sort of shocks that have occurred in recent years. By withstanding shocks, we are assuming that shocks will occur, but the key is how can supply chains adapt and respond to these shocks and return to 'normal' as quickly as possible? This requires supply chains to be more transparent, maybe less complex, and agile. We will provide a very brief outline of some of the ways which firms are considering in seeking to make supply chains more resilient.

Stockpiling Critical Inputs

The problem with the shortage of semiconductors referred to earlier illustrates how critical components can disrupt supply chains across a number of different products. One response to this is to identify those critical components and build stockpiles of them so that in the event of a disruption to supply, production and distribution can continue. What firms must do in this regard is assess the trade-off between the cost of acquiring and holding stocks and the benefits of being able to utilize those stocks to maintain production if and when disruption occurs.

Standardizing Components

One way of making supply chains more resilient is to make the components used more standardized. Not only can this standardization help improve understanding and clarity between all partners in the supply chain network, but it can also mean that components can be swapped more easily. We saw in the example of the production of chips earlier in the chapter that fabs were built and configured in the same way. This is one element of standardizing in that if the supplier in one country (for example) faced some disruption due to a shock then supplies can be sourced elsewhere and seamlessly substituted. A number of firms utilize this approach. The domestic appliance manufacturer Whirlpool, for example, identified ways in which it could reduce the number of unique parts in its appliances, achieving a 35 per cent reduction. Car manufacturers adopt a similar approach meaning that different models might use the same chassis, the same cockpit display units, the same seats and so on. If supply is disrupted again, it is relatively easy to divert components from different models to maintain production.

The Location of Business Processes

One of the ways in which supply chains have become more complex is through outsourcing. Outsourcing involves transferring some operations to external locations, sometimes across different continents, and is carried out to help reduce costs. A related process is referred to as offshoring where operations are relocated to another country. In some cases these are done to take advantage of cheaper labour costs or to gain more secure access to raw materials or supplies. Apple, for example, has a supplier list in excess of 200 enterprises spread across 43 countries and six continents. This inevitably increases the complexity of supply chains and increases the risk of disruption. In response to this, some firms have explored the options of nearshoring and onshoring. **Nearshoring** refers to the relocation or outsourcing of operations to countries nearer to the central business unit. This will often be to a country which shares a border with the country where the central business unit is located. In the event of disruption caused by a pandemic which disrupted air and sea freight, for example, transport by road could be continued and the impact on production reduced. **Onshoring** refers to the relocation of business activities and operations to the domestic country. There are some obvious challenges with this in that the cost of production may be much higher, access to skilled labour and raw materials may be lower and so on – all reasons why firms chose to outsource initially. However, these challenges may be offset by the reduced risk in the event of a shock. Again, firms will have to assess the trade-offs involved in decisions whether to pursue these options.

nearshoring the relocation or outsourcing of operations to countries nearer to the central business unit
onshoring the relocation of business activities and operations to the domestic country

JEOPARDY PROBLEM A manufacturing firm has relocated some of its operations to the UK from countries in Asia. While its supply chain has improved with fewer delays it is facing complaints about quality and reliability from its customers who are saying the product is not as good as it used to be. The company's CEO has requested a report from the operations director on how to resolve this dilemma. How would you advise the operations director in addressing the problem?

SUMMARY

- A supply chain is the network of firms that enable a product to be produced and distributed to the consumer.

- Over the years, supply chains have become more complex as globalization has led to the spread of business activity.

- As supply chains have become more complex, they have also become more susceptible to external shocks. The pandemic, the conflict in Ukraine, Brexit and natural disasters have all resulted in shocks to supply chains which have caused global economic disruption.

- Supply chains can be broken into three broad sections; procurement, operations management and the consumer.

- Procurement has become increasingly associated not simply with purchasing inputs but with a much broader range of activities associated with obtaining the support for all aspects of a business's operations.

- Procurement can be viewed through the lens of the 5-Rs and 3-Ps, which provide a guide to ensuring procurement policies and processes meet a company's and the environment's needs.

- A key element in the supply chain process is looking to add value. This refers to the ability of the firm to find ways in which it can establish a difference between the cost of factor inputs and the price that consumers are prepared to pay for the product.

- Value can be created in a variety of different ways.

- Operations management is concerned with analysing the operations that firms undertake to find ways in which efficiencies can be identified and realized.

- The disruptions to supply chains in recent years have led to firms analysing their supply chains to look at ways in which they can be made more transparent and resilient. There are three main ways this might be done, firstly through stockpiling critical inputs, secondly through standardizing components, and finally through the location of business processes.

IN THE NEWS

Back to Normal?

The disruptions to supply chains caused major economic effects across the world. As countries began to ease restrictions that were put in place during the pandemic, demand increased dramatically and because supply chains were so badly disrupted, supply simply could not keep up. Anyone with even a basic understanding of economics can appreciate that when demand is greater than supply prices rise. Many nations experienced an acceleration of inflation as a result. One of the key elements in the disruption was China. Its policy of zero tolerance of Covid-19 meant that manufacturing was shut down at various times, and because so much of the world's supply of goods is shipped from China, the supply constraints continued for longer than many anticipated.

According to some reports, the typical journey by sea from Asia to the United States, for example, should take around 14 days. This rose to around 120 days during and in the immediate aftermath of the pandemic and in some cases and caused goods to arrive at the right place but at the wrong time. Supply chains often follow seasonal patterns. For example, toy sellers start to think about placing orders for new stock months in advance of the Christmas selling season to ensure they have supplies in place for November and December. Goods typically bought during the

(*Continued*)

summer such as garden furniture, beachwear, barbecues, etc. similarly need to be ordered months in advance so that supplies arrive in time to meet the anticipated demand. As demand for shipping rose but supply could not increase at the same rate, the price of shipping containers also rose. The cost of transporting a 12-metre container was typically upwards of €10,000 in the aftermath of the pandemic. By December 2022, this had come down to nearer €1,900. This fall in shipping prices should begin to feed through to retail prices and ease the pressure on inflation.

As many countries get back to some normality post-pandemic, the challenges to supply chains are not over even if there are reports that they are easing. The conflict in Ukraine may continue to cause disruption to food and energy supplies. In China, restrictions have been eased as the government moves away from its zero tolerance policy but analysts are warning that this could have the effect of creating a wave of Covid-19 infections that could still result in disruption to manufacturing and, therefore, supplies.

China's zero tolerance of covid cases caused considerable disruption and China's leaders eventually relaxed the strict rules.

Questions

1 Explain how the article highlights the importance and role of supply chains to the health of the global economy.
2 The article notes that there are some aspects of global trade that are seasonal in nature. Explain how an understanding of procurement is an important element in ensuring the smooth operation of supply chains.
3 Comment on how the disruption to supply chains has resulted in accelerating inflation in many countries of the world. You should seek to use appropriate supply and demand diagrams and the contents of the article to illustrate your answer.
4 The article notes that there will still be potential challenges to the smooth running of supply chains in the coming years. Consider some options for businesses in improving the resilience of their supply chains.
5 Assume that you are an operations manager facing delays in deliveries and higher shipping costs caused by global supply chain disruptions. What options are open to you in managing this situation and improving efficiency?

Reference: www.businessinsider.com/supply-chain-crisis-over-risk-china-labor-2022-12?r=US&IR=T (accessed 9 June 2023).

QUESTIONS FOR REVIEW

1 Give a definition of the term 'supply chain'.
2 Why are efficient and smooth running supply chains essential to the implementation of just-in-time production processes?
3 Explain the meaning of the term 'integrated supply chain'.
4 Describe two ways in which supply chains can be disrupted.
5 What is meant by the term procurement?
6 What are the 5-Rs and 3-Ps of procurement and how might adherence to these be a potential source of competitive advantage for a firm?
7 Choose a product and consider three ways in which a firm might add value to the product.

8 Explain the difference between quality control and quality assurance.

9 What is meant by 'increasing supply chain resilience'?

10 How might the relocation of business processes help improve the resilience of a firm's supply chain?

PROBLEMS AND APPLICATIONS

1 A firm based in Ireland produces packaged quarter pounder beef burgers for supermarkets and grocery stores. The key ingredients for the burgers include beef, eggs and breadcrumbs all sourced in Ireland, onions from the Netherlands, seasoning from France, cellophane wrapping from England and cardboard packaging from Germany. Produce a supply chain diagram for this product.

2 Using the burger example from question 1, assume that the firm is experiencing falling sales as a result of competition from other burger suppliers. What sort of tactics might the firm use to seek to add value to this product to compete more effectively and reverse the decline in sales?

3 Many organizations have highly integrated supply chains. What potential problems might arise in having such integrated supply chains?

4 In February 2022, the Director of the European Coalition for Corporate Justice, Claudia Saller, was quoted as saying: 'Companies are increasingly under pressure to take their social and environmental duties seriously. But many hide behind their complex supply chains to avoid accountability and dodge difficult questions … a draft law [being introduced] would, for the first time, require EU companies with more than 500 employees and turnover of €150 million to prevent human rights and environmental abuses along their full supply chains, by carrying out so-called "due diligence". In industries where the risk of exploitation is higher like agriculture and fashion, only companies with more than 250 employees and turnover of €40 million would be covered, while SMEs would be exempt. Non-EU companies in the single market that exceed these turnover thresholds would also be covered.' Source: https://corporatejustice.org/news/dangerous-gaps-undermine-eu-commissions-new-legislation-on-sustainable-supply-chains/ (accessed 9 June 2023). Why do you think the European Commission has introduced this legislation and what might be the limitations in the legislation?

5 'The pandemic, Brexit and the conflict in the Ukraine have conspired to create a perfect storm for supply chains.' To what extent to you agree with this statement?

6 To what extent do you agree with the view that achieving the idea of the 3-Ps or triple bottom line is fundamentally incompatible with each other?

7 Comment on the view that adding value is simply creating a smoke screen to fool consumers into thinking that they are buying something they are not.

8 'Analysing the supply chain throughout its length is the key to a firm being able to identify ways in which it can generate competitive advantage.' Discuss this statement and state your position on its assertion.

9 Discuss whether it is possible for a firm to achieve productive, technical, allocative and social efficiency all at the same time. You should use examples to help illustrate your answer.

10 Consider the three approaches to making supply chains more resilient covered in this chapter. Discuss the advantages and disadvantages of each and suggest which may be the most important for a car manufacturing firm based in Germany.

PART 5
MICROECONOMICS: FACTOR MARKETS

18 LABOUR MARKETS

THE MARKETS FOR THE FACTORS OF PRODUCTION

Much of the content in this chapter relies on some of the basic information we covered when looking at costs and revenues and production functions earlier in the book. Recall that a firm's production function shows the amount of output which can be produced with a given amount of different combinations of factor inputs. The cost functions associated with different output levels were determined by the cost of factors of production. In this chapter we will look at how the price of factors of production, which in turn influence the costs of firms, are determined. For many businesses, one of the most significant costs they face is paying for labour. They also must pay interest on loans, pay rent for the factor land and buy raw materials.

The payments for factors of production provide one way of measuring the economic performance of an economy. Factor incomes are earned in various ways. Workers supply their labour in return for wages and salaries; the payment to landowners is called rent; and the owners of capital, the economy's stock of equipment and structures, receive interest. Rent, wages and interest are the prices paid for the supply of factors of production. The actual prices businesses pay for labour, capital and land are determined in part by the supply and demand of factors of production. When a computer firm produces a new software program, for example, it uses programmers' time (labour), the physical space on which its offices sit (land), and an office building and computer equipment (capital). Similarly, when a fuel station sells fuel, it uses attendants' time (labour), the physical space (land), and the fuel tanks and pumps (capital).

Although in many ways factor markets resemble the goods markets we have analyzed in previous chapters, they are different in one important way: the demand for a factor of production is a **derived demand**. That is, a firm's demand for a factor of production is derived (determined) from its decision to supply a good in another market. The demand for computer programmers is inextricably tied to the supply of computer software, and the demand for fuel station attendants is inextricably tied to the supply of fuel.

> **derived demand** when demand for a factor of production is derived (determined) from its decision to supply a good in another market

Our initial analysis will be based on the labour market and we will initially assume that firms operate in a competitive market, both for products and labour. Given this assumption, labour is free to enter and exit the market and firms are equally free to employ and shed labour at will. In other words people can move into and out of work easily and employers can 'hire and fire' workers when they need to. There are a number of imperfections in the labour market, but our initial analysis serves to act as a benchmark for looking at how labour markets work in reality.

 WHAT IF... labour markets were perfect markets. Would there ever be any unemployment, and would firms ever have problems accessing the labour market skills they need?

THE DEMAND FOR LABOUR

Labour markets, like other markets in the economy, are influenced by the forces of supply and demand. As we have already noted, the demand for labour is a derived demand. Most labour services are inputs into the production of other goods. To understand labour demand, we must remember that firms hire the labour to produce goods and services for sale. The link between the production of goods and the demand for labour provides an insight into the determination of the equilibrium wage rate.

> **PITFALL PREVENTION** Remember that the demand for factors of production, because of their very nature, are inextricably linked with the demand for the goods and services which they are associated with in production. This is one of the reasons why the workings of the economy as a whole is interdependent.

The Competitive Profit-Maximizing Firm

Assume that we are looking at a profit-maximizing firm operating under conditions of perfect competition. This firm will seek to employ labour to help it to produce goods and services for sale and to generate profit. The demand for labour (and any other factor of production), therefore, is determined by the productivity of labour and the value that labour adds to the production process. Under the assumptions of perfect competition, there are many other firms selling products in the market and seeking to hire labour. A single firm has little influence over the price it gets for its output or the wage it pays workers. The firm takes the price and the wage as given by market conditions. It only decides how many workers to hire and how many units of output to sell.

The assumption that the firm is *profit maximizing* means that the firm makes decisions to generate profit, which equals the total revenue from the sale of its output minus the total cost of producing this output. The firm's supply of output and its demand for workers are derived from its primary goal of maximizing profit.

The Production Function and the Marginal Product of Labour

To make its hiring decision, the firm must consider how the amount of labour employed affects the quantity of output it can produce and sell. Recall that the production function describes the relationship between the quantity of inputs used in production and the quantity of output from production. Let us assume that labour is the variable factor of production and all other factors are fixed in the short run.

Thinking at the margin is key to understanding how firms decide what quantity of labour to hire. The marginal product of labour is the increase in the amount of output from an additional unit of labour. Recall that when a firm adds additional units of a fixed factor, in this case labour, to a quantity of fixed factors in the short run, it will begin to experience diminishing marginal product. For this reason, the production function becomes flatter as the number of workers rises.

> **PITFALL PREVENTION** Calculating marginal product is not always easy especially when looking at service industries. Firms in these industries must think of how they can measure the productivity of their workers.

The Value of the Marginal Product and the Demand for Labour

When deciding how many workers to hire, the firm considers how much profit each worker will generate. Because profit is total revenue minus total cost, the profit from an additional worker is the worker's contribution to revenue minus the worker's wage. To find the worker's contribution to revenue, we convert the marginal product of labour (which is measured in units of output) into the *value* of the marginal product (measured in monetary terms).

The **value of the marginal product** of any input is the marginal product of that input multiplied by the market price of the output. If an additional worker is hired and adds 50 units of output per week to total production and the market value of each unit sold is €1 then the value of the marginal product of labour in our example is €50. Because the market price is constant for a competitive firm, the value of the marginal product (like the marginal product itself) diminishes as the number of workers rises. Economists sometimes call this the firm's *marginal revenue product*: it is the extra revenue the firm gets from hiring an additional unit of a factor of production.

 value of marginal product the marginal product of an input times the price of the output

To calculate how many workers the firm will hire we look at the value of marginal product in relation to the wage rate. Suppose that the market wage facing the firm is €500 per week, if the first worker yields €1,000 in revenue, this generates €500 in profit for the firm and it is worth employing that unit of labour. If a second worker is employed and generates €800 in additional revenue, or €300 in profit it is still worth employing that unit of labour. Similarly, if a third worker produces €600 in additional revenue, or €100 in profit, it is worth employing that unit of labour. However, if the fourth worker generates only €400 of additional revenue, because the worker's wage is €500, hiring the fourth worker would mean a €100 reduction in profit. Thus the firm would not employ this additional worker and employs only three workers.

It is instructive to consider the firm's decision graphically. Figure 18.1 graphs the value of the marginal product. This curve slopes downward because the marginal product of labour diminishes as the number of workers rises. The figure also includes a horizontal line at the market wage. To maximize profit, the firm employs workers up to the point where these two curves cross. Below this level of employment, the value of the marginal product exceeds the wage, so hiring another worker would increase profit. Above this level of employment, the value of the marginal product is less than the wage, so the marginal worker is unprofitable. Thus a competitive, profit-maximizing firm hires workers up to the point where the value of the marginal product of labour equals the wage.

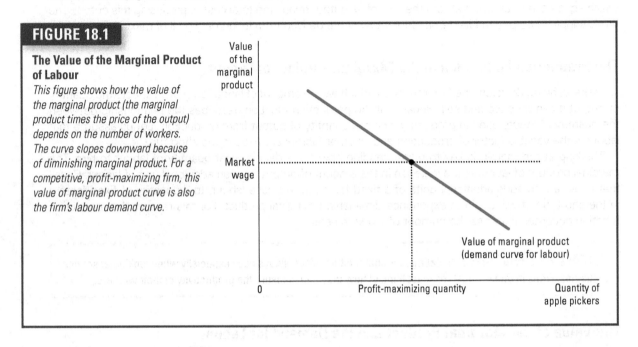

FIGURE 18.1

The Value of the Marginal Product of Labour

This figure shows how the value of the marginal product (the marginal product times the price of the output) depends on the number of workers. The curve slopes downward because of diminishing marginal product. For a competitive, profit-maximizing firm, this value of marginal product curve is also the firm's labour demand curve.

Having explained the profit-maximizing hiring strategy for a competitive firm, we can now offer a theory of labour demand. Recall that a firm's labour demand curve tells us the quantity of labour that a firm demands at any given wage. We have just seen in Figure 18.1 that the firm makes the decision by choosing the quantity of labour at which the value of the marginal product equals the wage. As a result, the value of the marginal product curve is the labour demand curve for a competitive, profit-maximizing firm.

What Causes the Labour Demand Curve to Shift?

The labour demand curve reflects the value of the marginal product of labour. With this insight in mind, let us consider a few of the things that might cause the labour demand curve to shift.

The Output Price The value of the marginal product is marginal product times the price of the firm's output. When the output price changes, the value of the marginal product changes and the labour demand curve shifts. An increase in the price of a good raises the value of the marginal product of each worker employed and, therefore, increases labour demand from the firms that supply this output. Conversely, a decrease in the price of a good reduces the value of the marginal product and decreases labour demand.

Technological Change Increases in labour productivity can be attributed in part to technological progress: scientists and engineers work on developing new and better ways of doing things. This has profound implications for the labour market. Technological advance raises the marginal product of labour, which in turn increases the demand for labour. Such technological advances allow firms to increase wages and employment but still make profits, providing productivity rises faster than labour costs.

The Supply of Other Factors The quantity available of one factor of production can affect the marginal product of other factors. If the amount of capital available falls, for example, it can reduce the marginal product of workers and thus the demand for those workers. We consider this linkage among the factors of production more fully later in the chapter.

FYI

Input Demand and Output Supply: Two Sides of the Same Coin

Remember that a competitive, profit-maximizing firm decides how much of its output to sell: it chooses the quantity of output at which the price of the good equals the marginal cost of production. We have just seen that a firm chooses the quantity of labour at which the wage equals the value of the marginal product. Because the production function links the quantity of inputs to the quantity of output, you should not be surprised to learn that the firm's decision about input demand is closely linked to its decision about output supply. In fact, these two decisions are two sides of the same coin.

To see this relationship more fully, let us consider how the marginal product of labour (*MPL*) and marginal cost (*MC*) are related. Suppose an additional worker costs €500 and has a marginal product of 50 units of output. In this case, producing 50 more units costs €500; the MC of a unit is €500/50, or €10. More generally, if *W* is the wage, and an extra unit of labour produces *MPL* units of output, then the MC of a unit of output is given by:

$$MC = W \div MPL$$

This analysis shows that diminishing marginal product is closely related to increasing MC. When additional units of labour are applied to a fixed number of other factor inputs, the firm becomes crowded with workers, each additional worker adds less to output and the *MPL* falls. Similarly, if the firm is producing a large quantity of output, the firm is already crowded with workers, so the MC of producing an additional unit of output rises.

Now consider our criterion for profit maximization. We determined earlier that a profit-maximizing firm chooses the quantity of labour so that the value of the marginal product ($P \times MPL$) equals the wage (*W*). We can write this mathematically as:

$$P \times MPL = W$$

If we divide both sides of this equation by *MPL*, we obtain:

$$P = \frac{W}{MPL}$$

We just noted that $W \div MPL$ equals MC. Therefore, we can substitute to obtain:

$$P = MC$$

This equation states that the price of the firm's output is equal to the MC of producing a unit of output. Thus, when a competitive firm hires labour up to the point at which the value of the marginal product equals the wage, it also produces up to the point at which the price equals MC. Our analysis of labour demand in this chapter is just another way of looking at production decisions.

THE SUPPLY OF LABOUR

Having analyzed labour demand let us turn to the other side of the market and consider labour supply.

The Trade-Off Between Work and Leisure

One of the more obvious or more important trade-offs in any individual's life is the trade-off between work and leisure. The more hours individuals spend working, the fewer hours are available to watch TV, socialize with friends or pursue hobbies. Firms are increasingly aware of the effect on productivity of the work-life balance and how employees view this trade-off. The development in technology has meant that many workers are in touch with their work more than ever before, and the temptation to put in ever more hours is considerable. This is not always a good thing for productivity. The trade-off between work and leisure lies behind the labour supply curve.

What must be given up to get an hour of leisure? An hour of work, which in turn means an hour of wages. Thus, if an individual's wage is €15 per hour, the opportunity cost of an hour of leisure is €15. If pay rises to €20 per hour, the opportunity cost of enjoying leisure increases.

The labour supply curve reflects how workers' decisions about the work–leisure trade-off respond to a change in opportunity cost. An upward sloping labour supply curve means that an increase in the wage induces workers to increase the quantity of labour hours they supply. Because time is limited, more hours of work means that workers are enjoying less leisure. That is, workers respond to the increase in the opportunity cost of leisure by taking less of it.

It is worth noting that the labour supply curve need not be upward sloping. If pay increases from €15 to €20 per hour, the opportunity cost of leisure is now greater, but the individual is also richer than before. They might decide that with the rise they can now afford to enjoy more leisure. That is, at the higher wage, the individual chooses to work fewer hours. If so, the labour supply curve would slope backwards.

What Causes the Labour Supply Curve to Shift?

The labour supply curve shifts whenever people change the amount they want to work at a given wage. Let us now consider some of the events that might cause such a shift.

Changes in Tastes   The proportion of women in the workforce in many countries is growing and has been since the 1960s. There are many explanations for this development, but one of them is changing tastes or attitudes towards work. A generation or two ago, it was more the norm for women to stay at home while raising children. Today, family sizes are smaller and more mothers choose to work. The result is an increase in the supply of labour.

Changes in Alternative Opportunities   The supply of labour in any one labour market depends on the opportunities available in other labour markets. If the wage earned by pear pickers suddenly rises, some apple pickers may choose to switch occupations. The supply of labour in the market for apple pickers falls.

Immigration   Movement of workers from region to region, or country to country, is an obvious and often important source of shifts in labour supply. When immigrants move from one European country to another, say from Poland to the UK, the supply of labour in the UK increases and the supply of labour in Poland contracts. In fact, much of the policy debate about immigration centres on its effect on labour supply and, thereby, equilibrium in the labour market.

SELF TEST   Who has a greater opportunity cost of enjoying leisure, a petrol station attendant or a brain surgeon? Explain. Can this help explain why doctors work such long hours?

JEOPARDY PROBLEM   A manufacturing firm wants to increase productivity and thinks that increasing wages is the way to achieve this. It has a system where workers have a basic working week of 35 hours and any additional hours are paid as overtime. The vast majority of its workers take advantage of the overtime opportunities whenever possible, especially when there are periods of high demand for the product. Overtime pay, especially at weekends and during periods classed as 'unsociable hours', attracts a higher rate than the normal basic pay, and the firm has noticed that productivity during these periods of overtime is higher than that recorded during the normal working week. The firm announces that all workers will receive a basic 20 per cent increase in pay for the normal working week, but that overtime pay will remain at previous rates. It hopes this increase in pay will boost productivity during the week. Six months after the increase, an internal review shows that productivity during the week has not changed, but that the amount of overtime workers are prepared to do has gone down. What could the explanation be for this situation?

Equilibrium in the Labour Market

So far, we have established two facts about how wages are determined in competitive labour markets:

- The wage adjusts to balance the supply and demand for labour.
- The wage equals the value of the MPL.

At first, it might seem surprising that the wage can do both these things at once. In fact, there is no real puzzle here, but understanding why there is no puzzle is an important step in understanding wage determination.

Figure 18.2 shows the labour market in equilibrium. The wage and the quantity of labour have adjusted to balance supply and demand. When the market is in this equilibrium, each firm has bought as much labour as it finds profitable at the equilibrium wage. That is, each firm has followed the rule for profit maximization: it has hired workers until the value of the marginal product equals the wage. Hence, the wage must equal the value of the MPL once it has brought supply and demand into equilibrium.

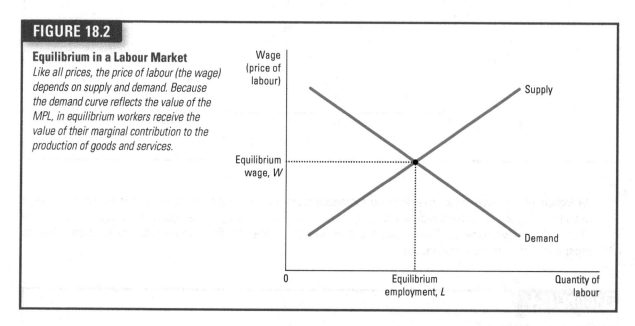

FIGURE 18.2

Equilibrium in a Labour Market
*Like all prices, the price of labour (the wage)
depends on supply and demand. Because
the demand curve reflects the value of the
MPL, in equilibrium workers receive the
value of their marginal contribution to the
production of goods and services.*

This brings us to an important lesson: any event that changes the supply or demand for labour must change the equilibrium wage and the value of the marginal product by the same amount, because these must always be equal. This can affect the costs of firms and influence their labour structures. To see how this works, let us consider some events that shift these curves.

Shifts in Labour Supply

Suppose that immigration increases the number of workers. As Figure 18.3 shows, the supply of labour shifts to the right from S_1 to S_2. At the initial wage W_1, the quantity of labour supplied now exceeds the quantity demanded. This surplus of labour puts downward pressure on the wage of existing workers, and the fall in the wage from W_1 to W_2 in turn makes it profitable for firms to hire more workers. As the number of workers employed rises, the marginal product of a worker falls, and so does the value of the marginal product. In the new equilibrium, both the wage and the value of the MPL are lower than they were before the influx of new workers.

Shifts in Labour Demand

If an industry experiences an increase in demand for its products, *ceteris paribus*, the price of goods in the industry rises. This price increase does not change the MPL for any given number of workers, but it does raise the *value* of the marginal product. With a higher price hiring more workers is now profitable.

FIGURE 18.3

A Shift in Labour Supply

When labour supply increases from S_1 to S_2, perhaps because of an influx of new workers, the equilibrium wage falls from W_1 to W_2. At this lower wage, firms hire more labour, so employment rises from L_1 to L_2. The change in the wage reflects a change in the value of the MPL: with more workers, the added output from an extra worker is smaller.

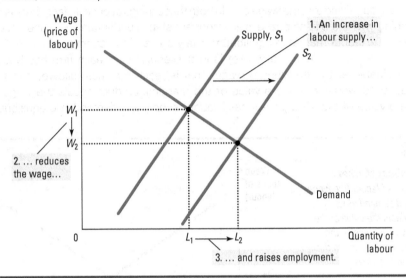

As Figure 18.4 shows, when the demand for labour shifts to the right from D_1 to D_2, the equilibrium wage rises from W_1 to W_2, and equilibrium employment rises from L_1 to L_2. Once again, the wage and the value of the MPL move together. This analysis shows that prosperity for firms in an industry is often linked to prosperity for workers in that industry.

FIGURE 18.4

A Shift in Labour Demand

When labour demand increases from D_1 to D_2, perhaps because of an increase in the price of the firm's output, the equilibrium wage rises from W_1 to W_2, and employment rises from L_1 to L_2. Again, the change in the wage reflects a change in the value of the MPL: with a higher output price, the added output from an extra worker is more valuable.

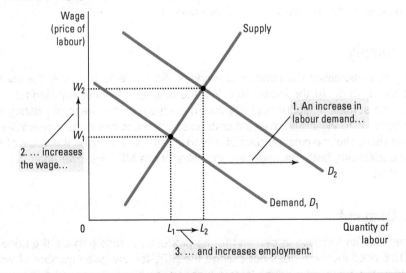

In competitive labour markets, therefore, labour supply and labour demand together determine the equilibrium wage, and shifts in the supply or demand curve for labour cause the equilibrium wage to change. At the same time, profit maximization by the firms that demand labour ensures that the equilibrium wage equals the value of the MPL.

SELF TEST How does the immigration of workers affect labour supply, labour demand, the MPL and the equilibrium wage?

Monopsony

We have built our analysis of the labour market with the tools of supply and demand. In doing so, we assumed that the labour market was competitive. That is, we assumed that there were many buyers of labour and many sellers of labour, so each buyer or seller had a negligible effect on the wage.

Imagine the labour market, however, in a small town dominated by a single large employer. That employer can exert a large influence on the going wage, and it may well use that market power to alter the outcome. Such a market in which there is a single buyer is called a *monopsony.*

A **monopsony** firm in a labour market hires fewer workers than would a competitive firm: by reducing the number of jobs available, the monopsony firm moves along the labour supply curve, reducing the wage it pays and raising its profits. Thus, both monopolists and monopsonists reduce economic activity in a market below the socially optimal level. In both cases, the existence of market power distorts the outcome and causes deadweight losses.

monopsony a market in which there is one dominant buyer and many sellers

In the real world, monopsonies are rare, although on a small scale, a number of towns in parts of Europe may be highly dependent on a major employer: a motor vehicle manufacturer, a steel works or chocolate manufacturer, for example. Other examples have been cited in relation to the plans by multinationals to expand into emerging markets. In such situations, the analysis may have to be amended to take into consideration the effect that the monopoly power of the employer has on the local labour market. In most labour markets, however, workers have many possible employers, and firms compete with one another to attract workers. In this case, the model of supply and demand is an appropriate one to use.

THE GIG ECONOMY

The development of the internet has promoted communication and connectivity in many different ways. The technology in smartphones is extremely sophisticated and has allowed innovation and entrepreneurship to generate new ways of doing business. This business is not necessarily completely new, as many of the developments that utilize connectivity technologies are based on traditional businesses, but they are taking them in different directions and improving the customer experience. For example, the growth of online retailing and the deregulation of markets has enabled firms who deliver parcels and packages to expand and improve the speed and efficiency with which they deliver parcels to customers. Customers not only receive their parcels quickly, they can track the progress of their packages from when they are despatched by the retailer, when they arrive in the delivery firm's warehouse, to when they are on the road, the anticipated time slot for delivery and who is delivering their package. Once delivered, the customer can be informed of what time it was received, who signed for it (if required), and where it was left if no one was in.

Firms that offer these types of services need highly flexible workers. Traditional contracts of work where employees are recruited on a wage or salary, and have various legal employment rights such as paid holidays, sick pay and pension contributions, are not suitable for some of the firms utilizing connectivity technologies as part of their business. The workers needed in these types of business are more like self-employed contractors of the firm rather than employees. Each employment task is like a mini-contract between firm and worker. This has resulted in the term **gig economy** to refer to a labour market in which workers do not have permanent jobs, but instead have a relationship with a firm which is characterized by short-term contracts, freelance work or zero hours contracts. The term 'gig' comes from the music industry where musicians provide a single performance. It is reputed to be derived from the word 'engagement' by jazz musicians in 1920s America.

For firms, the use of workers on these terms can mean greater flexibility for adjusting to changes in demand and can help control labour costs. For workers, the degree of independence and flexibility can be appealing. However, as with many issues in economics, the gig economy has some downsides which must be balanced against the benefits to firms and workers, and has been the subject of increasing debate. Governments have been considering the issues and looking at the extent to which employment law needs to be changed to take account of the developments in the labour market.

> **gig economy** a labour market in which workers have short-term, freelance or zero hours contracts with employers, more akin to being self-employed than employed

The Nature of the Gig Economy

The basic premise of workers in the gig economy is that they are self-employed or independent contractors. There are consequences of being defined as self-employed. Workers who are self-employed do not have the employment rights enjoyed by those who are classed as 'employed'. Employed workers in many European countries are entitled to paid holidays, to be paid the national minimum or living wage of the country they are working in, to be paid when off work through illness, and to receive the country's statutory redundancy pay. In addition, employed workers are protected against unfair dismissal. Workers in the gig economy have no such rights. Instead, they receive a payment for work carried out for the 'contractor'. They are then responsible for paying their income tax, any other employment taxes, such as National Insurance Contributions in the UK, and for making their own arrangements for their pension and any other financial protection they choose to take out.

The Benefits to Workers One of the reported benefits of working in the gig economy for individuals is the flexibility it affords. Workers are free to work as much or as little as they choose, to work when it is convenient for them, and equally to choose not to work when it is not convenient. Workers have the freedom and incentives that other self-employed people have who are running their own businesses, but for gig economy workers, the fact that they are working for contactors means they are not bearing all of the risks of running a business in the way that the contractor is.

The types of work in the gig economy include delivery work such as the delivery of fast foods, meals, parcels and packages, so called 'ride hailing' drivers (as distinct from a taxi), work doing household chores and maintenance, video production and property renting, right through to software development. Firms like Uber, Airbnb, TaskRabbit, Deliveroo, 90 Seconds, LiquidTalent and Evri are all part of the gig economy.

The Benefits to Firms Firms using workers in the gig economy can manage their workflows more effectively and manage their costs. Not only do they not have the full costs of employment, they have the flexibility to hire workers to carry out tasks as and when demand varies, and as a result can increase productivity. Because they are employing workers for particular tasks, such as carrying a passenger from one location to another, they can pay according to the task rather than the hour, and this can mean that they can legally pay workers less than the minimum wage in the country concerned, which is invariably expressed as an amount per hour.

Estimates of the numbers working in the gig economy vary, but the Chartered Institute for Professional Development (CIPD) in the UK notes that around 1.3 million people are employed in the gig economy. The UK government reported that 15 per cent, or 5 million people, are 'self-employed', which would include those working in the gig economy. It is expected that the number participating in the gig economy will continue to increase.

The Debate Over the Gig Economy

The advantages to both workers and firms of the gig economy have to be balanced by the disadvantages. The disadvantages to workers have been at the centre of the debate about the gig economy. Are these workers really self-employed? Should they be eligible for the same sort of employment rights that employed workers have? Are firms using the gig economy as a means of exploiting workers and paying low wages?

In October 2016, two UK-based Uber drivers argued that they should not be classed as self-employed, but as employed workers, at an employment tribunal. They won their case, although Uber has appealed against the decision. The tribunal noted: 'The notion that Uber in London is a mosaic of 30,000 small businesses linked by a common "platform" is to our mind faintly ridiculous.' Trades unions in the UK welcomed the decision, saying it represented greater protection for workers in this type of employment. Uber pointed to the flexibility and independence of decision making that its drivers have in organizing their own time and work commitments. Reports at the time of the decision seemed to suggest that Uber drivers themselves were split on whether the decision was a good thing or not. To meet the additional employment rights, Uber would have to charge customers more, and this could affect the business model and ultimately mean fewer jobs. Supporters of the judgement pointed to the control that Uber had over their lives in terms of what drives they do, and when they do them, making them more employed than self-employed.

The employment tribunal decision was repeated in January 2017 when an individual from London working for a courier firm, City Sprint, argued a similar case. City Sprint offered similar counter-arguments to the ruling as Uber, and also said it would appeal.

The UK government commissioned a report on the issues and in July 2017, the Taylor Report was published. Matthew Taylor was a former political strategist for Tony Blair and is Chief Executive of the Royal Society of Arts (RSA). The report was titled: *Good Work: The Taylor Review of Modern Working Practices*. The report noted that work was essential to well-being and happiness, but that it was also important that the terms under which people work are fair and help people to progress.

The report made seven recommendations. One of the main ones was that workers should be classed not as independent contractors but as 'dependent contractors'. The report noted that there is a distinction between these two terms, and that the law needed to be clearer about distinguishing between those who are genuinely self-employed and those who are dependent contractors. This, it noted, would ensure that the flexibility that is at the heart of the benefits to both firms and workers are maintained, but that workers can be treated fairly. The current state of affairs tended to be a 'one-sided flexibility'. Firms needed stronger incentives to treat workers fairly. Dependent workers would not be employees, but also not self-employed, and should be entitled to sick pay and paid holidays. Taylor's report also concluded that regulation was not necessarily the way to achieve 'better work', but responsible corporate governance and good management were also key.

The report was greeted in different ways, with trades unions welcoming the recommendations while some employment lawyers commented that the new definition of dependent contractor would merely complicate an already complex legal framework. In the United States, it has been suggested that transactions in the gig economy could be subject to a small tax which would be earmarked to help provide additional benefits for workers. This, it is argued, maintains the flexibility for firms and workers while at the same time providing benefits for workers. By supporting workers in this way, the gig economy could continue to expand and be successful.

Uber in London In the summer of 2017, Uber re-applied for its licence to operate in London. Transport for London rejected the application, stating that Uber was not a 'fit and proper' operator. The basis for the decision was centred on a number of alleged misdemeanours in the way Uber operated. This included the way the company reported serious criminal offences, the way it checked the background of its drivers for safety and security, and the alleged prevention and obfuscation of regulatory and legal checks on its operations.

Uber appealed the decision, and in June 2018 won a 15-month probationary licence to operate in the capital. Uber has also noted that it is willing to attempt to work with Transport for London and recognized that it was 'not perfect'. In March 2022, Uber came to an agreement with Transport for London which resulted in the granting of a two and a half-year private hire vehicle operator's licence.

Zero Hours Contracts

Workers on zero hours contracts and workers in the gig economy are often spoken of in the same breath, but zero hours contracts are different. As firms have sought greater labour flexibility to help manage demand and reduce costs, zero hours contracts help manage these elements of the labour market. A worker employed on a zero hours contract is offered work as and when the firm has a need. The worker can be called upon to carry out that work under the terms of the contract, but the worker does have the right to turn down the work. There is no compulsion for the firm to offer work under the contract. In addition, the firm has to pay at least the national minimum or living wage and workers under zero hours contracts are entitled to paid annual leave.

For workers, zero hours contracts give them some flexibility, because they cannot be prevented from seeking work with another employer. The fact that they can turn down work if it is not convenient provides further flexibility, although it may be the case that workers feel pressured to accept hours when offered.

In 2000, the number of workers on zero hours contracts in the UK, according to the Labour Force Survey of the Office for National Statistics (ONS), was just over 200,000 but this had risen to just over 900,000 by 2016, but fell back to 883,000 in the period April to June 2017. This represented 2.8 per cent of people in employment in the UK.

THE OTHER FACTORS OF PRODUCTION: LAND AND CAPITAL

We have seen how firms decide how much labour to hire and how these decisions determine workers' wages. At the same time that firms are hiring workers, they are also deciding about other inputs to production. These inputs include land and buildings, equipment and machinery (capital).

Equilibrium in the Markets for Land and Capital

What determines how much the owners of land and capital earn for their contribution to the production process? Before answering this question, we need to distinguish between two prices: the purchase price and the rental price. The *purchase price* of land or capital is the price a person pays to own that factor of production indefinitely. The *rental price* is the price a person pays to use that factor for a limited period of time. It is important to keep this distinction in mind because, as we will see, these prices are determined by different economic forces.

Having defined these terms, we can now apply the theory of factor demand that we developed for the labour market to the markets for land and capital. The wage is, after all, the rental price of labour. Therefore, much of what we have learned about wage determination applies also to the rental prices of land and capital. As Figure 18.5 illustrates, the rental price of land, shown in panel (a), and the rental price of capital, shown in panel (b), are determined by supply and demand. Moreover, the demand for land and capital is determined just like the demand for labour. For both land and capital, the firm increases the quantity hired until the value of the factor's marginal product equals the factor's price. Thus, the demand curve for each factor reflects the marginal productivity of that factor.

We can now explain how much income goes to labour, how much goes to landowners and how much goes to the owners of capital. As long as the firms using the factors of production are competitive and profit maximizing (important assumptions), each factor's rental price must equal the value of the marginal product for that factor: labour, land and capital each earn the value of their marginal contribution to the production process.

Now consider the purchase price of land and capital. The rental price and the purchase price are related: buyers are willing to pay more for a piece of land or capital if it produces a valuable stream of rental income. As we have just seen, the equilibrium rental income at any point in time equals the value of that factor's marginal product. Therefore, the equilibrium purchase price of a piece of land or capital depends on both the current value of the marginal product and the value of the marginal product expected to prevail in the future.

FIGURE 18.5

The Markets for Land and Capital

Supply and demand determine the compensation paid to the owners of land, as shown in panel (a), and the compensation paid to the owners of capital, as shown in panel (b). The demand for each factor, in turn, depends on the value of the marginal product of that factor.

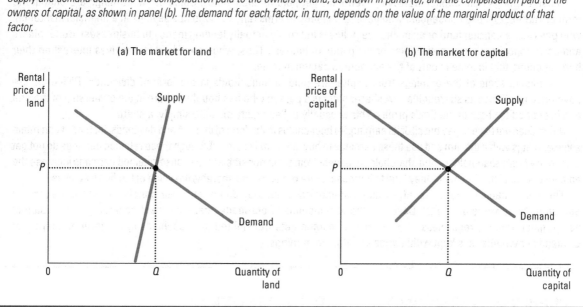

Linkages Between the Factors of Production

The price paid for any factor of production (labour, land or capital) equals the value of the marginal product of that factor. The marginal product of any factor depends on the quantity of that factor that is available. Because of diminishing marginal product, a factor in abundant supply has a low marginal product and thus a low price, and a factor in scarce supply has a high marginal product and a high price. As a result, when the supply of a factor falls, its equilibrium factor price rises and so firms' costs rise.

When the supply of any factor changes, however, the effects are not limited to the market for that factor. In most situations, factors of production are used together in a way that makes the productivity of each factor dependent on the quantities of the other factors available to be used in the production process. As a result, a change in the supply of any one factor alters the earnings of all the factors.

An event that changes the supply of any factor of production can alter the earnings of all the factors. The change in earnings of any factor can be found by analysing the impact of the event on the value of the marginal product of that factor.

FYI

What is Capital Income?

Labour income is a more familiar concept to understand: it is the wages and salaries that workers get from their employers. The income earned by capital, however, is less familiar.

In our analysis, we have been implicitly assuming that households own the economy's stock of capital (equipment, machinery, computers, warehouses and so forth) and rent it to the firms that use it. Capital income, in this case, is the rent that households receive for the use of their capital. This assumption simplified our analysis of how capital

(Continued)

owners are compensated, but it is not entirely realistic. In fact, firms usually own the capital they use and, therefore, they receive the earnings from this capital.

These earnings from capital, however, eventually get paid to households. Some of the earnings are paid in the form of interest to those households who have lent money to firms (anyone who has savings in a financial institution, who pays into a pension fund or an insurance policy is indirectly actually lending money to businesses). Bondholders and bank depositors are two examples of recipients of interest. Thus, when an individual receives interest on their bank account, that income is part of the economy's capital income.

In addition, some of the earnings from capital are paid to households in the form of dividends. Dividends are payments by a firm to its shareholders. A shareholder is a person who has bought a share in the ownership of the firm and is entitled to share in the firm's profits. This is usually called equity or, quite simply, a share.

A firm does not have to pay out all of its earnings to households in the form of interest and dividends. Instead, it can retain some earnings within the firm and use these earnings to buy additional capital. Although these retained earnings do not get paid to the firm's shareholders, the shareholders benefit from them nonetheless. Because retained earnings increase the amount of capital the firm owns, they tend to increase future earnings and, thereby, the value of the firm's equities.

These institutional details are interesting and important, but they do not alter our conclusion about the income earned by the owners of capital. Based on the assumptions of our model, capital is paid according to the value of its marginal product, regardless of whether this income gets transmitted to households in the form of interest or dividends or whether it is kept within firms as retained earnings.

IMPERFECTIONS IN THE LABOUR MARKET

Our analysis of the labour market so far has largely been based on an assumption of a competitive market. Imperfections in the market will lead to anomalies in the way in which workers are paid, and firms must face the issues and consequences that arise as a result of these imperfections. Governments pass laws and regulations aiming to reduce the effects of imperfections in the market, and firms are often the ones picking up the bill in terms of the additional costs of meeting legislation and regulation. In this section, we consider how the characteristics of workers and jobs affect labour supply, labour demand and equilibrium wages.

Compensating Differentials

The sort of jobs firms offer varies. The wage is only one of many job attributes that must be taken into account. Some jobs require few skills, and are 'easy' and safe; others might require considerable skill and experience; some may be very dull, while others can be very dangerous. The 'better' the job as gauged by these non-monetary characteristics, the more people there are who are willing (and able) to do the job at any given wage. In other words, the supply of labour for jobs requiring few skills or no experience is greater than the supply of labour for highly skilled and dangerous jobs. As a result, 'good' jobs will tend to have lower equilibrium wages than 'bad' jobs. Economists use the term **compensating differential** to refer to a difference in wages that arises from non-monetary characteristics of different jobs.

 compensating differential a difference in wages that arises to offset the non-monetary characteristics of different jobs

Human Capital

Human capital is the accumulation of investments in people. The most important type of human capital is education. Like all forms of capital, education represents an expenditure of resources at one point in time to raise productivity in the future. Unlike an investment in other forms of capital, an investment in education is tied to a specific person, and this linkage is what makes it human capital.

human capital the accumulation of investments in people, such as education and on-the-job training

Not surprisingly, workers with more human capital, on average, earn more than those with less human capital. University graduates in Europe and North America, for example, earn over their lifetimes more than those workers who end their education after secondary school. The difference tends to be even larger in less developed countries, where educated workers are in scarce supply.

Firms (the demanders of labour) are willing to pay more for the highly educated because highly educated workers have higher marginal products. Workers (the suppliers of labour) are willing to pay the cost of becoming educated only if there is a reward for doing so. In essence, the difference in wages between highly educated workers and less educated workers may be considered a compensating differential for the cost of becoming educated.

Ability, Effort and Chance

Natural ability is important for workers in all occupations. Because of heredity and upbringing, people differ in their physical and mental attributes. Some people have physical and mental strength whereas others have less of both. Some people are able to solve complex problems, others less so. Some people are outgoing, others awkward in social situations. These and many other personal characteristics determine how productive workers are and play a role in determining the wages they earn.

Closely related to ability is effort. Some people are prepared to put long hours and considerable effort into their work, whereas others are content to do what they are required to do and no more. We should not be surprised to find that those who put in more effort may be more productive and earn higher wages. To some extent, firms reward workers directly by paying people on the basis of what they produce. Sales people, for instance, are often paid based on a percentage of the sales they make. At other times, greater effort is rewarded less directly in the form of a higher annual salary or a bonus.

Chance also plays a role in determining wages. Workers in retail stores, for example, are finding that their skills are increasingly becoming redundant as new ways of shopping become more popular. Those workers affected have been in the wrong place at the wrong time.

How important are ability, effort and chance in determining wages? It is hard to say, because ability, effort and chance are hard to measure. Indirect evidence suggests that they are very important. When labour economists study wages, they relate a worker's wage to those variables that can be measured: years of schooling, years of experience, age and job characteristics. Although all of these measured variables affect a worker's wage as theory predicts, they account for less than half of the variation in wages in many economies. Because so much of the variation in wages is left unexplained, omitted variables, including ability, effort and chance, must play an important role.

An Alternative View of Education: Signalling

Earlier we discussed the human capital view of education, according to which schooling raises workers' wages because it makes them more productive. Although this view is widely accepted, some economists have proposed an alternative theory which emphasizes that firms use educational attainment as a way of sorting between high ability and low ability workers. According to this alternative view, when people earn a university degree, for instance, they do not become more productive (indeed there are often complaints that graduates leave university without the skills that business needs), but they do *signal* their high ability to prospective employers. Because it is easier for high ability people to earn a university degree than it is for low ability people, more high ability people get university degrees. As a result, it is rational for firms to interpret a university degree as a signal of ability.

In the signalling theory of education, schooling has no real productivity benefit, but the worker signals their innate productivity to employers by their willingness to spend years at school and university. In both cases, an action is being taken not for its intrinsic benefit, but because the willingness to take that action conveys private information to someone observing it.

With the human capital view, increasing educational levels for all workers would raise all workers' productivity and thereby their wages. According to the signalling view, education does not enhance productivity, so raising all workers' educational levels would not affect wages. Most likely, the truth lies somewhere between these two extremes. The benefits of education are probably a combination of the productivity enhancing effects of human capital and the productivity revealing effects of signalling. The open question is the relative size of these two effects.

Above-Equilibrium Wages: Minimum Wage Laws, Unions and Efficiency Wages

For some workers, wages are set above the level that brings supply and demand into equilibrium. Let us consider three reasons why this might be so.

The Minimum Wage Market wage rates are not always at a level which are deemed appropriate. A number of countries have adopted laws to set a minimum or living wage, including the United States, the UK and around 21 of the 27 EU states. A statutory minimum wage dictates the lowest price for labour that any employer may pay. To examine the effects of a minimum wage, we must consider the market for labour. Panel (a) of Figure 18.6 shows the labour market subject to the forces of supply and demand. Workers determine the supply of labour, and firms determine the demand. If the government doesn't intervene, the wage normally adjusts to balance labour supply and labour demand.

FIGURE 18.6

How the Minimum Wage Affects the Labour Market
Panel (a) shows a labour market in which the wage adjusts to balance labour supply and demand. Panel (b) shows the impact of a binding minimum wage. Because the minimum wage is a price floor, it causes a surplus: the quantity of labour supplied exceeds the quantity demanded. The result is unemployment.

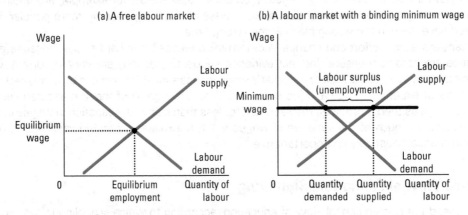

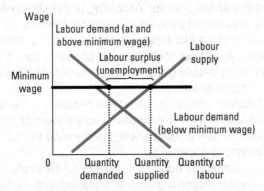

Panel (b) of Figure 18.6 shows the labour market with a minimum wage. The reason for setting a minimum wage is because there may be a perception that market wage rates for some workers are too low, and so the minimum wage is set above the equilibrium level. In panel (b), the minimum wage results in the quantity of labour supplied exceeding the quantity demanded. The result is unemployment. The minimum wage raises the incomes of those workers who have jobs, but the number of people who have work is less than the equilibrium wage shown in panel (a).

To fully understand the minimum wage, keep in mind that the economy contains not a single labour market, but many labour markets for different types of workers. The impact of the minimum wage depends on the skill and experience of the worker. Workers with high skills and much experience are not affected, because their equilibrium wages are most likely above the minimum. For these workers, the minimum wage is not binding. We would therefore expect a diagram such as that in panel (b) of Figure 18.6, where the minimum wage is above the equilibrium wage and unemployment results, to apply primarily to the market for low skilled and teenage labour. Note, however, that the *extent* of the unemployment that results depends upon the elasticities of the supply and demand for labour. It is often argued that the demand for unskilled labour is in fact likely to be highly elastic with respect to the price of labour, because employers of unskilled labour, such as fast food restaurants, usually face highly price elastic demand curves for their own product and so cannot easily pass on wage rises in the form of higher prices without seeing their revenue fall.

This is only true, however, if one firm raises its price while others do not. If all fast food companies are forced to raise prices slightly in order to pay the minimum wage to their staff, this may result in a much smaller fall in the demand for the output (e.g. burgers) of any one firm. If this is the case, then the imposition of a statutory minimum wage may actually lead to a rightward shift in the segment of the labour demand curve at or above the statutory minimum wage: a firm is able to pay the higher wage without drastically reducing its labour demand, because it can pass on the higher wage costs by charging a higher price for its product, safe in the knowledge that other firms in the industry will have to do the same and hence that it will not suffer a dramatic fall in demand for its output. In this case, as in panel (c) of Figure 18.6, although there is an increase in unemployment relative to the case with no minimum wage, this is mainly because the supply of labour is higher with the minimum wage imposed. Some workers will be attracted by the higher wage to enter the labour market: second earners, for example, or young people who otherwise would have stayed in full-time education. Businesses do face an increase in costs when having to pay the minimum wage if the minimum is higher than the market wage for those workers. Small businesses, in particular, may find the additional costs a burden and may have to defer hiring staff, let some go or, in some cases, they may find that the additional costs are too much and they have to close.

Advocates of minimum wage laws view the policy as one way to raise the income of those on the lowest incomes. They point out that workers who earn the minimum wage can afford only a meagre standard of living. They admit that it may have some adverse effects, including a possible rise in unemployment, but they believe that these effects are small and that, all things considered, a higher minimum wage makes those on lower incomes better off. In other words, they argue that the value of the benefits of a minimum wage are greater than the value of the costs, and so such a policy is worth putting into practice.

Opponents of the minimum wage contend that it is not the best way to combat poverty, since it affects only the income of those in employment and may raise unemployment. In addition, they point out that not all minimum wage workers are heads of households trying to help their families raise their overall income; some may be second or even third earners in relatively well-off households. To decide which is the more powerful argument, economists will try to find ways to measure the size of the contrasting effects, so that an informed decision can be made about the value of the benefits and the costs. This is often harder than it may at first appear, but is a crucial part of an economist's work.

Labour Unions A second reason that wages might rise above their equilibrium level is the market power of labour unions. A **union** is a worker association that bargains with employers over wages and working conditions. Unions often raise wages above the level that would prevail without a union, perhaps because they can threaten to withhold labour from the firm by calling a **strike**. Studies suggest that union workers earn about 10 to 20 per cent more than similar non-union workers.

union a worker association that bargains with employers over wages and working conditions
strike the organized withdrawal of labour from a firm by a union

Efficiency Wages A third reason for above equilibrium wages is suggested by the theory of **efficiency wages**. This theory holds that a firm can find it profitable to pay high wages because doing so increases the productivity of its workers. In particular, high wages may reduce worker turnover (hiring and training new workers is an expensive business), increase worker effort and raise the quality of workers who apply for jobs at the firm. A firm may feel it has to offer high wages in order to attract and keep the best people. If this theory is correct, then some firms may choose to pay their workers more than the equilibrium wage rate under the assumptions of perfect competition.

efficiency wages wages above the equilibrium wage paid by firms to increase worker productivity

Above equilibrium wages, whether caused by minimum wage laws, unions or efficiency wages, have similar effects on the labour market. Pushing a wage above the equilibrium level raises the quantity of labour supplied and reduces the quantity of labour demanded. The result is a surplus of labour, or unemployment.

> **SELF TEST** Define *compensating differential* and give an example. Give two reasons why more educated workers earn more than less educated workers.

CASE STUDY   Living Wage

Many European countries have introduced a minimum wage which stipulates the minimum amount that employers are legally allowed to pay workers. For many workers, the minimum wage is irrelevant as they will be earning above the minimum statutory level. The minimum wage is particularly relevant, however, for firms that tend to employ workers who are at the lower end of the pay range. For workers with limited skills or in jobs where the value of marginal product is relatively low, a minimum wage helps in boosting their earnings. For firms, however, the minimum wage can present financial challenges.

In the UK, for example, the government sets the minimum wage each April and in 2023 it was £10.42 (€11.95) for those aged 23 and over, £10.18 (€11.68) for those aged 21 to 22, £7.49 (€8.59) for those aged 18 to 20, and £5.28 (€6.06) for the under 18s and apprentices. The increase in the National Living Wage, as it is called in the UK, from 2022 for the over 23s was 9.68 per cent. This increase was much higher than the increase in average earnings in other parts of the economy. Critics pointed out that despite this seemingly generous increase, it was still not enough to help those on lower incomes. For firms, the increase put additional pressure on finances that, for many, were still weak following the pandemic and in the face of cost pressures elsewhere in the national and global economy due to supply chain problems and the conflict in Ukraine.

There is a considerable amount of publicity around the minimum wage. Representatives of those on the lowest incomes such as The Living Wage Foundation, an independent body consisting of businesses and individuals who campaign for better pay for those on the lowest incomes, argue that businesses have a responsibility to pay workers what they call a 'real living wage'. Businesses that are part of The Living Wage Foundation commit to paying their workers a 'real living wage'. In 2022, for example, the National Living Wage in the UK was £9.50 for the over 23s but the real living wage was set at £10.90 and £11.95

(Continued)

in London. This is 14.7 per cent higher than the National Living Wage. Businesses that are members of the Living Wage Foundation include well-known names such as Nestlé, Aviva, Burberry, the Nationwide, Oxfam and Ikea. In total, there are around 11,000 living wage employers in the UK.

The living wage causes heated debate on both sides as to its value and effects.

Questions

1 Think about a small business, for example a local grocery store, an independent hotel, a hairdresser and so on, that employs only a small number of workers but who must pay the minimum wage. What impact do you think such firms will face when the minimum wage rate is increased? Use the concept of marginal product and marginal value product to illustrate your answer.

2 Explain why critics of the minimum wage argue that it leads to increased unemployment. Use appropriate labour market diagrams to help illustrate your answer.

3 It is reported that a large number of the FTSE 100 companies have not volunteered to pay the real living wage. Why do you think this is?

4 If governments in the UK and Europe have a statutory minimum wage, does this mean that the neoclassical theory of distribution is one that should be consigned to history? Explain.

References: www.gov.uk/national-minimum-wage-rates (accessed 11 June 2023).
www.livingwage.org.uk/ (accessed 11 June 2023).

CONCLUSION

The theory developed in this chapter is called the *neoclassical theory of distribution*. According to the neoclassical theory, the amount paid to each factor of production depends on the supply and demand for that factor. The demand, in turn, depends on that particular factor's marginal productivity. In equilibrium, each factor of production earns the value of its marginal contribution to the production of goods and services.

At this point you can use the theory to answer the question that began this chapter: why are computer programmers paid more than fuel station attendants? It is because programmers can produce a good of greater market value than can a fuel station attendant. People are willing to pay relatively high prices for a good computer game, but they are willing to pay little to have their car hand washed at the supermarket. The wages of these workers reflect the market prices of the goods they produce.

In competitive markets, workers earn a wage equal to the value of their marginal contribution to the production of goods and services. There are, however, many things that affect the value of the marginal product. Firms pay more for workers who are more talented, more diligent, more experienced and more educated because these workers are more productive.

SUMMARY

- The economy's income is distributed in the markets for the factors of production. The three most important factors of production are labour, land and capital.

- The demand for factors, such as labour, is a derived demand that comes from firms that use the factors to produce goods and services. Competitive, profit-maximizing firms hire each factor up to the point at which the value of the marginal product of the factor equals its price.

- The supply of labour arises from individuals' trade-offs between work and leisure. An upward sloping labour supply curve means that people respond to an increase in the wage by enjoying less leisure and working more hours.

- The price paid to each factor adjusts to balance the supply and demand for that factor. Because factor demand reflects the value of the marginal product of that factor, in equilibrium each factor is compensated according to its marginal contribution to the production of goods and services.

- Because factors of production are used together, the marginal product of any one factor depends on the quantities of all factors that are available. As a result, a change in the supply of one factor alters the equilibrium earnings of all the factors.

- Changes in technology and the development of the internet have led to businesses changing the relationships they have with workers. Workers hired 'by the job' have become a feature of the gig economy.

- The gig economy has both advantages and disadvantages for both workers and firms. In many countries, governments are trying to assess the impact of the gig economy and amend legislation to adjust to the different circumstances it raises.

- Workers earn different wages for many reasons. To some extent, wage differentials compensate workers for job attributes. Other things being equal, workers in hard, unpleasant jobs get paid more than workers in easy, pleasant jobs.

- Workers with more human capital get paid more than workers with less human capital. The return on accumulating human capital is high and has increased in the twenty-first century.

- Although years of education, experience and job characteristics affect earnings as theory predicts, there is much variation in earnings that cannot be explained by things that economists can measure. The unexplained variation in earnings is largely attributable to natural ability, effort and chance.

- Some economists have suggested that more educated workers earn higher wages, not because education raises productivity but because workers with high natural ability use education as a way to signal their high ability to employers. If this signalling theory is correct, then increasing the educational attainment of all workers would not raise the overall level of wages.

- Wages are sometimes pushed above the level that brings supply and demand into balance. Three reasons for above-equilibrium wages are minimum wage laws, unions and efficiency wages.

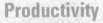

IN THE NEWS

Productivity

Productivity is a measure of the output per unit of input, per period of time. It is often cited as being one, if not the most, important factor in determining standards of living in a country. In our discussion of the neoclassical theory of distribution, productivity was an implied key factor in how firms decide to employ units of labour, or indeed, any factor of production. In recent years there has been some concern expressed that productivity levels in some economies have stalled and has been termed 'the productivity puzzle'. According to data provided by accounting firm PwC, the average growth in output per worker in the UK in the ten years prior to the 2007–2009 Financial Crisis was 2.0 per cent, but since the crisis the growth in output per worker has only averaged 0.6 per cent. If output per worker was increased to levels seen in Germany, for example, the PwC report estimates that UK GDP would increase by £180 billion (€207 billion) a year.

(Continued)

Figures from the UK Parliament show productivity measured as GDP per hour in US dollars in 2021. The UK was ranked fourth in the list of G7 countries. Productivity per hour in 2021 in the UK was $68, whereas in Germany it

was $81 per hour and in the United States, $85 per hour. In Italy the figure was $65 per hour and $62 and $49 per hour in Canada and Japan, respectively. Overall, productivity in the UK has been rising since 2000 albeit it took a significant downturn in 2020 due to lockdowns and the pandemic. In quarter three of 2022, productivity was around 1.4 per cent higher than in the same quarter in 2021 and around 1.4 per cent higher than the quarter four pre-pandemic level in 2019. However, many analysts see this growth rate as being too slow and a contributory factor to the UK's sluggish economic performance in the early 2020s. The Office for National Statistics shows data on labour productivity in the UK between 2012 and 2021 having risen by around 5.6 per cent. The conundrum facing policy makers is how to increase productivity. Investment in capital and infrastructure, improved education, focusing on skills, and better adoption of technologies are all potential options for improving productivity, but implementing these measures is easier said than done!

One of the challenges facing any economy is how to maximize productivity.

Questions

1 Explain why high levels of productivity are associated with improvements in a country's standard of living.
2 A trade union is in dispute with employers over pay. A rising cost of living has prompted the union to demand a pay rise for its members of 3 per cent above inflation, which is currently standing at 9 per cent. In negotiating with the union, the employer insists that productivity is considered as part of any negotiation on pay. Why might the employer insist on this as part of any pay deal?
3 Assume that in question 2, a deal is struck which gives workers in that industry a pay rise of 11 per cent but with measures in place to improve productivity by 15 per cent. What might be the effect on the supply of labour in that industry as a result of the agreement?
4 Assume that the increase in pay and productivity in question 2 takes place. How would this change impact on the marginal product of other factors used in the industry?
5 The article notes different policies that can be adopted to help improve productivity. Why do you think implementing these policies is 'easier said than done'?

References: www.pwc.co.uk/economic-services/ukeo/ukeo-november-2019-productivity-puzzle.pdf (accessed 11 June 2023).
https://commonslibrary.parliament.uk/research-briefings/sn02791/ (accessed 11 June 2023).
www.ons.gov.uk/employmentandlabourmarket/peopleinwork/labourproductivity/articles/ukproductivityintroduction/2022-10-07 (accessed 11 June 2023).

QUESTIONS FOR REVIEW

1 Explain how a firm's production function is related to its MPL, how a firm's MPL is related to the value of its marginal product, and how a firm's value of marginal product is related to its demand for labour.
2 Give one example of a factor that could shift the demand curve for labour to the left and one that could shift the demand curve of labour to the right, and show the effect on the wage rate and number of people employed of the changes. Use a supply and demand diagram to help illustrate your answer.
3 Give one example of a factor that could shift the supply curve for labour to the left and one that could shift the supply curve of labour to the right, and show the effect on the wage rate and number of people employed of the changes. Use a supply and demand diagram to help illustrate your answer.
4 Explain how the wage can adjust to balance the supply and demand for labour while simultaneously equalling the value of the MPL.

5 If the population of Belgium suddenly grew because of a large immigration, what would you expect to happen to wages? What would happen to the rents earned by the owners of land and capital?

6 What is meant by the term 'the gig economy'. What are the main advantages and disadvantages to firms and workers of the gig economy?

7 Why do divers employed by oil firms to survey, inspect and maintain oil rigs get paid more than other workers with similar amounts of education?

8 How might education raise a worker's wage without raising the worker's productivity?

9 Give three reasons why a worker's wage might be above the level that balances supply and demand.

10 Assume that a firm uses capital equipment that is dated and far less productive than modern capital equipment used by its rivals. How might this affect the marginal productivity of capital and labour in the firm and the wages of workers at the firm?

PROBLEMS AND APPLICATIONS

1 Suppose that the government proposes a new law aimed at reducing health care costs: all citizens are required to eat one apple daily.

   a. How would this apple a day law affect the demand and equilibrium price of apples?
   b. How would the law affect the marginal product and the value of the marginal product of apple pickers?
   c. How would the law affect the demand and equilibrium wage for apple pickers?

2 Show the effect of each of the following events on the market for labour in the smartphone manufacturing industry.

   a. The government buys smartphones pre-loaded with all their course materials for all university students.
   b. More university students graduate in engineering and computer science.
   c. Smartphone firms build new manufacturing factories.

3 Your enterprising uncle opens a book shop that employs seven people. The employees are paid €10 per hour and a book sells for an average of €17 each. If your uncle is maximizing his profit, what is the value of the marginal product of the last worker he hired? What is that worker's marginal product?

4 Suppose a harsh winter in Normandy destroys part of the French apple crop.

   a. Explain what happens to the price of apples and the marginal product of apple pickers as a result of the freeze. Can you say what happens to the demand for apple pickers? Why or why not?
   b. Suppose the price of apples doubles and the marginal product falls by 30 per cent. What happens to the equilibrium wage of apple pickers?
   c. Suppose the price of apples rises by 30 per cent and the marginal product falls by 50 per cent. What happens to the equilibrium wage of apple pickers?

5 In recent years, the UK has experienced a significant inflow of capital in the form of direct investment, especially from the Far East.

   a. Using a diagram of the UK capital market, show the effect of this inflow on the rental price of capital in the UK and on the quantity of capital in use.
   b. Using a diagram of the UK labour market, show the effect of the capital inflow on the average wage paid to UK workers.

6 Suppose that labour is the only input used by a perfectly competitive firm that can hire workers for €150 per day. The firm's production function is as follows:

Days of labour	Units of output
0	0
1	7
2	13
3	19
4	25
5	28
6	29

Each unit of output sells for €110. Plot the firm's demand for labour. How many days of labour should the firm hire? Show this point on your graph.

7 Assume that the supply of labour in a particular industry is determined by a union of workers.

  a. Explain why the situation faced by a labour union may resemble the situation faced by a monopoly firm.
  b. The goal of a monopoly firm is to maximize profits. Is there an analogous goal for labour unions?
  c. Now extend the analogy between monopoly firms and unions. How do you suppose that the wage set by a union compares with the wage in a competitive market? How do you suppose employment differs in the two cases?
  d. What other goals might unions have that make them different from monopoly firms?

8 Assume that a government announces an increase in the minimum wage beginning in the April of the following year. How might firms who employ workers on minimum wages be affected and how might they respond to the new wage level?

9 A minimum wage law distorts the market for low-wage labour. To reduce this distortion, some economists advocate a two-tiered minimum wage system, with a regular minimum wage for adult workers and a lower, 'sub-minimum' wage for teenage workers. Give two reasons why a single minimum wage might distort the labour market for teenage workers more than it would the market for adult workers.

10 Imagine that someone were to offer you a choice: you could spend four years studying at the world's best university, but you would have to keep your attendance there a secret. Or you could be awarded an official degree from the world's best university, but you could not actually attend (although no one need ever know this). Which choice do you think would enhance your future earnings more? What does your answer say about the debate over signalling versus human capital in the role of education?

19 FINANCIAL MARKETS

SOURCES OF BUSINESS FINANCE

Businesses, whether small or large, new or existing, require funds to invest in the purchase of factor inputs. An individual entrepreneur setting up a hairdressing salon will need to fund premises, chairs, wash basins, a till, mirrors, chemicals and equipment such as scissors, trolleys and razors among other inputs. A large business manufacturing chemicals must purchase plant and equipment, computer systems, buildings, chemical ingredients, vessels and containers, office space, transport equipment and testing laboratories.

The funds needed to purchase these inputs must come from somewhere. Individuals running small businesses might use savings or borrow money from a bank or from a friend or relative. Many businesses, both small and large, will raise the funds they need by convincing someone to provide the money for the business in exchange for a share of future profits. In either case, the investment in inputs is being financed by someone else's saving. In many economies, there are people who do not spend all their income and set aside the remainder as savings. At the same time, there will be people who borrow to finance investments in new and growing businesses. The aims of each of these two groups are different. Savers may want to defer current spending to provide income in the future and look for a return on their savings to provide a future stream of income. Borrowers need funds immediately to finance investment in inputs. These two groups are brought together by financial markets. **Financial markets** consist of those institutions in the economy that help to match one person's saving with another person's investment.

financial markets financial institutions through which savers can directly provide funds to borrowers

This chapter examines how firms can access funds for investment and how financial markets work.

New Business Start-Ups

A significant practical problem for a new business is raising sufficient initial finance to successfully launch the business. Even with a convincing business plan, the risk attached to new business start-ups can make potential investors wary of committing their funds. This can make it especially difficult for a new business to get the funds needed to get started.

A new business requires finance for two main purposes:

- Purchase of premises and equipment. Any business, whatever its size, will need to have some equipment and a base to begin trading.
- **Working capital** is the cash needed to keep the business working day to day, pay bills and so on. Many new businesses underestimate the importance of having sufficient cash for working capital and quickly find themselves short of cash when revenues are slow to come in. In some cases, it might be many months from the original setup to the time when cash from revenue starts to come into the business.

We can broadly classify the way in which a business will use finance in two ways:

- **Capital expenditure** is the money spent on purchasing fixed assets such as buildings, machinery and vehicles. Capital expenditure adds to the value of the company.
- **Revenue expenditure** is money used to help generate sales such as stock purchases, wages and so on. Revenue expenditure does not add fixed value to the company.

We will look at the main ways in which a business can raise money.

working capital the cash needed to keep the business working day to day
capital expenditure the money spent on fixed assets
revenue expenditure money used to help generate sales

Types of Business Finance

Ordinary Share Capital Private and public limited companies can raise finance through the sale of shares in the business. A share is a legal right to part ownership of the business and a claim on its future profits. For a private limited company, there needs to be a minimum of one shareholder and a maximum of 50. Public limited companies (PLCs) can issue shares to the general public. This allows them to be able to raise large sums of money. If a member of the general public owns shares in a listed PLC, they are able to trade them on a stock exchange, which provides the facility for the purchase and sale of shares. When share ownership is transferred through these exchanges, the company whose shares are being traded is not directly affected. The role of a stock exchange is to bring together those who wish to sell shares and those who wish to buy shares.

While raising finance in this way does give access to greater amounts of money, there are some drawbacks. The cost of planning and implementing a share issue can be expensive and time consuming. Specialist organizations such as merchant or investment banks might handle such a share issue on behalf of the company. These banks charge a fee for the service they provide. There are a number of legal requirements to be fulfilled in this process, and this can make such a method difficult.

For example, Typical plc is planning on setting up a new business venture in a related but different market from its existing one. The business plan and market research have all been carried out, and the sum needed to finance the new venture is €150 million. The company has decided to raise the funds through a new share issue. It has offered existing ordinary shareholders the opportunity of buying additional shares, and it will also be offering the shares on the stock exchange. They have hired an investment bank to organize the share sale for them. In addition, the company's solicitors have been drafting the agreements and contracts, and attending to the regulations that govern new share issues. Typical produced a prospectus to outline details of the share offer, to give information to prospective investors, and has given notice in the national press. The whole project has taken two years to plan and has cost the firm over €1 million. However, Typical is confident that it will be able to sell all the shares it is planning to issue. Even if it does not, the advantage in hiring an investment company is that it will underwrite the issue. That means that they will agree to buy any unsold shares. As a result, Typical will be able to raise the money it needs on time to get the business started as planned.

Loan Capital Businesses, large and small, will borrow money from banks to finance a start-up. In many cases, the loan will form part of the finance raised but not all of it. We will look at two main types of loan capital: bank loans and overdrafts.

A bank loan is a common form of start-up business finance. Most of the main high street banks will have a team of people working specifically on supporting businesses and managing business accounts. The size of a bank loan will be dependent on a variety of factors. The bank will want to consider the risks involved. These will include: the likelihood that the borrower will be able to pay back a loan, the type of business venture the loan is for, the quality of the planning that has gone into the application and the clients' banking history.

A bank loan is usually repaid monthly over a number of years. It can be medium or long term, and incurs interest charges. The interest payable can be either fixed or variable. With a variable rate loan, the interest rate may change in line with decisions made by central banks. If central banks change the rate at which they are prepared to lend to the banking system, it affects the structure of interest rates throughout the system. If the Bank of England, for example, raises interest rates, a business's interest payments will also rise: usually about a month after the announcement by the Bank. If rates are rising steadily over a period of time, this can make a significant difference to the costs of a business and to the viability of investment plans. This is something businesses must consider when taking out a loan. In the same way, a business might find its costs falling if there is a period where central banks are reducing interest rates.

When a business negotiates a fixed interest loan, they will be able to plan more effectively, and have a greater degree of certainty about their on-going costs. However, some loans only have a fixed rate for a set period. When that period ends the applicable rate could be quite a different rate from the fixed rate. This could be a major shock to the cash flow of the business.

Bank loans are relatively popular and easy to access. However, banks usually require some form of security on the loan. This is some asset which shows the bank that the borrower is serious about the loan and understands the consequences. Banks ask for security so that in the event the loan cannot be repaid, the asset put up as security can be sold to help meet the obligations the business has entered into. Assets which might be put up as security against the loan might be a building or, in the case of a sole trader, a personal asset such as a house. If the business is unable to repay the loan, the bank will seize this asset to cover its loan. This means that sole traders, who have unlimited liability, do have to think very carefully before committing themselves.

An overdraft is effectively a short-term bank loan. A bank will allow a business to withdraw from its account more money than it has deposited. Overdrafts are often used to cover cash shortages, so a business may be overdrawn only for a matter of days. Interest is paid only when the account is overdrawn. An overdraft is a flexible way for businesses to borrow small sums of money as and when required. The bank will usually agree a limit for the overdraft above which the business should not go. Businesses that do breach this limit are likely to be charged a higher fee, and also higher interest on the excess. Over a period of time, if the business cannot show that it can control its cash flow and keep within the overdraft, the bank may well withdraw the facility, or at the very least, want to have some serious discussions with the business.

Both loans and overdrafts tend to attract higher rates of interest. In many cases, small businesses might face very high rates of interest for loans and overdrafts. The riskier the business proposition is in the eyes of the bank, the higher the interest rate is likely to be.

For example, Emma is thinking of starting a business providing manicures and nail art. She has found a small shop in a town centre that is available for rent which would provide the ideal accommodation for her business. She has prepared a business plan and has approached her bank's business manager for a loan of €40,000 to help pay for some of the fixtures and fittings she requires for the shop. She has also asked for an overdraft facility to be arranged for €5,000. The bank has looked closely at her business plan and especially her projected cash flow figures. The bank is concerned that she has been over-confident in her revenue projections, although it believes the basic business idea is sound. Emma knows that the normal interest rate on loans for things like cars is 7.5 per cent and she has based her cost projections for the loan on this figure.

She had a bit of a shock when she had her meeting with the bank. It said that it would only be prepared to lend her €30,000, and that the interest rate would be 12.5 per cent. In addition, it was only prepared to offer an overdraft of €2,500, and the interest rate on this would be 15 per cent. That was very different from what she had expected. Emma had to go away and re-think and re-work her projections, as well as work out how to raise the additional €10,000 she needed. The bank had told her that if she could put up some form of security for at least €50,000, then it might be able to accommodate her original request. Having only just bought a ground floor flat, and getting sorted out in life, Emma was not keen to risk losing her home. Not only that, she was advised by the bank that she could also risk losing her business and personal assets to the bank if she was not able to repay her debt. She had some hard thinking to do in the coming weeks!

Venture Capital Venture capitalists are specialist finance providers. If a business is unable to raise sufficient funds, venture capital is often used. Venture capitalists usually invest in smaller, risky ventures and do not ask for security. Rather, they will loan a business money in return for a share of business ownership or of any eventual profits. Venture capital is capital contributed at an early stage in the development of a new enterprise, which may have a significant chance of failure, but also a significant chance of providing above average returns, especially where the provider of the capital expects to have some influence over the direction of the enterprise. Venture capital can be a high-risk strategy.

Business Angels Business angels are informal investors who are wealthy and entrepreneurial individuals looking to invest in new and growing businesses in return for a share of the equity. They usually have considerable experience of running businesses that they can place at the disposal of the companies in which they invest. Business angels invest at all stages of business development, but predominantly in start-up and early stage businesses.

The general profile of a business angel-style of relationship is that:

● The enterprise looking to raise between €10,000 and €600,000.
● The entrepreneur is prepared to give up some of the equity in the business and allow an investor to take a 'hands-on' role.
● The business has the potential to grow sufficiently to provide the business angel with a return on investment.
● The entrepreneur can offer the business angel an 'exit' (for example, through a trade sale or the repurchase of their equity stake) at some future date.

For example, Curtly Adams had an idea for a new business. He had prepared a business plan and visited his bank to get a loan to help start up. He was prepared to put in £40,000 of his own money, but needed another £120,000. He thought he had everything planned, and had offered his three-bedroomed house as security. He was therefore staggered when he read the bank's letter refusing to grant him a loan. The reason, it said, was that it felt the risk was too great that the business would not be a success. He tried three other banks but they all gave the same response.

Curtly's bank business adviser explained that his idea was indeed risky, but that he might try contacting the British Venture Capital Association (BVCA). Through its website, he identified a member and made an appointment to see them. The meeting was very productive. The BVCA pointed out that it was not a last resort of finance for a new business, but simply a different way of securing finance. It pointed to a number of advantages. If an agreement was reached, it did not always require security, and therefore took on the same risk as he did. The BVCA was in it for the long term: a bank's interest might be limited to the period of the loan. The return to the venture capitalist was not interest payments, but the success and profitability of the business and therefore they had an interest in making sure Curtly had all the support he needed. Curtly did have to accept that the venture capitalist would expect to have some say in the running of the business. This did reduce the amount of independence he had, but at the same time provided him with experience, skills and expertise that could be a real benefit in making sure the business was a success. Curtly was also told that he would have to convince the venture capitalist that there would be some form of exit for them. This might be in the form of a future management buyout, the ability to sell shares to another investor or another business, or possibly a future stock market listing.

Personal Sources Many people will start-up a business using their own money as the source of finance, or at least as part of the financing of the start-up. Such sources can include the personal savings of an individual, an inheritance, the proceeds of selling another business, or a redundancy settlement. Individuals might also ask friends and family if they will invest in the business. In such cases, it is important that the individual makes it very clear to the investor what the risks are and what the terms and conditions of the investment would be.

For example, Mike had been working as a technical engineer for a motor manufacturer for 25 years and had built up a considerable expertise in his field and was widely respected. However, when the business had to close due to the pressure of competition from China and Japan, Mike found himself redundant. Due to the number of years he had been with the company and the generous redundancy package they had offered, Mike had some time to be able to consider his next step. At 45, he knew that this was an important decision in his life. He looked around for jobs, but many of them paid less than he was earning before and did not fully make use of his skills. The more he looked, the more he felt that he could set himself up in business acting as a consultant for other engineering firms. He decided to use the €25,000 lump sum payment from his redundancy, which he had initially put into a savings account, as the main source of funds for the new venture. He was also able to get a further €15,000 backing from three contacts he had from his previous work. They knew how good Mike was at his job and believed he could make a success from his idea. The €40,000 was sufficient to be able to rent a small office and to equip himself to begin his new life.

FINANCIAL INSTITUTIONS IN THE ECONOMY

At the broadest level, the financial system moves the economy's scarce resources from savers, who could include individuals and businesses, to borrowers (people who spend more than they earn). Firms represent a significant group of these borrowers. In capitalist economic systems, savers supply their money to the financial system with the expectation that they will get it back with interest at a later date. Firms demand money from the financial system with the knowledge that they will be required to pay it back with interest at a later date. We will be exploring the workings of financial markets in a capitalist system. Not all firms will access funds through a capitalist market system. There is an increase in the role of Islamic finance, where the concept of interest is not part of the interaction between savers and borrowers. We will provide a brief outline of Islamic finance, but our main focus will be on capitalist financial markets.

Financial Markets

The institutions making up financial markets are the means through which a person who wants to save can directly supply funds to a person who wants to borrow. Two of the most important financial markets in capitalist economies are the bond market and the stock market.

The Bond Market When large corporations, national government, or local governments need to borrow to finance the purchase of a factory, jet fighter or school, for example, they often do so by issuing bonds. When BP, the energy company for example, wants to borrow to finance a major new solar development project, it can borrow directly from the public. It can do this by selling bonds. A **bond** is a certificate of indebtedness that specifies the obligations of the borrower to the holder of the bond. The buyer of a bond gives their money to BP in exchange for a promise of interest and eventual repayment of the amount borrowed (called the *principal*). The buyer can hold the bond until maturity or can sell the bond at an earlier date to someone else. A bond is an IOU. It identifies the time at which the loan will be repaid, called the *date of maturity*, and the rate of interest that will be paid periodically (called the *coupon*) until the loan matures.

> **bond** a certificate of indebtedness

Two characteristics of bonds are most important.

The first is a bond's *term,* the length of time until the bond matures. Some bonds have short terms, such as a few months, while others have terms as long as 30 years. The UK government has even issued more than one bond that never matures, called a *perpetuity.* This bond pays interest forever, but the principal is never repaid. The interest rate on a bond depends, in part, on its term. Long-term bonds are riskier than short-term bonds because holders of long-term bonds must wait longer for repayment of the principal. If a holder of a long-term bond needs their money earlier than the distant date of maturity, they have no choice but to sell the bond to someone else, perhaps at a reduced price. To compensate for this risk, long-term bonds usually (but not always) pay higher interest rates than short-term bonds.

The second important characteristic of a bond is its *credit risk,* the probability that the borrower will fail to pay some of the interest or principal. Such a failure to pay is called a *default.* Borrowers can (and sometimes do) default on their loans. When bond buyers perceive that the probability of default is high, they demand a higher interest rate to compensate them for this risk. Some government bonds are considered a safe credit risk, such as those from Germany, for example, and tend to pay low interest rates. Others are much riskier and the interest rate attached to these bonds is high, for example the government bonds issued by Greece, Portugal, Italy and Spain in 2011–2013. Financially shaky corporations raise money by issuing *junk bonds,* which pay very high interest rates; in recent years, some countries' debt has been graded as 'junk'. Sometimes, these bonds are referred to euphemistically but less graphically as *below investment grade bonds.* Buyers of bonds can judge credit risk by checking with various private agencies, such as Standard & Poor's, which rate the credit risk of different bonds.

The bond market brings together buyers and sellers of bonds. Bond buyers may be purchasing bonds as a means of saving for the future. Assume that an individual buys a bond with a €1,000 principal with a term of 10 years and a coupon of 3.5 per cent. The individual can keep the bond for the full term and take the interest of €35 each year and when the bond matures, receive the principal of €1,000 from the borrower. If our individual decided they wanted to sell their bond, the price they would get for it would be dependent on the demand and supply of that particular bond in the market. Demand for bonds will be determined by the returns that the bond will provide in relation to returns that could be provided by placing those funds elsewhere. The price of a bond in the market could be higher or lower than the principal. The yield of a bond (in simple terms) is given by the coupon divided by the price multiplied by 100. The price is quoted as a percentage of the principal:

$$\text{Yield} = \frac{\text{Coupon}}{\text{Price}} \times 100$$

Assume that our bond holder needs to access some cash quickly and decides to sell their bond. They sell the bond for €995. The yield on this bond is:

$$(35/995) \times 100 = 3.52\%$$

If the bond holder was able to sell the bond for €1,050, then the yield would be:

$$(35/1,050) \times 100 = 3.3\%$$

Notice that when the price of a second-hand bond rises, the yield falls. There is an inverse relationship between the price of a bond and its yield. Bond prices and yields are affected by the demand and supply of existing bonds in the market, the issue of new bonds, the likelihood of the bond issuer defaulting and the interest rates on other securities. A new bond issue will also be affected by these factors. If current interest rates are relatively high, new bond issues will require a coupon which will be competitive.

The Stock Market Another way for BP to raise funds for its solar development project is to sell stock in the company. **Shares** represents ownership in a firm and are, therefore, a claim on the future profits the firm makes. For example, if BP sells a total of 1,000,000 shares, each share represents ownership of 1/1,000,000 of the business. A share is also commonly referred to as a *stock* or *equity.* These terms can be used more or less interchangeably.

> **share** (or stock or equity) a claim to partial ownership in a firm

The sale of shares to raise money is called *equity finance*, whereas the sale of bonds is called *debt finance.* Although businesses use both equity and debt finance to raise money for new investments, shares and bonds are very different. The owner of BP shares is a part owner of BP; the owner of a BP bond is a creditor of the corporation. If BP is very profitable, the shareholders enjoy the benefits of these profits, whereas the bondholders get only the interest on their bonds. If BP runs into financial difficulty, the bondholders are paid what they are due before shareholders receive anything at all. Compared to bonds, shares offer the holder both higher risk and potentially higher return.

After a business issues shares to the public, these shares trade among shareholders on organized stock exchanges. In these transactions, the business itself receives no money when its shares change hands. Most of the world's countries have their own stock exchanges on which the shares of national and international companies trade.

The prices at which shares trade on stock exchanges are determined by the supply and demand for the shares in these companies. Because shares represent ownership in a business, the demand for a share (and thus its price) reflects investors' perceptions of the business's future profitability. When investors become optimistic about a company's future, they raise their demand for its shares and so bid up the price. Conversely, when investors come to expect a company's profitability to be declining the price of a share tends to fall.

Various stock indices are available to monitor the overall level of stock prices for any particular stock market. A *stock index* is computed as an average of a group of share prices. The Dow Jones Industrial Average has been computed regularly for the New York Stock Exchange since 1896. It is now based on the prices of the shares of 30 major US companies. The Financial Times Stock Exchange (FTSE) 100 Index is based on the top 100 companies (according to the total value of their shares) listed on the London Stock Exchange (LSE), while the FTSE All-Share Index is based on all companies listed on the LSE. Indices of prices on the Frankfurt stock market, based on 30 and 100 companies respectively, are the DAX 30 and DAX 100. The NIKKEI 225 (or just plain NIKKEI Index) is based on the largest 225 companies, in terms of market value of shares, traded on the Tokyo Stock Exchange.

Because share prices reflect expected profitability, stock indices are watched closely as possible indicators of future economic conditions.

Financial Intermediaries

Financial intermediaries are financial institutions through which savers can indirectly provide funds to borrowers. The term *intermediary* reflects the role of these institutions in standing between savers and borrowers. Here we consider two of the most important financial intermediaries: banks and investment funds.

> **financial intermediaries** financial institutions through which savers can indirectly provide funds to borrowers

Banks If the owners of a small restaurant want to finance an expansion of their business, they probably take a strategy quite different from BP. Unlike BP, a small business person would find it difficult to raise funds in the bond and stock markets. Most buyers of shares and bonds prefer to buy those issued by larger, more familiar companies. The small business person, therefore, most likely finances their business expansion with a loan from a bank.

Banks are the financial intermediaries with which people are most familiar. A primary function of banks is to take in deposits from people who want to save and use these deposits to make loans to people who want to borrow. Banks pay depositors interest on their deposits and charge borrowers slightly higher interest on their loans. The difference between these rates of interest covers the banks' costs and returns some profit to the owners of the banks.

Besides being financial intermediaries, banks play a second important role in the economy: they facilitate purchases of goods and services by allowing people to transfer money from their account to the account of the person or corporation they are buying something from. In other words, banks help create a special asset that people can use as a *medium of exchange*. A medium of exchange is an item that people can easily use to engage in transactions. A bank's role in providing a medium of exchange distinguishes it from many other financial institutions. Shares and bonds, like bank deposits, are a possible *store of value* for the wealth that people have accumulated in past saving.

Investment Funds An **investment fund** is an institution that sells shares to the public and uses the proceeds to buy a selection, or *portfolio*, of various types of shares, bonds or both shares and bonds. The shareholder of the investment fund accepts all the risk and return associated with the portfolio. If the value of the portfolio rises, the shareholder benefits; if the value of the portfolio falls, the shareholder suffers the loss. These intermediaries are important in providing the lifeblood of finance to businesses.

> **investment fund** an institution that sells shares to the public and uses the proceeds to buy a portfolio of stocks and bonds

We know that firms will raise finance in different ways and through different intermediaries. The decision about what to borrow, how much to borrow, from whom, for how long and at what price are key decisions that businesses need to take at some point in their existence, if not at the very outset. Invariably, a business will borrow money to finance activity which will only begin to yield streams of income at some point in the future. For example, a pharmaceutical company may spend many years researching and developing a new drug which may bring returns for a limited period of time, depending on whether it is able to take out a patent to protect its discovery.

Businesses take decisions on such investments on the basis of whether the expected returns over a period of time are greater than the cost of the investment and, in many cases, on the size of the difference between the expected return and the cost. For example, if an investment brought a return of 2 per cent over a 10-year period, a firm may decide that the return is not enough, but would go ahead with the investment if the expected return was 8 per cent over the same period.

One important factor here is time. Sums of money are not worth the same at different time periods. Firms not only make decisions based on borrowing money at a rate of interest today to gain returns over a period of time in the future, but on what the risk involved in making that decision might be. Such decisions might have a significant impact on the value of a company. We are now going to turn to these three topics. First, we discuss how to compare sums of money at different points in time. Second, we discuss how to manage risk. Third, we build on our analysis of time and risk to examine what determines the value of an asset, such as a share of stock.

> **SELF TEST** What factors might determine the source of funds for investment in inputs for a business?

MEASURING THE TIME VALUE OF MONEY

Imagine that someone offered to give you €100 today or €100 in 10 years. Which would you choose? Getting €100 today is better, because you can always deposit the money in a bank, still have it in 10 years, and earn interest on the €100 along the way. The lesson: money today is more valuable than the same amount of money in the future.

Now consider a harder question: imagine that someone offered you €100 today or €200 in 10 years. Which would you choose? To answer this question, you need some way to compare sums of money from different points in time. Economists do this with a concept called **present value**. The present value of any future sum of money is the amount today that would be needed, at current interest rates, to produce that future sum.

> **present value** the amount of money today that would be needed to produce, using prevailing interest rates, a given future amount of money

To learn how to use the concept of present value, let us work through a couple of examples.

Question: If a business put €100 in a bank account today, how much will it be worth in N years? That is, what will be the **future value** of this €100?

Answer: Let us use r to denote the interest rate expressed in decimal form (so an interest rate of 5 per cent means $r = 0.05$). Suppose that interest is paid annually and that the interest paid remains in the bank account to earn more interest, a process called **compounding**. Then the €100 will become:

$(1 + r)$ €100	after one year
$(1 + r)(1 + r)$ €100	after two years
$(1 + r)(1 + r)(1 + r)$ €100	after three years
$(1 + r)^N$ €100	after N years

For example, if we are investing at an interest rate of 5 per cent for 10 years, then the future value of the €100 will be $(1.05)^{10} \times$ €100, which is €163.

> **future value** the amount of money in the future that an amount of money today will yield, given prevailing interest rates
> **compounding** the accumulation of a sum of money in, say, a bank account where the interest earned remains in the account to earn additional interest in the future

Question: Now suppose the business was going to earn €200 in N years. What is the *present value* of this future payment? That is, how much would the business have to deposit in a bank right now to yield €200 in N years?

Answer: To answer this question, we turn the previous answer on its head. In the first question, we computed a future value from a present value by *multiplying* by the factor $(1 + r)^N$. To compute a present value from a future value, we *divide* by the factor $(1 + r)^N$. Thus, the present value of €200 in N years is €200/$(1 + r)^N$. For example, if the interest rate is 5 per cent, the present value of €200 in 10 years is €200/1.05^{10} = €123. €123 would have to be deposited into a bank at an interest rate of 5 per cent to generate a return of €200 in 10 years' time.

This illustrates the general formula: if r is the interest rate, then an amount X to be received in N years has present value of $X/(1 + r)^N$.

Let us now return to our earlier question: should you choose €100 today or €200 in 10 years? We can infer from our calculation of present value that if the interest rate is 5 per cent, you should prefer the €200 in 10 years. The future €200 has a present value of €123, which is greater than €100. You are better off waiting for the future sum.

Notice that the answer to our question depends on the interest rate. If the interest rate were 8 per cent, then the €200 in 10 years would have a present value of €200/1.08^{10}, which is only €93. In this case, the business should take the €100 today. Why should the interest rate matter? The answer is that the higher the interest rate, the more you can earn by depositing your money at the bank, so the more attractive getting €100 today becomes.

The concept of present value is useful in assessing the decisions that businesses face when evaluating investment projects. For instance, imagine that Citroën is thinking about building a new car factory. Suppose that the factory will cost €100 million today and will yield the company €200 million in 10 years. Should Citroën undertake the project? You can see that this decision is exactly like the one we have been studying. To make its decision, the company will compare the present value of the €200 million return to the €100 million cost.

The company's decision, therefore, will depend on the interest rate. If the interest rate is 5 per cent, then the present value of the €200 million return from the factory is €123 million, and the company will choose to pay the €100 million cost. By contrast, if the interest rate is 8 per cent, then the present value of the return is only €93 million, and the company will decide to forego the project. As a general principle, therefore, a company will undergo an investment if the net present value is positive and vice versa. Thus, the concept of present value helps explain why investment declines when the interest rate rises.

Here is another application of present value. Suppose a small business is the subject of a takeover. The business owners are given an option about the way the takeover will work. They could either remain as part of the business and take a guaranteed sum of money over a specified period, or take an upfront payment and leave the company. Imagine the owner is given the choice between €20,000 a year for 50 years (totalling €1,000,000) or an immediate payment of €400,000. Which should the owner choose? To make the right choice, they need to calculate the present value of the stream of payments. After performing 50 calculations similar to those above (one calculation for each payment) and adding up the results, they would learn that the present value of this stream of income totalling €1 million at a 7 per cent interest rate is only €276,000. The owner would be better off picking the immediate payment of €400,000. The €1 million may seem like more money, but the future cash flows, once discounted to the present, are worth far less.

> **SELF TEST** The interest rate is 7 per cent. What is the present value of €150 to be received in 10 years?

MANAGING RISK

Life is full of gambles. If you go skiing, you risk breaking your leg in a fall. If you cycle to work or university, you risk being knocked off your bike by a car. When a business makes an investment decision, it risks the decision failing and the value of the business falling as a result. The rational response to this risk is not necessarily to avoid it at any cost, but to take it into account in your decision making. Let us consider how a business might do that.

Risk Aversion

Many businesses are **risk averse**. This means more than businesses simply dislike bad things happening to them. It means that they dislike bad things more than they like comparable good things. (This is also reflected in *loss aversion:* research suggests that losing something makes people twice as miserable as gaining something makes them happy!)

 risk averse exhibiting a dislike of uncertainty

Economists have developed models of risk aversion using the concept of *utility*, the subjective measure of a person's well-being or satisfaction. Every level of wealth provides a certain amount of utility, as shown by the utility function in Figure 19.1. The function exhibits the property of diminishing marginal utility: the more wealth a person has, the less utility they get from an additional euro. Thus, in the figure, the utility function gets flatter as wealth increases. Because of diminishing marginal utility, the utility lost from losing the €1,000 bet is more than the utility gained from winning it. Diminishing marginal utility is one reason why businesses can be risk averse.

Risk aversion provides the starting point for explaining various things we observe in relation to how businesses operate in the economy.

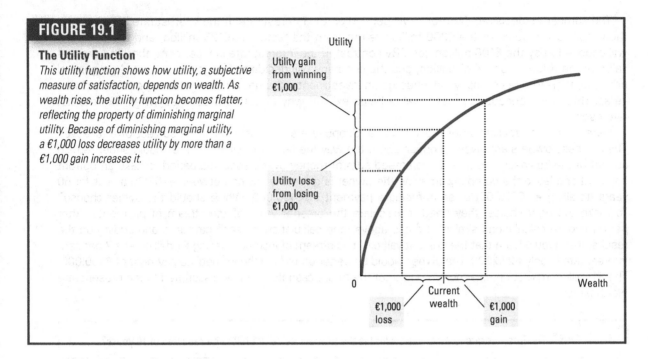

FIGURE 19.1

The Utility Function

This utility function shows how utility, a subjective measure of satisfaction, depends on wealth. As wealth rises, the utility function becomes flatter, reflecting the property of diminishing marginal utility. Because of diminishing marginal utility, a €1,000 loss decreases utility by more than a €1,000 gain increases it.

The Markets for Insurance

One way for a business to deal with risk is to buy insurance. The general feature of insurance contracts is that a business facing a risk pays a fee to an insurance company, which in return agrees to accept all or part of the risk. Firms have to take out different types of insurance. They can insure against the risk of their buildings catching fire, theft of goods and loss of revenue in certain circumstances. Businesses are also required to take out insurance to cover the risk of a customer or employees having an accident while on the premises, and cover for damage or loss to capital equipment.

In a sense, every insurance contract is a gamble. It is possible that none of the risks insured will happen. In most years, businesses pay the insurance company the premium and get nothing in return except peace of mind. Indeed, the insurance company is counting on the fact that most businesses will not make claims on their policies; otherwise, it could not pay out the large claims to those few who are unlucky and still stay in business.

From the standpoint of the economy as a whole, the role of insurance is not to eliminate the risks inherent in life but to spread them around more efficiently. Consider fire insurance on a business, for instance. Owning fire insurance does not reduce the risk of losing a business in a fire. If that unlucky event occurs, the insurance company compensates the business owners. The risk, rather than being borne by that business alone, is shared among the thousands of insurance company shareholders. Because people are risk averse, it is easier for 10,000 businesses to bear 1/10,000 of the risk than for one business to bear the entire risk itself.

The markets for insurance suffer from two types of problems that impede their ability to spread risk. One problem is *adverse selection*: a high-risk business is more likely to apply for insurance than a low-risk business. A second problem is *moral hazard*: after businesses buy insurance, they have less incentive to be careful about their risky behaviour. Insurance companies are aware of these problems, and the price of insurance reflects the actual risks that the insurance company will face after the insurance is bought. The high price of insurance is why some businesses, especially those who know themselves to be low risk, decide against buying insurance if it is not a legal requirement and, instead, endure some of life's uncertainty on their own.

SELF TEST Describe three ways by which a risk-averse business might reduce the risk they face.

ASSET VALUATION

Now that we have developed a basic understanding of the two building blocks of finance, time and risk, let us apply this knowledge. An **asset** is any tangible or intangible item controlled by an individual or business which has economic value, that is, it can be converted into cash. Business assets can include tangible items like plant and equipment, or intangible items such as a brand or the goodwill associated with a particular business, or the value of the skills inherent in the businesses employees. Valuing assets is an important part of any business activity. For large businesses, asset valuation can make a big difference to the financial accounts of the business when it reports to its shareholders. This section considers a simple question which applies to a range of assets. What determines the price of an asset? Like most prices, the answer is supply and demand.

asset a tangible or intangible item controlled by a business that has economic value

> **PITFALL PREVENTION** Always take into consideration the type of asset being analyzed and note its different characteristics. Shares in a business, for example, may have to be treated slightly differently, even if the same principles are applied, from a decision to launch a takeover bid for a rival firm (the asset in this case) or investing in new plant.

Fundamental Analysis

Let us imagine that a business has some cash reserves which it wants to put to use to earn a return. It is deciding how to allocate these cash reserves to different assets. These assets might include the acquisition of another firm and investing in new plant and equipment to improve efficiency. When buying any asset, it is natural to consider two things: the value of the asset and the price at which the asset is being sold. If the price is less than the value, the asset is said to be *undervalued*. If the price is more than the value, the asset is said to be *overvalued*. If the price and the value are equal, the asset is said to be *fairly valued*. When buying assets, the business should prefer undervalued assets; in such cases, the business would benefit by paying less than the asset is worth.

This is easier said than done. Learning the price is easy but determining the value of the asset is the hard part. The term **fundamental analysis** refers to the detailed analysis of an asset to determine its value. Many firms, especially those in the financial sector, hire analysts to conduct such fundamental analysis and offer advice about which assets to buy.

fundamental analysis the study of an asset to determine its value

The value of an asset to a business is what they get out of owning it, which includes the present value of the stream of income and the possible final sale price or scrap value. The stream of income an asset can generate depends on a large number of factors: the demand for the product that the asset helps produce; how quickly technology renders the asset obsolete; how flexible the asset is and how easily it can be used for other purposes; and so on. The job of fundamental analysts is to take all these factors into account to determine how much an asset is worth.

> **JEOPARDY PROBLEM** A business does detailed analysis of a rival firm which it is thinking of taking over. It arrives at a value for the company based on fundamentals such as the current share price, profitability, earnings, the volume of shares traded in recent months, the ratio of its share price to its earnings and dividend payments. Having undertaken this analysis, the firm believes the takeover target is under-priced, and that it would be beneficial to launch the takeover bid. When it announces its plans to do so, its own share price falls. What might be the reason, given the amount of analysis the firm has carried out?

SAVINGS AND INVESTMENTS IN THE NATIONAL INCOME ACCOUNTS

Access to funds for business development and growth is closely related to the rate of interest that firms must pay to borrow money. Whether there are funds available for firms to borrow is dependent on the number of people who are willing to save money. There is a market in loanable funds and the financial institutions we looked at earlier in the chapter play a big part in this market.

The Market for Loanable Funds

We are going to build a model of financial markets. Our purpose in building this model is to explain how financial markets coordinate the economy's saving and investment and thus help channel finance to businesses that need it. The model also gives us a tool with which we can analyze various government policies that influence saving and investment, which in turn can affect the amount of funds available to businesses. The supply and demand of loanable funds determines the price of loanable funds: the interest rate.

To keep things simple, we assume that the economy has only one financial market, called the **market for loanable funds**. All savers go to this market to deposit their savings, and all borrowers go to this market to get their loans. Thus, the term *loanable funds* refers to all income that people have chosen to save and lend out, rather than use for their own consumption. In the market for loanable funds, we assume there is one interest rate, which is both the return to saving and the cost of borrowing.

> **market for loanable funds** the market in which those who want to save supply funds and those who want to borrow to invest demand funds

We can identify two types of saving in the economy, **private saving** and **public saving**. Private saving is the amount of income that households have left after paying their taxes and for their consumption. In particular, because households receive income, which we denote as Y, pay taxes of T, and spend C on consumption, private saving is $Y - T - C$. Public saving is the amount of tax revenue that the government has left after paying for its spending. The government receives T in tax revenue and spends G on goods and services. If T exceeds G, the government runs a budget surplus because it receives more money than it spends. This surplus of $T - G$ represents public saving. If the government spends more than it receives in tax revenue, then G is larger than T. In this case, the government runs a budget deficit, and public saving $T - G$ is a negative number.

> **private saving** the income that households have left after paying for taxes and consumption
> **public saving** the tax revenue that the government has left after paying for its spending

Supply and Demand for Loanable Funds

The supply of loanable funds comes from those people who have some extra income they want to save and lend out. This lending can occur directly, such as when a household buys a bond, or it can occur indirectly, such as when a household makes a deposit in a bank, which in turn uses the funds to make loans. In both cases, saving is the source of the supply of loanable funds.

The demand for loanable funds comes from households and firms who wish to borrow to make investments. This demand includes people taking out mortgages to buy homes. It also includes firms borrowing to buy new equipment or build factories. In both cases, investment is the source of the demand for loanable funds.

The interest rate is the price of a loan. It represents the amount that borrowers pay for loans and the amount that lenders receive on their saving. Because a high interest rate makes borrowing more expensive, the quantity of loanable funds demanded falls as the interest rate rises. Similarly, because a high interest rate makes saving more attractive, the quantity of loanable funds supplied rises as the interest rate rises. In other words, the demand curve for loanable funds slopes downward, and the supply curve for loanable funds slopes upward.

Figure 19.2 shows the interest rate that balances the supply and demand for loanable funds. In the equilibrium shown, the interest rate is 5 per cent, and the quantity of loanable funds demanded and the quantity of loanable funds supplied both equal €500 billion.

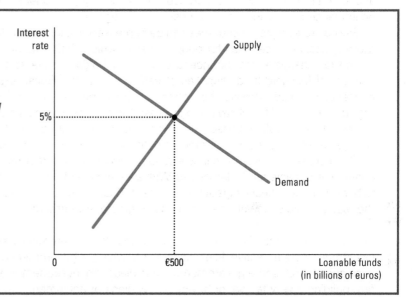

FIGURE 19.2

The Market for Loanable Funds
The interest rate in the economy adjusts to balance the supply and demand for loanable funds. The supply of loanable funds comes from national saving, including both private saving and public saving. The demand for loanable funds comes from firms and households that want to borrow for the purposes of investment. Here the equilibrium interest rate is 5 per cent, and €500 billion of loanable funds are supplied and demanded.

The adjustment of the interest rate to the equilibrium level occurs for the usual reasons. If the interest rate was lower than the equilibrium level, the quantity of loanable funds supplied would be less than the quantity of loanable funds demanded. The resulting shortage of loanable funds would encourage lenders to raise the interest rate they charge. A higher interest rate would encourage saving (thereby increasing the quantity of loanable funds supplied) and discourage borrowing for investment (thereby decreasing the quantity of loanable funds demanded). Conversely, if the interest rate was higher than the equilibrium level, the quantity of loanable funds supplied would exceed the quantity of loanable funds demanded. As lenders competed for the scarce borrowers, interest rates would be driven down. In this way, the interest rate approaches the equilibrium level at which the supply and demand for loanable funds exactly balance.

Economists distinguish between the real interest rate and the nominal interest rate. The **nominal interest rate** is the interest rate as usually reported: the monetary return on saving and cost of borrowing. The **real interest rate** is the nominal interest rate corrected for inflation; it equals the nominal interest rate minus the inflation rate. Because inflation erodes the value of money over time, the real interest rate more accurately reflects the real return on saving and cost of borrowing. Therefore, the supply and demand for loanable funds depend on the real (rather than nominal) interest rate, and the equilibrium in Figure 19.2 should be interpreted as determining the real interest rate in the economy.

> **nominal interest rate** the monetary return on saving and the cost of borrowing
> **real interest rate** the interest rate adjusted to take account of the effect of inflation, calculated as the nominal interest rate minus the inflation rate

This model of the supply and demand for loanable funds shows that financial markets work much like other markets in the economy. When the interest rate adjusts to balance supply and demand in the market for loanable funds, it coordinates the behaviour of people who want to save (the suppliers of loanable funds) and the behaviour of people who want to invest (the demanders of loanable funds). When the interest rate changes, it affects the risk involved in investment for a business and affects the value of the returns. We are likely to see firms reducing their investment plans when the interest rate rises but increasing them when the interest rate falls.

We can now use this analysis of the market for loanable funds to examine various government policies that affect the economy's saving and investment and in particular the ability of firms to borrow.

Policy 1: Saving Incentives If a country can raise its saving rate, the interest rate (other things being equal) will fall and firms can invest more. This in turn leads the growth rate of the economy to increase and, over time, the citizens of that country should enjoy a higher standard of living. The savings rate may be influenced by incentives, both positive and negative.

Savings rates in some countries can be depressed because of tax laws that discourage saving. What is more typical are incentives for people to save which shelter some of their saving from taxation.

The tax change alters the incentive for households to save *at any given interest rate*; it affects the quantity of loanable funds supplied at each interest rate. Because saving would be taxed less heavily, households would increase their saving by consuming a smaller fraction of their income. Households would use this additional saving to increase their deposits in banks or to buy more bonds. The supply of loanable funds would increase. The demand for loanable funds would remain the same, because the tax change would not directly affect the amount that borrowers want to borrow at any given interest rate.

The increased supply of loanable funds reduces the interest rate. The lower interest rate raises the quantity of loanable funds demanded. With a lower cost of borrowing, households and firms are motivated to borrow more to finance greater investment. Thus, if a reform of the tax laws encouraged greater saving, the result would be lower interest rates and greater investment.

Policy 2: Investment Incentives Suppose that the government passed a tax reform aimed at making investment more attractive. In essence, this is what the government does when it institutes an *investment allowance*, which some governments put in place. An investment allowance gives a tax advantage to any firm building a new factory or buying a new piece of equipment. Let us consider the effect of such a tax reform on the market for loanable funds, as illustrated in Figure 19.3.

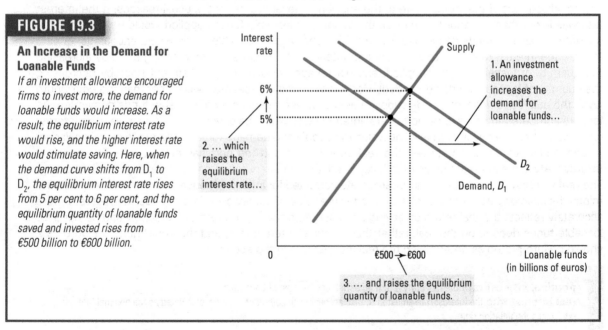

FIGURE 19.3

An Increase in the Demand for Loanable Funds

If an investment allowance encouraged firms to invest more, the demand for loanable funds would increase. As a result, the equilibrium interest rate would rise, and the higher interest rate would stimulate saving. Here, when the demand curve shifts from D$_1$ to D$_2$, the equilibrium interest rate rises from 5 per cent to 6 per cent, and the equilibrium quantity of loanable funds saved and invested rises from €500 billion to €600 billion.

The investment allowance rewards firms that borrow and invest in new capital; it would alter investment at any given interest rate and change the demand for loanable funds. Because firms would have an incentive to increase investment at any interest rate, the quantity of loanable funds demanded would be higher at any given interest rate. Thus, the demand curve for loanable funds would move to the right, as shown by the shift from D$_1$ to D$_2$ in the figure. By contrast, because the investment allowance would not affect the amount that households save at any given interest rate, it would not affect the supply of loanable funds.

In Figure 19.3, the increased demand for loanable funds raises the interest rate from 5 per cent to 6 per cent, and the higher interest rate in turn increases the quantity of loanable funds supplied from €500 billion to €600 billion, as households respond by increasing the amount they save.

This change in household behaviour is represented here as a movement along the supply curve. Thus, if a reform of the tax system encouraged greater investment, the result would be higher interest rates and greater saving.

Policy 3: Government Budget Deficits and Surpluses A *budget deficit* is an excess of government spending over tax revenue. Governments finance budget deficits by borrowing in the bond market, and the accumulation of past government borrowing is called the *government debt*. A *budget surplus*, an excess of tax revenue over government spending, can be used to repay some of the government debt. If government spending exactly equals tax revenue, the government is said to have a *balanced budget*.

Imagine that the government starts with a balanced budget and then, because of a tax cut or a spending increase, starts running a budget deficit. We can analyze the effects of the budget deficit as illustrated in Figure 19.4.

FIGURE 19.4

The Effect of a Government Budget Deficit

When the government spends more than it receives in tax revenue, the resulting budget deficit lowers national saving. The supply of loanable funds decreases, and the equilibrium interest rate rises. Thus, when the government borrows to finance its budget deficit, it crowds out households and firms who otherwise would borrow to finance investment. Here, when the supply shifts from S_1 to S_2, the equilibrium interest rate rises from 5 per cent to 6 per cent, and the equilibrium quantity of loanable funds saved and invested falls from €500 billion to €300 billion.

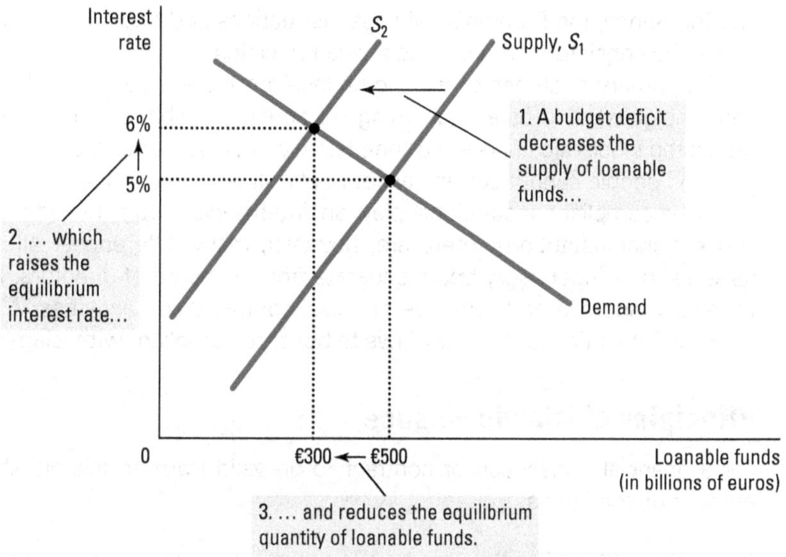

Interest rate

S_2 Supply, S_1

6%

5%

1. A budget deficit decreases the supply of loanable funds...

2. ... which raises the equilibrium interest rate...

Demand

0   €300 ◄— €500   Loanable funds (in billions of euros)

3. ... and reduces the equilibrium quantity of loanable funds.

Recall that national saving (the source of the supply of loanable funds) is composed of private saving and public saving. A change in the government budget balance represents a change in public saving and, thereby, in the supply of loanable funds. When the government runs a budget deficit, public saving is negative and this reduces national saving. In other words, when the government borrows to finance its budget deficit, it reduces the supply of loanable funds available to finance investment by households and firms. Thus a budget deficit shifts the supply curve for loanable funds to the left from S_1 to S_2, as shown in Figure 19.4. Because the budget deficit does not influence the amount that households and firms want to borrow to finance investment at any given interest rate, it does not alter the demand for loanable funds.

When the budget deficit reduces the supply of loanable funds, the interest rate rises from 5 per cent to 6 per cent. This higher interest rate alters the behaviour of the households and firms that participate in the loan market. In particular, many demanders of loanable funds are discouraged by the higher interest rate. Fewer families buy new homes and fewer firms choose to build new factories. The fall in investment because of government borrowing is called **crowding out** and is represented in Figure 19.4 by the movement along the demand curve from a quantity of €500 billion in loanable funds to a quantity of €300 billion. That is, when the government borrows to finance its budget deficit, it crowds out private borrowers who are trying to finance investment.

crowding out a decrease in investment that results from government borrowing

Government budget surpluses work just the opposite way to budget deficits. When government collects more in tax revenue than it spends, it saves the difference by retiring some of the outstanding government debt. This budget surplus, or public saving, contributes to national saving. Thus, a budget surplus increases the supply of loanable funds, reduces the interest rate and stimulates investment. Higher investment, in turn, means greater capital accumulation and more rapid economic growth.

AN OVERVIEW OF ISLAMIC FINANCE

Our analysis in this chapter has been based on financial markets working in a capitalist system. There is a growing interest in other types of financial market and the globalization of business now means that access to funds for investment can be explored through these other markets. Islamic finance is a financial system governed by Islamic sharia (an Arabic term often translated as Islamic law), comprising the principles and rules derived from Islam as a religion. Its primary sources are the holy Quran (also known as the holy book) and the Sunna, the Prophet's religious instructions and traditions. In Islamic finance, all financial contracts should be consistent with Islamic sharia principles.

The primary doctrines of Islamic finance are the avoidance of riba (fixed interest), gharar (uncertainty and ambiguity), and haram (anything religiously prohibited). Therefore, any interest-based transaction is prohibited in Islamic finance. Further, Islamic financial principles entail all parties sharing profits as well as risk, and people cannot sell any asset (real or financial) that they do not own.

Sharia-compliant institutions play an intermediary role by offering the same banking services as conventional institutions. There are, however, many differences. All sharia-compliant institutions should have a sharia supervisory board separate from its board of directors. The main task of the sharia board is to review, approve or disapprove financial contracts and activities. A number of European countries are reforming their financial and tax laws to become compliant with Islamic finance products and instruments.

Principles of Islamic Finance

For a financial transaction or contract to be valid from an Islamic sharia standpoint, it should satisfy a number of conditions.

To Be Halal (Permitted) In sharia, halal means permitted or legal. All financial transactions are allowed in Islamic sharia as long as they do not include riba and gharar. In other words, permission is the default status in any transaction. Practically, the sharia supervisory board takes responsibility for checking contracts and transactions against Islamic sharia principles.

Avoidance of Riba *Riba* means 'growth' or 'increase', and denotes the payment or receipt of interest for the use of money. By default, Islamic finance business and activities must be free from any interest element. Lending money for more money is forbidden because money is not a commodity in itself and cannot be rented out for a fee. It is seen as unfair that a borrower pays a fixed return (interest) regardless of the outcome of their investments or how such funds may have been used. Many Islamic practitioners believe that riba is exploitative and unproductive as it brings a gain to the lender, who has an excess of funds, and it passes all the risk onto the borrower, who is initially short of funds.

Avoidance of Gharar Gharar is interpreted as excessive uncertainty. Examples of gharar are selling fish in the sea, birds in the sky and gambling, all of which cause excessive uncertainty. Fish are common resources that cannot be owned by any one person; gambling can be seen as a zero-sum game in which one party benefits at the expense of another. Because gharar might lead to disputes caused by an unjustified term in the contract arising from fraud or misrepresentation, the contract should be clear with a full description of the subject matter, and the seller should own the assets that they intend to sell.

Islamic Versus Conventional Banks

There are many similarities between Islamic and conventional banks. An Islamic bank is expected to perform the same activities as a conventional bank and carries out the role of a financial intermediary. Unlike conventional banks, Islamic banks are not allowed to borrow and lend funds based on interest. The assets of an Islamic bank include funds on a profit and loss sharing (PLS) basis usually deriving from equity financing, asset financing and lease financing. On the liabilities side, Islamic banks mobilize agency contract funds; they can accept current, saving and investment deposits which are treated again on the basis of PLS.

Islamic Banking Sources and Uses

With a growing international profile, Islamic finance is evolving towards a fully fledged financial system offering a broad range of sharia-compliant products and services to satisfy the needs of individuals as well as businesses. As with any bank, Islamic banks aim to maximize shareholders' wealth and provide adequate return to the depositors who invest their savings in the bank. Islamic banks are required to pursue those objectives with a clear understanding of their role towards the development of society as a whole. Financially, Islamic banks will achieve these objectives by operating as an intermediary between depositors, who have excess funds, and fund seekers, who have a shortage of funds.

The Main Sources of Funds

Islamic banks' depositors are seeking safe custody for their money and/or looking to earn adequate returns on their deposits. The main sources of funds for Islamic banks are described below.

Shareholder Investments Islamic banks raise their initial capital by offering equity participation in which the shareholders are owners and partners in the bank's business. The shareholders expect a return in the form of a share of the bank's profit (if any).

Current Accounts The current account is an account that entitles the account holder to receive their funds on demand. The depositor can raise payments on the account to transfer legal ownership of funds to others. In this type of account there is no guaranteed return, but sometimes the bank rewards current account clients by hiba, or gift, which is at the bank's sole discretion. There is no limit for withdrawals from a current account.

Savings Accounts (Wadiah) When depositors put money into a bank they expect it to be kept safely. Banks can use these savings accounts (also called wadiah) provided the bank seeks the depositor's permission. Assuming this permission is granted the bank can employ the funds, although it guarantees the deposit principal against any damage or loss. As with the current account, the bank may pay hiba on these accounts at its discretion and without a predetermined agreement.

Investment Accounts Investment accounts are profit sharing accounts, also known as mudarabah, where banks accept deposits for a specific period. Mudarabah contracts are used as sources of funds for a bank as well as being used to finance other activities. In practice the bank pools the deposits with other funds while keeping a record of each individual account. The bank invests these funds in a sharia-compliant investment with the aim of maximizing the return. Any return on those funds will be shared with depositors according to a predetermined profit sharing ratio. Although these accounts are known as profit and loss sharing accounts, the depositors bear all the losses, except when the loss results from the bank's misconduct or negligence.

FINTECH

Fintech is short for financial technologies. It refers to technologies that are primarily used in the financial services industry and includes mobile payments, transferring money, loans, fund raising and asset management. It is of increasing relevance in financial markets, and more and more businesses are making use of fintech services.

> **fintech** financial technologies used in the financial services industry, including mobile payments, transferring money, loans, fund raising and asset management

The growth of fintech has, and is expected to continue to have, a significant impact on the traditional banking system and the way in which businesses handle transactions, and raise and manage loans.

One way in which fintech is changing how businesses start up is through the provision of an alternative way of raising funds. One such way is crowdfunding.

Crowdfunding **Crowdfunding** is the raising of finance using technology to secure individual contributions of small sums of money from a large number of people. Businesses seeking to raise funds in this way use the internet as a means of contacting a large number of potential investors. These investors may be willing to provide funds for a variety of reasons. The reasons may not always include an expected financial return, but could be a return in kind.

> **crowdfunding** the raising of finance using technology to secure individual contributions of small sums of money from a large number of people

Investors might choose to donate because they want to contribute to a good cause, such as the setup of businesses providing essential goods and services in less developed countries. Their motivation for investing is the social benefits that arise from the business activity, not any financial return. Financial returns can be gained in the case of equity crowdfunding, where investors acquire a small share in the business. A number of websites have developed to help put potential investors in touch with those looking for funds, for example, Kickstarter, Indiegogo, SeedInvest Technology and crowdcube.com.

Crowdfunding is not only beneficial in raising funds, but the funds can often be raised much quicker, without the administration and costs that are associated with raising funds through traditional means such as going through banks.

Payment Services Large businesses can have sophisticated payment services allowing customers to pay in different ways, but small businesses may not be able to access these services. In some cases, this is because the payment service charges the business a fee for the hire of equipment and a percentage of the transaction and this can make it unviable for small businesses, especially those which are just starting up. Fintech has resulted in a range of different payment systems which allow small firms to be able to increase the payment options to which their customers have access, and increase the potential size of their market as a result. Examples of such systems include PayPal and Square. Both these systems make payments much easier and more mobile for many businesses, and also makes international transactions easier. Traditional banks and firms such as Apple are also involved in payment services to provide easier ways in which customers can pay for goods and services with contactless cards, smartphone payment and ApplePay, meaning that customers can pay easily wherever they are.

Cryptocurrencies A currency such as the euro, pound sterling, dollar and yen have the characteristic of being widely acceptable as a medium of exchange. The value of these currencies is reflected in the amount of goods and services (and other currencies) they can buy. **Cryptocurrencies** are peer-to-peer networks facilitating transactions between users without an intermediary such as a bank. Cryptocurrencies can be exchanged for other currencies, goods and services.

> **cryptocurrencies** peer-to-peer networks facilitating transactions between users without an intermediary

Zippia Research estimates that there are around 20,000 cryptocurrencies in circulation, over 400,000 daily Bitcoin transactions and some 300 million global cryptocurrency users. The top three cryptocurrencies are Ethereum, Tether and the most popular, Bitcoin. Bitcoin was developed in 2008/2009. The name

Satoshi Nakamoto has been attached to the creation of bitcoin. This name could be an individual or to a group of people; nobody knows for sure.

Bitcoins are created through mining. Mining uses software to solve mathematical problems for which a number of bitcoins are issued in exchange. This means that the issue of bitcoins has some element of self-control since the mining process is not easy and helps maintain the stability of the currency, as in the way a central bank will seek to control a national currency through managing the quantity of the currency in circulation.

The issue of bitcoins through mining is done in a 'block' which is added to all other blocks, called a blockchain, and is then added to the network. The blockchain acts as a ledger recording all transactions of the currency, although there is no central ledger. As the technology develops, other cryptocurrencies are using the experience of bitcoin to develop more efficient and reliable systems. In 2020, the Bank of England in the UK published a discussion paper looking at the possible introduction of a Central bank digital currency (CBDC). The Bank received a large number of responses to the paper and has engaged in further research and exploration of the idea. Other central banks are also exploring the idea of a CBDC.

CASE STUDY | Crowdfunding

The music industry is one which seems to be perfectly orientated towards crowdfunding. There are often fans out there who would like to see new music, would pay to help bands produce albums and access merchandise. For bands and artists, getting closer to the people who like their music is a good way of building relationships. In 2009, Benji Rogers founded PledgeMusic to do just this – to provide a crowdfunding platform for musicians and artists to help them fund their work through contributions from fans. Fans could pledge different amounts of money which allowed them to access different experiences, including a download of the digital version of the album when it was finally released, through to a CD, have their names included in the production credits, have regular updates on progress sent to them, exclusive videos of the development of the work, and even have the artists give private concerts. For eight years it seemed to be successful, but in 2018, problems appeared. The business attempted to grow quickly and critics argued that there was not the infrastructure in place to support the number of projects it had taken on. Artists complained that they were not getting paid, had problems in communicating with PledgeMusic and that promotion of projects was weak. The business model was also criticized. The prices that

PledgeMusic put on the various products and experiences they were offering were insufficient to cover the true costs of them and it was rumoured that some existing campaigns were being funded by receipts from new campaigns. The company tried to restructure and brought back Rogers, who had stepped down in 2016, in a temporary role, but even his involvement was not enough to save the company and it declared insolvency in the summer of 2019. Reports suggested that artists were owed around €8.9 million in unpaid funds. Many fans also did not get what they had paid for.

Crowdfunding can be a useful way for artists to raise money to fund new projects but there are pitfalls.

Questions

1 **Many artists and musicians struggle to secure sufficient funds to create new albums and distributing their work. Does this suggest that traditional funding for small businesses such as these is fundamentally flawed?**

(Continued)

2 **One of the reasons for the failure of PledgeMusic is that it was using funds from new campaigns to pay for existing campaigns. Why does this make the business model unsustainable?**

3 **Does the failure of PledgeMusic suggest that crowdfunding is not an option that a business should follow in seeking to raise finance to start an enterprise?**

References: https://variety.com/2019/music/news/pledgemusic-owes-money-10-artists-1203146213/ (accessed 11 June 2023). www.digitalmusicnews.com/2019/10/25/rise-and-fall-of-pledgemusic/ (accessed 11 June 2023).

The Impact of Fintech

Fintech has been described as a disruptive technology in that it challenges the traditional way firms can raise funds, and the way financial markets work. Fintech has grown rapidly and is likely to continue to evolve. The Bank of England conducts what it calls the annual cyclical scenario (ACS) stress test framework. The purpose of the stress tests is to assess the ability of banks to withstand financial shocks. The tests were introduced following The Financial Crisis in 2007–2009 and now includes fintech. The Bank of England has noted how important fintech could be in the financial system and is working to understand how fintech might affect stability of the financial system, how it might affect the safety and soundness of firms and how fintech might affect macroeconomic policy making.

SUMMARY

- Businesses need to raise finance not only to start up but to grow and expand. Two major sources of finance for business are loan capital and share capital.

- The financial system of an advanced economy is made up of many types of financial institutions, such as the bond market, the stock market, banks and investment funds. These institutions act to direct the resources of households who want to save some of their income into the hands of households and firms who want to borrow.

- Because savings can earn interest, a sum of money today is more valuable than the same sum of money in the future. A person can compare sums from different times using the concept of present value. The present value of any future sum is the amount that would be needed today, given prevailing interest rates, to produce that future sum.

- Because of diminishing marginal utility, most people are risk averse. Risk-averse people can reduce risk using insurance.

- The value of an asset equals the present value of the income streams the owner will receive and the final sale price if appropriate.

- The interest rate is determined by the supply and demand for loanable funds. The supply of loanable funds comes from households who want to save some of their income and lend it out. The demand for loanable funds comes from households and firms who want to borrow for investment. To analyze how any policy or event affects the interest rate, you should consider how it affects the supply and demand for loanable funds.

- National saving equals private saving plus public saving. A government budget deficit represents negative public saving and, therefore, reduces national saving and the supply of loanable funds available to finance investment. When a government budget deficit crowds out investment, it reduces the growth of productivity and GDP.

- Islamic finance, which is based on profit and loss sharing rather than on interest, is a growing option for financing for some businesses and is growing in sophistication not only in Muslim countries.

- Fintech, financial technologies, offer different ways in which businesses can raise funds, manage their cash flows, make and receive payments and manage their finances. The effect of fintech is likely to grow as technologies continue to evolve.

IN THE NEWS

Small and Medium Enterprise Finance

One of the recurrent challenges facing small and medium-sized enterprises (SMEs) is accessing finance. In the UK, for example, the Department for Business, Energy, and Industrial Strategy (DBEIS) noted that 99 per cent of the 5.5 million private sector businesses registered in the UK at the start of 2022 were small, employing between 0 and 49 people. Despite these statistics pointing to the importance of SMEs to the UK economy, there are reports that around half of SMEs say they face challenges in accessing capital. The news magazine *Business Leader* writes that the disparity between the infrastructure to allow small businesses to access capital and their larger counterparts is widening and even suggests that: 'the existing credit landscape is not set up for SMEs to succeed'.

The magazine highlights the fact that many banks are closing high street branches as relationships with customers change. In addition, accelerating inflation and the likelihood of recession over much of 2023 will make it even harder for SMEs to access capital. *Business Leader* points out that one of the problems is that SMEs do not always explore different channels for obtaining finance. It suggests that many firms have assets which can be used to secure funding which they are not aware of. In addition, SMEs could take advantage of a relatively new scheme launched in 2021, the Merchant Cash Advance (MCA) or Business cash Advance (BCA). This offers SMEs between £10,000 and £300,000 in loans and is available to businesses that have been trading for at least six months, have a minimum turnover of £10,000 per month in credit or debit card sales, and is available through 365 Business Finance, a direct financial provider. Loans under this scheme are paid back as a percentage of card sales. This allows SMEs to manage their cash flow more effectively and in line with sales. SMEs might also utilize the services provided by business finance brokers, specialists in securing finance for SMEs.

Small businesses often face challenges in seeking to access funds to support their enterprises.

Questions

1 Why do you think that banks may be reluctant to lend to SMEs in times of economic uncertainty such as in recession and when inflation rates are accelerating?
2 To what extent do you agree with the view that the 'the existing credit landscape is not set up for SMEs to succeed'?
3 Many SMEs rely on sources of finance such as personal credit cards, overdrafts and personal savings. Why might these not be the right types of finance for SMEs?
4 Why is an efficient and effective funding mechanism for SMEs important to the health of an economy?
5 Do some research on the MCA, asset financing and finance brokers. To what extent do you think these approaches to financing SMEs are more appropriate and efficient compared to traditional sources of funding?

References: www.businessleader.co.uk/how-smes-can-overcome-the-barriers-to-accessing-finance/ (accessed 11 June 2023).
www.gov.uk/business-finance-support/merchant-cash-advance-uk (accessed 11 June 2023).
www.gov.uk/government/statistics/business-population-estimates-2022/business-population-estimates-for-the-uk-and-regions-2022-statistical-release-html (accessed 11 June 2023).
www.365businessfinance.co.uk/merchant-cash-advance/?utm_source=gov_uk&utm_medium=sitelink&utm_campaign=gov_uk (accessed 11 June 2023).

QUESTIONS FOR REVIEW

1 Distinguish between capital expenditure and revenue expenditure.

2 Distinguish between a loan and an overdraft as a source of finance.

3 What is the role of the financial system? Name and describe two markets that are part of the financial system in an economy. Name and describe two financial intermediaries.

4 What might be some of the advantages and disadvantages to a firm of issuing bonds or issuing shares as a source of finance?

5 A chemical processing manufacturer is considering investing in a new process to produce a constituent ingredient for an agricultural fertilizer. It expects the return on the investment to last for at least 10 years. How might it decide whether to proceed with the investment?

6 What is private saving? What is public saving? How are these two variables related?

7 What is investment? How is it related to national saving?

8 What is a government budget deficit? How does it affect interest rates, investment and economic growth?

9 What is the logic behind the prohibition of interest in Islamic finance?

10 What is fintech and in what way is it disrupting traditional banking models?

PROBLEMS AND APPLICATIONS

1 A small business involved with the manufacture of component parts for aircraft engines is contemplating expansion due to increased demand for its products.

   a. What might be an appropriate source of finance for such a business?
   b. What sort of risks would a bank consider in assessing a request by the business for finance?
   c. To what extent might alternative funding sources using fintech be appropriate for this firm?

2 A company has an investment project that would cost €10 million today and yield a pay-off of €18 million in four years.

   a. Should the firm undertake the project if the interest rate is 11 per cent? 10 per cent? 9 per cent? 8 per cent?
   b. Can you calculate the exact cut-off for the interest rate between profitability and non-profitability?

3 For which kind of asset would you expect to pay the higher average return: shares in an industry that is very sensitive to economic conditions (such as a car manufacturer) or shares in an industry that is relatively insensitive to economic conditions (such as a water company). Why?

4 Suppose that BP is considering exploring the development of large scale solar energy production.

   a. Assuming that BP needs to borrow money in the bond market to finance the purchase of plant equipment and machinery, why would an increase in interest rates affect BP's decision about whether to carry out the project?
   b. If BP has enough of its own funds to finance the development of the project without borrowing, so would an increase in interest rates still affect BP's decision about whether to undertake the new project? Explain.

5 Suppose the government borrows €5 billion more next year than this year.

   a. Use a supply and demand diagram to analyze this policy. Does the interest rate rise or fall?
   b. What happens to investment? To private saving? To public saving? Compare the size of the changes to the €5 billion of extra government borrowing.
   c. How does the elasticity of supply of loanable funds affect the size of these changes?
   d. How does the elasticity of demand for loanable funds affect the size of these changes?

Suppose households believe that greater government borrowing today implies higher taxes to pay off the government debt in the future. What does this belief do to private saving and the supply of loanable funds today? Does it increase or decrease the effects you discussed in parts a and b?

6 Since the turn of the century, new computer technology has enabled firms to substantially reduce the amount of inventories (stock) they hold for each unit of sales. Illustrate the effect of this change on the market for loanable funds. (Hint: expenditure on inventories is a type of investment.) What do you think has been the effect on investment in factories and equipment?

7 This chapter explains that investment can be increased both by reducing taxes on private saving and by reducing the government budget deficit.

   a. Why is it difficult to implement both of these policies at the same time?
   b. What would you need to know about private saving in order to judge which of these two policies would be a more effective way to raise investment?

8 The 2007–2009 Financial Crisis had a significant effect on many banks in financial markets in capitalist systems. In contrast, many Islamic financial institutions proved to be more resilient during this period. What do think might be some of the reasons for this contrast?

9 To what extent do you think that fintech has the capacity to significantly disrupt the traditional banking model with regard to the financing of SMEs?

10 In many countries, inflation rates have accelerated and central banks have increased interest rates to try to slow down the rate of growth of prices. As interest rates increase, what factors might businesses take into account in making decisions on investment?

PART 6
INTRODUCTION TO MACROECONOMICS

20 THE MACROECONOMIC ENVIRONMENT

LEARNING OUTCOMES

After reading this chapter you should be able to:

- Demonstrate why income equals expenditure equals output.
- Explain the key words and phrases in the definition of GDP.
- Define consumption, investment, government purchases and net exports.
- Calculate real and nominal GDP using base year and current year prices.
- List the five steps necessary to calculate the inflation rate.
- Discuss three reasons why the CPI may be biased.
- Describe two differences between the CPI and GDP deflator.
- Explain the relationship between the real interest rate, the nominal interest rate and the inflation rate.
- Use data on the number of employed, unemployed and not in the labour force to calculate the unemployment rate and the labour force participation rate.
- Explain the meaning of the balance of payments and describe its components.
- Explain why net exports must always equal net capital outflow.

INTRODUCTION

All businesses operate within an external economic environment which is largely out of an individual firm's control. In some years, firms throughout the economy are expanding their production of goods and services. This helps create more business activity for other firms who act as suppliers, distributors, provide financial services or advice, and act as wholesalers. When the economy expands, employment rises and households receive more income which is used to purchase goods and services. This can help generate further economic growth. In other years, firms cut back on production; as employment declines household spending gets cut back as incomes fall, and firms throughout the economy find that business activity has slowed and operating becomes increasingly challenging.

Because the condition of the overall economy profoundly affects businesses and individuals, changes in economic conditions are widely reported by the media. These reports include changes in the total income of everyone in the economy (gross domestic product), the rate at which average prices are rising (inflation), the percentage of the labour force that is out of work (unemployment), and the balance of trade between the domestic economy and the rest of the world (the balance of payments). All these statistics are *macroeconomic*. Rather than telling us about a particular household or firm, they tell us something about the entire economy. As a consequence, they are regarded as key economic indicators.

Firms pay close attention to macroeconomic data because it gives clues about the direction in which the economy, not only in their own country but around the world, is heading. This information can be factored into decision making so that the firm can try to anticipate events and be better prepared to be able to manage the changing macroeconomic environment as a result.

In this chapter, we will look at some key macroeconomic economic indicators: GDP, inflation, unemployment and the balance of payments.

KEY ECONOMIC INDICATORS

Gross Domestic Product

Recall that the economy is all the transactions that take place over a period of time. When judging the performance of the economy, a key economic indicator is how total transactions change over time. The measure typically used is gross domestic product (GDP). GDP measures the market value of all final goods and services produced within a country in a given period of time. There are three ways to measure this market value. First, we can add up all the incomes received in the economy as a result of transactions. These incomes will have been received by firms and households and represent expenditure by other firms and households, so expenditure on the economy's output of goods and services is the second way we can measure GDP. An economy's income is the same as its expenditure because every transaction has two parties: a buyer and a seller. Every euro of spending by some buyer is a euro of income for some seller. Finally, the goods and services transacted have a value, and the value of the output is the third way GDP can be measured. We will focus on the income and expenditure methods of measuring GDP.

The equality of income and expenditure can be represented as a diagram called the circular-flow as in Figure 20.1. This is a model which describes all the transactions between households and firms in a simple economy. In this economy, households buy goods and services from firms. These expenditures flow through the markets for goods and services. The firms in turn use the money they receive from sales to pay workers' wages, landowners' rent and firm owners' profit. This income flows through the markets for the factors of production. In this economy, money flows from households to firms and then back to households.

The actual economy is, of course, more complicated than the one illustrated in Figure 20.1. In particular, households do not spend all of their income. They pay some of it to the government in taxes, and they save some for use in the future. In addition, households do not buy all goods and services produced within the economy. Some goods and services are bought by governments, through taxes paid by households, which represent government spending. Some are bought by firms that plan to use them in the future to produce their own output, which represents investment. Some goods are bought from sellers in foreign countries (imports) and some domestic products are sold abroad (exports). Regardless of whether a household, government or firm buys a good or service, the transaction has a buyer and seller. Thus, for the economy as a whole, expenditure and income are always the same.

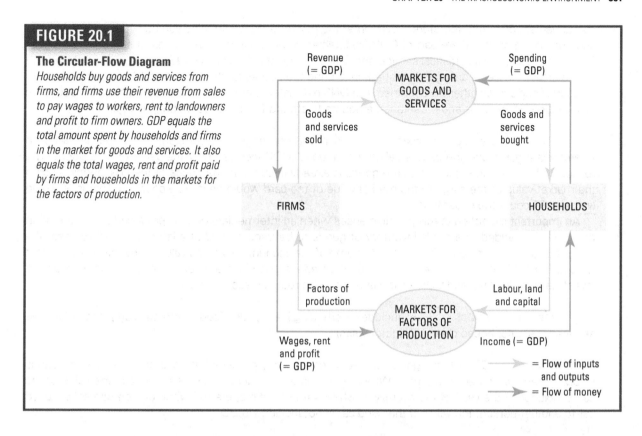

FIGURE 20.1

The Circular-Flow Diagram
Households buy goods and services from firms, and firms use their revenue from sales to pay wages to workers, rent to landowners and profit to firm owners. GDP equals the total amount spent by households and firms in the market for goods and services. It also equals the total wages, rent and profit paid by firms and households in the markets for the factors of production.

Revenue
(= GDP)

Spending
(= GDP)

MARKETS FOR GOODS AND SERVICES

Goods and services sold

Goods and services bought

FIRMS

HOUSEHOLDS

Factors of production

Labour, land and capital

MARKETS FOR FACTORS OF PRODUCTION

Wages, rent and profit
(= GDP)

Income (= GDP)

⟶ = Flow of inputs and outputs
⟶ = Flow of money

SELF TEST In theory, income and expenditure are mirror images of a transaction. Why might the authorities find that in measuring income and expenditure in the economy they get different results for each?

The Measurement of GDP

The following is a more detailed breakdown of how GDP is measured:

'GDP is the Market Value...' GDP adds together many different kinds of products into a single measure of the value of economic activity. To do this, it uses market prices. Because market prices measure the amount people are willing to pay for different goods, they reflect the value of those goods. If the price of an apple is twice the price of an orange, then an apple contributes twice as much to GDP as does an orange.

'... Of All...' GDP tries to be comprehensive. It includes all items produced in the economy and sold legally in markets. GDP measures the market value of not just apples and oranges, but also pears and grapefruit, books and films, haircuts and health care and so on.

GDP also includes the market value of the housing services provided by the economy's stock of housing. For rental housing, this value is easy to calculate. The rent equals both the tenant's expenditure and the landlord's income. Yet many people own the place where they live and, therefore, do not pay rent. The government includes this owner-occupied housing in GDP by estimating its rental value. That is, GDP is based on the assumption that the owner, in effect, pays rent to themselves, so the rent is included both in their expenditure and in their income.

There are some products, however, that GDP excludes because measuring them is so difficult. GDP excludes items which are not transacted through official channels such as when work is done on a cash-in-hand basis and is not declared as income by the receiver. It also excludes most items that are produced and consumed at home and, therefore, never enter the marketplace. Vegetables you buy at the greengrocer's shop or the supermarket are part of GDP; vegetables you grow in your garden are not. From September 2014, the UK's national statistical service, the Office for National Statistics (ONS) included estimates of the level of activity in illegal drugs and prostitution to bring the figures for the UK National Accounts in line with methods used across other EU countries. The ONS estimated that the average impact on the UK economy by including illegal drugs and prostitution amounts to around £10 billion (€11.7bn) per year.

'... **Final**...' When a paper company sells paper to a greetings card company, the paper is called an *intermediate good*, and the card is called a *final good*. GDP includes only the value of final goods. The reason is that the value of intermediate goods is already included in the prices of the final goods. Adding the market value of the paper to the market value of the card would be double counting. That is, it would (incorrectly) count the paper twice.

An important exception to this principle arises when an intermediate good is produced and, rather than being used, is added to a firm's inventory of goods to be used or sold at a later date. In this case, the intermediate good is taken to be 'final' at the time of the accounting, and its value as inventory investment is added to GDP. When the inventory of the intermediate good is later used or sold, the firm's inventory investment is negative, and GDP for the later period is reduced accordingly.

'... **Goods and Services**...' GDP includes both tangible goods (food, clothing, cars) and intangible services (haircuts, house cleaning, doctor visits).

'... **Produced**...' GDP includes goods and services currently produced. It does not include transactions involving items produced in the past. When Aston Martin produces and sells a new car, the value of the car is included in the GDP of the country in which Aston Martin operates. When one person sells a used car to another person, the value of the used car is not included in GDP.

'... **Within a Country**...' GDP measures the value of production within the geographic confines of a country. When an Australian citizen works temporarily in South Africa, their production is part of South African GDP. When a UK citizen owns a factory in Bulgaria, the production at their factory is not part of UK GDP: it is part of Bulgaria's GDP. Thus items are included in a nation's GDP if they are produced domestically, regardless of the nationality of the producer.

'... **in a Given Period of Time**' GDP measures the value of production that takes place within a specific interval of time. Usually that interval is a year or a quarter (three months). GDP measures the economy's flow of income and expenditure during that interval.

When GDP is reported for a quarter, it usually presents GDP 'at an annual rate'. This means that the figure is the amount of income and expenditure during the quarter multiplied by 4. This convention is used so that quarterly and annual figures on GDP can be compared more easily.

In addition, when quarterly GDP is reported, it presents data after being modified by a statistical procedure called *seasonal adjustment*. The unadjusted data show clearly that the economy produces more goods and services during some times of the year than during others. (As you might guess, December's holiday shopping season is a high point in many countries while the period before Ramadan is a high point for many Muslim countries.) When monitoring the condition of the economy, economists and policy makers often want to look beyond these regular seasonal changes. Therefore, national statisticians adjust the quarterly data to take out the seasonal cycle. The GDP data reported in the news are always seasonally adjusted.

 WHAT IF... a business receives a cash payment for a job. Does the value of the work carried out contribute to GDP? What might your answer depend upon?

THE COMPONENTS OF GDP

Spending in the economy takes many forms. At any moment, the Müller family may be having lunch in a Munich restaurant; Honda may be building a car factory on the banks of the Rhine; the German army may be procuring weapons from German arms manufacturers; and a New York investment company may be buying bonds from a German bank. German GDP includes all of these various forms of spending on domestically produced goods and services. Similarly, each country in Europe will monitor the forms of spending and income to arrive at the GDP for that country.

To understand how the economy is using its scarce resources and how this use affects business activity and planning, economists are often interested in studying the composition of GDP among various types of spending. To do this, GDP (which we denote as Y) is divided into four components: consumption (C), investment (I), government purchases (G) and net exports (NX):

$$Y \equiv C + I + G + NX$$

This equation is an *identity:* an equation that must be true by the way the variables in the equation are defined. (That is why we use the three-bar, 'identically equals' symbol, '$\equiv$', although for the most part we will follow normal practice in dealing with identities and use the usual equals sign, '$=$'). In this case, because each pound, dirham, rand or euro of expenditure included in GDP is placed into one of the four components of GDP, the total of the four components must be equal to GDP.

Consumption

Consumption is spending by households on goods and services. 'Goods' include household spending on durable goods, such as cars and appliances like washing machines and fridges, and non-durable goods, such as food and clothing. 'Services' include intangible items such as haircuts and insurance. Household spending on education is also included in consumption of services (although one might argue that it would fit better in the next component).

 consumption spending by households on goods and services, with the exception of purchases of new housing

Investment

Investment is the purchase of goods that will be used in the future to produce more goods and services. It is the sum of purchases of capital equipment, inventories and structures. Investment in structures include expenditure on new housing. By convention, the purchase of a new house is the one form of household spending categorized as investment rather than consumption.

It is worth remembering the way in which goods produced but not sold and added to inventories are treated in the national accounts. Inventories are treated this way because one aim of GDP is to measure the value of the economy's production, and goods added to inventory are part of that period's production.

Government Purchases

Government purchases include spending on goods and services by local and national governments. It includes the salaries of government workers and spending on public works.

 government purchases spending on goods and services by local, state and national governments

The meaning of 'government purchases' requires a little clarification. When the government pays the salary of an army general, that salary is part of government purchases. What happens when the government pays a social security benefit to a retired person? Such government spending is called a **transfer payment** because it is not made in exchange for a currently produced good or service. Transfer payments alter household income, but they do not reflect the economy's production. (From a macroeconomic standpoint, transfer payments are like negative taxes.) Because GDP is intended to measure income from, and expenditure on, the production of goods and services, transfer payments are not counted as part of government purchases.

transfer payment a payment for which no good or service is exchanged

Net Exports

Net exports equal the purchases of domestically produced goods by foreigners (exports) minus the domestic purchases of foreign goods (imports). A domestic firm's sale to a buyer in another country, such as the sale of textbooks produced in the UK to customers in South Africa, increases UK net exports.

net exports spending on domestically produced goods by foreigners (exports) minus spending on foreign goods by domestic residents (imports)

The 'net' in 'net exports' refers to the fact that the value of imports is subtracted from the value of exports. This subtraction is made because imports of goods and services are included in other components of GDP. For example, suppose that a UK household buys a £50,000 car from Volvo, the Swedish car maker. That transaction increases consumption in the UK by £50,000 because car purchases are part of consumer spending in the UK. It also reduces net exports by £50,000 because the car is an import (note it represents an export for Sweden). In other words, net exports include goods and services produced abroad (with a minus sign) because these goods and services are included in consumption, investment and government purchases (with a plus sign). Thus, when a domestic household, firm or government buys a good or service from abroad, the purchase reduces net exports, but because it also raises consumption, investment or government purchases, it does not affect GDP. The above example shows the importance of making sure that we focus on a particular country when discussing imports and exports because of the potential for confusion to arise.

REAL VERSUS NOMINAL GDP

If total spending rises from one year to the next, one of two things (or a combination of the two) must be true: (1) the economy is producing a larger output of goods and services, or (2) goods and services are being sold at higher prices. When studying changes in the economy over time, economists want to separate these two effects and businesses need to be able to have an accurate and stable picture of what is happening on which to base decision making. In particular, they want a measure of the total quantity of goods and services the economy is producing that is not affected by changes in the prices of those goods and services.

The answer is *real GDP*. Real GDP presents the value of goods and services and accounts for changes in prices. It does this by valuing goods and services at prices that prevailed in some specific year in the past. By evaluating current production using prices that are fixed at past levels, real GDP shows how the economy's overall production of goods and services changes over time.

To see more precisely how real GDP is constructed, let us consider an example. Table 20.1 shows some data for an economy that produces only two goods, burgers and pizzas. The table shows the quantities of the two goods produced and their prices in the years 2023, 2024 and 2025.

TABLE 20.1	**Real and Nominal GDP**

This table shows how to calculate nominal GDP, real GDP and the GDP deflator for a hypothetical economy that produces only burgers and pizzas.

	Prices and quantities			
Year	**Price of burgers (€)**	**Quantity of burgers**	**Price of pizzas (€)**	**Quantity of pizzas**
2023	1	100	2	50
2024	2	150	3	100
2025	3	200	4	150
Year	**Calculating nominal GDP**			
2023	(€1 per burger × 100 pizzas) + (€2 per pizza × 50 pizzas) = €200			
2024	(€2 per burger × 150 pizzas) + (€3 per pizza × 100 pizzas) = €600			
2025	(€3 per burger × 200 pizzas) + (€4 per pizza × 150 pizzas) = €1,200			
Year	**Calculating real GDP (base year 2023)**			
2023	(€1 per burger × 100 pizzas) + (€2 per pizza × 50 pizzas) = €200			
2024	(€1 per burger × 150 pizzas) + (€2 per pizza × 100 pizzas) = €350			
2025	(€1 per burger × 200 pizzas) + (€2 per pizza × 150 pizzas) = €500			
Year	**Calculating the GDP deflator**			
2023	(€200/€200) × 100 = 100			
2024	(€600/€350) × 100 = 171			
2025	(€1,200/€500) × 100 = 240			

To compute total spending in this economy, we would multiply the quantities of burgers and pizzas by their prices. In the year 2023, 100 burgers are sold at a price of €1 per burger, so expenditure on burgers equals €100. In the same year, 50 pizzas are sold for €2 per pizza, so expenditure on pizzas also equals €100. Total expenditure in the economy, the sum of expenditure on burgers and expenditure on pizzas, is €200. This amount, the production of goods and services valued at current prices, is called **nominal GDP**.

nominal GDP the production of goods and services valued at current prices

The table shows the calculation of nominal GDP for these three years. Total spending rises from €200 in 2023 to €600 in 2024 and then to €1,200 in 2025. Part of this rise is attributable to the increase in the quantities of burgers and pizzas, and part is attributable to the increase in the prices of burgers and pizzas.

To obtain a measure of the amount produced that is not affected by changes in prices, we use **real GDP**, which is the production of goods and services valued at constant prices. We calculate real GDP by first choosing one year as a *base year*. We then use the prices of burgers and pizzas in the base year to compute the value of goods and services in all of the years. In other words, the prices in the base year provide the basis for comparing quantities in different years.

real GDP a measure of the amount produced that is not affected by changes in prices

Suppose that we choose 2023 to be the base year in our example. We can then use the prices of burgers and pizzas in 2023 to compute the value of goods and services produced in 2023, 2024 and 2025. Table 20.1 shows these calculations. To compute real GDP for 2023 we use the prices of burgers and pizzas in 2023 (the base year) and the quantities of burgers and pizzas produced in 2023. (Thus for the base year, real GDP always equals nominal GDP.) To compute real GDP for 2024, we use the prices of burgers and pizzas in 2023 (the base year) and the quantities of burgers and pizzas produced in 2024. Similarly, to compute real GDP for 2025, we use the prices in 2023 and the quantities in 2023. When we find that real GDP has risen from €200 in 2023 to €350 in 2024 and then to €500 in 2025, we know that the increase is attributable to an increase in the quantities produced, because the prices are being held fixed at base year levels.

To sum up: nominal GDP uses current prices to place a value on the economy's production of goods and services, while real GDP uses constant base year prices to place a value on the economy's production of goods and services. Because real GDP is not affected by changes in prices, changes in real GDP reflect only changes in the amounts being produced. Thus, real GDP is a measure of the economy's production of goods and services.

Our goal in computing GDP is to gauge how well the overall economy is performing. Because real GDP measures the economy's production of goods and services, it reflects the economy's ability to satisfy people's needs and desires. Thus, real GDP is a better gauge of economic well-being than is nominal GDP. When economists talk about the economy's GDP, they usually mean real GDP rather than nominal GDP. And when they talk about growth in the economy, they measure that growth as the percentage change in real GDP from one period to another.

The GDP Deflator

Nominal GDP reflects both the prices of goods and services and the quantities of goods and services the economy is producing. In contrast, by holding prices constant at base year levels, real GDP reflects only the quantities produced. From these two statistics, we can compute a third, called the **GDP deflator**, which reflects the prices of goods and services but not the quantities produced.

The GDP deflator is calculated as follows:

$$\text{GDP deflator} = \left(\frac{\text{Nominal GDP}}{\text{Real GDP}} \right) \times 100$$

> **GDP deflator** a measure of the price level calculated as the ratio of nominal GDP to real GDP times 100

Because nominal GDP and real GDP must be the same in the base year, the GDP deflator for the base year always equals 100. The GDP deflator for subsequent years measures the change in nominal GDP from the base year that cannot be attributable to a change in real GDP.

The GDP deflator measures the current level of prices relative to the level of prices in the base year. To see why this is true, consider a couple of simple examples. First, imagine that the quantities produced in the economy rise over time but prices remain the same. In this case, both nominal and real GDP rise together, so the GDP deflator is constant. Now suppose, instead, that prices rise over time but the quantities produced stay the same. In this second case, nominal GDP rises but real GDP remains the same, so the GDP deflator rises as well. Notice that, in both cases, the GDP deflator reflects what is happening to prices, not quantities.

Let us now return to our numerical example in Table 20.1. The GDP deflator is computed at the bottom of the table. For year 2023, nominal GDP is €200 and real GDP is €200, so the GDP deflator is 100. For the year 2024, nominal GDP is €600 and real GDP is €350, so the GDP deflator is 171. Because the GDP deflator rose in year 2024 from 100 to 171, we can say that the price level increased by 71 per cent.

> **SELF TEST** Define real and nominal GDP. Which is a better measure of economic well-being? Why?

INFLATION: MEASURING THE COST OF LIVING

Distinguishing between real and nominal GDP is important, but this leads us to another question: how do we measure changes in prices over time, and the change in prices of all goods and services produced in the economy as opposed to the bundle of goods bought by the average household? If firms face increases in the price of component parts, raw materials and other supplies then they must consider whether to increase prices of finished goods to the consumer or maintain their selling price and accept lower profit margins. If they do pass on these price increases to consumers, what will rivals do and how will consumers respond?

To measure these changes in prices we use a statistic called the **consumer price index (CPI)**. The CPI is used to monitor changes in the cost of living over time and is a measure of inflation. It is a standard method of measuring changes in prices adopted in many countries. Economists use the term **inflation** to describe a situation in which the economy's overall price level is rising. The *inflation rate* is the percentage change in the price level from the previous period.

> **consumer price index (CPI)** a measure of the overall prices of the goods and services bought by a typical consumer
> **inflation** an increase in the overall price level in the economy

How the CPI Is Calculated

To calculate the CPI and the inflation rate, national statistics offices use data on the prices of thousands of goods and services. To see exactly how these statistics are constructed, let us revisit our simple economy in which consumers buy only two goods, burgers and pizzas. Table 20.2 shows the five steps that national statistics offices follow.

- *Fix the basket.* The first step in computing the CPI is to determine which prices are most important to the typical consumer. If the typical consumer buys more burgers than pizzas, then the price of burgers is more important than the price of pizzas and, therefore, should be given greater weight in measuring the cost of living. The statistics office sets these weights by surveying consumers and finding the basket of goods and services that the typical consumer buys. In the example in the table, the typical consumer buys a basket of four burgers and two pizzas.
- *Find the prices.* The second step in computing the CPI is to find the prices of each of the goods and services in the basket for each point in time. The table shows the prices of burgers and pizzas for three different years.
- *Compute the basket's cost.* The third step is to use the data on prices to calculate the cost of the basket of goods and services at different times. The table shows this calculation for each of the three years. Notice that only the prices in this calculation change. By keeping the basket of goods the same (four burgers and two pizzas), we are isolating the effects of price changes from the effect of any quantity changes that might be occurring at the same time.
- *Choose a base year and compute the index.* The fourth step is to designate one year as the base year, which is the benchmark against which other years are compared. To calculate the index, the price of the basket of goods and services in each year is divided by the price of the basket in the base year, and this ratio is then multiplied by 100. The resulting number is the CPI.

  In the example in the table, 2023 is the base year. In this year, the basket of burgers and pizzas costs €8. Therefore, the price of the basket in all years is divided by €8 and multiplied by 100. The CPI is 100 in 2023. (The index is always 100 in the base year.) The CPI is 175 in 2024. This means that the price of the basket in 2024 is 175 per cent of its price in the base year. Put differently, a basket of goods that costs €100 in the base year costs €175 in 2024. Similarly, the CPI is 250 in 2025, indicating that the price level in 2025 is 250 per cent of the price level in the base year.

- *Compute the inflation rate.* The fifth and final step is to use the CPI to calculate the **inflation rate**, which is the percentage change in the price index from the preceding period. That is, the inflation rate between two consecutive years is computed as follows:

$$\text{Inflation rate in year 2} = 100 \times \frac{(\text{CPI in year 2} - \text{CPI in year 1})}{\text{CPI in year 1}}$$

In our example, the inflation rate is 75 per cent in 2024 and 43 per cent in 2025.

> **inflation rate** the percentage change in the price index from the preceding period

| TABLE 20.2 | Calculating the CPI and the Inflation Rate: An Example |

This table shows how to calculate the CPI and the inflation rate for a hypothetical economy in which consumers buy only burgers and pizzas.

Step 1: Survey consumers to determine a fixed basket of goods

Four burgers, two pizzas

Step 2: Find the price of each good in each year

Year	Price of burgers €	Price of pizzas €
2023	1	2
2024	2	3
2025	3	4

Step 3: Compute the cost of the basket of goods in each year

2023	(€1 per burger × 4 burgers) + (€2 per pizza × 2 pizzas) = €8
2024	(€2 per burger × 4 burgers) + (€3 per pizza × 2 pizzas) = €14
2025	(€3 per burger × 4 burgers) + (€4 per pizza × 2 pizzas) = €20

Step 4: Choose one year as a base year (2017) and compute the CPI in each year

2023	(€8/€8) × 100 = 100
2024	(€14/€8) × 100 = 175
2025	(€20/€8) × 100 = 250

Step 5: Use the CPI to compute the inflation rate from previous year

2024	(175 − 100)/100 × 100 = 75%
2025	(250 − 175)/175 × 100 = 43%

Although this example simplifies the real world by including only two goods, it shows how statistics offices compute the CPI and the inflation rate. Statistics offices collect and process data on the prices of thousands of goods and services every month and, by following the five foregoing steps, determine how quickly the cost of living for the typical consumer is rising.

In addition to the CPI for the overall economy, statistics offices may calculate price indices for the sub-categories of 'goods' and of 'services' separately, as well as the **producer price index**, which measures the change in prices of a basket of goods and services bought by firms rather than consumers. Because firms eventually pass on their costs to consumers in the form of higher consumer prices, changes in the producer price index are often thought to be useful in predicting changes in the CPI.

 producer price index a measure of the change in prices of a basket of goods and services bought by firms

Problems in Measuring the Cost of Living

The goal of the CPI is to measure changes in the cost of living. In other words, the CPI tries to gauge how much incomes must rise to maintain a constant standard of living. The CPI, however, is not a perfect measure of the cost of living. Four problems with the index are widely acknowledged but difficult to solve.

Substitution Bias The first problem is called *substitution bias*. When prices change from one year to the next, they do not all change proportionately: some prices rise more than others and some prices fall. Consumers respond to these differing price changes by buying less of the goods whose prices have risen and by buying more of the goods whose prices have risen less or perhaps even have fallen. That is, consumers substitute towards goods that have become relatively less expensive. For businesses, this information is important to know as part of their overall planning. If a prices index is computed assuming a fixed basket of goods, it ignores the possibility of consumer substitution and, therefore, overstates the increase in the cost of living from one year to the next.

Let us consider a simple example. Imagine that in the base year apples are cheaper than pears, and so consumers buy more apples than pears. When the statistics office constructs the basket of goods, it will include more apples than pears. Suppose that next year pears are cheaper than apples. Consumers will respond to the price changes by buying more pears and fewer apples. Yet, when computing the CPI, the statistics office uses a fixed basket, which in essence assumes that consumers continue buying the now expensive apples in the same quantities as before. For this reason, the index will measure a much larger increase in the cost of living than consumers actually experience.

Introduction of New Goods When a new good is introduced, consumers have more variety from which to choose. Greater variety, in turn, makes each unit of currency more valuable, so consumers need fewer units to maintain any given standard of living. Yet because the CPI is based on a fixed basket of goods and services, it does not reflect this change in the purchasing power of the currency.

Unmeasured Quality Change If the quality of a good deteriorates from one year to the next, the effective value of a unit of currency falls, even if the price of the good stays the same. Similarly, if the quality rises from one year to the next, the effective value of a unit of currency rises. National statistics offices do try to account for quality change. When the quality of a good in the basket changes (for example, when a smartphone has a better quality camera) the statistics office adjusts the price of the good to account for the quality change. It is, in essence, trying to compute the price of a basket of goods of constant quality.

Statistics offices attempt to correct for this by a method known as *hedonic quality adjustment*. This involves working out the average characteristics of a product, for example a smartphone, and adjusting the price when one or more of these average characteristics increases. Despite these efforts, changes in quality remain a problem, because quality is so hard to measure.

Relevance A final problem with the index is that people may not see the reported CPI measure of inflation as relevant to their particular situation. This is because their spending patterns are individual and might not be typical of the representative pattern on which the official figures are based. For example, if an individual spent a high proportion of their income on fuel and their mortgage, the effect of price rises in gas, electricity, petrol and a rise in mortgage rates would have a disproportionate effect on their own experience of inflation.

The GDP Deflator Versus the CPI

Economists and policy makers monitor both the GDP deflator and the CPI to gauge how quickly prices are rising. Usually, these two statistics tell a similar story. Yet there are two important differences that can cause them to diverge.

The first difference is that the GDP deflator reflects the prices of all goods and services *produced domestically*, whereas the CPI reflects the prices of all goods and services *bought by consumers*. For example, suppose that the price of an aeroplane produced by Dassault, a French aerospace firm and sold to the French Air Force, rises. Even though the aeroplane is part of GDP in France, it is not part of the basket of goods and services bought by a typical consumer. Thus, the price increase shows up in the GDP deflator for France but not in the CPI.

This first difference between the CPI and the GDP deflator is particularly important when the price of oil changes. Although the UK does produce some oil, as with all of Europe and also North America, much of the oil used in the UK is imported from the Middle East. As a result, oil and oil products such as petrol and heating oil comprise a much larger share of consumer spending than they do of GDP. When the price of oil rises, the CPI rises by much more than the GDP deflator.

The second and subtler difference between the GDP deflator and the CPI concerns how various prices are weighted to yield a single number for the overall level of prices. The CPI compares the price of a *fixed* basket of goods and services with the price of the basket in the base year. Statistics offices revise this basket of goods on a regular basis. In contrast, the GDP deflator compares the price of *currently produced* goods and services with the price of the same goods and services in the base year. Thus the group of goods and services used to compute the GDP deflator changes automatically over time. This difference is not important when all prices are changing proportionately. If the prices of different goods and services are changing by varying amounts, the way we weight the various prices matters for the overall inflation rate.

Comparing Inflation Over Time

The purpose of measuring the overall level of prices in the economy is to permit comparisons of monetary figures from different points in time. A business might want to compare what it is paying for raw materials in 2024 with 2014, for example.

To do this we need to know the level of prices in 2014 and the level of prices in 2024. To compare prices, we need to inflate the 2014 prices to turn the 2014 unit of currency (euro in this example) into today's unit of currency. A prices index determines the size of this inflation correction.

The formula for turning currency figures from *year T* into today's currency is:

$$\text{Amount in today's currency} = \text{amount in year } T \text{ currency} \times \frac{\text{Price level today}}{\text{Price level in year } T}$$

A prices index such as the CPI measures the price level and determines the size of the inflation correction.

Real and Nominal Interest Rates

Correcting economic variables for the effects of inflation is particularly important, and somewhat tricky, when we look at data on interest rates. Firms have cash deposits in bank accounts which may earn interest. Conversely, when firms borrow from a bank to buy capital equipment, they will pay interest on the loan. Interest represents a payment in the future for a transfer of money in the past. As a result, interest rates always involve comparing amounts of money at different points in time. To fully understand interest rates, we need to know how to correct for the effects of inflation.

Suppose that a firm has cash deposits of €10,000 in a bank account that pays an annual interest rate of 2 per cent. After a year passes, the firm has accumulated €200 in interest. The firm then withdraws the €10,200. Is the firm €200 richer than a year earlier?

The answer depends on what we mean by 'richer'. The firm does have €200 more than before. In other words, the number of euros has risen by 2 per cent. If prices have risen at the same time, each euro now buys less than it did a year ago. Thus, the firm's purchasing power has not risen by 2 per cent. If the inflation rate was 1 per cent, then the amount of resources the firm can buy has increased by only 1 per cent. If the inflation rate was 5 per cent, then the price of goods has increased proportionately more than the number of euros in the account. In that case, the firm's purchasing power has actually fallen by 3 per cent.

The interest rate that the bank pays is called the nominal interest rate, and the interest rate corrected for inflation is called the real interest rate. We can write the relationship between the nominal interest rate, the real interest rate and inflation as follows:

$$\text{Real interest rate} = \text{Nominal interest rate} - \text{Inflation rate}$$

The real interest rate is the difference between the nominal interest rate and the rate of inflation. The nominal interest rate tells you how fast the number of units of currency in a bank account rises over time. The real interest rate tells you how fast the purchasing power of the bank account rises over time.

UNEMPLOYMENT

What is Unemployment?

The answer to this question may seem obvious: an unemployed person is someone who does not have a job. If you are in full-time education, however, you do not have a full-time job in the usual sense of the word, i.e. you are not in full-time paid employment and not available for work. If you were suffering from some long-term illness that meant that you were unfit for work, although you would not have a job, we would not say that you were unemployed because you would not be available for work. From these two examples, it seems clear that we need to qualify our original definition of an unemployed person as 'someone who does not have a job' to 'someone who does not have a job and who is available for work'.

We still need to be clear as to what we mean by 'available for work'. Suppose you were not in full-time employment and were offered a job as a research assistant for €1 a day. Would you take it? At this wage rate, probably not. At another extreme, suppose you won so much money on the Euro Millions Lottery that you decided you would leave university and live off your winnings for the rest of your life. Would you be unemployed? No, because you would still be unavailable for work, no matter what wage rate you were offered. Thus, being unemployed also depends upon whether you are willing to work (whether you are 'available for work') at going wage rates.

We are now in a position to give a more precise definition of what it means to be **unemployed**: the number unemployed in an economy is the number of people of working age who are able and available for work at current wage rates and who do not have a job.

unemployed the number unemployed in an economy is the number of people of working age who are able and available for work at current wage rates and who do not have a job

Normally, economists find it more convenient to speak of the *unemployment rate*. This expresses the number unemployed as a percentage of the *labour force*, which in turn can be defined as the total number of people who could possibly be employed in the economy at any given point in time. If you think about it, this must be equal to the total number of people who are employed plus the total number of people who are unemployed.

How is Unemployment Measured?

There are two basic ways that government agencies go about measuring the unemployment rate in the economy:

The Claimant Count One simple way is to count the number of people who, on any given day, are claiming unemployment benefit payments from the government: the so-called *claimant count*. Since a government agency is paying out the benefits, it will be easy to gather data on the number of claimants. The government also has a good idea of the total labour force in employment, since it is receiving income tax payments from them. Adding to this the number of unemployment benefit claimants is a measure of the total labour force, and expressing the claimant count as a proportion of the labour force is a measure of the unemployment rate.

Labour Force Surveys The second and probably more reliable method of measuring unemployment is through the use of surveys, in other words going out and asking people questions, based on an accepted definition of unemployment. In many countries, the government carries out Labour Force Surveys based on the standardized definition of unemployment from the International Labour Office, or ILO. The ILO's definition of an unemployed person is someone who is without a job and who is willing to start work within the next two weeks and either has been looking for work within the past four weeks or was waiting to start a job. The Labour Force Survey is carried out quarterly throughout Europe. The surveys are published in different languages, but scrutinized by statisticians to ensure comparability between the surveys carried out in each member state.

Once the government has placed all the individuals covered by the survey in a category, it computes various statistics to summarize the state of the labour market. The **labour force** is defined as the sum of the employed and the unemployed:

Labour force = Number of people employed + number of people unemployed

labour force the total number of workers, including both the employed and the unemployed

The **unemployment rate** can be measured as the percentage of the labour force that is unemployed:

$$\text{Unemployment rate} = \left(\frac{\text{Number of unemployed}}{\text{Labour force}}\right) \times 100$$

unemployment rate the percentage of the labour force that is unemployed

The government computes unemployment rates for the entire adult population and for more narrowly defined groups: men, women, youths and so on.

The same survey results are used to produce data on labour force participation. The **labour force participation rate** measures the percentage of the total adult population of the country that is in the labour force:

$$\text{Labour force participation rate} = \left(\frac{\text{Labour force}}{\text{Adult population}}\right) \times 100$$

labour force participation rate the percentage of the adult population that is in the labour force

This statistic tells us the fraction of the population that has chosen to participate in the labour market. The labour force participation rate, like the unemployment rate, is computed both for the entire adult population and for more specific groups.

Data on the labour market also allow economists and policy makers to monitor changes in the economy over time. The normal rate of unemployment, around which the unemployment rate fluctuates, is called the **natural rate of unemployment** and the deviation of unemployment from its natural rate is called **cyclical unemployment**.

natural rate of unemployment the normal rate of unemployment around which the unemployment rate fluctuates
cyclical unemployment the deviation of unemployment from its natural rate

Unemployment figures represent an important statistic for businesses because they give an indication of the performance of the economy as a whole. They are part of the jigsaw that businesses need to make more informed decisions about the state of the economy, whether to make investments, what the labour market is like and how this might impact on wage rates and costs, and how they might fill skill shortages.

> **SELF TEST** How is the unemployment rate measured? How might the unemployment rate overstate the amount of joblessness? How might it understate it?

THE BALANCE OF PAYMENTS

International trade involves all the purchases and sales of goods and services between firms from different countries. The record of the flows of money as part of the transactions of international trade is presented in the balance of payments. The **balance of payments** is the official account of international payments for the import and export of goods, services and capital. The balance of payments consists of three elements. In theory, the balance of payments must balance. We will see more of why this is so later in this section. The balance of trade, however, does not have to balance. It is also very difficult to collect fully accurate data and as a result there is usually a balancing item which takes into account the fact that there will be statistical discrepancies.

> **balance of payments** the official account of international payments for the import and export of goods, services and capital

The Current Account The current account of the balance of payments records the flows of money which represent payments for goods and services transacted between firms in the domestic economy and those in foreign economies. There will be the import and export of physical goods such as cars, steel, coal, clothing, food, oil and so on, and the value of the flows of funds for the import and export of services such as insurance, banking, tourism and leisure. The trade in physical goods is sometimes referred to as the visible trade balance and the trade in services is referred to as the invisible trade balance. Together, the difference between the value of imports and exports of visible and invisible items is recorded in the balance of trade.

The current account of the balance of payments also includes net income flows. That is the difference between flows of income such as wages and investment income between the domestic economy and foreigners. Net current transfers record secondary income flows such as transfers between governments or between governments and international bodies such as the EU.

The Financial Account The financial account records the flows of funds between the domestic economy and foreigners for investment. For example, if Nissan, a Japanese company, expands its car manufacturing facility in Sunderland in the UK, this would be recorded as an inflow on the financial account for the UK. Funds also flow between countries in payment for bonds, stocks and other financial instruments and these are classed as portfolio investment. The financial account will also include speculative money flows which occur as traders move funds from one country to another in search of returns. For example, if there is a hint that the US central bank, the Federal Reserve, is going to increase interest rates in the United States and interest rates elsewhere remain constant, traders may sell pounds and euros and buy dollars to invest in dollar denominated assets which attract higher interest rates. These flows of funds in response to changes in interest rates or exchange rates are sometimes called 'hot money flows'.

The Capital Account The capital account records the transfer of funds for the purchase and sale of non-financial assets such as land, the movement of funds for aid for capital works, the forgiveness of debt and the sale of embassies.

Factors Affecting the Balance of Payments

The trade between countries can be affected by a range of factors. Key among these are interest rates, exchange rates, government policies, productivity levels in different countries, the difference in inflation rates, and levels of consumer spending in different countries on imports and exports. Some countries will have to import raw materials and foodstuffs because they do not have the resources to produce those goods, while others might have very strong export sales, for example, Germany. The state of the economy in the country in comparison to its trading partners can also affect the balance of payments. If a country is going through a contraction in economic activity, this can mean that spending on imports goes down. If a foreign country is experiencing an upturn in economic activity, this might lead to increased export sales for the domestic economy.

The International Flows of Goods and Capital

Businesses in an economy buy and sell goods and services in world product markets and they buy and sell capital assets such as stocks and bonds in world financial markets. Here we discuss these two activities and the close relationship between them.

The Flow of Goods and Services: Exports, Imports and Net Exports **Exports** are domestically produced goods and services that are sold abroad, and **imports** are foreign-produced goods and services that are sold domestically. When Lloyd's of London insures a building in New York, it is paid an insurance premium for this service by the owner of the building. The sale of the insurance service provided by Lloyd's is an export for the UK and an import for the United States. When Volvo, the Swedish car manufacturer, makes a car and sells it to a Swiss resident, the sale is an import for Switzerland and an export for Sweden.

> **exports** goods produced domestically and sold abroad leading to an inflow of funds into a country
>
> **imports** goods produced abroad and purchased for use in the domestic economy leading to an outflow of funds from a country

> **PITFALL PREVENTION** It can be easy to get confused about imports and exports of services. For goods, it can be helpful to focus on the physical movement of the good. For services, we need to think about the direction of payment. For example, if a Dutch family decides to take a holiday in Dubai all members of the family physically travel to Dubai. However, what they are actually doing is buying a service, tourism in this case, from Dubai and so their visit represents an import to the Netherlands and an export to Dubai.

The net exports of any country are the value of its exports minus the value of its imports. The sale of insurance services abroad by Lloyd's raises UK net exports, and the Volvo sale reduces Swiss net exports. Because net exports tell us whether a country is, in total, a seller or a buyer in world markets for goods and services, net exports are also called the **trade balance**. If net exports are positive, exports are greater than imports, indicating that the country sells more goods and services abroad than it buys from other countries. In this case, the country is said to run a **trade surplus**. If net exports are negative, exports are less than imports, indicating that the country sells fewer goods and services abroad than it buys from other countries. In this case, the country is said to run a **trade deficit**. If net exports are zero, its exports and imports are exactly equal, and the country is said to have **balanced trade**.

> **trade balance** the value of a nation's exports minus the value of its imports; also called net exports
> **trade surplus** an excess of exports over imports
> **trade deficit** an excess of imports over exports
> **balanced trade** a situation in which exports equal imports

Some of the factors that might influence a country's exports, imports and net exports include the following:

- the tastes of consumers for domestic and foreign goods
- the prices of goods at home and abroad
- the exchange rates at which people can use domestic currency to buy foreign currencies
- the incomes of consumers at home and abroad
- the cost of transporting goods from country to country
- the policies of the government towards international trade.

As these variables change over time, so does the amount of international trade.

The Flow of Financial Resources: Net Capital Outflow Residents of an open economy participate in world financial markets. A UK resident with £50,000 could use that money to buy a car from BMW, but they could instead use that money to buy stock in the German BMW corporation. The first transaction would represent a flow of goods, whereas the second would represent a flow of capital.

The term **net capital outflow** refers to the purchase of foreign assets by domestic residents minus the purchase of domestic assets by foreigners. It is sometimes called *net foreign investment*. When a UK resident buys shares in BMW, the purchase raises UK net capital outflow. When a Japanese resident buys a bond issued by the UK government, the purchase reduces UK net capital outflow.

> **net capital outflow** the purchase of foreign assets by domestic residents minus the purchase of domestic assets by foreigners

Recall that the flow of capital abroad takes two forms. If the French car manufacturer Renault opens up a factory in Romania, that is an example of *foreign direct investment*. Alternatively, if a French citizen buys shares in a Romanian company, that is an example of *foreign portfolio investment*. In the first case, the French owner is actively managing the investment, whereas in the second case the French owner has a more passive role. In both cases, French residents are buying assets located in another country, so both purchases increase French net capital outflow.

Let us consider briefly some of the more important variables that influence net capital outflow:

- the real interest rates being paid on foreign assets
- the real interest rates being paid on domestic assets
- the perceived economic and political risks of holding assets abroad
- the government policies that affect foreign ownership of domestic assets.

For example, consider German investors deciding whether to buy Mexican government bonds or German government bonds. To make this decision, German investors compare the real interest rates offered on the two bonds. The higher a bond's real interest rate, the more attractive it is. While making this comparison, however, German investors must also take into account the risk that one of these governments might *default* on its debt (that is, not pay interest or principal when it is due), as well as any restrictions that the Mexican government has imposed, or might impose in the future, on foreign investors in Mexico.

The Equality of Net Exports and Net Capital Outflow

Net exports and net capital outflow each measure a type of imbalance in these markets. Net exports measure an imbalance between a country's exports and its imports. Net capital outflow measures an imbalance between the amount of foreign assets bought by domestic residents and the amount of domestic assets bought by foreigners.

An important but subtle fact of accounting states that, for an economy as a whole, these two imbalances must offset each other. That is, net capital outflow (NCO) always equals net exports (NX):

$$NCO = NX$$

This equation holds because every transaction that affects one side of this equation must also affect the other side by exactly the same amount. This equation is an *identity*, an equation that must hold because of the way the variables in the equation are defined and measured.

To see why this accounting identity is true, consider an example. Suppose that BP sells some aircraft fuel to a Japanese airline. In this sale, the UK company (BP) gives aircraft fuel to the Japanese company, and the Japanese company gives yen to the UK company. Notice that two things have occurred simultaneously. The UK has sold to a foreigner some of its output (the fuel), and this sale increases UK net exports. In addition, the UK has acquired some foreign assets (the yen), and this acquisition increases UK *NCO*.

Although BP most probably will not hold on to the yen it has acquired in this sale, any subsequent transaction will preserve the equality of net exports and *NCO*. For example, BP may exchange its yen for pounds with a UK investment fund that wants the yen to buy shares in Sony Corporation, the Japanese maker of consumer electronics. In this case, BP's net export of aircraft fuel equals the investment fund's *NCO* in Sony shares. Hence, *NX* and *NCO* rise by an equal amount.

Alternatively, BP may exchange its yen for pounds with another UK company that wants to buy computers from Toshiba, the Japanese computer maker. In this case, UK imports (of computers) exactly offset UK exports (of aircraft fuel). The sales by BP and Toshiba together affect neither UK net exports nor UK *NCO*. That is, *NX* and *NCO* are the same as they were before these transactions took place.

The equality of net exports and *NCO* follows from the fact that every international transaction is an exchange. When a seller country transfers a good or service to a buyer country, the buyer country gives up some asset to pay for this good or service. The value of that asset equals the value of the good or service sold. When we add everything up, the net value of goods and services sold by a country (*NX*) must equal the net value of assets acquired (*NCO*). The international flow of goods and services and the international flow of capital are two sides of the same coin.

CASE STUDY The UK Balance of Payments

Since the early 1980s, the UK balance of payments on current account has been in deficit. This means that the value of funds leaving the UK in payment for goods and services has been greater than the amount generated from selling goods and services abroad. Figure 20.2 shows that between 2003 and 2008, the deficit widened from around £23 billion to almost £50 billion before narrowing to around £30 billion in 2011. Thereafter, the deficit widened again through to 2016 when it reached around £110 billion but since then has been narrowing and at the end of 2022, the current account deficit was around £32 billion or 5.2 per cent of GDP. This figure, however, does not include trade in precious metals and when these are taken into account the current account deficit was around £19 billion or around 3 per cent of GDP. The reason for excluding the movements in precious metals is because that trade can be highly volatile and so removing this allows analysts to see the underlying trend in the balance of payments. The trade in goods in the third quarter of 2022 showed a deficit of £64 billion while the trade in services was in surplus for that period at £40.5 billion. One of the biggest influences on the balance of trade deficit was the cost of importing fuels, which increased by £8.8 billion to stand at £38.5 billion overall.

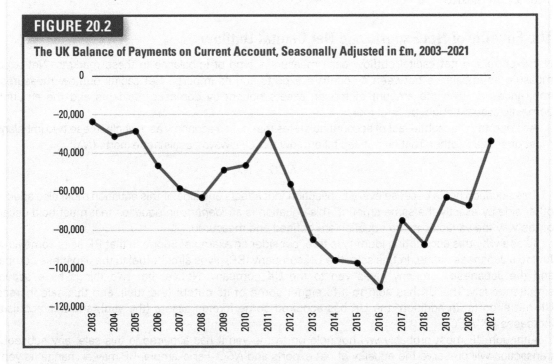

FIGURE 20.2

The UK Balance of Payments on Current Account, Seasonally Adjusted in £m, 2003–2021

(*Continued*)

Questions

1 The balance of payments must balance but the balance of trade need not balance. Explain why this is so.
2 Is a deficit on the balance of trade necessarily something that firms and the government should be worried about?
3 What factors might explain the narrowing of the deficit on the balance of payments on current account since 2016?

References: www.ons.gov.uk/economy/nationalaccounts/balanceofpayments/bulletins/balanceofpayments/julytoseptember2022 (accessed 11 June 2023).
www.ons.gov.uk/economy/nationalaccounts/balanceofpayments/timeseries/hbop/pnbp (accessed 11 June 2023).

Saving and Investment, and Their Relationship to the International Flows

A nation's saving and investment is crucial to its long run economic growth. Let us consider how these variables are related to the international flows of goods and capital as measured by net exports and *NCO*. We can do this most easily with the help of some simple mathematics.

Recall that the total expenditure on the economy's output of goods and services is the sum of expenditure on consumption, investment, government purchases and net exports ($Y = C + I + G + NX$). Recall that national saving is the income of the nation that is left after paying for current consumption and government purchases. National saving (S) equals $Y - C - G$. If we rearrange the first equation to reflect this fact, we obtain:

$$Y - C - G = I + NX$$
$$S = I + NX$$

Because net exports (NX) also equal NCO, we can write this equation as:

$$S = I + NCO$$
$$Saving = Domestic\ investment + NCO$$

This equation shows that a nation's saving must equal its domestic investment plus its *NCO*. In other words, when Dutch citizens save a euro of their income for the future, that euro can be used to finance accumulation of domestic capital or it can be used to finance the purchase of capital abroad.

In a closed economy (with no external trade), net capital outflow is zero ($NCO = 0$), so saving equals investment ($S = I$). In an open economy with trade there are two uses for its saving: domestic investment and *NCO*.

We can view the financial system as standing between the two sides of this identity. For example, suppose the Smith family decides to save some of its income for retirement. This decision contributes to national saving, the left-hand side of our equation. If the Smiths deposit their saving in an investment fund, the fund may use some of the deposit to buy shares issued by BP, which uses the proceeds to build solar energy projects. In addition, the investment fund may use some of the Smiths' deposit to buy shares issued by Toyota, which uses the proceeds to build a factory in Osaka. These transactions show up on the right-hand side of the equation. From the standpoint of UK accounting, the BP expenditure on a new solar project is domestic investment, and the purchase of Toyota stock by a UK resident is *NCO*. Thus, all saving in the UK economy shows up as investment in the UK economy or as UK *NCO*.

> **SELF TEST** Define *NX* and *NCO*. Explain how they are related.

SUMMARY

- Economic well-being can be measured by GDP.
- Because every transaction has a buyer and a seller, the total expenditure in the economy must equal the total income in the economy, and this must also be equal to the value of the output produced in the economy over a period of time.

- GDP measures an economy's total expenditure on newly produced goods and services, and the total income earned from the production of these goods and services. More precisely, GDP is the market value of all final goods and services produced within a country in a given period of time.

- The standard of living in an economy depends on the economy's ability to produce goods and services.

- Nominal GDP uses current prices to value the economy's production of goods and services. Real GDP uses constant base year prices to value the economy's production of goods and services. The GDP deflator (calculated from the ratio of nominal to real GDP) measures the level of prices in the economy.

- The CPI shows the changes in the prices of a basket of goods and services relative to the prices of the same basket in the base year. The index is used to measure the overall level of prices in the economy. The percentage change in the CPI measures the inflation rate.

- The CPI is an imperfect measure of the cost of living for four reasons. First, it does not take into account consumers' ability to substitute towards goods that become relatively cheaper over time. Second, it does not take into account increases in the purchasing power of money due to the introduction of new goods. Third, it is distorted by unmeasured changes in the quality of goods and services. A final problem with the index is that people may not see the reported CPI measure of inflation as relevant to their particular situation.

- The nominal interest rate is the interest rate usually reported; it is the rate at which the amount of money in a savings account increases over time. In contrast, the real interest rate takes into account changes in the value of money over time. The real interest rate equals the nominal interest rate minus the rate of inflation.

- An economy's saving can be used either to finance investment at home or to buy assets abroad. Thus, national saving equals domestic investment plus NCO.

- The unemployment rate is the percentage of those who would like to work who do not have jobs. The government calculates this statistic monthly based on a survey of thousands of households.

- The unemployment rate is an imperfect measure of joblessness. Some people who call themselves unemployed may actually not want to work, and some people who would like to work have left the labour force after an unsuccessful search.

- The balance of payments records the value of the transactions between nations. It is generally split into the current account and the capital account.

- The balance of trade records the value of visible imports and exports of a country.

- Net exports are the value of domestic goods and services sold abroad minus the value of foreign goods and services sold domestically. NCO is the acquisition of foreign assets by domestic residents minus the acquisition of domestic assets by foreigners. Because every international transaction involves an exchange of an asset for a good or service, an economy's NCO always equals its net exports.

IN THE NEWS

Economic Indicators in Europe

In January 2023, the unemployment rate in the Eurozone 19 countries was around 6.5 per cent. Inflation in the Eurozone had been accelerating throughout 2022 changing from 5.9 per cent in February 2022 to 10.1 per cent in December 2022. Quarter two of 2020 saw GDP growth in the Eurozone shrink by 11.5 per cent but by quarter two in 2021, growth had recovered to 2.0 per cent only to slow again into 2022 with quarter four of 2022 showing growth of 0.3 per cent. The current account of the Eurozone in February 2022 recorded a surplus of €54 million in February 2022 and just over €5 billion in March 2022, but thereafter the current account slipped into deficit reaching almost €24 billion in August 2022 before narrowing to almost €4 billion in October 2022.

(Continued)

The economic performance of Eurozone countries was affected by the Financial Crisis and also by Brexit not to mention issues like the pandemic and the conflict in Ukraine.

There were a number of economic shocks which hit the Eurozone from 2019 onwards, not least the adjustment and outcome of Brexit but then the pandemic and the conflict in Ukraine. Europe has, like many countries, suffered from global supply chain disruptions and this, along with a shortage of energy supplies, resulted in accelerating inflation. The European Central Bank had been increasing interest rates to try to combat inflation, but the risk was that this would provide a further drag on economic growth. Some commentators were expecting inflation to continue to be a challenge and that there was an increased likelihood of stagflation, a situation where inflation and low or negative growth occur at the same time. The elevated levels of inflation was expected to reduce consumers' real incomes resulting in lower levels of spending and, thus, reducing growth further.

Questions

1 Given the figures quoted in the article, what does this tell you about the economic performance of the Eurozone during 2022?
2 Given the figures quoted in the article, what conclusions would you draw about how businesses performed in the Eurozone in 2022?
3 What is meant by the phrase 'the deficit on the balance of payments on the current account widened in 2022'?
4 The article notes that the Eurozone is facing challenges into 2023 with the prospect of stagflation very real. Would you agree with this assessment based on the figures quoted? Explain.
5 What other data do you think would be useful in giving an assessment of the performance of the Eurozone economy in the last few years and its prospects for the future?

Reference: Eurostat. www2.deloitte.com/us/en/insights/economy/emea/eurozone-economic-outlook.html (accessed 11 June 2023).

QUESTIONS FOR REVIEW

1 Explain why an economy's income must equal its expenditure.
2 What does the level of a nation's GDP measure? What does the growth rate of GDP measure? Would you rather live in a nation with a high level of GDP and a low growth rate, or in a nation with a low level of GDP and a high growth rate?
3 A farmer sells wheat to a baker for €2. The baker uses the wheat to make bread, which is sold for €3. What is the total contribution of these transactions to GDP?
4 Which do you think has a greater effect on the CPI: a 10 per cent increase in the price of chicken or a 10 per cent increase in the price of caviar? Why?
5 Over a long period of time, the price of a chocolate bar rose from €0.10 to €0.60. Over the same period, the CPI rose from 150 to 300. Adjusted for overall inflation, how much did the price of the chocolate bar change?
6 Why do economists use real GDP rather than nominal GDP to gauge economic well-being?
7 What is the GDP deflator and how does it differ to the CPI?
8 Define net exports and NCO. Explain how and why they are related.
9 Describe how the balance of payments of a country is recorded.
10 What is the relationship between national saving and investment and international flows of funds?

PROBLEMS AND APPLICATIONS

1 Below are some data from the land of milk and honey.

   a. Compute nominal GDP, real GDP and the GDP deflator for each year, using 2023 as the base year.
   b. Compute the percentage change in nominal GDP, real GDP and the GDP deflator in 2024 and 2025 from the preceding year. For each year, identify the variable that does not change. Explain in words why your answer makes sense.
   c. Did economic well-being rise more in 2024 or 2025? Explain.

Year	Price of milk €	Quantity of milk (litres)	Price of honey €	Quantity of honey (litres)
2023	1	100	2	50
2024	1	200	2	100
2025	2	200	4	100

2 To what extent do you think that GDP is a good measure of economic welfare?

3 Suppose that a borrower and a lender agree on the nominal interest rate to be paid on a loan. Then inflation turns out to be higher than they both expected.

   a. Is the real interest rate on this loan higher or lower than expected?
   b. Does the lender gain or lose from this unexpectedly high inflation? Does the borrower gain or lose?

4 Do you think that firms in small towns or in cities have more market power in employing workers? Do you think that firms generally have more market power in employing today than in the 1970s, or less? Explain.

5 How would the following transactions affect UK NCO? Also, state whether each involves direct investment or portfolio investment.

   a. A British mobile telephone company establishes an office in the Czech Republic.
   b. A US company's pension fund buys shares in BP.
   c. Toyota expands its factory in Derby, England.
   d. A London-based investment trust sells its Volkswagen shares to a French investor.

6 How would the following transactions affect UK exports, imports and net exports?

   a. A British art lecturer spends the summer touring museums in Italy.
   b. Students in Paris flock to see the Royal Shakespeare Company perform *King Lear* on tour.
   c. The British art lecturer buys a new Volvo.
   d. A student in Munich buys a Manchester United official team shirt (in Munich).
   e. A British citizen goes to Calais for the day to stock up on French wine.

7 International trade in each of the following products has increased over time. Suggest some reasons why this might be so.

   a. wheat
   b. banking services
   c. computer software
   d. cars

8 Suppose that a car company owned entirely by South Korean citizens opens a new factory in the north of England.

   a. What sort of foreign investment would this represent?
   b. What would be the effect of this investment on UK GDP?
   c. Would the effect on UK GNP be larger or smaller?

9 The pound appreciates in value against the euro from £1 = €1.15 to £1 = €1.20. How does this change affect businesses in the UK that import a high proportion of raw materials from Europe for production? How does the change impact businesses in the UK that export the majority of their products to Europe? How would you expect the change in the exchange rate to affect the balance of payments of the UK and the balance of payments of Germany? Explain.

10 To what extent do you think that the economic indicators for any particular country covered in this chapter provide a picture of the way in which most businesses in that country are performing?

21 AGGREGATE DEMAND AND AGGREGATE SUPPLY AS A MODEL TO DESCRIBE THE ECONOMY

LEARNING OUTCOMES

After reading this chapter you should be able to:

- Outline three key facts about economic fluctuations.
- Explain the difference between the short run and the long run.
- Analyze at least three reasons why the aggregate demand and aggregate supply curve can shift.
- Assess the effect of a shift in either the aggregate demand curve or the aggregate supply curve.

INTRODUCTION

Economic activity fluctuates from year to year. In most years, the production of goods and services rises. Because of increases in the labour force, increases in the capital stock and advances in technological knowledge, the economy can produce more and more over time.

> **economic activity** the amount of buying and selling (transactions) that take place in an economy over a period of time

In some years, however, this normal growth does not occur. Firms find themselves unable to sell all of the goods and services they have to offer, so they cut back on production. Workers are laid off, unemployment rises and firms have excess capacity. With the economy producing fewer goods and services, real GDP and other measures of income fall. Such a period of falling incomes and rising unemployment is called a **recession** if it is relatively mild and a **depression** if it is more severe.

> **recession** a period of declining real incomes and rising unemployment. The technical definition gives recession occurring after two successive quarters of negative economic growth
> **depression** a severe recession

What causes short run fluctuations in economic activity? How are businesses affected by these fluctuations and how do they react? What, if anything, can public policy do to moderate swings in economic activity? These are the questions that we examine now.

The variables that we study in relation to these questions include GDP, unemployment and the price level. The main policy instruments include government spending, taxes, the money supply and interest rates. Many of these policies are designed to influence how the economy works in the short run.

Although there remains some debate among economists about how to analyze short run fluctuations, at an introductory level it is appropriate to use the *model of aggregate demand and aggregate supply*.

THREE KEY FACTS ABOUT ECONOMIC FLUCTUATIONS

Short run fluctuations in economic activity occur in all countries and throughout history. As a starting point for understanding these year to year fluctuations, let us discuss some of their most important properties.

Fact 1: Economic Fluctuations Are Irregular and Unpredictable

Fluctuations in the economy are often called the *business cycle*. As this term suggests, economic fluctuations correspond to changes in business conditions. When real GDP grows rapidly, firms find that customers are plentiful and that profits are growing. On the other hand, during periods of economic contraction, many firms experience declining sales and dwindling profits.

The term *business cycle* is somewhat misleading, however, because it implies that economic fluctuations follow a regular, predictable pattern. In fact, economic fluctuations are not at all regular, and they are almost impossible to predict with much accuracy. Over a period of time, the general trend in real GDP is to rise steadily in many countries, but the path of GDP is not always smooth. We can define a recession as occurring when real GDP falls for two successive quarters. From this definition, we can identify recessions in almost every decade since the 1960s in Europe and across other parts of the world. In recent times the 2007–2009 Financial Crisis caused a global recession, as did the Covid-19 pandemic in 2020.

Fact 2: Most Macroeconomic Quantities Fluctuate Together

Real GDP is the variable that is most commonly used to monitor short run changes in the economy because it is the most comprehensive measure of economic activity. Real GDP measures the total income (adjusted for inflation) of everyone in the economy.

In monitoring short run fluctuations, it does not really matter which measure of economic activity we look at. Most macroeconomic variables that measure some type of income, spending or production fluctuate closely together. When real GDP falls in a recession, so do personal incomes, corporate profits, consumer spending, investment spending, industrial production, retail sales, home sales, car sales and so on. Because recessions are economy-wide phenomena, they show up in many sources of macroeconomic data.

Although many macroeconomic variables fluctuate together, they fluctuate by different amounts. In particular, investment spending by businesses varies greatly over the business cycle. When economic conditions deteriorate, much of the decline is attributable to reductions in spending on new factories, housing and inventories.

Fact 3: As Output Falls, Unemployment Rises

Changes in the economy's output of goods and services are strongly correlated with changes in the economy's utilization of its labour force, so when real GDP declines unemployment rises. When firms choose to produce a smaller quantity of goods and services, they lay off workers, expanding the pool of unemployed. However, there is generally a time lag between any downturn in economic activity and a rise in unemployment and vice versa. Even when positive growth resumes, therefore, unemployment is likely to continue to rise for some time afterwards. For this reason, unemployment is referred to as a 'lagged indicator'.

> **SELF TEST** If economic activity falls, what would you expect to happen to the overall level of consumption, investment, government spending and net exports? What would you expect to happen to the price level?

EXPLAINING SHORT RUN ECONOMIC FLUCTUATIONS

Describing the patterns that economies experience as they fluctuate over time is easy. Explaining what causes these fluctuations is more difficult. The theory of economic fluctuations remains controversial.

How the Short Run Differs From the Long Run

There are a number of theories to explain what determines most important macroeconomic variables in the long run. Much of this analysis is based on two related ideas: the classical dichotomy and monetary neutrality. The classical dichotomy is the separation of variables into real variables (those that measure physical units, quantities or relative prices) and nominal variables (those measured in terms of money). Monetary neutrality refers to the assumption that changes in the money supply affect nominal variables but not real variables.

The Classical Dichotomy and Monetary Neutrality

The political philosopher David Hume (1711–1776) suggested that all economic variables should be divided into nominal variables and real variables. For example, the income of dairy farmers is a nominal variable because it is measured in euros, whereas the quantity of milk they produce is a real variable because it is measured in litres. Similarly, nominal GDP is a nominal variable because it measures the euro value of the economy's output of goods and services; real GDP is a real variable because it measures the total quantity of goods and services produced and is not influenced by the current prices of those goods and services. This separation of variables into these groups is now called the **classical dichotomy**. (A *dichotomy* is a division into two groups, and *classical* refers to the earlier economic thinkers or classical economists.)

classical dichotomy the theoretical separation of nominal and real variables

Application of the classical dichotomy is somewhat tricky when we turn to prices. Prices in the economy are normally quoted in terms of money and, therefore, are nominal variables. For instance, when we say that the price of barley is €2 a kilo or that the price of wheat is €1 a kilo, both prices are nominal variables. But what about a **relative price**, the price of one thing compared to another? In our example, we could say that the price of a kilo of barley is two kilos of wheat. Notice that this relative price is no longer measured in terms of money. When comparing the prices of any two goods, the euro signs cancel and the resulting number is measured in physical units. The lesson is that money prices (e.g. in pounds, euros, rand or dollars) are nominal variables, whereas relative prices are real variables.

relative price the ratio of the price of one good to the price of another

This lesson has several important applications. For instance, the real wage (the money wage adjusted for inflation) is a real variable because it measures the rate at which the economy exchanges goods and services for each unit of labour. Similarly, the real interest rate (the nominal interest rate adjusted for inflation) is a real variable because it measures the rate at which the economy exchanges goods and services produced today for goods and services produced in the future.

Why bother separating variables into these two groups? Hume suggested that the classical dichotomy is useful in analysing the economy because different forces influence real and nominal variables. In particular, he argued, nominal variables are heavily influenced by developments in the economy's monetary system, whereas the monetary system is largely irrelevant for understanding the determinants of important real variables.

Hume's idea is implicit in discussions of the real economy in the long run. Real GDP, saving, investment, real interest rates and unemployment are determined without any mention of the existence of money. The economy's production of goods and services depends on productivity and factor supplies, the real interest rate adjusts to balance the supply and demand for loanable funds, the real wage adjusts to balance the supply and demand for labour, and unemployment results when the real wage is for some reason kept above its equilibrium level. These important conclusions have nothing to do with the quantity of money supplied.

Changes in the supply of money, according to Hume, affect nominal variables but not real variables. When the central bank doubles the money supply, the price level doubles, the euro wage doubles and all other euro values double. Real variables, such as production, employment, real wages and real interest rates, are unchanged. This irrelevance of monetary changes for real variables is called **monetary neutrality**.

monetary neutrality the proposition that changes in the money supply do not affect real variables

An analogy sheds light on the meaning of monetary neutrality. As the unit of account, money is the yardstick we use to measure economic transactions. When a central bank doubles the money supply, other things being equal, all prices double and the value of the unit of account falls by half.

Is this conclusion of monetary neutrality a realistic description of the world in which we live? Most economists today believe that over short periods of time, within the span of a year or two, there is reason to think that monetary changes do have important effects on real variables. Hume himself also doubted that monetary neutrality would apply in the short run. Most economists today accept Hume's conclusion as a description of the economy in the long run. Over the course of a decade, for instance, monetary changes have important effects on nominal variables (such as the price level) but only negligible effects on real variables (such as real GDP). When studying long run changes in the economy, the neutrality of money offers a good description of how the world works.

Beyond a period of several years, changes in the money supply affect prices and other nominal variables but do not affect real GDP, unemployment or other real variables. When studying year to year changes in the economy, however, the assumption of monetary neutrality is no longer appropriate. Most economists believe that, in the short run, real and nominal variables are highly intertwined. In particular, changes in the money supply can temporarily push output away from its long run trend.

To understand the economy in the short run, therefore, we need a different model. To build this new model, we rely on many of the tools we have developed in previous chapters, but we must abandon the classical dichotomy and the neutrality of money.

The Basic Model of Economic Fluctuations

Our model of short run economic fluctuations focuses on the behaviour of two variables. The first variable is the economy's output of goods and services, as measured by real GDP. The second variable is the overall price level, as measured by the CPI or the GDP deflator. Output is a real variable, whereas the price level is a nominal variable. By focusing on the relationship between these two variables, we are highlighting the breakdown of the classical dichotomy.

We analyze fluctuations in the economy as a whole with the **model of aggregate demand and aggregate supply**, which is illustrated in Figure 21.1. On the vertical axis is the overall price level in the economy. On the horizontal axis is the overall quantity of goods and services. The **aggregate demand curve** shows the quantity of goods and services that households, firms and the government want to buy at each price level. The **aggregate supply curve** shows the quantity of goods and services that firms produce and sell at each price level. According to this model, the price level and the quantity of output adjust to bring aggregate demand and aggregate supply into balance.

model of aggregate demand and aggregate supply the model that many economists use to explain short run fluctuations in economic activity around its long run trend
aggregate demand curve a curve that shows the quantity of goods and services that households, firms and the government want to buy at each price level
aggregate supply curve a curve that shows the quantity of goods and services that firms choose to produce and sell at each price level

---

FIGURE 21.1

Aggregate Demand and Aggregate Supply

Economists use the model of aggregate demand and aggregate supply to analyze economic fluctuations. On the vertical axis is the overall level of prices. On the horizontal axis is the economy's total output of goods and services. Output and the price level adjust to the point at which the aggregate supply and aggregate demand curves intersect.

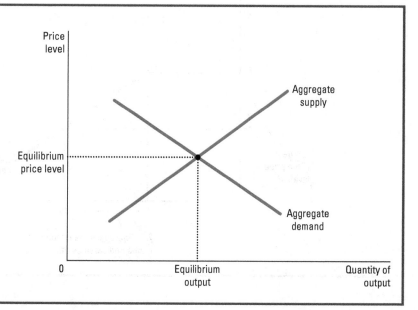

It may be tempting to view the model of aggregate demand and aggregate supply as nothing more than a macro version of the model of market demand and market supply. Yet in fact this model is quite different. When we consider demand and supply in a particular market, wheat, for instance, the behaviour of buyers and sellers depends on the ability of resources to move from one market to another. When the price of wheat rises, the quantity demanded falls because buyers will use their incomes to buy products other than wheat. Similarly, a higher price of wheat raises the quantity supplied, because firms that produce wheat can increase production by hiring workers away from other parts of the economy. This *microeconomic* substitution from one market to another is impossible when we are analysing the economy as a whole. After all, the quantity that our model is trying to explain (real GDP) measures the total quantity produced in all of the economy's markets.

SELF TEST How does the economy's behaviour in the short run differ from its behaviour in the long run? Draw the model of aggregate demand and aggregate supply. What variables are on the two axes?

THE AGGREGATE DEMAND CURVE

The aggregate demand curve tells us the quantity of all goods and services demanded in the economy at any given price level. As Figure 21.2 illustrates, the aggregate demand curve is downward sloping. This means that, other things equal, a fall in the economy's overall level of prices (from, say, P_1 to P_2) tends to raise the quantity of goods and services demanded (from Y_1 to Y_2).

FIGURE 21.2

The Aggregate Demand Curve

A decrease in the price level from P_1 to P_2 increases the quantity of goods and services demanded from Y_1 to Y_2. There are three reasons for this negative relationship. As the price level falls, real wealth rises, interest rates fall and the exchange rate depreciates. These effects stimulate spending on consumption, investment and net exports. Increased spending on these components of output means a larger quantity of goods and services demanded.

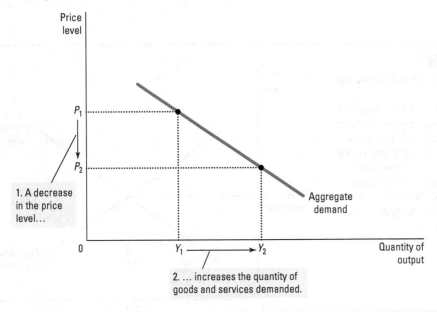

Why the Aggregate Demand Curve Slopes Downward

Why does a fall in the price level raise the quantity of goods and services demanded? To answer this question, it is useful to recall that $GDP = C + I + G + NX$. Let us assume that government spending is fixed by policy. The other three components of spending – consumption, investment and net exports – depend on economic conditions, particularly on the price level. To understand the downward slope of the aggregate demand curve we must examine how the price level affects the quantity of goods and services demanded for consumption, investment and net exports.

The Price Level and Consumption: The Wealth Effect Consider the money that you hold in your pocket and your bank account. The nominal value of this money is fixed, but its real value is not. When prices fall, this money is more valuable because then it can be used to buy more goods and services. Thus, a decrease in the price level makes consumers wealthier, which in turn encourages them to spend more. The increase in consumer spending means a larger quantity of goods and services demanded.

The Price Level and Investment: The Interest Rate Effect The price level is one determinant of the quantity of money demanded. The lower the price level, the less money households need to hold to buy the goods and services they want. When the price level falls, therefore, households try to reduce their holdings of money by lending some of it out. For instance, a household might use its excess money to buy interest bearing bonds. Or it might deposit its excess money in an interest bearing savings account, and the bank would use these funds to make more loans. In either case, as households try to convert some of their money into interest bearing assets, they drive down interest rates. Lower interest rates, in turn, encourage borrowing by firms that want to invest in new factories and equipment and by households who want to invest in new housing. Thus, a lower price level reduces the interest rate, encourages greater spending on investment goods, and thereby increases the quantity of goods and services demanded.

The Price Level and Net Exports: The Exchange Rate Effect As we have just discussed, a lower price level lowers the interest rate. In response, some investors will seek higher returns by investing abroad. For instance, as the interest rate on European government bonds falls, an investment fund might sell European government bonds to buy US government bonds. As the investment fund tries to convert its euros into dollars to buy the US bonds, it increases the supply of euros in the market for foreign currency exchange. The increased supply of euros causes the euro to depreciate relative to other currencies. Because each euro buys fewer units of foreign currencies, non-European goods (i.e. imports) become more expensive to European residents, but exporters find that foreign buyers get more euros for each unit of their currency. This change in the real exchange rate (the relative price of domestic and foreign goods) increases European exports of goods and services and decreases European imports of goods and services. Net exports, which equal exports minus imports, also increase. Thus when a fall in the European price level causes European interest rates to fall, the real value of the euro falls, and this depreciation stimulates European net exports and thereby increases the quantity of goods and services demanded in the European economy.

It is important to keep in mind that the aggregate demand curve (like all demand curves) is drawn holding 'other things equal'. In particular, our three explanations of the downward sloping aggregate demand curve assume that the money supply is fixed. That is, we have been considering how a change in the price level affects the demand for goods and services, holding the amount of money in the economy constant. As we will see, a change in the quantity of money shifts the aggregate demand curve. At this point, just keep in mind that the aggregate demand curve is drawn for a given quantity of money.

Why the Aggregate Demand Curve Might Shift

The downward slope of the aggregate demand curve shows that a fall in the price level raises the overall quantity of goods and services demanded. Many other factors, however, affect the quantity of goods and services demanded at a given price level. When one of these other factors changes, the aggregate demand curve shifts.

Shifts Arising from Consumption Suppose people suddenly become more concerned about saving for retirement and, as a result, reduce their current consumption. Because the quantity of goods and services demanded at any price level is lower, the aggregate demand curve shifts to the left. Conversely, imagine that a stock market boom makes people wealthier and less concerned about saving. The resulting increase in consumer spending means a greater quantity of goods and services demanded at any given price level, so the aggregate demand curve shifts to the right.

Thus, any event that changes how much people want to consume at a given price level shifts the aggregate demand curve. One policy variable that has this effect is the level of taxation. When the government cuts taxes, it encourages people and businesses to spend more, so the aggregate demand curve shifts to the right. When the government raises taxes, people and businesses cut back on their spending and the aggregate demand curve shifts to the left.

Shifts Arising from Investment Any event that changes how much firms want to invest at a given price level also shifts the aggregate demand curve. For instance, imagine that firms are optimistic about increased spending in the economy and invest in increasing capacity in anticipation. Because the quantity of goods and services demanded at any price level is higher, the aggregate demand curve shifts to the right. Conversely, if firms become pessimistic about future business conditions, they may cut back on investment spending, shifting the aggregate demand curve to the left.

Tax policy can also influence aggregate demand through investment. An investment allowance (a tax rebate tied to a firm's investment spending) increases the quantity of investment goods that firms demand at any given interest rate. It therefore shifts the aggregate demand curve to the right. The repeal of an investment allowance reduces investment and shifts the aggregate demand curve to the left.

Another policy variable that can influence investment and aggregate demand is the money supply. An increase in the money supply lowers the interest rate in the short run. This makes borrowing less costly, which stimulates investment spending and thereby shifts the aggregate demand curve to the right.

Conversely, a decrease in the money supply raises the interest rate, discourages investment spending and thereby shifts the aggregate demand curve to the left.

Shifts Arising from Government Purchases The most direct way that policy makers shift the aggregate demand curve is through government purchases. For example, suppose the government decides to reduce purchases of new weapons systems. Because the quantity of goods and services demanded at any price level is lower, the aggregate demand curve shifts to the left. Conversely, if the government starts building more motorways, the result is a greater quantity of goods and services demanded at any price level, so the aggregate demand curve shifts to the right.

Shifts Arising from Net Exports Any event that changes net exports for a given price level also shifts aggregate demand. For instance, when the United States experiences a recession, it buys fewer goods from Europe. This reduces European net exports and shifts the aggregate demand curve for the European economy to the left. When the United States recovers from its recession, it starts buying European goods again, shifting the aggregate demand curve to the right.

Net exports sometimes change because of movements in the exchange rate. Suppose, for instance, that international speculators bid up the value of the euro in the market for foreign currency exchange. This appreciation of the euro would make goods produced in the Eurozone more expensive compared to foreign goods, which would depress net exports and shift the aggregate demand curve to the left. Conversely, a depreciation of the euro stimulates net exports and shifts the Eurozone aggregate demand curve to the right.

> **SELF TEST** Explain the three reasons why the aggregate demand curve slopes downward. Give an example of an event that would shift the aggregate demand curve. Which way would this event shift the curve?

THE AGGREGATE SUPPLY CURVE

The aggregate supply curve tells us the total quantity of goods and services that firms produce and sell at any given price level. Unlike the aggregate demand curve, which is always downward sloping, the aggregate supply curve shows a relationship that depends crucially on the time horizon being examined. In the long run, the aggregate supply curve is vertical, whereas in the short run, the aggregate supply curve is upward sloping. To understand short run economic fluctuations, and how the short run behaviour of the economy deviates from its long run behaviour, we need to examine both the long run aggregate supply curve and the short run aggregate supply curve.

Why the Aggregate Supply Curve is Vertical in the Long Run

In the long run, an economy's production of goods and services (its real GDP) depends on its supplies of labour, capital, natural resources and the available technology used to turn these factors of production into goods and services. In the long run these resources are fixed and so there is a finite amount that can be produced with these given resources. Because the price level does not affect these long run determinants of real GDP, the long run aggregate supply curve is vertical, as in Figure 21.3.

The vertical long run aggregate supply curve is, in essence, just an application of the classical dichotomy and monetary neutrality. As we have already discussed, classical macroeconomic theory is based on the assumption that real variables do not depend on nominal variables. The long run aggregate supply curve is consistent with this idea because it implies that the quantity of output (a real variable) does not depend on the level of prices (a nominal variable). As noted earlier, there are economists who believe that this principle works well when studying the economy over a period of many years, but not when studying year to year changes. Thus, the aggregate supply curve is vertical only in the long run.

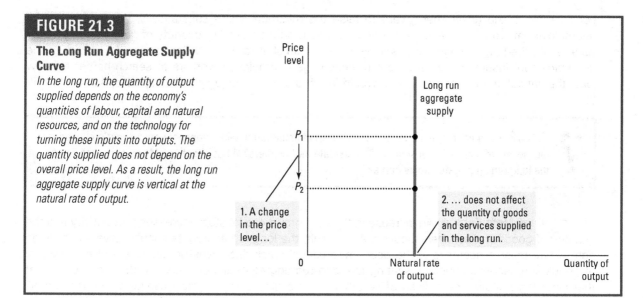

FIGURE 21.3

The Long Run Aggregate Supply Curve

In the long run, the quantity of output supplied depends on the economy's quantities of labour, capital and natural resources, and on the technology for turning these inputs into outputs. The quantity supplied does not depend on the overall price level. As a result, the long run aggregate supply curve is vertical at the natural rate of output.

You might wonder why supply curves for specific goods and services can be upward sloping if the long run aggregate supply curve is vertical. The reason is that the supply of specific goods and services depends on *relative prices,* the prices of those goods and services compared to other prices in the economy. For example, when the price of ice cream rises, holding other prices in the economy constant, there is an incentive for suppliers of ice cream to increase their production by taking labour, milk, chocolate and other inputs away from the production of other goods, such as frozen yoghurt. By contrast, the economy's overall production of goods and services is limited by its labour, capital, natural resources and technology. Thus, when all prices in the economy rise together, there is no change in the overall quantity of goods and services supplied because relative prices and thus incentives have not changed.

Why the Long Run Aggregate Supply Curve Might Shift

The position of the long run aggregate supply curve shows the quantity of goods and services predicted by classical macroeconomic theory. This level of production is sometimes called *potential output* or *full employment output.* To be more accurate, we call it the **natural rate of output** because it shows what the economy produces when unemployment is at its natural, or normal, rate. The natural rate of output is the level of production towards which the economy gravitates in the long run.

> **natural rate of output** the output level in an economy when all existing factors of production (land, labour, capital and technology resources) are fully utilized and where unemployment is at its natural rate

Any change in the economy that alters the natural rate of output shifts the long run aggregate supply curve. Because output in the classical model depends on labour, capital, natural resources and technological knowledge, we can categorize shifts in the long run aggregate supply curve as arising from these sources.

Shifts Arising from Labour   Imagine that an economy experiences an increase in immigration. Because there would be a greater number of workers, the quantity of goods and services supplied would increase. As a result, the long run aggregate supply curve would shift to the right. Conversely, if many workers left the economy to go abroad, the long run aggregate supply curve would shift to the left.

The position of the long run aggregate supply curve also depends on the natural rate of unemployment, so any change in the natural rate of unemployment shifts the long run aggregate supply curve.

For example, if the government were to raise the minimum wage substantially, the natural rate of unemployment would rise, and the economy would produce a smaller quantity of goods and services. As a result, the long run aggregate supply curve would shift to the left. Conversely, if a reform of the unemployment insurance system were to encourage unemployed workers to search harder for new jobs, the natural rate of unemployment would fall, and the long run aggregate supply curve would shift to the right.

WHAT IF... a country experiences a high level of immigration with people of poor education but sees high levels of emigration of some of its most talented workers? What effect would you expect to see on the long run aggregate supply curve?

Shifts Arising from Capital An increase in the economy's capital stock increases productivity and the quantity of goods and services supplied. As a result, the long run aggregate supply curve shifts to the right. Conversely, a decrease in the economy's capital stock decreases productivity and the quantity of goods and services supplied, shifting the long run aggregate supply curve to the left. Notice that the same logic applies regardless of whether we are discussing physical capital or human capital. An increase either in the number of machines or in the number of university degrees will raise the economy's ability to produce goods and services. Thus, either would shift the long run aggregate supply curve to the right.

This highlights the trade-off which many nations face in investment in infrastructure projects which boost future productive capacity and shift the long run aggregate supply curve to the right, but which take resources away from current consumption.

Shifts Arising from Natural Resources An economy's production depends on its natural resources, including its land, minerals and climate. A discovery of a new mineral deposit shifts the long run aggregate supply curve to the right. A change in weather patterns that makes farming more difficult shifts the long run aggregate supply curve to the left.

In many countries, important natural resources are imported from abroad. A change in the availability of these resources can also shift the aggregate supply curve.

Shifts Arising from Technological Knowledge Perhaps the most important reason that the economy today produces more than it did a generation ago is that technological knowledge has advanced. The invention of the computer, for instance, has allowed the production of more goods and services from any given amounts of labour, capital and natural resources. As a result, it has shifted the long run aggregate supply curve to the right.

Although not literally technological, there are many other events that act like changes in technology. Opening up international trade has effects similar to inventing new production processes, so it also shifts the long run aggregate supply curve to the right. Conversely, if the government passed new regulations preventing firms from using some production methods, perhaps because they were too dangerous for workers, the result would be a leftward shift in the long run aggregate supply curve.

A Way to Depict Long Run Growth and Inflation

Having introduced the economy's aggregate demand curve and the long run aggregate supply curve, we now have a way to describe the economy's long run trends. Figure 21.4 illustrates the changes that occur in the economy from decade to decade. Notice that both curves are shifting. Although there are many forces that govern the economy in the long run and can in principle cause such shifts, the two most important in practice are technology and monetary policy. Technological progress enhances the economy's ability to produce goods and services, and this continually shifts the long run aggregate supply curve to the right. At the same time, because the central bank increases the money supply over time, the aggregate demand curve also shifts to the right. As Figure 21.4 illustrates, the result is trend growth in output (as shown by increasing Y) and continuing inflation (as shown by increasing P).

FIGURE 21.4

Long Run Growth and Inflation in the Model of Aggregate Demand and Aggregate Supply
As the economy becomes better able to produce goods and services over time, primarily because of technological progress, the long run aggregate supply curve shifts to the right. At the same time, as the central bank increases the money supply, the aggregate demand curve also shifts to the right. In this figure, output grows from Y_{2005} to Y_{2015} and then to Y_{2025}, and the price level rises from P_{2005} to P_{2015} and then to P_{2025}. Thus the model of aggregate demand and aggregate supply offers a way to describe the classical analysis of growth and inflation.

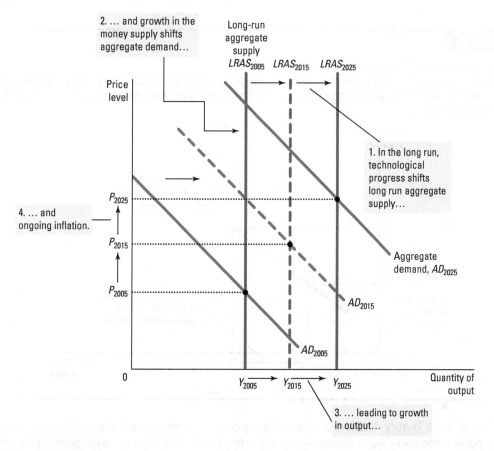

The purpose of developing the model of aggregate demand and aggregate supply is to provide a framework for short run analysis. As we develop the short run model, we keep the analysis simple by not showing the continuing growth and inflation depicted in Figure 21.4. Remember, however, that long run trends provide the background for short run fluctuations. Short run fluctuations in output and the **price level** should be viewed as deviations from the continuing long run trends.

price level the price of a basket of goods and services measured as the weighted arithmetic average of current prices

Why the Aggregate Supply Curve Slopes Upward in the Short Run

As we have already discussed, the long run aggregate supply curve is vertical. By contrast, in the short run, the aggregate supply curve is upward sloping, as shown in Figure 21.5. That is, over a period of a year or two, an increase in the overall level of prices in the economy tends to raise the quantity of goods and services supplied, and a decrease in the level of prices tends to reduce the quantity of goods and services supplied.

Macro-economists have proposed three theories for the upward slope of the short run aggregate supply curve. In each theory, a specific market imperfection causes the supply side of the economy to behave differently in the short run than it does in the long run. Although each of the following theories will differ in detail, they share a common theme: the quantity of output supplied deviates from its long run, or 'natural' level when the price level deviates from what people expected to prevail. When the price level rises above the expected level, output rises above its natural rate, and when the price level falls below the expected level, output falls below its natural rate.

FIGURE 21.5

The Short Run Aggregate Supply Curve

In the short run, a fall in the price level from P_1 to P_2 reduces the quantity of output supplied from Y_1 to Y_2. This positive relationship could be due to sticky wages, sticky prices or misperceptions. Over time, wages, prices and perceptions adjust, so this positive relationship is only temporary.

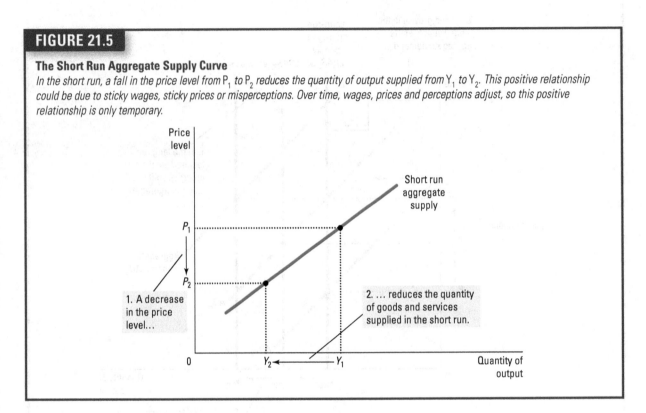

The Sticky Wage Theory The first and simplest explanation of the upward slope of the short run aggregate supply curve is the sticky wage theory. According to this theory, the short run aggregate supply curve slopes upward because nominal wages are slow to adjust, or are 'sticky', in the short run. To some extent, the slow adjustment of nominal wages is attributable to long-term contracts between workers and firms that fix nominal wages, sometimes for as long as three years. In addition, this slow adjustment may be attributable to social norms and notions of fairness that influence wage setting and change only slowly over time.

To see what sticky nominal wages mean for aggregate supply, imagine that a firm has agreed in advance to pay its workers a certain nominal wage based on what it expected the price level to be. The wage that a firm pays to a worker is closely related to the amount of output produced. Productivity measures the amount produced per time period per factor of production. Imagine that a picker in an online retail distribution centre processes 50 parcels per hour. Each parcel has a retail price of €25. The value of the output of the worker to the firm is 50 × €25 = €1,250. If the worker gets paid €20 per hour, then every €1 the firm pays the worker results in €62.50 worth of output to the firm. If the price of the goods fall from €25 to €22 but the wage and productivity stays the same at €20 per hour and 50 parcels, then each €1 the firm pays to the worker now only generates €50 worth of output. The cost of production to the firm has effectively increased.

If the price level *P* falls below the level that was expected and the nominal wage remains stuck at *W*, then the real wage rises above the level the firm planned to pay. The firm responds to these higher costs by hiring less labour and producing a smaller quantity of goods and services. In other words, because wages do not adjust immediately to the price level, a lower price level makes employment and production less profitable, so firms reduce the quantity of goods and services they supply.

FYI

Calculating Real Wages

Over time wages increase, but so does the price level. If wages increased at the same rate as prices, the amount of goods each euro, rand, pound or whatever unit of currency buys would stay the same. When prices rise at different rates to wages, purchasing power, or the real wage, will either rise or fall. In simple terms, if wages over a period rise by 2 per cent but prices rise over the same period by 4 per cent, people are worse off because their income cannot buy the same amount of goods at the end of the period as it did at the start.

The real wage is a measure of the wage measured in the currency of another year:

$$\text{Real wage rate} = \frac{\text{Nominal wage rate}}{\left(\dfrac{\text{Base CPI}}{\text{Current CPI}}\right)}$$

Imagine that in June 2015 you earned €6.66 an hour. How much would you have to earn in 2025 to buy the same amount of goods as €6.66 an hour would have bought in 2015? Assume that the CPI for June 2025 was 180 and that the CPI in June 2015 was 100 (the base year). The real wage would be calculated as follows:

$$\text{Real wage rate} = \frac{6.66}{\left(\dfrac{100}{180}\right)} \quad \text{Real wage rate} = \text{€12.00 (rounded up)}$$

This tells us that you would have to earn €12.00 per hour in 2025 to buy the same amount of goods that €6.66 would have bought in 2015. If your nominal wage is higher than €12.00 an hour in 2025, then you would be better off compared to 2015, as your wage will buy you more goods. But if your wage is less than €12.00 you would be worse off. You would be able to buy fewer goods compared to 2015.

We can also look at comparisons of yearly earnings over time. For example, assume that you currently earn €35,000 in 2025, but in 2005 you were on a salary of €12,000. Are you better off now than you were in 2005? To calculate this, you need to know the CPI in 2005. Assume that it was 65.

The formula used is:

$$\text{Real wage in 2005 currency} = \frac{\text{Current nominal wage}}{\left(\dfrac{\text{Current CPI}}{\text{Base (2005) CPI}}\right)}$$

Substituting the figures into the formula we get:

$$\text{Real wage in 2005 currency} = \frac{35,000}{\left(\dfrac{180}{65}\right)}$$

$$\text{Real wage in 2005 currency} = \frac{35,000}{2.77}$$

Real wage in 2005 currency = €12,635.38

The result tells you that you are better off than in 2005. Your real wage today buys €635.38 more goods than it would have done in 2005 and so the rate of growth of wages has increased by more than prices over the period.

CASE STUDY   Real Wages in the UK

While 2022 may have been the first full year without pandemic restrictions, for many it did not bring good economic news. The acceleration of inflation to double digit figures meant that large numbers of people saw their real incomes falling. The news media described it as a 'cost of living crisis'. Certainly, the vast majority of the population will have noticed prices rising on a range of goods and services. Energy prices in particular rose quickly largely as a result of the conflict in Ukraine, but prices of basic foodstuffs also rose partly due to that same conflict and partly due to the unwinding of supply chain problems following the pandemic.

To get an accurate picture of the cost of living, we also have to take into account what happens to wages. The Office for National Statistics (ONS) reported that median monthly pay (the middle number in a data set) was £2,181 (€2,483) in November 2022, an increase of 8.0 per cent compared to the same period in 2021. Figures from the ONS showed that annual growth in wages in the private sector was 6.9 per cent in the three months to October 2022 whereas public sector pay grew by 2.7 per cent in the same period. The growth in wage rates in the private sector may be partly driven by a tighter labour market where employers are having to offer higher wages to recruit staff. This could further fuel inflation and so the Bank of England increased interest rates, reaching 5.0 per cent in July 2023, to try to dampen inflationary pressures. While the 8.0 per cent increase in median monthly pay was relatively high in historical terms, the fact that inflation was in double digits for part of 2022 meant that many workers saw their real wages fall. A report by the accountancy firm, PwC noted that real wages in the UK in 2020 stood at £36,330 but would fall to £34,643 in 2023. PwC compared this to the situation in France where inflation is lower and as a result real wages there would only fall from £35,848 in 2021 to £35,462 in 2023.

As real incomes fall, many people have had to resort to 'tightening their belts' and managing their spending more effectively.

Questions

1   Figures from the ONS published in June 2023 show that inflation as measured by the Consumer Price Index (CPI) rose by 9.7 per cent in the 12 months to May 2023 down from 11.1 per cent in October. The CPI including owner occupiers' housing costs (CPIH) changed by the same amounts. Using these figures and the figures for wage increases in the case study, comment on the effect on real wages of workers in the UK.

2   The case study notes that as a result of a 'tight labour market' and the relatively sharp increase in wages, the Bank of England is likely to increase interest rates further. Use an aggregate demand and aggregate supply diagram to analyze the effect of an increase in interest rates on the UK economy.

3   Use an aggregate demand and aggregate supply diagram to show how rapidly rising wage costs can fuel further inflationary pressures.

4   Given the information in the case study and your response to question 1, to what extent should the news media be describing the situation in the UK as a cost of living 'crisis'? What other information would you want to see to help you address this question objectively?

References: www.ons.gov.uk/employmentandlabourmarket/peopleinwork/earningsandworkinghours/bulletins/earningsandemploymentfrompayasyouearnrealtimeinformationuk/december2022 (accessed 12 June 2023).
www.pwc.co.uk/press-room/press-releases/pwc-economic-predictions-2023.html (accessed 12 June 2023).

The Sticky Price Theory Some economists have advocated another approach to the short run aggregate supply curve, called the sticky price theory. As we just discussed, the sticky wage theory emphasizes that nominal wages adjust slowly over time. The sticky price theory emphasizes that the prices of some goods and services also adjust sluggishly in response to changing economic conditions. This slow adjustment of prices occurs in part because there are costs to adjusting prices, called **menu costs**. These menu costs include the cost of printing and distributing price lists or mail order and online catalogues, changes to prices in back-office systems which feed through to various accounting and supply chain systems, down to the physical time required to change price tags. As a result of these costs, prices as well as wages may be sticky in the short run.

menu costs the costs of changing prices

To see the implications of sticky prices for aggregate supply, suppose that each firm in the economy announces its prices in advance based on the economic conditions it expects to prevail. Then, after prices are announced, the economy experiences an unexpected contraction in the money supply, which will reduce the overall price level in the long run. Although some firms reduce their prices immediately in response to changing economic conditions, other firms may not want to incur additional menu costs and, therefore, may temporarily lag behind. Because these lagging firms have prices that are too high, their sales decline. Declining sales, in turn, cause these firms to cut back on production and employment. In other words, because not all prices adjust instantly to changing conditions, an unexpected fall in the price level leaves some firms with higher than desired prices, and these prices depress sales and induce firms to reduce the quantity of goods and services they produce.

The Misperceptions Theory A third approach to the short run aggregate supply curve is the misperceptions theory. According to this theory, changes in the overall price level can temporarily mislead suppliers about what is happening in the individual markets in which they sell their output. As a result of these short run misperceptions, suppliers respond to changes in the level of prices, and this response leads to an upward sloping aggregate supply curve.

To see how this might work, suppose the overall price level falls below the level that people expected. When suppliers see the prices of their products fall, they may mistakenly believe that their *relative* prices have fallen. For example, wheat farmers may notice a fall in the price of wheat before they notice a fall in the prices of the many items they buy as consumers. They may infer from this observation that the reward to producing wheat is temporarily low, and they may respond by reducing the quantity of wheat they supply. Similarly, workers may notice a fall in their nominal wages before they notice a fall in the prices of the goods they buy. They may infer that the reward to working is temporarily low and respond by reducing the quantity of labour they supply. In both cases, a lower price level causes misperceptions about relative prices, and these misperceptions induce suppliers to respond to the lower price level by decreasing the quantity of goods and services supplied.

PITFALL PREVENTION Misperception of changes in prices is not only a mistake that businesses and consumers make but also economics students. There is a difference between changes in the overall price level and particular prices of goods and services. There is always the danger of generalizing one from the other too easily.

Why the Short Run Aggregate Supply Curve Might Shift

When thinking about what shifts the short run aggregate supply curve, we have to consider all those variables that shift the long run aggregate supply curve plus a new variable, the expected price level. This influences sticky wages, sticky prices and misperceptions.

As we discussed earlier, shifts in the long run aggregate supply curve normally arise from changes in labour, capital, natural resources or technological knowledge. These same variables shift the short run aggregate supply curve. For example, when an increase in the economy's capital stock increases productivity, both the long run and short run aggregate supply curves shift to the right. If an increase in the minimum wage raises the natural rate of unemployment, both the long run and short run aggregate supply curves shift to the left.

The important new variable that affects the position of the short run aggregate supply curve is people's expectations of the price level. As we have discussed, the quantity of goods and services supplied depends, in the short run, on sticky wages, sticky prices and misperceptions. Yet wages, prices and perceptions are set on the basis of expectations of the price level. When expectations change, the short run aggregate supply curve shifts.

To make this idea more concrete, consider a specific theory of aggregate supply, the sticky wage theory. According to this theory, when workers and firms expect the price level to be high, they are more likely to negotiate high nominal wages. High wages raise firms' costs and, for any given actual price level, reduce the quantity of goods and services that firms supply. When the expected price level rises, wages are higher, costs increase and firms supply a smaller quantity of goods and services at any given actual price level. Thus the short run aggregate supply curve shifts to the left. Conversely, when the expected price level falls, wages are lower, costs decline, firms increase production at any given price level and the short run aggregate supply curve shifts to the right.

A similar logic applies in each theory of aggregate supply. The general lesson is that an increase in the expected price level reduces the quantity of goods and services supplied and shifts the short run aggregate supply curve to the left. A decrease in the expected price level raises the quantity of goods and services supplied and shifts the short run aggregate supply curve to the right. As we will see in the next section, this influence of expectations on the position of the short run aggregate supply curve plays a key role in reconciling the economy's behaviour in the short run with its behaviour in the long run. In the short run, expectations are fixed, and the economy finds itself at the intersection of the aggregate demand curve and the short run aggregate supply curve. In the long run, expectations adjust and the short run aggregate supply curve shifts. This shift ensures that the economy eventually finds itself at the intersection of the aggregate demand curve and the long run aggregate supply curve.

TWO CAUSES OF ECONOMIC FLUCTUATIONS

Now that we have introduced the model of aggregate demand and aggregate supply, we have the basic tools we need to analyze fluctuations in economic activity. In particular, we can use what we have learned about aggregate demand and aggregate supply to examine the two basic causes of short run fluctuations.

To keep things simple, we assume the economy begins in long run equilibrium, as shown in Figure 21.6. Equilibrium output and the price level are determined by the intersection of the aggregate demand curve and the long run aggregate supply curve, shown as point A in the figure. At this point, output is at its natural rate. The short run aggregate supply curve passes through this point as well, indicating that wages, prices and perceptions have fully adjusted to this long run equilibrium. That is, when an economy is in its long run equilibrium, wages, prices and perceptions must have adjusted so that the intersection of aggregate demand with short run aggregate supply is the same as the intersection of aggregate demand with long run aggregate supply.

The Effects of a Shift in Aggregate Demand

Suppose that for some reason a wave of pessimism suddenly overtakes the economy. The cause might be a government scandal, a banking crisis, a pandemic, a crash in the stock market, the outbreak of war, or uncertainty caused by increases in acts of terrorism across the world. Because of this event, many people lose confidence in the future and alter their plans. Households cut back on their spending and delay major purchases, and firms put off buying new equipment.

FIGURE 21.6

The Long Run Equilibrium
The long run equilibrium of the economy is found where the aggregate demand curve crosses the long run aggregate supply curve (point A). When the economy reaches this long run equilibrium, wages, prices and perceptions will have adjusted so that the short run aggregate supply curve crosses this point as well.

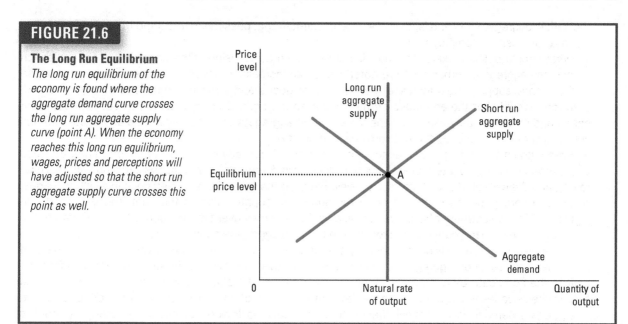

What is the impact of such a wave of pessimism on the economy? Such an event reduces the aggregate demand for goods and services. That is, for any given price level, households and firms now want to buy a smaller quantity of goods and services. As Figure 21.7 shows, the aggregate demand curve shifts to the left from AD_1 to AD_2.

FIGURE 21.7

A Contraction in Aggregate Demand
A fall in aggregate demand, which might be due to a wave of pessimism in the economy, is represented with a leftward shift in the aggregate demand curve from AD_1 to AD_2. The economy moves from point A to point B. Output falls from Y_1 to Y_2, and the price level falls from P_1 to P_2. Over time, as wages, prices and perceptions adjust, the short run aggregate supply curve shifts to the right from AS_1 to AS_2, and the economy reaches point C, where the new aggregate demand curve crosses the long run aggregate supply curve. The price level falls to P_3, and output returns to its natural rate, Y_1.

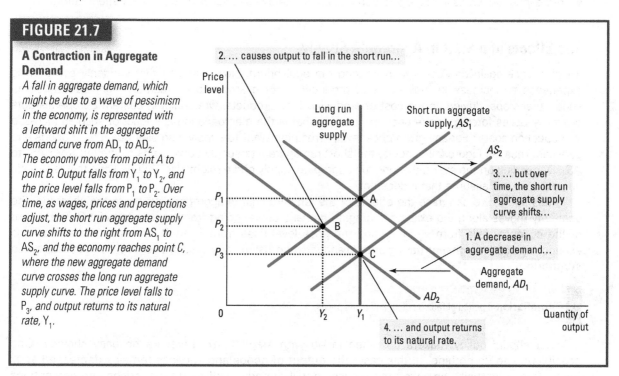

In this figure, we can examine the effects of the fall in aggregate demand. In the short run, the economy moves along the initial short run aggregate supply curve AS_1, going from point A to point B. As the economy moves from point A to point B, output falls from Y_1 to Y_2, and the price level falls from P_1 to P_2. The falling level of output indicates that the economy is in a recession. Although not shown in the figure, firms respond to lower sales and production by reducing employment. Thus, the pessimism that caused the shift in aggregate demand is, to some extent, self-fulfilling: pessimism about the future leads to falling incomes and rising unemployment.

What should policy makers do when faced with such a recession? One possibility is to take action to increase aggregate demand. As we noted earlier, an increase in government spending or an increase in the money supply would increase the quantity of goods and services demanded at any price and, therefore, would shift the aggregate demand curve to the right. If policy makers can act with sufficient speed and precision, they can offset the initial shift in aggregate demand, return the aggregate demand curve back to AD_1, and bring the economy back to point A.

Even without action by policy makers, the recession will remedy itself over a period of time. Because of the reduction in aggregate demand, the price level falls. Eventually, expectations catch up with this new reality, and the expected price level falls as well. Because the fall in the expected price level alters wages, prices and perceptions, it shifts the short run aggregate supply curve to the right from AS_1 to AS_2 in Figure 21.7. This adjustment of expectations allows the economy over time to approach point C, where the new aggregate demand curve (AD_2) crosses the long run aggregate supply curve.

In the new long run equilibrium, point C, output is back to its natural rate. Even though the wave of pessimism has reduced aggregate demand, the price level has fallen sufficiently (to P_3) to offset the shift in the aggregate demand curve. Thus, in the long run, the shift in aggregate demand is reflected fully in the price level and not at all in the level of output. In other words, the long run effect of a shift in aggregate demand is a nominal change (the price level is lower) but not a real change (output is the same).

To sum up, this story about shifts in aggregate demand has two important lessons:

- In the short run, shifts in aggregate demand cause fluctuations in the economy's output of goods and services.
- In the long run, shifts in aggregate demand affect the overall price level but do not affect output.

The Effects of a Shift in Aggregate Supply

Imagine once again an economy in its long run equilibrium. Now suppose that suddenly some firms experience an increase in their costs of production. For example, bad weather might destroy some agricultural crops, driving up the cost of producing food products. Or conflict in Eastern Europe disrupts energy supplies forcing up the price of energy. What is the macroeconomic impact of such an increase in production costs? For any given price level, firms now want to supply a smaller quantity of goods and services. Thus, as Figure 21.8 shows, the short run aggregate supply curve shifts to the left from AS_1 to AS_2. Depending on the event, the long run aggregate supply curve might also shift. To keep things simple, however, we will assume that it does not.

In this figure, we can trace the effects of the leftward shift in aggregate supply. In the short run, the economy moves along the existing aggregate demand curve, going from point A to point B. The output of the economy falls from Y_1 to Y_2, and the price level rises from P_1 to P_2. Because the economy is experiencing both *stagnation* (falling output) and *inflation* (rising prices), such an event is sometimes called **stagflation**.

stagflation a period of falling output and rising prices

What should policy makers do when faced with stagflation? There are no easy choices. One possibility is to do nothing. In this case, the output of goods and services remains depressed at Y_2 for a while. Eventually, however, the recession will remedy itself as wages, prices and perceptions adjust. A period of low output and high unemployment, for instance, puts downward pressure on workers' wages. Lower wages, in turn, increase the quantity of output supplied. Over time, as the short run aggregate supply curve shifts back towards AS_1, the price level falls and the quantity of output approaches its natural rate. In the long run, the economy returns to point A, where the aggregate demand curve crosses the long run aggregate supply curve. This is the view that believers of free markets might adopt.

FIGURE 21.8

An Adverse Shift in Aggregate Supply

When some event increases firms' costs, the short run aggregate supply curve shifts to the left from AS_1 to AS_2. The economy moves from point A to point B. The result is stagflation: output falls from Y_1 to Y_2, and the price level rises from P_1 to P_2.

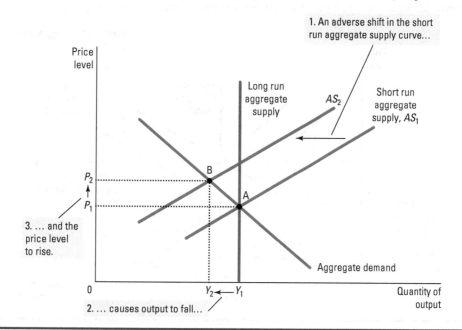

Alternatively, policy makers who control monetary and fiscal policy might attempt to offset some of the effects of the shift in the short run aggregate supply curve by shifting the aggregate demand curve. This possibility is shown in Figure 21.9. In this case, changes in policy shift the aggregate demand curve to the right from AD_1 to AD_2, exactly enough to prevent the shift in aggregate supply from affecting output. The economy moves directly from point A to point C. Output remains at its natural rate, and the price level rises from P_1 to P_3. In this case, policy makers are said to *accommodate* the shift in aggregate supply because they allow the increase in costs to permanently affect the level of prices. This intervention by policy makers would be seen as desirable by supporters of John Maynard Keynes. In 1936, Keynes published an influential book entitled *The General Theory of Employment, Interest and Money*, which attempted to explain short run fluctuations in economic activity. The fundamental idea Keynes put forward was that downturns in economic activity could occur because of a lack of aggregate demand. Policy makers, he argued, could manipulate fiscal policy to influence aggregate demand. Following the Second World War, a number of countries adopted demand management policies which reflected the ideas Keynes put forward. By the end of the 1970s, these policies seemed to be failing and attention turned to monetary and supply side policies. The recession which followed the 2007–2009 Financial Crisis led to a revival of interest in the use of Keynesian demand management. These different views on policy action form a key aspect of the debate between economists about action in the face of short run fluctuations in economic activity.

SELF TEST Suppose that the election of a popular prime minister suddenly increases people's confidence in the future. Use the model of aggregate demand and aggregate supply to analyze the effect on the economy.

JEOPARDY PROBLEM Over a period of 20 years an economy has found that despite periods of growth it has ended up with higher inflation rates and a level of unemployment no different from the one it started with at the beginning of the time period. Explain, using aggregate demand and supply diagrams, why this may have occurred.

FIGURE 21.9

Accommodating an Adverse Shift in Aggregate Supply

Faced with an adverse shift in aggregate supply from AS$_1$ to AS$_2$, policy makers who can influence aggregate demand might try to shift the aggregate demand curve to the right from AD$_1$ to AD$_2$. The economy would move from point A to point C. This policy would prevent the supply shift from reducing output in the short run, but the price level would permanently rise from P$_1$ to P$_3$.

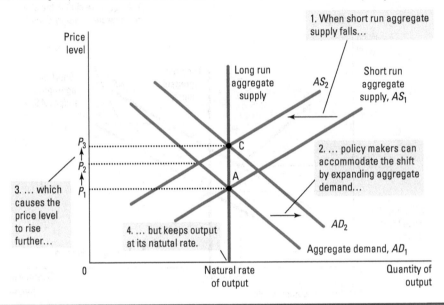

SUMMARY

- All societies experience short run economic fluctuations around long run trends. These fluctuations are irregular and largely unpredictable. When recessions do occur, real GDP and other measures of income, spending and production fall and unemployment rises.

- Economists analyze short run economic fluctuations using the model of aggregate demand and aggregate supply. According to this model, the output of goods and services and the overall level of prices adjust to balance aggregate demand and aggregate supply.

- The aggregate demand curve slopes downward for three reasons. First, a lower price level raises the real value of households' money holdings, which stimulates consumer spending. Second, a lower price level reduces the quantity of money households' demand. As households try to convert money into interest bearing assets, interest rates fall, which stimulates investment spending. Third, as a lower price level reduces interest rates, the local currency depreciates in the market for foreign currency exchange, which stimulates net exports.

- Any event or policy that raises consumption, investment, government purchases or net exports at a given price level increases aggregate demand. Any event or policy that reduces consumption, investment, government purchases or net exports at a given price level decreases aggregate demand.

- The long run aggregate supply curve is vertical. In the long run, the quantity of goods and services supplied depends on the economy's labour, capital, natural resources and technology, but not on the overall level of prices.

- Three theories have been proposed to explain the upward slope of the short run aggregate supply curve. According to the sticky wage theory, an unexpected fall in the price level temporarily raises real wages, which induces firms to reduce employment and production. According to the sticky price theory, an unexpected fall in the price level leaves some firms with prices that are temporarily too high, which reduces their sales and causes them to cut back production. According to the misperceptions theory, an unexpected fall in the price level leads suppliers to mistakenly believe that relative prices have fallen, which induces them to reduce production. All three theories imply that output deviates from its natural rate when the price level deviates from the price level that people expected.

- Events that alter the economy's ability to produce output, such as changes in labour, capital, natural resources or technology, shift the short run aggregate supply curve (and may shift the long run aggregate supply curve as well). In addition, the position of the short run aggregate supply curve depends on the expected price level.

- One possible cause of economic fluctuations is a shift in aggregate demand. When the aggregate demand curve shifts to the left, for instance, output and prices fall in the short run. Over time, as a change in the expected price level causes wages, prices and perceptions to adjust, the short run aggregate supply curve shifts to the right, and the economy returns to its natural rate of output at a new, lower price level.

- A second possible cause of economic fluctuations is a shift in aggregate supply. When the aggregate supply curve shifts to the left, the short run effect is falling output and rising prices, a combination called stagflation. Over time, as wages, prices and perceptions adjust, the price level falls back to its original level, and output recovers.

IN THE NEWS

Economic Theory Conundrum

Economic theory would suggest that when economic growth is strong, the rate of inflation will begin to accelerate and unemployment will fall. The thinking is that if aggregate demand is rising, businesses will be expanding and increasing output and to do that, they will need to employ more labour. As the demand for labour increases, other things being equal, the wage rate will rise as well. This puts pressure on firms' costs, which will lead to them increasing prices and so fuel further inflationary pressures. What this scenario is depicting is a situation where aggregate demand is rising faster than the ability of the economy to meet the demand.

What has actually happened in recent years? Economic growth across the Eurozone fell sharply as a result of the pandemic but bounced back sharply as restrictions were lifted before settling back to more modest growth rates into 2022. In the third quarter of 2022, economic growth was recorded at 0.3 per cent. Inflation had accelerated throughout 2022 and in November 2022 was recorded at 11.1 per cent. Throughout 2022, unemployment across the Eurozone had fallen from 6.9 per cent in January 2022 to 6.5 per cent in November 2022. Across the Eurozone, wage costs rose following the decline witnessed during the pandemic and reached around 3.8 per cent in the second quarter of 2022 before falling back to 2.9 per cent in the third quarter.

In the UK, inflation as measured by the Consumer Price Index did reach double digits for part of 2022. Like the rest of Europe, the UK economy shrank during the pandemic but bounced back as restrictions were eased but from quarter three of 2021, when growth was 1.7 per cent, it slowed thereafter. The Bank of England forecast that the UK would experience recession during 2023 and the quarter three figures for 2022 showed GDP shrank by 0.3 per cent. However, unemployment continued to fall over the same period. In October 2020, the unemployment rate was recorded at 5.2 per cent whereas in the three months to October 2022, it was recorded at 3.7 per cent. The case study highlighted wage growth in the UK during 2022.

How do these figures fit with the model of aggregate demand and aggregate supply presented in this chapter? In theory, periods of strong economic growth would be associated with accelerating inflation and wage rates and falling unemployment. In both the UK and across the Eurozone, economic growth could not really be described as 'strong' but inflation accelerated sharply. Sluggish economic growth might also not be compatible with falling unemployment and relatively strong wage rate growth, so what is happening? Is the model of aggregate demand and aggregate supply sufficiently robust to help explain modern economies or do we need a new model?

The experience of both the Eurozone economies and the UK in recent years seems at odds with traditional theory.

(*Continued*)

Questions

1 In both the Eurozone and the UK, inflation accelerated sharply in the aftermath of the pandemic. Use an aggregate supply and aggregate demand diagram to explain why this might have happened.

2 In the UK, the unemployment rate in 2022 was likely to have been below the natural rate. What would you expect to happen to wage rates in such a scenario? To what extent do figures on wage rate growth in the UK support the analysis you have provided?

3 The Bank of England and the European Central Bank increased interest rates during 2022 in response to accelerating inflation. Use an aggregate demand and aggregate supply diagram to analyze the impact of this tightening of monetary policy ensuring that you comment on the factors determining the likely extent of the changes you outline.

4 How might inflation be rising sharply but growth be sluggish in an economy? Use the model of aggregate demand and aggregate supply to help illustrate your answer and refer to the data provided in the article to support your answer.

5 To what extent do you think the model of aggregate demand and aggregate supply as depicted in this chapter accurately reflects a way of explaining what is happening to key economic indicators in your country?

QUESTIONS FOR REVIEW

1 Name two macroeconomic variables that decline when the economy goes into a recession. Name one macroeconomic variable that rises during a recession.

2 Draw a diagram with aggregate demand, short run aggregate supply and long run aggregate supply. Label the axes correctly.

3 List and explain the three reasons why the aggregate demand curve is downward sloping.

4 Explain why the long run aggregate supply curve is vertical.

5 List and explain the three theories for why the short run aggregate supply curve is upward sloping.

6 What might shift the aggregate demand curve to the left? Use the model of aggregate demand and aggregate supply to trace through the effects of such a shift.

7 What might shift the aggregate supply curve to the left? Use the model of aggregate demand and aggregate supply to trace through the effects of such a shift.

8 Use an aggregate supply and aggregate demand diagram to show how an economy can experience rising prices and falling growth (stagflation) at the same time.

9 Why do recessions ultimately come to an end?

10 What sort of policy do you think would be the most appropriate to bring about a reduction in a country's natural rate of unemployment?

PROBLEMS AND APPLICATIONS

1 Why do you think that investment is more variable over the business cycle than consumer spending? Which category of consumer spending do you think would be most volatile: durable goods (such as furniture and car purchases), non-durable goods (such as food and clothing) or services (such as haircuts and social care)? Why?

2 Suppose that the economy is in a long run equilibrium.

a. Use a diagram to illustrate the state of the economy. Be sure to show aggregate demand, short run aggregate supply and long run aggregate supply.

b. Now suppose that a pandemic causes aggregate demand to fall. Use your diagram to show what happens to output and the price level in the short run. What happens to the unemployment rate?

c. Use the sticky wage theory of aggregate supply to explain what will happen to output and the price level in the long run (assuming there is no change in policy). What role does the expected price level play in this adjustment? Be sure to illustrate your analysis with a graph.

3 Explain whether each of the following events will increase, decrease or have no effect on long run aggregate supply:

a. The country experiences a wave of immigration.
b. The government raises the minimum wage above the national average wage level.
c. A war leads to the destruction of a large number of factories.

4 In Figure 21.7, how does the unemployment rate at points B and C compare to the unemployment rate at point A? Under the sticky wage explanation of the short run aggregate supply curve, how does the real wage at points B and C compare to the real wage at point A?

5 Explain why the following statements are false:

a. 'The aggregate demand curve slopes downward because it is the horizontal sum of the demand curves for individual goods.'
b. 'The long run aggregate supply curve is vertical because economic forces do not affect long run aggregate supply.'
c. 'If firms adjusted their prices every day, then the short run aggregate supply curve would be horizontal.'
d. 'Whenever the economy enters a recession, its long run aggregate supply curve shifts to the left.'

6 For each of the three theories for the upward slope of the short run aggregate supply curve, explain:

a. How the economy recovers from a recession and returns to its long run equilibrium without any policy intervention.
b. What determines the speed of the recovery?

7 Suppose the central bank expands the money supply, but because the public expects this action, it simultaneously raises its expectation of the price level. What will happen to output and the price level in the short run? Compare this result to the outcome if the central bank expanded the money supply but the public did not change its expectation of the price level.

8 Suppose that the economy is currently in a recession. If policy makers take no action, how will the economy evolve over time? Explain in words and using an aggregate demand/aggregate supply diagram.

9 Suppose workers and firms suddenly believe that inflation will be quite high over the coming year. Suppose also that the economy begins in long run equilibrium, and the aggregate demand curve does not shift.

a. What happens to nominal wages? What happens to real wages?
b. Using an aggregate demand/aggregate supply diagram, show the effect of the change in expectations on both the short run and long run levels of prices and output.
c. Were the expectations of high inflation accurate? Explain.

10 Explain whether each of the following events shifts the short run aggregate supply curve, the aggregate demand curve, both or neither. For each event that does shift a curve, use a diagram to illustrate the effect on the economy.

a. Households decide to save a larger share of their income.
b. Cattle farmers suffer a prolonged period of foot and mouth disease which cuts average cattle herd sizes by 80 per cent.
c. Increased job opportunities overseas cause many people to leave the country.

GOVERNMENT ECONOMIC POLICY AND THE EFFECT ON BUSINESS: FISCAL, MONETARY AND SUPPLY SIDE POLICY

After reading this chapter you should be able to:

- Give a clear definition to outline the differences between monetary, fiscal and supply side policies.
- Explain the difference between planned and actual spending, saving and investment.
- Draw a diagram of the Keynesian cross and use it to show both an inflationary and deflationary gap.
- Be able to calculate the value of the multiplier given data on the marginal propensities to withdraw.
- Draw a diagram to explain the relevance of the slope of the expenditure line in relation to changes in autonomous expenditure.
- Show what an increase in the money supply does to the interest rate in the short run.
- Illustrate what an increase in the money supply does to aggregate demand.
- Analyze how fiscal policy affects interest rates and aggregate demand.
- Discuss the debate over whether policy makers should try to stabilize the economy.
- Describe how a change in the money supply (both increase and decrease) feeds through to the interest rate in the short run.
- Explain the idea of crowding out.

GOVERNMENT ECONOMIC POLICIES

In this chapter, we are going to examine three main policies used to control the economy. These policies are *monetary policy, fiscal policy* and *supply side policy*. In each case, policy is designed to influence economic activity in different ways. The heading of this section is 'government economic policies'. The policies we will discuss are not necessarily administered or actioned directly by governments. Monetary policy, for example, will invariably be carried out by a central bank, but the government frames the overall direction and aim of the policy.

The effects on business and consumer behaviour of these policies can be very different and the consequences for the economy will also vary. A change in monetary and fiscal policy can lead to short run fluctuations in output and prices. The effects of changes to supply side policy tend to be longer term. Fiscal and monetary policies tend to have an impact on aggregate demand, whereas supply side policies are focused on the aggregate supply curve.

Many factors influence aggregate demand besides monetary and fiscal policy. In particular, desired spending by households and firms determines the overall demand for goods and services. When desired spending changes, aggregate demand shifts. If policy makers do not respond, such shifts in aggregate demand cause short run fluctuations in output, employment and prices. As a result, monetary and fiscal policy makers sometimes use the policy levers at their disposal to try to offset these shifts in aggregate demand and thereby stabilize the economy. Here we discuss the theory behind these policy actions and some of the difficulties that arise in using this theory in practice.

MONETARY POLICY

Monetary policy refers to attempts to influence the level of economic activity (the amount of buying and selling in the economy) through changes to the amount of money in circulation and the price of money: short-term interest rates. The basis of the relationship between the money supply and inflation is set out in the classical quantity theory of money encapsulated in the formula:

$$MV = PY$$

where M = the money stock, V = velocity of circulation, P = price level and Y = level of national income. This can be stated more formally as:

$$M_d = kPY$$

where P is the price level, Y is the level of real national income, M_d is demand for money for transactions purposes and k = proportion of national income held as transactions balances.

In equilibrium $M_d = M_s$, so:

$$M_s = kPY$$

$$P = M_s (1/kY)$$

$$P = 1/kY \times Ms$$

It follows that a rise in M_s will lead to a proportional rise in P.

> **monetary policy** the set of actions taken by the central bank to influence the money supply and the price of money

The main weapon used to control the money supply is interest rates set by the central bank. Changes in the rate at which the central bank lends to the banking system helps determine the structure of interest rates throughout the financial system. The structure of interest rates then feeds through to different parts of the economy through the *interest rate transmission mechanism*. This transmission mechanism is summarized in Figure 22.1. In panel (a), changes in interest rates affect the amount of borrowing by businesses and individuals which in turn affect levels of consumption and investment. At the same time, businesses that have existing loans may find that the cost of servicing the loan changes if interest rates rise. Higher interest rates affect costs and margins, and may cause firms to cut back production or find other ways to reduce costs, such as shed employment. If workers lose their jobs and their incomes fall, this affects consumption.

In panel (b), the effect occurs through mortgages and savings. Changes to interest rates affect those with mortgages and can impact on disposable income thus affecting consumption. It will also affect the demand for new mortgages and can feed through to investment in housing stock. There might also be changes to property prices which can affect homeowners' equity. For example, if interest rates rise significantly, the demand for mortgages might fall. This may slow down the housing market causing a fall in house prices. The fall in house prices can leave some homeowners in a position where the value of their mortgage is greater than the value of the property. If they must sell, they end up saddled with debt, and this may lead to them cutting their consumption. There will also be effects from changes in interest rates on savings.

Panel (c) shows how changes in interest rates feed through to exchange rates. If the central bank changes interest rates and other countries' interest rates remain constant, then the difference in relative interest rates affects the demand and supply of currencies as traders look to move funds to higher interest rate countries to improve returns. This affects the demand and supply of currencies causing an appreciation or depreciation which in turn affects import and export prices (denoted by M_p and X_p respectively), and the demand for imports and exports. There will be a resulting effect on net exports.

FIGURE 22.1

The Interest Rate Transmission Mechanism

The three panels (a), (b) and (c) show the effect of changes in interest rates on different parts of the economy. In panel (a), the effect is traced through changes to borrowing by individuals and firms on consumption and investment. In panel (b) the effect is traced through mortgage holders and savers and in panel (c) the effect on exchange rates, import and export prices and the subsequent demand for imports and exports is shown, which together have an impact on net exports.

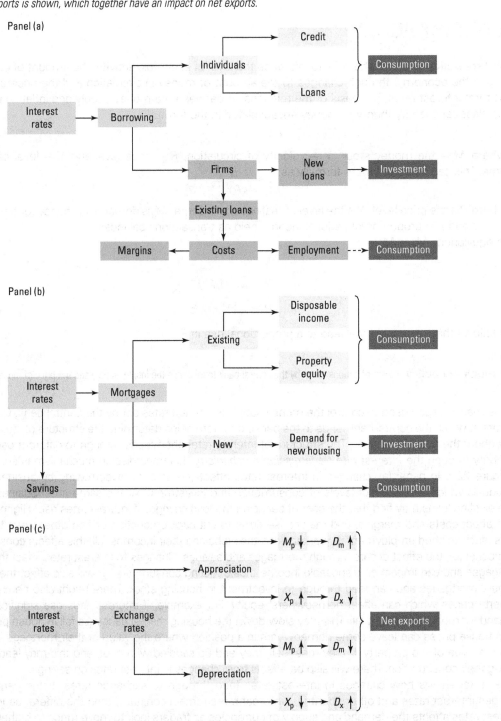

THE BANKING SYSTEM

Interest rates are at the heart of the banking system, at least in what might be termed the conventional banking system. Interest does not play a role in Islamic banking systems as we saw earlier in the book. The structure of interest rates in the banking system is heavily influenced by central banks, which play a crucial role in the monetary system.

Most firms in the banking sector exist to make a profit. While there are numerous differences between financial intermediaries which make up the banking sector, we will assume they all have in common the basic function of accepting deposits and making loans. Banks must monitor their balance sheets which consist of assets and liabilities. Most banks will earn interest on assets and must pay interest on liabilities. The difference between the average interest it earns on its assets and the average interest paid on its liabilities is termed the **spread** and is a primary determinant of the profit a bank makes.

spread the difference between the average interest banks earns on assets and the average interest paid on liabilities

A Bank's Balance Sheet

A bank's balance sheet consists of its assets and liabilities. A bank's assets might include reserves of cash, securities and loans it holds. Its liabilities include demand deposits, savings deposits, borrowings from other banks in the interbank market and, if it is a public limited company, equity capital. Its assets must equal its liabilities plus equity capital.

A bank keeps some money in its vault to cover possible withdrawals. Some of a bank's reserves are held at the central bank and the bank can instruct the central bank to transfer funds from its account to that of other banks in settling transactions. It is important to note that the amount of reserves do not, in themselves, act as a constraint to a bank in the amount it lends.

Broad measures of the money supply include bank deposits and currency. According to the Bank of England, bank deposits of various kinds account for around 97 per cent of broad money with currency making up the other 3 per cent. Banks do not sit around waiting for customers to walk through their doors and deposit money, and then use this money to lend to other people and businesses. Banks actively find ways of making new loans. This might be in the form of granting a loan to a business for expansion or the purchase of new plant and equipment, a loan to an individual to buy a car or the granting of a mortgage to someone seeking to buy a house. In granting a loan, the bank credits the account of the borrower with the funds. As far as the borrower is concerned, their bank statement now shows that they have 'money' to spend on whatever it is they arranged the loan for. At the point a new loan is agreed, new money is created and the money supply increases. These new loans represent assets to the bank (because the borrower must pay the loan plus interest to the bank) but at the same time increases liabilities by the same amount. The bank's balance sheet also expands.

The flip side of this is that when bank loans are repaid, the money supply contracts. For example, if an individual borrowed €10,000 to buy a new car, they pay monthly instalments which consist of the capital sum (the €10,000) and an element of the interest. If the capital element of the monthly payment is €300, the borrower's outstanding loan shrinks by this amount, effectively reducing the money supply.

It is not only consumers and businesses borrowing and paying back loans which impact on the money supply in this way. Banks buy and sell a range of assets including bonds. The purchase of government bonds is a way in which the banking system can hold assets which are relatively liquid, as they can be sold to the central bank. Banks will also buy and sell bonds on the bond market. If a bond is purchased from a non-banking sector holder (i.e. not purchased from another bank), the funds are credited to the seller's account. This increases the money supply. Equally, if banks sell bonds to the non-banking sector, the buyer's account is debited with the sum paid and the money supply contracts.

Banks will also be involved with borrowing funds over much longer terms and with more restrictions. These loans may be highly illiquid in that they cannot easily be converted into cash. Banks can take this type of debt onto its balance sheet because it represents a form of funding which helps protect the bank from external shocks. If banks became heavily exposed to paying short-term obligations, it can put them under severe stain and in some cases, cause them to collapse. This happened to some banks during the 2007–2009 Financial Crisis. If too many of a bank's liabilities are short term, they become more unstable in the event that borrowers demand their money. Having more long-term debt helps reduce the risk. Since the 2007–2009 Financial Crisis, a number of central banks have sought to regulate on the amount of long-term debt bank's hold as a way of improving security in the banking sector.

Constraints on Bank Lending While banks create money by lending, there are a number of constraints on their ability to do this at will. The crucial constraint is monetary policy and the interest rate set by the central bank. This rate sets the basis for the structure of interest rates throughout the economy, because it is the rate at which the central bank will lend to the banking system. If interest rates are increased, banks must increase the interest rate on lending and this leads to a reduction in the demand for loans. Similarly, a reduction in interest rates would be expected to stimulate the demand for loans. Exactly how much loans contract or increase in response to changes in interest rates depends on the interest elasticity of demand.

If bank lending is increasing and money growth is rising too fast, the central bank will look at the risk this poses in accelerating inflation over and above the target rate. If it is felt that the risk is too great, the central bank will increase interest rates, which is designed to slow down the rate of growth of money through reducing lending.

In addition, banks operate in a competitive market. To generate appropriate profits, banks must be mindful of the cost of seeking out and making loans against the returns they get. The profit they make is determined by the spread and this in turn is influenced by central bank monetary policy. To attract new loans, banks may have to offer rates which are lower than their competitors. This, in turn, affects the profitability of its operations. If a borrower banking with First European Bank takes out a loan of €15,000 to buy a car, the funds are transferred to the seller's bank (let us call it Second European Bank) from First's reserves at the central bank. This results in a reduction in First's reserves and an increase in Second's. First now faces a situation in which it has lower reserves and more loans in relation to its overall deposits. With lower reserves it is in a riskier position if it needs to meet potential withdrawals or payment obligations. Banks, therefore, cannot continue to lend indefinitely in this way. In addition, different institutions will have different cost structures and shareholder expectations of profit, not to mention the response of the public to the bank's activities. Whether it can attract new loans will be dependent on market forces and its profit requirements. Taking on more long-term debt, as outlined above, helps provide a further constraint. Long-term debt may provide the bank with more security, but attracting these funds requires a higher interest rate which in turn affects banks' spread. There is a trade-off between profitable lending and security, on which the bank needs to make a judgement.

Banks themselves must be mindful of the risk they take in making loans that borrowers will default (termed a **credit risk**). This might mean them securing funding (referred to, inaccurately, as setting aside reserves) which can absorb losses that might arise from default or wider bank sector problems which might threaten their ability to function.

credit risk the risk a bank faces in defaults on loans

Macroprudential Policy One of the criticisms of central banks during the 2007–2009 Financial Crisis was that they did not have sufficient powers to deal with systemic risk in the banking system. **Systemic risk** refers to the risk of failure across the whole of the financial sector rather than just to one or two institutions. The risk is increased because of the interconnectedness and interdependence of the financial system. Once problems begin to occur in one area of the banking system, it cascades down to others and results in a severe economic downturn.

systemic risk the risk of failure across the whole of the financial sector

In the UK, the Financial Policy Committee (FPC) has been set up to assess the risks inherent across the financial system. It has powers to take action to prevent or reduce these risks. This is referred to as **macroprudential policy**.

macroprudential policy policies designed to limit the risk across the financial sector by focusing on improving prudent standards of operation that enhance stability and reduce risk

Banks accept deposits from many people, invariably in the form of short-term deposits. Bank customers may want to take out loans over much longer durations and so banks 'transform' many short-term deposits into a smaller number of longer-term loans. A bank's assets are all the financial, physical and intangible assets they hold or are due to be paid at some point in the future. Financial assets include loans made to households and firms, mortgages, lending to other banks and the wholesale market (transactions between large financial institutions, for example merchant banks that might be arranging for the listing of a company on the stock exchange). Other assets include cash, holdings of bonds and reserves at the central bank. Physical assets include all the property the bank owns and intangible assets will include the brand value and reputation of the bank.

A bank's liabilities are what it owes to others. This includes all the deposits from households and firms, borrowings from other banks and wholesale markets, and its share capital. If a bank makes a loan it runs the risk that the loan will not be paid back, that the borrower will default. If defaults reach high levels the bank's assets fall and its liabilities increase. The other risk a bank faces is that it will be unable to meet demand for withdrawals. If withdrawals increase substantially (for example, through a bank run), the bank may have to sell off assets to raise funds and in doing so depresses the price of those assets. This is termed a **liquidity risk**. The failure of one bank can have cascade effects onto other banks and across the financial system.

As noted above, banks face a trade-off between risk and reward. They want to lend more money to make higher profits, but are constrained by the need to maintain liquidity to insulate themselves from the risk of insolvency. Banks must have sufficient sources of funding to meet their obligations. This means that if there were a sudden increase in demand for withdrawals, the bank would be in a position to secure sufficient funding to be able to meet that demand. Banks do not, therefore, have a large vault where funds are stored away to use in the event of a crisis, but instead must ensure that they are able to fund any such crisis event that occurs. This is the function of reserves.

liquidity risk the risk that a bank may not be able to fund demand for withdrawals

Banks structure their balance sheets to ensure they have a profile of assets and liabilities which enable them to respond to a rise in defaults and increased demand for withdrawals. Macroprudential regulation lays down minimum requirements banks must adhere to in structuring their balance sheets. Since share capital is the banks 'own money' rather than money it has borrowed from depositors, capital is important in being able to provide a buffer against shocks. The regulations encourage banks to take account of the risks they face, so that they themselves are capable of managing those risks rather than relying on the taxpayer to bail them out.

THE CENTRAL BANK'S TOOLS OF MONETARY CONTROL

Central banks in many developed economies have a central function of maintaining economic stability and stable inflation. The principal way they seek to achieve these objectives is through influencing the price of money in the economy through setting interest rates. In general, a central bank has three main tools in its monetary toolbox: open market operations, the refinancing rate and reserve requirements.

Open Market Operations

If the central bank wants to increase the money supply, it buys bonds from the public in the bond market. After the purchase, the extra currency is in the hands of the public. Thus an open market purchase of bonds by the central bank effectively increases broad money. If, on the other hand, the central bank wants to decrease broad money, it can sell bonds from its portfolio to the public. After the sale, the currency it receives for the bonds is out of the hands of the public. To be precise, the open market operations discussed in these simple examples are called **outright open market operations**, because they each involve an outright sale or purchase of non-monetary assets to or from the banking sector without a corresponding agreement to reverse the transaction at a later date.

> **outright open market operations** the outright sale or purchase of non-monetary assets to or from the banking sector by the central bank without a corresponding agreement to reverse the transaction at a later date

The Refinancing Rate

The central bank of an economy will set an interest rate at which it is willing to lend to commercial banks on a short-term basis. As we shall see, the name of this interest rate differs across central banks, although in general in this book we will follow the practice of the European Central Bank and refer to it as the *refinancing rate*.

The way in which the central bank lends to the banking sector is through a special form of open market operations. Although outright open market operations have traditionally been used by central banks to regulate broad money, central banks more often use a slightly more sophisticated form of open market operations that involves buying bonds or other assets from banks and at the same time agreeing to sell them back later. When it does this, the central bank has effectively made a loan and taken the bonds or other assets as collateral or security on the loan. The central bank will have a list of eligible assets that it will accept as collateral, 'safe' assets such as government bonds or assets issued by large corporations, on which the risk of default by the issuer is negligible. The interest rate that the central bank charges on the loan is the refinancing rate. Because the central bank has bought the assets but the seller has agreed to buy them back later at an agreed price, this kind of open market operation is often called a **repurchase agreement** or 'repo' for short.

> **repurchase agreement** the sale of a non-monetary asset together with an agreement to repurchase it at a set price at a specified future date

Banks need to structure their balance sheets to ensure they can meet credit and liquidity risks. Because deposits and withdrawals at banks can fluctuate randomly, some banks may find that they have an excess of reserves one day, while other banks may find that they are short of reserves. Therefore, the commercial banks in an economy will generally lend money to one another on a short-term basis, overnight to a couple of weeks, so that banks with excess reserves can lend them to banks that have inadequate reserves to cover their lending. This market for short-term reserves is called the **money market**. If there is a *general* shortage of liquidity in the money market (because the banks together have done a lot of lending), then the short-term interest rate at which they lend to one another will begin to rise, while it will begin to fall if there is excess liquidity among banks. The central bank closely monitors the money market and may intervene in it to affect the supply of liquidity to banks, which in turn affects their lending and hence affects the money supply.

> **money market** the market in which the commercial banks lend money to one another on a short-term basis

Suppose, for example, that there is a shortage of liquidity in the market because the banks have been increasing their lending. A commercial bank may then attempt to obtain liquidity by selling assets to the central bank and agreeing to purchase them back a short time later. As we said before, in this type of open market operation the central bank effectively lends money to the bank and takes the assets as collateral on the loan. Because the commercial bank is legally bound to repurchase the assets at a set price, this is called a *repurchase agreement*. The difference between the price the bank sells the assets to the central bank and the price at which it agrees to buy them back (expressed as an annualized percentage of the selling price) is called the repurchase or repo rate by the Bank of England and the refinancing rate by the European Central Bank. The ECB's **refinancing rate** is thus the rate at which it will lend to the banking sector of the euro area, while the **repo rate** or Bank Rate is the rate at which the Bank of England lends short term to the UK banking sector.

> **refinancing rate** the interest rate at which the European Central Bank lends on a short-term basis to the euro area banking sector
>
> **repo rate** the interest rate at which the Bank of England lends on a short-term basis to the UK banking sector

In the example given, the central bank added liquidity to the banking system by lending reserves to banks. This would have the effect of increasing broad money. Because the loans made through open market operations are typically very short term, with a maturity of at most two weeks, the banks are constantly having to repay the loans and borrow again, or refinance the loans. If the central bank wants to mop up liquidity, it can simply decide not to renew some of the loans. In practice, however, the central bank will set a reference rate of interest (the Bank of England's repo rate or the ECB's refinancing rate) and will conduct open market operations, adding to or mopping up liquidity, close to this reference rate.

In the United States, the interest rate at which the Federal Reserve lends to the banking sector (corresponding to the ECB's refinancing rate or the Bank of England's repo rate) is called the **discount rate** (also called the Federal Funds Rate).

> **discount rate** the interest rate at which the Federal Reserve lends on a short-term basis to the US banking sector

Now we can see why the setting of the central bank's refinancing rate is the key instrument of monetary policy. If the central bank raises the refinancing rate, commercial banks will try and pull in their lending rather than borrow reserves from the central bank, and so the money supply will fall. If the central bank lowers the refinancing rate, banks will feel freer to lend, knowing that they will be able to borrow more cheaply from the central bank to meet their reserve requirements, and so the money supply will tend to rise.

Quantitative Easing

During the 2007–2009 Financial Crisis, central banks adopted new tactics to try to support the economy, which involved market operations. One of the methods adopted was an asset purchasing facility (APF) or quantitative easing (QE).

The process of QE involves the central bank buying assets from private sector institutions financed by the creation of broad money. Private sector institutions might include banks, pension funds and insurance companies. The type of assets purchased varies from bonds and gilt-edged stock to commercial paper (short-term promissory notes issued by companies with a maturity ranging up to 270 days but with an average of 30 days), equities and possibly toxic assets. In selling assets to the central bank, institutions will hold more money in relation to other assets, and look to maintain their portfolios by using the money to buy bonds and shares of companies, which is in effect lending to firms. An example may serve to help understand the process (we will use pounds in this example and assume the central bank is the Bank of England).

Assume a pension fund has £1 billion worth of gilt-edged stock. It decides that it wants to sell £500 million worth. The Bank of England announces that it intends to purchase gilts at an auction and sets a specific date for the auction (normally a Monday and Wednesday each week for a specified period of time). The process takes place via what is called a 'reverse auction'. Rather than the buyer putting in bids for what they would be willing to pay for the item, the seller submits an electronic bid to the Bank stating what they would like to sell and at what price they would be willing to sell. The Bank itself has a specified amount that it intends to buy at that time. The bids coming in from banks and other institutions may mean that the auction is oversubscribed, i.e. more bids to sell are received than the Bank intends to buy. As a result the Bank is able to select which offers it will accept and at what price.

The pension fund in our example held government debt on its balance sheet, but following the sale of the debt to the central bank it now has a £500 million credit. This credit appears in its bank account, thus affecting the banking sector. The pension fund can use this £500 million to buy bonds and shares.

There will be further ripple effects in the bond market. Remember, companies use the bond market as a means of raising funds. Over a period of time, these bonds will mature and firms may issue new bonds to replace them. These new bond issues may have different coupon rates from existing ones, depending on current conditions in the bond market. Assume that a company has issued a 10-year bond with a coupon on issue of 5 per cent. The price at which the bond sells on the market will not necessarily be the same as its par value (what it was originally issued at). The ratio of coupon in relation to the price gives investors the yield $\left(\text{Yield}=\dfrac{\text{Coupon}}{\text{Price}}\right)$. For example, if the company issues a €100 bond, with a coupon (interest) rate of 5 per cent, the yield will also be 5 per cent. However, if demand for this bond rises then its price may rise (to €105 for example) and as a result the yield will fall:

$$\left(\frac{5\,\text{per cent}}{105}=4.76\,\text{per cent}\right)$$

There is an inverse relationship between bond prices and yield.

If the central bank intervenes to buy bonds, the supply of bonds will fall and bond prices will rise. As bond prices rise, yields fall. If our company now issues a new bond it can offer that bond at a lower coupon. There is no incentive not to buy it since buying existing bonds does not give any better return. Using the example above, if our company wanted to issue a new bond to replace the matured €100 bond, then it could offer the bond at a coupon of 4.76 per cent (or slightly higher) and have every chance of raising the finance. For the company, it is now raising funds at 4.76 per cent rather than 5 per cent. This means that firms are now able to borrow at cheaper rates. This provides an impetus for generating increased economic activity.

Problems in Controlling the Money Supply

Through the setting of its refinancing rate and the associated open market operations, the central bank can exert an important degree of control over the money supply. Yet the central bank's control of the money supply is not precise.

The first problem is that the central bank does not control the amount of money that households choose to hold as deposits in banks. To see why this is a problem, suppose that one day people begin to lose confidence in the banking system and decide to withdraw deposits and hold more cash. When this happens, the banking system's balance sheet changes, which affects their ability to go out and create loans. The money supply falls, even without any central bank action.

The second problem of monetary control is that the central bank does not control the amount that bankers choose to lend. For instance, suppose that one day bankers become more cautious about economic conditions and decide to make fewer loans. In this case, the banking system creates less money than it otherwise would. This is a situation that arose following the 2007–2009 Financial Crisis, and the consequence was that many businesses found it harder to secure vital loans for managing their business, or for expansion, or that the price of securing a loan was prohibitively high. Because of the bankers' decision, the money supply falls.

> **SELF TEST** If the ECB wanted to use all three of its policy tools to decrease the money supply, what would it do?

FISCAL POLICY

Fiscal policy involves influencing the level of economic activity though manipulation of government income and expenditure. It works through affecting key variables in aggregate demand, consumption, investment and government spending. In many developed countries, government spending accounts for around 40 per cent of total spending. This fact alone suggests that governments can have a significant effect on economic activity.

 fiscal policy influencing the level of economic activity through manipulation of government income and expenditure

In 1936, economist John Maynard Keynes published a book entitled *The General Theory of Employment, Interest and Money*, which attempted to explain short run economic fluctuations in general, and the Great Depression in particular. Keynes' primary message was that recessions and depressions can occur because of inadequate aggregate demand for goods and services. Keynes had long been a critic of classical economic theory because it could explain only the long run effects of policies.

When he published *The General Theory*, a number of the world's economies were suffering very high levels of unemployment. Keynes advocated policies to increase aggregate demand through the government manipulating its own income and expenditure by changing taxes and government spending on public works. Keynes argued that short run interventions in the economy could lead to improvements in the economy that would be beneficial, rather than waiting for the long run equilibrium to establish itself.

The Keynesian Cross

Classical economics placed a fundamental reliance on the efficiency of markets and the assumption that they would clear. At a macro level, this meant that if the economy was in disequilibrium and unemployment existed, wages and prices would adjust to bring the economy back into equilibrium at full employment. **Full employment** is defined as a point where those people who want to work at the going market wage level are able to find a job. Any unemployment that did exist would be classed as voluntary unemployment. The experience of the Great Depression of the 1930s brought the classical assumptions under closer scrutiny. The many millions suffering from unemployment could not all be volunteering to not take jobs at the going wage rates so some must have been involuntarily unemployed.

 full employment a point where those people who want to work at the going market wage level are able to find a job

Fundamental to Keynesian analysis is the distinction between planned and actual decisions by households and firms. **Planned spending, saving or investment** refers to the desired or intended actions of firms and households. A publisher may plan to sell 1,000 copies of a textbook in the first three months of the year, an individual may plan to go on holiday to Turkey in the summer and to save up to finance the trip, a person may intend to save €1,000 over the year to pay for a wedding in the following year.

 planned spending, saving or investment the desired or intended actions of households and firms

Actual spending, saving or investment refers to the realized, *ex post* (after the event) outcome. The publisher may only sell 800 copies in the first three months and so has a stock of 200 more than planned; the holidaymaker may fall ill and so is unable to go on holiday and so actual consumption is lower than planned (but actual saving is more than planned), and the plans for saving for the wedding may be compromised by the need to spend the money on repairing a house damaged by a flood.

 actual spending, saving or investment the realized or *ex post* outcome resulting from actions of households and firms

Planned and actual outcomes might be very different. As a result, Keynes argued that there was no reason why equilibrium national income would coincide with full employment output. Wages and prices might not adjust in the short run (due to sticky wages and prices) and so the economy could be at a position where the level of demand in the economy was insufficient to bring about full employment. Recall the model of the circular flow of income. Households and firms interact in the market for goods and services and in the factor market. Recall also the identity which described how a country's gross domestic product (national income, Y) is divided among four components, i.e. consumption spending, investment spending, spending by government and net exports. Figure 22.2 summarizes this analysis.

FIGURE 22.2

Deflationary and Inflationary Gaps
The 45° line shows all the points where consumption spending equals income. The vertical intercept of the expenditure line shows autonomous expenditure. The economy is in equilibrium where the expenditure line, C + I + G + NX, cuts the 45° line. In panel (a) this equilibrium is lower than full employment output Y_f; at Y_1 there is insufficient demand to maintain full employment output. The government would need to shift the expenditure line up to C + I + G + NX_1 to eliminate the deflationary gap as shown. In panel (b) the equilibrium is higher than full employment output. The economy does not have the capacity to meet demand. In this case the government needs to shift the C + I + G + NX line down to C + I + G + NX_2 to eliminate the inflationary gap.

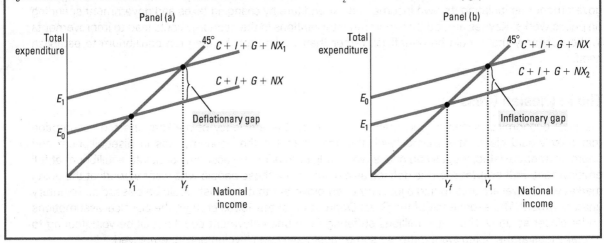

In panels (a) and (b), the 45° line connects all points where consumption spending would be equal to national income. This line can be thought of as the equivalent of the capacity of the economy, the aggregate supply (*AS*) curve. The economy is in equilibrium where the $C + I + G + NX$ line cuts the 45° line at Y_1. In panel (a) the equilibrium is less than that required to give full employment output (Y_f). At this equilibrium, there is spare capacity in the economy and unemployment will rise. The difference between full employment output and the expenditure required to meet it is termed the **deflationary gap**.

In panel (b) equilibrium is above full employment output and in this case the economy does not have the capacity to meet the demand.

This will trigger inflationary pressures in the economy. The difference between full employment output and the expenditure line here is called the **inflationary gap**. To eradicate these gaps governments can influence the components of aggregate demand through both fiscal and monetary policy to bring about an equilibrium that is closer to the desired full employment output.

 deflationary/inflationary gap the difference between full employment output and expenditure in the economy

The Multiplier Effect

When a government makes a purchase, say a contract for €20 billion to build a new nuclear power generating station, that purchase has repercussions. The immediate impact of the higher demand from the government is to raise employment and profits at the construction company (which we shall call Nucelec). Nucelec, in turn, buys resources from other contractors to carry out the job, and so these suppliers also experience an increase in orders. Then, as the workers see higher earnings and the firm owners see higher profits, they respond to this increase in income by raising their own spending on consumer goods. As a result, the government purchase from Nucelec raises the demand for the products of many other firms and consumers in the economy. Because each euro, pound, rand, etc. spent by the government can raise the aggregate demand for goods and services by more than the initial spending, government purchases are said to have a **multiplier effect** on aggregate demand.

> **multiplier effect** the additional shifts in aggregate demand that result when expansionary fiscal policy increases income and thereby increases consumer spending

This multiplier effect continues even after this first round. When consumer spending rises, the firms that produce these consumer goods hire more people and experience higher profits. Higher earnings and profits stimulate consumer spending once again and so on. Thus, there is positive feedback as higher demand leads to higher income, which in turn leads to even higher demand. Once all these effects are added together, the total impact on the quantity of goods and services demanded can be much larger than the initial impulse from higher government spending.

This multiplier effect arising from the response of consumer spending can be strengthened by the response of investment to higher levels of demand. For instance, Nucelec might respond to the higher demand for building services by buying more cranes and other mechanized building equipment. In this case, higher government demand spurs higher demand for investment goods. This positive feedback from demand to investment is sometimes called the investment accelerator.

A Formula for the Spending Multiplier

A little algebra permits us to derive a formula for the size of the multiplier effect that arises from consumer spending. An important number in this formula is the **marginal propensity to consume** (*MPC*), the fraction of extra income that a household spends rather than saves. For example, suppose that the MPC is ¾. This means that for every extra euro that a household earns, the household spends 75c of it and saves 25c. The **marginal propensity to save** is the fraction of extra income that a household saves rather than consumes. With an *MPC* of ¾, when the workers and owners of Nucelec earn €20 billion from the government contract, they increase their consumer spending by ¾ × €20 billion, or €15 billion.

> **marginal propensity to consume** the fraction of extra income that a household spends rather than saves
> **marginal propensity to save** the fraction of extra income that a household saves rather than consumes

To gauge the impact on aggregate demand of a change in government purchases, we follow the effects step-by-step. The process begins when the government spends €20 billion, which implies that national income (earnings and profits) also rises by this amount. This increase in income in turn raises consumer spending by *MPC* × €20 billion, which in turn raises the income for the workers and owners of the firms that produce the consumption goods. This second increase in income again raises consumer spending, this time by *MPC* × (*MPC* × €20 billion). These feedback effects go on and on.

To find the total impact on the demand for goods and services, we add up all these effects:

Change in government purchases	= €20 billion
First change in consumption	= MPC × €20 billion
Second change in consumption	= MPC^2 × €20 billion
Third change in consumption	= MPC^3 × €20 billion
Total change in demand	= $(1 + MPC + MPC^2 + MPC^3 = \ldots)$ × €20 billion

Thus we can write the multiplier as follows:

$$\text{Multiplier} = 1 + MPC + MPC^2 + MPC^3 + \cdots$$

Here, '...' represents an infinite number of similar terms. This multiplier tells us the demand for goods and services that each unit of currency of government purchases generates.

To simplify this equation for the multiplier, recall from your school algebra that this expression is an infinite geometric series. For x between −1 and 1:

$$1 + x + x^2 + x^3 + \ldots = \frac{1}{(1-x)}$$

The sum of this series, as the number of terms tends to infinity, is given by the expression:

$$\frac{1}{1-x}$$

In our case, $x = MPC$. Thus:

$$\text{Multiplier} = \frac{1}{(1-MPC)}$$

Note, the $MPC + MPS = 1$ so the multiplier can also be expressed as:

$$\text{Multiplier} = \frac{1}{MPS}$$

For example, if MPC is ¾, the multiplier is $1/(1-¾)$, which is 4. In this case, the €20 billion of government spending generates €80 billion of demand for goods and services.

This formula for the multiplier shows an important conclusion: the size of the multiplier depends on the MPC. While an MPC of ¾ leads to a multiplier of 4, an MPC of ½ leads to a multiplier of only 2. Thus, a larger MPC means a larger multiplier. To see why this is true, remember that the multiplier arises because higher income induces greater spending on consumption. The larger the MPC is, the greater is this induced effect on consumption, and the larger is the multiplier.

 WHAT IF... the government did some research and found that the MPC for the wealthiest 20 per cent of the population was 0.3 but that the MPC for the least well-off 20 per cent was 0.95. What might the explanation for this difference be? How might this affect policy decisions on tax changes to boost the economy?

Other Applications of the Multiplier Effect

Because of the multiplier effect, a euro of government purchases can generate more than a euro of aggregate demand. The logic of the multiplier effect, however, is not restricted to changes in government purchases. Instead, it applies to any event that alters spending on any component of GDP: consumption, investment, government purchases or net exports.

For example, suppose that a recession overseas reduces the demand for German net exports by €1 billion. This reduced spending on German goods and services depresses German national income, which reduces spending by German consumers. If the MPC is ¾ and the multiplier is 4, then the €1 billion fall in net exports means a €4 billion contraction in aggregate demand.

The multiplier is an important concept in macroeconomics because it shows how the economy can amplify the impact of changes in spending. A small initial change in consumption, investment, government purchases or net exports can end up having a large effect on aggregate demand and, therefore, on the economy's production of goods and services.

Another important concept in this analysis is that of **autonomous expenditure**, spending which does not depend on income. Government spending is a key element of this expenditure. The amount spent in each successive 'round' of spending is termed induced expenditure. The multiplier showed how the eventual change in income would be determined by the size of the MPC and the MPS, the proportion of an extra €1 spent or saved by consumers. The higher the MPC the greater the multiplier effect.

> **autonomous expenditure** spending which is not dependent on income

In an open economy, any extra €1 is not simply either spent or saved, some of the extra income may be spent on imported goods and services or go to the government in taxation. These are all classed as withdrawals from the circular flow of income. Withdrawals (W) from the circular flow are classed as endogenous, as they are directly related to changes in income. There are also injections to the circular flow of income. Governments receive tax revenue, but use it to spend on the goods and services they provide for citizens. Firms earn revenue from selling goods abroad (exports) and firms, as we have seen, use savings as a source of funds to borrow for investment. Injections into the circular flow are exogenous. They are not related to the level of output or income, and are investment (I), government spending (G) and export earnings (X).

The slope of the expenditure line, therefore, will be dependent on how much of each extra €1 is withdrawn. There will be a marginal propensity to taxation (MPT), a marginal propensity to import (MPM) in addition to the MPS. Collectively these are referred to as the marginal propensity to withdraw (MPW). The multiplier (k) would be expressed as:

$$k = \frac{1}{MPS + MPT + MPM}$$

or:

$$k = \frac{1}{MPW}$$

A higher MPW will reduce the value of the multiplier, and thus the impact on national income. In equilibrium, planned withdrawals would equal planned injections:

Planned $S + T + M$ = Planned $I + G + X$

At this point, all the output being produced by the economy would be 'bought' by households and firms. However, if actual withdrawals are greater than planned injections, then the economy would be experiencing a deficiency in demand. For example, assume that equilibrium output is €100 billion. Planned withdrawals amount to €60 billion. If this planned withdrawal level is not 'bought' by governments, firms and foreigners (i.e. planned injections) then firms will build up stocks and plan to cut back on output in the next period. This leads to a fall in income, and as withdrawals are endogenous, planned withdrawals for the next period will fall. The process will continue until planned withdrawals equal planned injections once again, and the economy is in equilibrium.

In situations where the economy is experiencing such demand deficiency, the government can budget for a deficit, and spend more than it receives in tax revenue by borrowing or cutting taxes to boost spending in the economy. It could also influence monetary policy to cut the cost of borrowing and so boost investment. There may also have been an incentive to find ways of boosting exports or cutting imports through imposing various trade barriers and offering export subsidies. However, if the emphasis is primarily on fiscal policy, the direct influence the government can have over tax and spending can mean that the effect is more immediate. The multiplier process means that the increase in government spending does not need to be as high as the size of the inflationary or deflationary gap. The steeper the slope of the expenditure line, the greater the size of the multiplier, as shown in Figure 22.3.

The Keynesian cross, as it is known, gives us a picture of the economy in short run equilibrium. If you look at a copy of Keynes' *General Theory* you might be surprised to see a complete absence of Keynesian cross diagrams. The use of these diagrams to explain Keynesian ideas was developed by later economists to help portray Keynes' ideas.

In equilibrium, planned expenditure (E), ($C + I + G +$ NX) equals actual income (GDP or national income (Y), ($E = Y$). This equilibrium is referred to as equilibrium in the goods market. Equilibrium in the money market is given by the intersection of the demand for money and the supply of **real money balances**. The goods market and the money market are both interrelated, linked by the interest rate.

FIGURE 22.3

The Slope of the Expenditure Line and Changes in Autonomous Expenditure
Panel (a) shows a relatively shallow expenditure line which would mean that the MPW would be high and the value of the multiplier relatively low. The impact on national income (ΔY) of a change in government spending (ΔG) would be more limited in comparison to the effect as shown in panel (b) where the expenditure line is much steeper, reflecting a higher value of the multiplier where the MPW was relatively low. In this case, it takes a smaller rise in government spending to achieve the same increase in national income.

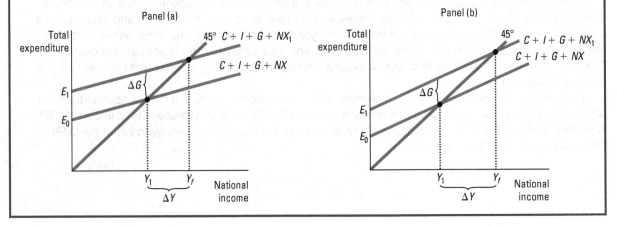

real money balances what money can actually buy given the ratio of the money supply to the price level

JEOPARDY PROBLEM Over a 30-year period a government adopts demand management policies as its primary weapon in managing its economy. After 20 years, politicians are congratulating themselves on maintaining low levels of inflation, consistent growth of around 2 per cent a year and unemployment below 5 per cent. However, in the next few years, things seem to go wrong. Unemployment starts to rise and inflation accelerates to over 9 per cent. What might have gone wrong?

CASE STUDY   Job Generation in Clusters

Governments are keen to point out the magic of the multiplier effect when making additional domestic purchases, encouraging inward investment or indeed when consumer spending increases, influenced by whatever macroeconomic policy is in force. The positive effect on employment and income is a multiple of the initial cause of change.

However, the geographical impact of the multiplier is not evenly felt. One argument put forward is that certain cities or regions gain while others are left behind. The regional imbalance in house price changes in a country might provide some evidence to support this view.

Research by Enrico Moretti in the United States points to a divergence between go-getting cities like Austin in Texas, Boston in Massachusetts and Seattle in Washington State, which are becoming engines of prosperity, and other cities and regions of the country. He points out that workers in these growing cities are producing two to three times the levels identical workers are making in cities that are losing ground.

He notes that job generation happens in clusters, because these growing cities have the 'right' industries and a solid base of human capital. They, in turn, attract growing companies. These often

(Continued)

high-tech companies can generate five times as many indirect jobs as direct ones. What's more, these indirect jobs include skilled work such as lawyers and teachers, as well as unskilled work such as restaurant service staff.

Moretti suggests that the innovation sector's multiplier effect is three times larger than for manufacturing. It implies that the best way to increase low skilled job opportunities in a city is to attract high-tech companies. However, can government really influence where these industries locate and create job hubs? Moretti doesn't think so. He has proposed that a government should encourage those out of work in areas of high unemployment to move to areas of stronger economic activity.

What would this mean for the UK? Since 2010 there has been a notable shift in jobs from the public sector to the private sector. Areas such as Wales and North East England, where dependency on public sector employment was higher than average, have suffered most. Wales and North East England had lower gross value added (GVA) per head figures on average than London and the South East. Birmingham has been close behind London. Liverpool and Bristol have tended to show a decline in GVA per head. What is more, unemployment rates are highest in several of the older northern industrial cities including those in North East England. It implies a problem, and according to Moretti the unemployed in these areas should be encouraged to move to where the growth is, such as London. But house prices in the capital are already well beyond the reach of many. Sorting out regional inequality is an enormous challenge.

Another option would be to shift capital spending north from London. The UK government committed to a £15 billion infrastructure investment plan in 2015 for five northern cities to make them better connected and create a 'northern powerhouse'. There have been problems in implementing the policy, and arguments that the funds are insufficient and misdirected. Looking at publicly funded infrastructure, far more is spent in London per person than anywhere else. The figure is £5,426 per head compared to £1,248 for the North West and £223 for the North East, according to a report by the Institute for Public Policy and Research (IPPR).

Does clustering mean that particular areas of a country like the North East of England suffer more than other areas?

Questions

1 Analyze the case for the UK government investing significantly in infrastructure for high-tech businesses in the North of England to encourage businesses in the sector to invest in and locate to the area. What factors might limit the potential success of such a policy?

2 What is the relevance of the multiplier to the decision by the UK government to invest in infrastructure in the North of England.

3 To what extent do you think that the sort of investment outlined in the case study will succeed in 'levelling up' the UK economy. Refer to the research of Moretti in your answer.

References: sloanreview.mit.edu/article/the-multiplier-effect-of-innovation-jobs/ (accessed 12 June 2023).
www.gov.uk/government/uploads/system/uploads/attachment_data/file/396740/bis-15-4-growth-dashboard.pdf (accessed 12 June 2023).
www.publicfinance.co.uk/news/2014/08/ippr-north-seeks-infrastructure-ideas/ (accessed 12 June 2023).

SUPPLY SIDE POLICIES

Supply side policy is a macroeconomic policy that seeks to improve the efficiency of the operation of markets to increase the capacity of the economy. The aim of such a policy is to shift the aggregate supply curve to the right and in so doing generate economic growth (and thus reduce unemployment) but without creating inflationary pressures.

 Supply side policy policy aimed at influencing the level of aggregate supply in the economy

This is illustrated in Figure 22.4. The AS curve is shown as a curve which gets steeper as it approaches full employment output Y_f, where the long run AS would be vertical. At very low levels of output, the aggregate supply curve is almost horizontal. The reason for this is that there would be a great deal of spare capacity in the economy at low levels of output and it would be relatively easy for firms to expand output without any significant effect on the price level. The closer national output gets to full employment output, the steeper the AS curve becomes because resource inputs start to become scarcer and can only be utilized at higher price levels. Assume equilibrium output is initially at a price level of 2.3 per cent and an output level of Y_0 where the AD curve cuts the AS curve.

FIGURE 22.4

Shifting Aggregate Supply
Successful supply side policies could increase the capacity of the economy by shifting the AS curve to the right to AS$_1$. Given aggregate demand(AD), the economy could now support an increased level of capacity from Y$_f$ to Y$_{f2}$ and lower inflation from 2.3 per cent to 2.0 per cent.

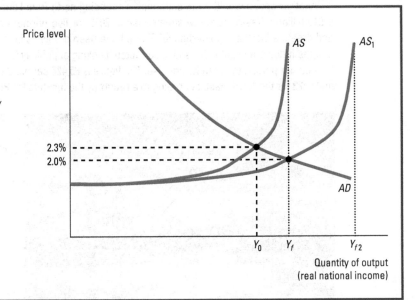

If the capacity of the economy was increased by policies which shift the AS curve to the right to AS_1, then the economy could not only support a higher level of output (and hence reduce unemployment) but also reduce the price level to 2.0 per cent.

Supply side policies are characterized by a number of features detailed in the following sections.

Deregulation Deregulation refers to the removal of controls, laws or rules governing a particular market aimed at improving the economic efficiency of that market and therefore the performance of the economy at the microeconomic level. An example would be the abandonment of a licensing system for taxis, or reducing the processes, procedures and paperwork that entrepreneurs need to go through in order to set up a new business. **Deregulation** aims to help promote enterprise, risk and incentives and create a climate where private businesses can go about their activities unencumbered by bureaucracy and distractions.

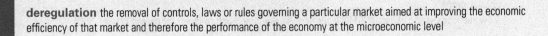 **deregulation** the removal of controls, laws or rules governing a particular market aimed at improving the economic efficiency of that market and therefore the performance of the economy at the microeconomic level

Tax Laws Reducing the tax burden on individuals and companies is seen as a key part of supply side policy, with the aim of promoting incentives which may include inducements to work rather than claim benefits, to be entrepreneurial, to invest and to expand. Part of such tax changes might include reductions in business taxes on profits and payroll, and reductions in income taxes. The emphasis may instead be switched from direct to indirect taxes. People would have choices as to whether they spent money on items that attract indirect taxes such as value added tax (VAT), but do not have such choices with regard to their income. There is disagreement about the extent of the effect of reducing tax rates on incentives. Much of the outcome may depend on the size of the relevant elasticities. The more elastic supply and demand are in any market, the more taxes distort behaviour.

Welfare Reform The welfare policies adopted by countries are designed to help support those in society who are most vulnerable. Welfare benefits may include some sort of health insurance, unemployment insurance, disability and housing benefits and so on. However, while the system is designed to support the most vulnerable, it is invariably also open to abuse and accusations that some individuals in society come to rely on state benefits rather than helping themselves. When this happens, long-term unemployment becomes more likely. Not only is the opportunity cost of lost output a factor in reducing the efficiency of the economy, but government spending increases.

Adjustments to welfare policy, therefore, aim to reverse these incentives and to encourage those out of work to try to find employment rather than rely on the state. This might include amendments to the tax and benefits system that make the hoops people have to go through to claim benefits harder, as well as making the financial incentive of getting work more significant. Such a policy is fraught with problems because every individual who feels they have a need which society should help them with expects some support. The definition of what those needs are and what level of support is required vary tremendously. There is also the problem of the poverty trap, the problems people face when moving from state support to work. Tax systems may mean an individual can be worse off by having a job, because they become liable for paying tax and do not qualify for benefits. Every government is very aware of the potential for damaging news headlines about how policies have left families 'in need' hungry, destitute and worse off.

Flexible Labour Markets Flexible labour markets focus on the ease with which the demand and supply of labour responds to changing wage conditions. This determines the extent to which unemployment or underemployment will exist in the economy. **Underemployment** is a situation where a worker has a job but may not be working to full capacity, or does not have all their skills utilized, or is working for a lower income than their qualifications, training or experience might suggest.

> **underemployment** a situation where a worker has a job but may not be working to full capacity, or does not have all their skills utilized, or is working for a lower income than their qualifications, training or experience might suggest

Elements of reforming the labour market to make it more flexible might include new employment regulations or legislation relating to the hiring, firing and dealing with employees. A firm with a very seasonal operation, for example, may need large numbers of workers at certain times of the year but very few at others. If the market mechanism is working effectively then, in theory, the firm will be able to do this, but if there are restrictions to the working of the labour market then this may not be possible. Workers may be left without jobs that technically are available. A firm may have labour which is underutilized because they have to be retained and paid even if there is insufficient work for them.

The more flexibility firms have to match the workforce to their output needs, the more efficient they can be, but this can mean that workers' rights can be compromised. Measures may be taken to help improve job searches by helping both **geographical mobility**, the ease with which people can move to different parts of the country where jobs may be available, and **occupational mobility**, the ease with which people are able to move from occupation to occupation, including the degree to which skills and qualifications are transferable between occupations.

> **geographical mobility** the ease with which people can move to different parts of the country where jobs may be available
> **occupational mobility** the ease with which people are able to move from occupation to occupation, including the degree to which skills and qualifications are transferable between occupations

Education and Training Investment in human capital can help improve productivity. Innovation and creativity are factors we have mentioned earlier in the book. However, important questions emerge about who should pay for training: the state or the employer? What type of qualifications structure should a country put in place? Should science and engineering courses be prioritized at the expense of arts and humanities courses? Should education and training be aimed at preparing people for work or is education more than that? Should students in higher education pay for their studies or should the state subsidize it?

Whatever the answers to these questions, the importance of having a well-educated workforce is crucial to the economic well-being of a country and it is generally agreed that the link between high standards and levels of education in a country and productive capacity (aggregate supply in other words) is clear.

Infrastructure Investment in infrastructure can take on many forms, but ultimately the aim is to help the economy operate more efficiently. This might be through:

- improved transport links which help speed up delivery and distribution
- reducing congestion
- providing better schools
- providing better medical facilities, to keep the population healthy, reducing days missed at work through ill-health
- promoting entrepreneurship
- creating reliable energy supplies, or
- creating technology solutions and communications.

The latter is particularly important in an economy that is based around knowledge and information exchange, like many service industry economies. Having fast broadband access, good telephone links, and widespread and strong mobile phone signals is essential for knowledge-based economies and service industries.

Investment in new technologies for information exchange, for example, can also help job search by providing help to both employers and employees seeking information about vacancies and skills available, as well as helping improve geographical mobility.

Trade Unions While trade unions exist to represent workers who may not have any market power themselves, some economists note that trade union activity can distort the working of the labour market. Partly because some politicians believed that trade unions had become too powerful and that the distorting effects were too significant, and partly because of changed working practices, the role of trade unions in many countries has changed since the early 1990s. Unions now tend to take on roles that help support workers in legal disputes, and give welfare and financial advice, as well as representing the views of workers in national policy debates.

Summary

The three main policies outlined above are not used independently of each other, nor exclusively. The extent to which a country has control over fiscal and monetary policy does depend on particular circumstances. In Europe, for example, governments in the Eurozone have surrendered control of monetary policy to the European Central Bank, and discussions are ongoing regarding greater fiscal unity within the Eurozone. In the UK, South Africa and parts of the Middle East, governments have control over fiscal policy, but have given control of monetary policy to the country's central bank.

Where countries do have some control over fiscal policy, decisions are not simply designed to influence macroeconomic variables like growth, unemployment or inflation, but also to focus on specific microeconomic goals associated with a broader supply side policy. Examples include increasing funds available for research into science and technology, or improving transport and communication networks which are publicly funded.

> **PITFALL PREVENTION** Remember that monetary, fiscal and supply side policies tend to be used together to target not only macroeconomic objectives but also microeconomic objectives which may help boost the overall efficiency of the economy. Given the prevailing economic orthodoxy of the day, one policy might have more prominence over another, but the reality is that the three must work in harmony.

HOW MONETARY POLICY INFLUENCES AGGREGATE DEMAND

In this next section, we are going to look at how monetary and fiscal policy affect aggregate demand. To understand how policy influences aggregate demand, we need to examine the interest rate effect in more detail. Here we develop a theory of how the interest rate is determined, called the **theory of liquidity preference**, which was originally developed by John Maynard Keynes in the 1930s.

> **theory of liquidity preference** Keynes' theory that the interest rate adjusts to bring money supply and money demand into balance

The Theory of Liquidity Preference

The theory is, in essence, just an application of supply and demand. According to Keynes, the interest rate adjusts to balance the supply and demand for money. In the analysis that follows, we hold constant the expected rate of inflation. This assumption is reasonable for studying the economy in the short run. Thus when the nominal interest rate rises or falls, the real interest rate that people expect to earn rises or falls as well. For the rest of this chapter, when we refer to changes in the interest rate, you should envision the real and nominal interest rates moving in the same direction.

Money Supply The first element of the theory of liquidity preference is the supply of money. The money supply is assumed to be controlled by the central bank which can alter the money supply through the purchase and sale of government bonds in outright open market operations. In addition to these open market operations, the central bank can alter the refinancing rate. For the purpose of our analysis we are going to assume that the quantity of money supplied in the economy is fixed at whatever level the central bank decides to set it.

Because the quantity of money supplied is fixed by central bank policy, it does not depend on other economic variables. In particular, it does not depend on the interest rate. Once the central bank has made its policy decision, the quantity of money supplied is the same, regardless of the prevailing interest rate. We represent a fixed money supply with a vertical supply curve in Figure 22.5.

Money Demand The second element of the theory of liquidity preference is the demand for money. Any asset's *liquidity* refers to the ease with which that asset is converted into the economy's medium of exchange. Money is the economy's medium of exchange, so it is by definition the most liquid asset available. The liquidity of money explains the demand for it. Businesses and people choose to hold money instead of other assets that offer higher rates of return because money can be used to buy raw materials, equipment and goods and services.

Although many factors determine the quantity of money demanded, the one emphasized by the theory of liquidity preference is the interest rate. The reason is that the interest rate is the opportunity cost of holding money. That is, when wealth is held as cash, instead of as an interest bearing bond or bank account, the benefits of the interest which could have been earned (the opportunity cost) are foregone. An increase in the interest rate raises the opportunity cost of holding money. Figure 22.5 shows the money demand curve sloping downward. At higher interest rates the opportunity cost in terms of foregone interest is higher and so demand for money as cash is lower than at lower interest rates.

FIGURE 22.5

Equilibrium in the Money Market

According to the theory of liquidity preference, the interest rate adjusts to bring the quantity of money supplied and the quantity of money demanded into balance. If the interest rate is above the equilibrium level (such as at r_1), the quantity of money people want to hold (M_1^d) is less than the quantity the central bank has created, and this surplus of money puts downward pressure on the interest rate. Conversely, if the interest rate is below the equilibrium level (such as at r_2), the quantity of money people want to hold (M_2^d) is greater than the quantity the central bank has created, and this shortage of money puts upward pressure on the interest rate. Thus the forces of supply and demand in the market for money push the interest rate towards the equilibrium interest rate, at which people are content holding the quantity of money the central bank has created.

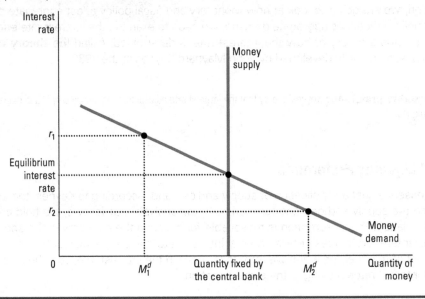

Equilibrium in the Money Market According to the theory of liquidity preference, the interest rate adjusts to balance the supply and demand for money. There is one interest rate, called the *equilibrium interest rate*, at which the quantity of money demanded exactly balances the quantity of money supplied. If the interest rate is at any other level, businesses and people will try to adjust their portfolios of assets and, as a result, drive the interest rate towards the equilibrium.

For example, suppose that the interest rate is above the equilibrium level, such as r_1 in Figure 22.5. In this case, the quantity of money that businesses and people want to hold, M_1^d, is less than the quantity of money that the central bank has supplied. Those who are holding the surplus of money will try to get rid of it by buying interest bearing bonds or by depositing it in an interest bearing bank account. Because bond issuers and banks prefer to pay lower interest rates, they respond to this surplus of money by lowering the interest rates they offer. As the interest rate falls, people become more willing to hold money until, at the equilibrium interest rate, businesses and people are happy to hold exactly the amount of money the central bank has supplied.

Conversely, at interest rates below the equilibrium level, such as r_2 in Figure 22.5, the quantity of money that people want to hold, M_2^d, is greater than the quantity of money that the central bank has supplied. Businesses and people try to increase holdings of money by reducing their holdings of bonds and other interest bearing assets. As holdings of bonds are reduced, bond issuers find that they must offer higher interest rates to attract buyers. Thus the interest rate rises and approaches the equilibrium level.

The Downward Slope of the Aggregate Demand Curve Suppose that the overall level of prices in the economy rises. What happens to the interest rate that balances the supply and demand for money, and how does that change affect the quantity of goods and services demanded?

The price level is one determinant of the quantity of money demanded. At higher prices, more money is exchanged every time a good or service is sold. As a result, businesses and people will choose to hold a larger quantity of money. That is, a higher price level increases the quantity of money demanded for any given interest rate. Thus, an increase in the price level from P_1 to P_2 shifts the money demand curve to the right from MD_1 to MD_2, as shown in panel (a) of Figure 22.6.

FIGURE 22.6

The Money Market and the Slope of the Aggregate Demand Curve

An increase in the price level from P_1 to P_2 shifts the money demand curve to the right, as in panel (a). This increase in money demand causes the interest rate to rise from r_1 to r_2. Because the interest rate is the cost of borrowing, the increase in the interest rate reduces the quantity of goods and services demanded from Y_1 to Y_2. This negative relationship between the price level and quantity demanded is represented with a downward sloping aggregate demand curve, as in panel (b).

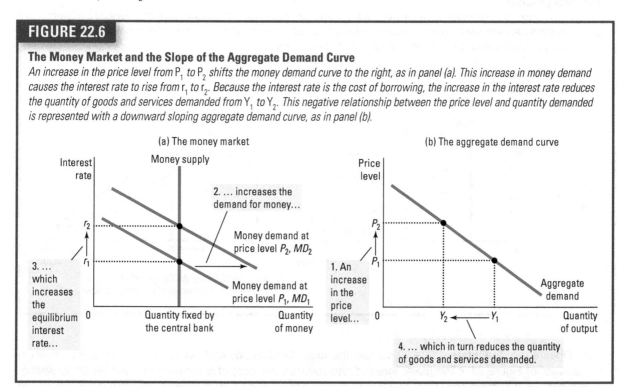

Notice how this shift in money demand affects the equilibrium in the money market. For a fixed money supply, the interest rate must rise to balance money supply and money demand. The higher price level has increased the amount of money businesses and people want to hold, and has shifted the money demand curve to the right. Yet the quantity of money supplied is unchanged, so the interest rate must rise from r_1 to r_2 to discourage the additional demand.

This increase in the interest rate has ramifications not only for the money market but also for the quantity of goods and services demanded, as shown in panel (b). At a higher interest rate, the cost of borrowing and the return to saving are greater. Fewer households choose to borrow to buy a new house, and those who do buy smaller houses, so the demand for residential investment falls. Fewer firms choose to borrow to build new factories and buy new equipment, so business investment falls. Thus when the price level rises from P_1 to P_2, increasing money demand from MD_1 to MD_2 and raising the interest rate from r_1 to r_2, the quantity of goods and services demanded falls from Y_1 to Y_2.

Of course, the same logic works in reverse as well: a lower price level reduces money demand, which leads to a lower interest rate, and this in turn increases the quantity of goods and services demanded. The result of this analysis is a negative relationship between the price level and the quantity of goods and services demanded, which is illustrated with a downward sloping aggregate demand curve.

Changes in the Money Supply

Whenever the quantity of goods and services demanded changes *for a given price level*, the aggregate demand curve shifts. Suppose that the central bank increases the money supply by buying government bonds in open market operations. As panel (a) of Figure 22.7 shows, an increase in the money supply shifts the money supply curve to the right from MS_1 to MS_2. Because the money demand curve has not changed, the interest rate falls from r_1 to r_2 to balance money supply and money demand. That is, the interest rate must fall to induce people to hold the additional money that the central bank has created.

FIGURE 22.7

A Monetary Injection

In panel (a), an increase in the money supply from MS_1 to MS_2 reduces the equilibrium interest rate from r_1 to r_2. Because the interest rate is the cost of borrowing, the fall in the interest rate raises the quantity of goods and services demanded at a given price level from Y_1 to Y_2. Thus, in panel (b), the aggregate demand curve shifts to the right from AD_1 to AD_2.

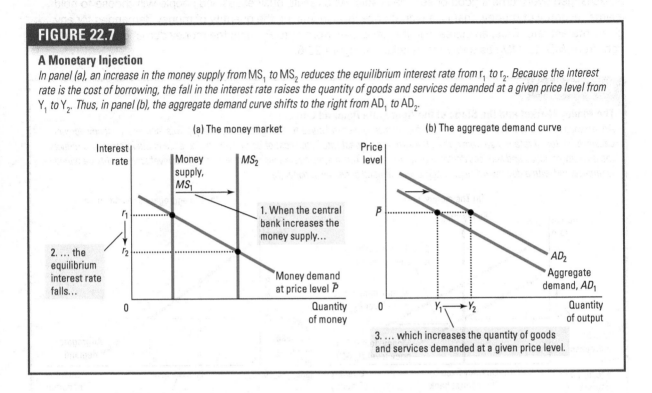

Once again, the interest rate influences the quantity of goods and services demanded, as shown in panel (b) of Figure 22.7. The lower interest rate reduces the cost of borrowing and the return to saving. Households buy more and larger houses, stimulating the demand for residential investment. Firms spend more on new factories and new equipment, stimulating business investment. The quantity of goods and services demanded at a given price level $\bar{P}$, rises from Y_1 to Y_2. Of course, there is nothing special about $\bar{P}$: the monetary injection raises the quantity of goods and services demanded at every price level. The entire aggregate demand curve shifts to the right. Conversely, when the central bank contracts the money supply, the interest rate rises to bring the money market into equilibrium and reduces the quantity of goods and services demanded for any given price level, shifting the aggregate demand curve to the left.

The Role of Interest Rates

Our discussion so far in this chapter has treated the money supply as the central bank's policy instrument. When the central bank buys government bonds in open market operations, it increases the money supply and expands aggregate demand. When the central bank sells government bonds in open market operations, it decreases the money supply and contracts aggregate demand.

Often, however, discussions of central bank policy treat the interest rate, rather than the money supply, as the central bank's policy instrument. However, as we have seen, in practice the key tool of monetary policy is the interest rate. The central bank's decision to set interest rates rather than target a certain level (or rate of growth) of the money supply does not fundamentally alter our analysis of monetary policy. The theory of liquidity preference illustrates an important principle: monetary policy can be described either in terms of the money supply or in terms of the interest rate. When the central bank sets a target for the refinancing rate of, say, x per cent, the central bank's bond traders are told: 'Conduct whatever open market operations are necessary to ensure that the equilibrium interest rate equals x per cent.' In other words, when the central bank sets a target for the interest rate, it commits itself to adjusting the money supply to make the equilibrium in the money market hit that target.

Thus changes in monetary policy can be viewed either in terms of a changing target for the interest rate or in terms of a change in the money supply.

SELF TEST Use the theory of liquidity preference to explain how a decrease in the money supply affects the equilibrium interest rate. How does this change in monetary policy affect the demand curve?

HOW FISCAL POLICY INFLUENCES AGGREGATE DEMAND

In the short run, the primary effect of fiscal policy is on the aggregate demand for goods and services.

Changes in Government Purchases

We have seen that changes in autonomous spending can have an effect on the level of spending in the economy which is greater than the initial injection. The multiplier effect means that aggregate demand will shift by a larger amount than the increase in government spending. However, the **crowding out effect** suggests that the shift in aggregate demand could be *smaller* than the initial injection.

> **crowding out effect** the offset in aggregate demand that results when expansionary fiscal policy raises the interest rate and thereby reduces investment spending

The Crowding Out Effect To see why crowding out occurs, let us consider what happens in the money market when the government invests in a nuclear power station from Nucelec. As we have discussed, this increase in demand raises the incomes of the workers and owners of this firm (and, because of the multiplier effect, of other firms as well). As incomes rise, households plan to buy more goods and services and, as a result, choose to hold more of their wealth in liquid form. That is, the increase in income caused by the fiscal expansion raises the demand for money.

The effect of the increase in money demand is shown in panel (a) of Figure 22.8.

Because the central bank has not changed the money supply, the vertical supply curve remains the same. When the higher level of income shifts the money demand curve to the right from MD_1 to MD_2, the interest rate must rise from r_1 to r_2 to keep supply and demand in balance.

The increase in the interest rate, in turn, reduces the quantity of goods and services demanded. In particular, because borrowing is more expensive, the demand for residential and business investment goods declines. That is, as the increase in government purchases increases the demand for goods and services, it may also crowd out investment. This crowding out effect partially offsets the impact of government purchases on aggregate demand, as illustrated in panel (b) of Figure 22.8. The initial impact of the increase in government purchases is to shift the aggregate demand curve from AD_1 to AD_2, but once crowding out takes place, the aggregate demand curve drops back to AD_3.

To sum up: when the government increases its purchases by €20 billion, the aggregate demand for goods and services could rise by more or less than €20 billion, depending on whether the multiplier effect or the crowding out effect is larger.

Changes in Taxes

The other important instrument of fiscal policy, besides the level of government purchases, is the level of taxation. When the government cuts personal income taxes, for instance, it increases households' take-home pay. Households will save some of this additional income, but they will also spend some of it on consumer goods. Because it increases consumer spending, the tax cut shifts the aggregate demand curve to the right. Similarly, a tax increase depresses consumer spending and shifts the aggregate demand curve to the left.

FIGURE 22.8

The Crowding Out Effect

Panel (a) shows the money market. When the government increases its purchases of goods and services, the resulting increase in income raises the demand for money from MD_1 to MD_2, and this causes the equilibrium interest rate to rise from r_1 to r_2. Panel (b) shows the effects on AD. The initial impact of the increase in government purchases shifts the aggregate demand curve from AD_1 to AD_2. Yet because the interest rate is the cost of borrowing, the increase in the interest rate tends to reduce the quantity of goods and services demanded, particularly for investment goods. This crowding out of investment partially offsets the impact of the fiscal expansion on AD. In the end, the aggregate demand curve shifts only to AD_3.

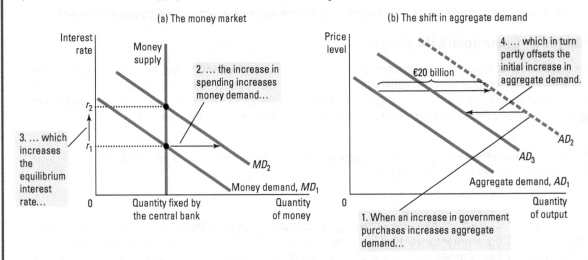

The size of the shift in aggregate demand resulting from a tax change is also affected by the multiplier and crowding out effects. When the government cuts taxes and stimulates consumer spending, earnings and profits rise, which further stimulates consumer spending. This is the multiplier effect. At the same time, higher income leads to higher money demand, which tends to raise interest rates. Higher interest rates make borrowing more costly, which reduces investment spending. This is the crowding out effect. Depending on the size of the multiplier and crowding out effects, the shift in aggregate demand could be larger or smaller than the tax change that causes it.

In addition to the multiplier and crowding out effects, there is another important determinant of the size of the shift in aggregate demand that results from a tax change: households' perceptions about whether the tax change is permanent or temporary. For example, suppose that the government announces a tax cut of €1,000 per household. In deciding how much of this €1,000 to spend, households must ask themselves how long this extra income will last. If households expect the tax cut to be permanent, they will view it as adding substantially to their financial resources and increase their spending by a large amount. In this case, the tax cut will have a large impact on aggregate demand. By contrast, if households expect the tax change to be temporary, they will view it as adding only slightly to their financial resources and will increase their spending by only a small amount. In this case, the tax cut will have a small impact on aggregate demand.

SELF TEST Suppose that the government reduces spending on motorway construction by €1 billion. Which way does the aggregate demand curve shift? Explain why the shift might be larger than €1 billion. Explain why the shift might be smaller than €1 billion.

FYI

The Accelerator Principle

The accelerator principle relates the rate of change of aggregate demand to the rate of change in investment. To produce goods, a firm needs equipment. Imagine that a machine is capable of producing 1,000 DVDs per week. Demand for DVDs is currently 800. A rise in demand for DVDs of up to 200 is capable of being met without any further investment in new machinery. However, if the rate of growth of demand continues to rise, it may be necessary to invest in a new machine.

Imagine that in year 1, demand for DVDs rises by 10 per cent to 880. The business can meet this demand through existing equipment. In year 2, demand increases by 20 per cent and is now 1,056. The existing capacity of the machine means that this demand cannot be met, but the shortage is only 56 units so the firm decides that it might increase price rather than invest in a new machine. In year 3, demand rises by a further 25 per cent. Demand is now 1,320, but the machine is only capable of producing a maximum of 1,000 DVDs. The firm decides to invest in a new machine. The manufacturers of the new machine will see a rise in their order books as a result of the increase in demand. An increase in demand of 25 per cent has led to an accelerated rise in investment of 100 per cent. Investment is a component of aggregate demand, and so economists are interested in the way investment adjusts to changes in demand in the economy. As this brief example shows, the relationship between an increase in demand and an increase in investment is not a simple one.

SUMMARY

- The three main policies used to affect economic activity are monetary policy, fiscal policy and supply side policy.
- Keynes developed the general theory as a response to the mass unemployment which existed in the 1930s. He advocated governments intervene to boost demand through influencing aggregate demand.
- The Keynesian cross diagram shows how the economy can be in equilibrium when $E = Y$.
- This equilibrium may not be sufficient to deliver full employment output, and so the government can attempt to boost demand to help achieve full employment.
- Supply side policies aim to improve the efficiency of the economy and increase the capacity of the economy by shifting the aggregate supply curve to the right.
- Key elements of a supply side policy include tax and welfare reforms, improving the flexibility of labour markets including trade union reform, education and training, and investing in improved infrastructure.
- In developing a theory of short run economic fluctuations, Keynes proposed the theory of liquidity preference to explain the determinants of the interest rate. According to this theory, the interest rate adjusts to balance the supply and demand for money.
- An increase in the price level raises money demand and increases the interest rate that brings the money market into equilibrium. Because the interest rate represents the cost of borrowing, a higher interest rate reduces investment and the quantity of goods and services demanded. The downward sloping aggregate demand curve expresses this negative relationship between the price level and the quantity demanded.
- Policy makers can influence aggregate demand with monetary policy. An increase in the money supply reduces the equilibrium interest rate for any given price level. Because a lower interest rate stimulates investment spending, the aggregate demand curve shifts to the right. Conversely, a decrease in the money supply raises the equilibrium interest rate for any given price level and shifts the aggregate demand curve to the left.
- Policy makers can also influence aggregate demand with fiscal policy. An increase in government purchases or a cut in taxes shifts the aggregate demand curve to the right. A decrease in government purchases or an increase in taxes shifts the aggregate demand curve to the left.
- When the government alters spending or taxes, the resulting shift in aggregate demand can be larger or smaller than the fiscal change. The multiplier effect tends to amplify the effects of fiscal policy on aggregate demand. The crowding out effect tends to dampen the effects of fiscal policy on aggregate demand.

IN THE NEWS

Economic Policy in China

In December 2017, a meeting of the Central Economic Work Conference (CEWC) in China set the agenda for fiscal and monetary policy in the country for 2018. The CEWC is an annual meeting of around 200 of the members of the Central Committee of the Communist Party, around 170 alternate members and other invited guests such as the governor of the People's Bank of China, the country's central bank.

At the 2017 meeting, the CEWC maintained plans to use fiscal policy to invest in key areas of the economy while seeking to maintain a prudent monetary policy. A post-meeting CEWC statement noted: 'The proactive orientation of fiscal policy will be maintained, while the structure of fiscal spending should be optimized.' Commentators noted that fiscal policy was likely to be targeted at poverty reduction, partly through income redistribution, the environment, innovation and entrepreneurship. It was also expected that investment in infrastructure would not be as aggressive as it was following the 2007–2009 Financial Crisis.

On monetary policy, the desire to be prudent was designed to help improve the stability of the financial sector, prevent future crashes and ensure that the financial system was capable of withstanding potential shocks. Since the 2007–2009 Financial Crisis, monetary policy has been described as being 'looser' but is now expected to 'tighten'.

In summarizing the outcomes of the CEWC, Zhao Xijun, Associate Dean of the School of Finance from Renmin University of China, said: 'Proactive fiscal policy and prudent monetary policy, both major macroeconomic policies, will pave a solid foundation for China's economic restructuring and deepening supply side reform next year.'

Economic policy in China is heavily influenced by the leadership of the country.

Questions

1   What do you think is meant by a 'proactive fiscal policy'?
2   How do you think the 'optimization of fiscal spending' could be measured in terms of the stated aims of Chinese fiscal policy at the CEWC?
3   Why might spending on infrastructure be scaled back in favour of poverty reduction schemes? Would not spending on infrastructure provide multiplier effects which would help the poor?
4   Since the 2007–2009 Financial Crisis, the Chinese government 'loosened' monetary policy. What do think this means and what effects might it have had on the Chinese economy?
5   Referring to the comment by Zhao Xijun, what do you think the plans for fiscal and monetary policy in providing a 'solid foundation for … deepening supply side reform' means?

Reference: www.xinhuanet.com/english/2017–12/25/c_136851284.htm (Reference correct at time of writing. Web page has since been removed.)

QUESTIONS FOR REVIEW

1 Define monetary policy, fiscal policy and supply side policy.

2 Explain how the interest rate transmission mechanism works to bring about changes in the components of aggregate demand and helps to boost growth.

3 Distinguish between planned expenditure and actual expenditure.

4 Draw a Keynesian cross diagram to show the effects of a rise in autonomous expenditure on an economy operating below full employment output.

5 Explain how the marginal propensity to withdraw affects the outcome of a rise in autonomous expenditure.

6 How can supply side policies help an economy to produce greater output, reduce unemployment but reduce the price level at the same time?

7 Why are flexible labour markets such an important element in supply side policies?

8 What is the theory of liquidity preference? How does it help explain the downward slope of the aggregate demand curve?

9 Use the theory of liquidity preference to explain how a decrease in the money supply affects the aggregate demand curve.

10 A government spends €50 million to buy a new fleet of police cars. Explain why aggregate demand might increase by more than €50 million. Explain why aggregate demand might increase by less than €50 million.

PROBLEMS AND APPLICATIONS

1 Prior to national elections, the existing government says that if elected again it wants to focus on delivering the following:

   a. A reduction in child poverty.
   b. Improvements in productivity in manufacturing industries.
   c. Increases in investment by businesses.
   d. A reduction in the rate of inflation.

What policy options would you suggest this government uses to deliver these objectives?

2 Explain, using an appropriate diagram, how a deflationary gap can occur and how this gap can be eliminated.

3 Suppose economists observe that an increase in government spending of €10 billion raises the total demand for goods and services by €30 billion.

   a. If these economists ignore the possibility of crowding out, what would they estimate the marginal propensity to consume (MPC) to be?
   b. Now suppose the economists allow for crowding out. Would their new estimate of the MPC be larger or smaller than their initial one? Explain your answer.

4 Suppose the government reduces taxes by €2 billion, that there is no crowding out, and that the MPC is 0.75:

   a. What is the initial effect of the tax reduction on aggregate demand?
   b. What additional effects follow this initial effect? What is the total effect of the tax cut on aggregate demand?
   c. How does the total effect of this €2 billion tax cut compare to the total effect of a €2 billion increase in government purchases? Why?

5 Explain how each of the following developments would affect the supply of money, the demand for money and the interest rate. Illustrate your answers with diagrams.

   a. The central bank's bond traders buy bonds in open market operations.
   b. An increase in credit card availability reduces the cash people hold.
   c. The central bank reduces banks' reserve requirements.
   d. Households decide to hold more money to use for holiday shopping.
   e. A wave of optimism boosts business investment and expands aggregate demand.
   f. An increase in oil prices shifts the short run aggregate supply curve to the left.

6 Suppose banks install automatic teller machines on every street corner and, by making cash readily available, reduce the amount of money people want to hold.

    a. Assume the central bank does not change the money supply. According to the theory of liquidity preference, what happens to the interest rate? What happens to aggregate demand?

    b. If the central bank wants to stabilize aggregate demand, how should it respond?

7 Consider two policies: a tax cut that will last for only one year, and a tax cut that is expected to be permanent. Which policy will stimulate greater spending by consumers? Which policy will have the greater impact on aggregate demand? Explain.

8 The economy is in a recession with high unemployment and low output.

    a. Use a graph of aggregate demand and aggregate supply to illustrate the current situation. Be sure to include the aggregate demand curve, the short run aggregate supply curve and the long run aggregate supply curve.

    b. Identify an open market operation that would restore the economy to its natural rate.

    c. Use a graph of the money market to illustrate the effect of this open market operation. Show the resulting change in the interest rate.

    d. Use a graph similar to the one in part a. to show the effect of the open market operation on output and the price level. Explain in words why the policy has the effect that you have shown in the graph.

9 In which of the following circumstances is expansionary fiscal policy more likely to lead to a short run increase in investment? Explain.

    a. When the effect on investment is large, or when it is small?

    b. When the interest sensitivity of investment is large, or when it is small?

10 Assume the economy is in a recession. Explain how each of the following policies would affect consumption and investment. In each case, indicate any direct effects, any effects resulting from changes in total output, any effects resulting from changes in the interest rate and the overall effect. If there are conflicting effects making the answer ambiguous, say so.

    a. An increase in government spending.

    b. A reduction in taxes.

    c. An expansion of the money supply.

PART 7
GLOBAL BUSINESS AND ECONOMICS

23 BUSINESS AND TRADE

LEARNING OUTCOMES

After reading this chapter you should be able to:

- Explain the principle of absolute and comparative advantage.
- Describe the main advantages and disadvantages of international trade.
- Explain at least three reasons why governments impose trade barriers.
- Outline at least two other theories of international trade.
- Distinguish between real and nominal exchange rates.
- Outline the principles of purchasing power parity as a theory of exchange rate determination.

INTERNATIONAL TRADE

Consider this typical day. You wake up in the morning and make some coffee from beans grown in Kenya, or tea from leaves grown in Sri Lanka. Over breakfast, you listen to a radio programme on a device made in China. You get dressed in clothes manufactured in Thailand. You drive to the university in a car made of parts manufactured in more than a dozen countries around the world. Then you open up your economics textbook published by a company located in Hampshire in the UK, printed on paper made from trees grown in Finland and written by authors from the United States and the UK.

Every day you rely on many people from around the world, most of whom you do not know, to provide you with the goods and services that you enjoy. Such interdependence is possible because people trade with one another. One of the early insights from economists like Adam Smith and David Ricardo was that trade can be beneficial and this insight is something that many economists still hold dear. In this chapter, we will look at the benefits to trade and also at arguments which cast doubt on the extent to which trade benefits everyone.

A Parable for the Modern Economy

We are going to use a simple example to illustrate how trade can lead to benefits. Imagine that there are two goods in the world, beef and potatoes, and two people in the world (our analogy for two different countries), a cattle farmer named Silvia and a market gardener named Johan, each of whom would like to eat both beef and potatoes.

Assume that the farmer and the gardener are each capable of producing both beef and potatoes. Further assume that the market gardener can rear cattle and produce meat, but that he is not very good at it and that the cattle farmer is able to grow potatoes, but her land is not very well suited to this crop. We can represent the situation facing Johan and Silvia by using a production possibility frontier (PPF). You might also see this referred to as a production possibilities boundary or production possibilities curve, they are the same thing. The **production possibilities frontier** is a graph that shows the various combinations of output, capital goods and consumer goods, that the economy can produce given the available factors of production and technology that firms can use to turn these factors into output.

> **production possibilities frontier** a graph that shows the combinations of output that the economy can possibly produce given the available factors of production and technology

The PPF for Johan and Silvia would look like those in Figure 23.1. Panel (a) shows Silvia's PPF and panel (b) shows Johan's. If Silvia devoted all her time and resources to producing meat she could produce Q_M, the vertical intercept. If she devotes all her resources to producing potatoes, she can produce the quantity Q_p, the horizontal intercept. The curve connecting these two extremes is the PPF. Similarly, if Johan devotes all his resources to producing meat, he can produce Q_M and if he devotes all his resources to producing potatoes, he can produce Q_p. The line connecting these two extremes is Johan's PPF.

FIGURE 23.1

Differing Opportunity Cost Ratios
Panels (a) and (b) show Silvia and Johan's PPFs respectively. Silvia is more skilled in producing meat while Johan is more skilled in producing potatoes, although both could divert resources to produce the other good. The opportunity cost ratios for each are different – the opportunity cost for Silvia of diverting resources from meat to potatoes is high while for Johan the opportunity cost of diverting resources from potatoes to meat is high.

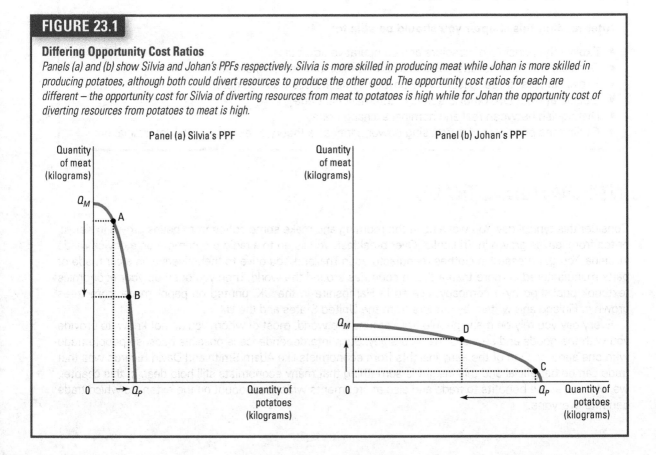

If Silvia makes the decision to divert resources to the production of meat the sacrifice in terms of lost meat output is relatively high compared to the gains in output of potatoes. This is shown by the movement from point A to point B. Because Silvia is more efficient in the production of meat than she is in producing potatoes, the shape of the PPF reflects the opportunity cost of any decision to divert more of her resources away from producing meat to producing potatoes. The opportunity cost is expressed as a ratio of the sacrifice in one good in terms of the gain in the other:

$$\text{Opportunity cost of good } y = \frac{\text{Sacrifice of good } x}{\text{Gain in good } y}$$

The opportunity cost in terms of good x would be:

$$\text{Opportunity cost of good } x = \frac{\text{Sacrifice of good } y}{\text{Gain in good } x}$$

Johan's situation is the reverse of Silvia's and is shown in panel (b). If Johan diverts resources away from potato production towards meat production he sacrifices a relatively large amount of output of potatoes to gain a relatively small amount of meat as shown by the movement from C to D. The opportunity cost of diverting resources to meat for Johan is high, therefore.

Economically, it would be more efficient for Johan and Silvia to co-operate with each other, specialize in what they both do best and benefit from trading with each other at some mutually agreeable rate of exchange. For example, they might agree to a rate of exchange of 1 kg of meat for every 5 kg of potatoes.

The gains from trade are less obvious, however, when one person is better at producing *every* good. For example, suppose that Silvia is better at rearing cattle *and* better at growing potatoes than Johan. In this case, should the farmer or gardener choose to remain self-sufficient, or is there still reason for them to trade with each other?

Production Possibilities

Suppose that Johan and Silvia each work 8 hours a day 6 days a week (a working week of 48 hours) and take Sunday off. They can spend their time growing potatoes, rearing cattle, or a combination of the two. Table 23.1 shows the amount of time each person takes to produce 1 kg of each good. The gardener can produce 1 kg of meat in 6 hours and 1 kg of potatoes in 1½ hours. The farmer, who is more productive in both activities, can produce 1 kg of meat in 2 hours and 1 kg of potatoes in 1 hour. The last columns in Table 23.1 show the amounts of meat or potatoes the gardener and farmer can produce in a 48-hour working week, producing only that good.

TABLE 23.1	The Production Opportunities of Johan the Gardener and Silvia the Farmer			
	Time needed to make 1 kg of		Amount of meat or potatoes produced in 48 hours	
	Meat	**Potatoes**	**Meat**	**Potatoes**
Johan	6 hrs/kg	1.5 hrs/kg	8 kg	32 kg
Silvia	2 hrs/kg	1 hr/kg	24 kg	48 kg

Panel (a) of Figure 23.2 illustrates the amounts of meat and potatoes that Johan can produce. If he devotes all 48 hours of his time to potatoes, he produces 32 kg of potatoes (measured on the horizontal axis) and no meat. If he devotes all his time to meat, he produces 8 kg of meat (measured on the vertical axis) and no potatoes. If Johan divides his time equally between the two activities, spending 24 hours a week on each, he produces 16 kg of potatoes and 4 kg of meat. The figure shows these three possible outcomes and all others in between.

FIGURE 23.2

The Production Possibilities Frontier

Panel (a) shows the combinations of meat and potatoes that Johan can produce. Panel (b) shows the combinations of meat and potatoes that Silvia can produce. Both production possibilities frontiers are derived from Table 23.1 and the assumption that the gardener and farmer each work 8 hours a day.

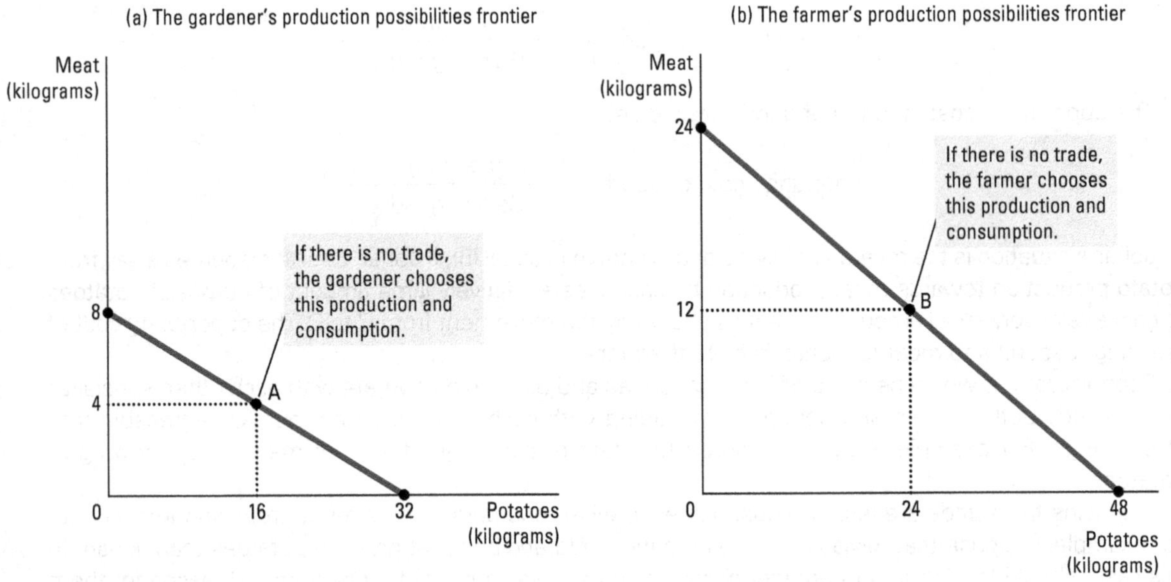

(a) The gardener's production possibilities frontier

(b) The farmer's production possibilities frontier

This graph is Johan's PPF. Note that in this case, the PPF is a straight line, indicating that the slope is constant and thus the opportunity cost to Johan of switching between potatoes and meat is constant. Johan faces a trade-off between producing meat and producing potatoes. If Johan devotes an extra hour to producing meat, he sacrifices potato production. Assume Johan starts at point A producing 4 kg of meat and 16 kg of potatoes. If he then devoted all resources to producing potatoes, he would produce 32 kg of potatoes and sacrifice 4 kg of meat. The opportunity cost of one additional kilo of potatoes is 0.25 kg of meat. Every additional 1 kg of potatoes produced would involve a trade-off of ¼ kg of meat. Conversely, if Johan chose to increase meat production by 1 kg he would have to sacrifice 4 kg of potatoes.

Panel (b) of Figure 23.2 shows the PPF for Silvia. If she devotes all 48 hours of her working week to potatoes, she produces 48 kg of potatoes and no meat. If she devotes all her time to meat production, she produces 24 kg of meat and no potatoes. If Silvia divides her time equally, spending 24 hours a week on each activity, she produces 24 kg of potatoes and 12 kg of meat. If Silvia moved from devoting half her time to producing each product to producing all potatoes, the opportunity cost of the additional 24 kg of potatoes is 12 kg of meat. Silvia would sacrifice ½ kg of meat for every 1 kg of additional potatoes. The slope of this PPF is, therefore, 0.5. If Silvia shifted production to meat from potatoes, the opportunity cost of an additional 1 kg of meat would be 2 kg of potatoes sacrificed.

If the gardener and farmer choose to be self-sufficient, rather than trade with each other, then each consumes exactly what they produce. In this case, the PPF is also the consumption possibilities frontier. That is, without trade, Figure 23.2 shows the possible combinations of meat and potatoes that Johan and Silvia can each consume.

Although these production possibilities frontiers are useful in showing the trade-offs that the gardener and farmer face, they do not tell us what Johan and Silvia will actually choose to do. To determine their choices, we need to know the tastes of the gardener and the farmer. Assume they choose the combinations identified by points A and B in Figure 23.2. Johan produces and consumes 16 kg of potatoes and 4 kg of meat, while Silvia produces and consumes 24 kg of potatoes and 12 kg of meat.

Specialization and Trade

After several years of feeding her family on combination B, Silvia gets an idea and she goes to talk to Johan:

SILVIA: Johan, I have a proposal to put to you. I know how to improve life for both of us. I think you should stop producing meat altogether and devote all your time to growing potatoes. According to my calculations, if you devote all of your working week to growing potatoes, you'll produce 32 kg of potatoes. If you give me 15 of those 32 kg, I'll give you 5 kg of meat in return. You will have 17 kg of potatoes left to enjoy and 5 kg of meat every week, instead of the 16 kg of potatoes and 4 kg of meat you now make do with. If you go along with my plan, you'll have more of *both* foods. (To illustrate her point, Silvia shows Johan panel (a) of Figure 23.3.)

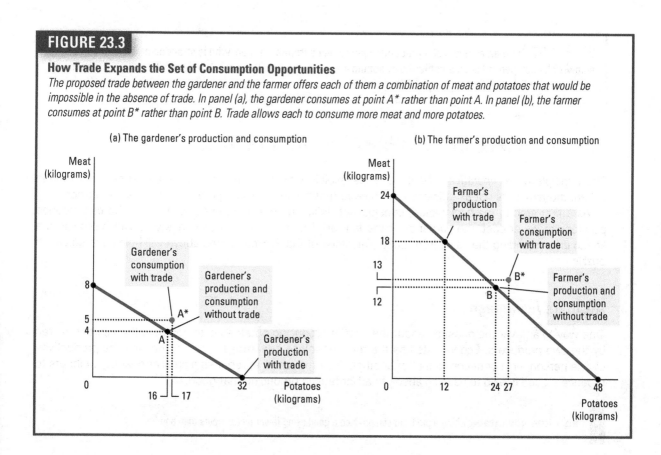

FIGURE 23.3

How Trade Expands the Set of Consumption Opportunities
The proposed trade between the gardener and the farmer offers each of them a combination of meat and potatoes that would be impossible in the absence of trade. In panel (a), the gardener consumes at point A* rather than point A. In panel (b), the farmer consumes at point B* rather than point B. Trade allows each to consume more meat and more potatoes.

JOHAN: That seems like a good deal for me, Silvia, but how is it that we can both benefit?
SILVIA: Suppose I spend 12 hours a week growing potatoes and 36 hours rearing cattle. Then I can produce 12 kg of potatoes and 18 kg of meat. You will give me 15 kg of your potatoes in exchange for the 5 kg of my meat. This means I end up with 27 kg of potatoes and 13 kg of meat. I will also be able to consume more of both foods than I do now. (She points out panel (b) of Figure 23.3.) To help, I've summarized my proposal for you in a simple table. (The farmer hands the gardener a copy of Table 23.2.)
JOHAN: *(after pausing to study the table)* These calculations seem correct. So we can both be better off?
SILVIA: Yes, because trade allows each of us to specialize in doing what we do best. You will spend more time growing potatoes and less time rearing cattle. I will spend more time rearing cattle and less time growing potatoes. As a result of specialization and trade, each of us can consume more meat and more potatoes without working any more hours.

TABLE 23.2   **The Gains from Trade: A Summary**

	Johan		Silvia	
	Meat	**Potatoes**	**Meat**	**Potatoes**
Without trade:				
Production and consumption	4 kg	16 kg	12 kg	24 kg
With trade:				
Production	0 kg	32 kg	18 kg	12 kg
Trade	Gets 5 kg	Gives 15 kg	Gives 5 kg	Gets 15 kg
Consumption	5 kg	17 kg	13 kg	27 kg
Gains from trade:				
Increase in consumption	+1 kg	+1 kg	+1 kg	+3 kg

SELF TEST Draw an example of a production possibilities frontier for Jon, who is stranded on an island after a shipwreck and spends his time gathering coconuts and catching fish. Does this frontier limit Jon's consumption of coconuts and fish if he lives by himself? Does he face the same limits if he can trade with natives on the island?

THE PRINCIPLE OF COMPARATIVE ADVANTAGE

The principle of *comparative advantage* helps explain why benefits from trade can arise even though Johan, the farmer, is not as efficient in both rearing cattle and growing potatoes as Silvia the farmer.

As a first step in the explanation, consider the following question: in our example, who can produce potatoes at lower cost: the gardener or the farmer? There are two possible answers which provide the key to understanding the gains from trade. The slope of the PPF discussed above will help us to solve the puzzle.

Absolute Advantage

One way to answer the question about the cost of producing potatoes is to compare the inputs required by the two producers. Economists use the term **absolute advantage** when comparing the productivity of one person, firm or nation to that of another. The producer that requires a smaller quantity of inputs to produce a good is said to have an absolute advantage in producing that good.

 absolute advantage where a producer can produce a good using fewer factor inputs than another

In our example, the farmer has an absolute advantage both in producing meat and in producing potatoes, because she requires less time than the gardener to produce a unit of either good. The farmer needs to input only 2 hours in order to produce a kilogram of meat, whereas the gardener needs 6 hours. Similarly, Silvia needs only 1 hour to produce a kilogram of potatoes, whereas Johan needs 1½ hours. Based on this information, we can conclude that the farmer has the lower cost of producing potatoes, if we measure cost in terms of the quantity of inputs.

Opportunity Cost and Comparative Advantage

There is another way to look at the cost of producing potatoes. Rather than comparing inputs required, we can compare the opportunity costs. Let's first consider Silvia's opportunity cost in relation to the number of hours she needs to work. According to Table 23.1, producing 1 kg of potatoes takes her 1 hour of work. When Silvia spends that 1 hour producing potatoes, she spends 1 hour less producing meat. Because

Silvia needs 2 hours to produce 1 kg of meat, 1 hour of work would yield ½ kg of meat. Hence, the farmer's opportunity cost of producing 1 kg of potatoes is ½ kg of meat.

Now consider Johan's opportunity cost. Producing 1 kg of potatoes takes him 1½ hours. Because he needs 6 hours to produce 1 kg of meat, 1½ hours of work would yield ¼ kg of meat. Hence, the gardener's opportunity cost of 1 kg of potatoes is ¼ kg of meat.

Table 23.3 shows the opportunity costs of meat and potatoes for the two producers. Remember that the opportunity cost of meat is the inverse of the opportunity cost of potatoes. Because 1 kg of potatoes costs the farmer ½ kg of meat, 1 kg of meat costs the farmer 2 kg of potatoes. Similarly, because 1 kg of potatoes costs the gardener ¼ kg of meat, 1 kg of meat costs the gardener 4 kg of potatoes.

TABLE 23.3   **The Opportunity Cost of Meat and Potatoes**

	Opportunity cost of:	
	1 kg of meat	**1 kg of potatoes**
Gardener	4 kg potatoes	0.25 kg meat
Farmer	2 kg potatoes	0.5 kg meat

Comparative advantage describes the opportunity cost of two producers. The producer who gives up less of other goods to produce good X has the smaller opportunity cost of producing good X and is said to have a comparative advantage in producing it. In our example, the gardener has a lower opportunity cost of producing potatoes than does the farmer: a kilogram of potatoes costs the gardener only ¼ kg of meat, while it costs the farmer ½ kg of meat. Conversely, Silvia has a lower opportunity cost of producing meat than does Johan: a kilogram of meat costs Silvia 2 kg of potatoes, while it costs Johan 4 kg of potatoes. Thus the gardener has a comparative advantage in growing potatoes, and the farmer has a comparative advantage in producing meat.

> **comparative advantage** the comparison among producers of a good according to their opportunity cost. A producer is said to have a comparative advantage in the production of a good if the opportunity cost is lower than that of another producer

Although it is possible for one person to have an absolute advantage in both goods (as Silvia does in our example), it is impossible for one person to have a comparative advantage in both goods. Because the opportunity cost of one good is the inverse of the opportunity cost of the other, if a person's opportunity cost of one good is relatively high, their opportunity cost of the other good must be relatively low. Comparative advantage reflects the relative opportunity cost. Unless two people have exactly the same opportunity cost, one person will have a comparative advantage in one good, and the other will have a comparative advantage in the other good.

Comparative Advantage and Trade

In theory, differences in opportunity cost and comparative advantage create the gains from trade. The theory predicts that when each person specializes in producing the good for which they have a comparative advantage, total production in the economy rises, and this increase in the size of the economic cake can be used to make everyone better off.

Consider the proposed deal from the viewpoint of Johan. He gets 5 kg of meat in exchange for 15 kg of potatoes. In other words, Johan buys each kilogram of meat for a price of 3 kg of potatoes. This price of meat is lower than his opportunity cost for 1 kg of meat, which is 4 kg of potatoes. Thus the gardener benefits from the deal because he gets to buy meat at a good price.

Now consider the deal from Silvia's viewpoint. The farmer buys 15 kg of potatoes for a price of 5 kg of meat. That is, the price of potatoes is ⅓ kg of meat. This price of potatoes is lower than her opportunity cost of 1 kg of potatoes, which is ½ kg of meat. The farmer benefits because she can buy potatoes at a good price.

These benefits arise because each person concentrates on the activity for which they have the lower opportunity cost: the gardener spends more time growing potatoes, and the farmer spends more time producing meat. As a result, the total production of potatoes and the total production of meat both rise. In our example, potato production rises from 40 to 44 kg, and meat production rises from 16 to 18 kg. The gardener and farmer share the benefits of this increased production.

SELF TEST Jon can gather ten coconuts or catch one fish per hour. His friend, Marie, can gather 30 coconuts or catch two fish per hour. What is Jon's opportunity cost of catching one fish? What is Marie's? Who has an absolute advantage in catching fish? Who has a comparative advantage in catching fish?

Should Countries in Europe Trade with other Countries?

Our model of Johan and Silvia can be extended to represent whole countries. Many of the goods that Europeans enjoy are produced abroad, and many of the goods produced across Europe are sold abroad. Goods produced abroad and purchased for use in the domestic economy are called imports. An import leads to a flow of money from the country in payment. Goods produced domestically and sold abroad are called exports.

To see how countries can benefit from trade, suppose there are two countries (Germany and the Netherlands) and two goods (machine tools and cut flowers). Imagine that the two countries produce cut flowers equally well: a German worker and a Dutch worker can each produce 1 tonne per month. By contrast, because Germany has more land suitable for manufacturing, it is better at producing machine tools: a German worker can produce 2 tonnes of machine tools per month, whereas a Dutch worker can produce only 1 tonne of machine tools per month.

The principle of comparative advantage implies that each good should be produced by the country that has the smaller opportunity cost of producing that good. Because the opportunity cost of an additional 1 tonne of cut flowers is 2 tonnes of machine tools in Germany but only 1 tonne of machine tools in the Netherlands, the Dutch have a comparative advantage in producing cut flowers. The Netherlands should produce more cut flowers than it wants for its own use and export some of them to Germany. Similarly, because the opportunity cost of a tonne of cut flowers is 1 tonne of machine tools in the Netherlands but only ½ a tonne of machine tools in Germany, the Germans have a comparative advantage in producing machine tools. Germany should produce more machine tools than it wants to consume and export some to the Netherlands. Through specialization and trade, both countries can have more machine tools and more cut flowers.

In reality, the issues involved in trade among nations are more complex than this simple example suggests. Most important among these issues is that each country has many citizens with different interests. International trade can make some individuals worse off, even as it makes the country as a whole better off. When Germany exports machine tools and imports cut flowers, the impact on a German worker is not the same as the impact on a German cut flower worker.

SELF TEST Suppose that the world's fastest typist happens to be trained in brain surgery. Should they do their own typing or hire a personal assistant? Explain.

THE DETERMINANTS OF TRADE

Having seen that there are benefits to countries of trading, in this next section we look at the gains and losses of international trade. Consider the market for olive oil. The olive oil market is well suited to examining the gains and losses from international trade: it is made in many countries around the world, and there is much world trade in it. Moreover, the olive oil market is one in which policymakers often consider (and sometimes implement) trade restrictions to protect domestic producers from foreign competitors. We examine here the olive oil market in the imaginary country of Isoland.

The Equilibrium Without Trade

Assume that the Isolandian olive oil market is isolated from the rest of the world. By government decree, no one in Isoland is allowed to import or export olive oil, and the penalty for violating the decree is so large that no one dares try.

Because there is no international trade, the market for olive oil in Isoland consists solely of Isolandian buyers and sellers. As Figure 23.4 shows, the domestic price adjusts to balance the quantity supplied by domestic sellers and the quantity demanded by domestic buyers. The figure shows the consumer and producer surplus in the equilibrium without trade. The sum of consumer and producer surplus measures the total benefits that buyers and sellers receive from the olive oil market.

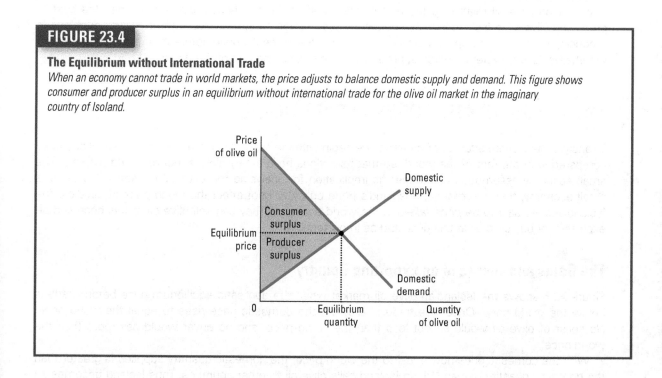

FIGURE 23.4

The Equilibrium without International Trade
When an economy cannot trade in world markets, the price adjusts to balance domestic supply and demand. This figure shows consumer and producer surplus in an equilibrium without international trade for the olive oil market in the imaginary country of Isoland.

From this basic position we can ask three questions:

- If the government allowed Isolandians to import and export olive oil, what would happen to the price and quantity sold in the domestic market?
- Who would gain from free trade in olive oil and who would lose? Would the gains exceed the losses?
- Should a tariff (a tax on olive oil imports) or an import quota (a limit on olive oil imports) be part of the new trade policy?

The World Price and Comparative Advantage

The first question focuses on whether Isoland is likely to become an olive oil importer or exporter. In other words, if free trade were allowed, would Isolandians end up buying or selling olive oil in world markets?

To answer this question, compare the current Isolandian price with those in other countries. We call the price prevailing in world markets the **world price**. If the world price of olive oil is higher than the domestic price, then Isoland would become an exporter once trade is permitted. Isolandian producers would be eager to receive the higher prices available abroad, and would start selling their olive oil to buyers in other countries. Conversely, if the world price of olive oil is lower than the domestic price, then Isoland would become an importer. Because foreign sellers offer a better price, Isolandian consumers would buy olive oil from other countries.

world price the price that prevails in the world market for that good

In essence, comparing the world price and the domestic price before trade indicates whether Isoland has a comparative advantage in producing olive oil. The domestic price reflects the opportunity cost of olive oil: it tells us how much an Isolandian must give up to get one unit of olive oil. If the domestic price is low, the cost of producing olive oil in Isoland is low, suggesting that Isoland has a comparative advantage in producing olive oil relative to the rest of the world. If the domestic price is high, then the cost of producing olive oil in Isoland is high, suggesting that foreign countries have a comparative advantage in producing olive oil. By comparing the world price and the domestic price before trade, we can determine whether Isoland is better or worse at producing olive oil than the rest of the world.

THE WINNERS AND LOSERS FROM TRADE

To analyze the welfare effects of free trade, we begin with the assumption that Isoland is a small economy compared with the rest of the world, so that its actions have a negligible effect on world markets. The small economy assumption has a specific implication for analysing the olive oil market: if Isoland is a small economy, then the change in Isoland's trade policy will not affect the world price of olive oil. The Isolandians are said to be *price takers* in the world economy. They can sell olive oil at this price and be exporters, or buy olive oil at this price and be importers.

The Gains and Losses of an Exporting Country

Figure 23.5 shows the Isolandian olive oil market when the domestic equilibrium price before trade is below the world price. Once free trade is allowed, the domestic price rises to equal the world price. No seller of olive oil would accept less than the world price, and no buyer would pay more than the world price.

With the domestic price now equal to the world price, the domestic quantity supplied is greater than the domestic quantity demanded, so Isoland sells olive oil to other countries. Thus Isoland becomes an olive oil exporter. Although domestic quantity supplied and domestic quantity demanded differ, the olive oil market is still in equilibrium, because there is now another participant in the market: the rest of the world. We can view the horizontal line at the world price as representing the demand for olive oil from the rest of the world. This demand curve is perfectly price elastic because Isoland, as a small economy, can sell as much olive oil as it wants at the world price.

Now consider the gains and losses from opening up trade. Clearly, not everyone benefits. Trade forces the domestic price to rise to the world price. Domestic producers of olive oil are better off, because they can now sell at a higher price, but domestic consumers are worse off because they must buy olive oil at a higher price.

To measure these gains and losses, we look at the changes in consumer and producer surplus, which are shown in the graph and table in Figure 23.6. Before trade is allowed, the price of olive oil adjusts to balance domestic supply and domestic demand. Consumer surplus, the area between the demand curve and the before trade price, is area A + B. Producer surplus, the area between the supply curve and the before trade price, is area C. Total surplus before trade, the sum of consumer and producer surplus, is area A + B + C.

FIGURE 23.5

International Trade in an Exporting Country
Once trade is allowed, the domestic price rises to equal the world price. The supply curve shows the quantity of olive oil produced domestically, and the demand curve shows the quantity consumed domestically. Exports from Isoland equal the difference between the domestic quantity supplied and the domestic quantity demanded at the world price.

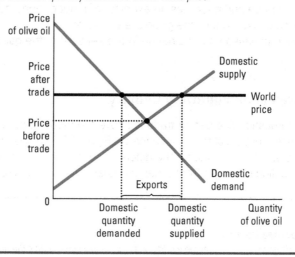

FIGURE 23.6

How Free Trade Affects Welfare in an Exporting Country
When the domestic price rises to equal the world price, sellers are better off (producer surplus rises from C to B + C + D), and buyers are worse off (consumer surplus falls from A + B to A). Total surplus rises by an amount equal to area D, indicating that trade raises the economic well-being of the country as a whole.

	Before trade	After trade	Change
Consumer surplus	A + B	A	−B
Producer surplus	C	B + C + D	+(B + D)
Total surplus	A + B + C	A + B + C + D	+D

The area D shows the increase in total surplus and represents the gains from trade.

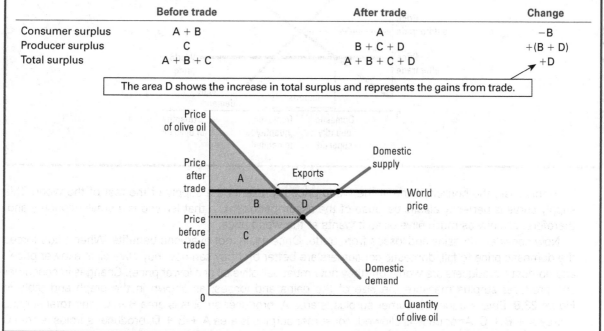

After trade is allowed, the domestic price rises to the world price. Consumer surplus is area A (the area between the demand curve and the world price). Producer surplus is area B + C + D (the area between the supply curve and the world price). Thus total surplus with trade is area A + B + C + D.

These welfare calculations show who wins and who loses from trade in an exporting country given the assumptions of the model. Sellers benefit because producer surplus increases by the area B + D. Buyers are worse off because consumer surplus decreases by the area B. Because the gains of sellers exceed the losses of buyers by the area D, total surplus in Isoland increases.

This analysis of an exporting country yields two conclusions:

- When a country allows trade and becomes an exporter of a good, domestic producers of the good are better off and domestic consumers of the good are worse off.
- Trade raises the economic well-being of a nation in the sense that the gains of the winners exceed the losses of the losers.

The Gains and Losses of an Importing Country

Now suppose that the domestic price before trade is above the world price. Once again, after free trade is allowed, the domestic price must equal the world price. As Figure 23.7 shows, the domestic quantity supplied is less than the domestic quantity demanded. The difference between the domestic quantity demanded and the domestic quantity supplied is bought from other countries, and Isoland becomes an olive oil importer.

FIGURE 23.7

International Trade in an Importing Country
Once trade is allowed, the domestic price falls to equal the world price. The supply curve shows the amount produced domestically, and the demand curve shows the amount consumed domestically. Imports equal the difference between the domestic quantity demanded and the domestic quantity supplied at the world price.

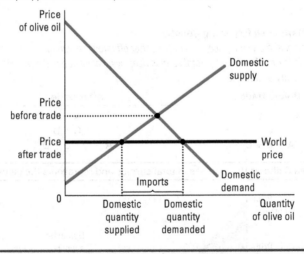

In this case, the horizontal line at the world price represents the supply of the rest of the world. This supply curve is perfectly elastic because of the assumptions made that Isoland is a small economy and, therefore, can buy as much olive oil as it wants at the world price.

Now consider the gains and losses from trade. Once again, not everyone benefits. When trade forces the domestic price to fall, domestic consumers are better off (they can now buy olive oil at a lower price), and domestic producers are worse off (they now must sell olive oil at a lower price). Changes in consumer and producer surplus measure the size of the gains and losses, as shown in the graph and table in Figure 23.8. Before trade, consumer surplus is area A, producer surplus is area B + C, and total surplus is area A + B + C. After trade is allowed, consumer surplus is area A + B + D, producer surplus is area C and total surplus is area A + B + C + D.

These welfare calculations show who wins and who loses from trade in an importing country given the assumptions of the model. Buyers benefit because consumer surplus increases by the area B + D. Sellers are worse off because producer surplus falls by the area B. The gains of buyers exceed the losses of sellers, and total surplus increases by the area D.

FIGURE 23.8

How Free Trade Affects Welfare in an Importing Country
When the domestic price falls to equal the world price, buyers are better off (consumer surplus rises from A to A + B + D), and sellers are worse off (producer surplus falls from B + C to C). Total surplus rises by an amount equal to area D, indicating that trade raises the economic well-being of the country as a whole.

	Before trade	After trade	Change
Consumer surplus	A	A + B + D	+(B + D)
Producer surplus	B + C	C	−B
Total surplus	A + B + C	A + B + C + D	+D

The area D shows the increase in total surplus and represents the gains from trade.

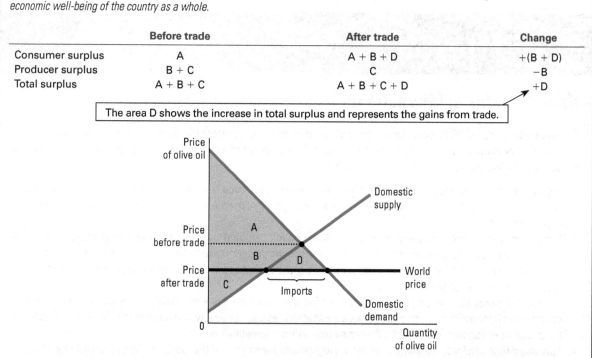

This analysis of an importing country yields two conclusions parallel to those for an exporting country:

- When a country allows trade and becomes an importer of goods, domestic consumers of the good are better off and domestic producers of the good are worse off.
- Trade raises the economic well-being of a nation in the sense that the gains of the winners exceed the losses of the losers.

Having completed our analysis of trade, we can draw a conclusion that trade can make everyone better off. If Isoland opens up its olive oil market to international trade, the change will create winners and losers regardless of whether Isoland ends up exporting or importing olive oil. Notice that in our analysis we have not made a judgement about the winners and losers: whether the gain to the producers is more valuable than the loss to the consumers. In this analysis, the key is the effect on total welfare, which in this case has risen for Isoland. In the real world, policy makers may have to take into consideration the power which resides with different groups. If domestic consumers of olive oil in Isoland had considerable lobbying power compared with olive oil producers, then policy decisions may be affected which distort outcomes and reduce total welfare.

The effect on consumers, for example, might be limited in comparison with the gains to producers, but presenting arguments in this way does not always win political points! This is something that must always be considered because while economic analysis may point to a clear policy decision and outcome, there are many other factors that decision makers must take into account, as exemplified when we look at the arguments for restricting trade.

In our example, the gains of the winners exceed the losses of the losers, so the winners could compensate the losers and still be better off. In this sense, trade *can* make everyone better off. But *will* trade make everyone better off? Probably not. In practice, compensation for the losers from international trade is rare. Without such compensation, opening up to international trade is a policy that expands the size of the economic cake, while perhaps leaving some participants in the economy with a smaller slice.

We can now see why the debate over trade policy is so often contentious. Whenever a policy creates winners and losers, the stage is set for a political battle. Nations sometimes fail to enjoy the gains from trade simply because the losers from free trade have more political influence than the winners. The losers lobby for trade restrictions, such as tariffs and import quotas.

FYI

Other Benefits of International Trade

Our conclusions so far have been based on the standard analysis of international trade. There are several other economic benefits of trade beyond those emphasized in the standard analysis which can be taken into account. Here, in a nutshell, are some of these other benefits:

- *Increased variety of goods.* Goods produced in different countries are not exactly the same. German beer, for instance, is not the same as US beer. Free trade gives consumers in all countries greater variety from which to choose.
- *Lower unit costs through economies of scale.* Some goods can be produced at low unit or average cost only if they are produced in large quantities. A firm in a small country cannot take full advantage of economies of scale if it can sell only in a small domestic market. Free trade gives firms access to larger world markets and allows them to realize economies of scale more fully.
- *Increased competition.* A company shielded from foreign competitors is more likely to have market power, which in turn gives it the ability to raise prices above competitive levels. This is a type of market failure. Opening up trade fosters competition with the benefits that arise from more competitive markets.
- *Enhanced flow of ideas.* The transfer of technological advances around the world is often thought to be linked to international trade in the goods that embody those advances. The best way for a lower income agricultural nation to learn about the computer revolution, for instance, is to buy some computers from abroad, rather than trying to make them domestically.
- *Generating economic growth.* For lower income countries, the increase in output can be a trigger to generating economic growth, which may also bring an improvement in the standard of living for its citizens.

RESTRICTIONS ON TRADE

Despite the benefits that can arise from trade, the fact that there will always be winners and losers means that arguments for restricting trade in some way are regularly promoted. We will look at three main methods of restricting trade: tariffs, quotas and non-tariff barriers, and then some of the arguments for trade.

The Effects of a Tariff

A **tariff** is a tax on imported goods. The tariff matters only if Isoland becomes an olive oil importer. We can compare welfare with and without the tariff.

> **tariff** a tax on goods produced abroad and sold domestically

The graph in Figure 23.9 shows the Isolandian market for olive oil. Under free trade, the domestic price equals the world price. A tariff raises the price of imported olive oil above the world price by the amount of the tariff. Domestic suppliers of olive oil, who compete with suppliers of imported olive oil, can now sell their olive oil for the world price plus the amount of the tariff. Thus the price of olive oil, both imported and domestic, rises by the amount of the tariff and is, therefore, closer to the price that would prevail without trade.

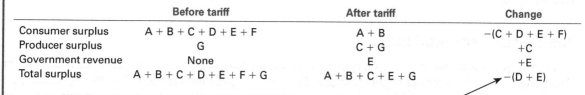

FIGURE 23.9

The Effects of a Tariff

A tariff reduces the quantity of imports and moves a market closer to the equilibrium that would exist without trade. Total surplus falls by an amount equal to area D + F. These two triangles represent the deadweight loss from the tariff.

Before the tariff, the domestic price equals the world price. Consumer surplus, the area between the demand curve and the world price, is area A + B + C + D + E + F. Producer surplus, the area between the supply curve and the world price, is area G. Government revenue equals zero. Total surplus – the sum of consumer surplus, producer surplus and government revenue – is area A + B + C + D + E + F + G.

	Before tariff	After tariff	Change
Consumer surplus	A + B + C + D + E + F	A + B	−(C + D + E + F)
Producer surplus	G	C + G	+C
Government revenue	None	E	+E
Total surplus	A + B + C + D + E + F + G	A + B + C + E + G	−(D + E)

The area D + F shows the fall in total surplus and represents the deadweight loss of the tariff.

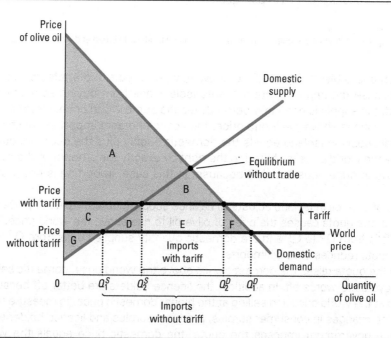

The change in price affects the behaviour of domestic buyers and sellers. Because the tariff raises the price of olive oil, it reduces the domestic quantity demanded from Q_1^D to Q_2^D and raises the domestic quantity supplied from Q_1^S to Q_2^S. Thus, the tariff reduces the quantity of imports and moves the domestic market closer to its equilibrium without trade.

Now consider the gains and losses from the tariff. Because the tariff raises the domestic price, domestic sellers are better off and domestic buyers are worse off. In addition, the government raises revenue. To measure these gains and losses, we look at the changes in consumer surplus, producer surplus and government revenue. These changes are summarized in the table in Figure 23.9.

Once the government imposes a tariff, the domestic price exceeds the world price by the amount of the tariff. Consumer surplus is now area A + B. Producer surplus is area C + G. Government revenue, which is the quantity of after tariff imports times the size of the tariff, is the area E. Thus total surplus with the tariff is area A + B + C + E + G.

To determine the total welfare effects of the tariff, we add the change in consumer surplus (which is negative), the change in producer surplus (positive) and the change in government revenue (positive). We find that total surplus in the market decreases by the area D + F. This fall in total surplus is the *deadweight loss* of the tariff.

A tariff causes a deadweight loss simply because a tariff is a type of tax and can distort incentives and change the allocation of resources. In this case, we can identify two effects. Firstly, the tariff on olive oil raises the price that domestic producers can charge above the world price and, as a result, encourages them to increase production (from Q_1^S to Q_2^S). Secondly, the tariff raises the price that domestic olive oil buyers must pay and, therefore, encourages them to reduce consumption of olive oil (from Q_1^D to Q_2^D). Area D represents the deadweight loss from the overproduction of olive oil, and area F represents the deadweight loss from the underconsumption. The total deadweight loss of the tariff is the sum of these two triangles.

The Effects of an Import Quota

An **import quota** is a limit on the quantity of imports. In particular, imagine that the Isolandian government distributes a limited number of import licences. Each licence gives the licence holder the right to import 1 tonne of olive oil into Isoland from abroad. We can compare welfare under a policy of free trade and welfare with the addition of this import quota.

import quota a limit on the quantity of a good that can be produced abroad and sold domestically

The graph and table in Figure 23.10 show how an import quota affects the Isolandian market for olive oil. Because the import quota prevents Isolandians from buying as much olive oil as they want from abroad, the supply is no longer perfectly elastic at the world price. Instead, as long as the price of olive oil in Isoland is above the world price, the licence holders import as much as they are permitted, and the total supply in Isoland equals the domestic supply plus the quota amount. That is, the supply curve above the world price is shifted to the right by exactly the amount of the quota. The supply curve below the world price does not shift because, in this case, importing is not profitable for the licence holders.

The price of olive oil in Isoland adjusts to balance supply (domestic plus imported) and demand. As the figure shows, the quota causes the price of olive oil to rise above the world price. The domestic quantity demanded falls from Q_1^D to Q_2^D and the domestic quantity supplied rises from Q_1^S to Q_2^S. Not surprisingly, the import quota reduces olive oil imports.

Because the quota raises the domestic price above the world price, domestic sellers are better off, and domestic buyers are worse off. In addition, the licence holders are better off because they make a profit from buying at the world price and selling at the higher domestic price. To measure these gains and losses, we look at the changes in consumer surplus, producer surplus and licence holder surplus.

Before the government imposes the quota, the domestic price equals the world price. Consumer surplus, the area between the demand curve and the world price, is area A + B + C + D + E' + E'' + F. Producer surplus, the area between the supply curve and the world price, is area G. The surplus of licence holders equals zero because there are no licences. Total surplus, the sum of consumer, producer and licence holder surplus, is area A + B + C + D + E' + E'' + F + G.

After the government imposes the import quota and issues the licences, the domestic price exceeds the world price. Domestic consumers get surplus equal to area A + B, and domestic producers get surplus equal to area C + G. The licence holders make a profit on each unit imported equal to the difference between the Isolandian price of olive oil and the world price. Their surplus equals this price differential times the quantity of imports. Thus, it equals the area of the rectangle E' + E''. Total surplus with the quota is the area A + B + C + E' + E'' + G.

To see how total welfare changes with the imposition of the quota, we add the change in consumer surplus (which is negative), the change in producer surplus (positive) and the change in licence holder surplus (positive). We find that total surplus in the market decreases by the area D + F. This area represents the deadweight loss of the import quota.

FIGURE 23.10

The Effects of an Import Quota

An import quota, like a tariff, reduces the quantity of imports and moves a market closer to the equilibrium that would exist without trade. Total surplus falls by an amount equal to area D + F. These two triangles represent the deadweight loss from the quota. In addition, the import quota transfers E′ + E″ to whoever holds the import licences.

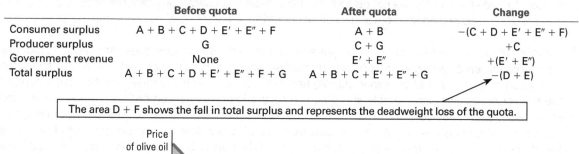

	Before quota	After quota	Change
Consumer surplus	A + B + C + D + E′ + E″ + F	A + B	−(C + D + E′ + E″ + F)
Producer surplus	G	C + G	+C
Government revenue	None	E′ + E″	+(E′ + E″)
Total surplus	A + B + C + D + E′ + E″ + F + G	A + B + C + E′ + E″ + G	−(D + E)

The area D + F shows the fall in total surplus and represents the deadweight loss of the quota.

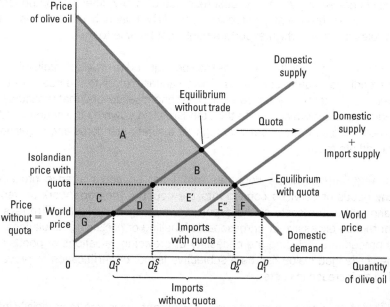

This analysis should seem somewhat familiar. Indeed, if you compare the analysis of import quotas in Figure 23.10 with the analysis of tariffs in Figure 23.9, you will see that they are essentially identical. Both tariffs and import quotas raise the domestic price of the good, reduce the welfare of domestic consumers, increase the welfare of domestic producers and cause deadweight losses. There is only one difference between these two types of trade restriction: a tariff raises revenue for the government (area E in Figure 23.9), whereas an import quota creates surplus for licence holders (area E′ + E″ in Figure 23.10).

Tariffs and import quotas can be made to look even more similar. Suppose that the government tries to capture the licence holder surplus for itself by charging a fee for the licences. A licence to sell 1 tonne of olive oil is worth exactly the difference between the Isolandian price of olive oil and the world price, and the government can set the licence fee as high as this price differential. If the government does this, the licence fee for imports works exactly like a tariff: consumer surplus, producer surplus and government revenue are exactly the same under the two policies.

Although in our analysis so far import quotas and tariffs appear to cause similar deadweight losses, a quota can potentially cause an even larger deadweight loss, depending on the mechanism used to allocate the import licences. Suppose that when Isoland imposes a quota, everyone understands that the licences will go to those who spend the most resources lobbying the Isolandian government. In this case, there is an implicit licence fee, the cost of lobbying. The revenues from this fee, however, rather than being collected by the government, are spent on lobbying expenses. The deadweight losses from this type of quota include not only the losses from overproduction (area D) and underconsumption (area F) but also whatever part of the licence holder surplus (area E' + E") is wasted on the cost of lobbying.

Non-Tariff Barriers (NTBs)

Barriers to trade are sometimes not obvious but nevertheless present significant restrictions on the ability of firms to buy and sell goods from and to other countries. We will briefly outline some of the main ones.

Complex or Discriminatory Rules of Origin and Quality Conditions Countries may impose strict rules on the production of goods in its domestic market relating to technical specifications, health and safety, production standards and so on. Exporters may find it difficult to meet these rules, or if they can it increases the cost of production considerably and thus makes the imports less competitive against domestically produced goods. In addition, firms may be required to give precise details as to where goods come from, something which is not easy given the widespread use of many different component parts from across the globe in many cases. The country establishing the NTB may only allow goods to be imported if they adhere to strict rules of origin, which exporters might not be able to meet.

Sanitary or Phyto Sanitary Conditions Firms may be required to provide details of food and plant exports which again must adhere to strict conditions. Phyto sanitary refers to the health of plants, and exporting firms may have to show that plants are free from pest and disease, and that measures have been taken to ensure the conditions of growth adhere to the standards laid down by the country setting the NTB. In the case of food exports, a country may set very high food safety standards and regulations which exporters find difficult or costly to meet.

Administrative Regulations Some countries might set up administrative procedures that must be met prior to any goods or services coming into the country. The paperwork or 'red tape' involved can be excessive and add to the costs of the exporter, which again make the firm less competitive. Some countries might require excessive or unreasonable labelling or packaging regulations, or set burdensome customs entry procedures including the necessity of providing valuations of goods at the point of entry which might be challenged (value can be a subjective issue) or certification to prove authenticity, which again can lead to an increase in costs.

Currency Manipulation Some countries might implement measures to artificially influence the value of their currency, leading to exporters finding the price they face being higher than it would otherwise be and, as a result, reducing their competitiveness against domestic producers. We will see later in this chapter how exchange rates behave in response to government policies.

SELF TEST Draw the supply and demand curve for wool suits in the country of Autarka. When trade is allowed, the price of a suit falls from 300 to 200 grams of gold. In your diagram, what is the change in consumer surplus, the change in producer surplus and the change in total surplus? How would a tariff on suit imports alter these effects?

The Arguments for Restricting Trade

Despite the benefits to free trade, the vast majority of countries around the world impose some restrictions on trade. The following outlines the main reasons put forward for such restrictions.

The Jobs Argument Opponents of free trade often argue that trade with other countries destroys domestic jobs. In our example, free trade in olive oil would cause the price to fall, reducing the quantity produced in Isoland and thus reducing employment in the Isolandian olive oil industry. Some Isolandian olive oil workers would lose their jobs.

The counter-argument to this is that trade can create jobs at the same time that it destroys them. When Isolandians buy olive oil from other countries, those countries obtain the resources to buy other goods from Isoland. Isolandian workers would move from the olive oil industry to those industries in which Isoland has a comparative advantage. This assumes that workers can move easily between different jobs, which of course, is possible but by no means cost free. The movement of workers between industries does impose hardship in the short run, but in the long run it can be argued that it allows Isolandians as a whole to enjoy a higher standard of living.

The National Security Argument

When an industry is threatened with competition from other countries, opponents of free trade often argue that the industry is vital for national security. Free trade would allow Isoland to become dependent on foreign countries to supply vital resources. If a war later broke out, Isoland might be unable to produce enough to defend itself and remain self-sufficient.

Some economists acknowledge that protecting key industries may be appropriate when there are legitimate concerns over national security. It is also possible that this argument may be used too quickly by producers eager to gain at consumers' expense. Certainly, it is tempting for those in an industry to exaggerate their role in national defence to obtain protection from foreign competition.

The Infant Industry Argument

New industries sometimes argue for temporary trade restrictions to help them get started. After a period of protection, the argument goes, these industries will mature and can compete with foreign competitors. Similarly, older industries sometimes argue that they need protection to help them adjust to new conditions. In 2002, for example, when US President George Bush imposed steep tariffs on the import of steel from the EU, he argued that the industry needed protection in order to be able to afford to pay the pensions and health care costs of its retired workers, and while it was going through a period of adjustment to make its production more efficient in order to be able to cope with intense foreign competition.

Some economists are sceptical about such claims. The primary reason is that the infant industry argument is difficult to implement in practice. To apply protection successfully, the government would need to decide which industries would eventually be profitable and whether the benefits of establishing these industries exceed the costs to consumers of protection. Yet 'picking winners' is extraordinarily difficult. It is made even more difficult by the political process, which often awards protection to those industries that are politically powerful. Once a powerful industry is protected from foreign competition, the 'temporary' policy is hard to remove.

In addition, some economists are sceptical about the infant industry argument even in principle. Suppose, for instance, that the Isolandian olive oil industry is young and unable to compete profitably against foreign rivals, but there is reason to believe that the industry can be profitable in the long run. In this case, the owners of the firms should be willing to incur temporary losses to obtain the eventual profits. Protection is not necessary for an industry to grow. Firms in various industries, such as many internet firms today, incur temporary losses in the hope of growing and becoming profitable in the future. Many of them succeed, even without protection from foreign competition.

The Unfair Competition Argument

A common argument is that free trade is desirable only if all countries play by the same rules. If firms in different countries are subject to different laws and regulations, then it is unfair (the argument goes) to expect the firms to compete in the international marketplace. For instance, suppose that the government of Neighbourland subsidizes its olive oil industry by giving olive oil companies large tax breaks. The Isolandian olive oil industry might argue that it should be protected from this foreign competition because Neighbourland is not competing fairly.

Would it, in fact, hurt Isoland to buy olive oil from another country at a subsidized price? Certainly, Isolandian olive oil producers would suffer, but Isolandian olive oil consumers would benefit from the low price. Moreover, the case for free trade is no different: the gains of the consumers from buying at the low price would exceed the losses of the producers. Neighbourland's subsidy to its olive oil industry may be a bad policy, but it is the taxpayers of Neighbourland who bear the burden. Isoland can benefit from the opportunity to buy olive oil at a subsidized price.

The Protection as a Bargaining Chip Argument

Another argument for trade restrictions concerns the strategy of bargaining. Many policy makers claim to support free trade but, at the same time, argue that trade restrictions can be useful when we bargain with our trading partners. They claim that the threat of a trade restriction can help remove a trade restriction already imposed by a foreign government. For example, Isoland might threaten to impose a tariff on olive oil unless Neighbourland removes its tariff on wheat. If Neighbourland responds to this threat by removing its tariff, the result can be freer trade.

The problem with this bargaining strategy is that the threat may not work. If it doesn't work, the country has a difficult choice. It can carry out its threat and implement the trade restriction, which would reduce its own economic welfare. Or it can back down from its threat, which would cause it to lose prestige in international affairs. Faced with this choice, the country would probably wish that it had never made the threat in the first place.

CASE STUDY   Legitimate Restrictions or Barriers to Trade?

Palm oil is a vegetable oil that is extracted from the fruit of oil palms. It is a key ingredient in thousands of products from ice cream to lipstick. Indonesia and Malaysia account for around 85 per cent of global palm oil exports. Because the trees require a tropical climate, there have been concerns that expanding palm oil production has gone hand-in-hand with deforestation. The EU has expressed concerns about this and has imposed restrictions on both countries using the argument that more needs to be done to stop deforestation in the drive to expand palm oil production. Malaysia and Indonesia argue that they have both taken steps to improve the sustainability of palm oil production and that the EU is seeking to impose increasing trade restrictions on their exports of palm oil as a measure to try to protect its own soft-oils industry, which is mostly derived from plants such as sunflowers, rape, canola and soybeans. The EU denies this accusation. The dispute between the EU and Malaysia and Indonesia threatened to escalate when, in early January 2023, Malaysia announced that it could cease exports of palm oil to the EU and would enter negotiations with Indonesia on the issue. The EU accounts for around 9 per cent of Malaysia's total global export of palm oil but the amount sold across the EU has declined by around 40 per cent since 2015.

The debate over the challenges posed by palm oil production has spilt over into disagreements between the EU and Malaysia and Indonesia.

Questions

1 If Malaysia and Indonesia did seek to prevent exports of palm oil to the EU, what methods might they employ to achieve this?

2 Assume that the EU is seeking to restrict palm oil imports to protect its soft-oils industry. Use diagrams to show the possible effects of this policy on domestic (i.e. EU) producers of soft-oils and on Malaysian and Indonesian producers of palm oil. What might determine the size of the effect on both?

3 How does the issue in the case study highlight the difficulties of regulating and promoting free trade across nations?

Reference: www.euronews.com/next/2023/01/13/malaysia-palm-oil-eu-explainer (accessed 9 June 2023).

CRITICISMS OF COMPARATIVE ADVANTAGE THEORY

The theory of comparative advantage has appeal and intuitively makes sense. In some surveys of economists, there seems to be a considerable number who agree that free trade is essentially a 'good' thing. The belief in free trade is based on the benefits espoused by the theory of comparative advantage. There have been criticisms of the theory because of the context in which it was developed and that its assumptions are too simplistic to describe modern economies.

For example, countries with a large supply of unskilled labour and land might reasonably be expected to have a comparative advantage in the production of primary products, and to trade the surplus of these with other more developed nations who may have a comparative advantage in the production of manufactured goods. In Africa, this scenario applies to many countries, but these countries seem to have failed to reap the benefits of trade in the way that the theory suggests and remain extremely poor.

Other developing economies like India, China and South Korea, in contrast, have seen more rapid growth and improvement in their citizen's well-being. China's leaders have invested heavily in manufacturing industry, and South Korea in large enterprises. India has a reputation in software and computer program development. Given that there are plenty of other countries in the world that had developed industries in these fields, it can be argued that India, China and South Korea were not exploiting comparative advantage. Rather, a conscious decision by the authorities to invest and build skills in industries where they did not have a comparative advantage has helped them to develop at a faster rate than many countries in Africa.

Rather than focus on comparative advantage, a more relevant point is that countries may make active decisions to specialize not in those industries in which it has the factor endowments that give them comparative advantage but in industries where the benefits to the population as a whole are likely to be greatest. For countries like China, South Korea and India, these decisions might be based on what is called the **Prebisch–Singer hypothesis**. This hypothesis states that as incomes rise, spending on manufactured goods rises, while spending on primary products fall. For countries focusing on primary products like many in Africa, which have appropriate resource endowments, they are likely to become poorer over time compared to those which invest in manufactured goods production.

> **Prebisch–Singer hypothesis** a theory suggesting that the rate at which primary products exchange for manufactured goods declines over time, meaning that countries specializing in primary good production become poorer

Attempts to impose free trade on countries based on the theory of comparative advantage, therefore, could lead to countries not gaining the benefits the theory predicts. Joan Robinson noted that Ricardo's analysis focused on Britain and Portugal and used cloth and wine as the two goods concerned, with Britain having the comparative advantage in cloth production and Portugal in wine production. In specializing in wine production, the cloth industry in Portugal withered, but the benefits from exporting wine were also limited because the global market for wine was not expanding quickly.

Empirical research into the Prebisch–Singer hypothesis, published in 2013 by Arezki, Hadri, Lougani and Rao for the International Monetary Fund, looked at 25 primary products since 1650 and found that their results on the Prebisch–Singer hypothesis were mixed, but that 'in the majority of cases, the Prebisch–Singer hypothesis is not rejected'. Critics of the theory of comparative advantage thus point to historical evidence that gains from trade can be garnered through investment in goods that have higher value in world trade markets rather than in goods where resource endowments suggest they have a comparative advantage.

OTHER THEORIES OF INTERNATIONAL TRADE

Over the years there have been a number of other theories of international trade which have developed. We will provide an overview of some of these in the next section.

Factor Endowments: The Hecksher–Ohlin Theory

This theory derives from work by two Swedish economists, Eli Hecksher and Bertil Ohlin, the latter being jointly awarded the Nobel Prize in Economics in 1979 (with James Meade) for his work on the theory of international trade. Hecksher and Ohlin's theory was based around the idea that any produced good or service represents a bundle of factors of production which go into their production. Different countries have different endowments of factors of production. Some have abundant supplies of raw materials such as oil, copper, iron ore and so on, whereas others might have greater supplies of productive land and labour. This means that different countries will have a comparative advantage in the production of goods and services in which they have relevant factor endowments. Saudi Arabia, for example, has a comparative advantage in the production of oil given the large reserves of oil it has, whereas Bangladesh has a comparative advantage in the production of goods which utilize labour intensive production methods.

Of course, most countries will import raw materials, component parts and semi-finished products, and use these to help produce goods and services which they then export. Countries have different patterns of trade depending on the relative proportions of imports and exports. This pattern of trade will be partly dependent on the relative factor endowments that countries have. The Hecksher–Ohlin theory offers a prediction on what this pattern of trade is likely to be. In simple terms, it is likely that a country will tend to import goods and services where the factor endowments to produce those goods and services in that country are relatively scarce. Equally, where a country has a relative abundance of factor endowments which enable it to produce goods and services, it is likely to export those goods and services. There are benefits to trade, therefore, between countries with different factor endowments.

For example, assume two countries which use only capital and labour in the production of two goods, X and Y. Country A is a capital abundant country, having a greater factor endowment of capital in relation to labour, whereas Country B is endowed with a greater amount of labour in relation to capital. The amount of capital per unit of labour is higher in Country A whereas the amount of labour per unit of capital is greater in Country B. If we now look at the two goods, assume that the production of good X requires more units of capital per unit of labour to produce. Good X, therefore, is relatively capital intensive. Good Y, on the other hand, requires more labour per unit of capital in production and so is the more labour intensive good.

The Hecksher–Ohlin theory predicts that Country A would produce good X, the capital intensive good and Country B would produce good Y, the labour intensive good. Country A would export good X and import good Y and Country B would export good Y and import good X. Both countries benefit from trade. In summary, the theory predicts that a country will export goods that are intensive in the factor in which it has an abundance, and import goods which are intensive in the factor in which its factor endowment is, in relative terms, more limited.

Patterns of trade can change as a result of changes in relative factor endowments. In China, for example, the existence of large quantities of relatively cheap labour meant that China was able to export goods which were relatively labour intensive. In recent years, the innovation and investment in capital in China is shifting the relative factor endowments of the country and its trading pattern is changing as a consequence. These factor endowments are not set and governments can adjust them through judicious investment and incentives, as suggested earlier in the cases of India and South Korea.

The Imitation Gap or Imitation Lag Hypothesis

Countries may have different factor endowments, but dynamic events in the economy can result in one country innovating at a different rate from others. When new products are developed, it may take time before these products are replicated and/or developed further by other countries, hence the term 'gap' or 'lag' in this hypothesis. This hypothesis was developed by Michael V. Posner (1931–2006), a UK economist who worked at the University of Cambridge and was also an adviser to the UK government.

When a new product is developed, the innovation may be centred in a particular country and this country has an advantage in the production of this good. Assuming it is successful, there will be a period of time before rival firms are able to also produce variants of the same good and thus compete. The time lag will be dependent on the nature of the technology involved, the resources needed and the investment required to enable the product to be commercially viable and available.

In addition to the supply side of the equation, there will also be demand-side lags. It might take time for the product to become known and accepted. If and when an alternative supply does become available from other countries, consumers in different countries may take time to come to accept and embrace the substitute products, if indeed they do at all. For example, Apple has introduced a number of innovative products which have resulted in 'imitations', most notably in smartphones and the associated operating systems which run applications. Other technology companies have attempted to replicate Apple products and developed rival mobile operating systems such as Android (developed by Google), Windows Phone, BlackBerry 10 and Ubuntu Touch. Some of these systems have been accepted by the market and others have not and have been discontinued. Even if new products are introduced which are very good imitations, it may be more challenging to gain market penetration because of existing brand loyalty and familiarity.

The imitation lag hypothesis, therefore, suggests that international trade and the pattern of imports and exports in different countries can be affected by the development of new products, and highlights the importance of innovation to improving and maintaining export performance. Economic development can be driven by export-led growth and the imitation lag hypothesis points to the importance for countries of the need to support and encourage innovation, research and development, and entrepreneurship if the country is to maintain its position in international trade.

Product Cycle Theory

The basic principles of the product life cycle can be extended to international trade theory. Product cycle theory has become an extension of the imitation lag hypothesis in explaining changes in trade patterns. Product cycle theory was developed by the US Economist, Raymond Vernon (1913–1999). Recall that in product life cycle theory, products are developed and go through an early growth stage (assuming they are successful). Product cycle theory notes that at this stage in the development of a product, it is most likely that sales will take place in the country in which the product was developed and so international trade in the product will be non-existent.

As the product enters the maturity stage, techniques of mass production and commercialization of the product will have been developed and firms producing the product will be able to benefit from economies of scale. As the product becomes more competitive, it will begin to generate sales abroad as firms enter negotiations to develop trading agreements and contracts. If the product is one introduced in an already developed economy, it is likely that the trading opportunities will be with other similarly developed economies. However, it is also likely that less developed economies will begin copying these products, and if they have cheaper labour costs, for example, they can offer similar products for sale around the world at lower prices than those which may be in force in the country of origin. Trade patterns thus begin to change as countries with advantages in certain factor endowments begin to take market share. The domestic country in which the product originated might begin to find that exports of the product begin to slow and even decline, while imports of the imitation products grow and gain greater market share.

As the product continues along the product life cycle (a stage Vernon referred to as the 'standardized product stage'), production may have transferred almost entirely to developing countries and developed economies will have shifted their focus onto developing other new products which would help generate export revenue and growth. Product cycle theory reflects the dynamics of international trade and changing trade patterns.

Consumer Tastes: The Linder Theory

Countries in the world can be classified as high income, middle income and low income. Consumers in these different countries will have different purchasing habits and patterns, and this can be reflected in the types of goods and services produced in the country. For example, in a high income country, the type of goods and services domestic firms produce might cater for more sophisticated financial products, more technology based luxuries, more highly processed foods. In low income countries, these types of goods would not be in such high demand, and firms in these countries would tend to produce goods and services which might be regarded as basic necessities. As a consequence, the trade which different countries engage in is a function of the goods and services it produces.

A Swedish economist, Hans Martin Staffan Burenstam Linder (1931–2000), argued that trade patterns are influenced by the extent to which there is an overlap in the demand from consumers across countries with different income levels. In the theory of comparative advantage, we stated that it was not possible for a country to have a comparative advantage in all goods because the opportunity cost of one good is the inverse of the opportunity cost of another. The Linder hypothesis argues that trade can take place in the same good and be beneficial to both countries provided consumer tastes overlap. This is observed in the UK which both imports and exports oil. Linder argued that even if countries have different income levels, there can be instances where there is a common demand for goods which can mean trade in those goods can take place and be beneficial to both countries.

THE PRICES FOR INTERNATIONAL TRANSACTIONS: REAL AND NOMINAL EXCHANGE RATES

Just as the price in any market serves the important role of coordinating buyers and sellers in that market, international prices help coordinate the decisions of consumers and producers as they interact in world markets.

Nominal Exchange Rates

The **nominal exchange rate** is the rate at which a person can trade the currency of one country for the currency of another. For example, a business in Belgium trading with one in Japan might be quoted an exchange rate of 125 yen per euro. If the business gives up one euro, it would get 125 Japanese yen in return.

 nominal exchange rate the rate at which a person can trade the currency of one country for the currency of another

An exchange rate can always be expressed in two ways. If the exchange rate is 125 yen per euro, it is also 1/125 (= 0.008) euro per yen. If a euro is worth £0.88, a pound is worth 1/0.88 (= 1.136) euros. This can be a source of confusion, and there is no real hard and fast convention that people use. For example, it is customary to quote the US dollar–pound exchange rate as dollars per pound, e.g. $1.50 if £1 exchanges for $1.50. On the other hand, the pound–euro exchange rate can be quoted either way, as pounds per euro or euros per pound. In this book, we shall for the most part think of the exchange rate as being the quantity of foreign currency that exchanges for one unit of domestic currency, or the foreign price of a unit of domestic currency. For example, if we are thinking of the UK as the domestic economy and the USA as the foreign economy, then the exchange rate is expressed as $1.35 per pound. If we are thinking of, say, Germany as the domestic economy, then we could express the exchange rate as dollars per euro, e.g. $1.23 per euro.

The exchange of any particular currency is determined by the supply and demand of that currency on foreign exchange markets. When the exchange rate changes so that a euro buys more of another currency, this is referred to as an **appreciation** of the euro. When the exchange rate changes so that a euro buys less of another currency, this is referred to as a **depreciation** of the euro. For example, when the exchange rate rises from 125 to 127 yen per euro, the euro is said to appreciate. At the same time, because a Japanese yen now buys less of the European currency, the yen is said to depreciate. When the exchange rate falls from 125 to 123 yen per euro, the euro is said to depreciate, and the yen to appreciate.

appreciation an increase in the value of a currency as measured by the amount of foreign currency it can buy
depreciation a decrease in the value of a currency as measured by the amount of foreign currency it can buy

At times, you may have heard the media report that the pound or the euro is either strong or weak. These descriptions usually refer to recent changes in the nominal exchange rate. When a currency appreciates, it is said to *strengthen* because it can then buy more foreign currency. Similarly, when a currency depreciates, it is said to *weaken*. If the individual gets more of the foreign currency in exchange for the same amount of the domestic currency, the domestic currency is stronger. If the individual has to give up more of the domestic currency to get the same amount of the foreign currency, then the domestic currency is weaker.

For any currency, there are many nominal exchange rates. The euro can be used to buy US dollars, UAE dirham, South African rand, British pounds, Mexican pesos and so on. When economists study changes in the exchange rate, they often use indices that average these many exchange rates. Just as the CPI turns the many prices in the economy into a single measure of the price level, an exchange rate index turns these many exchange rates into a single measure of the international value of the currency. When economists talk about the euro or the pound appreciating or depreciating, they often are referring to an exchange rate index that takes into account many individual exchange rates.

Real Exchange Rates

The **real exchange rate** is the rate at which a person can trade the goods and services of one country for the goods and services of another. For example, suppose that you go shopping and find that a kilo of Swiss cheese is twice as expensive as a kilo of English Cheddar cheese. We would then say that the real exchange rate is a ½ kilo of Swiss cheese per kilo of English cheese. Notice that, like the nominal exchange rate, we express the real exchange rate as units of the foreign item per unit of the domestic item. But in this instance the item is a good rather than a currency.

> **real exchange rate** the rate at which a person can trade the goods and services of one country for the goods and services of another

Real and nominal exchange rates are closely related. To see how, consider an example. Suppose that a kilo of British wheat sells for £1, and a kilo of European wheat sells for €3. What is the real exchange rate between British and European wheat? To answer this question, we must first use the nominal exchange rate to convert the prices into a common currency. If the nominal exchange rate is €2 per pound, then a price for British wheat of £1 per kilo is equivalent to €2 per kilo. European wheat, however, sells for €3 a kilo, so British wheat is only ⅔ as expensive as European wheat. The real exchange rate is ⅔ of a kilo of European wheat per kilo of British wheat.

We can summarize this calculation for the real exchange rate with the following formula, where we are measuring the exchange rate as the amount of foreign currency needed to buy one unit of domestic currency:

$$\text{Real exchange rate} = \frac{(\text{Nominal exchange rate} \times \text{Domestic price})}{(\text{Foreign price})}$$

Using the numbers in our example, the formula applies as follows:

$$\text{Real exchange rate} = \frac{(\text{€2 per pound}) \times (\text{£1 per kilo of UK wheat})}{(\text{€3 per kilo of European wheat})}$$

$$= \tfrac{2}{3} \text{ kilo of European wheat per kilo of UK wheat}$$

Thus the real exchange rate depends on the nominal exchange rate and on the prices of goods in the two countries measured in the local currencies.

The real exchange rate is a key determinant of how much a country exports and imports. For example, when a UK bread company is deciding whether to buy British or European wheat to make into flour and use in making its bread, it will ask which wheat is cheaper. The real exchange rate gives the answer.

When studying an economy as a whole, macroeconomists focus on overall prices rather than the prices of individual items. That is, to measure the real exchange rate, they use price indices, such as the CPI, which measure the prices of a basket of goods and services. By using a prices index for a European basket (P), a prices index for a foreign basket (P^*) and the nominal exchange rate between the euro and foreign currencies (e = foreign currency per euro), we can compute the overall real exchange rate between Europe and other countries as follows:

$$\text{Real exchange rate} = \frac{(e \times P)}{P^*}$$

This real exchange rate measures the price of a basket of goods and services available domestically relative to a basket of goods and services available abroad.

A country's real exchange rate is a key determinant of its net exports of goods and services. A depreciation (fall) in the real exchange rate of the euro means that EU goods have become cheaper relative to foreign goods. This change encourages consumers both at home and abroad to buy more EU goods and fewer goods from other countries. Businesses in the EU selling goods to South Africa, for example, will benefit from the depreciation whereas those buying goods and services from South Africa will find the depreciation has increased their costs. As a result, EU exports rise and EU imports fall, and both of these changes raise EU net exports. Conversely, an appreciation (rise) in the euro real exchange rate means that EU goods have become more expensive compared to foreign goods, so EU net exports fall.

It is important to remember that while we are talking about the prices of exports and imports changing, the domestic price for these goods and services may not change. For example, a French wine producer may have wine for sale priced at €10 per bottle. If the exchange rate between the euro and the South African rand is €1 = R9.9 then a South African buyer of wine must give up R99 to buy a bottle of wine. If the euro exchange rate appreciates to €1 = R10.5 then the South African buyer now must give up R105 to buy the bottle of wine. The euro price of the wine has not changed, but to the South African buyer the price has risen. Equally, if the euro exchange rate depreciated from €1 = R9.9 to €1 = R9.0 then the South African buyer would now have to give up R90 to buy the wine. Again, the euro price of the wine has not changed but the price to the South African buyer has fallen because the exchange rate between the rand and the euro has changed.

SELF TEST Define nominal exchange rate and real exchange rate, and explain how they are related. If the nominal exchange rate changes from 100 to 120 yen per euro, has the euro appreciated or depreciated? Explain.

JEOPARDY PROBLEM A firm based in the Netherlands buys raw materials from firms in South Africa and Saudi Arabia and sells its output to firms elsewhere in the EU and to the United States. The exchange rate between the euro and those other currencies in which it trades depreciates significantly over a period of a year. The Dutch firm finds that far from benefiting from the depreciation its profits are falling. Why might this happen?

A MODEL OF EXCHANGE RATE DETERMINATION: PURCHASING POWER PARITY

Exchange rates vary substantially over time. Economists have developed many models to explain how exchange rates are determined, each emphasizing just some of the many forces at work. Here we develop the simplest theory of exchange rates, called purchasing power parity. This theory states that a unit of any given currency should be able to buy the same quantity of goods in all countries. Some economists believe that **purchasing power parity** describes the forces that determine exchange rates in the long run. We now consider the logic on which this long run theory of exchange rates is based, as well as the theory's implications and limitations.

purchasing power parity a theory of exchange rates whereby a unit of any given currency should be able to buy the same quantity of goods in all countries

The Basic Logic of Purchasing Power Parity

The theory of purchasing power parity is based on a principle called the *law of one price*. This law asserts that a good must sell for the same price in all locations. Otherwise, there would be opportunities for profit left unexploited. For example, suppose that coffee beans sold for less in Munich than in Frankfurt. A person could buy coffee in Munich for, say, €4 a kilo and then sell it in Frankfurt for €5 a kilo, making a profit of €1 per kilo from the difference in price. The process of taking advantage of differences in prices in different markets is called *arbitrage*. In our example, as people took advantage of this arbitrage opportunity, they would increase the demand for coffee in Munich and increase the supply in Frankfurt. The price of coffee would rise in Munich (in response to greater demand) and fall in Frankfurt (in response to greater supply). This process would continue until, eventually, the prices were the same in the two markets.

Now consider how the law of one price applies to the international marketplace. If a euro (or any other currency) could buy more coffee in Germany than in Japan, international traders could profit by buying coffee in Germany and selling it in Japan. This export of coffee from Germany to Japan would drive up the German price of coffee and drive down the Japanese price. Conversely, if a euro could buy more coffee in Japan than in Germany, traders could buy coffee in Japan and sell it in Germany. This import of coffee into Germany from Japan would drive down the German price of coffee and drive up the Japanese price. In the end, the law of one price tells us that a euro must buy the same amount of coffee in all countries.

This logic leads us to the theory of purchasing power parity. According to this theory, a currency must have the same purchasing power in all countries. That is, a euro must buy the same quantity of goods in Germany and Japan, and a Japanese yen must buy the same quantity of goods in Japan as in Germany. Indeed, the name of this theory describes it well. *Parity* means equality, and *purchasing power* refers to the value of money. *Purchasing power parity* states that a unit of all currencies must have the same real value in every country.

Implications of Purchasing Power Parity

What does the theory of purchasing power parity say about exchange rates? It tells us that the nominal exchange rate between the currencies of two countries depends on the price levels in those countries. If a euro buys the same quantity of goods in Germany (where prices are measured in euros) as in Japan (where prices are measured in yen), then the number of yen per euro must reflect the prices of goods in Germany and Japan. For example, if a kilo of coffee is priced at 500 yen in Japan and €5 in Germany, then the nominal exchange rate must be 100 yen per euro (500 yen/€5 = 100 yen per euro). Otherwise, the purchasing power of the euro would not be the same in the two countries.

To see more fully how this works, it is helpful to use just a little mathematics. Think of Germany as the home or domestic economy. Suppose that P is the price of a basket of goods in Germany (measured in euros), P^* is the price of a basket of goods in Japan (measured in yen), and e is the nominal exchange rate (the number of yen needed to buy one euro). Now consider the quantity of goods a euro can buy at home (in Germany) and abroad. At home, the price level is P, so the purchasing power of €1 at home is $1/P$. Abroad, a euro can be exchanged into e units of foreign currency, which in turn have purchasing power e/P^*. For the purchasing power of a euro to be the same in the two countries, it must be the case that:

$$\frac{1}{P} = \frac{e}{P^*}$$

With rearrangement, this equation becomes:

$$1 = \frac{eP}{P^*}$$

Notice that the left-hand side of this equation is a constant, and the right-hand side is the real exchange rate. Thus, if the purchasing power of the euro is always the same at home and abroad, then the real exchange rate (the relative price of domestic and foreign goods) cannot change.

To see the implication of this analysis for the nominal exchange rate, we can rearrange the last equation to solve for the nominal exchange rate:

$$e = \frac{P^*}{P}$$

That is, the nominal exchange rate equals the ratio of the foreign price level (measured in units of the foreign currency) to the domestic price level (measured in units of the domestic currency). According to the theory of purchasing power parity, the nominal exchange rate between the currencies of two countries must reflect the different price levels in those countries.

Limitations of Purchasing Power Parity

The theory of purchasing power parity is not completely accurate. That is, exchange rates do not always move to ensure that a euro has the same real value in all countries all the time. There are two reasons why the theory of purchasing power parity does not always hold in practice.

The first reason is that many goods are not easily traded. Imagine, for instance, that haircuts are more expensive in Paris than in New York. International travellers might avoid getting their haircuts in Paris, and some hairdressers might move from New York to Paris. Yet such arbitrage would probably be too limited to eliminate the differences in prices. Thus the deviation from purchasing power parity might persist, and a euro (or dollar) would continue to buy less of a haircut in Paris than in New York.

The second reason that purchasing power parity does not always hold is that even tradable goods are not always perfect substitutes when they are produced in different countries. For example, some consumers prefer German cars and others prefer Japanese cars. Moreover, consumer tastes can change over time. If German cars suddenly become more popular, the increase in demand will drive up the price of German cars compared to Japanese cars. But despite this difference in prices in the two markets, there might be no opportunity for profitable arbitrage because consumers do not view the two cars as equivalent.

Thus both because some goods are not tradable and because some tradable goods are not perfect substitutes with their foreign counterparts, purchasing power parity is not a perfect theory of exchange rate determination. For these reasons, real exchange rates fluctuate over time. Nonetheless, the theory of purchasing power parity does provide a useful first step in understanding exchange rates. The basic logic is persuasive: as the real exchange rate drifts from the level predicted by purchasing power parity, people have greater incentive to move goods across national borders. Even if the forces of purchasing power parity do not completely fix the real exchange rate, they provide a reason to expect that changes in the real exchange rate are most often small or temporary. As a result, large and persistent movements in nominal exchange rates typically reflect changes in price levels at home and abroad.

SUMMARY

- A production possibilities frontier can be used as a model to identify the benefits of specialization and trade.
- The principle of comparative advantage shows that countries can benefit from trade if they specialize in goods in which they have lower opportunity costs.
- International trade can be beneficial, but as with much in economics, there will be winners and losers in trade.
- Despite the benefits of trade, many countries impose restrictions on trade and there are a number of reasons given for doing so.
- Key barriers to trade are tariffs, quotas and non-tariff or hidden barriers.
- The theory of comparative advantage is one theory of international trade. It has its critics, and other theories to explain international trade have been proposed over time since the 1920s.
- International trade necessitates international payments. Exchange rates between currencies are determined, in part, by the demand and supply of currencies on foreign exchange markets arising from the demand and supply of imports and exports.
- It is important to distinguish between nominal and real exchange rates.
- According to the theory of purchasing power parity, a unit of currency should be able to buy the same quantity of goods in all countries. This theory implies that the nominal exchange rate between the currencies of two countries should reflect the price levels in those countries. As a result, countries with relatively high inflation should have depreciating currencies, and countries with relatively low inflation should have appreciating currencies.

IN THE NEWS

The Egyptian Currency

The global nature of trade may bring benefits but it can also bring challenges. Egypt purchases wheat and oil from Russia, but the conflict in Ukraine has meant that prices have risen and Egyptian traders have had to give up more Egyptian pounds to buy these goods. Russians were an important source of exports for Egypt through tourism from the country, but the conflict severely restricted export earnings from this source. By the end of 2022, inflation in Egypt was running at around 16 per cent. Egypt sought a loan from the International Monetary Fund (IMF) to help with economic reforms aimed at cutting inflation, reducing public sector debt growth, and other structural reforms of its economy. In late 2022, the IMF announced that it had come to an agreement with the Egyptian government on a $3 billion loan which was tied to some of these reforms but which also required the government to commit to allowing the value of the Egyptian pound (EGP) to be determined by market forces, a so-called freely floating exchange rate.

On news of the IMF loan and the floating of the currency, the exchange rate between the Egyptian pound and the US dollar weakened. In the autumn of 2022, the currency stood at around $1 = EGP19. Following the announcement of the IMF loan and the commitment to float the currency, the Egyptian pound weakened and by mid-January 2023 was at $1 = EGP29.

External events can weigh heavily on a country's currency as Egypt has discovered.

Questions

1 Assume that the conflict in Ukraine led to oil and wheat prices rising by 25 per cent. If importers of wheat and oil from Russia in Egypt continue to buy similar amounts of the two goods, how might this affect the value of imports into Egypt and the supply and demand of the Egyptian currency?

2 The article notes that tourism to Egypt was badly affected by the conflict in Ukraine. Is tourism an import or an export to the Egyptian economy? Explain.

3 How might the conflict in Ukraine affect inflation rates in Egypt?

4 Prior to the agreement with the IMF, the Egyptian government sought to manage the exchange rate. How might the government and the Central Bank of Egypt 'manage' the level of its currency?

5 Consider the change in the exchange rate between the Egyptian pound and the US dollar between November 2022 and January 2023. Analyze the effect on importers and exporters in Egypt and on the domestic economy. Who might be the winners and who might be the losers in the change in the exchange rate and on what does the extent of the effects on both depend?

References: www.imf.org/en/News/Articles/2022/12/16/pr22441-egypt-imf-executive-board-approves-46-month-usd3b-extended-arrangement (accessed 9 June 2023).
www.reuters.com/business/finance/egypts-central-bank-raises-key-interest-rates-by-200-basis-points-2022-10-27/ (accessed 9 June 2023).

QUESTIONS FOR REVIEW

1 Draw a PPF for a country producing only computers and wheat. What determines the shape and position of the PPF you have drawn? Use your diagram to show the opportunity cost of different output combinations.

2 What does the domestic price that prevails without international trade tell us about a nation's comparative advantage?

3 Explain how absolute advantage and comparative advantage differ.

4 Can two countries gain from trade if the opportunity cost ratios relating to production of goods they can both produce is the same? Explain.

5 Explain how a country with an absolute advantage in the production of oranges and lemons could gain from trade if it specialized in the product in which it had the lowest opportunity cost.

6 Describe what a tariff is and its economic effects. What is an import quota? Compare its economic effects with those of a tariff.

7 If there are so many benefits to international trade, why do governments impose trade barriers?

8 Which of the theories of international trade covered in this chapter do you find the most convincing and why?

9 How does an appreciation of the exchange rate against the US dollar affect a UK-based firm that buys raw materials from the United States for products it sells in the UK?

10 What effect would you expect a tariff to have on the real exchange rate? Explain using appropriate diagrams.

PROBLEMS AND APPLICATIONS

1 Draw the PPF for a country which produces just oranges and cars. Assume that the country is better at producing oranges than cars.

  a. What can you say about the opportunity cost of the country diverting more resources into producing cars?

  b. The country discovers new resources which will mean that its ability to produce cars is significantly improved. What happens to the shape of the PPF as a result of this discovery?

  c. What can you say about the opportunity cost facing the country after this new discovery?

2 Look at the table below which shows the production possibilities for two products, pens and pencils.

Point	Pens	Pencils
A	10	0
B	5	10
C	2	25

  a. Calculate the opportunity cost of producing 1 additional pen between points A and B.

  b. Calculate the opportunity cost of producing 1 additional pencil between points A and B.

  c. Calculate the opportunity cost of producing 1 additional pen between points B and C. What conclusions can you come to about this opportunity cost compared to the calculation you made in a. above?

  d. Calculate the opportunity cost of producing 1 additional pencil between points B and C. What conclusions can you come to about this opportunity cost compared to the calculation you made in b. above?

3 International trade in each of the following products has increased over time. Suggest some reasons why this might be so.

  a. Wheat
  b. Banking services
  c. Computer software
  d. Cars

4 The UK and Poland both produce cakes and coats. Suppose that a UK worker can produce 50 cakes per hour or 1 coat per hour. Suppose that a Polish worker can produce 40 cakes per hour or 2 coats per hour.

   a. Which country has the absolute advantage in the production of each good? Which country has the comparative advantage?

   b. If the UK and Poland decided to trade, which commodity will Poland trade to the UK? Explain.

   c. If a Polish worker could produce only 1 coat per hour, would Poland still gain from trade? Would the UK still gain from trade? Explain.

5 Would each of the following groups be happy or unhappy if the euro appreciated against all currencies? Explain.

   a. US pension funds holding French government bonds.

   b. German manufacturing industries.

   c. Australian tourists planning a trip to Europe.

   d. A UK firm trying to purchase property overseas.

6 What is happening to the Swiss real exchange rate in each of the following situations? Explain.

   a. The Swiss nominal exchange rate is unchanged, but prices rise faster in Switzerland than abroad.

   b. The Swiss nominal exchange rate is unchanged, but prices rise faster abroad than in Switzerland.

   c. The Swiss nominal exchange rate declines, and prices are unchanged in Switzerland and abroad.

   d. The Swiss nominal exchange rate declines, and prices rise faster abroad than in Switzerland.

7 The world price of wine is below the price that would prevail in France in the absence of trade.

   a. Assuming that French imports of wine are a small part of total world wine production, draw a graph for the French market for wine under free trade. Identify consumer surplus, producer surplus and total surplus in an appropriate table.

   b. Now suppose that an outbreak of phyloxera (a sap sucking insect which damages grape vines) in California and South America destroys much of the grape harvest there. What effect does this shock have on the world price of wine? Using your graph and table from a., show the effect on consumer surplus, producer surplus and total surplus in France. Who are the winners and losers? Is France better or worse off?

8 'The theory of comparative advantage may have been able to explain international trade in the late nineteenth century but it is a theory that is outdated and should be consigned to history books. There are more relevant and reliable theories to explain international trade.' Do you agree with this statement? Explain.

9 European and Chinese workers can each produce 4 capital goods a year. A European worker can produce 10 tonnes of grain a year, whereas a Chinese worker can produce 5 tonnes of grain a year. To keep things simple, assume that Europe and China have 100 million workers each.

   a. For this situation, construct a table analogous to Table 23.1.

   b. Graph the production possibilities frontier of the European and Chinese economies.

   c. For Europe, what is the opportunity cost of a car? Of grain? For China, what is the opportunity cost of a car? Of grain? Put this information in a table analogous to Table 23.3.

   d. Which has an absolute advantage in producing capital goods? In producing grain?

   e. Which has a comparative advantage in producing capital goods? In producing grain?

   f. Without trade, half of Europe and China's workers produce capital goods and half produce grain. What quantities of capital goods and grain do Europe and China produce?

   g. Starting from a position without trade, give an example in which trade makes both Europe and China better off.

10 Suppose that EU countries impose a common tariff on imported cars to protect the European car industry from foreign competition. Assuming that Europe is a price taker in the world car market, show on a diagram: the change in the quantity of imports, the loss to European consumers, the gain to European car manufacturers, government revenue and the deadweight loss associated with the tariff. The loss to consumers can be decomposed into three pieces: a transfer to domestic producers, a transfer to the government and a deadweight loss. Use your diagram to identify these three pieces.

24 GLOBAL INFLUENCES ON BUSINESS BEHAVIOUR

LEARNING OUTCOMES

After reading this chapter you should be able to:

- Distinguish between the terms globalization and internationalization.
- Outline the main reasons for the development of globalization.
- Discuss some of the main costs and benefits of globalization.
- Define the concept of 'emerging markets' and describe the characteristics, and importance of, emerging markets.
- Describe the main features and importance of Industry 4.0.
- Consider some of the issues associated with cybercrime and how businesses are seeking to combat this problem.
- Outline the main purpose and principles of corporate governance.

GLOBALIZATION AND INTERNATIONALIZATION

The term **globalization** refers to the growth of interdependence among world economies, usually seen as resulting from the removal of many international regulations affecting financial flows. In one respect, this means that it is becoming easier for firms to conduct business across national boundaries and to engage in trade around the world. This clearly opens up major opportunities but also presents difficulties and challenges that must be recognized and managed, not least the ethical and cultural issues of carrying out business in a global market.

> **globalization** the growth of interdependence among world economies, usually seen as resulting from the removal of many international regulations affecting financial flows

Doing business globally means that a firm can get its product and brand positioned anywhere in the world. It is highly likely that regardless of where you are in the world, for example, you will be able to find a store that sells Coca-Cola. Many businesses have expanded their reach by setting up operations in different countries but are headquartered in their country of origin. These types of organizations are referred to as **multinationals** or multinational corporations (MNCs). These firms have developed, and seek to exploit, a global brand presence. It is not only firms in product markets who have such a global presence, other markets, such as commodity and financial markets, could be argued to be even more global.

> **multinationals** organizations characterized by having operations in a number of countries, although their main headquarters will be in one country, normally the country in which the firm originally developed

Internationalization is considered an element of globalization. It refers to the increase in the way in which organizations produce goods and services which are intended for use in many different countries. In doing this, organizations have had to adapt and change the way they do things to meet different needs and to become involved in trade in more complex ways. To finance and produce these goods and services, organizations have had to adopt different types of design and structure and have had to engage far more in the development of global networks.

> **internationalization** the increase in the way in which organizations produce goods and services which are intended for use in many different countries

> **PITFALL PREVENTION** Ensure that you always provide clear definitions and do not confuse terms – globalization and internationalization can be used interchangeably but they refer to different things.

The Reasons for Globalization

One of the main reasons for the development of global markets has been technological change, particularly the internet, but also transport and other forms of communication. Firms have been able to exploit the developments in these technologies to increase efficiency, gain economies of scale, and produce and communicate 365 days of the year. The main reasons for globalization can be summarized as follows.

Transport and Logistics Investing in production facilities in different countries can present challenges, but the developments in low cost transport systems and improvements in infrastructure in many countries around the world mean that component parts can travel across the globe many times during a production process. Crucially, the cost of producing in this way has not increased at the same rate as the productivity benefits. As a result unit costs are kept low, which means that firms are able to offer consumers high quality products at relatively low competitive prices.

Developments in transport infrastructures mean that firms can analyze and devise logistics to increase productivity. In particular, the advancements in containerization as a means of transporting goods enables firms to move far more goods per hour, with much lower levels of labour than in the 1970s. Containers come in standard sizes and can be loaded in very large quantities from ships onto freight trains and lorries to be delivered to factories, warehouses and distribution hubs.

A paper published in 2016 by Bernhofen, El-Sahli and Kneller on 'Estimating the effects of the container revolution on world trade' (Bernhofen, D., El-Sahli, Z. and Kneller, R. Estimating the Effects of the Container Revolution on World Trade. *Journal of International Economics* 98(C) 36–50 https://www.sciencedirect.com/science/article/abs/pii/S0022199615001403.) suggested that containerization increased bilateral trade (the trade of goods between two countries) between developed countries in the northern hemisphere by some 700 per cent in the period between 1966 and 1990. For developments in technologies like containerization to be commercially viable, there must be appropriate infrastructure available. Investment in port facilities to handle the size of ships that carry containers is essential. Once containers arrive in port, there need to be road and rail systems available for the onward journey of cargo to distribution hubs, warehouses and finally retail outlets. The importance of having this infrastructure is highlighted by the fact that countries which have developed ports to cope with the demands of containerization are most likely to see the economic benefits of increased trade. For lower income countries, the inability to invest in this sort of infrastructure holds them back in their development.

Capital Mobility Trade requires a medium of exchange. Countries where regulations and laws associated with their currencies make it harder to engage in international trade will benefit less from that trade. Since the 1970s, many countries have relaxed currency laws and regulations, which has meant that capital is able to flow more freely between countries. This has increased the ability of firms to invest in developing operations in other countries and to move funds around to maximize returns. As a result, the benefits of international trade are shared across more countries.

The Expansion of Global Credit Markets The complexity of financial markets has increased, partly due to the development of new products designed to boost access to credit for businesses across the globe. Firms looking to borrow funds for investment and expansion can increasingly look at global financial markets to access cheaper credit. Products developed to help firms insure their debt more effectively have also improved the creditworthiness of global businesses and, as a result, they can benefit from financial economies of scale.

The Collapse of the Soviet Bloc and Emerging Markets A significant proportion of the world's countries operated under a different economic system until the early part of the 1990s. Social, political and economic change in Eastern Europe has led to countries gaining independence, embracing the market economy and opening up their borders to trade. It is not only the former Soviet Bloc countries which have increased trade with the rest of the world. Many countries in South America, Africa and Asia, some of which are classed as emerging economies, have seen their share of trade as a percentage of national income increase. The ratio of exports plus imports to national income is called **trade openness**. The extent to which trade openness leads to wider economic benefits for the countries involved is debated, but there has been empirical research which suggests a causal link between increased trade openness and improved economic growth. Of course, the extent to which all citizens share in the improved economic growth must be investigated if broader conclusions on the benefits are to be drawn.

> **trade openness** the ratio of exports plus imports to gross domestic product

The Growth of Multinational Companies (MNCs) Sometimes, statistics can tell a story with far more clarity than words. The World Trade Organisation (WTO) has noted that the top 500 MNCs account for almost 70 per cent of global trade. If the turnovers of MNCs were compared to the GDP of countries, then 69 of the 100 largest economies of the world are corporations. The revenues of US grocery retailer, Walmart, for example, is larger than the GDP of Spain, Australia and the Netherlands. The revenues of Volkswagen and Toyota are larger than the GDPs of Russia and Belgium. (Source: www.weforum.org/agenda/2016/10/corporations-not-countries-dominate-the-list-of-the-world-s-biggest-economic-entities/ and www.globaljustice.org.uk/news/69-richest-100-entities-planet-are-corporations-not-governments-figures-show/.) These statistics highlight the importance of MNCs in global trade and the way in which they have contributed to the growth in trade across borders since the 1970s.

Globalization has brought benefits to billions of people, but the extent to which everyone can share in these benefits is still open to question.

The Benefits of Globalization

Choice and Price The opportunity to expand sales globally means that many businesses can invest in production systems that result in economies of scale. The lower unit costs can be passed on to consumers in the form of lower prices. In addition, consumers have access to a much wider choice of goods and services. Assuming the principle of 'more is preferred to less' this improves standards of living.

Shareholder Value Businesses can exploit global markets to source cheaper factor inputs, which not only lowers unit costs but improves the flexibility of firms to improve their competitiveness around the world. The wider access to markets means firms can increase revenues and with lower unit costs can improve profitability.

Inward Investment As businesses expand in different countries, investment can create a multiplier effect which not only improves the living standards of local people but also generates opportunities for local businesses to expand as suppliers, and in turn increase employment. Inward investment also means that technologies and knowledge are more widely shared and this is also likely to bring economic benefits.

The Costs of Globalization

The links between globalization and the benefits outlined above have been the subject of research, and it is not clear just how far these benefits extend. Figures published by The World Bank show that around half the world's population have difficulties meeting basic needs. The rates of extreme poverty have, however, fallen from 36 per cent in 1990 to 10 per cent in 2015. Some 46 per cent of the world's population live on less than $5.50 (€5.17) per day. (Source: www.worldbank.org/en/news/press-release/2018/10/17/nearly-half-the-world-lives-on-less-than-550-a-day.) The United Nations Department of Economic and Social Affairs also notes that progress on reducing poverty was impacted by the Covid-19 pandemic. Given these figures, we must be mindful of the costs of globalization.

The Power of Multinationals The statistic that 69 of the top 100 'economies' is a corporation is an indicator of the size and global reach of MNCs. While their size can bring benefits, the power that these corporations can wield has been highlighted as a cause for concern. This power might manifest itself in pressure on governments to make decisions on investment and planning which may not be in the best interests of the majority of citizens. The desire to secure inward investment might be transitory, with MNCs capable of switching investments from country to country seeking out the most favourable returns. Knowledge of this may lead to some governments relaxing the regulatory environment, which may not always improve the welfare of the population as a whole. MNCs are also criticized for driving down wages and for using suppliers who may seek to exploit workers to maintain lucrative contracts. The pay and conditions of workers in factories in developing and emerging countries is often publicized, although most MNCs claim that they have rigorous and robust codes of practice in place which seek to minimize such exploitation. Consumers also have a role to play here. Many consumers are willing to buy goods at low prices without necessarily considering the pay and conditions of the workers who make these products.

There are arguments which suggest that inward investment by MNCs can help to create employment and increase standards of living. The size of such an effect will depend on the nature of the business and the number and type of people employed. If the MNC is capital intensive, then the effect on job creation might be relatively small. It might also depend on the number of local people employed and how many high skilled workers the MNC brings in from its own ranks. If MNCs are producing goods which are also produced in the domestic economy, the competition they bring in might be too great for local firms, leading to them close down and putting domestic labour out of work. The dynamics of inward investment by MNCs is complex and the relative costs and benefits need to be considered on a case-by-case basis.

 WHAT IF... a multinational business invests heavily in a developing economy and existing businesses cannot compete. How likely is it that those who worked in the domestic industry will find their skills and abilities employed in the multinational?

Standardization One feature of global business is the increase in standardization; wherever you go in the world, the customer experiences of many products are very similar. Whether it be a McDonald's burger, Windows operating system, Apple's iPad, Coca-Cola, Head and Shoulders shampoo, Colgate toothpaste or BMW cars, regardless of where you are in the world these are highly standardized products. In one respect, it might be argued that this is a good thing in that quality can be assured and all customers get the same experience, but standardization also results in a lack of product diversity and sets up barriers to entry for domestic businesses to compete effectively.

Climate Change The idea that human-made increases in carbon dioxide emissions is resulting in changes in the climate, which could bring devastating effects to some countries, is argued as being exacerbated by globalization. Agreement between global leaders to reduce carbon emissions have been extremely difficult to secure, partly because developing countries seeking to improve living standards for their populations through economic growth are being asked by the wealthier nations to cut their carbon emissions, compromising their attempts at growth. Many developing nations take the view that the extent of the problem has been caused by the wealthier nations' profligacy since the 1920s. Developing nations want to see the developed world take far more responsibility for their actions and have much greater involvement in solving the problem.

Interdependence The 2007–2009 Financial Crisis highlighted the extent to which financial institutions around the world are highly interdependent. The expansion of global credit and the reduction in the barriers to flows of capital across borders mean that, more than ever before, shocks which occur in one country can very quickly affect businesses across the globe and exacerbate the effects of the shock.

In product markets, there are similar problems. Many businesses rely on complex logistics and supply chains, as we have seen, and disruptions to supply chains can have significant consequences for national economies and the global economy.

Inequality and Equity Most economics textbooks would point to the benefits that international trade can bring to individuals and communities. The benefits of trade, however, are not shared equally between all citizens in a country or even between countries. Trade between countries in the northern hemisphere and many countries in the southern hemisphere will tend to favour the wealthier northern countries, while it may be that within countries a relatively small number of people will become ever more wealthy while the majority remain in relative poverty. When the gap between the well-off and the less well-off increases, and where poverty persists, there is unrest and the potential for civil and political turmoil and terrorism. Less well-off people may see that they are not sharing in wealth creation and in some cases see no other option but to resort to violence to advance their cause, or simply to survive. Levels of inequality might also be a driver to the increase in migration that has caused major problems for a number of European countries.

The Wider Implications of Globalization

There are wider social and environmental implications of globalization in addition to those outlined above, not least the potential damage to eco-systems, the increasing use of non-renewable resources and damage to indigenous cultures. Firms are increasingly aware of these potential difficulties, making attempts to demonstrate transparency in their actions and be accountable. Many large firms produce social and environmental accountability reports, which aim to highlight how they are managing their operations to limit the negative effects of their activities on stakeholders.

Cultural and Religious Sensitivities Cultural and religious differences present challenges to businesses trading abroad. There are many examples of different cultural sensitivities which need to be taken into account, such as how to greet people, how the use of colour can have different meanings in different parts of the world, and how certain gestures and body language can be interpreted very differently throughout the world. For example, showing the soles of the feet is considered highly offensive in many Muslim countries. Touching has different interpretations in different parts of the world. Touching the head in parts of Asia is not polite, because the head houses the soul. In Islamic and Hindu cultures, the use of the left hand for social interaction is considered insulting. Having hands in pockets or sitting cross-legged is considered disrespectful in Turkey. Making eye contact is expected in the West and in some Arabic cultures but not in Japan, parts of Africa, the Caribbean and parts of Latin America. For firms doing business in different parts of the world and individuals travelling to conduct business, it is imperative to understand, appreciate and respect local cultures and sensitivities to trade successfully.

Foreign Direct Investment

Globalization has led to an increase in the investments firms make abroad. These investments might include the construction of new plant and equipment abroad, the development of new or expanded production facilities and the acquisition of businesses. This investment leads to funds flowing into the host country and is termed **foreign direct investment (FDI)**. The World Bank defines FDI as: 'Net inflows of investment to acquire a lasting management interest (defined as 10 per cent or more of voting stock) in an enterprise operating in an economy other than that of the investor.' FDI has been made easier because of the opening up of trade borders, the growth in the internet and communications technologies which makes it easier for different regional operations to keep in touch, and by the deregulation of capital markets.

 foreign direct investment (FDI) inflows of investment into a host country from external businesses

The sums of money involved in FDI are difficult to comprehend. The OECD notes that the level of FDI in 2007 was around $2,170 billion ($2.1 trillion), but fell back following the Financial Crisis 2007–2009 and amounted to around $1,600 billion ($1.6 trillion) in 2011. The UK House of Commons reported in 2022 that world flows of inward FDI reached a record high of $2.0 trillion in 2015 but has fallen back since and was significantly affected by the pandemic. Global FDI flows in the first half of 2020, for example, were down by almost a half compared to the first six months of 2019.

Features of FDI The growth in FDI is closely linked to the growth in MNCs and many of the costs and benefits of FDI also mirror the costs and benefits of MNCs. For the investing firms, there are the potential benefits of new markets, new distribution channels, access to new technology, skills and finance, and the potential for lower unit costs. In addition, FDI can help a firm avoid trade barriers, especially given the growth in free trade agreements between countries (trading blocs). There may also be tax benefits, or access to grants and allowances to firms investing in foreign countries. For the host countries, the investments can lead to higher living standards for its citizens, access to new technologies, capital, processes, products and skills, the potential for an expansion in employment and the development of infrastructure to further boost economic growth.

One feature of FDI has been the investment in new technology start-ups. These are often small firms which have grown in a country, in some cases having arisen out of the research and development which takes place at universities. The spin-offs from this research and development can take the form of small businesses set up by the researchers. Firms from abroad then acquire these start-ups or engage in licensing and technology transfer arrangements which allows the start-ups to expand. For larger firms the risk associated with research and development is reduced, as this risk is assumed by these start-ups. The large firm comes in when a lot of the development work has taken place and its resources can be used to build commercially viable production. In some cases, large firms may collaborate with researchers on projects. Changes to rules on intellectual property ownership have meant that researchers in universities who develop new products or processes can issue licence agreements to commercial businesses to further develop the ideas, with some of the funding feeding back into the university. In some countries, the close links between business and higher education institutions are fostered by the development of science and innovation parks constructed in and around university towns and cities. In Cambridge, in the UK, the high-quality research carried out by academics at the University of Cambridge is particularly attractive, and the Cambridge Science Park located on the outskirts of the city is an example of this sort of relationship.

In some cases, two firms in a similar industry may enter into an agreement to use their distribution networks and logistics systems to distribute each other's products. For example, two brewery businesses in different countries may agree to a regional distribution agreement whereby their respective beers are made available in pubs and clubs in both countries. This saves both firms the costs of investment in new distribution networks in the foreign country and utilizes local knowledge, expertise and market access of the host firm. In each case, the firms get access to new markets, but at lower unit costs and with reduced competition.

Joint ventures involve partnerships between firms with different opportunities, markets or skills, allowing the partners to develop new products or exploit new markets. Such ventures are justified by exploiting synergies and economies of scale, reducing average costs and reducing some of the need to spend large sums on research and development. Despite these potential benefits, the success of joint ventures is not strong, with relatively high failure rates recorded.

SELF TEST Using your knowledge of economics, explain why you think that the success of joint ventures is relatively low. (Hint: recall what you have learned about game theory.)

BUSINESS IN EMERGING MARKETS

The economies of the developed world tend to dominate textbooks and the global news media. However, since the turn of the century political and economic changes have meant that increasing focus is now centred on economies in other countries termed 'emerging economies' or 'emerging markets'. An **emerging market economy** is one where the per capita income of the population is in the middle to low range compared to other global economies.

> **emerging market economy** a country where the per capita income of the population is in the middle to low range compared to other global economies

Each country differs in its state of development, but major attention has been focused in recent years on the so-called BRICS countries, Brazil, Russia, India, China and South Africa. These are countries with huge productive potential, due in part to their respective size, population and resource endowment. However, there are a growing number of countries which deserve to be classed in a similar category to these countries in terms of their increasing GDP per capita. These countries include Turkey, Mexico, Malaysia, Taiwan, Hungary, Poland, Czech Republic, Chile, Indonesia, Philippines, Thailand, the United Arab Emirates, Saudi Arabia, Egypt, Colombia, Peru and Morocco.

Characteristics of Emerging Markets

One of the reasons why these countries are categorized in the terms outlined above is because of their state of economic development. It is not just size that matters. The internal economic structures are important. Countries like China, Russia, Saudi Arabia and Poland, for example, have been under different types of political regime which have shaped their economic development since the 1920s. Russia and Poland were former states within the Union of Soviet Socialist Republics (USSR) where a planned market economy determined resource allocation. China was similarly governed by a communist regime, although would claim to be following a different brand of communism. In a planned economy, state planning authorities sought to answer the three basic questions of any economic system: what is to be produced, how is it going to be produced and who gets what is produced?

Many of these countries are changing and making economic reforms. The establishment of institutions and bodies which reflect broader international standards and regulations are being developed. Many of the emerging economies are embracing market reforms, engaging in trade, establishing private property and opening up their economies to outside investment. For these countries to take a growing part in the global economy it is essential that they have institutions and governance which reflect those of the developed world. Why would a business risk investing in setting up operations in these countries if it believed there was not the same or at least similar rules of governance that existed in their home country? It is accepted that there are still, in some cases, major obstacles to the integration of many emerging countries into the global economic system. There are problems with corruption, questions over human rights and issues over corporate governance and the rule of law, particularly in relation to intellectual property. However, it is also recognized that no country can move from being an essentially closed economy to a fully integrated market economy overnight. This is part of the reason why these economies are referred to as emerging.

Many emerging economies will also have specific advantages which their respective governments are recognizing have some economic value. It might be something to do with resource endowment such as the reserves of oil and gas that exist in Russia, discoveries of oil off the Brazilian coast, copper in Zambia and minerals in other parts of Africa. Or it might be something to do with the huge human resources at the disposal of many emerging economies: China and India both have populations in excess of one billion and this provides huge reserves of relatively cheap labour.

Some of the changes which have brought emerging economies into the global business environment have included a greater degree of political stability. Western governments may disagree fundamentally with the political systems in China and Saudi Arabia, for example, but these countries are stable and this provides an incentive for investment by businesses. The development of banking and financial sectors, systems and institutions to settle commercial disputes, having more harmonized business law as well as stock markets, have further helped accelerate investment into emerging economies.

Why are Emerging Markets So Important?

There is a simple answer to this question: opportunity. Businesses in the developed world are finding that many of the 'traditional' markets they are operating in are mature. The opportunities for growth in these markets are limited; growth is likely to occur in some but only at low rates. Take mobile (cell) phones, for example. In the UK, United States, Canada and countries of northern Europe and Scandinavia, penetration into the market is almost total. Virtually every person who wants a phone has now got (at least) one device, and this limits the potential for growth. Opportunities exist if new more sophisticated models are brought out, but unless they do something very different the incentive for an individual to give up their existing phone and buy a new one is limited.

However, in a country like Vietnam, for example, phone ownership has been growing at a rapid rate. Its 97.4 million people, therefore, represent a huge market for mobile phone manufacturers and service operators. This is a crucial reason for firms seeking to do business in emerging markets: there are billions of potential customers. Equally important, many of these people are becoming wealthier and entering the middle classes where spending on the sort of consumer goods which could be classed as luxuries is likely to rise dramatically in the next few decades.

The links between the increasing development of these economies and the rise in wages of workers in the countries has not been lost on businesses in the developed world. As they continue to industrialize and expand, workers will add more value, get paid more and will have more disposable income. The process may not be rapid, but businesses must look ahead to the next couple of decades for sustained revenue and sales growth rather than just the next few short years.

It is not only businesses selling consumer goods that see the opportunities for securing new markets and growth in sales. Business-to-business (B2B) operations are also recognizing that part of the continued development of emerging economies rests on improved infrastructure. Investment in energy supplies, telecommunications, internet supplies, construction plant, distribution networks, road and transport networks, and water and sewerage systems are all vital to the continued growth of emerging economies, and firms in the developed world have looked to invest heavily in such opportunities.

Firms that see and seize first mover opportunities may find that there are numerous problems in setting up and doing business in emerging economies, but despite these challenges, if they are in a position to become established, the medium and longer-term benefits in terms of growth opportunities can be extensive. Mistakes will be made, but the experience they gain and the scale opportunities that exist mean most want to be involved sooner rather than later for fear of missing the chances that exist.

Problems Facing Business in Emerging Markets

The opportunities for future growth may be large, but there are many challenges. One of the biggest is the fact that businesses need to understand the markets they are getting into. Typical of the early forays into emerging markets have been attempts to replicate successful business models in Western developed market economies.

Many businesses have found that this replication model has not worked and that major changes are needed to the way in which the business operates in these countries. Part of the reason may be the different political, cultural and religious systems and norms in place in some emerging economies. Another reason may be that assumptions about the markets and consumers within that market are flawed. Selling hi-tech gadgets in a country where there are very few people who own these may present a huge potential opportunity. This opportunity may only exist if there are enough people who are wealthy enough to have the disposable income to be able to afford (and want) these gadgets along with the infrastructure that is necessary. It may be that other products are deemed more important or valuable to these consumers. The way consumers in developed economies see the products may not be the same as those in emerging economies. The needs of customers in these markets may not be the same as those in developed economies, and so the business may find that its model is fundamentally flawed.

This sort of problem was discussed by C.K. Prahalad, the noted management thinker who died in 2010. In his book, *The Fortune at the Bottom of the Pyramid: Eradicating Poverty Through Profits* (2004), Prahalad sought to show how poverty could be tackled by focusing products on the world's least wealthy people, around five billion of them. Not only could firms make a real difference to those on the lowest incomes in the world, but they could also secure new profits and growth in the process. The key questions businesses need to ask in this regard are whether a market exists, and if it does what sort of scale is it? Does the market and the scale enable profits to be made? If the answers to these questions are 'Yes', then there are opportunities to be exploited. This means that firms can look at generating revenue from people who may only be earning very small incomes. One example is the market for shampoo. Do consumers in emerging markets want to buy shampoo in the same way as those in the Netherlands, for example? Prahalad suggested that these consumers may have a lot in common, not least their desire to purchase well-respected branded items. However, while consumers in the Netherlands may want to purchase their shampoo in 500 ml bottles for around €5, for some consumers in India this may represent a week's wages. The solution might be to supply the same product in single serve sachets so that the shampoo market in India (which in terms of size is potentially as large as in the United States) can be served.

SELF TEST Does the conflict in Ukraine suggest that businesses need to be cautious about doing business in emerging economies like Russia?

Business Strategies in Emerging Markets

There are a number of different but often complementary strategies that have been identified for conducting business in emerging markets.

Hit and Run Strategies Firms might enter a market with the intention of 'creaming off' the value from the market and then getting out. They sell their products to those that can afford them, take the profits and then leave the market. The advantage is a boost to short-term profits, but the disadvantage is that long-term growth prospects and business relationships are sacrificed. These relationships may be more profitable in the long run.

Enclave Strategies This is often associated with firms doing business in emerging economies exploiting natural resources. The intention is to set up operations which do not depend on local supply networks, and where local businesses and people have minimal involvement in the operation. This may be because the firm believes the local business environment is less efficient and reliable, but might also be because of concerns over security. Firms may engage with the local military to help provide that security. One of the problems of this is that such involvement can raise ethical questions about how the firm operates and the extent to which the payment to the local military is transparent. In addition, it can also attract attention to the business, especially in more politically volatile areas where local conflicts and terrorism might be problematic. It also alienates the firm from local stakeholders.

Learn to Earn Committing to investing in emerging markets for the long term may involve the firm having to accept that in the short run profits will be slim, or non-existent. By being involved in the economy, however, the firm will learn, and as it does it develops longer-term relationships and a better understanding of the market. In the long term, it is hoped that this improved understanding and experience will lead to higher and more consistent profits.

Outsourcing

The existence of emerging economies with large labour resources which often have high literacy levels but low wage costs has encouraged a number of companies to look to move parts of their operations to these countries. The contracting out of a part of the business's operations to another organization is referred to as **outsourcing**. While the focus has been on outsourcing labour operations to low wage economies, outsourcing also refers to any operation. This might include accountancy activities, IT, various human resources activities such as payroll management, recruitment and training. Outsourcing does not have to mean the operation goes abroad. Many businesses will outsource operations to other organizations within their own country.

 outsourcing contracting out of a part of the business's operations to another organization

The main reason for outsourcing is to reduce costs and improve efficiency. Taking advantage of the expertise of other organizations that may specialize in particular operations is a major factor in decision making. By outsourcing production and obtaining supplies from low-cost manufacturers, companies can focus their attention on their core competencies: the key strengths that they have. This leads to a more efficient operation while allowing the business to benefit from economies of scale.

The benefit to the consumer is that they get good quality products, and more of them, at lower prices. The clothing industry is an excellent example of where these changes have been happening. Primark is one business that has adopted this business model. Owned by Associated British Foods, Primark has placed itself as a 'value retailer' offering low-priced but good quality clothing, and along with other value retailers like Matalan they now account for around a quarter of total fashion spending in the UK.

The benefits of outsourcing must be weighed against the possible disadvantages. There are costs associated with outsourcing, not least of which is the setting up of the agreement with the contractor, but also the cost of closing down operations which the outsourced activity is replacing. Outsourcing call centre operations, for example, has led to domestic workers losing their jobs to outsourced operations in countries like India, where labour costs are significantly lower. The ethics of the decision to outsource have been questioned and the effect on the firm's reputation must be considered.

Some firms have found that the expected benefits have not been as large as they anticipated. There are complex issues that have arisen which may not have been foreseen. Customers, for example, have complained about the service they are receiving from outsourced services. Outsourced workers may not have the 'local' knowledge and understanding necessary to meet customer needs. Training of outsourced workers has also been a problem for some firms, which has led companies like Newcastle Building Society and Lloyds TSB to move some operations back to the UK. In other cases, firms in financial services have found that security is an issue. Handling and protecting customer data is an important part of the business of financial services, and something which is highly regulated.

There are also problems associated with how some outsourced operations do business. The development of social networking sites and the ease with which individuals can post information and videos onto the internet have meant that firms are acutely aware of the damage to their reputation from stories about abuse of workers in outsourced operations. A number of firms have attempted to counter stories that workers in plants in China are working long hours for low wages. A series of apparent suicides in a factory in Shenzhen in China, which makes products for Apple, Nokia, Dell, Sony and Nintendo, were linked to the stresses imposed as a result of the conditions for workers. These types of companies have a main demographic of young, socially aware individuals. When reports such as these filter through, the company must draw a balance between the benefits of the low cost of using outsourced manufacture and the potential for the image of the company to be damaged. Similar reports have been released about worker abuse in clothing factories supplying big name Western retailers, which can be equally as damaging. The speed with which many of these firms react to the claims is perhaps testament to the potential for damage to the firm.

CASE STUDY   Problems in Emerging Markets

Emerging markets have been seen as being important engines of global economic growth. However, a number of the countries classed as emerging markets have experienced considerable challenges in recent years. Russia's participation in the global economy has been affected by the sanctions that a number of countries have imposed following the country's military operations in Ukraine. China had been seeking to implement a zero Covid policy which had resulted in supply disruptions as areas and regions were in lockdown. The government relaxed restrictions in the latter part of 2022 but this did result in an increase in the number of cases of Covid-19 being reported. Brazil faced political instability that resulted in the election of a more socialist-leaning government facing challenges around combatting inflation. India's economy was badly affected by the pandemic and, in 2022, the country also faced challenges around its agriculture industry as a lack of rain hit output. South Africa's economy was hit by the restrictions on tourism, internal political disagreement and challenges to energy supplies which led to 'load-shedding', the cutting of energy supplies to try to manage overall capacity. This not only disrupts production but also affects business confidence and potential inward investment.

Emerging markets still face considerable challenges but may yet prove to the economic stars of the future.

Questions

1 **One of the problems for the global economy of Russia's actions in Ukraine was the disruption to energy supplies. How does this illustrate how reliance on emerging markets can be problematic?**
2 **Comment on the issues faced by China, Brazil and South Africa outlined in the case study and how these problems might influence the extent of investment decisions from firms in developed countries.**
3 **Do the problems outlined in the case study suggest that the optimism surrounding emerging markets is misplaced?**

Reference: www.investopedia.com/emerging-markets-rebound-2023-6835105 (accessed 9 June 2023).

INDUSTRY 4.0

Industry 4.0 (I4.0) refers to the developments in technology that result in a significant increase in the degree of connectedness with the digital world. Machines and computers are becoming more and more connected and this is resulting in what has been termed the fourth industrial revolution. The key features of I4.0 include artificial intelligence, the industrial internet of things (IIoT), machine learning, big data, autonomous robots, augmented reality, digital twins and blockchain, among other developments.

These 'cyber-physical systems' provide major opportunities for businesses to improve the efficiency of all aspects of their operations throughout the supply chain. This also includes opportunities for understanding customers, their needs and behaviour more effectively. The technologies mean that machines, equipment and devices are all interconnected far more and able to share information. This means that an increasing number of processes can be automated; raw materials, inputs, inventory and goods can be tracked through the supply chain; maintenance schedules can be automated; and problems and breakdowns can be identified before they occur. Payments can be tracked far more accurately and the analysis of the huge amounts of data that are produced through cyber-physical systems can be used to identify hidden patterns that can improve clarity and understanding of businesses processes and behaviour.

I4.0 in many respects represents a natural development from advances in computer technologies since the 1970s. There are few businesses these days that do not make some use of computer technology in some way or another, even if they sometimes may not realize it! Through the digitization of information many firms have been able to change their business model, and new firms have taken advantage of digitization to create new business opportunities. Many of the social networks that so many people now use and rely on could reasonably be included in the process of digitization.

Features of Industry 4.0

What follows is a brief introduction to some of the core elements of I4.0. It must be remembered that the topic is vast and ever changing but what follows gives a flavour of the subject area.

The Industrial Internet of Things The IIoT consists of physical things, including people, that can be connected to the internet, and data shared between these things to improve communication, understanding, decision making, choices, managing processes and even daily life. On a simple level, some domestic fridges can be connected to the internet and help the householder manage the stock in their fridge. Usage of products from the fridge can trigger orders from retailers to ensure that the household does not run out of those products. The IIoT is also bringing massive change to the agricultural sector. Farmers can utilize sensors in and around their fields that communicate with onboard computers in tractors and can help in the management of depth of tilling of the soil, seed sowing, harvesting information, irrigation and many other elements of the growing and harvesting process.

Augmented Reality Augmented reality gives people a means of experiencing the physical world through different sensory means. One example is the developments in GPS technology which allow people to not only see a map of where they are going on their car display screens but to actually see a visual representation of the area they are travelling in, rather than just a map with routes, road names, junctions and so on. The driver sees a 3D visual representation of where they are driving, along with the directions they are advised to use to get to their destination. The addition of this technology to vehicles allows a firm to add value and to make the car not only safer but a more attractive purchasing option, thus improving its value proposition. This technology can be applied to a wide range of manufacturing applications helping users to (for example) identify where faults may lie in equipment and helping pinpoint problems more quickly and efficiently.

Big Data Many computer systems are capable of collecting and generating massive amounts of data. Big data refers to the analysis of these data to find patterns, trends and other useful information which firms can then use to their advantage in some way. It might manifest itself in completely different ways of understanding customer behaviour and tailoring offers and advertising to customers, but it can also be utilized in manufacturing to help improve processes and systems, reduce costs and increase efficiencies. Big data has a major role to play in supply chains, helping to improve the efficiency and speed with which firms are able to get goods and services to their customers.

Artificial Intelligence and Machine Learning The digital connectedness that characterizes much of I4.0 also provides the opportunity for technologies to work together and for machines to process information and learn from that information. In doing so, machines can then put this new learning into action to provide more functionality, improve processes and make decisions. In effect, machines can emulate some elements of human intelligence and do tasks that humans do. Many people experience artificial intelligence (AI) in the home through the use of smart speakers and other devices, including 'smart assistants' like Apple's Siri, Amazon's Alexa, Microsoft's Cortana and Google's Assistant. Firms are using AI as a means of communicating with customers more effectively. Chatbots, for example, can be used to engage with consumers answering simple questions 24/7. In industry more broadly, AI is increasingly being used for predictive analytics, which can help to reduce equipment and machine malfunctions or breakdowns, improve performance and assist in maintenance and repair, forecasting and scheduling, and workforce training.

> **SELF TEST** Think about the way businesses contact you through social media, much of which is done through analysis of big data and artificial intelligence. Is this a benefit to consumers or an invasion of privacy?

Blockchain Blockchain is a form of database which differs from standard databases in that it stores information in blocks that are linked. Firms are increasingly using blockchain technology as a means of facilitating and recording transactions. Because the transactions are recorded on a network of computers throughout the world and not just on a firm's own computer network, the risks associated with network breakdown, downtime, human error or interference and so on are reduced and so represents a safer way of recording and storing data. Each transaction is processed and stored as blocks and then linked together. This provides a record of all transactions, which are viewable but not editable. These transactions can be financial, relate to legal documentation or inventory, or occur in the energy industry, where those who have surplus energy can feed it into the grid and those who need energy can purchase it. They can also be in the housing market, where rental and property purchase transactions can be made via blockchain technology, and in advertising, where customer targeting can be more focused and effective.

The Implications of Industry 4.0

As noted we have only been able to provide a very brief overview of I4.0. Many of the technological developments that can be classed as being part of I4.0 are not necessarily new. AI, for example, has been worked on for many years (Alan Turing was one of the early proponents of AI through his work on code breaking during World War II), but the way in which these technologies are now being applied to a wide range of industries is truly revolutionizing the way in which these technologies can influence productivity and efficiency and generate new and more effective products and services. To this extent, I4.0 will no doubt spawn winners and losers. The winners will be those that adapt and adopt the technologies quickly and effectively. The losers will see their existing business models become redundant. Firms will have to think carefully about hiring staff, about the skills they need, about training and development of staff, and about the purpose and function of their business. I4.0 offers tremendous opportunities but also challenges. One major challenge is ensuring the security of these connected systems and so cyber security is set to be a growth area in the future.

Cybercrime and Cyber Security

The developments in technology bring significant benefits to both businesses and consumers. However, as with many technological developments there are always those that seek to exploit them for illicit purposes. Many businesses have to be aware of, and put systems in place to combat, cybercrime. Cybercrime refers to criminal activity which targets computers or computer systems and networks in some way. The criminal typically seeks to gain some financial benefit from their actions, or access information which will allow them to financially benefit, or to use information for other reasons, for example for political purposes.

Typical examples of cybercrime include email and internet fraud such as phishing, identity theft, the theft and sale of sensitive corporate data, money laundering, ransom and malware attacks, cryptojacking and distributed denial of service attacks (DDoS), among many others. Some estimates put the cost of cybercrime at around €1.79 million per minute! *Cybercrime* magazine reported in 2020 that cybercrime was set to increase by around 15 per cent a year and reach €9.8 trillion by 2025. This value not only includes the cost of the theft of personal and corporate data but losses in productivity, theft of intellectual property, disruption to business activity, the cost of restoring systems affected by cybercrime, and the reputational damage that can be caused.

By its very nature, the costs of cybercrime are likely to be underestimated, but clearly they are significant and organizations have to find ways to protect themselves from cyber threats. One key way is to provide training for staff to help them work more securely and to make employees aware of the potential threats that exist. IT functions will have various systems in place to improve the security of data, software patches and updates, two-factor authentication systems and digital forensic tools. However, these can be compromised if staff ultimately do not take care over how they process digital information. Seeking to understand how cybercriminals operate is vital to helping develop more effective defences. Firms must try to keep one step ahead of the criminals, which is not easy. Isolation is an example of how some firms are seeking to develop such understanding. Here, the attack, for example a malware, ransomware, or spyware attack, is moved to an area on a firm's system where it can do no harm and is then analyzed to learn information about it to help develop more sophisticated and effective defences.

CORPORATE GOVERNANCE

Any organization is, at its heart, a collection of people. Some of these people are workers, some are managers or supervisors, some are leaders, some are owners or shareholders. The fact that organizations bring together groups of people from disparate backgrounds for the purpose of carrying out business activity means that ways of effectively supervising the activities of all these people are essential. This is the purpose of corporate governance. It looks at how organizations oversee their operations to ensure they comply with legal, regulatory, and moral and ethical obligations to meet the interests of all stakeholders. It involves analysing the business to identify and manage potential risks, ensure that activities comply with legal requirements, adhere to codes of conduct and codes of practice, and demonstrate the competence of those in charge and of decision makers to act appropriately, in part, to maintain the organization's integrity.

Legislation and Regulation of Corporate Governance

Corporate governance could be left to the discretion of individual businesses but there are also regulations and legislation in place to set standards for appropriate governance. In the UK, for example, the Financial Reporting Council (FRC) acts as an independent regulator for auditors, accountants and actuaries. It also sets UK corporate governance and stewardship codes. The FRC notes that its work is targeted at investors and those who use financial reports. Legislation covers the legal requirements for running a business and making decisions and the consequences of inappropriate or illegal decision making. Many countries have passed legislation covering bribery and corruption, and modern slavery and forced labour practices. In the UK, the main legislation relating to company behaviour are the Companies Act 2006, The Bribery Act 2010 and The Modern Slavery Act 2015.

The UK Corporate Governance Code covers such issues as the responsibilities of the board of directors and how they set the values and strategy of the business. How the board of directors is made up is also covered. There is an expectation that the board will include people with appropriate skills and competencies. How directors are appointed, policies around their remuneration and the transparency of reporting their remuneration, how the voices of employees are heard at board level, and policies to reflect commitment to diversity and inclusion are also covered.

Legislation around bribery and corruption includes requirements to have a clear anti-bribery policy, how staff are trained in understanding the issues around bribery, having an appropriate policy around whistleblowing, and clear guidance around policies associated with hospitality and gifts. Modern slavery legislation requires companies to publish annual statements about how they have sought to tackle and prevent slavery and forced labour practices in their supply chains. In the UK, the legislation applies to companies with an annual turnover above £36 million.

JEOPARDY PROBLEM An online retailer of clothing is subject to a report published in social media that notes that three of its manufacturing suppliers employ children under the age of 12 and that there is evidence of sexual favours being demanded by managers from both women and men working in one of the factories. The suppliers are critical to the business model of the retailer. What should the retailer do?

SUMMARY

- Globalization refers to the growth in interdependence between world economies. Internationalization is the increase in the way in which organizations produce goods and services which are intended for use in many different countries.

- The main reasons for the development of globalization are the reduced cost of transport and logistics, increased capital mobility, the expansion of global credit markets, the collapse of the Soviet Union and growth of emerging markets, and the growth of multinationals.

- There are a number of benefits of globalization including wider choice and lower prices, increases in shareholder value, and inward investment, but these have to be balanced against the costs. These costs include widening inequality, the power of multinationals, standardization, the impact on the climate and the environment, and interdependence.

- Foreign direct investment can lead to benefits to countries receiving such investment but there can also be costs and limitations to FDI.

- There are a number of countries classed as emerging markets that are likely to play an increasingly important part in global economic development in the few decades.

- Firms from developed countries looking to invest in emerging markets face a number of challenges and the countries themselves can also suffer negative consequences.

- Industry 4.0, or the fourth industrial revolution, is having an increasing influence on the way businesses operate and behave. The technologies can provide significant benefits to both firms and consumers, but as technology develops and businesses become more reliant on it, the problems of cyber security become more prevalent.

- A number of countries have introduced regulations and legislation to improve corporate governance to ensure that businesses act in the interests of wider stakeholders and have both the skills and competencies to carry out business effectively and fairly.

IN THE NEWS

Crypto Collapse

At the beginning of 2022, FTX, a cryptocurrency exchange run by Sam Bankman-Fried, was valued at around €30 billion. The exchange facilitated the buying and trading of cryptocurrencies. Mr Bankman-Fried set up FTX when he was 28 and rapidly became an important player in the cryptocurrency market with around one million users by 2021. It was reported that Mr Bankman-Fried's personal wealth was valued at around €15 billion. However, in November, a news site dedicated to cryptocurrencies called CoinDesk published an article which raised questions about the integrity of FTX. The article noted that another of Mr Bankman-Fried's financial trading companies, Alameda Research, had a large number of assets made up of a cryptocurrency called FTT which had been developed by FTX. This raised questions that there could be conflicts of interest between FTX and FTT with the potential for the value of FTT to be artificially inflated. There were also other reports circulating that Alameda Research was using customer funds from FTX as loans to facilitate trades. The reports led to investors seeking to withdraw their funds. The scale of the withdrawal led to FTX becoming insolvent in only a few days with large numbers of investors owed millions. Mr Bankman-Fried expressed his surprise at the speed at which the situation developed and also his sorrow at the events and his determination to rectify the situation. However, he was arrested in December 2022 over accusations of fraud. Later reports suggested a catalogue of potentially damaging issues at the company. In addition to the accusations of fraud, there were accusations that Mr Bankman-Fried had overseen 'greenwashing' and there were reports of 'unauthorized transactions' within FTX.

(Continued)

Confidence in cryptocurrencies can be badly affected by events such as the collapse of FTX.

A review of the problems raised by the collapse of FTX by global credit rating agency AM Best noted that FTX suffered from 'poor strategic decision-making associated with weak corporate governance' and that FTX 'suffered from a concentration of power in the hands of a single individual, combined with a lack of experience amongst its senior management team. A lack of transparency with external parties in terms of financial reporting or making misleading public statements is a powerful indicator of poor corporate governance and can precede a substantial decline in a company's financial strength.'

Questions

1 'Developments in technology such as the rise of cryptocurrencies have been made more likely as a result of globalization.' To what extent do you agree with this statement?

2 Businesses such as FTX rely on forensic analysis of big data generated by digital networks. How does the story of FTX illustrate the potential advantages and disadvantages of this type of technology?

3 One of the accusations against FTX was around 'unauthorized transactions' amounting to some €450 million. What does this suggest about the effectiveness of legislation and regulation in improving corporate governance?

4 Mr Bankman-Fried has been reported as suggesting he could set up another company which could help to pay back creditors who lost money in FTX. Do you think he should be allowed to do so? Justify your reasoning.

5 Look at the quote provided in the article and comment on why corporate governance is seen as being such an important aspect in business behaviour.

References: www.businesswire.com/news/home/20221205005680/en/Best%E2%80%99s-Commentary-Corporate-Governance-Lessons-for-Insurers-in-the-Wake-of-the-Failure-of-FTX (accessed 9 June 2023).
www.theverge.com/2022/11/30/23484331/ftx-explained-cryptocurrency-sbf-sam-bankman-fried (accessed 9 June 2023).

QUESTIONS FOR REVIEW

1 Explain the difference between globalization and internationalization.

2 Outline the main causes of globalization.

3 Describe two benefits and two costs of globalization.

4 Explain why foreign direct investment can be an important factor in developing economies achieving economic growth.

5 What are the main characteristics of a country classed as an emerging market economy?

6 Describe two reasons why emerging markets are important and two challenges that businesses face in entering emerging markets.

7 Using appropriate examples, describe two possible business strategies in emerging markets.

8 What is meant by the term 'Industry 4.0' and why is this movement important?

9 Why is cybercrime a concern for businesses?

10 Explain the reasons why many countries have developed laws and regulations around corporate governance.

PROBLEMS AND APPLICATIONS

1 In the UK, a decision has been made to go ahead with the construction of a high-speed railway called HS2 that will link London and the North West of England. The project has been controversial. Explain why this sort of investment might be important in helping firms in the UK to take advantage of globalization.

2 The Covid-19 pandemic forced many businesses to rethink their business models. Prior to the pandemic, a number of European countries (and the United States) were subject to so-called populist influences which centred on national economies rather than on the global economy. These influences have led some to argue that the world is entering a period of reverse globalization. Do you think that this might be a temporary trend or something more permanent?

3 Do some research to assess the accuracy of the statement that globalization has resulted in an increase in global inequality.

4 The political regimes in countries like China, Russia and Saudi Arabia are very different from those in many Western countries. Does this fact limit the potential benefits of the growth of emerging markets for businesses?

5 A firm has a degree of monopoly power in an emerging economy where it was a first mover. As economic growth gathers pace in the emerging economy, the firm decides to increase its prices to generate additional profits. Over a period of five years, it sees a large increase in the number of firms entering its market. The increase in supply drove down profits and after a further five years, the firm finds it is once again one of the dominant suppliers in the market. How does this scenario highlight the advantages and disadvantages of business strategies in emerging markets?

6 A firm closes its call centre operation in Belgium with the loss of 1,000 jobs, which has a significant impact on the local economy where the call centre was located. It outsources the operation to Malaysia and its press release says that it will reduce costs as a result by €1 million a year. After the first six months, the firm begins to receive complaints from customers that they are not happy with the level of service they receive from the new call centre operation. What should the firm do in this situation? (Hint: you might want to consider as part of your answer why customers use the call centre in the first place.)

7 One of the industries that is benefiting from the application of Industry 4.0 technologies is agriculture. Do some research on the use of either drones in farming or the idea of vertical farming. Comment on the potential costs and benefits of this type of technology.

8 If the value of cybercrime is such that it would rank in the top five global economies, are businesses powerless to prevent cybercrime growing further? Justify your reasoning.

9 Does the fact that countries must pass legislation and set up regulations and codes of practice prove that companies cannot be trusted to implement sound corporate governance?

10 In order to be able to get permission to obtain a licence to do business in an emerging economy, senior managers have been left in no doubt that a private payment to local administrative officials will be necessary. The opportunity to do business in this country is seen as being essential to the survival of the business in the medium term and to the security of 2,000 jobs in the home country. How should the senior managers handle this situation? Explain your answer.

25 BUSINESS AND EUROPE

LEARNING OUTCOMES

After reading this chapter you should be able to:

- Explain the key features of a currency area and a single market.
- Explain and illustrate with diagrams the macroeconomic effects of asymmetric shocks in a common currency area, wherein exchange rate adjustment is not possible.
- Explain and illustrate with diagrams how fiscal policy could be used for macroeconomic stabilization in the absence of exchange rate adjustment and independent monetary policy.
- Outline the key issues arising as a result of the decision by the UK to leave the EU.

THE SINGLE EUROPEAN MARKET AND THE EURO

Following the devastation of two world wars in the first half of the twentieth century, each of which had initially centred on European conflicts, some of the major European countries (in particular France and Germany) expressed a desire to make further wars impossible between them through a process of strong economic integration that, it was hoped, would lead to greater social and political harmony. This led to the development of the European Economic Community (EEC), now referred to as the European Union, or EU. The official website of the European Union defines the EU as 'a family of democratic European countries, committed to working together for peace and prosperity'.

Initially the EU consisted of just six countries: Belgium, Germany, France, Italy, Luxembourg and the Netherlands. In 1973, Denmark, Ireland and the UK joined. Greece joined in 1981, Spain and Portugal in 1986, and Austria, Finland and Sweden in 1995. In 2004 the biggest ever enlargement took place with ten new countries joining. Croatia became a member in 2013 and by June 2023 there were eight 'candidate countries' on the road to membership. These countries are Albania, Bosnia and Herzegovina, Moldova, Montenegro, the Republic of North Macedonia, Serbia, Turkey and Ukraine. Kosovo is classed as a 'potential candidate' and Georgia also applied for EU membership in March 2022. In June 2016, the UK held a referendum in which its people voted to begin the process of leaving the EU and the UK's withdrawal from the EU was formally completed in January 2020.

The EU has certainly been successful in its original central aim of ensuring European peace: countries such as France, Germany, Italy and Spain, who have been at war with each other on and off for centuries, now work together for mutual benefit. This has led to greater emphasis being given to the EU's second objective, prosperity. To this end, a desire became to create a **Single European Market (SEM)** throughout which labour, capital, goods and services could move freely. As member states removed obstacles to trade between themselves, it was argued, companies would start to enjoy economies of scale as they expanded their markets across Europe. At the same time, inefficient firms would be exposed to more cross-border competition, either forcing them out of business or forcing them to improve their efficiency. The aim was to provide businesses with an environment of fair competition in which economies of scale could be reaped and a strong consumer base developed from which they could expand into global markets. Households, on the other hand, would benefit from lower prices, greater choice of goods and services, and work opportunities across a wide area, while the economy in general would benefit from the enhanced economic growth that would result.

> **Single European Market (SEM)** a (still not complete) EU-wide market throughout which labour, capital, goods and services can move freely

Early steps towards the creation of the SEM included the abolition of internal EU tariff and quota barriers in 1968, and a movement towards greater harmonization in areas such as indirect taxation, industrial regulation and, in common EU-wide policies, towards agriculture and fisheries.

Nevertheless, it proved difficult to make progress on the more intangible barriers to free movement of goods, services, capital and labour. For example, even though internal tariffs and quotas had been abolished in the EU, local tax systems and technical regulations on goods and services still differed from country to country so that it was, in practice, often difficult to export from one country to another. A qualified engineer might find that their qualifications, obtained in Italy, were not recognized in Germany. The result was that during the 1970s and early 1980s, growth in the EU member states began to lag seriously behind that of international competitors, especially the United States and Japan. Therefore, in 1985 a discussion document (in the jargon, a 'White Paper') was produced by the European Commission that subsequently led to a European Act of Parliament, the 1986 Single European Act. This identified some 300 measures that would have to be addressed in order to complete the SEM and set 31 December 1992 as the deadline for completion. The creation of the SEM was to be brought about by EU Directives telling the governments of member states what changes needed to be put into effect to achieve four goals:

- The free movement of goods, services, labour and capital between EU member states.
- The approximation of relevant laws, regulations and administrative provisions between member states.
- A common, EU-wide competition policy, administered by the European Commission.
- A system of common external tariffs implemented against countries who were not members of the EU.

But today, more than 37 years since the Single European Act, the SEM is still far from complete. In particular, there still exist strong differences in national fiscal systems, while academic and professional qualifications are not easily transferable and labour mobility across EU countries is generally low. Some of the reasons for this are hard to overcome: language barriers and relative levels of economic development hamper the movement of factors, and member states continue to compete with one another economically, at times seeking their own national interests rather than the greater good of the EU.

Nevertheless, the years between 1985 and 1992 did see some important steps in the development of the SEM and the resulting achievements of the SEM project were not negligible: the European Commission estimates that the SEM helped create 2.5 million new jobs and generated €800 billion in additional wealth in the ten years or so following 1993.

In the context of the SEM project, the creation of a single European currency was seen as a final step towards 'completing the market', by which was meant two things: (a) getting rid of the transaction costs from intra-EU trade that result from different national currencies (and which act much as a tariff); and (b) removing the uncertainty and swings in national competitiveness among members that result from exchange rate movements. Before European Economic and Monetary Union (EMU), most EU countries participated in the Exchange Rate Mechanism (ERM), a system designed to limit the variability of exchange rates between members' currencies. However, the ERM turned out not to be a viable way of reducing volatility in exchange rates and, in any case, had no effect on the transaction costs arising from bank charges associated with changing currencies when engaging in intra-EU trade.

COMMON CURRENCY AREAS AND EUROPEAN MONETARY UNION

During the 1990s, a number of European nations decided to give up their national currencies and use a new, common currency called the *euro*.

A **common currency area** is a geographical area throughout which a single currency circulates as the medium of exchange. Another term for a common currency area is a *currency union*, and a closely related phenomenon is a *monetary union*: a monetary union is, strictly speaking, a group of countries that have adopted permanently and irrevocably fixed exchange rates among their various currencies. Nevertheless, the terms common currency area, currency union and monetary union are often used more or less interchangeably, and in this chapter, we will follow this practice.

> **common currency area (or currency union or monetary union)** a geographical area throughout which a single currency circulates as the medium of exchange

Usually we speak of common currency areas when the people of a number of economies, generally corresponding to different nation states, have taken a decision to adopt a common currency as their medium of exchange, as was the case with the euro.

The Euro

All member states of the EU are part of **European Economic and Monetary Union (EMU)**. Note that 'EMU' stands for 'Economic and Monetary Union', not European Monetary Union, as is often supposed. As of June 2023, 20 of the 27 member states had agreed to replace their national currencies with the euro. The countries that form the Euro Area or Eurozone are Austria, Belgium, Croatia, Cyprus, Estonia, Finland, France, Germany, Greece, Ireland, Italy, Latvia, Lithuania, Luxembourg, Malta, the Netherlands, Portugal, Slovenia, Slovakia and Spain. The move towards a single European currency has a very long history, but we can set out the main landmarks in its formation, starting in 1992 with the Maastricht Treaty (formally known as the Treaty on European Union), which laid down, among other things, various criteria for being eligible to join the proposed currency union. To participate in the new currency, member states had to meet strict criteria such as a government budget deficit of less than 3 per cent of GDP, a government debt to GDP ratio of less than 60 per cent, combined with low inflation and interest rates close to the EU average. The Maastricht Treaty also laid down a timetable for the introduction of the new single currency and rules concerning the setting up of a European Central Bank (ECB). The ECB came into existence in June 1998 and forms, together with the national central banks of the countries making up the common currency area, the European System of Central Banks (ESCB), which is given responsibility for ensuring price stability and implementing the single European monetary policy.

> **European Economic and Monetary Union (EMU)** the European currency union that has adopted the euro as its common currency

The single European currency (the euro) officially came into existence on 1 January 1999 when 12 countries adopted it (although Greece did not join the EMU until 1 January 2001). On this date, exchange rates between the old national currencies of Euro Area countries were irrevocably locked, and a few days later the financial markets began to trade the euro against other currencies such as the US dollar, as well as to trade securities denominated in euros.

The period from the beginning of 1999 until the beginning of 2002 was a transitional phase, with national currencies still circulating within the Euro Area countries and prices in shops displayed in both euros and local currency. On 1 January 2002, the first euro notes and coins came into circulation and within a few months the switch to the euro as the single medium of exchange was complete throughout the Euro Area. The launch of the euro also saw monetary policy become the responsibility of the independent ECB.

 WHAT IF... a country joins a single currency but is at a different stage in the business cycle to other countries in the single currency area. Is it still possible for the country to successfully embrace the single currency?

Benefits of a Single Currency

Elimination of Transaction Costs One obvious and direct benefit of a common currency is that it makes trade easier between members and, in particular, there is a reduction in the transaction costs involved in trade between members of the common currency area. When a German company imports French wine, it no longer pays a charge to a bank for converting German marks into French francs with which to pay the wine producer; it can just pay in euros. Of course, the banking sector loses out on the commission it used to charge for converting currencies, but this does not affect the fact that the reduction in transaction costs is a net gain. This is because paying a cost to convert currencies is in fact a deadweight loss in the sense that companies pay the transaction cost but get nothing tangible in return.

Reduction in Price Discrimination It is sometimes argued that a second, albeit indirect, gain to the members of a common currency area results from the reduction in price discrimination that should ensue when there is a single currency. If goods are priced in a single currency it should be much harder to disguise price differences across countries. This argument assumes that the transparency in prices that results from a common currency will lead to arbitrage in goods across the common currency area: people will buy goods where they are cheaper (tending to raise their price in that location) and reduce their demand for goods where they are more expensive (tending to reduce the price in that location).

Overall, however, EMU seems unlikely to bring an end to price discrimination across Euro Area countries. For items like groceries, having a single currency is unlikely to be much of an impetus to price convergence across the common currency area because of the large transaction costs (mainly related to travelling) involved in arbitraging, relative to the prices of the goods themselves.

Reduction in Foreign Exchange Rate Variability A third argument relates to the reduction in exchange rate variability and the consequent reduction in uncertainty that results from having a single currency. Exchange rates can fluctuate substantially on a day-to-day basis. Before EMU, when a German supermarket imported wine from France to be delivered, say, three months later, it had to worry about how much a French franc would be worth in terms of German marks in three months' time and therefore what the total cost of the wine would be in marks. This uncertainty might deter the supermarket company from importing wine at all, and instead lead them to concentrate on selling German wines, thereby foregoing gains from trade and reducing economic welfare. The supermarket could have eliminated the uncertainty by getting a bank to agree to sell the francs at an agreed rate against marks to be delivered three months later (an example of a forward foreign exchange contract). The bank would charge for this service, and this charge would be equivalent to a tariff on the imported wine and so would represent a deadweight loss to society.

The reduction in uncertainty arising from the removal of exchange rate fluctuations may also affect investment in the economy. This would clearly be the case for companies that export a large amount of their output to other Euro Area countries, since less uncertainty concerning the receipts from their exports means that they are able to plan for the future with less risk, so that investment projects such as building new factories appear less risky. An increase in investment will benefit the whole economy because it is likely to lead to higher economic growth.

Costs of a Single Currency

The major cost to an economy in joining a common currency area relates to the fact that it gives up its national currency and thereby relinquishes its freedom to set its own monetary policy and the possibility of macroeconomic adjustment coming about through movements in the external value of its currency. Clearly, if the nations of the Euro Area have only one money, they can have only one monetary policy, which is set and implemented by the ECB. This must be the case because, since there is only one currency, it is not possible to have a different set of interest rates in different countries. Why is this a potential problem?

Suppose, for example, that there is a shift in consumer preferences across the common currency area away from goods and services produced in one country (Germany, say) and towards goods and services produced in another country (France, say). This situation is depicted in Figure 25.1, which shows a leftward shift in the German short run aggregate demand curve and a rightward shift in the French short run aggregate demand curve. What should policy makers in France and Germany do about this? One answer is to do nothing: in the long run, each economy will return to its natural rate of output. In Germany, this will occur as the price level falls and wages, prices and perceptions adjust. In particular, as unemployment rises in Germany, wages eventually begin to fall. Lower wages reduce firms' costs and so, for any given price level, the amount supplied will be higher. In other words, the German short run aggregate supply curve will shift to the right, until eventually it intersects with the new short run aggregate demand curve at the natural rate of output. The opposite happens in France, with the short run aggregate supply curve shifting to the left. The adjustment to the new equilibrium levels of output are also shown in Figure 25.1.

FIGURE 25.1

A Shift in Consumer Preferences Away from German Goods Towards French Goods

The German fall in aggregate demand leads to a fall in output from Y_1^G to Y_2^G, and a fall in the price level from P_1^G to P_2^G. The increase in French aggregate demand raises output from Y_1^F to Y_2^F. Over time, however, wages and prices will adjust, so that German and French output return to their natural levels, Y_1^G and Y_1^F, with lower prices in Germany, at P_3^G, and higher prices in France, at P_3^F.

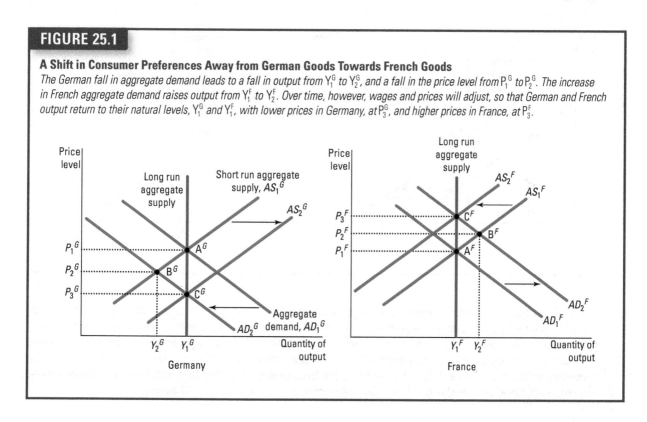

Note that, if Germany and France had maintained their own currencies and a flexible foreign exchange rate, then the short-term fluctuations in aggregate demand would be alleviated by a movement in the exchange rate: as the demand for French goods rises and falls for German goods, this would increase the demand for French francs and depress the demand for German marks, making the value of francs rise in terms of marks in the foreign currency exchange market. This would make French goods more expensive to German residents since they now must pay more marks for a given number of French francs. Similarly, German goods become less expensive to French residents. Therefore, French net exports would fall, leading to a fall in aggregate demand. This is shown in Figure 25.2, where the French aggregate demand schedule shifts back to the left until equilibrium is again established at the natural rate of output. Conversely, and also shown in Figure 25.2, German net exports rise and the German aggregate demand schedule shifts to the right until equilibrium is again achieved in Germany.

In a currency union, however, this automatic adjustment mechanism is not available, since, of course, France and Germany have the same currency (the euro). The best that can be done is to wait for wages and prices to adjust in France and Germany so that the aggregate supply shifts in each country, as in Figure 25.1. The resulting fluctuations in output and unemployment in each country will tend to create tensions within the monetary union, as unemployment rises in Germany and inflation rises in France. German policy makers, dismayed at the rise in unemployment, will favour a cut in interest rates to boost aggregate demand in their country, while their French counterparts, worried about rising inflation, will be calling for an increase in interest rates to curtail French aggregate demand. The ECB will not be able to keep both countries happy. Most likely, it will set interest rates higher than the German desired level and lower than the French desired level.

FIGURE 25.2

A Shift in Consumer Preferences With Flexible Exchange Rates

The fall in German aggregate demand leads, before prices have had time to adjust, to a fall in output from Y_1^G to Y_3^G. However, because this is due to a fall in net foreign demand, the value of the German currency falls, making German goods cheaper abroad. This raises net exports and restores aggregate demand. The converse happens in France: the increase in net foreign demand raises the external value of the French currency, making French goods more expensive abroad and choking off aggregate demand to its former level.

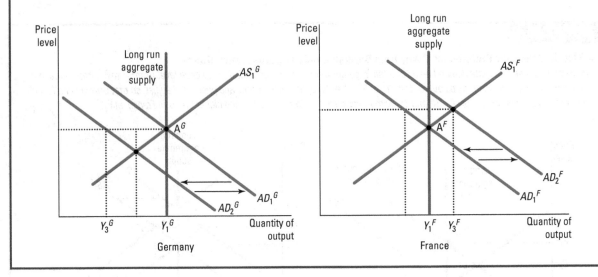

Germany
France

The ECB pursues an inflation targeting strategy, and the inflation rate it targets is based upon a consumer price index constructed as an average across the Euro Area. If a country's inflation rate (or expected inflation rate) is below the Euro Area average, the ECB's monetary policy will be too tight for that country; if it is above the average, the ECB's monetary policy will be too loose for it. All that is possible is a 'one size fits all' monetary policy. It is for this reason that entry to the Eurozone is restricted to those countries that can meet the criteria outlined above where inflation and interest rates are close to the EU average.

SELF TEST A business based in Spain generates a high proportion of its revenues from selling goods to buyers in the United States. In response to weak economic growth in the Euro Area, the ECB cuts interest rates. Over the next nine months, the euro–dollar exchange rate changes from €1 = \$1.15 to €1 = \$1.05. What effect might this change in the exchange rate have on the Spanish firm?

CASE STUDY   Croatia and the Euro

On 1 January 2023, Croatia formally joined the Eurozone becoming its 20th member. The process of joining the single currency had been five years in the making and for some time before that, the value of the Croatian kuna had been tied to that of the euro. In joining the single currency, Croatia hopes that it will improve the financial stability of the country and help the economy grow stronger. Around a quarter of Croatia's GDP is generated through tourism and some 70 per cent of tourists come from Eurozone countries. In an interview, the Governor of the Central Bank of Croatia, Boris Vujcic, commented that being a member of the single currency would also help make the economy more attractive to foreign investors.

(Continued)

Of course, one of the supposed disadvantages of adopting the euro is giving up the ability to control domestic monetary policy. However, Vujcic noted that this had not been a major problem for the country because Croatia had tied the value of the kuna initially to the German Deutschmark and then to the euro, so in effect it had already abandoned the sovereignty it had over monetary policy. Residents of Croatia seem to have mixed feelings about giving up the kuna, as might be imagined. Some say they fear that prices will rise, but in the first months of 2023, this fear seems to have been unfounded.

Croatia is the latest member of the EU to join the euroarea.

Questions

1 How might joining the euro help 'improve financial stability and help the economy to grow'?
2 Tourism and manufacturing are both important constituents of the Croatian economy. How might joining the euro help both these industries?
3 Why might joining a single currency like the euro lead to rising prices in an economy like that of Croatia?
4 One of the comments made by the governor of the central bank in relation to giving up the independence over monetary policy was 'it's about losing something that we didn't have to start with'. Does this mean that for any other countries thinking of joining the euro in the future, this supposed disadvantage is irrelevant?

Reference: www.euronews.com/next/2023/01/11/how-is-croatia-adapting-to-the-euro (accessed 10 June 2023).

Characteristics That Increase the Benefits of a Single Currency

High Degree of Trade Integration The greater the amount of trade that takes place between a group of countries (the greater the degree of trade integration) the more they will benefit from adopting a common currency. One of the principal benefits of a currency union, and the most direct benefit, is the reduction in transaction costs that are incurred in trade transactions between the various countries when there is a constant need to switch one national currency into another on the foreign currency exchange market. Clearly, therefore, the greater the amount of international trade and resulting foreign currency transactions that are carried out between member countries, the greater the reduction in transaction costs that having a common currency entails.

Currency unions can also help reduce exchange rate volatility, and this reduction will also be larger the greater the degree of intra-union trade, since more firms will benefit from knowing with certainty exactly the revenue generated from their sales to other currency union members, rather than having to bear the uncertainty associated with exchange rate fluctuations.

FISCAL POLICY AND COMMON CURRENCY AREAS

While adopting a common currency does mean that countries will have to give up autonomy in monetary policy, there is nothing in the adoption of a common currency that implies that members of the currency union should not still retain independence in fiscal policy. For instance, in our example of an asymmetric demand shock that expands demand in France and contracts aggregate demand in Germany, the French government could reduce government spending to offset the demand shock, while the German government could expand government spending. In fact, even if France and Germany did not make up an optimal currency area because wages were sticky and labour mobility was low between the countries, national fiscal policy could, in principle, still be used to ameliorate the loss of monetary policy autonomy.

Fiscal Federalism

Suppose that a currency union had a common fiscal policy in the sense of having a single, common fiscal budget covering tax and spending decisions across the common currency area. This means that fiscal policy in the currency union would work much as fiscal policy in a single national economy works, with a surplus of government tax revenue over government spending in one region used to pay for a budget deficit in another region. Return again to our example of an asymmetric demand shock that expands aggregate demand in France and contracts aggregate demand in Germany, as in Figure 25.2. Since almost all taxes are closely related to the level of economic activity in the economy, tax revenue will automatically decline in Germany as a result of the aggregate demand shock that shifts it into recession. At the same time, transfer payments in the form of unemployment benefit and other social security benefits will rise in Germany. These effects are referred to as automatic stabilizers built into the fiscal policy of an economy that automatically stimulate aggregate demand when the economy goes into recession without policy makers having to take any deliberate action. The opposite will be true in France, where the automatic stabilizers will be operating in reverse as transfer payments fall and tax receipts rise with the level of economic activity. These changes will tend to expand aggregate demand in Germany and contract it in France, to some extent offsetting the asymmetric demand shock.

Now, if the governments of France and Germany have a common budget, then the increased net government revenue in France can be used to offset the reduction in net government revenue in Germany. If the resulting movements in aggregate are not enough to offset the demand shock, then the French and German governments may even go further and decide to increase government expenditure further in Germany and pay for it by reducing spending and perhaps raising taxes in France.

This kind of arrangement, a fiscal system for a group of countries involving a common fiscal budget and a system of taxes and fiscal transfers across countries, is known as **fiscal federalism**. The problem with it is that the taxpayers of one country (here France) may not be happy about paying for government spending and transfer payments in another country (in this example, Germany).

> **fiscal federalism** a fiscal system for a group of countries involving a common fiscal budget and a system of taxes and fiscal transfers across countries

> **PITFALL PREVENTION** Being a member of a single currency does not mean that control over fiscal policy must be surrendered. In a country like the United States, for example, although all states use the dollar, each has control over its own fiscal policy. The drive to a greater degree of fiscal coordination in Europe, in some critics' eyes, is an attempt to move to a European super-state and is primarily political rather than economic.

National Fiscal Policies in a Currency Union: The Free-Rider Problem

During 2010 and 2011, difficulties in Greece, Ireland, Portugal, Spain and Italy led to EU leaders having to negotiate successive bailouts because of problems arising from the sovereign debt crisis where there were fears that these governments might be at risk of defaulting on their respective sovereign debt (bond issues). The Greek government borrowed heavily during the first decade of the twentieth century, but the 2007–2009 Financial Crisis and subsequent recession hit the country hard. The government did not have sufficient funds to pay off loans as they became due. The government accepted a deal to help provide it with financial support from the EU in return for cuts in public spending and increases in taxes to impose financial discipline. These so-called austerity measures have had wide-ranging effects on the Greek population, with unemployment rising and standards of living for many falling significantly. The difficulties experienced by the population led to political instability in the country and across the EU.

Similar problems were experienced by Portugal, Italy, Ireland and Spain. The ECB can control short-term interest rates, but not those on long-term 10- to 20-year bonds. As the stresses inside the Euro Area built up, interest rates on debt finance were pushed up. At a time of fragile economic activity, that was not good news for longer-term economic recovery. If the economy stalls then tax revenues go down, government spending on benefits increases and the debt problem intensifies.

One explanation for the debt problem in countries like Greece is the *free-rider problem*. Given that there is a single currency in the EU but there is no fiscal federalism, there is the possibility of individual members of the currency union using fiscal policy to offset asymmetric macroeconomic shocks that cannot be dealt with by the common monetary policy. For example, Spain might choose to run a big government budget deficit to counteract a fall in aggregate demand and borrow heavily to finance its deficit. The effects of Spain's decision impact on other members of the currency union.

Whenever a government raises its debt to very high levels, there is an increased risk of default. In general, this can be done in one of two ways. Where a country is not a member of a currency union and controls its own monetary policy, it can engineer inflation by increasing the money supply, so that the real value of the debt shrinks. When there is a sharp rise in the price level, this will usually be accompanied by a sharp fall in the foreign currency value of the domestic currency. This means that, valued in foreign currency, the stock of government debt will now be worth far less. Thus the government has in effect defaulted on a large portion of its debt by reducing its value both internally and externally.

If a country is part of a currency union and has no control over its own monetary policy then if a member country does engage in excessive debt issuance, it will tend to force up interest rates throughout the whole of the common currency area. However, interest rates may not be pushed up high enough to discipline the profligate country because markets believe that the other members of the currency union would not allow it to default. If the markets believe in this possibility, then the debt will not be seen as risky as it otherwise would be and so the interest rates charged to the debtor country on its debt will not be as high as they otherwise might be. The net effect is for that government to pay interest rates on its large stock of debt that are lower. This is because of the implicit belief that it will be bailed out if it has problems servicing the debt. All other members of the currency union pay higher interest rates on their debt because the financial markets become flooded with euro-denominated government bonds. This is the free-rider problem; a government is enjoying the benefits of a fiscal expansion without paying the full costs.

In addition, if that government is using the proceeds of its borrowing to fund a strong fiscal expansion, this may undo or work against the anti-inflationary monetary policy of the ECB by stoking up aggregate demand throughout the whole of the Euro Area.

To circumvent some of these problems, the currency union members can enter into a 'no bailout' agreement, which states that member countries cannot expect other members to come to their rescue if their debt levels become unsustainable as an attempt to convince the markets to charge profligate spend-and-borrow countries higher interest rates on their debt. In fact, exactly such a no bailout agreement existed among members of EMU, but applying it in practice is more difficult than describing it in theory.

In the aftermath of the 2007–2009 Financial Crisis, the sovereign debt crisis presented significant challenges to the continued existence of the euro. Two concepts are important to identify in this respect. A **cyclical deficit** occurs when government spending and income are disrupted by the 'normal' economic cycle. In times of strong economic growth government revenue from taxes will rise and spending on welfare and benefits will fall and so public finances will move into surplus (or the deficit shrinks appreciably). In times of economic slowdown, the opposite occurs and the size of the budget deficit will rise (or the surplus shrinks). A **structural deficit** refers to a situation where the deficit is not dependent on movements in the economic cycle but where a government is 'living beyond its means': spending what it has not got. New rules set up by the EU to try to avoid future crises of the sort experienced in the aftermath of the 2007–2009 Financial Crisis led to the setting up of the Fiscal Compact. This stated that structural deficits must not exceed 0.5 per cent of GDP at market prices although this can rise to 1 per cent provided government debt as a whole is 'significantly' less than 60 per cent of GDP at market prices. If countries breach this limit fines will be imposed of up to 0.1 per cent of GDP and 'a correction mechanism' designed to correct any imbalance will be automatically triggered. The Treaty also required countries to report in advance plans for major bond sales and economic reforms to EU institutions and for Euro Area summits to be held at least twice a year.

> **cyclical deficit** a situation when government spending and income is disrupted by the 'normal' economic cycle
> **structural deficit** a situation where the deficit is not dependent on movements in the economic cycle

> **JEOPARDY PROBLEM** A country with very high levels of sovereign debt announces that it is aiming to raise funds by borrowing on the bond market. It needs to raise €7 billion. As the time nears for the auction, the price of its existing debt starts to fall and yields rise. At the same time, the price of sovereign debt bonds of a country with a low level of debt starts to rise and yields fall. Why might this be happening?

BREXIT

On 23 June 2016, the UK went to the polls to vote in a referendum. The question they voted on was simple. Should the United Kingdom remain a member of the European Union or leave the European Union? Voters were given two options, one to tick a box saying, 'Remain a member of the European Union' and the second saying, 'Leave the European Union'. The result of the referendum was 17,410,742 votes cast to leave the EU (51.9 per cent) and 16,141,241 votes in favour of remaining in the EU (48.1 per cent). In Wales and England, the majority voted to leave the EU, while in Scotland and Northern Ireland, the majority voted to remain.

The referendum result was widely seen as a surprise. That process associated with the UK leaving the EU was formally started on 29 March 2017 when the UK government triggered Article 50 of the Treaty of Lisbon, which provides the right of an EU member to unilaterally declare its intention to leave the Union. Having triggered Article 50, a two-year period for the negotiations regarding the exit took place. In the event, the negotiations were protracted and difficult for both sides and aroused much debate and disagreement. Eventually, the UK formally left the EU on 31 January 2020.

The Impact of Brexit

There is much debate about the effect of Brexit on both the UK and EU economies. Politicians from different wings of the political spectrum trade claims and counter claims, much of which are based on simplistic data and do not provide the complete picture. One of the problems of assessing the impact of Brexit is that it is probably still too early to identify clear trends and in addition the pandemic, coming as it did around the same time as Brexit, has muddied the waters to a considerable extent. This has been further compounded by the developments in Ukraine from February 2022.

If we look at exports of goods and services to the EU from the UK, data from the Office for National Statistics suggests that in quarter one of 2016, the total value of exports of goods and services was around £57 billion. By quarter one of 2019, the value stood at just over £77 billion but then fell sharply to just over £57 billion in quarter two of 2020. From that point, the trend has been upwards and in quarter three of 2022, stood at almost £90 billion. How much of this increase has been due to any benefits that Brexit might bring to businesses and how much to a natural bounce back from the pandemic? These values are current prices and so do not take into consideration the effect of inflation. In quarter one of 2019, the value of exports to the rest of the world, not including the EU, stood at around £95.5 billion and by quarter three of 2022, stood at £128.3 billion. These figures are adjusted for inflation. Do these figures point to a greater ease and willingness of businesses to seek out trade with the rest of the world now that 'EU shackles' have been removed? Would exports to the rest of the world have increased by this amount whether Brexit had happened or not?

In its 'Brexit analysis', the Office for Budget Responsibility noted that its forecast assumption (note the language here) was for long run productivity to 'fall by 4 per cent relative to [the UK] remaining in the EU' (https://obr.uk/forecasts-in-depth/the-economy-forecast/brexit-analysis/#assumptions accessed 10 June 2023). It further stated its assumption was that both imports and exports would be around 15 per cent lower in the long run than if the UK had remained in the EU and that new trade deals would not have any major impact because many would be just replicate deals that already existed. At this stage, it is very difficult to tell and it may be impossible to disentangle all the various factors that could account for these, and other figures relating to the UK and the EU's economic performance post-Brexit. Perhaps it is safe to say that the debate around the wisdom of the decision by the UK to leave the EU will continue. What is important, however, it to look at any reports on the impact of Brexit with a critical eye. Those supporting Brexit may present 'evidence' that supports their view of the benefits of Brexit; those against Brexit will present 'evidence' to highlight what a disaster it has been. It is important, therefore, to try to take into consideration these conscious or unconscious biases in reports and statements to arrive at a more considered and informed view.

BUSINESS AND THE EUROPEAN MARKET

The EU represents a significant force in the global economy. It has a combined population of around 450 million and accounts for around 30 per cent of global GDP. The members states vary significantly in size and in individual populations. Cyprus, for example, has a population of around 900,000 whereas Germany's population is just over 83 million. The economic performance of each country also varies, and growth, inflation and unemployment rates differ across the EU. In general, EU members subscribe to market economies based on liberal democracy. While the EU can rightly claim some achievements throughout its history such as the development of the single market, freedom of movement throughout the so-called Schengen Area, the establishment of the euro and its development and humanitarian aid programmes, there are still major challenges and tensions that exist. There are barriers to the trade in services, co-operation on energy supplies is questionable and there are challenges around the availability of skills and productivity levels across the EU. One of the principles of the EU is **intergovernmentalism**, a situation where member states co-operate with each other on matters of common interest. However, while this is a fundamental principle in theory, in practice achieving intergovernmental agreement is difficult.

> **intergovernmentalism** a situation where member states cooperate with each other on matters of common interest

Challenges Facing the EU

The decision by the UK to leave was clearly a challenge to the EU and will have ongoing effects, but there are also a number of other challenges facing the EU and businesses operating in the EU.

Supply Chains Brexit and the Covid-19 pandemic highlighted problems in supply chain networks. As the EU project developed, supply chains became more and more integrated and complex and as Brexit and the pandemic developed, firms found increasing challenges in meeting demand and supply shortages forced up prices. While supply chain issues were also a global problem, the challenges across the EU were contributory factors in the acceleration of inflation across the EU and in the UK. This has led to firms re-examining their supply chains and looking at ways to simplify them to make them more resilient in the future.

Internal Country Problems Some of the key members of the EU face considerable economic and political challenges. In France, protests over the rising cost of living by the so-called 'Gilet Jaunes' in 2019 highlighted major discontent at the French government and the EU, and forced the government to introduce major public spending plans and the cancellation of planned tax increases, which put pressure on its fiscal position. Public spending in France is one of the highest in the Organization for Economic Cooperation and Development (OECD). Questions have been raised at how sustainable French debt levels are.

Italy faces similar debt challenges. The country is split into two halves: a relatively prosperous north and a much poorer south. The country has suffered from political instability and frequent changes in government. There are weaknesses in the banking system and the way in which banks are funded and this puts the country at risk of financial problems. It has a relatively high level of inequality and productivity levels are relatively low compared to other developed nations. The overall economic performance of Italy compared to other EU states and those of the OECD is poor.

Migration Migration to and across the countries of the EU is not a new thing, but in recent years pressure has increased on economies and social support systems as the number of migrants from Africa and parts of Asia has increased. Free movement of people is a fundamental principal of the EU enshrined in the establishment of the Schengen area. The **Schengen area** consists of 27 (23 member and 4 associate) countries: Austria, Belgium, Czech Republic, Croatia, Denmark, Estonia, Finland, France, Germany, Greece, Hungary, Italy, Latvia, Lithuania, Luxembourg, Malta, the Netherlands, Poland, Portugal, Slovakia, Slovenia, Spain and Sweden with associate membership for Iceland, Norway, Switzerland and Liechtenstein. Ireland is not a member, neither are Romania, Bulgaria and Cyprus, although these countries plan on joining. Members of the area have agreed to abolish internal borders facilitating the free and unrestricted movement of people.

> **Schengen area** an agreement by members to abolish internal borders facilitating the free and unrestricted movement of people

Many migrants seeking to enter the EU are seeking to escape from conflict or violence, but there are also many who are economic migrants looking for jobs and seeking to escape from poverty. The numbers have been such that some members of the EU have sought to close their borders, creating tensions across the EU. Trying to deal with the number of migrants has put pressure on social services, housing and education across the EU. In addition, there has been an increasing risk of 'importing' terrorism, the problems of trafficking and the criminal elements that can be associated with migrants. These have created political tensions in a number of countries with far-right political groups securing more support in some of these countries. The issue is somewhat ironic given that a number of EU countries suffer from declining and ageing populations and a lack of skills. However, it is not necessarily the case that the people coming into the EU are those who are able to fill the jobs that are needed and available.

Energy and the Environment The EU is the planet's largest importer of energy. With an annual import energy bill around €350 billion, around two-fifths of the gas and a quarter of the oil used across Europe was imported from Russia. The conflict in Ukraine has put energy supplies under pressure and contributed to the acceleration in inflation. The EU has targets to try to achieve carbon neutrality by 2050, but the energy crisis triggered by the conflict in Ukraine has made that target look challenging.

The EU has an Environmental Action Programme (EAP) which aims to push towards a climate-neutral, resource efficient and regenerative economy. The EU's share of global CO_2 emissions has been falling and accounts for around 18 per cent of global cumulative emissions. The reason for the fall in emissions is the fact that France produces around 80 per cent of its energy needs through nuclear and around a third of EU energy production is accounted for by renewable energy.

One of the key challenges now facing the EU is energy security. Prior to the conflict in Ukraine, there were plans to open a new gas pipeline, Nord Steam II, which would provide around a third of the EU's import needs. The pipeline was a €10.5 billion project to double capacity to 110 billion cubic metres squared of gas to Europe, which was started in 2011 and completed in September 2021. On completion it was awaiting certification from Germany and the EU to commence supply; however, the Russian announcement of independence for Donetsk and Luhansk in February 2022 led to the certification being suspended and the pipeline was effectively redundant.

Gas is less CO_2 intensive than coal, which accounted for around a fifth of energy use, but is still a carbon emitter. The Nord Stream construction project was controversial in any event given the commitment that the EU has made to seeking to become carbon neutral by 2050, but the need for a reliable source of energy seemed to trump this. Opponents also warned against becoming too reliant on Russia for energy. The EU, therefore, faces real challenges around energy security and the trade-offs that might have to be made in terms of its environmental and climate change targets.

The EU's energy policy has five main aims:

- Diversify Europe's sources of energy, ensuring energy security through solidarity and cooperation between EU countries.
- Ensure the functioning of a fully integrated internal energy market, enabling the free flow of energy through the EU through adequate infrastructure and without technical or regulatory barriers.
- Improve energy efficiency and reduce dependence on energy imports, cut emissions, and drive jobs and growth.
- Decarbonise the economy and move towards a low-carbon economy in line with the Paris Agreement.
- Promote research in low-carbon and clean energy technologies, and prioritise research and innovation to drive the energy transition and improve competitiveness.

(Source: www.europarl.europa.eu/factsheets/en/sheet/68/energy-policy-general-principles accessed 10 June 2023.)

However, there are a number of factors limiting the extent to which the EU can achieve these aims. Firstly, the time period before renewables can be fully exploited can be lengthy. Secondly, there are disagreements between member states on policy (such disagreements were highlighted over the Nord Stream II project). Thirdly, the conflict in Ukraine has affected fuel supplied to member states.

Social Inequality and Food Safety While it is generally accepted that the EU has been reasonably successful in increasing general prosperity, there are still considerable challenges around food and energy poverty across the EU. Food poverty or insecurity is measured by the Food Insecurity Experience Scale, which is a self-report scale asking questions around the extent to which people have felt worried or unable to eat or feed themselves adequately. The results of this measure show that between 3 and 20 per cent of people across Europe report problems with food insecurity.

Energy poverty occurs where 'a household is said to be fuel poor if it needs to spend more than 10 per cent of its income on fuel to maintain an adequate level of warmth' (Source: https://energy.ec.europa.eu/ topics/markets-and-consumers/energy-consumer-rights/energy-poverty-eu_en (accessed 4 August 2023). Between 50 and 125 million people are unable to afford 'proper indoor thermal comfort'.

The Common Agricultural Policy (CAP) was launched in 1962 and had five key aims:

- support farmers and improve agricultural productivity, ensuring a stable supply of affordable food
- safeguard EU farmers to make a reasonable living
- help tackle climate change and the sustainable management of natural resources
- maintain rural areas and landscapes across the EU
- keep the rural economy alive by promoting jobs in farming, agri-food industries and associated sectors.

There are disagreements around the extent of the success of CAP, but the cost is extensive. Around €58 billion per year is spent in support of the policy, around 40 per cent of the total EU budget.

The EU, therefore, faces considerable challenges in the coming years and the solutions to these challenges are neither simple nor without cost.

SUMMARY

- A common currency area (currency union or monetary union) is a geographical area through which one currency circulates and is accepted as the medium of exchange.

- The formation of a common currency area can bring significant benefits to the members of the currency union, particularly if there is already a high degree of international trade among them (i.e. a high level of trade integration). This is primarily because of the reductions in transaction costs in trade and the reduction in exchange rate uncertainty.

- There are, however, costs to joining a currency union, namely the loss of independent monetary policy and of the exchange rate as a means of macroeconomic adjustment. Given a long run vertical supply curve, the loss of monetary policy and the lack of exchange rate adjustment affect mainly short run macroeconomic adjustment.

- These adjustment costs will be lower the greater the degree of real wage flexibility, labour mobility and capital market integration across the currency union, and also the less the members of the currency union suffer from asymmetric demand shocks.

- The problems of adjustment within a currency union may be alleviated by fiscal federalism: a common fiscal budget and a system of taxes and fiscal transfers across member countries. In practice, however, fiscal federalism may be difficult to implement for political reasons.

- The national fiscal policies of the countries making up a currency union may be subject to a free-rider problem, whereby one country issues a large amount of government debt and pays a lower interest rate on it than it might otherwise have paid, but also leads to other member countries having to pay higher interest rates. It is for this reason that a currency union may wish to impose rules on the national fiscal policies of its members.

- The decision by UK voters to leave the EU in June 2016 has resulted in a great deal of uncertainty.

IN THE NEWS

Brexit

The decision by the UK population to vote to leave the EU has had widespread implications, perhaps none more so than the issue around the so-called Northern Ireland Protocol. One of the sticking points in the negotiations over the withdrawal of the UK was what to do about the border between the Republic of Ireland and Northern Ireland. In theory, firms moving goods across a border to a country which is not a member of the EU would have to submit to various checks, but given the delicacies of the political situation in Northern Ireland, this was not an option. Negotiators had to find a way round this problem and eventually, it was agreed that Northern Ireland would remain inside the EU's single market, which meant that

The Irish protocol has been the source of disagreement and renegotiation since the conclusion of the Brexit process.

goods being traded across the border between the Republic and Northern Ireland could move freely.

However, this then meant that goods moving from Northern Ireland to the rest of the UK would be subject to checks and controls. In effect, the border between the EU and the UK was now across the Irish Sea. Certain businesses are affected more significantly by the protocol than others. Firms that sell goods into the Republic, for example, are subject to checks at Northern Ireland ports before moving through Northern Ireland and then into the Republic without any further checks at the border. Some of the checks that have to be made are designed to ensure that any goods coming from a country that is not a member of the EU meet the standards set in the EU. Prior to Brexit, goods being shipped from the UK to Ireland would have met those standards because the UK was a member of the EU and firms were required to adhere to EU standards. Now that the UK is not a member of the EU, firms may adopt different standards and so have to undergo checks. These checks impose additional costs and time on the firms involved.

The reality for many firms, both those in Ireland shipping goods to the UK and UK firms shipping goods to Ireland, is that the checks and controls can become extremely complex. This is because the origin of goods is not always simple. For example, if a UK-based food processor wanted to sell food products into Ireland and the product contained ingredients sourced outside the UK, then the firm has to show that those ingredients meet EU standards before the processed end product could be shipped to Ireland, even though the manufacturing of the product was in the UK.

(Continued)

Given the complex nature of supply chains, this sort of issue can become very complex, require significant bureaucracy and time, and result in higher costs of production.

Discussions around the protocol between the UK and the EU have been in progress almost since the day the agreement came into being. Some see the protocol as unworkable and requiring reform. Some argue that the UK must accept that there are some side-effects of Brexit that are not palatable but that is one of the consequences of the decision made to leave the EU. The chances are that some sort of renegotiation of the protocol will be necessary to make it more practical and to benefit firms from both the EU and the UK, not to mention the importance of the political ramifications in Northern Ireland which have arisen since the UK left the EU. In late February 2023, it was announced that progress was being made between the UK and the EU on renegotiating the Northern Ireland protocol. In March 2023, an agreement was reached termed 'The Windsor Agreement' but at the time of writing problems still remain and not everyone is convinced the new agreement will resolve the key issues of contention.

Questions

1 The EU is an example of a trading bloc. What is the purpose of a trading bloc and in what ways do members of a trading bloc benefit?
2 Why do you think that the issue around the border between Northern Ireland and Ireland was such a challenging problem for Brexit negotiators?
3 Many of the firms that are selling into Ireland and buying goods from Ireland prior to Brexit are the same, so why do you think it is necessary to introduce checks and controls which would not have been in place prior to Brexit?
4 Many firms that trade between the UK and Ireland have noted that the protocol has increased costs and resulted in more time having to be devoted to bureaucracy. How do these firms manage these challenges?
5 How important do you think it is for the protocol to be renegotiated and what might be some of the problems in doing so?

Reference: www.bbc.co.uk/news/uk-northern-ireland-64268451 (accessed 10 June 2023).

QUESTIONS FOR REVIEW

1 Outline three of the main economic benefits that have arisen from the establishment and development of the Single European Market.
2 What are the main reasons why the Single European Market is still not complete?
3 Explain the main principles of a common currency area.
4 What are the main advantages and disadvantages of forming a currency union? Are these advantages and disadvantages long run or short run in nature?
5 Consider the Eurozone as an example of a common currency area. Assume that Germany faces an economic shock which is not felt in other countries of the EU. Use aggregate supply and aggregate demand diagrams to show the possible effects of this shock on the German and EU economies in the short run and what might happen in the long run.
6 Why would a high degree of trade integration increase the benefit of a common currency area?
7 What is fiscal federalism? How might the problems of macroeconomic adjustment in a currency union be alleviated by fiscal federalism?
8 What is meant by the 'free-rider' problem and why can this cause problems for a common currency area?
9 What is the difference between a structural and a cyclical deficit?
10 Using examples, outline two challenges facing the EU in the coming years.

PROBLEMS AND APPLICATIONS

1 Suppose Techoland and Cornsylvania form a currency union and adopt the electrocarrot as their common currency. Now suppose again that there is an increase in demand for electronic goods in both countries, and a simultaneous decline in demand for agricultural goods. As president of the central bank for the currency union, would you raise or lower the electrocarrot interest rate or keep it the same? Explain. (Hint: you are charged with maintaining low and stable inflation across the electrocarrot area.)

2 Suppose that Techoland and Cornsylvania decide to engage in fiscal federalism and adopt a common fiscal budget.

   a. Show, using the AD/AS model, how fiscal policy can be used to alleviate the short run fluctuations generated by the asymmetric demand shock.
   b. Given the typical lags in the implementation of fiscal policy, would you advise the use of federal fiscal policy to alleviate short run macroeconomic fluctuations? (Hint: distinguish between automatic stabilizers and discretionary fiscal policy.)

3 Would each of the following groups be happy or unhappy if the euro appreciated against all currencies? Explain.

   a. US pension funds holding French government bonds.
   b. German manufacturing industries.
   c. Australian tourists planning a trip to Europe.
   d. A British firm trying to purchase property overseas.

4 The United States can be thought of as a non-trivial currency union as, although it is a single country, it encompasses many states that have economies comparable in size to those of some European countries. Given that the United States has had a single currency for 200 years, it may be thought of as a successful currency union. Yet many of the US states produce very different products and services, so that they are likely to be impacted by different kinds of macroeconomic shocks (expansionary and recessionary) over time. For example, Texas produces oil, while Kansas produces agricultural goods. How do you explain the long-term success of the US currency union given this diversity? Are there any lessons or predictions for Europe that can be drawn from the US experience?

5 Explain, giving reasons, whether the following statements are true or false.

   a. A high degree of trade among a group of countries implies that there would be benefits from them adopting a common currency and forming a currency union.
   b. A high degree of trade among a group of countries implies that they should definitely adopt a common currency and form a currency union.

6 Do you think that the free-rider problem associated with national fiscal policies in a currency union is likely to be a problem in actual practice? Justify your answer.

7 Members of the Eurozone have forsaken monetary independence. This means they are not able to manipulate their currency to help manage asymmetric shocks. How does currency manipulation help in the case of asymmetric shocks and is such a policy a long-term solution to overcoming a country's economic problems?

8 Many firms across Europe and the UK complain that they are short of labour both skilled and unskilled. If this is the case, why is the migrant problem in the EU and the UK seen as being such a problem?

9 To what extent do you think that the EU has, overall, been of benefit to businesses? Justify your argument.

10 'The impact of Brexit on both the UK and the EU has proved to be far more damaging than anyone anticipated.' Use your knowledge of the current state of the EU and UK economies to address this statement.

26 SUSTAINABILITY

INTRODUCTION

It is difficult to imagine anyone being unaware of the issue of global warming or climate change (the two phrases are often used interchangeably but are not the same thing), issues around the availability of water, and biodiversity and the environment in general. The conventional wisdom is that economic growth (powered by human activity) has led to the creation of negative externalities that have resulted in average temperatures rising around the globe. Global warming, in turn, will lead to changes in the climate and include more instances of extreme weather events which together will result in widespread and 'disastrous' consequences. Human-generated carbon dioxide emissions have been cited as the main reason for the changes predicted. Continued human activity without changes to the way we do things will result in increasingly harmful effects on the environment and the loss of biodiversity and species extinction. The consequence of this analysis is that governments, firms and individuals around the world must take the lead in finding ways to cut carbon emissions and to approach the way we live, work and produce in different ways to help mitigate the potential damage we are inflicting on the planet. It is argued that only drastic and lasting cuts in carbon emissions can forestall the impending disaster which millions of people will experience.

Recall the transformation process, the process whereby firms use inputs to produce goods and services, and then distribute and sell these goods and services to consumers. This process is at the heart of almost every business. The implications are considerable. Firms take scarce resources and convert them into goods and services which are then sold to different customers. Some of these customers are individuals, some are other businesses, both at home and abroad, and some are other organizations such as charities, NGOs and governments. The reality is that resources are scarce and some resources are scarcer than others. When many resources are used up, they are no longer available for use elsewhere and, in many cases, these resources are not renewable. Future generations, therefore, may find that what we take for granted today may not be available, and the planet might be a very different place for them because of our actions.

This is the essence of sustainability. **Sustainability** refers to the capacity of economic activity to produce goods and services for current use without compromising the ability of future generations to also meet their economic needs. Recognizing that economic activity has a wider cost than simply the factor inputs that go into producing output is fundamental to the concept of externalities we discussed earlier in the book. The idea that production can have both benefits and costs to a third party (or parties) which are not accounted for in production decisions has been around since the nineteenth century when Henry Sidgwick (1838–1900), an English philosopher and economist in the utilitarian tradition, considered the notion of 'spillover costs and benefits'. Developments in the theory of externalities did enable firms to begin to produce reports which took into consideration the external costs and benefits of their immediate actions. However, the full impact of the actions of businesses on the environment, on ecosystems, on natural resources and biodiversity, was impaired by the limitations on fully understanding the impacts and being able to price them accurately. It is difficult for businesses to factor in how sustainable they are if they are unable to accurately estimate the value of the costs and benefits of their actions.

> **sustainability** the capacity of economic activity to produce goods and services for current use without compromising the ability of future generations to also meet their economic needs

Key Questions About Sustainability

Perhaps the first thing to say on sustainability is that it is extremely complex. It is also highly subjective. It arouses passions on both sides of the debate, but one of the important things to remember when looking at the issue is to approach it from an economist's perspective. That is, we must seek out the facts, understand the issues, focus on the evidence and try to quantity the costs and benefits and, as a result, adopt a positive rather than normative stance on the issue, in other words approach the issue thinking like an economist. As with any issue that arouses passions and feelings, there are always plenty of misinformation, disinformation, hearsay and speculation, and the economist's job is to work with others to understand the issues more effectively and to present policy options that are based on objectivity and not subjectivity.

There are a number of key questions that have to be considered when looking at sustainability. Some of these questions that need to be considered include the following:

1. How do we balance the need for economic activity to satisfy the wants and needs of today, and to positively impact on standards of living, with the wants and needs of future generations?
2. How do we measure these intertemporal choices? For example, to have a positive effect on reducing the level of emissions of greenhouse gases which will limit the effects of climate change, we will need to adopt behavioural changes today which involve a cost to enable future generations to receive benefits. How do we value the costs of choices made today with benefits that might accrue in 20, 50, 100 years' time?
3. Efficiency means reducing waste to a minimum, but how do we define efficiency in the context of sustainability? To get global change which improves sustainability there must be a collective understanding of what we are trying to achieve and that implies a global understanding of a definition of efficiency that we can all work towards.
4. Who should be responsible for designing and implementing the changes that will need to be made to improve sustainability and who should bear the cost? Should it be governments and, if so, which governments bear the most responsibility? Those that contributed to the increase in greenhouse gas emissions over the last 200 years of rapid industrialization? Those seeking to 'catch up' now and who are trying to help take millions out of poverty but are using technologies that are not sustainable according to the definition we have provided? Should firms take the leading role, or is it all our responsibilities as dwellers on planet Earth to change our behaviour?

The answers to the questions are not easy and there are considerable disagreements over them, but they have to be confronted if sustainability is to become more than just a 'buzzword'.

Changes in Approach to Sustainability

As noted, recognition that firms' activities have a wider impact on society and the environment is not new. The awareness of the public about the extent to which business activity has an impact is perhaps more recent. The developments in news media, the expansion of social media and improvements in education have combined to bring to the fore the issues facing the planet and its future. Politicians have spent many hours debating the problems, what to do about them and who should bear the cost and responsibility. As expectations on businesses in relation to their 'social and environmental footprint' increased, some began to produce environmental and social responsibility reports in addition to the more traditional finance and accounting reports.

Some firms faced accusations that the act was largely a marketing exercise. The irony of global firms generating billions in revenue and using massive quantities of resources was not lost on those who criticized these attempts at corporate social responsibility (CSR). Many of these reports seemed to be keen on demonstrating how they were seeking to cut costs by using resources more efficiently and reducing the environmental footprint of their operations. Ultimately, in a shareholder capitalist society, these firms are judged by traditional measures of success which are based on their ability to generate returns on investment and make profits. It was in their interests to find ways of cutting costs, but cutting costs and having a deep commitment to sustainability are different things.

One effect of these reports was to encourage firms to think more carefully about their costs, and indeed what they consider as costs. Do firms simply value the costs they immediately incur in production, or should external costs (and benefits) be considered, and if so how far should this process continue? If external costs and benefits are to be factored in, then how are they to be accurately valued? Many firms operate in relatively mature markets where growth is not easy. Expanding globally is one option as a means of increasing revenue and profit, but looking at the whole value chain might provide opportunities for improving profits, returns and efficiencies. The value chain refers to all the processes which add value for the firm. These processes are not simply the transformation process of factor inputs into output, but the goodwill the firm generates, its marketing activities, its brand development and recognition, customer services and back-office activities.

As firms delved further into their value chains, some sought to understand more fully the relationship between their operations and broader aspects of the environment and ecosystems. For example, food production depends on growing basic ingredients such as cereals, vegetables and fruit which are then used in other food products. In some cases, a successful harvest can be dependent on insects and animals pollinating plants. Did food production firms ever take into account the value of the positive externalities provided by insects and animals in food production costs? Certainly not in the past, but in the future many more firms will do so because of the importance of pollination in the growing process.

The Intergovernmental Science-policy Platform on Biodiversity and Ecosystem Services (IPBES), in a report published in 2017, estimated that 35 per cent of global food production by volume was dependent on insect and animal pollination. This 'service' provided by insects and animals, therefore, has a value which firms can seek to account for. The question is, how can these elements of the value chain be priced? The IPBES has reported the market value linked to pollinators at between $235 and $577 billion (€217 to €533 billion). With information on the value of this type of positive externality, it is logical that firms should look to find ways in which it can protect pollinators.

Similar arguments apply to other aspects of the environment, particularly regarding the use of non-renewable resources, energy, forests, wetlands, rivers, the oceans and so on. These are all factors which, in different ways, contribute to global production of goods and services. They are part of firms' value chains and it is now more widely recognized that these have an economic value which perhaps was not fully appreciated in the past.

Firms interested in sustainability and who are taking seriously ways of fully pricing their value chains are looking beyond the idea of sustainability reports as being a useful marketing tool. Incorporating and understanding the costs and benefits associated with sustainable production becomes an economic proposition, and one which is vital in generating profits not just in the present but in the future. More firms are recognizing that profit can be equated with minimizing their impact on the environment. This is increasingly becoming a driver in the way firms are planning future output and investment programmes and considering the circular economy. Sustainability is becoming associated with longer-term survival.

Socially Responsible Investing To plan for future production, take into account external costs and benefits and ensure longer-term profitable survival, firms need to invest. There is a trade-off associated with the short-term adjustment processes which may result in higher costs and lower profits with long-term survival, competitive advantage and profits in the future. Investment in innovation and value chain analysis requires funding, and another external benefit that firms are taking advantage of through sustainability is in securing investment funds.

Socially responsible investing is where individuals and firms with funds to invest make decisions based on the ethical and sustainable credentials of the investment. Firms that outsource operations to firms who employ child labour, those involved in gambling, paying low wages, supplying arms and weapons, and firms who cannot show that they are taking sustainability seriously may not be chosen for investment. The sums of money involved are not insignificant. The Forum for Sustainable and Responsible Investment report that funds devoted to socially responsible investment in the United States alone was around $8.4 trillion (€7.8 trillion) in 2022.

> **socially responsible investment** investment decisions which take into account sustainability, ethical and governance factors

Sustainability has evolved to become something which firms see has having real long-term economic value. Understanding the value chain, pricing the whole value chain, including the external costs and benefits, can help firms develop longer-term profitability and resilience.

WHAT IF... a business was alerted to a source of raw materials that are 100 per cent sustainable and could be substituted with existing ones. However, compared to the current raw materials used, the cost is 24 per cent higher. What factors might the firm seek to take into account in making a decision over whether to purchase the sustainable raw materials or not?

SELF TEST How might firms adjust their production processes to improve their sustainability?

The Broader Issues Around Sustainability

While we have defined sustainability as conducting business activity without affecting future generations, the idea has become more broadly associated with other issues. The consideration of the resources used and how their use will affect future generations is only one aspect of the potential impact of business activity. Business activity can have effects on social injustice, decisions can contribute to inequality and, equally, business decisions can promote or limit diversity and inclusion. In addition, what sort of contribution does business make to the community, both its local one and the national or international community? The broader social and environmental conscience of firms is often judged against what is called environmental, social and governance (ESG) standards. ESG standards are what some investor groups use as the basis for making decisions around sustainable investment. Businesses that seek to take into consideration these broader issues can be deemed more likely to survive in the longer term.

Advantages to Business of Sustainability

It may seem obvious that if businesses make decisions based around sustainability in its broadest terms, then there can be significant benefits not only to the environment but to society in general. The advantages can be self-serving but can also bestow wider benefits, and many argue that it is increasingly important for businesses to appreciate and work towards their wider responsibilities.

Increases in Profitability It may seem ironic that the first advantage being considered is very much focused on the business itself and how it can increase profitability. However, behind this bald statement there are some subtle and important influences. As we have seen, profit is the difference between a firm's revenue and its costs. Anything the firm can do to increase efficiency, reduce waste and cut costs can all impact on profit regardless of whether sales increase. We have seen how firms are re-examining supply chains and investing in Industry 4.0 technology to help improve efficiency and reduce waste and this is, in part, the drive to improving profitability. On the sales side, there have been accusations as noted, that some firms may engage in sustainability as a marketing ploy. Sustainability and high ESG standards *can* be used in marketing campaigns, but firms are increasingly realizing that their claims have to be supported by facts and evidence, otherwise customers relatively quickly find out and adverse publicity can negatively impact on sales. The act of seeking to use marketing or advertising to make inaccurate or misleading claims about the extent to which a firm's activities are sustainable is termed **greenwashing** or 'green sheening'.

> **greenwashing** the use of marketing or advertising to make inaccurate or misleading claims about the extent to which a firm's activities are sustainable

Many firms are finding that consumer demographics are increasingly influencing purchasing decisions. Certain types of consumers may be heavily influenced by ethical considerations in their purchasing, and if firms are able to offer convincing marketing campaigns and support these with facts and evidence of their sustainability credentials, then they can increase sales. Some of these customers may be willing to pay higher prices to access goods and services which are sustainable, and firms are able to develop increased customer loyalty and repeat purchase. It is therefore possible for firms to not only cut costs and improve efficiency but to also increase revenue and, thus, profitability.

Effects on the Labour Market Firms that take a broader view of sustainability may also find some benefits through their approach to managing human resources or its people. The Covid-19 pandemic helped to highlight a number of issues that some firms were already working on, not least remote and more flexible working arrangements, being more aware of the health and well-being of staff, of improving diversity and inclusivity, and improving the support networks for staff. These could all help with improving productivity but also help retain staff and reduce the costs of recruitment and selection, which can be extensive. Broadening the recruitment net to be more diverse and inclusive might also widen the talent pool and increase the sharing of ideas within the business. In addition to the internal benefits the firm can generate as noted above, there might also be benefits from reduced industrial action and fewer days lost to illness. However, firms may also need to recognize some of the potential disadvantages associated with inclusivity and diversity. Such an approach may require more training of existing staff to understand the changed approach. There is also some evidence that more diversity and inclusivity does not always translate into more harmonious and productive working relationships, but can stifle team working with so many different backgrounds, cultures, ideas and approaches, which can cause internal conflict and slow decision making.

Accessing New Markets Firms that embrace sustainability may find that new markets open up to them that they either were not aware of or did not have access to previously. For example, a firm that adopts sustainable production methods may find that their goods meet national standards set by other countries or trading blocs and means they can get access into those markets, whereas without these methods and without the means to certificate and show evidence of adherence to the standards, they would not gain access.

> **PITFALL PREVENTION** Remember that sustainability now encompasses more than just the idea of assessing the impact of a firm's activities on the environment. While the environmental impact is still vitally important, sustainability has become a much broader term to include other aspects of business operations, including people.

Disadvantages to Business of Sustainability

As with any business development, there are disadvantages to firms seeking to adopt a sustainable approach to their operations. These must be balanced against the advantages and the extent of the costs and benefits clearly identified and planned for. The main areas of disadvantage are discussed next.

The Cost of Implementation For many businesses, adopting sustainable strategies is not without its cost. Existing systems, relationships, agreements, processes, supply chains and so on may all have to be changed, and this will inevitably involve the need to set aside investment funds to achieve the desired outcome. In the short run the cost of these investments could be significant and can even lead to short-term losses being made. The patience and understanding of shareholders and wider stakeholders is necessary to make the shift towards sustainable production, as many of the benefits might take a number of years to realize.

Change Management Issues One of the biggest challenges facing many firms is in instituting change. There is lots of literature around change management and a number of different change management models proposed, but as with any model these tend to simplify the reality. Many firms find that introducing and then managing change can be extremely challenging, can create hostility and conflict, increase costs and, ultimately, the change programme does not deliver what it initially set out to do. In making the change the firm might also find that the longer-term nature of becoming more sustainable is eclipsed by the short-term imperatives they face, and so systemic inertia can result in stalled progress and ultimately the change being abandoned.

Understanding of Customers Any firm seeking to become more sustainable must not only take its staff with them on the journey but also its customers. While some customers are more aware of sustainability issues, not all are. If sustainable practices are employed which increase cost and necessitate increased prices, the firm must be confident that it understands its customers sufficiently to be able to communicate the journey and not lose customers on the way. This not only applies to business-to-customer (B2C) firms but equally to business-to-business (B2B) firms. New production and supply chain processes, for example, might require building new relationships with customer agents and suppliers, and customers need to be made aware of, and understand, the reasons for the decisions being made.

Internal Business Capability Shifting to a more sustainable business model is not a simple process. It requires a firm to understand the whole process, to have a clear strategy and, crucially, to have the people and processes to enable their strategies to be realized. Some firms have appointed specialists in the field of sustainable supply chain management, or have a dedicated team for its sustainability journey. Without the right knowledge, skills, understanding and tools, a firm can find the benefits of sustainability may not be achievable.

Definitions of Efficiency

Economics focuses on how we make use of scarce resources which have competing uses. It could be argued that 'waste' would be one of the things that economists most dislike. Waste implies extravagance, of things having no purpose or value, or something that is unusable in some way. Waste can be the by-product of production, but it can also be inherent in production processes and the elimination, or at the very least, the reduction and minimisation, of waste might be argued to be central to economics. Efficiency implies that waste is reduced to a minimum or eliminated. We have seen in earlier chapters that under conditions of perfect competition, in long run equilibrium, firms produce at the lowest point on their average cost curve. This is referred to as **productive efficiency**. At this point, output is maximized using the minimum amount of inputs. Finding the optimum combination of factor inputs to produce a given output is referred to as **technical efficiency**. However, there is little benefit in a firm producing according to these definitions of efficiency if consumers do not place a value on what is being produced. In other words, goods and services are produced and distributed according to consumer wants and needs and this is reflected, in turn, by the price they are willing to pay. **Allocative efficiency** occurs where the value placed on a unit of output, measured by the marginal utility gained in consuming that output, is equal to the marginal cost of producing that unit of output.

> **productive efficiency** a measure of efficiency where firms produce a given output level at lowest cost
> **technical efficiency** a measure of efficiency where firms produce a given output level using the least amount of factor inputs
> **allocative efficiency** a measure of efficiency where the value placed on a unit of output, measured by the marginal utility gained in consuming that output, is equal to the marginal cost of producing that unit of output

We have also seen that firms can produce efficiently but may not take into consideration the external costs and benefits of their production decisions. **Social efficiency**, therefore, occurs where the private and social costs and benefits of production are equal to the private and social benefits of consumption.

> **social efficiency** a measure of efficiency where the private and social costs and benefits of production are equal to the private and social benefits of consumption

SELF TEST Is it possible for a firm to achieve all measures of efficiency at any time?

CASE STUDY   Agriculture and Methane

The United Nations Environment Programme, in an article published in August 2021, noted that emissions from manure and gastroenteric releases account for almost a third of human-caused methane emissions. Methane is said to be 80 times more potent than carbon as a greenhouse gas over a 20-year period. Producers of meat and rice (paddy fields are also a source of methane emission) may not take into account the damage to the environment that methane output imposes. The price of meat and rice, therefore, may not reflect the social costs of producing meat and rice. There will, as a result, be overconsumption of meat and rice. The socially efficient output level would be lower, and so efforts to encourage farmers to find ways of making methane 'useful' in some way and reducing its environmental impact, along with an encouragement to consumers to reduce their meat and rice consumption, would result in a more socially efficient outcome.

Of course, this sounds simple in theory but in practice raises many questions. If farmers reduce output of meat and rice, what happens to their livelihoods? Should governments (by which we really mean the taxpayer) compensate farmers for reducing meat and rice output and/or finding ways to invest in making methane 'useful' rather than simply a 'waste' product (according to our definition above)? What are the

Paddy fields are a source of methane production but how can we control the generation and effects of methane more effectively?

ethical issues around persuading consumers to reduce meat and rice consumption? What right have governments or any other body or organization, to tell individuals what they should and should not eat? Are individuals sufficiently informed about the external costs and benefits of consumption to make appropriate and informed choices? These are all challenges which arouse different opinions and highlight the difficulties of confronting issues of sustainability.

Technology can assist in the task of reducing methane emissions. For example, farmers can use more nutritious feed so that meat production becomes more 'efficient'. Different types of feed might be used which would help

(Continued)

reduce methane production by livestock and improved management of manure might also help. Methane could be 'harvested' to produce biogas. The flooding of rice fields could be managed more effectively to reduce methane output. In November 2022, the Methane Alert and Response System (MARS) was launched at the 27th United Nations Climate Change Conference. The system is designed to detect emissions of methane, increase information and thus be in a better position to take action to reduce these emissions. These might all be ways in which methane generation could be managed more efficiently and help to manage the target of limiting global warming to the 1.5 degree Celsius target of the Paris climate change agreement.

Questions

1   Use a supply and demand diagram similar to the ones used in Chapter 7 to show how the output of meat could be socially inefficient.

2   Consider some of the questions posed in the case study around dealing with the issue of reducing methane emissions. What might be some of the practical and ethical issues which would arise that are associated with these questions?

3   If farmers are encouraged to use more nutritious feed for their animals and this reduces methane generation, what type of efficiency would this represent? Explain.

4   To what extent do you think methane is a 'waste' product as defined in this chapter? (Hint: consider ways in which methane might be used for other purposes such as that suggested in the case study.) Consider the costs and benefits associated with such approaches.

References: www.unep.org/news-and-stories/story/methane-emissions-are-driving-climate-change-heres-how-reduce-them (accessed 10 June 2023).
www.unep.org/explore-topics/energy/what-we-do/methane/imeo-action/methane-alert-and-response-system-mars (accessed 10 June 2023).

Sustainability Strategies

If a firm wishes to make the shift to sustainability, it needs to devise appropriate strategies to help it get to where it needs to be in X years' time, however long that time frame is estimated to be. As noted above, changing the business to become more sustainable is not without its challenges, and so the strategies that the business develops and seeks to put in place are important if the benefits are to be reaped. There are a number of steps that might need to be taken in establishing a suitable strategy.

Understand the Business At the start of the process, it will be important, as with any strategy development, for the firm to understand its current position and to define where it wants to be at a point in the future. This means analysing the firm to understand what the firm currently does, what its carbon and environmental footprint is, where waste occurs, the nature of its human resources activities including recruitment and selection policies, the firm's culture and so on. Like a medical diagnosis, the 'cure' cannot be suitably applied if the problem is not clear in the first place.

Establish Clear Goals To get to where the business wants to get to, it must understand what its goals are and have some plans in place for how it is going to try to achieve those goals. This may involve deciding how the firm is going to define sustainability, how far it wants and can go given current technology, and how it intends to communicate these plans and goals to all stakeholders. In some cases, this may mean revisiting the firm's value, vision and mission statements and revising them accordingly, or creating such statements if it does not currently have them. A check of many leading firm's websites can reveal the extent to which sustainability has become part of the core reason for its existence. Of course, having these types of statements is one thing but acting on them and ensuring all in the business understand them and act on them is another.

Aligning the Business As the business begins to move towards its goals, it will need to carry out a wide range of tasks and activities. In some cases, whole processes will need to be changed or adapted.

Negotiations with suppliers, customers, other parts of the supply chain, the redesign of IT systems and even the business model itself might need to be addressed. It is almost inevitable that these types of change will require significant investment by the business and decisions will have to be made about the priorities attached to different investments. It will have to be recognized that it is unlikely everything can be changed at once and so a clear path, perhaps guided by strategic intents, should be laid out. In making decisions about what changes to institute, it may be necessary to look at where the 'quick wins' can be gained and what part of the business can be changed quickly to make the greatest impact. This is where understanding the business is so important; a strategy aimed at improving sustainability is unlikely to succeed if it is carried out with limited understanding on a piecemeal basis. Aligning the business with the strategies is unlikely to succeed if the organization's people are not involved and if they do not 'buy into' the strategies. This requires skilled leadership and equally skilled management. Some businesses will choose to subscribe to the so-called **triple bottom line**. Rather than the emphasis being on profit, decisions are taken with three standards or measures in mind: people, planet and profit. Using these measures as a benchmark for the firm's success, the firm can not only seek to achieve profits which secure its long-term survival but also to ensure that it measures the impact of its social and environmental impacts. This might mean that the firm's principal responsibility shifts from generating shareholder value to creating stakeholder value. Again, communication is key and shareholders may need to be convinced that the strategies the firm is seeking to put in place also protect both their short-term and long-term interests. As noted above, increasingly investors are subscribing to the idea of sustainable investment and so having measures on the triple bottom line may help them to make decisions on where to place investments more effectively.

> **triple bottom line** a basis for decision making to help measure the impact of a firm's activities on people, planet and profit

Many larger businesses now produce sustainability reports where they seek to communicate and disclose their impact on society and the environment, and what it is doing to reduce the impact and to achieve greater levels of sustainability. Some of these reports look very impressive and are clearly carefully planned and presented. Publishing such information is one thing, but how far can stakeholders trust the information that they contain? How far are they just a marketing exercise? A study by Papoutsi and Sodhi in 2020 (Papoutsi, A. and Sodhi, M.M. (2020) Does disclosure in sustainability reports indicate actual sustainability performance? *Journal of Cleaner Performance*, 260: 121049) looked at 331 companies' sustainability reports and sought to link these to 51 sustainability indicators to assess the extent to which disclosures in sustainability reports actually indicate sustainable performance. Their research suggested that, given this sample, sustainability reports do indicate actual sustainability performance. This may point to the increased awareness among business leaders that empty promises and misleading information are no longer accepted, will be analyzed and if the business is found to be making claims that are inaccurate, that the potential damage to its reputation can be significant.

> **JEOPARDY PROBLEM** A firm adopts a policy to broaden the diversity and inclusivity of its workforce but finds that its decision making is 20 per cent slower and that there are an increased number of internal conflicts being generated in the business. How does this policy of diversity and inclusion for the workforce square with the definitions of efficiency provided in this chapter?

Sustainability and Small to Medium Business Enterprises

As we have noted elsewhere in the book, the vast majority of businesses in many countries are SMEs. While many large and well-known businesses are actively seeking to address sustainability, SMEs also have a role to play. Many new start-ups are based on sustainability first principles and those that have been in existence for some time can also make progress to improving sustainability. The British Business Bank, a national development bank set up to help SMEs, has noted that most of the principles that apply to large business apply in equal measure to SMEs. Considering sustainable options and the circular economy, it argues, can help attract more eco-aware customers; improve supply chain requirements, especially if the SME is working with governments or larger firms where they are required to comply with changing standards and regulations; help employee engagement; reduce waste; have a positive impact on costs; and make the business more attractive to investment.

SUMMARY

- Sustainability looks at how we use resources today to satisfy wants and needs in a way which does not compromise the ability of people in the future also being able to satisfy their wants and needs.

- There are four important questions that need to be answered in relation to sustainability: how do we balance current and future needs; how do we measure intertemporal choices; how do we define what we mean by 'efficiency'; and who should bear the costs and gain the benefits of the design and implementation of changes in behaviour to achieve sustainability?

- Many firms are now taking an increasing interest in, and recognizing, their role in sustainability and the definition of sustainability is becoming broader.

- Socially responsible investing refers to the process whereby individuals and firms with funds to invest make decisions based on the ethical and sustainable credentials of the investment.

- Advantages of adopting sustainability principles can include increased profitability, benefits of investing in people and access to new markets.

- Disadvantages of adopting sustainable principles include potential impacts on costs, the need for investment, challenges in managing change, ensuring that customers are understood and the extent to which the business is internally capable of achieving its goals.

- Efficiency can be viewed in different ways: productive, technical, allocative and social efficiency.

- To implement sustainability strategies, firms need to understand their business, establish clear goals and take steps to ensure all stakeholders are aligned with the business's goals.

- Sustainability principles and benefits are equally as applicable to small and medium sized enterprises as they are to large firms.

IN THE NEWS

Challenges to Sustainability

Progress towards a more sustainable business environment was severely impacted by the events of 2022. Not only was the world still recovering from the effects of the pandemic but the events in Ukraine shook the whole world. Some of the effects of the conflict pushed up global prices, resulted in energy shortages and shortages of some types of foodstuffs, and further disrupted supply chains. These challenges led to questions being asked about the progress to a more sustainable future. For example, given the energy shortages and the increase in fuel poverty across many countries in Europe and the UK, governments looked at relaxing some of the plans around investing in fossil fuels to plug the gap in energy supplies. Countries across Western Europe pledged military aid to Ukraine, which necessitated greater investment in defence equipment. Can both of these be defended in the light of ESG targets? Many firms faced challenges across their supply chains and in meeting customer needs. Should they respond by reducing their plans around sustainability to address these short-term issues, or should the longer term still be the main focus of decision making? Reports also highlighted how some firms were linking remuneration packages for senior leaders of businesses to ESG targets and CSR goals. Is this ethical and what sort of challenges might such policies generate?

(Continued)

A report published in 2023 by the SustainAbility Institute of the Environmental Resources Management (ERM), a multinational consultancy, outlined some of the trends in sustainable business. The report highlighted some of the challenges noted above but also suggested that there was still a momentum behind the evolution of sustainability. One aspect it noted was the idea of stakeholder capitalism. This is the idea that the activities of business should be designed to serve all a business's stakeholders and not just shareholders. In other words, profitability is not the sole focus of business decision making but the much wider issues highlighted in this chapter. The report noted that the concept was becoming increasingly popular and was not simply a 'fad'. The report included a quote from Larry Fink, the CEO of BlackRock, an investment company, who is reported to have said '[stakeholder capitalism] is not political or "woke", rather it is capitalism focused on the very company–stakeholder relationships that enable business success'. For sustainability to continue to evolve, this concept will become increasingly important.

Issues such as the conflict in Ukraine have raised new questions about how to manage energy supplies effectively.

Questions

1 **How might the pandemic have affected the approaches businesses had to implementing sustainability policies?**
2 **The conflict in Ukraine disrupted energy supplies and resulted in increases in energy poverty across Europe. To what extent do you agree with the view that investment in fossil fuel energies is essential to plug shortages in energy supplies?**
3 **How might firms involved with supplying military equipment to countries like Ukraine and to countries which have been accused of human rights abuses defend their activities in the light of ESG targets?**
4 **What might be the ethical issues associated with the decision by firms to link remuneration packages of senior leaders to ESR and CSR targets?**
5 **Consider the concept of stakeholder capitalism. To what extent do you agree with the view expressed by Larry Fink in the article?**

Reference: www.sustainability.com/globalassets/sustainability.com/thinking/pdfs/2023/2023_sustainability_trends_report.pdf (accessed 10 June 2023).

REVIEW QUESTIONS

1 What do you understand by the term 'sustainability'?
2 Outline the four key questions related to sustainability.
3 How has the approach to sustainability changed in recent years?
4 Explain how improved understanding of the value of value chains can contribute towards sustainability.
5 What is socially responsible investing and what benefits do you think it brings in relation to meeting sustainability targets?
6 Outline three possible advantages to firms of adopting sustainable practices.
7 Outline three possible disadvantages to firms of adopting sustainable practices.
8 What do you understand by the term 'greenwashing'? Can you find an example of 'greenwashing'?

9 Define and give examples of four different measures of efficiency. Which do you think is the most appropriate definition in relation to achieving sustainability?

10 Outline some steps that a business might have to take in adopting more sustainable practices in its business.

PROBLEMS AND APPLICATIONS

1 In February 2022, conflict began in the Eastern European country of Ukraine. The conflict affected other countries as supplies of energy to other parts of Europe began to be affected and contributed to rising energy prices for businesses and households. In response, some countries began to look again at proposals by firms to open up new coal fields and investing into fossil fuels as a means of improving energy security. Critique this situation in the context of the debate around sustainability.

2 Sustainability seeks to take account of the impact of business activities on the welfare and well-being of future generations. How might we measure the value of the costs of implementing sustainable practices today with the benefits to people at some point in the future?

3 A firm is considering adopting more sustainable practices across its key operations. The leaders of the business are debating what measure of efficiency they should adopt to help them measure progress towards achieving their goal. What measure would you advise them to adopt and why?

4 To what extent do you think that issues around diversity and inclusion, social inequality and people should be part of the definition of sustainability, or has the concept been hijacked by broader interest groups?

5 Consider a business which manufactures breakfast cereals. One of its senior directors reads the reports about the importance and value of pollinators and suggests to the board of directors that it must urgently reassess its accounts to take into consideration the cost of the continued decline in the bee population in the next ten years. The director notes that they have done some initial calculations and factoring in this external cost reduces forecast profits by 10 per cent a year for the next five years. How should the business respond to this suggestion?

6 Given the complexity of supply chains, to what extent do you think that it is really possible to invest in a socially responsible way?

7 There are a number of advantages that can arise from adopting sustainable practices, but to what extent do you agree with the view that sustainability is just a bandwagon that firms are jumping on to help them generate more profits?

8 Research suggests that around 70 per cent of change management programmes fail, with the main reasons being employee resistance and a lack of management support (Source: McKinsey and Company). What steps can business leaders take to reduce the incidence of failure in relation to implementing sustainability practices?

9 Do some research to find a sustainability report from a company of your choice. From your research, outline the main ways in which the company is seeking to achieve increased levels of sustainability and assess the success the firm has in achieving their goals.

10 To what extent do you think that the triple bottom line is a valid measure of sustainability, and what might be the problems in using such a framework for firms seeking to achieve sustainability?

GLOSSARY

abnormal profit the profit over and above normal profit

absolute advantage where a producer can produce a good using fewer factor inputs than another

accounting profit total revenue minus total explicit cost

actual spending, saving or investment the realized or *ex post* outcome resulting from actions of households and firms

added value the difference between the cost of factor inputs into production and the amount consumers are prepared to pay (the value placed on the product by consumers)

adverse selection the tendency for the mix of unobserved attributes to become undesirable from the standpoint of an uninformed party

agency theory where managers act as the agents of shareholders and as a result there may be a divorce between ownership and control such that managers pursue their own self-interests rather than the interests of shareholders

agent a person who is performing an act for another person, called the principal

aggregate demand curve a curve that shows the quantity of goods and services that households, firms and the government want to buy at each price level

aggregate supply curve a curve that shows the quantity of goods and services that firms choose to produce and sell at each price level

aims the long-term goals of a business

allocative efficiency a measure of efficiency where the value placed on a unit of output, measured by the marginal utility gained in consuming that output, is equal to the marginal cost of producing that unit of output

appreciation an increase in the value of a currency as measured by the amount of foreign currency it can buy

asset a tangible or intangible item controlled by a business that has economic value

autonomous expenditure spending which is not dependent on income

average fixed cost fixed costs divided by the quantity of output

average total cost total cost divided by the quantity of output

average variable cost total variable cost divided by the quantity of output

balance of payments the official account of international payments for the import and export of goods, services and capital

B2B business business activity where the business sells goods and services to another business

B2C business business activity where the business sells goods and services to a final consumer

balanced trade a situation in which exports equal imports

bond a certificate of indebtedness

bounded rationality the idea that humans make decisions under the constraints of limited, and sometimes unreliable, information that they are unable to fully process

branding the means by which a business creates an identity for itself and highlights the way in which it differs from its rivals

budget constraint the limit on the consumption bundles that a consumer can afford

C2C business business activity where consumers exchange goods and services, often facilitated by a third party such as an online auction site

capital any item used in production which is not used for its own sake but for what it contributes to production

capitalist economies systems where resource inputs are largely owned by private individuals and where the motive for exchange takes place primarily for profit

capital expenditure the money spent on fixed assets

cartel a group of firms acting in unison

classical dichotomy the theoretical separation of nominal and real variables

club goods goods that are excludable but non-rival

collusion an agreement among firms in a market about quantities to produce or prices to charge

common currency area (or currency union or monetary union) a geographical area throughout which a single currency circulates as the medium of exchange

common resources goods that are rival but not excludable

communist economies systems where resource inputs are largely owned by the state and exchange and trade is based on social, political and economic motives which may be primarily based on a belief of greater equality

comparative advantage the comparison among producers of a good according to their opportunity cost. A producer is said to have a comparative advantage in the production of a good if the opportunity cost is lower than that of another producer

compensating differential a difference in wages that arises to offset the non-monetary characteristics of different jobs

competition a market situation when two or more firms are rivals for customers

competitive advantage the advantages firms can gain over another which have the characteristics of being both distinctive and defensible

complements two goods for which an increase in the price of one leads to a decrease in the demand for the other (and vice versa)

compounding the accumulation of a sum of money in, say, a bank account where the interest earned remains in the account to earn additional interest in the future

concentration ratio the proportion of total sales in an industry accounted for by a given number of firms

constant returns to scale the property whereby long run average total cost stays the same as the quantity of output changes

consumer price index (CPI) a measure of the overall prices of the goods and services bought by a typical consumer

consumer surplus the amount a buyer is willing to pay for a good minus the amount the buyer actually pays for it

consumption spending by households on goods and services, with the exception of purchases of new housing

contingency theory a theory of organizations which suggests there is no one way to organize a business but that leaders and managers need to respond to situations (or contingencies) as they arise

contribution the difference between the selling price and the variable cost per unit

core competencies the things a business does which are the source of competitive advantage over its rivals

corporate social responsibility a business philosophy that recognizes combining the need to generate profit with the wider responsibilities to the environment, communities, ethical considerations, and society in general

cost the payment to factor inputs in production

cost leadership a strategy to gain competitive advantage through reducing costs below competitors

cream-skimming a situation where a firm identifies parts of a market that are high in value added and seeks to exploit those markets

credit risk the risk a bank faces in defaults on loans

cross-price elasticity of demand a measure of how much the quantity demanded of one good responds to a change in the price of another good, computed as the percentage change in quantity demanded of the first good divided by the percentage change in the price of the second good

crowdfunding the raising of finance using technology to secure individual contributions of small sums of money from a large number of people

crowding out a decrease in investment that results from government borrowing

crowding out effect the offset in aggregate demand that results when expansionary fiscal policy raises the interest rate and thereby reduces investment spending

cryptocurrencies peer-to-peer networks facilitating transactions between users without an intermediary

cyclical deficit a situation when government spending and income is disrupted by the 'normal' economic cycle

cyclical unemployment the deviation of unemployment from its natural rate

deadweight loss the fall in total surplus that results from a market distortion, such as a tax

deflationary/inflationary gap the difference between full employment output and the expenditure in the economy

demand curve a graph of the relationship between the price of a good and the quantity demanded

demand schedule a table that shows the relationship between the price of a good and the quantity demanded

depreciation a decrease in the value of a currency as measured by the amount of foreign currency it can buy

depression a severe recession

deregulation the removal of controls, laws or rules governing a particular market aimed at improving the economic efficiency of that market and therefore the performance of the economy at the microeconomic level

derived demand when demand for a factor of production is derived (determined) from its decision to supply a good in another market

differentiation the way in which a firm seeks to portray or present itself as being different or unique in some way

diminishing marginal product the property whereby the marginal product of an input declines as the quantity of the input increases

diminishing marginal utility a 'law' that states that marginal utility will fall as consumption increases

direct tax taxes levied on income and wealth with the responsibility for payment lying with the individual or organization

discount rate the interest rate at which the Federal Reserve lends on a short-term basis to the US banking sector

discrimination the offering of different opportunities to similar individuals who differ only by race, ethnic group, sex, age or other personal characteristics

diseconomies of scale where long run average total cost rises as the quantity of output increases

dominant strategy a strategy that is best for a player in a game regardless of the strategies chosen by the other players

economic activity the amount of buying and selling (transactions) that take place in an economy over a period of time

economic growth the increase in the amount of goods and services in an economy over a period of time

economic profit total revenue minus total cost, including both explicit and implicit costs

economics the study of how society makes decisions in managing scarce resources

economies of scale the advantages of large scale production that result in lower cost per unit produced

efficiency wages wages above the equilibrium wage paid by firms to increase worker productivity

efficient scale the quantity of output that minimizes average total cost

elasticity a measure of the responsiveness of quantity demanded or quantity supplied to one of its determinants

emerging market economy a country where the per capita income of the population is in the middle to low range compared to other global economies

enterprise the act of taking risks in the organization of factors of production to generate business activity

entry limit pricing a situation where a firm will keep prices lower than they could be in order to deter new entrants

equilibrium price the price that balances quantity supplied and quantity demanded, otherwise known as market clearing price

equilibrium quantity the quantity supplied and the quantity demanded at the equilibrium price

ethical responsibility the moral basis for business activity and whether what the business does 'is right' and is underpinned by some moral purpose, doing what is 'right'

European Economic and Monetary Union (EMU) the European currency union that has adopted the euro as its common currency

excludable the property of a good whereby a person can be prevented from using it or gaining benefit when they do not pay for it

expected utility theory the idea that buyers can rank preferences from best to worst (or vice versa)

explicit costs input costs that require an outlay of money by the firm

exports goods produced domestically and sold abroad leading to an inflow of funds into a country

externality the uncompensated impact of one person's actions on the well-being of a bystander or third party

factors of production a classification of inputs used in business activity which includes land, labour, capital and enterprise

financial intermediaries financial institutions through which savers can indirectly provide funds to borrowers

financial markets financial institutions through which savers can directly provide funds to borrowers

fintech financial technologies used in the financial services industry, including mobile payments, transferring money, loans, fund raising and asset management

fiscal federalism a fiscal system for a group of countries involving a common fiscal budget and a system of taxes and fiscal transfers across countries

fiscal policy influencing the level of economic activity through manipulation of government income and expenditure

fixed costs costs that are not determined by the quantity of output produced

foreign direct investment (FDI) inflows of investment into a host country from external businesses

free cash flow the cash generated from the firm's operations minus that spent on capital assets

full employment a point where those people who want to work at the going market wage level are able to find a job

fundamental analysis the study of an asset to determine its value

future value the amount of money in the future that an amount of money today will yield, given prevailing interest rates

game theory the study of how people behave in strategic situations

GDP deflator a measure of the price level calculated as the ratio of nominal GDP to real GDP times 100

geographical mobility the ease with which people can move to different parts of the country where jobs may be available

gig economy a labour market in which workers have short-term, freelance or zero-hours contracts with employers, more akin to being self-employed than employed

globalization the growth of interdependence among world economies, usually seen as resulting from the removal of many international regulations affecting financial flows

government purchases spending on goods and services by local, state and national governments

greenwashing the use of marketing or advertising to make inaccurate or misleading claims about the extent to which a firm's activities are sustainable

gross domestic product (GDP) the market value of all final goods and services produced within a country in a given period of time

gross domestic product (GDP) per head the market value of all final goods and services produced within a country in a given period of time divided by the population of a country to give a per capita figure

heuristics rules of thumb or shortcuts used in decision making

human capital the accumulation of investments in people, such as education and on-the-job training

implicit costs input costs that do not require an outlay of money by the firm

imports goods produced abroad and purchased for use in the domestic economy leading to an outflow of funds from a country

import quota a limit on the quantity of a good that can be produced abroad and sold domestically

income effect the change in consumption that results when a price change moves the consumer to a higher or lower indifference curve

income elasticity of demand a measure of how much the quantity demanded of a good responds to a change in consumers' income, computed as the percentage change in quantity demanded divided by the percentage change in income

indifference curve a curve that shows consumption bundles that give the consumer the same level of satisfaction

indirect tax tax levied on consumption and invariably paid by businesses to tax authorities, but where some or all of the tax can be passed on to a consumer

inferior good a good for which, other things being equal, an increase in income leads to a decrease in demand (and vice versa)

inflation an increase in the overall level of prices in the economy

inflation rate the percentage change in the price index from the preceding period

intergovernmentalism a situation where member states co-operate with each other on matters of common interest

internalizing an externality altering incentives so that people take account of the external effects of their actions

internal economies of scale the advantages of large scale production that arise through the growth of the firm

internationalization the increase in the way in which organizations produce goods and services which are intended for use in many different countries

investment making money available to develop a project which will generate future returns including increasing future productive capacity

investment fund an institution that sells shares to the public and uses the proceeds to buy a portfolio of stocks and bonds

just-in-time management an approach to inventory management which seeks to ensure inputs arrive at a firm only when they are needed

labour all the human effort, mental and physical, which is used in production

labour force the total number of workers, including both the employed and the unemployed

labour force participation rate the percentage of the adult population that is in the labour force

land all the natural resources of the Earth which can be used in production

law of demand the claim that, other things being equal, the quantity demanded of a good falls when the price of the good rises

law of supply the claim that, other things being equal, the quantity supplied of a good rises when its price rises

law of supply and demand the claim that the price of any good adjusts to bring the quantity supplied and the quantity demanded for that good into balance

limited liability a legal principle where an owner's liability for the debts of a company are limited to the amount they have agreed to subscribe

liquidity risk the risk that a bank may not be able to fund demand for withdrawals

long run the period of time in which all factors of production can be altered

macroeconomic environment the national or global economy within which the business operates

macroprudential policy policies designed to limit the risk across the financial sector by focusing on improving prudent standards of operation that enhance stability and reduce risk

margin the amount of profit a firm makes on each sale

margin of safety the distance between the break-even output and current production where total revenue is greater than total cost

marginal changes small incremental adjustments to a plan of action

marginal cost the increase in total cost that arises from an extra unit of production

marginal product the increase in output that arises from an additional unit of input

marginal propensity to consume the fraction of extra income that a household spends rather than saves

marginal propensity to save the fraction of extra income that a household saves rather than consumes

marginal utility the addition to total utility as a result of one extra unit of consumption

market a group of buyers and sellers of a particular good or service who come together to agree a price for exchange

market clearing price the price that balances quantity demanded and quantity supplied, otherwise known as equilibrium price

market economy an economy that allocates resources through the decentralized decisions of many firms and households as they interact in markets for goods and services

market equilibrium a situation in which the price has reached the level where quantity supplied equals quantity demanded

market failure a situation in which a market left on its own fails to allocate resources efficiently

market for loanable funds the market in which those who want to save supply funds and those who want to borrow to invest demand funds

market niche a small segment of an existing market with specific wants and needs which are not currently being met by the market

market power the ability of a single economic agent (or small group of agents) to have a substantial influence on market prices

market segmentation the separating out of a group of customers according to particular needs, attitudes, behaviours or shared characteristics

market share the proportion of total sales accounted for by a product/business in a market

menu costs the costs of changing prices

merit good a good which could be provided by the private sector, but which may also be offered by the public sector because it is believed that a less than optimal amount would be available to the public if resource allocation was left entirely to the private sector

microeconomic environment factors and issues that affect an individual firm operating in a particular market or industry

minimum efficient plant size the point where increasing the scale of production of an individual plant in an industry further yields no significant unit cost benefits

minimum efficient scale the point at which further increases in the scale of production will not yield any significant unit cost benefits

mixed economies economic systems that include elements of both private and public ownership of resources to answer the fundamental questions

model of aggregate demand and aggregate supply the model that many economists use to explain short run fluctuations in economic activity around its long run trend

monetary neutrality the proposition that changes in the money supply do not affect real variables

monetary policy the set of actions taken by the central bank in order to affect the money supply

money market the market in which the commercial banks lend money to one another on a short-term basis

monopolistic competition a market structure in which many firms sell products that are similar but not identical

monopoly a firm that is the sole seller of a product without close substitutes

monopsony a market in which there is one dominant buyer and many sellers

moral hazard the tendency of a person who is imperfectly monitored to engage in dishonest or otherwise undesirable behaviour

multinationals organizations characterized by having operations in a number of countries, although their main headquarters will be in one country, normally the country in which the firm originally developed

multiplier effect the additional shifts in aggregate demand that result when expansionary fiscal policy increases income and thereby increases consumer spending

Nash equilibrium a situation in which economic actors interacting with one another each choose their best strategy given the strategies that all the other actors have chosen

natural monopoly a monopoly that arises because a single firm can supply a good or service to an entire market at a smaller cost than could two or more firms

natural rate of output the output level in an economy when all existing factors of production (land, labour, capital and technology resources) are fully utilized and where unemployment is at its natural rate

natural rate of unemployment the normal rate of unemployment around which the unemployment rate fluctuates

nearshoring the relocation or outsourcing of operations to countries nearer to the central business unit

net capital outflow the purchase of foreign assets by domestic residents minus the purchase of domestic assets by foreigners

net exports spending on domestically produced goods by foreigners (exports) minus spending on foreign goods by domestic residents (imports)

nominal exchange rate the rate at which a person can trade the currency of one country for the currency of another

nominal GDP the production of goods and services valued at current prices

nominal interest rate the monetary return on saving and the cost of borrowing

nominal variables variables measured in monetary units

normal good a good for which, other things being equal, an increase in income leads to an increase in demand (and vice versa)

normal profit the minimum amount required to keep factors of production in their current use

objectives the means by which a business will be able to achieve its aims

occupational mobility the ease with which people are able to move from occupation to occupation, including the degree to which skills and qualifications are transferable between occupations

oligopoly competition among the few, a market structure in which only a few sellers offer similar or identical products and dominate the market

onshoring the relocation of business activities and operations to the domestic country

opportunity cost the cost expressed in terms of the benefits sacrificed of the next best alternative

organizational culture the shared beliefs, values, behaviours and actions that exist within an organization

organization design the alignment between the purposes and aims of the organization and how its people and resources are structured to help achieve its goals

outright open market operations the outright sale or purchase of non-monetary assets to or from the banking sector by the central bank without a corresponding agreement to reverse the transaction at a later date

outsourcing contracting out of a part of the business' operations to another organization

patent the exclusive right to manufacture and sell a product for a fixed number of years

Pigouvian tax a tax enacted to correct the effects of a negative externality

planned spending, saving or investment the desired or intended actions of households and firms

Prebisch–Singer hypothesis a theory suggesting that the rate at which primary products exchange for manufactured goods declines over time, meaning that countries specializing in primary good production become poorer

predatory or destroyer pricing a situation where firms hold price below average cost for a period to try and force out competitors or prevent new firms from entering the market

present value the amount of money today that would be needed to produce, using prevailing interest rates, a given future amount of money

price the amount of money a buyer (a business or a consumer) has to give up in order to acquire something

price discrimination the business practice of selling the same good at different prices to different customers

price elasticity of demand a measure of how much the quantity demanded of a good responds to a change in the price of that good, computed as the percentage change in quantity demanded divided by the percentage change in price

price elasticity of supply a measure of how much the quantity supplied of a good responds to a change in the price of that good, computed as the percentage change in quantity supplied divided by the percentage change in price

price level the price of a basket of goods and services measured as the weighted arithmetic average of current prices

principal a person for whom another person, called the agent, is performing some act

prisoners' dilemma a particular 'game' between two prisoners that illustrates why co-operation is difficult to maintain even when it is mutually beneficial

private goods goods that are both excludable and rival

private saving the income that households have left after paying for taxes and consumption

private sector business activity which is owned, financed and organized by private individuals

procurement a process that encompasses all the activities associated with obtaining the necessary support for its business

producer price index a measure of the change in prices of a basket of goods and services bought by firms

producer surplus the amount a seller is paid minus the cost of production

product life cycle a diagram representing the life cycle of a product from launch through to growth, maturity and decline

production function the relationship between the quantities of inputs used to make a good and the quantity of output of that good

production possibilities frontier a graph that shows the combinations of output that the economy can possibly produce given the available factors of production and technology

productive efficiency a measure of efficiency where firms produce a given output level at lowest cost

productivity the quantity of goods and services produced from each hour of a worker, or other factor of production's, time

profit the reward for taking risk in carrying out business activity

property rights the exclusive right of an individual, group or organization to determine how a resource is used

public goods goods that are neither excludable nor rival

public saving the tax revenue that the government has left after paying for its spending

public sector business activity owned, financed and organized by the state on behalf of the population as a whole

purchasing power parity a theory of exchange rates whereby a unit of any given currency should be able to buy the same quantity of goods in all countries

quality assurance a holistic approach to quality where ensuring appropriate standards is the responsibility of everyone in the organization

quality control a process where checks are carried out on products at different stages of the production process to determine whether the output being produced meets required standards

quantity demanded the amount of a good buyers are willing and able to purchase at different prices

quantity supplied the amount of a good that sellers are willing and able to sell

real exchange rate the rate at which a person can trade the goods and services of one country for the goods and services of another

real GDP a measure of the amount produced that is not affected by changes in prices

real interest rate the interest rate adjusted to take account of the effect of inflation, calculated as the nominal interest rate minus the inflation rate

real money balances what money can actually buy given the ratio of the money supply to the price level

real variables variables measured in physical units

recession a period of declining real incomes and rising unemployment. The technical definition gives recession occurring after two successive quarters of negative economic growth

refinancing rate the interest rate at which the European Central Bank lends on a short-term basis to the euro area banking sector

relative prices the ratio of the price of one good to the price of another

repo rate the interest rate at which the Bank of England lends on a short-term basis to the UK banking sector

repurchase agreement the sale of a non-monetary asset together with an agreement to repurchase it at a set price at a specified future date

revenue expenditure money used to help generate sales

risk the extent to which a decision leading to a course of action will result in some loss, damage, adverse effect or otherwise undesirable outcome to the decision maker

risk averse exhibiting a dislike of uncertainty

rival the property of a good whereby one person's use diminishes other people's use

scarcity the limited nature of society's resources in relation to wants and needs

Schengen area an agreement by members to abolish internal borders facilitating the free and unrestricted movement of people

screening an action taken by an uninformed party to induce an informed party to reveal information

share (or stock or equity) a claim to partial ownership in a firm

shareholder value the overall value delivered to the owners of business in the form of cash generated and the reputation and potential of the business to continue growing over time

short run the period of time in which some factors of production cannot be changed

shortage a situation in which quantity demanded is greater than quantity supplied

signalling an action taken by an informed party to reveal private information to an uninformed party

Single European Market (SEM) a (still not complete) EU-wide market throughout which labour, capital, goods and services can move freely

social efficiency a measure of efficiency where the private and social costs and benefits of production are equal to the private and social benefits of consumption

socially responsible investment investment decisions which take into account sustainability, ethical and governance factors

social responsibility the responsibility a firm has for the impact of their product and activities on society

spread the difference between the average interest banks earns on assets and the average interest paid on liabilities

stagflation a period of falling output and rising prices

stakeholders groups or individuals with an interest in a business, such as workers, managers, suppliers, the local community, customers and owners

standard of living a measure of welfare based on the amount of goods and services a person's income can buy

strategic intent a framework for establishing and sharing a vision of where a business wants to be at some point in the future and encouraging all those involved in the business to understand and work towards achieving this vision

strategy a series of actions, decisions and obligations that lead to the firm gaining a competitive advantage and exploiting the firm's core competencies

strike the organized withdrawal of labour from a firm by a union

structural deficit a situation where the deficit is not dependent on movements in the economic cycle

subsidy a payment to buyers and sellers to supplement income or lower costs and which thus encourages consumption or provides an advantage to the recipient

substitutes two goods for which an increase in the price of one leads to an increase in the demand for the other (and vice versa)

substitution effect the change in consumption that results when a price change moves the consumer along a given indifference curve to a point with a new marginal rate of substitution

sunk cost a cost that has already been committed and cannot be recovered

supply chain a network of firms that facilitate the production and distribution of a good or service to consumers

supply curve a graph of the relationship between the price of a good and the quantity supplied

supply schedule a table that shows the relationship between the price of a good and the quantity supplied

supply side policy policy aimed at influencing the level of aggregate supply in the economy

surplus a situation in which quantity supplied is greater than quantity demanded

sustainability the capacity of economic activity to produce goods and services for current use without compromising the ability of future generations to also meet their economic needs

SWOT analysis an analysis of the firm's strengths, weaknesses, opportunities and threats

synergy a situation where the combination of two or more businesses or business operations brings total benefits which are greater than those which would arise from the separate business entities

systemic risk the risk of failure across the whole of the financial sector

tactic short-term framework for decision making

tariff a tax on goods produced abroad and sold domestically

tax avoidance the legal use of the tax system to minimize the amount of tax paid

tax evasion the deliberate and illegal activity by an individual or organization not to pay the required statutory tax due

tax incidence the manner in which the burden of a tax is shared among participants in a market

technical efficiency a measure of efficiency where firms produce a given output level using the least amount of factor inputs

technology the application or use of knowledge in some way which enables individuals or businesses to have greater control over their environment

the economy the collective interaction between individuals in the process of production and exchange in a defined area

theory of liquidity preference Keynes' theory that the interest rate adjusts to bring money supply and money demand into balance

third sector business activity owned, financed and organized by private individuals, but with the primary aim of providing needs and not making profit

total cost the market value of the inputs a firm uses in production

total expenditure the amount paid by buyers, computed as the price of the good times the quantity purchased

total revenue the amount received by sellers of a good, computed as the price of the good times the quantity sold

trade balance the value of a nation's exports minus the value of its imports; also called net exports

trade deficit an excess of imports over exports

trade-off the loss of the benefits from a decision to forego or sacrifice one option, balanced against the benefits incurred from the choice made

trade openness the ratio of exports plus imports to gross domestic product

trade surplus an excess of exports over imports

transfer payment a payment for which no good or service is exchanged

transformation process the process in which businesses take factor inputs and process them to produce outputs which are then sold

triple bottom line a basis for decision making to help measure the impact of a firm's activities on people, planet and profit

underemployment a situation where a worker has a job but may not be working to full capacity, or does not have all their skills utilized, or is working for a lower income than their qualifications, training or experience might suggest

unemployed the number unemployed in an economy is the number of people of working age who are able and available for work at current wage rates and who do not have a job

unemployment rate the percentage of the labour force that is unemployed

unintended consequences the outcomes of decision making or policy changes which are not anticipated and are unforeseen

unlimited liability a situation where the owner of a business is legally responsible for all the debts of the business

union a worker association that bargains with employers over wages and working conditions

utility the satisfaction derived from consumption

value the worth to an individual of owning an item represented by the satisfaction derived from its consumption

value chain how value is added at each stage in the activities and operations which a firm carries out

value for money a situation (mostly subjective) where the satisfaction gained from purchasing and consuming a product is equal to or greater than the amount of money the individual had to hand over to acquire it (the price)

value of marginal product the marginal product of an input times the price of the output

value proposition the reason why consumers should buy a product rather than those of a rival or competitor

variable costs costs that are dependent on the quantity of output produced

willingness to pay a measure of how much a buyer values a good by the amount they are prepared to pay to acquire the good

working capital the cash needed to keep the business working day to day

world price the price that prevails in the world market for that good

X-inefficiency the failure of a firm to operate at maximum efficiency due to a lack of competitive pressure and reduced incentives to control costs

INDEX

FORMULAS

1. **Average Revenue:**

$$AR = \frac{\text{Total revenue } (TR)}{\text{Output } (Q)}$$

2. **Average Total Cost:**

Average total cost = Total cost/Quantity

$$ATC = \frac{TC}{Q}$$

3. **Break-Even Output:**

$$\text{Break-even} = \frac{\text{Fixed costs}}{\text{Contribution per unit}}$$

4. **Calculating the Inflation Rate between Consecutive Years:**

$$\text{Inflation rate in year 2} = 100 \times \frac{(\text{CPI in year 2} - \text{CPI in year 1})}{\text{CPI in year 1}}$$

5. **Classical Quantity Theory of Money:**

$$MV = PY$$

$$M_d = kPY$$

6. **Comparing Inflation Over Time:**

$$\text{Amount in today's currency} = \text{Amount in year } T \text{ currency} \times \frac{\text{Price level today}}{\text{Price level in year } T}$$

7. **Consumer Optimum in the Standard Economic Model:**

$$\frac{MU_x}{P_x} = \frac{MU_y}{P_y}$$

8. **Cross-Price Elasticity of Demand:**

$$\text{Cross-price elasticity of demand} = \frac{\text{Percentage change in quantity demanded of good 1}}{\text{Percentage change in the price of good 2}}$$

9. **Demand Function:**

$$D = f(P_n, P_n \ldots P_{n-1}, Y, T, P, A, E)$$

Where:

- P_n = Price
- $P_n \ldots P_{n-1}$ = Prices of other goods (substitutes and complements)
- Y = Incomes (the level and distribution of income)
- T = Tastes and fashions
- P = The level and structure of the population
- A = Advertising
- E = Expectations of consumers

10. **Desired Margin Level:**

$$\text{Selling price} = \frac{\text{Total cost per unit}}{(1 - \text{Margin})}$$

11. Entry Point:

$$\text{Enter if } P > ATC$$

12. Equilibrium of the Economy:

$$\text{Planned } S + T + M = \text{Planned } I + G + X$$

13. Exit Point:

$$\text{Exit if } P < ATC$$

14. Gross Domestic Product (Expenditure Method):

$$GDP(Y) = C + I + G + NX$$

15. GDP Deflator:

$$GDP \text{ deflator} = \left(\frac{\text{Nomimal GDP}}{\text{Real GDP}}\right) \times 100$$

16. Income Elasticity of Demand:

$$\text{Income elasticity of demand} = \frac{\text{Percentage change in quantity demanded}}{\text{Percentage change in income}}$$

17. Labour Force:

$$\text{Labour force} = \text{Number of people employed} + \text{number of people unemployed}$$

18. Labour Force Participation Rate:

$$\text{Labour force participation rate} = \left(\frac{\text{Labour force}}{\text{Adult population}}\right) \times 100$$

19. Least Cost Input Combination:

$$\frac{MP_K}{P_K} = \frac{MP_L}{P_L}$$

20. Marginal Cost:

$$\text{Marginal cost} = \text{Change in total cost/Change in quantity}$$

$$MC = \frac{\Delta TC}{\Delta Q}$$

21. Marginal Propensity to Consume:

$$MPC = \frac{\Delta C}{\Delta Y}$$

22. Marginal Propensity to Save:

$$MPS = \frac{\Delta S}{\Delta Y}$$

23. Marginal Rate of Substitution:

$$MRS = \frac{\Delta P_x}{\Delta P_y}$$

24. Marginal Revenue:

$$MR = \frac{\Delta TR}{\Delta Q}$$

25. Market Equilibrium:

Market equilibrium occurs where $Qd = Qs$

26. Mark-Up:

$$\text{Mark-up (per cent)} = \left(\frac{\text{Selling price} - \text{Total cost per unit}}{\text{Total cost per unit}} \right) \times 100$$

27. Midpoint Method of Calculating Price Elasticity of Demand:

$$\text{Price elasticity of demand} = \frac{(Q_2 - Q_1)/([Q_2 + Q_1]/2)}{(P_2 - P_1)/([P_2 + P_1]/2)}$$

28. Midpoint Method of Calculating Price Elasticity of Supply:

$$\text{Price elasticity of supply} = \frac{(Q_2 - Q_1)/([Q_2 + Q_1]/2)}{(P_2 - P_1)/([P_2 + P_1]/2)}$$

29. Multiplier (k):

$$\text{Multiplier} = \frac{1}{(1 - MPC)}$$

$$\text{Multiplier} = \frac{1}{MPS}$$

$$k = \frac{1}{MPS + MPT + MPM}$$

$$k = \frac{1}{MPW}$$

30. Opportunity Cost:

$$\text{Opportunity cost} = \frac{\text{Sacrifice}}{\text{Gain}}$$

31. Percentage Growth Rate:

$$\text{Percentage growth rate} = (V_{present} - V_{past})/V_{past} \times 100$$

32. Price Elasticity of Demand:

$$\text{Price elasticity of demand} = \frac{\text{Percentage change in quantity demanded}}{\text{Percentage change in price}}$$

33. Price Elasticity of Supply:

$$\text{Price elasticity of supply} = \frac{\text{Percentage change in quantity supplied}}{\text{Percentage change in price}}$$

34. Production Function (Assuming Two Factor Inputs, Land and Capital):

$$Q = f(L_1, K_1)$$

35. Productivity:

$$\text{Productivity} = \frac{\text{Total output}}{\text{Units of the factor}}$$

36. Profit:

$$\text{Profit} = \text{Total revenue} - \text{Total cost} \ (\pi = TR - TC)$$

37. Profit-Maximizing Output:

$$\text{where } MC = MR$$

38. Real Exchange Rate:

$$\text{Real exchange rate} = \frac{(\text{Nominal exchange rate} \times \text{Domestic price})}{(\text{Foreign price})}$$

$$\text{Real exchange rate} = \left(\frac{e \times P}{P*} \right)$$

39. Real Interest Rate:

$$\text{Real interest rate} = \text{Nominal interest rate} - \text{Inflation rate}$$

40. Real Money Balances:

$$\frac{M}{P}$$

41. Real Wage:

$$\text{Real wage rate} = \frac{\text{Nominal wage rate}}{\left(\dfrac{\text{Base CPI}}{\text{Current CPI}} \right)}$$

42. Saving:

$$S \quad = \quad I \quad + \quad NCO$$
$$\text{Saving} = \text{Domestic investment} + \text{Net capital outflow}$$

43. Shut-Down Point:

$$\text{Shut down if } P < AVC$$

44. Supply Function:

$$S = f(P_n,\ P_n \dots P_{n-1},\ H,\ N,\ F_1 \dots F_m,\ E,\ S_f)$$

Where:

- P_n = Price
- $P_n \dots P_{n-1}$ = Profitability of other goods in production and prices of goods in joint supply
- H = Technology
- N = Natural shocks
- $F_1 \dots F_m$ = Costs of production
- E = Expectations of producers
- S_f = Social factors

45. Total Cost:

$$\text{Total cost} = \text{Fixed costs} + \text{Variable cost } (TC = FC + VC)$$

46. Total Revenue:

$$TR = P \times Q$$

47. Unemployment Rate:

$$\text{Unemployment rate} = \left(\frac{\text{Number of unemployed}}{\text{Labour force}} \right) \times 100$$

48. Yield on a Bond:

$$\text{Yield} = \frac{\text{Coupon}}{\text{Price}} \times 100$$

CREDITS